Born in Edinburgh in 1740, the son of a distinguished Scottish judge, JAMES BOSWELL was educated at the universities of Edinburgh, Glasgow, and Utrecht. Trained as a lawyer, he became moderately successful in his profession; but his real interests were writing and the London circles of "the great, the gay, and the ingenious." In 1763, his meeting in London with Samuel Johnson provided him with both a lifelong hero and a subject for a projected biography. During his Grand Tour of Europe (1764–66), he visited the then remote island of Corsica, and became internationally known for his account of the Corsicans and their ruler, Pasquale de Paoli. Later he was a familiar figure in the literary world of London, and dabbled unsuccessfully in politics. He succeeded his father in 1782 as laird of Auchinleck, the large family estate in Ayrshire. In 1785, a year after Johnson's death, Boswell's *Journal of a Tour to the Hebrides with Samuel Johnson,* and in 1791, the publication of *The Life of Samuel Johnson, LL. D.* marked the fruition of a project that had matured for almost thirty years. Boswell died in 1795, his biography already recognized as a masterpiece. In recent years, the posthumous publication of his private papers and journals has further increased the stature of this delightful personality and wonderfully acute observer.

THE LIFE OF
SAMUEL JOHNSON

by James Boswell

Edited and Abridged, with an
Introduction, by *Frank Brady*

◯

A SIGNET CLASSIC
NEW AMERICAN LIBRARY
TIMES MIRROR
NEW YORK AND SCARBOROUGH, ONTARIO
THE NEW ENGLISH LIBRARY LIMITED, LONDON

SIGNET, SIGNET CLASSICS, SIGNETTE, MENTOR and
PLUME BOOKS are published *in the United States* by
The New American Library, Inc.,
1301 Avenue of the Americas, New York, New York 10019,
in Canada by The New American Library of Canada Limited,
81 Mack Avenue, Scarborough, 704, Ontario,
in the United Kingdom by The New English Library Limited,
Barnard's Inn, Holborn, London E.C. 1, England

3 4 5 6 7 8 9 10 11

First Printing, January, 1968

PRINTED IN THE UNITED STATES OF AMERICA

CONTENTS

CONTENTS

INTRODUCTION

I

The only period in English literature since the Renaissance to be named after a writer is the Age of Johnson. This label is a misnomer, since no period shows more divergent literary trends; nor is Johnson clearly the greatest writer of his time as Shakespeare and Milton are of theirs. But the name attests to the fascination Johnson exerted over his contemporaries. As he himself remarked to Boswell, "I believe there is hardly a day in which there is not something about me in the newspapers." The fascination endures, caught forever in the light and shade of Boswell's biography.

Eighteenth-century and modern views of Johnson, however, overlap rather than coincide; they emphasize different aspects of his varied career. Born in 1709, the son of a provincial bookseller, Johnson was in turn a humiliatingly poor Oxford student, an unsuccessful schoolmaster, a Grub Street hack, and then suddenly the author of *London* (1738), a poem so powerful that Pope, the greatest poet of the century, acutely and generously acknowledged its merit. Eleven more years passed, notable mainly for his striking "Life of Savage" (1744), before Johnson published his second great poem, *The Vanity of Human Wishes* (1749). Almost simultaneously his only play, *Irene,* was staged unsuccessfully. But it was his series of periodical essays, *The Rambler* (1750–52), and, more important, the *Dictionary of the English Language* (1755), which established him as the dominant literary figure of his time. *Rasselas* (1759), his edition of Shakespeare (1765), the *Journey to the Western Islands of Scotland* (1775), and the *Lives of the Poets* (1779–81) confirmed this position.

To his contemporaries, Johnson was primarily a lexicographer and moralist. (The *Lives of the Poets* was published too late in his career to alter his general reputation much.) Why

7

his *Dictionary* made him so famous is likely to seem puzzling; who today except a specialist could name the editors of the *Oxford English Dictionary?* Apart from its excellence, the fame of Johnson's *Dictionary* rests on an historical accident: it appeared at the right linguistic moment. Today native English speakers assume unselfconsciously that English is the world's dominant language, but in the mid-eighteenth century, French was the international language. English, as the language of Shakespeare, Milton, Dryden, and Pope, was certainly respectable, but it had no authoritative basis. We smile a little at the idea of a prescriptive basis for a language, but the educated Englishman of the time, trained in the fixities of Latin, was looking for an equivalent to the monumental dictionary of the French Academy. This, Johnson's *Dictionary* provided.

A remark in his "Life of Milton" defines what Johnson meant as a "moralist" to his contemporaries: "We are perpetually moralists, but we are geometricians only by chance." Johnson is not distinguishing humanist from scientist here, but man facing the common range of ethical problems from man as specialist or technician. And the Johnson of *The Rambler* and *Rasselas* shows a mind unequaled among English writers for penetrating common sense. His judgment is sometimes arbitrary or limited by the prejudices of his age, and it is always suspicious of the romantic or imaginative. But even at their most unreasonable, Johnson's views can never be dismissed as absurd; they demand answers. And time and again, they are impressive in their insight, an insight based on Johnson's insistence on thinking for himself. As he told Boswell:

> My dear friend, clear your *mind* of cant. You may *talk* as other people do: you may say to a man, "Sir, I am your most humble servant." You are *not* his most humble servant. You may say, "These are sad times; it is a melancholy thing to be reserved to such times." You don't mind the times. . . . You may *talk* in this manner; it is a mode of talking in Society: but don't *think* foolishly.

For the eighteenth century, the moral and the aesthetic were as inseparable as content and form are today thought to be: the moral was a work's content and the aesthetic its form. Modern critics tend to separate the two and to emphasize the aesthetic, which accounts in part for our considering Johnson today mainly as a critic, poet, and quasi-novelist. To approach Johnson in the modern manner, to ask, "What is the structure of *Rasselas?*" or "What is the function of the portrait in *The Vanity of Human Wishes?*" (a couple of tired

8

but useful questions) can surely lead to a better grasp of his technique. Johnson himself would have taken a professional interest in such questions, or even in what he might have called "the niceties of verbal criticism," as his discussion of Pope's epitaphs illustrates. But he would have dismissed any attempt at purely aesthetic criticism as having only limited significance, just as he would have found the idea of "art for art's sake" incomprehensible.

Among Johnson's best works, *The Vanity of Human Wishes* and *Rasselas* particularly insist on his moral concern. They express a somber though always orthodox outlook in powerful and moving language, notable for its precise use of abstractions to enforce general truths. The *Lives of the Poets*, that masterpiece of his old age, focused Johnson's talent for seeing a man's life and work as a unity, and for seizing the central issues that they posed. The "Life of Cowley" includes the most memorable discussion of metaphysical poetry in English. The lives of Dryden and Pope gave opportunity for extended illustration and defense of the neoclassical view of literature. Even where Johnson is unsympathetic, as in his treatment of "Lycidas" or Gray's odes, his views must always be reckoned with. As Macaulay said, "At the very worst, they mean something, a praise to which much of what is called criticism in our time has no pretensions."

It was "Dictionary Johnson," the author of the *Rambler* essays and *Rasselas*, that Boswell venerated as a young man. The Johnson whom he met on that famous day in the back parlor of Tom Davies' bookshop was naturally a far more complex figure. Readers of the *Life* may be forgiven for thinking that it presents the "whole" Johnson, but it is important to remember that it is Johnson refracted through Boswell's eyes. Boswell himself was well aware of this obvious fact, and he delighted, as he says, in including as many other views of Johnson as he could. Fanny Burney tells an amusing story of how Boswell pursued her from the Chapel to the Queen's Lodge at Windsor, saying,

> Yes, madam; you must give me some of your choice little notes of the Doctor's; we have seen him long enough upon stilts; I want to show him in a new light. Grave Sam, and great Sam, and solemn Sam, and learned Sam,—all these he has appeared over and over. Now I want to entwine a wreath of the graces across his brow; I want to show him as gay Sam, agreeable Sam, pleasant Sam.

His lack of success with prim Miss Burney was not typical.

Boswell was born in 1740, the son of an eminent Scottish judge who bore the judicial title of Lord Auchinleck. Educated at Edinburgh, Glasgow, and Utrecht universities, he became a moderately successful advocate at the Scottish bar, and eventually inherited a large but encumbered estate in Ayrshire. His fondest desire was a seat in the House of Commons, which would have enabled him to assert the consequence of the Boswells of Auchinleck and to live part of each year in London, a city he loved. He never reached this goal, and his transfer to the English bar in 1786 proved a disastrous end to his legal career. But as a writer, he early achieved great success with his *Account of Corsica* (1768), which was notable for its "Memoirs" of Pascal Paoli, the Corsican George Washington. This portrait, based on an adventurous trip to the then isolated island of Corsica, provided a brief but important model for Boswell's later depiction of Johnson.

Fundamentally, Boswell regarded himself neither as an advocate nor as a writer, but as "a gentleman of ancient blood, the pride of which was his predominant passion." Yet he wrote all his life, and as instinctively as he breathed: lyric poems, an allegorical novel, unfinished plays, political pamphlets and ballads, and any number of newspaper squibs on subjects that caught his attention. Most important he kept extensive journals. Of the works published during his lifetime, only *Corsica* and his two books on Johnson were to endure. As soon as Johnson died in December, 1784, Boswell, who had long made known an intention to write his life, was pressed for a full-length biography. He determined instead to print first his *Journal of a Tour to the Hebrides*, which could be quickly prepared for the press and which would demonstrate, in its detailed, authentic account of Johnson's conversation, his claim to be Johnson's authoritative biographer. Published in the fall of 1785, after the usual delays unanticipated by authors, the *Tour* was highly successful, and it encouraged Boswell to persist with the greater work through six long, intermittent, and often distressing years of work. For months at a time the biography was forgotten while Boswell pursued legal and political projects that never materialized. Periods of dissipation and depression also intervened. Indeed, it is possible, though unlikely, that the *Life* would never have been finished without the sustained prodding and assistance of his close friend, the eminent Shakespearean scholar, Edmond Malone. But for all of Malone's considerable help, Boswell deserves full credit for the book that was published on May 16, 1791, the twenty-eighth anniversary of his first meeting with Johnson.

The reception of the *Life* was all Boswell could have hoped for. Though the two quarto volumes cost a substantial two guineas, the first edition of 1,750 copies was almost sold out within a year. A second edition was published in 1793, and

Boswell was preparing the third at the time of his death in May, 1795. This popularity partly reflected a *succès de scandale:* the overlapping literary and social worlds of London saw themselves depicted with a brilliant and, in the opinion of many, unseemly frankness. Boswell had suppressed certain names and exchanges, but he was an erratic censor. Relatively trivial incidents were heavily disguised, while embarrassing scenes were presented in detail or so lightly veiled that no one could be in doubt as to who was involved.

But the inclusion of amusing gossip could never explain even the *Life*'s contemporary reception, to say nothing of its enduring popularity. From the beginning, its readers were agreed on one matter: it was readable to the point of fascination. Edmund Burke told George III that it was the most entertaining book he had ever read. Some of these readers also recognized that it was a very fine, indeed a great, book. And a few very discerning critics realized that Boswell was a great writer. For one of the most impressive aspects of the *Life* was the art with which Boswell concealed art.

II

George Bernard Shaw's comment that Boswell was the dramatist who invented Johnson points to the basic critical problem raised by the *Life:* the necessity of realizing that it is more than a biographical record, that it is a work of art. So much of its material, for example, we now know was taken from Boswell's journals that it is possible to consider the journals themselves as the larger work of which the *Life* represents a selection centered on Johnson. Even so, the *Life* remains a distinct entity, conceived of and published as such, and one that, of course, takes much from sources other than the journals.

Long before the existence of these journals became known in this century, however, critics found the *Life* a puzzle. *Why* is it the greatest biography ever written? The plain if general answer that a great writer treated his perfect subject in an appropriate manner would have been thought absurd by most nineteenth-century critics. Their tendency to confuse author with character, poet with poem, fatally disqualified them for understanding many eighteenth-century works. If Swift is Gulliver, then Thackeray had reason to denounce his depraved imagination. In dealing with "factual" biography, this difficulty is naturally compounded. If there is no distinction between Boswell the author and Boswell the character, then Boswell was indeed an innocent, even a simpleton. This confusion of author and character already was evident in Boswell's time, and he specifically warned against it at the end of the Dedication to Reynolds. There still are readers who pay no attention.

Boswell brought on part of this trouble by his self-presentation as intellectually and morally inferior to Johnson. Famous nineteenth-century critics of the *Life* like Macaulay and, especially, Carlyle had their heroes, but ordinarily they were heroes of the past, and neither Macaulay nor Carlyle usually betrays any sign that he felt at all inferior to his subjects. (My guess is that Carlyle would have found Frederick the Great as intolerable at close quarters as Voltaire did.) Exaggerating Boswell's dependence upon Johnson and his humility before him, they treated him with outrageous condescension. Macaulay even stated that if Boswell "had not been a great fool, he would never have been a great writer." But great fools do not write great books.

Carlyle took a similar, as well as characteristic, line: the greatness of the *Life* inhered in Johnson himself, the outstanding man of his age. Boswell he credited with a loving heart open to wisdom, but little else. (With a skill in physiognomy denied to lesser visionaries, Carlyle discovered that "the under part of Boswell's face is of a low, almost brutish character.") Here, Boswell's insistence on the accuracy of his record misled critics. Carlyle and others seem to assume, in spite of explicit evidence to the contrary in the *Life*, that Boswell was a kind of stenographer, who recorded Johnson's wit and wisdom on the spot. But such a practice is contrary to the customs of any age, would have paralyzed conversation, and would have led to Boswell's speedy exclusion from polite society. In fact, Boswell did not operate in this way. He was sometimes days, and more often weeks, behind in keeping his journals, which vary from being fully written to being so condensed and cryptic that where he failed to expand the record in the *Life*, his modern editors often cannot reconstruct his meaning. What Boswell really asserted was the *essential* accuracy of his record; only some device like a tape recorder could precisely preserve every word. The most telling evidence in support of Boswell's assertion is that apart from a few obviously self-involved pleaders, no one who knew Johnson well attacked the *Life* as inaccurate. But the simplest answer to Carlyle's dismissal of Boswell is that great books are not written by stenographers either.

Another puzzling aspect of the *Life* was its originality. It was quite unlike any previous biography in English, especially in its extensively reproduced conversations. Though Boswell praised Johnson as the greatest of biographers, it had little or nothing in common with his "Life of Savage" or "Life of Pope"—to cite two quite different models—in struc-

12

ture or presentation of material. Boswell does mention Mason's "Memoirs of Gray" as a model for its "plan," its chronological interweaving of materials, but Mason's work actually consists of a large selection of Gray's letters thinly interspersed with commentary. At most, it was a justification for Boswell's procedure rather than a pattern. The one biographer who did influence Boswell greatly was Plutarch, "the prince of ancient biographers," but Plutarch's influence was mainly indirect, one of spirit rather than technique.

To the extent that the *Life* has a model, it is an eighteenth-century novel like *Clarissa*. Both emphasize scene, conversation, trivial but characteristic detail; both use tone of voice, gesture, and bodily attitude as important clues to states of mind as well as to the meaning of speech and action. In addition, the casting of conversation dramatically derives perhaps from printed plays, and a couple of scenes that involve "irrelevant" association of ideas and breakdowns in communication may recall his early enthusiasm for *Tristram Shandy*.

Yet no model or analogue is of decisive importance. Boswell's modes of presentation follow from his clearly stated desire to give a "Flemish picture" of Johnson, one that allowed Johnson to emerge from the accretion of minute circumstances. The accumulation of Johnsonian material in his journals not only permitted this unusual procedure, it demanded it. Boswell never doubted the unique value of this material. "I will venture to promise," he wrote to Hugh Blair (April 21, 1786), "that my Life of my revered friend will be the richest piece of biography that has ever appeared. The bullion will be immense, whatever defects there may be in the workmanship." Where he had his fully written journals to go on, Boswell worked carefully but with instinctive assurance. Often tearing pages directly from them for printer's copy, he provided introductions and transitions, cut irrelevant material, changed an occasional phrase, and little else was necessary. Even where the journals were scanty, he often could reconstruct scene and conversation in confident detail.

In contrast to this handling of specific scenes in the *Life*, Boswell found that the inclusion of other material into its general structure offered certain problems. His solutions to these problems were simple to the point of seeming primitive. Johnson's correspondence, for example, was ordinarily just inserted according to date; the reminiscences he acquired from Johnson's friends, if not chronological, were usually inserted where Boswell's journals were thin or nonexistent. William Maxwell's recollections, for example, are grouped under 1770, one of the years in which Johnson and Boswell did not meet. Other material might be placed to create narra-

13

tive suspense, such as the imitations of Johnson's style, which appear just before the account of his last illness.

So "primitive" an arrangement gives the effect of being natural to the point of artlessness. It is not really surprising that J. W. Croker thought the *Life* just a grab bag of all available material, and so calmly inserted into his edition of 1831 all the various Johnsonian accounts he found of interest, including the whole of the *Tour of the Hebrides!* The distended product was its own refutation, though Macaulay's savage attack on it drove the nails into the coffin.

Actually, Boswell had not included everything at his disposal. Some accounts he rejected as trivial or uninteresting; some as improbable; some, such as Mrs. Desmoulins' vivid and still unprinted description of Johnson's sexual feelings, as unacceptable to contemporary taste. (One such conversation about marital infidelity was not canceled until the *Life* was in proof. It was "mighty good stuff," Boswell told Malone regretfully.) And some material he apparently rejected on artistic grounds. For example, he learned that on Johnson's last visit to the Reverend John Taylor in 1784, one of Taylor's friends maliciously urged Johnson to eat so much that it was feared he would die, and a drastic remedy was applied. Boswell hardly could have doubted the truth of this story, but it was omitted. It didn't fit his pattern.

Whatever the defects of Boswell's apparently unselective and sometimes discontinuous presentation of material, it enabled him to handle one major structural problem, that of fullness of presentation, with brilliance. Boswell's aim, as his conversation with Fanny Burney illustrates, was to present Johnson as totally and from as many perspectives as possible. The diverse material of his "Flemish picture"—selections from published works, diaries, letters, unprinted poems, legal opinions, and conversations—showed Johnson in many roles, ranging from the most public, as literary and moral arbiter, to something close to the most intimate self.

More remarkably, though Johnson is always at the center of the picture, he is constantly qualified by the perspectives of others. In the series of linked scenes that composes so much of the *Life,* Johnson is defined by his relationships: as Dr. Major to Goldsmith's Dr. Minor; as Garrick's constant critic and jealous "proprietor"; as Burke's intellectual equal and antagonist; as Langton's loving but amused friend. And the comments of his contemporaries define him directly: Goldsmith's "if you were to make little fishes talk, they would talk like WHALES"; Garrick's "Who's for *poonsh?*"; Lord Pembroke's comment on "his *bow-wow way*"; Dr. Bos-

14

well's description, "a robust genius, born to grapple with whole libraries."

No biography compares with Boswell's in the vividness and firmness of outline of its background figures. They never seem to exist simply to provide perspective on Johnson; Boswell's presentation makes them live for themselves. What, for example, could better define Topham Beauclerk, that elegant and worldly aristocrat, than his saying "he could not conceive a more humiliating situation than to be clapped on the back" by the actor-bookseller-bankrupt, Tom Davies? Or more accurately suggest a minor character like Johnson's Oxford contemporary, Oliver Edwards, than his immortal contrast between philosophy and cheerfulness? Even the unnamed writer of the *Ode to the Warlike Genius of Britain* (he was the Reverend William Tasker) is made memorable in a description Dickens might have envied:

> the bard was a lank bony figure, with short black hair; he was writhing himself in agitation, while Johnson read, and shewing his teeth in a grin of earnestness, exclaimed in broken sentences, and in a keen sharp tone, "Is that poetry, Sir? —Is it Pindar?"

Boswell's title page promised "a view of literature and literary men in Great-Britain, for near half a century," but the work provides more: a view of eighteenth-century character equal in immediacy to that in any contemporary novel, and far greater in scope and variety.

By far the most important background figure is, of course, Boswell himself. And his "character," instead of being an obstacle to understanding the *Life,* is a significant clue to the way in which a mass of biographical material is shaped into a work of art. The central relationship in the *Life* involves two men widely differing in age. Usually this is described as a father-son relationship, which it is among others. More important, Boswell is in search of the moral and intellectual education a great teacher can provide. This student-teacher pattern can be illustrated by a sequence of remarks all taken from the first two months of their acquaintance:

> BOSWELL: "It is benevolent to allow me to sit and hear you." "Wishing to avail myself of the opportunity which I fortunately had of consulting a sage. . . ." JOHNSON: "There is a good deal of Spain that has not been perambulated. I would have you go thither." BOSWELL: "I . . . asked his advice as to my studies." "I was so wrapt up in admiration of his extraordinary colloquial talents. . . ." JOHNSON: "A young man should read five hours in a day, and so may acquire a great deal of knowledge." BOSWELL: "He advised me,

15

when abroad, to be as much as I could with the Professors in the Universities. . . ." "He recommended to me to keep a journal of my life, full and unreserved."

(This last piece of advice, which confirmed Boswell's own practice, was the most important Johnson ever gave him.) And, in spite of occasional irritability, Johnson thoroughly enjoyed the role of master. As F. A. Pottle remarks, he usually *liked* being asked why a fox's tail was bushy.

But Johnson's major role in the *Life* is as a moralist, and it is the one Boswell's relationship with him most clearly emphasizes. The *Life*, Boswell declared, is like the *Odyssey:* the heroes of both works exemplify the power of virtue and wisdom. But for Johnson virtue and wisdom were acquired and sustained through an intense struggle, which took place not in the supernatural world of the Greek epic but in the daily confusion of ordinary existence. His weaknesses and limitations, his fundamental doubts—like the fear of eternal damnation passionately expressed just a few months before his death—in the end underline the strength of his character and achievement. The necessity of Christian fortitude is as much the theme of the *Life* as it is of that more conventional moral epic, *Paradise Lost*.

No subject or theme, however, assures the greatness of a work; the power of the *Life* finally depends on its style. Mr. Pottle has remarked that "Boswell's interpretation moves on the plane of average or normal experience, with the result that in him we seem to see the past through no kind of medium at all, or at most through plate glass." In the *Life* this style operates as a masterpiece of *trompe d'oeil:* the reader mistakes art for nature. Ironically, the continuous depreciation of Boswell has resulted from this ultimate triumph. "It is all *true*," said Carlyle, as if truth itself, and not a human being, had written the *Life*. Yet there is no more difficult art than to give the impression that nothing intervenes between the reader and what is being described.

A brief look at a dinner given by Boswell (October 16, 1769) will illustrate:

> Garrick played round him [Johnson] with a fond vivacity, taking hold of the breasts of his coat, and, looking up into his face with a lively archness, complimented him on the good health which he seemed then to enjoy; while the sage, shaking his head, beheld him with a gentle complacency. . . . Goldsmith, to divert the tedious minutes, strutted about, bragging of his dress, and I believe was seriously vain of it, for his mind was wonderfully prone to such impressions.

16

All this is Boswell, not merely the selection of gestures and actions, but the attribution of motives, and the balance of the figures: Garrick's "lively archness" against Johnson's "gentle complacency." In turn, these two, with their thorough knowledge of each other, are contrasted to Goldsmith caught up in his wonderfully blind vanity. The strong, direct words used to describe Goldsmith—"strutted about, bragging"—modulate into the tentative, calm comment of the narrator, "and I believe was seriously vain of it." And we believe it, all of it, as much as if we had been present.

FRANK BRADY

New York
September 1, 1967

17

A NOTE ON THE TEXT

The text of *The Life of Samuel Johnson* presented here is based on that of the third edition, which Boswell presumably was revising at the time of his death in 1795. The revision was completed by Malone and published in 1799. Cuts in the text are indicated by ellipses or by footnotes. Those of Boswell's notes that have been retained are signed "B." Other notes are by scholars ranging from Malone to the late R. W. Chapman, but the great standard edition of the *Life*, edited by G. B. Hill and revised by L. F. Powell, is the source for most of the annotation. I have added a few notes based on my research in the Boswell Papers at Yale.

Apart from classical quotations, which are translated and identified, sources for quotations and allusions are seldom indicated. Only those anonymous figures whose identity is both certain and important are named in the notes. Readers interested in further detail should, of course, consult the Hill-Powell edition.

No abridgment does justice to the *Life*. Hopefully, as readers become "impregnated with the Johnsonian aether," they will give themselves the pleasure of reading the entire work. The best one-volume edition is that edited by R. W. Chapman in the Oxford Standard Authors series.

I should like to thank the Editorial Committee of the Yale Editions of the Private Papers of James Boswell and the McGraw-Hill Book Company, Inc. for permission to quote from Boswell's letter to Hugh Blair (April 21, 1786).

THE LIFE OF

SAMUEL JOHNSON, LL.D.

COMPREHENDING

AN ACCOUNT OF HIS STUDIES

AND NUMEROUS WORKS

IN CHRONOLOGICAL ORDER;

A SERIES OF HIS EPISTOLARY CORRESPONDENCE

AND CONVERSATIONS WITH MANY EMINENT PERSONS;

AND

VARIOUS ORIGINAL PIECES OF HIS COMPOSITION,

NEVER BEFORE PUBLISHED:

THE WHOLE EXHIBITING A VIEW OF LITERATURE AND
LITERARY MEN IN GREAT-BRITAIN, FOR NEAR
HALF A CENTURY, DURING WHICH HE
FLOURISHED.

By James Boswell, Esq.

————————Quò fit ut OMNIS
Votiva pateat veluti descripta tabella
VITA SENIS.———— HORAT.

THE THIRD EDITION, REVISED AND AUGMENTED

DEDICATION TO
SIR JOSHUA REYNOLDS

MY DEAR SIR,—Every liberal motive that can actuate an Authour in the dedication of his labours, concurs in directing me to you, as the person to whom the following Work should be inscribed.

If there be a pleasure in celebrating the distinguished merit of a contemporary, mixed with a certain degree of vanity not altogether inexcusable, in appearing fully sensible of it, where can I find one, in complimenting whom I can with more general approbation gratify those feelings? Your excellence not only in the Art over which you have long presided with unrivalled fame, but also in Philosophy and elegant Literature, is well known to the present, and will continue to be the admiration of future ages. Your equal and placid temper, your variety of conversation, your true politeness, by which you are so amiable in private society, and that enlarged hospitality which has long made your house a common centre of union for the great, the accomplished, the learned, and the ingenious; all these qualities I can, in perfect confidence of not being accused of flattery, ascribe to you.

If a man may indulge an honest pride, in having it known to the world, that he has been thought worthy of particular attention by a person of the first eminence in the age in which he lived, whose company has been universally courted, I am justified in availing myself of the usual privilege of a Dedication, when I mention that there has been a long and uninterrupted friendship between us.

If gratitude should be acknowledged for favours received, I have this opportunity, my dear Sir, most sincerely to thank you for the many happy hours which I owe to your kindness,

21

—for the cordiality with which you have at all times been pleased to welcome me,—for the number of valuable acquaintances to whom you have introduced me,—for the *noctes cœnæque Deûm,*[1] which I have enjoyed under your roof.

If a work should be inscribed to one who is master of the subject of it, and whose approbation, therefore, must ensure it credit and success, the *Life of Dr. Johnson* is, with the greatest propriety, dedicated to Sir Joshua Reynolds, who was the intimate and beloved friend of that great man; the friend, whom he declared to be 'the most invulnerable man he knew; whom, if he should quarrel with him, he should find the most difficulty how to abuse.' You, my dear Sir, studied him, and knew him well: you venerated and admired him. Yet, luminous as he was upon the whole, you perceived all the shades which mingled in the grand composition; all the little peculiarities and slight blemishes which marked the literary Colossus. Your very warm commendation of the specimen which I gave in my *Journal of a Tour to the Hebrides,* of my being able to preserve his conversation in an authentick and lively manner, which opinion the Publick has confirmed, was the best encouragement for me to persevere in my purpose of producing the whole of my stores.

In one respect, this Work will, in some passages, be different from the former. In my *Tour,* I was almost unboundedly open in my communications, and from my eagerness to display the wonderful fertility and readiness of Johnson's wit, freely shewed to the world its dexterity, even when I was myself the object of it. I trusted that I should be liberally understood, as knowing very well what I was about, and by no means as simply unconscious of the pointed effects of the satire. I own, indeed, that I was arrogant enough to suppose that the tenour of the rest of the book would sufficiently guard me against such a strange imputation. But it seems I judged too well of the world; for, though I could scarcely believe it, I have been undoubtedly informed, that many persons, especially in distant quarters, not penetrating enough into Johnson's character, so as to understand his mode of treating his friends, have arraigned my judgement, instead of seeing that I was sensible of all that they could observe.

It is related of the great Dr. Clarke, that when in one of his leisure hours he was unbending himself with a few friends in the most playful and frolicksome manner, he observed Beau Nash approaching; upon which he suddenly stopped:

[1] 'Nights and banquets of the gods.' Horace, *Satires,* II. vi. 65.

—'My boys, (said he,) let us be grave: here comes a fool.' The world, my friend, I have found to be a great fool, as to that particular, on which it has become necessary to speak very plainly. I have, therefore, in this Work been more reserved; and though I tell nothing but the truth, I have still kept in my mind that the whole truth is not always to be exposed. This, however, I have managed so as to occasion no diminution of the pleasure which my book should afford; though malignity may sometimes be disappointed of its gratifications.

I am, my dear Sir,
Your much obliged friend,
And faithful humble servant,
JAMES BOSWELL.

London,
April 20, 1791.

... took fraud to... for to the publisher I announce to
The world my resolve never again to be a great landing capitalist... have thousand has I been... they of my own
... publicity... have thousands... to talk with... have town...
... and again I call nothing but the truth. I have will
... in my integrity, the whole... is not life worth to be
... paged... This answer I have managed so as to occasion no
examination of the case and which particular should which
... further indignity may sometimes be as possible of the true
... citizens.

I am my dear Sir,
Your much obliged friend,
And most humble servant,
JAMES BOSWELL.

London,
April 20, 1791.

ADVERTISEMENT TO
THE FIRST EDITION

I at last deliver to the world a Work which I have long promised, and of which I am afraid, too high expectations have been raised. The delay of its publication must be imputed, in a considerable degree, to the extraordinary zeal which has been shewn by distinguished persons in all quarters to supply me with additional information concerning its illustrious subject; resembling in this the grateful tribes of ancient nations, of which every individual was eager to throw a stone upon the grave of a departed Hero, and thus to share in the pious office of erecting an honourable monument to his memory.

The labour and anxious attention with which I have collected and arranged the materials of which these volumes are composed, will hardly be conceived by those who read them with careless facility. The stretch of mind and prompt assiduity by which so many conversations were preserved, I myself, at some distance of time, contemplate with wonder; and I must be allowed to suggest, that the nature of the work, in other respects, as it consists of innumerable detached particulars, all which, even the most minute, I have spared no pains to ascertain with a scrupulous authenticity, has occasioned a degree of trouble far beyond that of any other species of composition. Were I to detail the books which I have consulted, and the inquiries which I have found it necessary to make by various channels, I should probably be thought ridiculously ostentatious. Let me only observe, as a specimen of my trouble, that I have sometimes been obliged to run half over London, in order to fix a date correctly; which, when I had accomplished, I well knew would obtain me no praise, though a failure would have been to my discredit. And after all, perhaps, hard as it may be, I shall not be surprized if omissions or mistakes be pointed out with invidious severity. I have also been extremely careful as to the exactness of my quotations; holding that there is a respect due to the publick which should oblige every Authour to attend to this, and never to presume to introduce them with,—'I think I have read;'—or,—'If I remember right;'—when the originals may be examined.

I beg leave to express my warmest thanks to those who have been pleased to favour me with communications and advice in the conduct of my Work. But I cannot sufficiently acknowledge my obligations to my friend Mr. Malone, who was so good as to allow me to read to him almost the whole of my manuscript, and made such remarks as were greatly for the advantage of the Work; though it is but fair to him to mention, that upon many occasions I differed from him, and followed my own judgement. I regret exceedingly that I was deprived of the benefit of his revision, when not more than one half of the book had passed through the press. . . .

ADVERTISEMENT TO
THE SECOND EDITION

That I was anxious for the success of a Work which had employed much of my time and labour, I do not wish to conceal: but whatever doubts I at any time entertained, have been entirely removed by the very favourable reception with which it has been honoured. That reception has excited my best exertions to render my Book more perfect; and in this endeavour I have had the assistance not only of some of my particular friends, but of many other learned and ingenious men, by which I have been enabled to rectify some mistakes, and to enrich the Work with many valuable additions. . . .

In reflecting that the illustrious subject of this Work, by being more extensively and intimately known, however elevated before, has risen in the veneration and love of mankind, I feel a satisfaction beyond what fame can afford. We cannot, indeed, too much or too often admire his wonderful powers of mind, when we consider that the principal store of wit and wisdom which this Work contains, was not a particular selection from his general conversation, but was merely his occasional talk at such times as I had the good fortune to be in his company; and, without doubt, if his discourse at other periods had been collected with the same attention, the whole tenor of what he uttered would have been found equally excellent.

His strong, clear, and animated enforcement of religion, morality, loyalty, and subordination, while it delights and improves the wise and the good, will, I trust, prove an effectual antidote to that detestable sophistry which has been lately imported from France, under the false name of Philosophy, and with a malignant industry has been employed against the

27

peace, good order, and happiness of society, in our free and prosperous country; but thanks be to GOD, *without producing the pernicious effects which were hoped for by its propagators.*

It seems to me in my moments of self-complacency, that this extensive biographical work, however inferior in its nature may in one respect be assimilated to the ODYSSEY. *Amidst a thousand entertaining and instructive episodes the* HERO *is never long out of sight; for they are all in some degree connected with him; and* HE, *in the whole course of the History, is exhibited by the Author for the best advantage of his readers.*

—Quid virtus et quid sapientia possit,
Utile proposuit nobis exemplar Ulyssen.[1]

Should there be any cold-blooded and morose mortals who really dislike this Book, I will give them a story to apply. When the great Duke of Marlborough, *accompanied by* Lord Cadogan, *was one day reconnoitering the army in Flanders, a heavy rain came on, and they both called for their cloaks. Lord Cadogan's servant, a good humoured alert lad, brought his Lordship's in a minute. The Duke's servant, a lazy sulky dog, was so sluggish, that his Grace being wet to the skin, reproved him, and had for answer with a grunt, 'I came as fast as I could,' upon which the Duke calmly said, 'Cadogan, I would not for a thousand pounds have that fellow's temper.'*

There are some men, I believe, who have, or think they have, a very small share of vanity. Such may speak of their literary fame in a decorous style of diffidence. But I confess, that I am so formed by nature and by habit, that to restrain the effusion of delight, on having obtained such fame, to me would be truly painful. Why then should I suppress it? Why 'out of the abundance of the heart' should I not speak? Let me then mention with a warm, but no insolent exultation, that I have been regaled with spontaneous praise of my work by many and various persons eminent for their rank, learning, talents and accomplishments; much of which praise I have under their hands to be reposited in my archives at Auchinleck. An honourable and reverend friend speaking of the favourable reception of my volumes, even in the circles of fashion and elegance, said to me, 'you have made them all talk Johnson,'—*Yes, I may add, I have* Johnsonised *the land; and I trust they will not only talk, but think,* Johnson. . . .

[1] 'To show what virtue and wisdom can do, he displays Ulysses, an instructive pattern.' Horace, *Epistles*, I. ii. 17–18.

THE LIFE OF
SAMUEL JOHNSON, LL.D.

To write the Life of him who excelled all mankind in writing the lives of others, and who, whether we consider his extraordinary endowments, or his various works, has been equalled by few in any age, is an arduous, and may be reckoned in me a presumptuous task.

Had Dr. Johnson written his own life, in conformity with the opinion which he has given, that every man's life may be best written by himself; had he employed in the preservation of his own history, that clearness of narration and elegance of language in which he has embalmed so many eminent persons, the world would probably have had the most perfect example of biography that was ever exhibited. But although he at different times, in a desultory manner, committed to writing many particulars of the progress of his mind and fortunes, he never had persevering diligence enough to form them into a regular composition. Of these memorials a few have been preserved; but the greater part was consigned by him to the flames, a few days before his death.

As I had the honour and happiness of enjoying his friendship for upwards of twenty years; as I had the scheme of writing his life constantly in view; as he was well apprised of this circumstance, and from time to time obligingly satisfied my inquiries, by communicating to me the incidents of his early years; as I acquired a facility in recollecting, and was very assiduous in recording, his conversation, of which the extraordinary vigour and vivacity constituted one of the first features of his character; and as I have spared no pains in obtaining materials concerning him, from every quarter where I could discover that they were to be found, and have been favoured with the most liberal communications by his friends; I flatter myself that few biographers have entered upon such a work as this, with more advantages; independent of literary abilities, in which I am not vain enough to compare myself with some great names who have gone before me in this kind of writing.

Since my work was announced, several Lives and Memoirs of Dr. Johnson have been published, the most voluminous of which is one compiled for the booksellers of London, by Sir John Hawkins, Knight, a man, whom, during my long intimacy with Dr. Johnson, I never saw in his company, I think but once, and I am sure not above twice. Johnson might have esteemed him for his decent, religious demeanour, and his knowledge of books and literary history; but from the rigid formality of his manners, it is evident that they never could have lived together with companionable ease and familiarity; nor had Sir John Hawkins that nice perception which was necessary to mark the finer and less obvious parts of Johnson's character. His being appointed one of his executors, gave him an opportunity of taking possession of such fragments of a diary and other papers as were left; of which, before delivering them up to the residuary legatee, whose property they were, he endeavoured to extract the substance. In this he has not been very successful, as I have found upon a perusal of those papers, which have been since transferred to me. Sir John Hawkins's ponderous labours, I must acknowledge, exhibit a *farrago,* of which a considerable portion is not devoid of entertainment to the lovers of literary gossiping; but besides its being swelled out with long unnecessary extracts from various works (even one of several leaves from Osborne's Harleian Catalogue, and those not compiled by Johnson, but by Oldys), a very small part of it relates to the person who is the subject of the book; and, in that, there is such an inaccuracy in the statement of facts, as in so solemn an authour is hardly excusable, and certainly makes his narrative very unsatisfactory. But what is still worse, there is throughout the whole of it a dark uncharitable cast, by which the most unfavourable construction is put upon almost every circumstance in the character and conduct of my illustrious friend; who, I trust, will, by a true and fair delineation, be vindicated both from the injurious misrepresentations of this authour, and from the slighter aspersions of a lady who once lived in great intimacy with him.[1] . . .

Instead of melting down my materials into one mass, and constantly speaking in my own person, by which I might

<hr/>

[1] Mrs. Thrale.

have appeared to have more merit in the execution of the work, I have resolved to adopt and enlarge upon the excellent plan of Mr. Mason, in his Memoirs of Gray. Wherever narrative is necessary to explain, connect, and supply, I furnish it to the best of my abilities; but in the chronological series of Johnson's life, which I trace as distinctly as I can, year by year, I produce, wherever it is in my power, his own minutes, letters or conversation, being convinced that this mode is more lively, and will make my readers better acquainted with him, than ever most of those were who actually knew him, but could know him only partially; whereas there is here an accumulation of intelligence from various points, by which his character is more fully understood and illustrated.

Indeed I cannot conceive a more perfect mode of writing any man's life, than not only relating all the most important events of it in their order, but interweaving what he privately wrote, and said, and thought; by which mankind are enabled as it were to see him live, and to 'live o'er each scene' with him, as he actually advanced through the several stages of his life. Had his other friends been as diligent and ardent as I was, he might have been almost entirely preserved. As it is, I will venture to say that he will be seen in this work more completely than any man who has ever yet lived.

And he will be seen as he really was; for I profess to write, not his panegyrick, which must be all praise, but his Life; which, great and good as he was, must not be supposed to be entirely perfect. To be as he was, is indeed subject of panegyrick enough to any man in this state of being; but in every picture there should be shade as well as light, and when I delineate him without reserve, I do what he himself recommended, both by his precept and his example.

'If the biographer writes from personal knowledge, and makes haste to gratify the publick curiosity, there is danger lest his interest, his fear, his gratitude, or his tenderness overpower his fidelity, and tempt him to conceal, if not to invent. There are many who think it an act of piety to hide the faults or failings of their friends, even when they can no longer suffer by their detection; we therefore see whole ranks of characters adorned with uniform panegyrick, and not to be known from one another but by extrinsick and casual circumstances. "Let me remember, (says Hale,) when I find myself inclined to pity a criminal, that there is likewise a pity due to the country." If we owe regard to the memory of the dead, there is yet more respect to be paid to knowledge, to virtue and to truth.'

What I consider as the peculiar value of the following work, is, the quantity it contains of Johnson's conversation; which is universally acknowledged to have been eminently instructive and entertaining; and of which the specimens that I have give upon a former occasion, have been received with so much approbation, that I have good grounds for supposing that the world will not be indifferent to more ample communications of a similar nature.

That the conversation of a celebrated man, if his talents have been exerted in conversation, will best display his character, is, I trust, too well established in the judgment of mankind, to be at all shaken by a sneering observation of Mr. Mason, in his *Memoirs of Mr. William Whitehead,* in which there is literally no *Life,* but a mere dry narrative of facts. I do not think it was quite necessary to attempt a depreciation of what is universally esteemed, because it was not to be found in the immediate object of the ingenious writer's pen; for in truth, from a man so still and so tame, as to be contented to pass many years as the domestick companion of a superannuated lord and lady, conversation worth recording could no more be expected, than from a Chinese mandarin on a chimney-piece, or the fantastick figures on a gilt leather skreen.

If authority be required, let us appeal to Plutarch, the prince of ancient biographers. . . . 'Nor is it always in the most distinguished atchievements that men's virtues or vices may be best discerned; but very often an action of small note, a short saying, or a jest, shall distinguish a person's real character more than the greatest sieges, or the most important battles.'

To this may be added the sentiments of the very man whose life I am about to exhibit.

'The business of the biographer is often to pass slightly over those performances and incidents which produce vulgar greatness, to lead the thoughts into domestick privacies, and display the minute details of daily life, where exteriour appendages are cast aside, and men excel each other only by prudence and by virtue. The account of Thuanus is with great propriety said by its authour to have been written, that it might lay open to posterity the private and familiar character of that man, *cujus ingenium et candorem ex ipsius scriptis sunt olim semper miraturi,* whose candour and genius will to the end of time be by his writings preserved in admiration.

'There are many invisible circumstances, which whether we read as enquirers after natural or moral knowledge, whether we intend to enlarge our science, or increase our virtue, are more important than publick occurrences. Thus Sallust, the great master of nature, has not forgot in his account of Catiline to remark, that his walk was now quick, and again slow, as an indication of a mind revolving with violent commotion. Thus the story of Melancthon affords a striking lecture on the value of time, by informing us, that when he had made an appointment, he expected not only the hour, but the minute to be fixed, that the day might not run out in the idleness of suspense; and all the plans and enterprises of De Wit are now of less importance to the world than that part of his personal character, which represents him as careful of his health, and negligent of his life.

'But biography has often been allotted to writers, who seem very little acquainted with the nature of their task, or very negligent about the performance. They rarely afford any other account than might be collected from publick papers, but imagine themselves writing a life, when they exhibit a chronological series of actions or preferments; and have so little regard to the manners or behaviour of their heroes, that more knowledge may be gained of a man's real character, by a short conversation with one of his servants, than from a formal and studied narrative, begun with his pedigree, and ended with his funeral.

'There are, indeed, some natural reasons why these narratives are often written by such as were not likely to give much instruction or delight, and why most accounts of particular persons are barren and useless. If a life be delayed till interest and envy are at an end, we may hope for impartiality, but must expect little intelligence; for the incidents which give excellence to biography are of a volatile and evanescent kind, such as soon escape the memory, and are transmitted by tradition. We know how few can pourtray a living acquaintance, except by his most prominent and observable particularities, and the grosser features of his mind; and it may be easily imagined how much of this little knowledge may be lost in imparting it, and how soon a succession of copies will lose all resemblance of the original.'

I am fully aware of the objections which may be made to the minuteness on some occasions of my detail of Johnson's conversation, and how happily it is adapted for the petty exercise of ridicule, by men of superficial understanding and ludicrous fancy; but I remain firm and confident in my opinion, that minute particulars are frequently characteristick, and always amusing, when they relate to a distinguished man. I am therefore exceedingly unwilling that any thing, however slight, which my illustrious friend thought it worth his while to express, with any degree of point, should perish. For this almost superstitious reverence, I have found very old and venerable authority, quoted by our great modern prelate, Secker, in whose tenth sermon there is the following passage:

'*Rabbi David Kimchi,* a noted Jewish Commentator, who lived above five hundred years ago, explains that passage in the first Psalm, *His leaf also shall not wither,* from Rabbins yet older than himself, thus: That *even the idle talk,* so he expresses it, *of a good man ought to be regarded;* the most superfluous things he saith are always of some value. And other ancient authours have the same phrase, nearly in the same sense.'

Of one thing I am certain, that considering how highly the small portion which we have of the table-talk and other anecdotes of our celebrated writers is valued, and how earnestly it is regretted that we have not more, I am justified in preserving rather too many of Johnson's sayings, than too few; especially as from the diversity of dispositions it cannot be known with certainty beforehand, whether what may seem trifling to some, and perhaps to the collector himself, may not be most agreeable to many; and the greater number that an authour can please in any degree, the more pleasure does there arise to a benevolent mind.

To those who are weak enough to think this a degrading task, and the time and labour which have been devoted to it misemployed, I shall content myself with opposing the authority of the greatest man of any age, JULIUS CÆSAR, of whom Bacon observes, that 'in his book of Apothegms which he collected, we see that he esteemed it more honour to make himself but a pair of tables, to take the wise and pithy words of others, than to have every word of his own to be made an apothegm or an oracle.'

Having said thus much by way of introduction, I commit the following pages to the candour of the Publick.

SAMUEL JOHNSON was born at Lichfield, in Staffordshire, on the 18th of September, N.S., 1709; and his initiation into the Christian Church was not delayed; for his baptism is recorded, in the register of St. Mary's parish in that city, to have been performed on the day of his birth. His father is there stiled *Gentleman,* a circumstance of which an ignorant panegyrist has praised him for not being proud; when the truth is, that the appellation of Gentleman, though now lost in the indiscriminate assumption of *Esquire,* was commonly taken by those who could not boast of gentility. His father was Michael Johnson, a native of Derbyshire, of obscure extraction, who settled in Lichfield as a bookseller and stationer. His mother was Sarah Ford, descended of an ancient race of substantial yeomanry in Warwickshire. They were well advanced in years when they married, and never had

34

more than two children, both sons; Samuel, their first born, who lived to be the illustrious character whose various excellence I am to endeavour to record, and Nathanael, who died in his twenty-fifth year.

Mr. Michael Johnson was a man of a large and robust body, and of a strong and active mind; yet, as in the most solid rocks veins of unsound substance are often discovered, there was in him a mixture of that disease, the nature of which eludes the most minute enquiry, though the effects are well known to be a weariness of life, an unconcern about those things which agitate the greater part of mankind, and a general sensation of gloomy wretchedness. From him then his son inherited, with some other qualities, 'a vile melancholy,' which in his too strong expression of any disturbance of the mind, 'made him mad all his life, at least not sober.' Michael was, however, forced by the narrowness of his circumstances to be very diligent in business, not only in his shop, but by occasionally resorting to several towns in the neighbourhood, some of which were at a considerable distance from Lichfield. At that time booksellers' shops in the provincial towns of England were very rare, so that there was not one even in Birmingham, in which town old Mr. Johnson used to open a shop every market-day. He was a pretty good Latin scholar, and a citizen so creditable as to be made one of the magistrates of Lichfield; and, being a man of good sense, and skill in his trade, he acquired a reasonable share of wealth, of which however he afterwards lost the greatest part, by engaging unsuccessfully in a manufacture of parchment. He was a zealous high-churchman and royalist, and retained his attachment to the unfortunate house of Stuart, though he reconciled himself, by casuistical arguments of expediency and necessity, to take the oaths imposed by the prevailing power. . . .

Johnson's mother was a woman of distinguished understanding. I asked his old school-fellow, Mr. Hector, surgeon, of Birmingham, if she was not vain of her son. He said, 'she had too much good sense to be vain, but she knew her son's value.' Her piety was not inferiour to her understanding; and to her must be ascribed those early impressions of religion upon the mind of her son, from which the world afterwards derived so much benefit. He told me, that he remembered distinctly having had the first notice of Heaven, 'a place to which good people went,' and hell, 'a place to which bad people went,' communicated to him by her, when a little child in bed with her; and that it might be the better fixed in his memory, she sent him to repeat it to Thomas Jackson, their man-servant; he not being in the way, this was not done; but

35

there was no occasion for any artificial aid for its preservation.

In following so very eminent a man from his cradle to his grave, every minute particular, which can throw light on the progress of his mind, is interesting. That he was remarkable, even in his earliest years, may easily be supposed; for to use his own words in his Life of Sydenham,

'That the strength of his understanding, the accuracy of his discernment, and ardour of his curiosity, might have been remarked from his infancy, by a diligent observer, there is no reason to doubt. For, there is no instance of any man, whose history has been minutely related, that did not in every part of life discover the same proportion of intellectual vigour.'

In all such investigations it is certainly unwise to pay too much attention to incidents which the credulous relate with eager satisfaction, and the more scrupulous or witty enquirer considers only as topicks of ridicule: Yet there is a traditional story of the infant Hercules of toryism, so curiously characteristick, that I shall not withhold it. It was communicated to me in a letter from Miss Mary Adye, of Lichfield.

'When Dr. Sacheverel was at Lichfield, Johnson was not quite three years old. My grandfather Hammond observed him at the cathedral perched upon his father's shoulders, listening and gaping at the much celebrated preacher. Mr. Hammond asked Mr. Johnson how he could possibly think of bringing such an infant to church, and in the midst of so great a croud. He answered, because it was impossible to keep him at home; for, young as he was, he believed he had caught the publick spirit and zeal for Sacheverel, and would have staid for ever in the church, satisfied with beholding him.'

Nor can I omit a little instance of that jealous independence of spirit, and impetuosity of temper, which never forsook him. The fact was acknowledged to me by himself, upon the authority of his mother. One day, when the servant who used to be sent to school to conduct him home, had not come in time, he set out by himself, though he was then so near-sighted, and he was obliged to stoop down on his hands and knees to take a view of the kennel before he ventured to step over it. His school-mistress, afraid that he might miss his way, or fall into the kennel, or be run over by a cart followed him at some distance. He happened to turn about and perceive her. Feeling her careful attention as an insult to his manliness, he ran back to her in a rage, and beat her, as well as his strength would permit.

Of the power of his memory, for which he was all his life eminent to a degree almost incredible, the following early instance was told me in his presence at Lichfield, in 1776, by his step-daughter, Mrs. Lucy Porter, as related to her by his mother. When he was a child in petticoats, and had learnt to read, Mrs. Johnson one morning put the common prayer-book into his hands, pointed to the collect for the day, and said, 'Sam, you must get this by heart.' She went up stairs, leaving him to study it: But by the time she had reached the second floor, she heard him following her. 'What's the matter?" said she. 'I can say it,' he replied; and repeated it distinctly, though he could not have read it over more than twice.

But there has been another story of his infant precocity generally circulated, and generally believed, the truth of which I am to refute upon his own authority. It is told, that, when a child of three years old, he chanced to tread upon a duckling, the eleventh of a brood, and killed it; upon which, it is said, he dictated to his mother the following epitaph:

> 'Here lies good master duck,
>   Whom Samuel Johnson trod on;
> If it had liv'd, it had been *good luck*,
>   For then we'd had an *odd one*.'

There is surely internal evidence that this little composition combines in it, what no child of three years old could produce, without an extension of its faculties by immediate inspiration; yet Mrs. Lucy Porter, Dr. Johnson's stepdaughter, positively maintained to me, in his presence, that there could be no doubt of the truth of this anecdote, for she had heard it from his mother. So difficult is it to obtain an authentick relation of facts, and such authority may there be for errour; for he assured me, that his father made the verses, and wished to pass them for his child's. He added, 'my father was a foolish old man; that is to say, foolish in talking of his children.'

Young Johnson had the misfortune to be much afflicted with the scrophula, or king's evil, which disfigured a countenance naturally well formed, and hurt his visual nerves so much, that he did not see at all with one of his eyes, though its appearance was little different from that of the other. There is amongst his prayers, one inscribed *'When my* EYE *was restored to its use,'* which ascertains a defect that many of his friends knew he had, though I never perceived it. I supposed him to be only near-sighted; and indeed I must observe, that in no other respect could I discern any defect in his vision; on the contrary, the force of his attention and perceptive quickness made him see and distinguish all manner of objects, whether of nature or of art, with a nicety that is rarely to be found. When he and I were travelling in the High-lands of Scotland, and I pointed out to him a mountain which I observed resembled a cone, he corrected my inaccuracy, by shewing me, that it was indeed pointed at the top, but that one side of it was larger than the other. And the ladies with whom he was acquainted agree, that no man was more nicely and minutely critical in the elegance of female dress. When I found that he saw the romantick beauties of Islam, in Derbyshire, much better than I did, I told him that he resembled an able performer upon a bad instrument. How false and contemptible then are all the remarks which have been made to the prejudice either of his candour or of his philosophy, founded upon a supposition that he was almost blind. It has been said, that he contracted this grievous malady from his nurse. His mother yielding to the superstitious notion, which, it is wonderful to think, prevailed so long in this country, as to the virtue of the regal touch; a notion, which our kings encouraged, and to which a man of such inquiry and such judgement as Carte could give credit; carried him to London, where he was actually touched by Queen Anne. Mrs. Johnson indeed, as Mr. Hector informed me, acted by the advice of the celebrated Sir John Floyer, then a physician in Lichfield. Johnson used to talk of this very frankly; and Mrs. Piozzi has preserved his very picturesque description of the scene, as it remained upon his fancy. Being asked if he could remember Queen Anne, 'He had (he said) a confused, but somehow a sort of solemn recollection of a lady in diamonds, and a long black hood.' This touch, however, was without any effect. I ventured to say to him, in allusion to the political principles in which he was educated, and of which he ever retained some odour, that 'his mother had not carried him far enough; she should have taken him to ROME.'

He was first taught to read English by Dame Oliver, a widow, who kept a school for young children in Lichfield. He told me she could read the black letter, and asked him to borrow for her, from his father, a bible in that character. When he was going to Oxford, she came to take leave of him, brought him, in the simplicity of her kindness, a present of gingerbread, and said, he was the best scholar she had ever had. He delighted in mentioning this early compliment: adding, with a smile, that 'this was as high a proof of his merit as he could conceive.' His next instructor in English was a master, whom, when he spoke of him to me, he familiarly called Tom Brown, who, said he, 'published a spelling-book, and dedicated it to the UNIVERSE; but, I fear, no copy of it can now be had.'

He began to learn Latin with Mr. Hawkins, usher, or under-master of Lichfield school, 'a man (said he) very skilful in his little way.' With him he continued two years, and then rose to be under the care of Mr. Hunter, the head-master, who, according to his account, 'was very severe, and wrong-headedly severe. He used (said he) to beat us unmercifully; and he did not distinguish between ignorance and negligence; for he would beat a boy equally for not knowing a thing, as for neglecting to know it. He would ask a boy a question; and if he did not answer it, he would beat him, without considering whether he had an opportunity of knowing how to answer it. For instance, he would call up a boy and ask him Latin for a candlestick, which the boy could not expect to be asked. Now, Sir, if a boy could answer every question, there would be no need of a master to teach him.' . . .

Indeed Johnson was very sensible how much he owed to Mr. Hunter. Mr. Langton one day asked him how he had acquired so accurate a knowledge of Latin, in which, I believe, he was exceeded by no man of his time; he said, 'My master whipt me very well. Without that, Sir, I should have done nothing.' He told Mr. Langton, that while Hunter was flogging his boys unmercifully, he used to say, 'And this I do to save you from the gallows.' Johnson, upon all occasions, expressed his approbation of enforcing instruction by means of the rod. 'I would rather (said he) have the rod to be the general terrour to all, to make them learn, than tell a child, if you do thus, or thus, you will be more esteemed than your brothers or sisters. The rod produces an effect which terminates in itself. A child is afraid of being whipped, and gets his task, and there's an end on't; whereas, by exciting emulation and comparisons of superiority, you lay the foundation of lasting mischief; you make brothers and sisters hate each other.'

When Johnson saw some young ladies in Lincolnshire who were remarkably well behaved, owing to their mother's strict discipline and severe correction, he exclaimed, in one of Shakespeare's lines a little varied,

'Rod, I will honour thee for this thy duty.'

That superiority over his fellows, which he maintained with so much dignity in his march through life, was not assumed from vanity and ostentation, but was the natural and constant effect of those extraordinary powers of mind, of which he could not but be conscious by comparison; the intellectual difference, which in other cases of comparison of characters is often a matter of undecided contest, being as clear in his case as the superiority of stature in some men above others. Johnson did not strut or stand on tiptoe: He only did not stoop. From his earliest years his superiority was perceived and acknowledged. He was from the beginning . . . a king of men. His school-fellow, Mr. Hector, has obligingly furnished me with many particulars of his boyish days: and assured me that he never knew him corrected at school, but for talking and diverting other boys from their business. He seemed to learn by intuition; for though indolence and procrastination were inherent in his constitution, whenever he made an exertion he did more than any one else. In short, he is a memorable instance of what has been often observed, that the boy is the man in miniature: and that the distinguishing characteristicks of each individual are the same, through the whole course of life. His favourites used to receive very liberal assistance from him; and such was the submission and deference with which he was treated, such the desire to obtain his regard, that three of the boys, of whom Mr. Hector was sometimes one, used to come in the morning as his humble attendants, and carry him to school. One in the middle stooped, while he sat upon his back, and one on each side supported him; and thus he was borne triumphant. Such a proof of the early predominance of intellectual vigour is very remarkable, and does honour to human nature. Talking to me once himself of his being much distinguished at school, he told me, 'they never thought to raise me by comparing me to any one; they never said, Johnson is as good a scholar as such a one; but such a one is as good a scholar as Johnson; and this was said but of one, but of Lowe; and I do not think he was as good a scholar.'

He discovered a great ambition to excel, which roused him to counteract his indolence. He was uncommonly inquisitive; and his memory was so tenacious, that he never forgot any thing that he either heard or read. Mr. Hector remembers having recited to him eighteen verses, which, after a little pause, he repeated *verbatim*, varying only one epithet, by which he improved the line.

He never joined with the other boys in their ordinary diversions: his only amusement was in winter, when he took a pleasure in being drawn upon the ice by a boy barefooted, who pulled him along by a garter fixed round him; no very easy operation, as his size was remarkably large. His defective sight, indeed, prevented him from enjoying the common sports; and he once pleasantly remarked to me, 'how wonderfully well he had contrived to be idle without them.' Lord Chesterfield, however, has justly observed in one of his letters, when earnestly cautioning a friend against the pernicious effects of idleness, that active sports are not to be reckoned idleness in young people; and that the listless torpor of doing nothing, alone deserves that name. Of this dismal inertness of disposition, Johnson had all his life too great a share. Mr. Hector relates, that 'he could not oblige him more than by sauntering away the hours of vacation in the fields, during which he was more engaged in talking to himself than to his companion.'

Dr. Percy, the Bishop of Dromore, who was long intimately acquainted with him, and has preserved a few anecdotes concerning him, regretting that he was not a more diligent collector, informs me, that 'when a boy he was immoderately fond of reading romances of chivalry, and he retained his fondness for them through life; so that (adds his Lordship) spending part of a summer at my parsonage-house in the country, he chose for his regular reading the old Spanish romance of *Felixmarte of Hircania,* in folio, which he read quite through. Yet I have heard him attribute to these extravagant fictions that unsettled turn of mind which prevented his ever fixing in any profession.'

1725: ÆTAT. 16.—AFTER having resided for some time at the house of his uncle, Cornelius Ford, Johnson was, at the age of fifteen, removed to the school of Stourbridge, in Worcestershire, of which Mr. Wentworth was then master. This step was taken by the advice of his cousin, the Reverend Mr. Ford, a man in whom both talents and good dispositions were disgraced by licentiousness, but who was a very able judge of what was right. At this school he did not receive so much benefit as was expected. It has been said, that he acted in the capacity of an assistant to Mr. Wentworth, in teaching the younger boys. 'Mr. Wentworth (he told me) was a very able man, but an idle man, and to me very severe; but I cannot blame him much. I was then a big boy; he saw I did not reverence him; and that he should get no honour by me. I had brought enough with me, to carry me through; and all I should get at his school would be ascribed to my own labour, or to my former master. Yet he taught me a great deal.'

He thus discriminated, to Dr. Percy, Bishop of Dromore, his progress at his two grammar-schools. 'At one, I learnt much in the school, but little from the master; in the other, I learnt much from the master, but little in the school.'

The Bishop also informs me, that 'Dr. Johnson's father, before he was received at Stourbridge, applied to have him admitted as a scholar and assistant to the Reverend Samuel Lea, M.A., head master of Newport school, in Shropshire' (a very diligent, good teacher, at that time in high reputation, under whom Mr. Hollis is said, in the Memoirs of his Life, to have been also educated). This application to Mr. Lea was not successful; but Johnson had afterwards the gratification to hear that the old gentleman, who lived to a very advanced age, mentioned it as one of the most memorable events of his life, that 'he was *very near* having that great man for his scholar.'

He remained at Stourbridge little more than a year, and then returned home, where he may be said to have loitered, for two years, in a state very unworthy his uncommon abilities. He had already given several proofs of his poetical genius, both in his school-exercises and in other occasional compositions. Of these I have obtained a considerable collection, by the favour of Mr. Wentworth, son of one of his masters, and of Mr. Hector, his school-fellow and friend; from which I select the following specimens.[1]

The two years which he spent at home, after his return from Stourbridge, he passed in what he thought idleness, and was scolded by his father for his want of steady application. He had no settled plan of life, nor looked forward at all, but merely lived from day to day. Yet he read a great deal in a desultory manner, without any scheme of study, as chance threw books in his way, and inclination directed him through them. He used to mention one curious instance of his casual reading, when but a boy. Having imagined that his brother had hid some apples behind a large folio upon an upper shelf in his father's shop, he climbed up to search for them. There were no apples; but the large folio proved to be Petrarch, whom he had seen mentioned in some preface, as one of restorers of learning. His curiosity having been thus excited, he sat down with avidity, and read a great part of the book. What he read during these two years he told me, was not works of mere amusement, 'not voyages and travels, but all literature, Sir, all ancient writers, all manly: though but little Greek, only some of Anacreon and Hesiod; but in this irregular manner (added he) I had looked into a great many books, which were not commonly known at the Universities, where they seldom read any books but what are put into their hands by their tutors; so that when I came to Oxford, Dr. Adams, now master of Pembroke College, told me I was the best qualified for the University that he had ever known come there.'

In estimating the progress of his mind during these two years, as well as in future periods of his life, we must not regard his own hasty confession of idleness; for we see, when he explains himself, that he was acquiring various stores; and,

[1] Omitted here.

42

indeed, he himself concluded the account with saying, 'I would not have you think I was doing nothing then.' He might, perhaps, have studied more assiduously; but it may be doubted whether such a mind as his was not more enriched by roaming at large in the fields of literature than if it had been confined to any single spot. The analogy between body and mind is very general, and the parallel will hold as to their food, as well as any other particular. The flesh of animals who feed excursively, is allowed to have a higher flavour than that of those who are cooped up. May there not be the same difference between men who read as their taste prompts and men who are confined in cells and colleges to stated tasks?

That a man in Mr. Michael Johnson's circumstances should think of sending his son to the expensive University of Oxford, at his own charge, seems very improbable. The subject was too delicate to question Johnson upon. But I have been assured by Dr. Taylor that the scheme never would have taken place had not a gentleman of Shropshire, one of his schoolfellows, spontaneously undertaken to support him at Oxford, in the character of his companion; though, in fact, he never received any assistance whatever from that gentleman.

He, however, went to Oxford, and was entered a Commoner of Pembroke College on the 31st of October, 1728, being then in his nineteenth year.

The Reverend Dr. Adams, who afterwards presided over Pembroke College with universal esteem, told me he was present, and gave me some account of what passed on the night of Johnson's arrival at Oxford. On that evening, his father, who had anxiously accompanied him, found means to have him introduced to Mr. Jorden, who was to be his tutor. His being put under any tutor reminds us of what Wood says of Robert Burton, authour of the 'Anatomy of Melancholy,' when elected student of Christ Church: 'For form's sake, *though he wanted not a tutor,* he was put under the tuition of Dr. John Bancroft, afterwards Bishop of Oxon.'

His father seemed very full of the merits of his son, and told the company he was a good scholar, and a poet, and wrote Latin verses. His figure and manner appeared strange to them; but he behaved modestly, and sat silent, till upon something which occurred in the course of conversation, he suddenly struck in and quoted Macrobius; and thus he gave the first impression of that more extensive reading in which he had indulged himself.

His tutor, Mr. Jorden, fellow of Pembroke, was not, it seems, a man of such abilities as we should conceive requisite for the instructor of Samuel Johnson, who gave me the following account of him. 'He was a very worthy man, but a heavy man, and I did not profit much by his instructions. Indeed, I did not attend him much. The first day after I came to college I waited upon him, and then staid away four. On the sixth, Mr. Jorden asked me why I had not attended. I answered I had been sliding in Christ-Church meadow. And this I said with as much *nonchalance* as I am now talking to you. I had no notion that I was wrong or irreverent to my tutor. BOSWELL: 'That, Sir, was great fortitude of mind.' JOHNSON: 'No, Sir; stark insensibility.' [1]

The fifth of November was at that time kept with great solemnity at Pembroke College, and exercises upon the subject of the day were required. Johnson neglected to perform his, which is much to be regretted; for his vivacity of imagination, and force of language, would probably have produced something sublime upon the gunpowder plot. To apologise for his neglect, he gave in a short copy of verses, entitled *Somnium*, containing a common thought; 'that the Muse had come to him in his sleep, and whispered, that it did not become him to write on such subjects as politicks; he should confine himself to humbler themes:' but the versification was truly Virgilian.

He had a love and respect for Jorden, not for his literature, but for his worth. 'Whenever (said he) a young man becomes Jorden's pupil, he becomes his son.'

Having given such a specimen of his poetical powers, he was asked by Mr. Jorden to translate Pope's Messiah into Latin verse, as a Christmas exercise. He performed it with uncommon rapidity, and in so masterly a manner, that he obtained great applause from it, which ever after kept him high in the estimation of his College, and, indeed, of all the University.

It is said, that Mr. Pope expressed himself concerning it in terms of strong approbation. Dr. Taylor told me, that it was first printed for old Mr. Johnson, without the knowledge of his son, who was very angry when he heard of it. . . .

The 'morbid melancholy,' which was lurking in his constitution, and to which we may ascribe those particularities, and that aversion to regular life, which, at a very early period, marked his character, gathered such strength in his twentieth year, as to afflict him in a dreadful manner. While he was at Lichfield, in the college vacation of the year 1729, he felt

[1] It ought to be remembered, that Dr. Johnson was apt, in his literary as well as moral exercises, to overcharge his defects. Dr. Adams informed me, that he attended his tutor's lectures, and also the lectures in the College Hall, very regularly—B.

44

himself overwhelmed with an horrible hypochondria, with perpetual irritation, fretfulness, and impatience; and with a dejection, gloom, and despair, which made existence misery. From this dismal malady he never afterwards was perfectly relieved; and all his labours, and all his enjoyments, were but temporary interruptions of its baleful influence. How wonderful, how unsearchable are the ways of GOD! Johnson, who was blest with all the powers of genius and understanding in a degree far above the ordinary state of human nature, was at the same time visited with a disorder so afflictive, that they who know it by dire experience, will not envy his exalted endowments. That it was, in some degree, occasioned by a defect in his nervous system, that inexplicable part of our frame, appears highly probable. He told Mr. Paradise that he was sometimes so languid and inefficient, that he could not distinguish the hour upon the town-clock.

Johnson, upon the first violent attack of this disorder, strove to overcome it by forcible exertions. He frequently walked to Birmingham and back again, and tried many other expedients, but all in vain. His expression concerning it to me was, 'I did not then know how to manage it.' His distress became so intolerable, that he applied to Dr. Swinfen, physician in Lichfield, his god-father, and put into his hands a state of his case, written in Latin. Dr. Swinfen was so much struck with the extraordinary acuteness, research, and eloquence of this paper, that in his zeal for his godson he shewed it to several people. His daughter, Mrs. Desmoulins, who was many years humanely supported in Dr. Johnson's house in London, told me, that upon his discovering that Dr. Swinfen had communicated his case, he was so much offended, that he was never afterwards fully reconciled to him. He indeed had good reason to be offended; for though Dr. Swinfen's motive was good, he inconsiderately betrayed a matter deeply interesting and of great delicacy, which had been entrusted to him in confidence; and exposed a complaint of his young friend and patient, which, in the superficial opinion of the generality of mankind, is attended with contempt and disgrace.

But let not little men triumph upon knowing that Johnson was an HYPOCHONDRIACK, was subject to what the learned, philosophical, and pious Dr. Cheyne has so well treated under the title of 'The English Malady.' Though he suffered severely from it, he was not therefore degraded. The powers of his great mind might be troubled, and their full exercise suspended at times; but the mind itself was ever entire. As a proof of this, it is only necessary to consider, that, when he was at the very worst, he composed that state of his own case, which shewed an uncommon vigour, not only of fancy and taste, but of judgement. I am aware that he himself was too ready to call such a complaint by the name of *madness;* in conformity with which notion, he has traced its gradations, with exquisite nicety, in one of the chapters of his RASSELAS. But there is surely a clear distinction between a disorder which affects only the imagination and spirits, while the judgement is sound, and a disorder by which the judgement itself is impaired. This distinction was made to me by the late Professor Gaubius of Leyden, physician to the Prince of Orange, in a conversation which I had with him several years ago, and he expanded it thus: 'If (said he) a man tells me that he is grievously disturbed, for that he *imagines* he sees a ruffian coming against him with a drawn sword, though at the same time he is *conscious* it is a delusion, I pronounce him to have a disordered imagination; but if a man tells me that he *sees* this, and in consternation calls to me to look at it, I pronounce him to be *mad.*'

It is a common effect of low spirits or melancholy, to make those who are afflicted with it imagine that they are actually suffering those evils which happen to be most strongly presented to their minds. Some have fancied themselves to be deprived of the use of their limbs, some to labour under acute diseases, others to be in extreme poverty; when, in truth, there was not the least reality in any of the suppositions; so that when the vapours were dispelled, they were convinced of the delusion. To Johnson, whose supreme enjoyment was the exercise of his reason, the disturbance or obscuration of that faculty was the evil most to be dreaded. Insanity, therefore, was the object of his most dismal apprehension; and he fancied himself seized by it, or approaching to it, at the very time when he was giving proofs of a more than ordinary soundness and vigour of judgement. That his own diseased imagination should have so far deceived him, is strange; but it is stranger still that some of his friends should have given credit to his groundless opinion, when they had such undoubted proofs that it was totally fallacious; though it is by no means surprising that those who wish to depreciate him, should, since his death, have laid hold of this circumstance, and insisted upon it with very unfair aggravation.

Amidst the oppression and distraction of a disease which very few have felt in its full extent, but many have experienced in a slighter degree, Johnson, in his writings, and in his conversation, never failed to display all the varieties of intellectual excellence. In his march through this world to a better, his mind still appeared grand and brilliant, and impressed all around him with the truth of Virgil's noble sentiment—

The history of his mind as to religion is an important article. I have mentioned the early impressions made upon his tender imagination by his mother, who continued her pious care with assiduity, but, in his opinion, not with judgement. 'Sunday (said he) was a heavy day to me when I was a boy. My mother confined me on that day, and made me read *The Whole Duty of Man*, from a great part of which I could derive no instruction. When, for instance, I had read the chapter on theft, which from my infancy I had been taught was wrong, I was no more convinced that theft was wrong than before; so there was no accession of knowledge. A boy should be introduced to such books, by having his attention directed to the arrangement, to the style, and other excellencies of composition; that the mind being thus engaged by an amusing variety of objects, may not grow weary.'

He communicated to me the following particulars upon the subject of his religious progress. 'I fell into an inattention to religion, or an indifference about it, in my ninth year. The church at Lichfield, in which we had a seat, wanted reparation, so I was to go and find a seat in other churches; and having bad eyes, and being awkward about this, I used to go and read in the fields on Sunday. This habit continued till my fourteenth year; and still I find a great reluctance to go to church. I then became a sort of lax *talker* against religion, for I did not much *think* against it; and this lasted till I went to Oxford, where it would not be *suffered*. When at Oxford, I took up Law's *Serious Call to a Holy Life,* expecting to find it a dull book (as such books generally are), and perhaps to laugh at it. But I found Law quite an overmatch for me; and this was the first occasion of my thinking in earnest of religion, after I became capable of rational inquiry.' From this time forward religion was the predominant object of his thoughts; though, with the just sentiments of a conscientious Christian, he lamented that his practice of its duties fell far short of what it ought to be. . . .

How seriously Johnson was impressed with a sense of religion, even in the vigour of his youth, appears from the following passage in his minutes kept by way of diary: Sept. 7, 1736. I have this day entered upon my twenty-eighth year. 'Mayest thou, O God, enable me, for JESUS CHRIST'S sake, to spend this in such a manner that I may receive comfort from it at the hour of death, and in the day of judgement! Amen.'

The particular course of his reading while at Oxford, and

[1] 'These seeds have a fiery strength and a heavenly origin.' Virgil, *Aeneid*, vi. 730.

during the time of vacation which he passed at home, cannot be traced. Enough has been said of his irregular mode of study. He told me that from his earliest years he loved to read poetry, but hardly ever read any poem to an end; that he read Shakespeare at a period so early, that the speech of the ghost in Hamlet terrified him when he was alone; that Horace's Odes were the compositions in which he took most delight, and it was long before he liked his Epistles and Satires. He told me what he read *solidly* at Oxford was Greek; not the Grecian historians, but Homer and Euripides, and now and then a little Epigram; that the study of which he was the most fond was Metaphysicks, but he had not read much, even in that way. I always thought that he did himself injustice in his account of what he had read, and that he must have been speaking with reference to the vast portion of study which is possible, and to which a few scholars in the whole history of literature have attained; for when I once asked him whether a person, whose name I have now forgotten, studied hard, he answered 'No, Sir; I do not believe he studied hard. I never knew a man who studied hard. I conclude, indeed, from the effects, that some men have studied hard, as Bentley and Clarke.' Trying him by that criterion upon which he formed his judgement of others, we may be absolutely certain, both from his writings and his conversation, that his reading was very extensive. Dr. Adam Smith, than whom few were better judges on this subject, once observed to me that 'Johnson knew more books than any man alive.' He had a peculiar facility in seizing at once what was valuable in any book, without submitting to the labour of perusing it from beginning to end. He had, from the irritability of his constitution, at all times, an impatience and hurry when he either read or wrote. A certain apprehension, arising from novelty, made him write his first exercise at College twice over; but he never took that trouble with any other composition; and we shall see that his most excellent works were struck off at a heat, with rapid exertion.

Yet he appears, from his early notes or memorandums in my possession, to have at various times attempted, or at least planned, a methodical course of study, according to computation, of which he was all his life fond, as it fixed his attention steadily upon something without, and prevented his mind from preying upon itself. Thus I find in his handwriting the number of lines in each of two of Euripides' Tragedies, of the Georgicks of Virgil, of the first six books of the Æneid, of Horace's Art of Poetry, of three of the books of Ovid's Metamorphosis, of some parts of Theocritus, and of the tenth Satire of Juvenal; and a table, shewing at the rate of various numbers a day (I suppose verses to be read), what would be, in each case, the total amount in a week, month, and year.

No man had a more ardent love of literature, or a higher respect for it than Johnson. His apartment in Pembroke College was that upon the second floor, over the gateway. The enthusiasts of learning will ever contemplate it with veneration. One day, while he was sitting in it quite alone, Dr. Panting, then master of the College, whom he called 'a fine Jacobite fellow,' overheard him uttering this soliloquy in his strong, emphatick voice: 'Well, I have a mind to see what is done in other places of learning. I'll go and visit the Universities abroad. I'll go to France and Italy. I'll go to Padua.—And I'll mind my business. For an *Athenian* blockhead is the worst of all blockheads.'

Dr. Adams told me that Johnson, while he was at Pembroke College, 'was caressed and loved by all about him, was a gay and frolicksome fellow, and passed there the happiest part of his life.' But this is a striking proof of the fallacy of appearances, and how little any of us know of the real internal state even of those whom we see most frequently; for the truth is, that he was then depressed by poverty, and irritated by disease. When I mentioned to him this account as given me by Dr. Adams, he said, 'Ah, Sir, I was mad and violent. It was bitterness which they mistook for frolick. I was miserably poor, and I thought to fight my way by my literature and my wit; so I disregarded all power and all authority.'

The Bishop of Dromore observes in a letter to me,

'The pleasure he took in vexing the tutors and fellows has been often mentioned. But I have heard him say, what ought to be recorded to the honour of the present venerable master of that College, the Reverend William Adams, D.D., who was then very young, and one of the junior fellows; that the mild but judicious expostulations of this worthy man, whose virtue awed him, and whose learning he revered, made him really ashamed of himself, "though I fear (said he) I was too proud to own it."

'I have heard from some of his contemporaries that he was generally seen lounging at the College gate, with a circle of young students round him, whom he was entertaining with wit, and keeping from their studies, if not spiriting them up to rebellion against the College discipline, which in his maturer years he so much extolled.'

He very early began to attempt keeping notes or memorandums, by way of a diary of his life. I find, in a parcel of loose leaves, the following spirited resolution to contend against his natural indolence:

'*Oct.* 1729. . . . I bid farewell to Sloth, being resolved

49

henceforth not to listen to her syren strains.' I have also in my possession a few leaves of another *Libellus,* or little book, entitled ANNALES, in which some of the early particulars of his history are registered in Latin.

I do not find that he formed any close intimacies with his fellow-collegians. But Dr. Adams told me that he contracted a love and regard for Pembroke College, which he retained to the last. A short time before his death he sent to that College a present of all his works, to be deposited in their library; and he had thoughts of leaving to it his house at Lichfield; but his friends who were about him very properly dissuaded him from it, and he bequeathed it to some poor relations. He took a pleasure in boasting of the many eminent men who had been educated at Pembroke. . . . Being himself a poet, Johnson was peculiarly happy in mentioning how many of the sons of Pembroke were poets; adding, with a smile of sportive triumph, 'Sir, we are a nest of singing birds.'

He was not, however, blind to what he thought the defects of his own College; and I have, from the information of Dr. Taylor, a very strong instance of that rigid honesty which he ever inflexibly preserved. Taylor had obtained his father's consent to be entered of Pembroke, that he might be with his schoolfellow Johnson, with whom, though some years older than himself, he was very intimate. This would have been a great comfort to Johnson. But he fairly told Taylor that he could not, in conscience, suffer him to enter where he knew he could have not have an able tutor. He then made inquiry all round the University, and having found that Mr. Bateman, of Christ Church, was the tutor of highest reputation, Taylor was entered of that College. Mr. Bateman's lectures were so excellent, that Johnson used to come and get them at second-hand from Taylor, till his poverty being so extreme that his shoes were worn out, and his feet appeared through them, he saw that this humiliating circumstance was perceived by the Christ Church men, and he came no more. He was too proud to accept of money, and somebody having set a pair of new shoes at his door, he threw them away with indignation. How must we feel when we read such an anecdote of Samuel Johnson! . . . .

The *res angusta domi*[1] prevented him from having the advantage of a complete academical education. The friend to whom he had trusted for support had deceived him. His debts in College, though not great, were increasing; and his scanty remittances from Lichfield, which had all along been made with great difficulty, could be supplied no longer, his

[1] 'Narrow means at home.' Juvenal, *Satires,* iii. 165.

father having fallen into a state of insolvency. Compelled, therefore, by irresistible necessity, he left the College in autumn, 1731, without a degree, having been a member of it little more than three years.

Dr. Adams, the worthy and respectable master of Pembroke College, has generally had the reputation of being Johnson's tutor. The fact, however, is, that in 1731 Mr. Jorden quitted the College, and his pupils were transferred to Dr. Adams; so that had Johnson returned, Dr. Adams *would have been his tutor.* It is to be wished, that this connection had taken place. His equal temper, mild disposition, and politeness of manners, might have insensibly softened the harshness of Johnson, and infused into him those more delicate charities, those *petites morales,* in which, it must be confessed, our great moralist was more deficient than his best friends could fully justify. Dr. Adams paid Johnson this high compliment. He said to me at Oxford, in 1776, 'I was his nominal tutor; but he was above my mark.' When I repeated it to Johnson, his eyes flashed with grateful satisfaction, and he exclaimed, 'That was liberal and noble.'

And now (I had almost said *poor*) Samuel Johnson returned to his native city, destitute, and not knowing how he should gain even a decent livelihood. His father's misfortunes in trade rendered him unable to support his son; and for some time there appeared no means by which he could maintain himself. In the December of this year his father died.

The state of poverty in which he died, appears from a note in one of Johnson's little diaries of the following year, which strongly displays his spirit and virtuous dignity of mind.

'1732, *Julii* 15. . . . I layed by eleven guineas on this day, when I received twenty pounds, being all that I have reason to hope for out of my father's effects, previous to the death of my mother; an event which I pray GOD may be very remote. I now therefore see that I must make my own fortune. Meanwhile, let me take care that the powers of my mind may not be debilitated by poverty, and that indigence do not force me into any criminal act.'

Johnson was so far fortunate, that the respectable character of his parents, and his own merit, had, from his earliest years, secured him a kind reception in the best families at Lichfield. Among these I can mention Mr. Howard, Dr. Swinfen, Mr. Simpson, Mr. Levett, Captain Garrick, father of the great ornament of the British stage; but above all, Mr. Gilbert Walmsley, Register of the Prerogative Court of Lichfield, whose character, long after his decease, Dr. Johnson has, in his Life of Edmund Smith, thus drawn in the glowing colours of gratitude:

51

'Of Gilbert Walmsley, thus presented to my mind, let me indulge myself in the remembrance. I knew him very early; he was one of the first friends that literature procured me, and I hope that, at least, my gratitude made me worthy of his notice.

'He was of an advanced age, and I was only not a boy, yet he never received my notions with contempt. He was a whig, with all the virulence and malevolence of his party; yet difference of opinion did not keep us apart. I honoured him, and he endured me.

'He had mingled with the gay world without exemption from its vices or its follies; but had never neglected the cultivation of his mind. His belief of revelation was unshaken; his learning preserved his principles; he grew first regular, and then pious.

'His studies had been so various, that I am not able to name a man of equal knowledge. His acquaintance with books was great, and what he did not immediately know, he could, at least, tell where to find. Such was his amplitude of learning, and such his copiousness of communication, that it may be doubted whether a day now passes, in which I have not some advantage from his friendship.

'At this man's table I enjoyed many cheerful and instructive hours, with companions, such as are not often found— with one who has lengthened, and one who has gladdened life; with Dr. James, whose skill in physick will be long remembered; and with David Garrick, whom I hoped to have gratified with this character of our common friend. But what are the hopes of man! I am disappointed by that stroke of death, which has eclipsed the gaiety of nations, and impoverished the publick stock of harmless pleasure.'

In these families he passed much time in his early years. In most of them, he was in the company of ladies, particularly at Mr. Walmsley's, whose wife and sisters-in-law, of the name of Aston, and daughters of a Baronet, were remarkable for good breeding; so that the notion which has been industriously circulated and believed, that he never was in good company till late in life, and, consequently had been confirmed in coarse and ferocious manners by long habits, is wholly without foundation. Some of the ladies have assured me, they recollected him well when a young man, as distinguished for his complaisance.

And that this politeness was not merely occasional and temporary, or confined to the circles of Lichfield, is ascertained by the testimony of a lady, who, in a paper with which I have been favoured by a daughter of his intimate friend and physician, Dr. Lawrence, thus describes Dr. Johnson some years afterwards:

'As the particulars of the former part of Dr. Johnson's life do not seem to be very accurately known, a lady hopes that the following information may not be unacceptable.

'She remembers Dr. Johnson on a visit to Dr. Taylor, at Ashbourn, some time between the end of the year 37, and the middle of the year 40; she rather thinks it to have been after he and his wife were removed to London. During his stay at Ashbourn, he made frequent visits to Mr. Meynell, at Bradley, where his company was much desired by the ladies of the family, who were, perhaps, in point of elegance and accomplishments, inferiour to few of those with whom he was afterwards acquainted. Mr. Meynell's eldest daughter was afterwards married to Mr. Fitzherbert, father to Mr. Alleyne Fitzherbert, lately minister to the court of Russia. Of her, Dr. Johnson said, in Dr. Lawrence's study, that she had the best understanding he ever met with in any human being. At Mr. Meynell's he also commenced that friendship with Mrs. Hill Boothby, sister to the present Sir Brook Boothby, which continued till her death. *The young woman whom he used to call Molly Aston,* was sister to Sir Thomas Aston, and daughter to a Baronet; she was also sister to the wife of his friend Mr. Gilbert Walmsley. Besides his intimacy with the above-mentioned persons, who were surely people of rank and education, while he was yet at Lichfield he used to be frequently at the house of Dr. Swinfen, a gentleman of a very ancient family in Staffordshire, from which, after the death of his elder brother, he inherited a good estate. He was, besides, a physician of very extensive practice; but for want of due attention to the management of his domestick concerns, left a very large family in indigence. One of his daughters, Mrs. Desmoulins, afterwards found an asylum in the house of her old friend, whose doors were always open to the unfortunate, and who well observed the precept of the Gospel, for he "was kind to the unthankful and to the evil." '

In the forlorn state of his circumstances, he accepted of an offer to be employed as usher in the school of Market-Bosworth, in Leicestershire, to which it appears, from one of his little fragments of a diary, that he went on foot, on the 16th of July. . . .

This employment was very irksome to him in every respect, and he complained grievously of it in his letters to his friend Mr. Hector, who was now settled as a surgeon at Birmingham. The letters are lost; but Mr. Hector recollects his writing 'that the poet had described the dull sameness of his existence in these words, *"Vitam continet una dies"* (one day contains the whole of my life); that it was unvaried as the note of the cuckow; and that he did not know whether it was more disagreeable for him to teach, or the boys to learn, the grammar rules.' His general aversion to this painful drudgery was greatly enhanced by a disagreement between him and Sir Wolstan Dixey, the patron of the school, in whose house, I have been told, he officiated as a kind of domestick chaplain, so far, at least, as to say grace at table, but was treated with what he represented as intolerable harshness; and, after suffering for a few months such complicated misery, he relinquished a situation which all his life afterwards he recollected with the strongest aversion, and even a degree of horrour. But it is probable that at this period, whatever uneasiness he may have endured, he laid the foundation of much future eminence by application to his studies.

Being now again totally unoccupied, he was invited by Mr. Hector to pass some time with him at Birmingham, as his guest, at the house of Mr. Warren, with whom Mr. Hector lodged and boarded. Mr. Warren was the first established bookseller in Birmingham, and was very attentive to Johnson, who he soon found could be of much service to him in his trade, by his knowledge of literature; and he even obtained the assistance of his pen in furnishing some numbers of a periodical Essay printed in the news-paper, of which Warren was proprietor. After diligent inquiry, I have not been able to recover those early specimens of that particular mode of writing by which Johnson afterwards so greatly distinguished himself.

He continued to live as Mr. Hector's guest for about six months, and then hired lodgings in another part of the town, finding himself as well situated at Birmingham as he supposed he could be anywhere, while he had no settled plan of life, and very scanty means of subsistence. He made some valuable acquaintances there, amongst whom were Mr. Porter, a mercer, whose widow he afterwards married, and Mr. Taylor, who by his ingenuity in mechanical inventions, and his success in trade, acquired an immense fortune. But the comfort of being near Mr. Hector, his old schoolfellow and intimate friend, was Johnson's chief inducement to continue here.

In what manner he employed his pen at this period, or whether he derived from it any pecuniary advantage, I have not been able to ascertain. He probably got a little money from Mr. Warren; and we are certain, that he executed here one piece of literary labour, of which Mr. Hector has favoured me with a minute account. Having mentioned that he had read at Pembroke College a Voyage to Abyssinia, by

Lobo, a Portuguese Jesuit, and that he thought an abridgement and translation of it from the French into English might be an useful and profitable publication, Mr. Warren and Mr. Hector joined in urging him to undertake it. He accordingly agreed; and the book not being to be found in Birmingham, he borrowed it of Pembroke College. A part of the work being very soon done, one Osborn, who was Mr. Warren's printer, was set to work with what was ready, and Johnson engaged to supply the press with copy as it should be wanted; but his constitutional indolence soon prevailed, and the work was at a stand. Mr. Hector, who knew that a motive of humanity would be the most prevailing argument with his friend, went to Johnson, and represented to him, that the printer could have no other employment till this undertaking was finished, and that the poor man and his family were suffering. Johnson upon this exerted the powers of his mind, though his body was relaxed. He lay in bed with the book, which was a quarto, before him, and dictated while Hector wrote. Mr. Hector carried the sheets to the press, and corrected almost all the proof sheets, very few of which were even seen by Johnson. In this manner, with the aid of Mr. Hector's active friendship, the book was completed, and was published in 1735, with LONDON upon the title-page, though it was in reality printed in Birmingham, a device too common with provincial publishers. For this work he had from Mr. Warren only the sum of five guineas.

This being the first prose work of Johnson, it is a curious object of inquiry how much may be traced in it of that style which marks his subsequent writings with such peculiar excellence; with so happy an union of force, vivacity, and perspicuity. I have perused the book with this view, and have found that here, as I believe in every other translation, there is in the work itself no vestige of the translator's own style; for the language of translation being adapted to the thoughts of another person, insensibly follows their cast, and, as it were, runs into a mould that is ready prepared. . . .

But, in the Preface, the Johnsonian style begins to appear; and though use had not yet taught his wing a permanent and equable flight, there are parts of it which exhibit his best manner in full vigour. I had once the pleasure of examining it with Mr. Edmund Burke, who confirmed me in this opinion, by his superiour critical sagacity, and was, I remember, much delighted with the following specimen:

'The Portuguese traveller, contrary to the general vein of his countrymen, has amused his reader with no romantick absurdity, or incredible fictions; whatever he relates, whether true or not, is at least probable; and he who tells nothing exceeding the bounds of probability, has a right to demand that they should believe him who cannot contradict him.

'He appears, by his modest and unaffected narration, to have described things as he saw them, to have copied nature from the life, and to have consulted his senses, not his imagination. He meets with no basilisks that destroy with their eyes, his crocodiles devour their prey without tears, and his cataracts fall from the rocks without deafening the neighbouring inhabitants.

'The reader will here find no regions cursed with irremediable barrenness, or blessed with spontaneous fecundity; no perpetual gloom, or unceasing sunshine; nor are the nations here described either devoid of all sense of humanity, or consummate in all private or social virtues. Here are no Hottentots without religious polity or articulate language; no Chinese perfectly polite, and completely skilled in all sciences; he will discover, what will always be discovered by a diligent and impartial enquirer, that wherever human nature is to be found, there is a mixture of vice and virtue, a contest of passion and reason; and that the Creator doth not appear partial in his distributions, but has balanced, in most countries, their particular inconveniences by particular favours.'

Here we have an early example of that brilliant and energetick expression, which, upon innumerable occasions in his subsequent life, justly impressed the world with the highest admiration. . . .

It is reasonable to suppose, that his having been thus accidentally led to a particular study of the history and manners of Abyssinia, was the remote occasion of his writing, many years afterwards, his admirable philosophical tale, the principal scene of which is laid in that country.

Johnson returned to Lichfield early in 1734, and in August that year he made an attempt to procure some little subsistence by his pen; for he published proposals for printing by subscription the Latin Poems of Politian. . . . It appears that his brother Nathanael had taken up his father's trade; for it is mentioned that 'subscriptions are taken in by the Editor, or N. Johnson, bookseller, of Lichfield.' Notwithstanding the merit of Johnson, and the cheap price at which this book was offered, there were not subscribers enough to insure a sufficient sale; so the work never appeared, and probably, never was executed. . . .

Johnson, had, from his early youth, been sensible to the influence of female charms. When at Stourbridge school, he was much enamoured of Olivia Lloyd, a young quaker, to whom he wrote a copy of verses, which I have not been able to recover; but with what facility and elegance he could warble the amorous lay, will appear from the following lines which he wrote for his friend Mr. Edmund Hector.[1]

His juvenile attachments to the fair sex were, however, very transient; and it is certain that he formed no criminal connection whatsoever. Mr. Hector, who lived with him in his younger days in the utmost intimacy and social freedom, has assured me, that even at that ardent season his conduct was strictly virtuous in that respect; and that though he loved to exhilarate himself with wine, he never knew him intoxicated but once.

In a man whom religious education has secured from licentious indulgences, the passion of love, when once it has seized him, is exceedingly strong; being unimpaired by dissipation, and totally concentrated in one object. This was experienced by Johnson, when he became the fervent admirer of Mrs. Porter, after her first husband's death. Miss Porter told me, that when he was first introduced to her mother, his appearance was very forbidding: he was then lean and lank, so that his immense structure of bones was hideously striking to the eye, and the scars of the scrophula were deeply visible. He also wore his hair, which was straight and stiff, and separated behind: and he often had, seemingly, convulsive starts and odd gesticulations, which tended to excite at once surprize and ridicule. Mrs. Porter was so much engaged by his conversation that she overlooked all these external disadvantages, and said to her daughter, 'this is the most sensible man that I ever saw in my life.'

Though Mrs. Porter was double the age of Johnson, and her person and manner, as described to me by the late Mr. Garrick, were by no means pleasing to others, she must have had a superiority of understanding and talents, as she certainly inspired him with a more than ordinary passion; and she having signified her willingness to accept of his hand, he went to Lichfield to ask his mother's consent to the marriage, which he could not but be conscious was a very imprudent scheme, both on account of their disparity of years, and her want of fortune. But Mrs. Johnson knew too well the ardour of her son's temper, and was too tender a parent to oppose his inclinations.

I know not for what reason the marriage ceremony was not performed at Birmingham; but a resolution was taken that it should be at Derby, for which place the bride and bridegroom set out on horseback, I suppose in very good humour. But though Mr. Topham Beauclerk used archly to mention Johnson's having told him, with much gravity, 'Sir,

[1] Omitted here.

57

it was a love-marriage upon both sides,' I have had from my illustrious friend the following curious account of their journey to church upon the nuptial morn:

9th JULY:—'Sir, she had read the old romances, and had got into her head the fantastical notion that a woman of spirit should use her lover like a dog. So, Sir, at first she told me that I rode too fast, and she could not keep up with me; and, when I rode a little slower, she passed me, and complained that I lagged behind. I was not to be made the slave of caprice; and I resolved to begin as I meant to end. I therefore pushed on briskly, till I was fairly out of her sight. The road lay between two hedges, so I was sure she could not miss it; and I contrived that she should soon come up with me. When she did, I observed her to be in tears.'

This, it must be allowed, was a singular beginning of connubial felicity; but there is no doubt that Johnson, though he thus shewed a manly firmness, proved a most affectionate and indulgent husband to the last moment of Mrs. Johnson's life: and in his *Prayers and Meditations* we find very remarkable evidence that his regard and fondness for her never ceased, even after her death.

He now set up a private academy, for which purpose he hired a large house, well situated near his native city. In the *Gentleman's Magazine* for 1736, there is the following advertisement:

'At Edial, near Lichfield, in Staffordshire, young gentlemen are boarded and taught the Latin and Greek languages, by SAMUEL JOHNSON.'

But the only pupils that were put under his care were the celebrated David Garrick and his brother George, and a Mr. Offely, a young gentleman of good fortune who died early. As yet, his name had nothing of that celebrity which afterwards commanded the highest attention and respect of mankind. Had such an advertisement appeared after the publication of his *London,* or his *Rambler,* or his *Dictionary,* how would it have burst upon the world! with what eagerness would the great and the wealthy have embraced an opportunity of putting their sons under the learned tuition of SAMUEL JOHNSON. The truth, however, is, that he was not so well qualified for being a teacher of elements, and a conductor in learning by regular gradations, as men of inferiour powers of mind. His own acquisitions had been made by fits and starts, by violent irruptions into the regions of knowledge; and it could not be expected that his impatience would be subdued, and his impetuosity restrained, so as to fit him for a quiet guide to novices. The art of communicating instruction, of whatever kind, is much to be valued; and I have ever thought

58

that those who devote themselves to this employment, and do their duty with diligence and success, are entitled to very high respect from the community, as Johnson himself often maintained. Yet I am of opinion that the greatest abilities are not only not required for this office, but render a man less fit for it. . . .

Johnson was not more satisfied with his situation as the master of an academy, than with that of the usher of a school; we need not wonder, therefore, that he did not keep his academy above a year and a half. From Mr. Garrick's account he did not appear to have been profoundly reverenced by his pupils. His oddities of manner, and uncouth gesticulations, could not but be the subject of merriment to them; and, in particular, the young rogues used to listen at the door of his bed-chamber, and peep through the key-hole, that they might turn into ridicule his tumultuous and awkward fondness for Mrs. Johnson, whom he used to name by the familiar appellation of *Tetty* or *Tetsey,* which, like *Betty* or *Betsey,* is provincially used as a contraction for *Elisabeth,* her christian name, but which to us seems ludicrous, when applied to a woman of her age and appearance. Mr. Garrick described her to me as very fat, with a bosom of more than ordinary protuberance, with swelled cheeks of a florid red, produced by thick painting, and increased by the liberal use of cordials; flaring and fantastick in her dress, and affected both in her speech and her general behaviour. I have seen Garrick exhibit her, by his exquisite talent of mimickry, so as to excite the heartiest bursts of laughter; but he, probably, as is the case in all such representation, considerably aggravated the picture. . . .

While Johnson kept his academy, there can be no doubt that he was insensibly furnishing his mind with various knowledge; but I have not discovered that he wrote any thing except a great part of his tragedy of *Irene.* Mr. Peter Garrick, the elder brother of David, told me that he remembered Johnson's borrowing the *Turkish History* of him, in order to form his play from it. When he had finished some part of it, he read what he had done to Mr. Walmsley, who objected to his having already brought his heroine into great distress, and asked him, 'How can you possibly contrive to plunge her into deeper calamity?' Johnson, in sly allusion to the supposed oppressive proceedings of the court of which Mr. Walmsley was register, replied, 'Sir, I can put her into the Spiritual Court!'

Mr. Walmsley, however, was well pleased with this proof of Johnson's abilities as a dramatick writer, and advised him to finish the tragedy, and produce it on the stage.

Johnson now thought of trying his fortune in London, the great field of genius and exertion, where talents of every kind have the fullest scope, and the highest encouragement. It is a memorable circumstance that his pupil David Garrick went thither at the same time,[1] with intention to complete his education, and follow the profession of the law, from which he was soon diverted by his decided preference for the stage. . . .

How he employed himself upon his first coming to London is not particularly known. I never heard that he found any protection or encouragement by the means of Mr. Colson, to whose academy David Garrick went. Mrs. Lucy Porter told me, that Mr. Walmsley gave him a letter of introduction to Lintot his bookseller, and that Johnson wrote some things for him; but I imagine this to be a mistake, for I have discovered no trace of it, and I am pretty sure he told me that Mr. Cave was the first publisher by whom his pen was engaged in London.

He had a little money when he came to town, and he knew how he could live in the cheapest manner. His first lodgings were at the house of Mr. Norris, a staymaker, in Exeter-street, adjoining Catherine-street, in the Strand. 'I dined (said he) very well for eight-pence, with very good company, at the Pine Apple in New-street, just by. Several of them had travelled. They expected to meet every day; but did not know one another's names. It used to cost the rest a shilling, for they drank wine; but I had a cut of meat for six-pence, and bread for a penny, and gave the waiter a penny; so that I was quite well served, nay, better than the rest, for they gave the waiter nothing.' He at this time, I believe, abstained entirely from fermented liquors: a practice to which he rigidly conformed for many years together, at different periods of his life.

His Ofellus in the *Art of Living in London,* I have heard him relate, was an Irish painter, whom he knew at Birmingham, and who had practised his own precepts of œconomy for several years in the British capital. He assured Johnson,

---

[1] Both of them used to talk pleasantly of this their first journey to London. Garrick, evidently meaning to embellish a little, said one day in my hearing, 'we rode and tied.' And the Bishop of Killaloe informed me, that at another time, when Johnson and Garrick were dining together in a pretty large company, Johnson humorously ascertaining the chronology of something, expressed himself thus: 'that was the year when I came to London with two-pence half-penny in my pocket.' Garrick overhearing him, exclaimed, 'eh? what do you say? with two-pence half-penny in your pocket?'—JOHNSON, 'Why yes; when I came with two-pence half-penny in *my* pocket, and thou, Davy, with three half-pence in thine'—B.

who, I suppose, was then meditating to try his fortune in London, but was apprehensive of the expence, 'that thirty pounds a year was enough to enable a man to live there without being contemptible. He allowed ten pounds for clothes and linen. He said a man might live in a garret at eighteen-pence a week; few people would inquire where he lodged; and if they did, it was easy to say, 'Sir, I am to be found at such a place.' By spending three-pence in a coffee-house, he might be for some hours every day in very good company; he might dine for six-pence, breakfast on bread and milk for a penny, and do without supper. On *clean-shirt-day* he went abroad, and paid visits.' I have heard him more than once talk of this frugal friend, whom he recollected with esteem and kindness, and did not like to have any one smile at the recital. 'This man (said he, gravely) was a very sensible man, who perfectly understood common affairs: a man of a great deal of knowledge of the world, fresh from life, not strained through books. He borrowed a horse and ten pounds at Birmingham. Finding himself master of so much money, he set off for West Chester, in order to get to Ireland. He returned the horse, and probably the ten pounds too, after he got home.'

Considering Johnson's narrow circumstances in the early part of his life, and particularly at the interesting æra of his launching into the ocean of London, it is not to be wondered at, that at an actual instance, proved by experience, of the possibility of enjoying the intellectual luxury of social life, upon a very small income, should deeply engage his attention, and be ever recollected by him as a circumstance of much importance. He amused himself, I remember, by computing how much more expence was absolutely necessary to live upon the same scale with that which his friend described, when the value of money was diminished by the progress of commerce. It may be estimated that double the money might now with difficulty be sufficient.

Amidst this cold obscurity, there was one brilliant circumstance to cheer him; he was well acquainted with Mr. Henry Hervey, one of the branches of the noble family of that name, who had been quartered at Lichfield as an officer of the army, and had at this time a house in London, where Johnson was frequently entertained, and had an opportunity of meeting genteel company. Not very long before his death, he mentioned this, among other particulars of his life, which he was kindly communicating to me; and he described this early friend, 'Harry Hervey,' thus: 'He was a vicious man, but very kind to me. If you call a dog HERVEY, I shall love him.'

He told me he had now written only three acts of his *Irene*, and that he retired for some time to lodgings at Greenwich, where he proceeded in it somewhat further, and used to compose, walking in the Park; but did not stay long enough at that place to finish it. . . .

In the course of the summer he returned to Lichfield, where he had left Mrs. Johnson, and there he at last finished his tragedy, which was not executed with his rapidity of composition upon other occasions, but was slowly and painfully elaborated. A few days before his death, while burning a great mass of papers, he picked out from among them the original unformed sketch of this tragedy, in his own hand-writing, and gave it to Mr. Langton, by whose favour a copy of it is now in my possession. It contains fragments of the intended plot, and speeches for the different persons of the drama, partly in the raw materials of prose, partly worked up into verse; as also a variety of hints for illustration, borrowed from the Greek, Roman, and modern writers. The hand-writing is very difficult to read, even by those who were best acquainted with Johnson's mode of penmanship, which at all times was very particular. The King having graciously accepted of this manuscript as a literary curiosity, Mr. Langton made a fair and distinct copy of it, which he ordered to be bound up with the original and the printed tragedy; and the volume is deposited in the King's library. His Majesty was pleased to permit Mr. Langton to take a copy of it for himself. . . .

Johnson's residence at Lichfield, on his return to it at this time, was only for three months; and as he had as yet seen but a small part of the wonders of the Metropolis, he had little to tell his townsmen. He related to me the following minute anecdote of this period: 'In the last age, when my mother lived in London, there were two sets of people, those who gave the wall, and those who took it; the peaceable and the quarrelsome. When I returned to Lichfield, after having been in London, my mother asked me, whether I was one of those who gave the wall, or those who took it. *Now* it is fixed that every man keeps to the right; or, if one is taking the wall, another yields it; and it is never a dispute.'

He now removed to London with Mrs. Johnson; but her daughter, who had lived with them at Edial, was left with her relations in the country. His lodgings were for some time in Woodstock-street, near Hanover-square, and afterwards in Castle-street, near Cavendish-square. As there is something pleasingly interesting, to many, in tracing so great a man through all his different habitations, I shall, before this work is concluded, present my readers with an exact list of his lodgings and houses, in order of time, which, in placid condescension to my respectful curiosity, he one evening dictated to me, but without specifying how long he lived at each. In the progress of his life I shall have occasion to mention some of them as connected with particular incidents, or with the writing of particular parts of his works. To some, this minute attention may appear trifling; but when we consider the punctilious exactness with which the different houses in which Milton resided have been traced by the writers of his life, a similar enthusiasm may be pardoned in the biographer of Johnson.

His tragedy being by this time, as he thought, completely finished and fit for the stage, he was very desirous that it should be brought forward. Mr. Peter Garrick told me, that Johnson and he went together to the Fountain tavern, and read it over, and that he afterwards solicited Mr. Fleetwood, the patentee of Drury-lane theatre, to have it acted at his house; but Mr. Fleetwood would not accept it, probably because it was not patronized by some man of high rank; and it was not acted till 1749, when his friend David Garrick was manager of that theatre.

The Gentleman's Magazine, begun and carried on by Mr. Edward Cave, under the name of SYLVANUS URBAN, had attracted the notice and esteem of Johnson, in an eminent degree, before he came to London as an adventurer in literature. He told me, that when he first saw St. John's Gate, the place where that deservedly popular miscellany was originally printed, he 'beheld it with reverence.' I suppose, indeed, that every young authour has had the same kind of feeling for the magazine or periodical publication which has first entertained him, and in which he has first had an opportunity to see himself in print, without the risk of exposing his name. I myself recollect such impressions from *The Scots Magazine*, which was begun at Edinburgh in the year 1739, and has been ever conducted with judgement, accuracy, and propriety. I yet cannot help thinking of it with an affectionate regard. Johnson has dignified the *Gentleman's Magazine*, by the importance with which he invests the life of Cave; but he has given it still greater lustre by the various admirable Essays which he wrote for it.[1] . . .

[1] While in the course of my narrative I enumerate his writings, I shall take care that my readers shall not be left to waver in doubt, between certainty and conjecture, with regard to their authenticity; and, for that purpose, shall mark with an *asterisk* (*) those which he acknowledged to his friends, and with a *dagger* (†) those which are ascertained to be his by internal evidence. When any other pieces are ascribed to him, I shall give my reasons—B.

His first performance in the *Gentleman's Magazine*, which for many years was his principal resource for employment and support, was a copy of Latin verses, in March 1738, addressed to the editor in so happy a style of compliment, that Cave must have been destitute both of taste and sensibility had he not felt himself highly gratified. . . .

It appears that he was now enlisted by Mr. Cave as a regular coadjutor in his magazine, by which he probably obtained a tolerable livelihood. At what time, or by what means, he had acquired a competent knowledge both of French and Italian, I do not know; but he was so well skilled in them, as to be sufficiently qualified for a translator. That part of his labour which consisted in emendation and improvement of the productions of other contributors, like that employed in levelling ground, can be perceived only by those who had an opportunity of comparing the original with the altered copy. What we certainly know to have been done by him in this way, was the Debates in both houses of Parliament, under the name of 'The Senate of Lilliput,' sometimes with feigned denominations of the several speakers, sometimes with denominations formed of the letters of their real names, in the manner of what is called anagram, so that they might easily be decyphered. Parliament then kept the press in a kind of mysterious awe, which made it necessary to have recourse to such devices. In our time it has acquired an unrestrained freedom, so that the people in all parts of the kingdom have a fair, open, and exact report of the actual proceedings of their representatives and legislators, which in our constitution is highly to be valued; though, unquestionably, there has of late been too much reason to complain of the petulance with which obscure scribblers have presumed to treat men of the most respectable character and situation.

This important article of the *Gentleman's Magazine* was, for several years, executed by Mr. William Guthrie, a man who deserves to be respectably recorded in the literary annals of this country. . . . The debates in Parliament, which were brought home and digested by Guthrie, whose memory, though surpassed by others who have since followed him in the same department, was yet very quick and tenacious, were sent by Cave to Johnson for his revision; and, after some time, when Guthrie had attained to greater variety of employment, and the speeches were more and more enriched by the accession of Johnson's genius, it was resolved that he should do the whole himself, from the scanty notes furnished by persons employed to attend in both houses of Parliament. Sometimes, however, as he himself told me, he had nothing more communicated to him than the names of the several speakers, and the part which they had taken in the debate.

Thus was Johnson employed, during some of the best years of his life, as a mere literary labourer 'for gain not glory,' solely to obtain an honest support. He however indulged himself in occasional little sallies, which the French so happily express by the term *jeux d'esprit,* and which will be noticed in their order, in the progress of this work.

But what first displayed his transcendent powers, and 'gave the world assurance of the MAN,' was his *London, a Poem, in Imitation of the Third Satire of Juvenal:* which came out in May this year, and burst forth with a splendour, the rays of which will for ever encircle his name. Boileau had imitated the same satire with great success, applying it to Paris; but an attentive comparison will satisfy every reader, that he is much excelled by the English Juvenal. Oldham had also imitated it, and applied it to London; all which performances concur to prove, that great cities, in every age, and in every country, will furnish similar topicks of satire. . . .

To us who have long known the manly force, bold spirit, and masterly versification of this poem, it is a matter of curiosity to observe the diffidence with which its authour brought it forward into publick notice, while he is so cautious as not to avow it to be his own production; and with what humility he offers to allow the printer[1] to 'alter any stroke of satire which he might dislike.' That any such alteration was made, we do not know. If we did, we could not but feel an indignant regret; but how painful is it to see that a writer of such vigorous powers of mind was actually in such distress, that the small profit which so short a poem, however excellent, could yield, was courted as a 'relief.' . . .

Johnson's *London* was published in May, 1738; and it is remarkable, that it came out on the same morning with Pope's satire, entitled '1738;' so that England had at once its Juvenal and Horace as poetical monitors. The Reverend Dr. Douglas, now Bishop of Salisbury, to whom I am indebted for some obliging communications, was then a student at Oxford, and remembers well the effect which *London* produced. Every body was delighted with it; and there being no name to it, the first buz of the literary circles was 'here is an unknown poet, greater even than Pope.' And it is recorded in the *Gentleman's Magazine* of that year, that it 'got to the second edition in the course of a week.' . . .

Pope, who then filled the poetical throne without a rival, it may reasonably be presumed, must have been particularly

[1] Cave.

struck by the sudden appearance of such a poet; and, to his credit, let it be remembered, that his feelings and conduct on the occasion were candid and liberal. He requested Mr. Richardson, son of the painter, to endeavour to find out who this new authour was. Mr. Richardson, after some inquiry, having informed him that he had discovered only that his name was Johnson, and that he was some obscure man, Pope said, 'he will soon be *déterré.*' We shall presently see, from a note written by Pope, that he was himself afterwards more successful in his inquiries than his friend.

That in this justly-celebrated poem may be found a few rhymes which the critical precision of English prosody at this day would disallow, cannot be denied; but with this small imperfection, which in the general blaze of its excellence is not perceived, till the mind has subsided into cool attention, it is, undoubtedly, one of the noblest productions in our language, both for sentiment and expression. The nation was then in that ferment against the court and the ministry, which some years after ended in the downfall of Sir Robert Walpole; and as it has been said, that Tories are Whigs when out of place, and Whigs, Tories when in place; so, as a Whig administration ruled with what force it could, a Tory opposition had all the animation and all the eloquence of resistance to power, aided by the common topicks of patriotism, liberty, and independence! Accordingly, we find in Johnson's *London* the most spirited invectives against tyranny and oppression, the warmest predilection for his own country, and the purest love of virtue; interspersed with traits of his own particular character and situation, not omitting his prejudices as a 'true-born Englishman,' not only against foreign countries, but against Ireland and Scotland. . . .

Yet, while we admire the poetical excellence of this poem, candour obliges us to allow, that the flame of patriotism and zeal for popular resistance with which it is fraught, had no just cause. There was, in truth, no 'oppression;' the 'nation' was *not* 'cheated.' Sir Robert Walpole was a wise and a benevolent minister, who thought that the happiness and prosperity of a commerical country like ours, would be best promoted by peace, which he accordingly maintained, with credit, during a very long period. Johnson himself afterwards honestly acknowledged the merit of Walpole, whom he called 'a fixed star;' while he characterised his opponent, Pitt, as a 'a meteor.' But Johnson's juvenile poem was naturally impregnated with the fire of opposition, and upon every account was universally admired.

Though thus elevated into fame, and conscious of uncommon powers, he had not that bustling confidence, or, I may rather say, that animated ambition, which one might have supposed would have urged him to endeavour at rising in life. But such was his inflexible dignity of character, that he could not stoop to court the great; without which, hardly any man has made his way to high station. He could not expect to produce many such works as his *London*, and he felt the hardship of writing for bread; he was, therefore, willing to resume the office of a schoolmaster, so as to have a sure, though moderate income for his life; and an offer being made to him of the mastership of a school, provided he could obtain the degree of Master of Arts, Dr. Adams was applied to, by a common friend, to know whether that could be granted him as a favour from the University of Oxford. But though he had made such a figure in the literary world, it was then thought too great a favour to be asked.

Pope, without any knowledge of him but from his *London*, recommended him to Earl Gower, who endeavoured to procure for him a degree from Dublin, by the following letter to a friend of Dean Swift.[1]

It was, perhaps, no small disappointment to Johnson that this respectable application had not the desired effect; yet how much reason has there been, both for himself and his country, to rejoice that it did not succeed, as he might probably have wasted in obscurity those hours in which he afterwards produced his incomparable works.

About this time he made one other effort to emancipate himself from the drudgery of authourship. He applied to Dr. Adams, to consult Dr. Smalbroke of the Commons, whether a person might be permitted to practice as an advocate there, without a doctor's degree in Civil Law. 'I am (said he) a total stranger to these studies; but whatever is a profession, and maintains numbers, must be within the reach of common abilities, and some degree of industry.' Dr. Adams was much pleased with Johnson's design to employ his talents in that manner, being confident he would have attained to great eminence. And, indeed, I cannot conceive a man better qualified to make a distinguished figure as a lawyer; for, he would have brought to his profession a rich store of various knowledge, an uncommon acuteness, and a command of language, in which few could have equalled, and none have surpassed him. He who could display eloquence and wit in defence of the decision of the House of Commons upon Mr. Wilkes's election for Middlesex, and of the unconstitutional taxation of our fellow-subjects in America, must have been a powerful

[1] Omitted here.

advocate in any cause. But here, also, the want of a degree was an insurmountable bar.

He was, therefore, under the necessity of persevering in that course, into which he had been forced; and we find that his proposal from Greenwich to Mr. Cave, for a translation of Father Paul Sarpi's History, was accepted.[1] . . .

In the *Gentleman's Magazine* of this year, Johnson gave a Life of Father Paul;* and he wrote the Preface to the Volume,† which, though prefixed to it when bound, is always published with the Appendix, and is therefore the last composition belonging to it. The ability and nice adaptation with which he could draw up a prefatory address, was one of his peculiar excellencies. . . . His separate publications were, 'A Complete Vindication of the Licensers of the Stage, from the malicious and scandalous Aspersions of Mr. Brooke, Authour of Gustavus Vasa,'* being an ironical Attack upon them for their Suppression of that Tragedy; and, 'Marmor Norfolciense; or an Essay on an ancient prophetical Inscription in monkish Rhyme, lately discovered near Lynne in Norfolk, by PROBUS BRITANNICUS.' * In this performance, he, in a feigned inscription, supposed to have been found in Norfolk, the county of Sir Robert Walpole, then the obnoxious prime minister of this country, inveighs against the Brunswick succession, and the measures of government consequent upon it. To this supposed prophecy he added a Commentary, making each expression apply to the times, with warm Anti-Hanoverian zeal.

This anonymous pamphlet, I believe, did not make so much noise as was expected, and, therefore, had not a very extensive circulation. Sir John Hawkins relates, that, 'warrants were issued, and messengers employed to apprehend the authour; who, though he had forborne to subscribe his name to the pamphlet, the vigilance of those in pursuit of him had discovered;' and we are informed, that he lay concealed in Lambeth-marsh till the scent after him grew cold. This, however, is altogether without foundation; for Mr. Steele, one of the Secretaries of the Treasury, who amidst a variety of important business, politely obliged me with his attention to my inquiry, informs me, that 'he directed every possible search to be made in the records of the Treasury and Secretary of State's Office, but could find no trace whatever of any warrant having been issued to apprehend the authour of this pamphlet.' . . .

As Mr. Pope's note concerning Johnson, alluded to in a former page, refers both to his *London,* and his *Marmor*

---

[1] The translation was later dropped.

Norfolciense, I have deferred inserting it till now. I am in-debted for it to Dr. Percy, the Bishop of Dromore, who per-mitted me to copy it from the original in his possession. It was presented to his Lordship by Sir Joshua Reynolds, to whom it was given by the son of Mr. Richardson the painter, the person to whom it is addressed. I have transcribed it with minute exactness, that the peculiar mode of writing, and im-perfect spelling of that celebrated poet, may be exhibited to the curious in literature. It justifies Swift's epithet of 'paper-sparing Pope,' for it is written on a slip no larger than a com-mon message-card, and was sent to Mr. Richardson, along with the *Imitation of Juvenal.*

'This is imitated by one Johnson who put in for a Publick-school in Shropshire, but was disappointed. He has an infirmi-ty of the convulsive kind, that attacks him sometimes, so as to make him a sad Spectacle. Mr. P. from the Merit of this Work which was all the knowledge he had of him endea-vour'd to serve him without his own application; & wrote to my L^d gore, but he did not succeed. Mr. Johnson published afterw^{ds} another Poem in Latin with Notes the whole very Humerous call'd the Norfolk Prophecy. P.'

Johnson had been told of this note; and Sir Joshua Reyn-olds informed him of the compliment which it contained, but, from delicacy, avoided shewing him the paper itself. When Sir Joshua observed to Johnson that he seemed very desirous to see Pope's note, he answered, 'Who would not be proud to have such a man as Pope so solicitous in inquiring about him?'

The infirmity to which Mr. Pope alludes, appeared to me also, as I have elsewhere observed, to be of the convulsive kind, and of the nature of that distemper called St. Vitus's dance; and in this opinion I am confirmed by the description which Sydenham gives of that disease. 'This disorder is a kind of convulsion. It manifests itself by halting or unsteadi-ness of one of the legs, which the patient draws after him like an ideot. If the hand of the same side be applied to the breast, or any other part of the body, he cannot keep it a mo-ment in the same posture, but it will be drawn into a different one by a convulsion, notwithstanding all his efforts to the contrary.' Sir Joshua Reynolds, however, was of a different opinion, and favoured me with the following paper.

'Those motions or tricks of Dr. Johnson are improperly called convulsions. He could sit motionless, when he was told so to do, as well as any other man; my opinion is that it pro-ceeded from a habit which he had indulged himself in, of accompaning his thoughts with certain untoward actions, and those actions always appeared to me as if they were meant to reprobate some part of his past conduct. Whenever he was not engaged in conversation, such thoughts were sure to rush into his mind; and, for this reason, any company, any employment whatever, he preferred to being alone. The great business of his life (he said) was to escape from himself; this disposition he considered as the disease of his mind, which nothing cured but company.

'One instance of his absence and particularity, as it is characteristick of the man, may be worth relating. When he and I took a journey together into the West, we visited the late Mr. Banks, of Dorsetshire; the conversation turning upon pictures, which Johnson could not well see, he retired to a corner of the room, stretching out his right leg as far as he could reach before him, then bringing up his left leg, and stretching his right still further on. The old gentleman observing him, went up to him, and in a very courteous manner assured him, that though it was not a new house, the flooring was perfectly safe. The Doctor started from his reverie, like a person waked out of his sleep, but spoke not a word.'

While we are on this subject, my readers may not be displeased with another anecdote, communicated to me by the same friend, from the relation of Mr. Hogarth.

Johnson used to be a pretty frequent visitor at the house of Mr. Richardson, authour of *Clarissa,* and other novels of extensive reputation. Mr. Hogarth came one day to see Richardson, soon after the execution of Dr. Cameron, for having taken arms for the house of Stuart in 1745–6; and being a warm partisan of George the Second, he observed to Richardson, that certainly there must have been some very unfavourable circumstances lately discovered in this particular case, which had induced the King to approve of an execution for rebellion so long after the time when it was committed, as this had the appearance of putting a man to death in cold blood, and was very unlike his Majesty's usual clemency. While he was talking, he perceived a person standing at a window in the room, shaking his head, and rolling himself about in a strange ridiculous manner. He concluded that he was an ideot, whom his relations had put under the care of Mr. Richardson, as a very good man. To his great surprize, however, this figure stalked forwards to where he and Mr. Richardson were sitting, and all at once took up the argument, and burst out into an invective against George the Second, as one, who, upon all occasions, was unrelenting and barbarous; mentioning many instances, particularly, that when an officer of high rank had been acquitted by a Court Martial, George the Second had, with his own hand, struck his name off the list. In short, he displayed such a power of eloquence, that Hogarth looked at him with astonishment, and actually imagined that this ideot had been at the moment inspired. Neither Hogarth nor Johnson were made known to each other at this interview.

1740: ÆTAT. 31.]—IN 1740 he wrote for the *Gentleman's Magazine* the 'Preface,'† 'Life of Sir Francis Drake,' * and the first parts of those of 'Admiral Blake,' * and of 'Philip Baretier,' * both which he finished the following year. He also wrote an 'Essay on Epitaphs,'† and an 'Epitaph on Philips, a Musician,' * which was afterwards published with some other pieces of his, in Mrs. Williams's *Miscellanies*. This Epitaph is so exquisitely beautiful, that I remember even Lord Kames, strangely prejudiced as he was against Dr. Johnson, was compelled to allow it very high praise. . . .

In 1741 he wrote for the *Gentleman's Magazine* 'the Preface,' * 'Conclusion of his lives of Drake and Baretier,' † 'A free translation of the Jests of Hierocles, with an Introduction;' † and, I think, the following pieces: 'Debate on the Proposal of Parliament to Cromwell, to assume the Title of King, abridged, methodised, and digested;' † 'Translation of Abbé Guyon's Dissertation on the Amazons;' † 'Translation of Fontenelle's Panegyrick on Dr. Morin.' † Two notes upon this appear to me undoubtedly his. He this year, and the two following, wrote the *Parliamentary Debates*. He told me himself, that he was the sole composer of them for those three years only. He was not, however, precisely exact in his statement, which he mentioned from hasty recollection; for it is sufficiently evident, that his composition of them began November 19, 1740, and ended February 23, 1742–3. . . . Johnson told me that as soon as he found that the speeches were thought genuine, he determined that he would write no more of them; for 'he would not be accessary to the propagation of falsehood.' And such was the tenderness of his conscience, that a short time before his death he expressed his regret for his having been the authour of fictions, which had passed for realities.

He nevertheless agreed with me in thinking, that the debates which he had framed were to be valued as orations upon questions of publick importance. They have accordingly been collected in volumes, properly arranged, and recommended to the notice of parliamentary speakers by a preface, written by no inferior hand. I must, however, observe, that although there is in those debates a wonderful store of political information, and very powerful eloquence, I cannot agree that they exhibit the manner of each particular speaker, as Sir John Hawkins seems to think. But, indeed, what opinion can we have of his judgement, and taste in publick speaking, who presumes to give, as the characteristicks of two celebrated orators, 'the deep-mouthed rancour of Pulteney, and the yelping pertinacity of Pitt. . . .

1742: ÆTAT. 33.]—In 1742 he wrote for the *Gentleman's Magazine* the 'Preface,' † the 'Parliamentary Debates,' * 'Essay on the Account of the conduct of the Duchess of Marlborough,' * then the popular topick of conversation. This 'Essay' is a short but masterly performance. We find him, in No. 13 of his *Rambler,* censuring a profligate sentiment in that 'Account;' and again insisting upon it strenuously in conversation. 'An account of the Life of Peter Burman,' * I believe chiefly taken from a foreign publication; as, indeed, he could not himself know much about Burman; 'Additions to his Life of Baretier;' * 'The Life of Sydenham,' * afterwards prefixed to Dr. Swan's edition of his works; 'Proposals for Printing Bibliotheca Harleiana, or a Catalogue of the Library of the Earl of Oxford.' * His account of that celebrated collection of books, in which he displays the importance to literature of what the French call a *catalogue raisonné,* when the subjects of it are extensive and various, and it is executed with ability, cannot fail to impress all his readers with admiration of his philological attainments. It was afterwards prefixed to the first volume of the Catalogue, in which the Latin accounts of books were written by him. He was employed in this business by Mr. Thomas Osborne the bookseller, who purchased the library for 13,000*l.,* a sum which Mr. Oldys says, in one of his manuscripts, was not more than the binding of the books had cost; yet, as Dr. Johnson assured me, the slowness of the sale was such, that there was not much gained by it. It has been confidently related, with many embellishments, that Johnson one day knocked Osborne down in his shop, with a folio, and put his foot upon his neck. The simple truth I had from Johnson himself. 'Sir, he was impertinent to me, and I beat him. But it was not in his shop: it was in my own chamber.' . . .

I would also ascribe to him an 'Essay on the Description of China, from the French of Du Halde.' †

His writings in the *Gentleman's Magazine* in 1743, are, the 'Preface,' † the 'Parliamentary Debates,' † 'Considerations on the Dispute between Crousaz and Warburton, on Pope's Essay on Man;' † in which, while he defends Crousaz, he shews an admirable metaphysical acuteness and temperance in controversy; 'Ad Lauram parituram Epigramma;'* and, 'A

72

Latin Translation of Pope's Verses on his Grotto;' * and, as he could employ his pen with equal success upon a small matter as a great, I suppose him to be the authour of an advertisement for Osborne, concerning the great Harleian Catalogue. . . .

Johnson had now an opportunity of obliging his schoolfellow Dr. James, of whom he once observed, 'no man brings more mind to his profession.' James published this year his *Medicinal Dictionary*, in three volumes folio. Johnson, as I understood from him, had written, or assisted in writing, the proposals for this work; and being very fond of the study of physick, in which James was his master, he furnished some of the articles. He, however, certainly wrote for it the Dedication to Dr. Mead,† which is conceived with great address, to conciliate the patronage of that very eminent man. . . .

His circumstances were at this time much embarrassed; yet his affection for his mother was so warm, and so liberal, that he took upon himself a debt of her's, which, though small in itself, was then considerable to him. This appears from the following letter which he wrote to Mr. Levett, of Lichfield, the original of which lies now before me.

'*To* Mr. LEVETT; *in Lichfield*.
    'SIR,   'December 1, 1743.
'I am extremely sorry that we have encroached so much upon your forbearance with respect to the interest, which a great perplexity of affairs hindered me from thinking of with that attention that I ought, and which I am not immediately able to remit to you, but will pay it (I think twelve pounds,) in two months. I look upon this, and on the future interest of that mortgage, as my own debt; and beg that you will be pleased to give me directions how to pay it, and not mention it to my dear mother. If it be necessary to pay this in less time, I believe I can do it; but I take two months for certainty, and beg an answer whether you can allow me so much time. I think myself very much obliged to your forbearance, and shall esteem it a great happiness to be able to serve you. I have great opportunities of dispersing any thing that you may think it proper to make publick. I will give a note for the money, payable at the time mentioned, to any one here that you shall appoint. I am, Sir, your most obedient, and most humble servant,

                                              'SAM. JOHNSON.
    'At Mr. Osborne's, bookseller, in Gray's Inn.'

1744: ÆTAT. 35.]—It does not appear that he wrote any thing in 1744 for the *Gentleman's Magazine,* but the Preface.† His *Life of Baretier* was now re-published in a pamphlet by itself. But he produced one work this year, fully sufficient to maintain the high reputation which he had acquired. This was *The Life of Richard Savage;*[*] a man, of whom it is difficult to speak impartially, without wondering that he was for some time the intimate companion of Johnson; for his character was marked by profligacy, insolence, and ingratitude: yet, as he undoubtedly had a warm and vigorous, though unregulated mind, had seen life in all its varieties, and been much in the company of the statesmen and wits of his time, he could communicate to Johnson an abundant supply of such materials as his philosophical curiosity most eagerly desired; and as Savage's misfortunes and misconduct had reduced him to the lowest state of wretchedness as a writer for bread, his visits to St. John's Gate naturally brought Johnson and him together.

It is melancholy to reflect, that Johnson and Savage were sometimes in such extreme indigence,[1] that they could not pay for a lodging; so that they have wandered together whole nights in the streets. Yet in these almost incredible scenes of distress, we may suppose that Savage mentioned many of the anecdotes with which Johnson afterwards enriched the life of his unhappy companion, and those of other Poets.

He told Sir Joshua Reynolds, that one night in particular, when Savage and he walked round St. James's-square for want of a lodging, they were not at all depressed by their situation; but in high spirits and brimful of patriotism, traversed the square for several hours, inveighed against the minister, and 'resolved they would *stand by their country.*'

I am afraid, however, that by associating with Savage, who was habituated to the dissipation and licentiousness of the town, Johnson, though his good principles remained steady, did not entirely preserve that conduct, for which, in days of greater simplicity, he was remarked by his friend Mr. Hector; but was imperceptibly led into some indulgencies which occasioned much distress to his virtuous mind.

That Johnson was anxious that an authentick and favourable account of his extraordinary friend should first get possession of the publick attention, is evident from a letter which he wrote in the *Gentleman's Magazine* for August of the year preceding its publication.[2]

---

[1] Soon after Savage's *Life* was published, Mr. Harte dined with Edward Cave, and occasionally praised it. Soon after, meeting him, Cave said, 'You made a man very happy t'other day.'—'How could that be,' says Harte; 'nobody was there but ourselves.' Cave answered, by reminding him that a plate of victuals was sent behind a screen, which was to Johnson, dressed so shabbily, that he did not choose to appear; but on hearing the conversation, was highly delighted with the encomiums on his book.

[2] Omitted here.

In February, 1744, it accordingly came forth from the shop of Roberts, between whom and Johnson I have not traced any connection, except the casual one of this publication. In Johnson's *Life of Savage,* although it must be allowed that its moral is the reverse of—'*Respicere exemplar vitæ morumque jubebo,*'[1] a very useful lesson is inculcated, to guard men of warm passions from a too free indulgence of them; and the various incidents are related in so clear and animated a manner, and illuminated throughout with so much philosophy, that it is one of the most interesting narratives in the English language. Sir Joshua Reynolds told me, that upon his return from Italy he met with it in Devonshire, knowing nothing of its authour, and began to read it while he was standing with his arm leaning against a chimney-piece. It seized his attention so strongly, that, not being able to lay down the book till he had finished it, when he attempted to move, he found his arm totally benumbed. The rapidity with which this work was composed, is a wonderful circumstance. Johnson has been heard to say, 'I wrote forty-eight of the printed octavo pages of the *Life of Savage* at a sitting; but then I sat up all night. . . .

It is remarkable, that in this biographical disquisition there appears a very strong symptom of Johnson's prejudice against players; a prejudice which may be attributed to the following causes: first, the imperfection of his organs, which were so defective that he was not susceptible of the fine impressions which theatrical excellence produces upon the generality of mankind; secondly, the cold rejection of his tragedy; and, lastly, the brilliant success of Garrick, who had been his pupil, who had come to London at the same time with him, not in a much more prosperous state than himself, and whose talents he undoubtedly rated low, compared with his own. His being outstripped by his pupil in the race of immediate fame, as well as of fortune, probably made him feel some indignation, as thinking that whatever might be Garrick's merits in his art, the reward was too great when compared with what the most successful efforts of literary labour could attain. At all periods of his life Johnson used to talk contemptuously of players; but in this work he speaks of them with peculiar acrimony; for which, perhaps, there was formerly too much reason from the licentious and dissolute manners of those engaged in that profession. It is but justice to add, that in our own time such a change has taken place, that there is no longer room for such an unfavourable distinction.

His schoolfellow and friend, Dr. Taylor, told me a pleasant

[1] 'I counseled him to take real life and customs as his model.' Horace, *Art of Poetry,* l. 317.

anecdote of Johnson's triumphing over his pupil David Garrick. When that great actor had played some little time at Goodman's-fields, Johnson and Taylor went to see him perform, and afterwards passed the evening at a tavern with him and old Giffard. Johnson, who was ever depreciating stage-players, after censuring some mistakes in emphasis which Garrick had committed in the course of that night's acting, said, 'The players, Sir, have got a kind of rant, with which they run on, without any regard either to accent or emphasis.' Both Garrick and Giffard were offended at this sarcasm, and endeavoured to refute it; upon which Johnson rejoined, 'Well now, I'll give you something to speak, with which you are little acquainted, and then we shall see how just my observation is. That shall be the criterion. Let me hear you repeat the ninth Commandment, "Thou shalt not bear false witness against thy neighbour." ' Both tried at it, said Dr. Taylor, and both mistook the emphasis, which should be upon *not* and *false witness*. Johnson put them right, and enjoyed his victory with great glee. . . .

Johnson's partiality for Savage made him entertain no doubt of his story, however extraordinary and improbable. It never occurred to him to question his being the son of the Countess of Macclesfield, of whose unrelenting barbarity he so loudly complained, and the particulars of which are related in so strong and affecting a manner in Johnson's life of him. Johnson was certainly well warranted in publishing his narrative, however offensive it might be to the lady and her relations, because her alledged unnatural and cruel conduct to her son, and shameful avowal of guilt, were stated in a *Life of Savage* now lying before me, which came out so early as 1727, and no attempt had been made to confute it, or to punish the authour or printer as a libeller: but for the honour of human nature, we should be glad to find the shocking tale not true; and, from a respectable gentleman connected with the lady's family, I have received such information and remarks, as joined to my own inquiries, will, I think, render it at least somewhat doubtful, especially when we consider that it must have originated from the person himself who went by the name of Richard Savage. . . .

He [Johnson] this year wrote the Preface to the *Harleian Miscellany*.* The selection of the pamphlets of which it was composed was made by Mr. Oldys, a man of eager curiosity and indefatigable diligence, who first exerted that spirit of inquiry into the literature of the old English writers, by which the works of our great dramatick poet have of late been so signally illustrated.

In 1745 he published a pamphlet entitled *Miscellaneous*

*Observations on the Tragedy of Macbeth, with remarks on Sir T. H.'s (Sir Thomas Hanmer's) Edition of Shakspeare.** To which he affixed, proposals for a new edition of that poet.

As we do not trace any thing else published by him during the course of this year, we may conjecture that he was occupied entirely with that work. But the little encouragement which was given by the publick to his anonymous proposals for the execution of a task which Warburton was known to have undertaken, probably damped his ardour. His pamphlet, however, was highly esteemed, and was fortunate enough to obtain the approbation even of the supercilious Warburton himself, who, in the Preface to his *Shakspeare* published two years afterwards, thus mentioned it: 'As to all those things which have been published under the titles of *Essays, Remarks, Observations,* &c. on Shakspeare, if you except some critical notes on *Macbeth,* given as a specimen of a projected edition, and written, as appears, by a man of parts and genius, the rest are absolutely below a serious notice.'

Of this flattering distinction shewn to him by Warburton, a very grateful remembrance was ever entertained by Johnson, who said, 'He praised me at a time when praise was of value to me.'

1746: ÆTAT. 37.]—IN 1746 it is probable that he was still employed upon his *Shakspeare,* which perhaps he laid aside for a time, upon account of the high expectations which were formed of Warburton's edition of that great poet. It is somewhat curious, that his literary career appears to have been almost totally suspended in the years 1745 and 1746, those years which were marked by a civil war in Great-Britain, when a rash attempt was made to restore the House of Stuart to the the throne. That he had a tenderness for that unfortunate House, is well known; and some may fancifully imagine, that a sympathetick anxiety impeded the exertion of his intellectual powers: but I am inclined to think, that he was, during this time, sketching the outlines of his great philological work.

None of his letters during those years are extant, so far as I can discover. This is much to be regretted. It might afford some entertainment to see how he then expressed himself to his private friends, concerning State affairs. Dr. Adams informs me, that 'at this time a favourite object which he had in contemplation was 'The Life of Alfred'; in which, from the warmth with which he spoke about it, he would, I believe, had he been master of his own will, have engaged himself, rather than on any other subject.'

1747: ÆTAT. 38.]—IN 1747 it is supposed that the *Gentleman's Magazine* for May was enriched by him with five short poetical pieces, distinguished by three asterisks. The first is a

77

translation, or rather a paraphrase, of a Latin Epitaph on Sir Thomas Hanmer. Whether the Latin was his, or not, I have never heard, though I should think it probably was, if it be certain that he wrote the English; as to which my only cause of doubt is, that his slighting character of Hanmer as an editor, in his *Observations on Macbeth,* is very different from that in the 'Epitaph.' It may be said, that there is the same contrariety between the character in the *Observations,* and that in his own Preface to Shakspeare; but a considerable time elapsed between the one publication and the other, whereas the *Observations* and the 'Epitaph' came close together. The others are 'To Miss——, on her giving the Authour a gold and silk net-work Purse of her own weaving;' 'Stella in Mourning;' 'The Winter's Walk;' 'An Ode;' and, 'To Lyce, an elderly Lady.' I am not positive that all these were his productions; but as 'The Winter's Walk' has never been controverted to be his, and all of them have the same mark, it is reasonable to conclude that they are all written by the same hand. . . .

This year his old pupil and friend, David Garrick, having become joint patentee and manager of Drury-lane theatre, Johnson honoured his opening of it with a Prologue, * which for just and manly dramatick criticism, on the whole range of the English stage, as well as for poetical excellence, is unrivalled. Like the celebrated Epilogue to the *Distressed Mother,* it was, during the season, often called for by the audience. The most striking and brilliant passages of it have been so often repeated, and are so well recollected by all the lovers of the drama and of poetry, that it would be superfluous to point them out. In the *Gentleman's Magazine* for December this year, he inserted an 'Ode on Winter,' which is, I think, an admirable specimen of his genius for lyrick poetry.

But the year 1747 is distinguished as the epoch, when Johnson's arduous and important work, his DICTIONARY OF THE ENGLISH LANGUAGE, was announced to the world, by the publication of its Plan or *Prospectus.*

How long this immense undertaking had been the object of his contemplation, I do not know. I once asked him by what means he had attained to that astonishing knowledge of our language, by which he was enabled to realise a design of such extent, and accumulated difficulty. He told me, that 'it was not the effect of particular study; but that it had grown up in his mind insensibly.' I have been informed by Mr. James Dodsley, that several years before this period, when Johnson was one day sitting in his brother Robert's shop, he heard his brother suggest to him, that a Dictionary of the English Language would be a work that would be well received by the publick; that Johnson seemed at first to catch at the proposition, but, after a pause, said, in his abrupt decisive manner, 'I believe I shall not undertake it.' That he, however, had bestowed much thought upon the subject, before he published his *Plan*, is evident from the enlarged, clear, and accurate views which it exhibits; and we find him mentioning in that tract, that many of the writers whose testimonies were to be produced as authorities, were selected by Pope; which proves that he had been furnished, probably by Mr. Robert Dodsley, with whatever hints that eminent poet had contributed towards a great literary project, that had been the subject of important consideration in a former reign.

The booksellers who contracted with Johnson, single and unaided, for the execution of a work, which in other countries has not been effected but by the co-operating exertions of many, were Mr. Robert Dodsley, Mr. Charles Hitch, Mr. Andrew Millar, the two Messieurs Longman, and the two Messieurs Knapton. The price stipulated was fifteen hundred and seventy-five pounds.

The *Plan* was addressed to Philip Dormer, Earl of Chesterfield, then one of his Majesty's Principal Secretaries of State; a nobleman who was very ambitious of literary distinction, and who, upon being informed of the design, had expressed himself in terms very favourable to its success. There is, perhaps in every thing of any consequence, a secret history which it would be amusing to know, could we have it authentically communicated. Johnson told me, 'Sir, the way in which the *Plan* of my *Dictionary* came to be inscribed to Lord Chesterfield, was this: I had neglected to write it by the time appointed. Dodsley suggested a desire to have it addressed to Lord Chesterfield. I laid hold of this as a pretext for delay, that it might be better done, and let Dodsley have his desire. I said to my friend, Dr. Bathurst, "Now if any good comes of my addressing to Lord Chesterfield, it will be ascribed to deep policy, when, in fact it was only a casual excuse for laziness."' . . .

'With regard to questions of purity or propriety, (says he) I was once in doubt whether I should not attribute to myself too much in attempting to decide them, and whether my province was to extend beyond the proposition of the question, and the display of the suffrages on each side; but I have been since determined by your Lordship's opinion, to interpose my own judgement, and shall therefore endeavour to support what appears to me most consonant to grammar and reason. Ausonius thought that modesty forbade him to plead inability for a task to which Cæsar had judged him equal:

And I may hope, my Lord, that since you, whose authority in our language is so generally acknowledged, have commissioned me to declare my own opinion, I shall be considered as exercising a kind of vicarious jurisdiction; and that the power which might have been denied to my own claim, will be readily allowed me as the delegate of your Lordship.'

This passage proves, that Johnson's addressing his *Plan* to Lord Chesterfield was not merely in consequence of the result of a report by means of Dodsley, that the Earl favoured the design; but that there had been a particular communication with his Lordship concerning it. Dr. Taylor told me, that Johnson sent his *Plan* to him in manuscript, for his perusal; and that when it was lying upon his table, Mr. William Whitehead happened to pay him a visit, and being shewn it, was highly pleased with such parts of it as he had time to read, and begged to take it home with him, which he was allowed to do; that from him it got into the hands of a noble Lord, who carried it to Lord Chesterfield. When Taylor observed this might be an advantage, Johnson replied, 'No, Sir; it would have come out with more bloom, if it had not been seen before by any body.' . . .

That he was fully aware of the arduous nature of the undertaking, he acknowledges; and shews himself perfectly sensible of it in the conclusion of his *Plan,* but he had a noble consciousness of his own abilities, which enabled him to go on with undaunted spirit.

Dr. Adams found him one day busy at his *Dictionary,* when the following dialogue ensued. 'ADAMS. This is a great work, Sir. How are you to get all the etymologies? JOHNSON. Why, Sir, here is a shelf with Junius, and Skinner, and others; and there is a Welch gentleman who has published a collection of Welch proverbs, who will help me with the Welch. ADAMS. But, Sir, how can you do this in three years? JOHNSON. Sir, I have no doubt that I can do it in three years. ADAMS. But the French Academy, which consists of forty members, took forty years to compile their Dictionary. JOHNSON. Sir, thus it is. This is the proportion. Let me see; forty times forty is sixteen hundred. As three to sixteen hundred, so is the proportion of an Englishman to a Frenchman.' With so much ease and pleasantry could he talk of that prodigious labour which he had undertaken to execute.

The publick has had, from another pen, a long detail of what had been done in this country by prior Lexicographers;

[1] 'Why should I say I cannot do what he thinks that I can?' Ausonius, *Epigrams,* i. 12.

80

and no doubt Johnson was wise to avail himself of them, so far as they went: but the learned, yet judicious research of etymology, the various, yet accurate display of definition, and the rich collection of authorities, were reserved for the superior mind of our great philologist. For the mechanical part he employed, as he told me, six amanuenses; and let it be remembered by the natives of North-Britain, to whom he is supposed to have been so hostile, that five of them were of that country. There were two Messieurs Macbean; Mr. Shiels, who we shall hereafter see partly wrote the *Lives of the Poets* to which the name of Cibber is affixed; Mr. Stewart, son of Mr. George Stewart, bookseller at Edinburgh; and a Mr. Maitland. The sixth of these humble assistants was Mr. Peyton, who, I believe, taught French, and published some elementary tracts.

To all these painful labourers, Johnson shewed a never-ceasing kindness, so far as they stood in need of it. The elder Mr. Macbean had afterwards the honour of being Librarian to Archibald, Duke of Argyle, for many years, but was left without a shilling. Johnson wrote for him a Preface to *A System of Ancient Geography;* and, by the favour of Lord Thurlow, got him admitted a poor brother of the Charterhouse. For Shiels, who died of a consumption, he had much tenderness; and it has been thought that some choice sentences in the *Lives of the Poets* were supplied by him. Peyton, when reduced to penury, had frequent aid from the bounty of Johnson, who at last was at the expense of burying both him and his wife.

While the *Dictionary* was going forward, Johnson lived part of the time in Holborn, part in Gough-square, Fleet-street; and he had an upper room fitted up like a counting-house for the purpose, in which he gave to the copyists their several tasks. The words, partly taken from other dictionaries, and partly supplied by himself, having been first written down with spaces left between them, he delivered in writing their etymologies, definitions, and various significations. The authorities were copied from the books themselves, in which he had marked the passages with a black-lead pencil, the traces of which could easily be effaced. I have seen several of them, in which that trouble had not been taken; so that they were just as when used by the copyists. It is remarkable, that he was so attentive in the choice of the passages in which words were authorised, that one may read page after page of his *Dictionary* with improvement and pleasure; and it should not pass unobserved, that he has quoted no authour whose writings had a tendency to hurt sound religion and morality.

The necessary expence of preparing a work of such magnitude for the press, must have been a considerable deduction from the price stipulated to be paid for the copy-right. I understand that nothing was allowed by the booksellers on that account; and I remember his telling me, that a large portion of it having by mistake been written upon both sides of the paper, so as to be inconvenient for the compositor, it cost him twenty pounds to have it transcribed upon one side only.

He is now to be considered as 'tugging at his oar,' as engaged in a steady continued course of occupation, sufficient to employ all his time for some years; and which was the best preventive of that constitutional melancholy which was ever lurking about him, ready to trouble his quiet. But his enlarged and lively mind could not be satisfied without more diversity of employment, and the pleasure of animated relaxation. He therefore not only exerted his talents in occasional composition very different from Lexicography, but formed a club in Ivy-lane, Paternoster-row, with a view to enjoy literary discussion, and amuse his evening hours. The members associated with him in this little society were his beloved friend Dr. Richard Bathurst, Mr. Hawkesworth, afterwards well known by his writings, Mr. John Hawkins, an attorney, and a few others of different professions.

In the *Gentleman's Magazine* for May of this year he wrote a 'Life of Roscommon,'* with Notes, which he afterwards much improved, indented the notes into text, and inserted it amongst his *Lives of the English Poets*.

Mr. Dodsley this year brought out his *Preceptor,* one of the most valuable books for the improvement of young minds that has appeared in any language; and to this meritorious work Johnson furnished 'The Preface,'* containing a general sketch of the book, with a short and perspicuous recommendation of each article; as also, 'The Vision of Theodore the Hermit, found in his Cell,'* a most beautiful allegory of human life, under the figure of ascending the mountain of Existence. The Bishop of Dromore heard Dr. Johnson say, that he thought this was the best thing he ever wrote.

1749: ÆTAT. 40.]—IN January, 1749, he published *The Vanity of Human Wishes, being the Tenth Satire of Juvenal imitated.* He, I believe, composed it the preceding year. Mrs. Johnson, for the sake of country air, had lodgings at Hampstead, to which he resorted occasionally, and there the greatest part, if not the whole, of this *Imitation* was written. The fervid rapidity with which it was produced, is scarcely credible. I have heard him say, that he composed seventy lines of it in one day, without putting one of them upon paper till they were finished. I remember when I once regretted to him that he had not given us more of Juvenal's *Satires,* he said he

82

probably should give more, for he had them all in his head; by which I understood that he had the originals and correspondent allusions floating in his mind, which he could, when he pleased, embody and render permanent without much labour. Some of them, however, he observed were too gross for imitation.

The profits of a single poem, however excellent, appear to have been very small in the last reign, compared with what a publication of the same size has since been known to yield, I have mentioned, upon Johnson's own authority, that for his *London* he had only ten guineas; and now, after his fame was established, he got for his *Vanity of Human Wishes* but five guineas more, as is proved by an authentick document in my possession.

It will be observed, that he reserves to himself the right of printing one edition of this satire, which was his practice upon occasion of the sale of all his writings; it being his fixed intention to publish at some period, for his own profit, a complete collection of his works.

His *Vanity of Human Wishes* has less of common life, but more of a philosophick dignity than his *London*. More readers, therefore, will be delighted with the pointed spirit of *London*, than with the profound reflection of *The Vanity of Human Wishes*. Garrick, for instance, observed in his sprightly manner, with more vivacity than regard to just discrimination, as is usual with wits, 'When Johnson lived much with the Herveys, and saw a good deal of what was passing in life, he wrote his *London*, which is lively and easy. When he became more retired, he gave us his *Vanity of Human Wishes*, which is as hard as Greek. Had he gone on to imitate another satire, it would have been as hard as Hebrew.'

But *The Vanity of Human Wishes* is, in the opinion of the best judges, as high an effort of ethick poetry as any language can shew. The instances of variety of disappointment are chosen so judiciously and painted so strongly, that, the moment they are read, they bring conviction to every thinking mind. That of the scholar must have depressed the too sanguine expectations of many an ambitious student. That of the warrior, Charles of Sweden, is, I think, as highly finished a picture as can possibly be conceived.

Were all the other excellencies of this poem annihilated, it must ever have our grateful reverence from its noble conclusion; in which we are consoled with the assurance that happiness may be attained, if we 'apply our hearts' to piety. . . .

Garrick being now vested with theatrical power by being manager of Drury-lane theatre, he kindly and generously made use of it to bring out Johnson's tragedy, which had been long kept back for want of encouragement. But in this benevolent purpose he met with no small difficulty from the temper of Johnson, which could not brook that a drama which he had formed with much study, and had been obliged to keep more than the nine years of Horace, should be revised and altered at the pleasure of an actor. Yet Garrick knew well, that without some alterations it would not be fit for the stage. A violent dispute having ensued between them, Garrick applied to the Reverend Dr. Taylor to interpose. Johnson was at first very obstinate. 'Sir, (said he) the fellow wants me to make Mahomet run mad, that he may have an opportunity of tossing his hands and kicking his heels.' He was, however, at last, with difficulty, prevailed on to comply with Garrick's wishes, so as to allow of some changes; but still there were not enough.

Dr. Adams was present the first night of the representation of *Irene,* and gave me the following account: 'Before the curtain drew up, there were catcalls whistling, which alarmed Johnson's friends. The Prologue, which was written by himself in a manly strain, soothed the audience, and the play went off tolerably, till it came to the conclusion, when Mrs. Pritchard, the heroine of the piece, was to be strangled upon the stage, and was to speak two lines with the bow-string round her neck. The audience cried out *"Murder! Murder!"* She several times attempted to speak; but in vain. At last she was obliged to go off the stage alive.' This passage was afterwards struck out, and she was carried off to be put to death behind the scenes, as the play now has it. The Epilogue, as Johnson informed me, was written by Sir William Yonge. I know not how his play came to be thus graced by the pen of a person then so eminent in the political world.

Notwithstanding all the support of such performers as Garrick, Barry, Mrs. Cibber, Mrs. Pritchard, and every advantage of dress and decoration, the tragedy of *Irene* did not please the publick. Mr. Garrick's zeal carried it through for nine nights, so that the authour had his three nights' profits; and from a receipt signed by him, now in the hands of Mr. James Dodsley, it appears that his friend Mr. Robert Dodsley gave him one hundred pounds for the copy, with his usual reservation of the right of one edition.

Irene, considered as a poem, is intitled to the praise of superiour excellence. Analysed into parts, it will furnish a rich store of noble sentiments, fine imagery, and beautiful language; but it is deficient in pathos, in that delicate power of touching the human feelings, which is the principal end of the drama. Indeed Garrick has complained to me, that Johnson not only had not the faculty of producing the impressions of tragedy, but that he had not the sensibility to perceive them. His great friend Mr. Walmsley's prediction, that he would 'turn out a fine tragedy-writer,' was, therefore, ill-founded. Johnson was wise enough to be convinced that he had not the talents necessary to write successfully for the stage, and never made another attempt in that species of composition.

When asked how he felt upon the ill success of his tragedy, he replied, 'Like the Monument;' meaning that he continued firm and unmoved as that column. And let it be remembered, as an admonition to the *genus irritabile*[1] of dramatick writers, that this great man, instead of peevishly complaining of the bad taste of the town, submitted to its decision without a murmur. He had, indeed, upon all occasions, a great deference for the general opinion: 'A man (said he) who writes a book, thinks himself wiser or wittier than the rest of mankind; he supposes that he can instruct or amuse them, and the publick to whom he appeals, must, after all, be the judges of his pretensions.'

On occasion of his play being brought upon the stage, Johnson had a fancy that as a dramatick authour his dress should be more gay than what he ordinarily wore; he therefore appeared behind the scenes, and even in one of the side boxes, in a scarlet waistcoat, with rich gold lace, and a gold-laced hat. He humourously observed to Mr. Langton, 'that when in that dress he could not treat people with the same ease as when in his usual plain clothes.' Dress indeed, we must allow, has more effect even upon strong minds than one should suppose, without having had the experience of it. His necessary attendance while his play was in rehearsal, and during its performance, brought him acquainted with many of the performers of both sexes, which produced a more favourable opinion of their profession than he had harshly expressed in his *Life of Savage*. With some of them he kept up an acquaintance as long as he ,and they lived, and was ever ready to shew them acts of kindness. He for a considerable time used to frequent the *Green Room*, and seemed to take delight in dissipating his gloom, by mixing in the sprightly chit-chat of the motley circle then to be found there. Mr. David Hume related to me from Mr. Garrick, that Johnson at last denied himself this amusement, from considerations of rigid virtue; saying, 'I'll come no more behind your scenes, David; for the silk stockings and white bosoms of your actresses excite my amorous propensities.'

1750: ÆTAT. 41.]—IN 1750 he came forth in the character for which he was eminently qualified, a majestick teacher of moral and religious wisdom. The vehicle which he chose was

---

[1] 'Irritable race.' Horace, *Epistles*, II. ii. 102.

that of a periodical paper, which he knew had been, upon former occasions, employed with great success. *The Tatler, Spectator,* and *Guardian,* were the last of the kind published in England, which had stood the test of a long trial; and such an interval had now elapsed since their publication, as made him justly think that, to many of his readers, this form of instruction would, in some degree, have the advantage of novelty. A few days before the first of his *Essays* came out, there started another competitor for fame in the same form, under the title of *The Tatler Revived,* which I believe was 'born but to die.' Johnson was, I think, not very happy in the choice of his title, *The Rambler,* which certainly is not suited to a series of grave and moral discourses; which the Italians have literally, but ludicrously, translated by *Il Vagabondo;* and which has been lately assumed as the denomination of a vehicle of licentious tales, *The Rambler's Magazine.* He gave Sir Joshua Reynolds the following account of its getting this name: 'What *must* be done, Sir, *will* be done. When I was to begin publishing that paper, I was at a loss how to name it. I sat down at night upon my bedside, and resolved that I would not go to sleep till I had fixed its title. *The Rambler* seemed the best that occurred, and I took it.' . . .

The first paper of *The Rambler* was published on Tuesday the 20th of March, 1750; and its authour was enabled to continue it, without interruption, every Tuesday and Friday, till Saturday the 17th of March, 1752, on which day it closed. This is a strong confirmation of the truth of a remark of his, which I have had occasion to quote elsewhere, that 'a man may write at any time, if he will set himself doggedly to it;' for, notwithstanding his constitutional indolence, his depression of spirits, and his labour in carrying on his *Dictionary,* he answered the stated calls of the press twice a week from the stores of his mind, during all that time; having received no assistance, except four billets in No. 10, by Miss Mulso, now Mrs. Chapone; No. 30, by Mrs. Catharine Talbot; No. 97, by Mr. Samuel Richardson, whom he describes in an introductory note as 'An author who has enlarged the knowledge of human nature, and taught the passions to move at the command of virtue;' and Nos. 44 and 100 by Mrs. Elizabeth Carter.

Posterity will be astonished when they are told, upon the authority of Johnson himself, that many of these discourses, which we should suppose had been laboured with all the slow attention of literary leisure, were written in haste as the moment pressed, without even being read over by him before they were printed. It can be accounted for only in this way; that by reading and meditation, and a very close inspection of life, he had accumulated a great fund of miscellaneous knowledge, which, by a peculiar promptitude of mind, was ever ready at his call, and which he had constantly accustomed himself to clothe in the most apt and energetick expression. Sir Joshua Reynolds once asked him by what means he had attained his extraordinary accuracy and flow of language. He told him, that he had early laid it down as a fixed rule to do his best on every occasion, and in every company; to impart whatever he knew in the most forcible language he could put it in; and that by constant practice, and never suffering any careless expressions to escape him, or attempting to deliver his thoughts without arranging them in the clearest manner, it became habitual to him.

Yet he was not altogether unprepared as a periodical writer; for I have in my possession a small duodecimo volume, in which he has written, in the form of Mr. Locke's Common-Place Book, a variety of hints for essays on different subjects. He has marked upon the first blank leaf of it, 'To the 128th page, collections for *The Rambler;*' and in another place, 'In fifty-two there were seventeen provided; in 97—21; in 190—25.' At a subsequent period (probably after the work was finished) he added, 'In all, taken of provided materials, 30.' . . .

This scanty preparation of materials will not, however, much diminish our wonder at the extraordinary fertility of his mind; for the proportion which they bear to the number of essays which he wrote, is very small; and it is remarkable, that those for which he had made no preparation, are as rich and as highly finished as those for which the hints were lying by him. It is also to be observed, that the papers formed from his hints are worked up with such strength and elegance, that we almost lose sight of the hints, which become like 'drops in the bucket.' Indeed, in several instances, he has made a very slender use of them, so that many of them remain still unapplied. . . .

As *The Rambler* was entirely the work of one man, there was, of course, such a uniformity in its texture, as very much to exclude the charm of variety; and the grave and often solemn cast of thinking, which distinguished it from other periodical papers, made it, for some time, not generally liked. So slowly did this excellent work, of which twelve editions have now issued from the press, gain upon the world at large, that even in the closing number the authour says, 'I have never been much a favourite of the publick.' . . .

Johnson told me, with an amiable fondness, a little pleasing circumstance relative to this work. Mrs. Johnson, in whose judgement and taste he had great confidence, said to him, after a few numbers of *The Rambler* had come out, 'I thought very well of you before; but I did not imagine you could have written any thing equal to this.' Distant praise, from whatever quarter, is not so delightful as that of a wife whom a man loves and esteems. Her approbation may be said to 'come home to his *bosom;*' and being so near, its effect is most sensible and permanent. . . .

The Rambler has increased in fame as in age. Soon after its first folio edition was concluded, it was published in six duodecimo volumes; and its authour lived to see ten numerous editions of it in London, beside those of Ireland and Scotland.

I profess myself to have ever entertained a profound veneration for the astonishing force and vivacity of mind which *The Rambler* exhibits. That Johnson had penetration enough to see, and seeing would not disguise the general misery of man in this state of being, may have given rise to the superficial notion of his being too stern a philosopher. But men of reflection will be sensible that he has given a true representation of human existence, and that he has, at the same time, with a generous benevolence displayed every consolation which our state affords us; not only those arising from the hopes of futurity, but such as may be attained in the immediate progress through life. He has not depressed the soul to despondency and indifference. He has every where inculcated study, labour, and exertion. Nay, he has shewn, in a very odious light, a man whose practice is to go about darkening the views of others, by perpetual complaints of evil, and awakening those considerations of danger and distress, which are, for the most part, lulled into a quiet oblivion. This he has done very strongly in his character of Suspirius, from which Goldsmith took that of Croaker, in his comedy of *The Good-Natured Man*, as Johnson told me he acknowledged to him, and which is, indeed, very obvious. . . .

The style of this work has been censured by some shallow criticks as involved and turgid, and abounding with antiquated and hard words. So ill-founded is the first part of this objection, that I will challenge all who may honour this book with a perusal, to point out any English writer whose language conveys his meaning with equal force and perspicuity. It must, indeed, be allowed, that the structure of his sentences is expanded, and often has somewhat of the inversion of Latin; and that he delighted to express familiar thoughts in philosophical language; being in this the reverse of Socrates, who, it was said, reduced philosophy to the simplicity of common life. But let us attend to what he himself says in his concluding paper: 'When common words were less pleasing

to the ear, or less distinct in their signification, I have famil-
iarised the terms of philosophy, by applying them to popular
ideas.' And, as to the second part of this objection, upon a
late careful revision of the work, I can with confidence say,
that it is amazing how few of those words, for which it has
been unjustly characterised, are actually to be found in it; I
am sure, not the proportion of one to each paper. This idle
charge has been echoed from one babbler to another, who
have confounded Johnson's Essays with Johnson's *Dictionary;*
and because he thought it right in a Lexicon of our language
to collect many words which had fallen into disuse, but were
supported by great authorities, it has been imagined that all
of these have been interwoven into his own compositions.
That some of them have been adopted by him unnecessarily,
may, perhaps, be allowed; but, in general they are evidently
an advantage, for without them his stately ideas would be
confined and cramped. 'He that thinks with more extent than
another, will want words of larger meaning.' He once told
me, that he had formed his style upon that of Sir William
Temple, and upon Chambers's Proposal for his *Dictionary.*
He certainly was mistaken; or if he imagined at first that he
was imitating Temple, he was very unsuccessful; for nothing
can be more unlike than the simplicity of Temple, and the
richness of Johnson. Their styles differ as plain cloth and bro-
cade. Temple, indeed, seems equally erroneous in supposing
that he himself had formed his style upon Sandys's *View of
the State of Religion in the Western parts of the World.*

The style of Johnson was, undoubtedly, much formed upon
that of the great writers in the last century, Hooker, Bacon,
Sanderson, Hakewell, and others; those 'GIANTS,' as they
were well characterised by A GREAT PERSONAGE, [1] whose authority, were I to name him, would stamp a reverence on the
opinion. . . .

Sir Thomas Brown, whose life Johnson wrote, was remarkably fond of Anglo-Latian diction; and to his example we are
to ascribe Johnson's sometimes indulging himself in this kind
of phraseology. Johnson's comprehension of mind was the
mould for his language. Had his conceptions been narrower,
his expression would have been easier. His sentences have a
dignified march; and, it is certain, that his example has given
a general elevation to the language of his country, for many
of our best writers have approached very near to him; and,
from the influence which he has had upon our composition,
scarcely any thing is written now that is not better expressed
than was usual before he appeared to lead the national
taste. . . .

[1] George III.

His just abhorrence of Milton's political notions was ever strong. But this did not prevent his warm admiration of Milton's great poetical merit, to which he has done illustrious justice, beyond all who have written upon the subject. And this year he not only wrote a Prologue, which was spoken by Mr. Garrick before the acting of *Comus* at Drury-lane theatre, for the benefit of Milton's grand-daughter, but took a very zealous interest in the success of the charity. . . .

1751: ÆTAT. 42.]—IN 1751 we are to consider him as carrying on both his *Dictionary* and *Rambler*. But he also wrote 'The Life of Cheynel,'* in the miscellany called *The Student;* and the Reverend Dr. Douglas having, with uncommon acuteness, clearly detected a gross forgery and imposition upon the publick by William Lauder, a Scotch schoolmaster, who had, with equal impudence and ingenuity, represented Milton as a plagiary from certain modern Latin poets, Johnson, who had been so far imposed upon as to furnish a Preface and Postscript to his work, now dictated a letter for Lauder, addressed to Dr. Douglas, acknowledging his fraud in terms of suitable contrition.

Though Johnson's circumstances were at this time far from being easy, his humane and charitable dispositon was constantly exerting itself. Mrs. Anna Williams, daughter of a very ingenious Welsh physician, and a woman of more than ordinary talents and literature, having come to London in hopes of being cured of a cataract in both her eyes, which afterwards ended in total blindness, was kindly received as a constant visitor at his house while Mrs. Johnson lived; and after her death, having come under his roof in order to have an operation upon her eyes performed with more comfort to her than in lodgings, she had an apartment from him during the rest of her life, at all times when he had a house.

1752: ÆTAT. 43.]—IN 1752 he was almost entirely occupied with his *Dictionary*. The last paper of his *Rambler* was published March 2, this year; after which, there was a cessation for some time of any exertion of his talents as an essayist. But, in the same year, Dr. Hawkesworth, who was his warm admirer, and a studious imitator of his style, and then lived in great intimacy with him, began a periodical paper, entitled *The Adventurer*, in connection with other gentlemen, one of whom was Johnson's much-loved friend, Dr. Bathurst; and, without doubt, they received many valuable hints from his conversation, most of his friends having been so assisted in the course of their works.

That there should be a suspension of his literary labours during a part of the year 1752, will not seem strange, when it is considered that soon after closing his *Rambler,* he suffered a loss which, there can be no doubt, affected him with the deepest distress. For on the 17th of March, O.S., his wife died. Why Sir John Hawkins should unwarrantably take upon him even to *suppose* that Johnson's fondness for her was *dissembled* (meaning simulated or assumed,) and to assert, that if it was not the case, 'it was a lesson he had learned by rote,' I cannot conceive; unless it proceeded from a want of similar feelings in his own breast. To argue from her being much older than Johnson, or any other circumstances, that he could not really love her, is absurd; for love is not a subject of reasoning, but of feeling, and therefore there are no common principles upon which one can persuade another concerning it. Every man feels for himself, and knows how he is affected by particular qualities in the person he admires, the impressions of which are too minute and delicate to be substantiated in language.

The following very solemn and affecting prayer was found after Dr. Johnson's decease, by his faithful servant, Mr. Francis Barber, who delivered it to my worthy friend the Reverend Mr. Strahan, Vicar of Islington, who at my earnest request has obligingly favoured me with a copy of it, which he and I compared with the original. I present it to the world as an undoubted proof of a circumstance in the character of my illustrious friend, which though some whose hard minds I never shall envy, may attack as superstitious, will I am sure endear him more to numbers of good men. I have an additional, and that a personal motive for presenting it, because it sanctions what I myself have always maintained and am fond to indulge.

'April 26, 1752, being after 12 at Night of the 25th.
'O Lord! Governour of heaven and earth, in whose hands are embodied and departed Spirits, if thou hast ordained the Souls of the Dead to minister to the Living, and appointed my departed Wife to have care of me, grant that I may enjoy the good effects of her attention and ministration, whether exercised by appearance, impulses, dreams or in any other manner agreeable to thy Government. Forgive my presumption, enlighten my ignorance, and however meaner agents are employed, grant me the blessed influences of thy holy Spirit, through Jesus Christ our Lord. Amen.'

What actually followed upon this most interesting piece of devotion by Johnson, we are not informed; but I, whom it had pleased GOD to afflict in a similar manner to that which occasioned it, have certain experience of benignant communication by dreams.

That his love for his wife was of the most ardent kind,

and, during the long period of fifty years, was unimpaired by the lapse of time, is evident from various passages in the series of his *Prayers and Meditations,* published by the Reverend Mr. Strahan, as well as from other memorials, two of which I select, as strongly marking the tenderness and sensibility of his mind.

'March 28, 1753. I kept this day as the anniversary of my Tetty's death, with prayer and tears in the morning. In the evening I prayed for her conditionally, if it were lawful.'

'April 23, 1753. I know not whether I do not too much indulge the vain longings of affection; but I hope they intenerate my heart, and that when I die like my Tetty, this affection will be acknowledged in a happy interview, and that in the mean time I am incited by it to piety. I will, however, not deviate too much from common and received methods of devotion.'

Her wedding-ring, when she became his wife, was, after her death, preserved by him, as long as he lived, with an affectionate care, in a little round wooden box, in the inside of which he pasted a slip of paper, thus inscribed by him in fair characters, as follows:

'Eheu!
Eliz. Johnson,
Nupta Jul. 9º 1736,
Mortua, eheu!
Mart. 17º 1752.'

After his death, Mr. Francis Barber, his faithful servant and residuary legatee, offered this memorial of tenderness to Mrs. Lucy Porter, Mrs. Johnson's daughter; but she having declined to accept of it, he had it enamelled as a mourning ring for his old master, and presented it to his wife, Mrs. Barber, who now has it. . . .

I have, indeed, been told by Mrs. Desmoulins, who, before her marriage, lived for some time with Mrs. Johnson at Hampstead, that she indulged herself in country air and nice living, at an unsuitable expense, while her husband was drudging in the smoke of London, and that she by no means treated him with that complacency which is the most engaging quality in a wife. But all this is perfectly compatible with his fondness for her, especially when it is remembered that he had a high opinion of her understanding, and that the impression which her beauty, real or imaginary, had orginally made upon his fancy, being continued by habit, had not been effaced, though she herself was doubtless much altered for the worse. The dreadful shock of separation took place in the night; and he immediately dispatched a letter to his friend, the Reverend Dr. Taylor, which, as Taylor told me, expressed grief in the strongest manner he had ever read; so that it is much to be regretted it has not been preserved. The letter was brought to Dr. Taylor, at his house in the Cloisters, Westminster, about three in the morning; and as it signified an earnest desire to see him, he got up, and went to Johnson as soon as he was dressed, and found him in tears and in extreme agitation. After being a little while together, Johnson requested him to join with him in prayer. He then prayed extempore, as did Dr. Taylor; and thus, by means of that piety which was ever his primary object, his troubled mind was, in some degree, soothed and composed.

The next day he wrote as follows:

'To THE REVEREND DR. TAYLOR

'DEAR SIR,—Let me have your company and instruction. Do not live away from me. My distress is great.

'Pray desire Mrs. Taylor to inform me what mourning I should buy for my mother and Miss Porter, and bring a note in writing with you.

'Remember me in your prayers, for vain is the help of man. I am, dear Sir, &c.

'March 18, 1752.'   'SAM. JOHNSON.'

That his sufferings upon the death of his wife were severe, beyond what are commonly endured, I have no doubt, from the information of many who were then about him, to none of whom I give more credit than to Mr. Francis Barber, his faithful negro servant, who came into his family about a fortnight after the dismal event. These sufferings were aggravated by the melancholy inherent in his constitution; and although he probably was not oftener in the wrong than she was, in the little disagreements which sometimes troubled his married state, during which, he owned to me, that the gloomy irritability of his existence was more painful to him than ever, he might very naturally, after her death, be tenderly disposed to charge himself with slight omissions and offences, the sense of which would give him much uneasiness. Accordingly we find, about a year after her decease, that he thus addressed the Supreme Being: 'O LORD, who givest the grace of repentance, and hearest the prayers of the penitent, grant that by true contrition I may obtain forgiveness of all the sins committed, and of all duties neglected in my union which the wife whom thou hast taken from me; for the neglect of joint devotion, patient exhortation, and mild instruction.' The kindness of his heart, notwithstanding the impetuosity of his temper, is well known to his friends; and I cannot trace the smallest foundation for the following dark and uncharitable assertion by Sir John Hawkins: 'The apparition of his departed wife was altogether of the terrifick kind, and hardly afforded him a hope that she was in a state of happiness.' That he, in conformity with the opinion of many of the most able, learned, and pious Christians in all ages, supposed that there was a middle state after death, previous to the time at which departed souls are finally received to eternal felicity, appears, I think, unquestionably from his devotions: 'And, O LORD, so far as it may be lawful in me, I commend to thy fatherly goodness *the soul of my departed wife;* beseeching thee to *grant* her whatever is best in her *present state,* and *finally to receive her to eternal happiness.*' But this state has not been looked upon with horrour, but only as less gracious.

He deposited the remains of Mrs. Johnson in the church of Bromley, in Kent, to which he was probably led by the residence of his friend Hawkesworth at that place. The funeral sermon which he composed for her, which was never preached, but having been given to Dr. Taylor, has been published since his death, is a performance of uncommon excellence, and full of rational and pious comfort to such as are depressed by that severe affliction which Johnson felt when he wrote it. When it is considered that it was written in such an agitation of mind, and in the short interval between her death and burial, it cannot be read without wonder.

From Mr. Francis Barber I have had the following authentick and artless account of the situation in which he found him recently after his wife's death:

'He was in great affliction. Mrs. Williams was then living in his house, which was in Gough-square. He was busy with the Dictionary. Mr. Shiels, and some others of the gentlemen who had formerly written for him, used to come about him. He had then little for himself, but frequently sent money to Mr. Shiels when in distress. The friends who visited him at that time, were chiefly Dr. Bathurst, and Mr. Diamond, an apothecary in Cork-street, Burlington-gardens, with whom he and Mrs. Williams generally dined every Sunday. There was a talk of his going to Iceland with him, which would probably have happened had he lived. There were also Mr. Cave, Dr. Hawkesworth, Mr. Ryland, merchant on Tower Hill, Mrs. Masters, the poetess, who lived with Mr. Cave, Mrs. Carter, and sometimes Mrs. Macaulay, also Mrs. Gardiner, wife of a tallow-chandler on Snow-hill, not in the learned way, but a worthy good woman; Mr. (now Sir Joshua) Reynolds: Mr. Millar, Mr. Dodsley, Mr. Bouquet, Mr. Payne of

Paternoster-row, booksellers; Mr. Strahan, the printer; the Earl of Orrery, Lord Southwell, Mr. Garrick.'

Many are, no doubt, omitted in this catalogue of his friends, and, in particular, his humble friend Mr. Robert Levet, an obscure practiser in physick amongst the lower people, his fees being sometimes very small sums, sometimes whatever provisions his patients could afford him; but of such extensive practice in that way, that Mrs. Williams has told me, his walk was from Houndsditch to Marybone. It appears from Johnson's diary that their acquaintance commenced about the year 1746; and such was Johnson's predilection for him, and fanciful estimation of his moderate abilities, that I have heard him say he should not be satisfied, though attended by all the College of Physicians, unless he had Mr. Levet with him. Ever since I was acquainted with Dr. Johnson, and many years before, as I have been assured by those who knew him earlier, Mr. Levet had an apartment in his house, or his chambers, and waited upon him every morning, through the whole course of his late and tedious breakfast. He was of a strange grotesque appearance, stiff and formal in his manner, and seldom said a word while any company was present.

The circle of his friends, indeed, at this time was extensive and various, far beyond what has been generally imagined. To trace his acquaintance with each particular person, if it could be done, would be a task, of which the labour would not be repaid by the advantage. But exceptions are to be made; one of which must be a friend so eminent as Sir Joshua Reynolds, who was truly his *dulce decus*,[1] and with whom he maintained an uninterrupted intimacy to the last hour of his life. When Johnson lived in Castle-street, Cavendish-square, he used frequently to visit two ladies, who lived opposite to him, Miss Cotterells, daughters of Admiral Cotterell. Reynolds used also to visit there, and thus they met. Mr. Reynolds, as I have observed above, had, from the first reading of his *Life of Savage*, conceived a very high admiration of Johnson's powers of writing. His conversation no less delighted him; and he cultivated his acquaintance with the laudable zeal of one who was ambitious of general improvement. Sir Joshua, indeed, was lucky enough at their very first meeting to make a remark, which was so much above the common-place style of conversation, that Johnson at once perceived that Reynolds had the habit of thinking for himself. The ladies were regretting the death of a friend, to whom they owed great obligations; upon which Reynolds observed, 'You have, however, the comfort of being relieved from a

[1] 'Cherished glory.' Horace, *Odes*, I. i. 2.

95

burthen of gratitude.' They were shocked a little at this alleviating suggestion, as too selfish; but Johnson defended it in his clear and forcible manner, and was much pleased with the *mind,* the fair view of human nature, which it exhibited, like some of the reflections of Rochefaucault. The consequence was, that he went home with Reynolds, and supped with him.

Sir Joshua told me a pleasant characteristical anecdote of Johnson about the time of their first acquaintance. When they were one evening together at the Miss Cotterells', the then Duchess of Argyle and another lady of high rank came in. Johnson thinking that the Miss Cotterells were too much engrossed by them, and that he and his friend were neglected, as low company of whom they were somewhat ashamed, grew angry; and resolving to shock their supposed pride, by making their great visitors imagine that this friend and he were low indeed, he addressed himself in a loud tone to Mr. Reynolds, saying, 'How much do you think you and I could get in a week, if we were to *work as hard* as we could?'—as if they had been common mechanicks.

His acquaintance with Bennet Langton, Esq. of Langton, in Lincolnshire, another much valued friend, commenced soon after the conclusion of his *Rambler;* which that gentleman, then a youth, had read with so much admiration, that he came to London chiefly with the view of endeavouring to be introduced to its authour. By a fortunate chance he happened to take lodgings in a house where Mr. Levet frequently visited; and having mentioned his wish to his landlady, she introduced him to Mr. Levet, who readily obtained Johnson's permission to bring Mr. Langton to him; as, indeed, Johnson, during the whole course of his life, had no shyness, real or affected, but was easy of access to all who were properly recommended, and even wished to see numbers at his *levee,* as his morning circle of company might, with strict propriety, be called. Mr. Langton was exceedingly surprised when the sage first appeared. He had not received the smallest intimation of his figure, dress, or manner. From perusing his writings, he fancied he should see a decent, well-drest, in short, a remarkably decorous philosopher. Instead of which, down from his bed-chamber, about noon, came, as newly risen, a huge uncouth figure, with a little dark wig which scarcely covered his head, and his clothes hanging loose about him. But his conversation was so rich, so animated, and so forcible, and his religious and political notions so congenial with those in which Mr. Langton had been educated, that he conceived for him that veneration and attachment which he ever preserved. Johnson was not the less ready to love Mr. Langton, for his being of a very ancient family; for I have heard him say, with pleasure, 'Langton, Sir, has a grant of free warren from Henry the Second; and Cardinal Stephen Langton, in King John's reign, was of this family.'

Mr. Langton afterwards went to pursue his studies at Trinity College, Oxford, where he formed an acquaintance with his fellow student, Mr. Topham Beauclerk; who, though their opinions and modes of life were so different, that it seemed utterly improbable that they should at all agree, had so ardent a love of literature, so acute an understanding, such elegance of manners, and so well discerned the excellent qualities of Mr. Langton, a gentleman eminent not only for worth and learning, but for an inexhaustible fund of entertaining conversation, that they became intimate friends.

Johnson, soon after this acquaintance began, passed a considerable time at Oxford. He at first thought it strange that Langton should associate so much with one who had the character of being loose, both in his principles and practice; but, by degrees, he himself was fascinated. Mr. Beauclerk's being of the St. Alban's family, and having, in some particulars, a resemblance to Charles the Second, contributed, in Johnson's imagination, to throw a lustre upon his other qualities; and, in a short time, the moral, pious Johnson, and the gay, dissipated Beauclerk, were companions. 'What a coalition! (said Garrick, when he heard of this;) I shall have my old friend to bail out of the Round-house.' But I can bear testimony that it was a very agreeable association. Beauclerk was too polite, and valued learning and wit too much, to offend Johnson by sallies of infidelity or licentiousness; and Johnson delighted in the good qualities of Beauclerk, and hoped to correct the evil. Innumerable were the scenes in which Johnson was amused by these young men. Beauclerk could take more liberty with him, than any body with whom I ever saw him; but, on the other hand, Beauclerk was not spared by his respectable companion, when reproof was proper. Beauclerk had such a propensity to satire, that at one time Johnson said to him, 'You never open your mouth but with intention to give pain; and you have often given me pain, not from the power of what you said, but from seeing your intention.' At another time applying to him, with a slight alteration, a line of Pope, he said,

'Thy love of folly, and thy scorn of fools—
Every thing thou dost shews the one, and every thing thou say'st the other.' At another time he said to him, 'Thy body is all vice, and thy mind all virtue.' Beauclerk not seeming to relish the compliment, Johnson said, 'Nay, Sir, Alexander the

Great, marching in triumph into Babylon, could not have desired to have had more said to him.'

Johnson was some time with Beauclerk at his house at Windsor, where he was entertained with experiments in natural philosophy. One Sunday, when the weather was very fine, Beauclerk enticed him, insensibly, to saunter about all the morning. They went into a church-yard, in the time of divine service, and Johnson laid himself down at his ease upon one of the tombstones. 'Now, Sir, (said Beauclerk) you are like Hogarth's Idle Apprentice.' When Johnson got his pension, Beauclerk said to him, in the humorous phrase of Falstaff, 'I hope you'll now purge and live cleanly like a gentleman.'

One night when Beauclerk and Langton had supped at a tavern in London, and sat till about three in the morning, it came into their heads to go and knock up Johnson, and see if they could prevail on him to join them in a ramble. They rapped violently at the door of his chambers in the Temple, till at last he appeared in his shirt, with his little black wig on the top of his head, instead of a nightcap, and a poker in his hand, imagining, probably, that some ruffians were coming to attack him. When he discovered who they were, and was told their errand, he smiled, and with great good humour agreed to their proposal: 'What, is it you, you dogs! I'll have a frisk with you.' He was soon drest, and they sallied forth together into Covent-Garden, where the greengrocers and fruiterers were beginning to arrange their hampers, just come in from the country. Johnson made some attempts to help them; but the honest gardeners stared so at his figure and manner, and odd interference, that he soon saw his services were not relished. They then repaired to one of the neighbouring taverns, and made a bowl of that liquor called *Bishop,* which Johnson had always liked; while in joyous contempt of sleep, from which he had been roused, he repeated the festive lines,

'Short, O short then be thy reign,
And give us to the world again!'

They did not stay long, but walked down to the Thames, took a boat, and rowed to Billingsgate. Beauclerk and Johnson were so well pleased with their amusement, that they resolved to persevere in dissipation for the rest of the day: but Langton deserted them, being engaged to breakfast with some young Ladies. Johnson scolded him for 'leaving his social friends, to go and sit with a set of wretched *un-idea'd* girls.' Garrick being told of this ramble, said to him smartly, 'I heard of your frolick t'other night. You'll be in the Chronicle.' Upon which Johnson afterwards observed, '*He* durst not do such a thing. His *wife* would not *let* him!'

1753: ÆTAT. 44.]—HE entered upon this year 1753 with his usual piety, as appears from the following prayer, which I transcribed from that part of his diary which he burnt a few days before his death:

'Jan. 1, 1753, N.S. which I shall use for the future.

'Almighty GOD, who hast continued my life to this day, grant that, by the assistance of thy Holy Spirit, I may improve the time which thou shalt grant me, to my eternal salvation. Make me to remember, to thy glory, thy judgements and thy mercies. Make me so to consider the loss of my wife, whom thou hast taken from me, that it may dispose me, by thy grace, to lead the residue of my life in thy fear. Grant this, O LORD, for JESUS CHRIST'S sake. Amen.'

He now relieved the drudgery of his *Dictionary*, and the melancholy of his grief, by taking an active part in the composition of *The Adventurer*. . . .

Johnson's papers in *The Adventurer* are very similar to those of *The Rambler*; but being rather more varied in their subjects, and being mixed with essays by other writers, upon topicks more generally attractive than even the most elegant ethical discourses, the sale of the work, at first, was more extensive. Without meaning, however, to depreciate *The Adventurer*, I must observe that as the value of *The Rambler* came, in the progress of time, to be better known, it grew upon the publick estimation, and that its sale has far exceeded that of any other periodical papers since the reign of Queen Anne. . . .

1754: ÆTAT. 45.]—IN 1754 I can trace nothing published by him, except his numbers of *The Adventurer*, and 'The Life of Edward Cave,' * in the *Gentleman's Magazine* for February. In biography there can be no question that he excelled, beyond all who have attempted that species of composition; upon which, indeed, he set the highest value. To the minute selection of characteristical circumstances, for which the ancients were remarkable, he added a philosophical research, and the most perspicuous and energetick language. Cave was certainly a man of estimable qualities, and was eminently diligent and successful in his own business, which, doubtless, entitled him to respect. But he was peculiarly fortunate in being recorded by Johnson, who, of the narrow life of a printer and publisher, without any digressions or adventitious circumstances, has made an interesting and agreeable narrative.

The *Dictionary*, we may believe, afforded Johnson full occupation this year. As it approached to its conclusion, he probably worked with redoubled vigour, as seamen increase their exertion and alacrity when they have a near prospect of their haven.

Lord Chesterfield, to whom Johnson had paid the high compliment of addressing to his Lordship the *Plan* of his *Dictionary,* had behaved to him in such a manner as to excite his contempt and indignation. The world has been for many years amused with a story confidently told, and as confidently repeated with additional circumstances, that a sudden disgust was taken by Johnson upon occasion of his having been one day kept long in waiting in his Lordship's antechamber, for which the reason assigned was, that he had company with him; and that at last, when the door opened, out walked Colley Cibber; and that Johnson was so violently provoked when he found for whom he had been so long excluded, that he went away in a passion, and never would return. I remember having mentioned this story to George Lord Lyttelton, who told me, he was very intimate with Lord Chesterfield; and holding it as a well-known truth, defended Lord Chesterfield, by saying, that 'Cibber, who had been introduced familiarly by the back-stairs, had probably not been there above ten minutes.' It may seem strange even to entertain a doubt concerning a story so long and so widely current, and thus implicitly adopted, if not sanctioned, by the authority which I have mentioned; but Johnson himself assured me, that there was not the least foundation for it. He told me, that there never was any particular incident which produced a quarrel between Lord Chesterfield and him; but that his Lordship's continued neglect was the reason why he resolved to have no connection with him. When the *Dictionary* was upon the eve of publication, Lord Chesterfield, who, it is said, had flattered himself with expectations that Johnson would dedicate the work to him, attempted, in a courtly manner, to sooth, and insinuate himself with the Sage, conscious, as it should seem, of the cold indifference with which he had treated its learned authour; and further attempted to conciliate him, by writing two papers in *The World,* in recommendation of the work; and it must be confessed, that they contain some studied compliments, so finely turned, that if there had been no previous offence, it is probable that Johnson would have been highly delighted. Praise, in general, was pleasing to him; but by praise from a man of rank and elegant accomplishments, he was peculiarly gratified. . . .

This courtly device failed of its effect. Johnson, who thought that 'all was false and hollow,' despised the honeyed words, and was even indignant that Lord Chesterfield should, for a moment, imagine that he could be the dupe of such an artifice. His expression to me concerning Lord Chesterfield, upon this occasion, was, 'Sir, after making great professions, he had, for many years, taken no notice of me; but when my *Dictionary* was coming out, he fell a scribbling in *The World* about it. Upon which, I wrote him a letter expressed in civil terms, but such as might shew him that I did not mind what he said or wrote, and that I had done with him.'

This is that celebrated letter of which so much has been said, and about which curiosity has been so long excited, without being gratified. I for many years solicited Johnson to favour me with a copy of it, that so excellent a composition might not be lost to posterity. He delayed from time to time to give it me; till at last in 1781, when we were on a visit at Mr. Dilly's, at Southill in Bedfordshire, he was pleased to dictate it to me from memory. He afterwards found among his papers a copy of it, which he had dictated to Mr. Baretti, with its title and corrections, in his own handwriting. This he gave to Mr. Langton; adding that if it were to come into print, he wished it to be from that copy. By Mr. Langton's kindness, I am enabled to enrich my work with a perfect transcript of what the world has so eagerly desired to see.

'To The Right Honourable the Earl of Chesterfield
'My Lord,   February 1755.

'I have been lately informed, by the proprietor of *The World,* that two papers, in which my Dictionary is recommended to the publick, were written by your Lordship. To be so distinguished, is an honour, which, being very little accustomed to favours from the great, I know not well how to receive, or in what terms to acknowledge.

'When, upon some slight encouragement, I first visited your Lordship, I was overpowered, like the rest of mankind, by the enchantment of your address; and could not forbear to wish that I might boast myself *Le vainqueur du vainqueur de la terre;*—that I might obtain that regard for which I saw the world contending; but I found my attendance so little encouraged, that neither pride nor modesty would suffer me to continue it. When I had once addressed your Lordship in publick, I had exhausted all the art of pleasing which a retired and uncourtly scholar can possess. I had done all that I could; and no man is well pleased to have his all neglected, be it ever so little.

'Seven years, my Lord, have now past, since I waited in your outward rooms, or was repulsed from your door; during which time I have been pushing on my work through difficulties, of which it is useless to complain, and have brought it, at last, to the verge of publication, without one act of

101

assistance,[1] one word of encouragement, or one smile of favour. Such treatment I did not expect, for I never had a Patron before.

'The shepherd in Virgil grew at last acquainted with Love, and found him a native of the rocks.

'Is not a Patron, my Lord, one who looks with unconcern on a man struggling for life in the water, and, when he has reached ground, encumbers him with help? The notice which you have been pleased to take of my labours, had it been early, had been kind; but it has been delayed till I am indifferent, and cannot enjoy it; till I am solitary, and cannot impart it; till I am known, and do not want it. I hope it is no very cynical asperity not to confess obligations where no benefit has been received, or to be unwilling that the Publick should consider me as owing that to a Patron, which Providence has enabled me to do for myself.

'Having carried on my work thus far with so little obligation to any favourer of learning, I shall not be disappointed though I should conclude it, if less be possible, with less; for I have been long wakened from that dream of hope, in which I once boasted myself with so much exultation, my Lord, your Lordship's most humble, most obedient servant,

'SAM. JOHNSON.'

'While this was the talk of the town, (says Dr. Adams, in a letter to me) I happened to visit Dr. Warburton, who finding that I was acquainted with Johnson, desired me earnestly to carry his compliments to him, and to tell him, that he honoured him for his manly behaviour in rejecting these condescensions of Lord Chesterfield, and for resenting the treatment he had received from him, with a proper spirit. Johnson was visibly pleased with this compliment, for he had always a high opinion of Warburton. Indeed, the force of mind which appeared in this letter, was congenial with that which Warburton himself amply possessed.'

There is a curious minute circumstance which struck me, in comparing the various editions of Johnson's imitations of Juvenal. In the tenth Satire, one of the couplets upon the vanity of wishes even for literary distinction stood thus:

'Yet think what ills the scholar's life assail,
Pride, envy, want, the *garret,* and the jail.'

[1] The following note is subjoined by Mr. Langton:—'Dr. Johnson, when he gave me this copy of his letter, desired that I would annex to it his information to me, that whereas it is said in the letter that "no assistance has been received," he did once receive from Lord Chesterfield the sum of ten pounds; but as that was so inconsiderable a sum, he thought the mention of it could not properly find place in a letter of the kind that this was.'—B.

But after experiencing the uneasiness which Lord Chesterfield's fallacious patronage made him feel, he dismissed the word *garret* from the sad group, and in all the subsequent editions the line stands

'Toil, envy, want, the *Patron,* and the jail.'

That Lord Chesterfield must have been mortified by the lofty contempt, and polite, yet keen satire with which Johnson exhibited him in this letter, it is impossible to doubt. He, however, with that glossy duplicity which was his constant study, affected to be quite unconcerned. Dr. Adams mentioned to Mr. Robert Dodsley that he was sorry Johnson had written his letter to Lord Chesterfield. Dodsley, with the true feelings of trade, said 'he was very sorry too; for that he had a property in the *Dictionary,* to which his Lordship's patronage might have been of consequence.' He then told Dr. Adams, that Lord Chesterfield had shewn him the letter. 'I should have imagined (replied Dr. Adams) that Lord Chesterfield would have concealed it.' 'Poh! (said Dodsley) do you think a letter from Johnson could hurt Lord Chesterfield? Not at all, Sir. It lay upon his table, where any body might see it. He read it to me; said, "this man has great powers," pointed out the severest passages, and observed how well they were expressed.' This air of indifference, which imposed upon the worthy Dodsley, was certainly nothing but a specimen of that dissimulation which Lord Chesterfield inculcated as one of the most essential lessons for the conduct of life. His Lordship endeavoured to justify himself to Dodsley from the charges brought against him by Johnson; but we may judge of the flimsiness of his defence, from his having excused his neglect of Johnson, by saying that 'he had heard he had changed his lodgings, and did not know where he lived;' as if there could have been the smallest difficulty to inform himself of that circumstance, by inquiring in the literary circle with which his Lordship was well acquainted, and was, indeed, himself one of its ornaments.

Dr. Adams expostulated with Johnson, and suggested, that his not being admitted when he called on him, was, probably, not to be imputed to Lord Chesterfield; for his Lordship had declared to Dodsley, that 'he would have turned off the best servant he ever had, if he had known that he denied him to a man who would have been always more than welcome;' and, in confirmation of this, he insisted on Lord Chesterfield's general affability and easiness of access, especially to literary men. 'Sir, (said Johnson) that is not Lord Chesterfield; he is the proudest man this day existing.' 'No, (said Dr. Adams) there is one person, at least, as proud; I think, by your own account, you are the prouder man of the two.' 'But mine (replied Johnson, instantly) was *defensive* pride.' This, as Dr. Adams well observed, was one of those happy turns for which he was so remarkably ready.

Johnson having now explicity avowed his opinion of Lord Chesterfield, did not refrain from expressing himself concerning that nobleman with pointed freedom: 'This man (said he) I thought had been a Lord among wits; but, I find, he is only a wit among Lords!' And when his *Letters* to his natural son were published, he observed, that 'they teach the morals of a whore, and the manners of a dancing master.'

The character of 'a respectable Hottentot,' in Lord Chesterfield's letters, has been generally understood to be meant for Johnson, and I have no doubt that it was. But I remember when the *Literary Property* of those letters was contested in the Court of Session in Scotland, and Mr. Henry Dundas, one of the counsel for the proprietors, read this character as an exhibition of Johnson, Sir David Dalrymple, Lord Hailes, one of the Judges, maintained, with some warmth, that it was not intended as a portrait of Johnson, but of a late noble Lord, distinguished for abstruse science. I have heard Johnson himself talk of the character, and say that it was meant for George Lord Lyttelton, in which I could by no means agree; for his Lordship had nothing of that violence which is a conspicuous feature in the composition. Finding that my illustrious friend could bear to have it supposed that it might be meant for him, I said, laughingly, that there was one trait which unquestionably did not belong to him; 'he throws his meat any where but down his throat.' 'Sir, (said he,) Lord Chesterfield never saw me eat in his life.'

On the 6th of March came out Lord Bolingbroke's works, published by Mr. David Mallet. The wild and pernicious ravings, under the name of *Philosophy*, which were thus ushered into the world, gave great offence to all well-principled men. Johnson, hearing of their tendency, which nobody disputed, was roused with a just indignation, and pronounced this memorable sentence upon the noble authour and his editor. 'Sir, he was a scoundrel, and a coward: a scoundrel, for charging a blunderbuss against religion and morality; a coward, because he had not resolution to fire it off himself, but left half a crown to a beggarly Scotchman, to draw the trigger after his death!' . . .

Johnson this year found an interval of leisure to make an excursion to Oxford, for the purpose of consulting the libraries there. Of this, and of many interesting circumstances concerning him, during a part of his life when he conversed but little with the world, I am enabled to give a particular account, by the liberal communications of the Reverend Mr. Thomas Warton. . . .

Of his conversation while at Oxford at this time, Mr. Warton preserved and communicated to me the following memorial, which, though not written with all the care and attention which that learned and elegant writer bestowed on those compositions which he intended for the publick eye, is so happily expressed in an easy style, that I should injure it by any alteration:

'When Johnson came to Oxford in 1754, the long vacation was beginning, and most people were leaving the place. This was the first time of his being there, after quitting the University. The next morning after his arrival, he wished to see his old College, *Pembroke*. I went with him. He was highly pleased to find all the College-servants which he had left there still remaining, particularly a very old butler; and expressed great satisfaction at being recognised by them, and conversed with them familiarly. He waited on the master, Dr. Radcliffe, who received him very coldly. Johnson at least expected, that the master would order a copy of his Dictionary, now near publication: but the master did not choose to talk on the subject, never asked Johnson to dine, nor even to visit him, while he stayed at Oxford. After we had left the lodgings, Johnson said to me, "*There* lives a man, who lives by the revenues of literature, and will not move a finger to support it. If I come to live at Oxford, I shall take up my abode at Trinity." We then called on the Reverend Mr. Meeke, one of the fellows, and of Johnson's standing. Here was a most cordial greeting on both sides. On leaving him, Johnson said, "I used to think Meeke had excellent parts, when we were boys together at the College: but, alas!

'Lost in a convent's solitary gloom!'

I remember, at the classical lecture in the Hall, I could not bear Meeke's superiority, and I tried to sit as far from him as I could, that I might not hear him construe."

'As we were leaving the College, he said, "Here I translated Pope's Messiah. Which do you think is the best line in it?—My own favourite is,

'*Vallis aromaticas fundit Saronica nubes.*' " [1]

I told him, I thought it a very sonorous hexameter. I did not tell him, it was not in the Virgilian style. He much regretted that his *first* tutor was dead; for whom he seemed to retain the greatest regard. He said, "I once had been a whole morn-

[1] 'See spicy clouds from lowly Saron rise.' (Pope, 1. 27.)

105

ing sliding in Christ-Church Meadow, and missed his lecture in logick. After dinner, he sent for me to his room. I expected a sharp rebuke for my idleness, and went with a beating heart. When we were seated, he told me he had sent for me to drink a glass of wine with him, and to tell me, he was *not* angry with me for missing his lecture. This was, in fact, a most severe reprimand. Some more of the boys were then sent for, and we spent a very pleasant afternoon." Besides Mr. Meeke, there was only one other Fellow of Pembroke now resident: from both of whom Johnson received the greatest civilities during this visit, and they pressed him very much to have a room in the College.

'In the course of this visit (1754,) Johnson and I walked, three or four times, to Ellsfield, a village beautifully situated about three miles from Oxford, to see Mr. Wise, Radclivian librarian, with whom Johnson was much pleased. At this place, Mr. Wise had fitted up a house and gardens, in a singular manner, but with great taste. Here was an excellent library; particularly, a valuable collection of books in Northern literature, with which Johnson was often very busy. One day Mr. Wise read to us a dissertation which he was preparing for the press, intitled, "A History and Chronology of the fabulous Ages." Some old divinities of Thrace, related to the Titans, and called the CABIRI, made a very important part of the theory of this piece; and in conversation afterwards, Mr. Wise talked much of his CABIRI. As we returned to Oxford in the evening, I out-walked Johnson, and he cried out *Sufflamina,* a Latin word which came from his mouth with peculiar grace, and was as much as to say, *Put on your drag chain.* Before we got home, I again walked too fast for him; and he now cried out, "Why, you walk as if you were pursued by all the CABIRI in a body." In an evening, we frequently took long walks from Oxford into the country, returning to supper. Once, in our way home, we viewed the ruins of the abbies of Oseney and Rewley, near Oxford. After at least half an hour's silence, Johnson said, "I viewed them with indignation!" We had then a long conversation on Gothick buildings; and in talking of the form of old halls, he said, "In these halls, the fire place was anciently always in the middle of the room, till the Whigs removed it on one side."—About this time there had been an execution of two or three criminals at Oxford on a Monday. Soon afterwards, one day at dinner, I was saying that Mr. Swinton the chaplain of the gaol, and also a frequent preacher before the University, a learned man, but often thoughtless and absent, preached the condemnation-sermon on repentance, before the convicts, on the preceding day, Sunday; and that in the close he told his audience, that he should give them the remainder of what he had to say on the subject, the next Lord's Day. Upon which, one of our company, a Doctor of Divinity, and a plain matter-of-fact man, by way of offering an apology for Mr. Swinton, gravely remarked, that he had probably preached the same sermon before the University: "Yes, Sir, (says Johnson) but the University were not to be hanged the next morning."

'I forgot to observe before that when he left Mr. Meeke, (as I have told above) he added, "About the same time of life, Meeke was left behind at Oxford to feed on a Fellowship, and I went to London to get my living: now, Sir, see the difference of our literary characters!"' . . .

The degree of Master of Arts, which, it has been observed, could not be obtained for him at an early period of his life, was now considered as an honour of considerable importance, in order to grace the title-page of his *Dictionary;* and his character in the literary world being by this time deservedly high, his friends thought that, if proper exertions were made, the University of Oxford would pay him the compliment. . . .

1755: ÆTAT. 46.]—IN 1755 we behold him to great advantage; his degree of Master of Arts conferred upon him, his *Dictionary* published, his correspondence animated, his benevolence exercised.[1] . . .

Mr. Andrew Millar, bookseller in the Strand, took the principal charge of conducting the publication of Johnson's *Dictionary;* and as the patience of the proprietors was repeatedly tried and almost exhausted, by their expecting that the work would be completed within the time which Johnson had sanguinely supposed, the learned authour was often goaded to dispatch, more especially as he had received all the copy-money, by different drafts, a considerable time before he had finished his task. When the messenger who carried the last sheet to Millar returned, Johnson asked him, 'Well, what did he say?'—'Sir, (answered the messenger) he said, thank GOD I have done with him.' 'I am glad (replied Johnson, with a smile) that he thanks GOD for any thing.' It is remarkable that those with whom Johnson chiefly contracted for his literary labours were Scotchmen, Mr. Millar and Mr. Strahan. Millar, though himself no great judge of literature, had good sense enough to have for his friends very able men to give him their opinion and advice in the purchase of copyright; the consequence of which was his acquiring a very large fortune, with great liberality. Johnson said of him, 'I respect Millar, Sir; he has raised the price of literature.' . . .

[1] The M. A. degree was awarded that winter.

The *Dictionary*, with a Grammar and History of the English Language, being now at length published, in two volumes folio, the world contemplated with wonder so stupendous a work atchieved by one man, while other countries had thought such undertakings fit only for whole academies. Vast as his powers were, I cannot but think that his imagination deceived him, when he supposed that by constant application he might have performed the task in three years. Let the Preface be attentively perused, in which is given, in a clear, strong, and glowing style, a comprehensive, yet particular view of what he had done; and it will be evident, that the time he employed upon it was comparatively short. I am unwilling to swell my book with long quotations from what is in every body's hands, and I believe there are few prose compositions in the English language that are read with more delight, or are more impressed upon the memory, than that preliminary discourse. One of its excellencies has always struck me with peculiar admiration: I mean the perspicuity with which he has expressed abstract scientifick notions. . . .

The extensive reading which was absolutely necessary for the accumulation of authorities, and which alone may account for Johnson's retentive mind being enriched with a very large and various store of knowledge and imagery, must have occupied several years. The Preface furnishes an eminent instance of a double talent, of which Johnson was fully conscious. Sir Joshua Reynolds heard him say, 'There are two things which I am confident I can do very well: one is an introduction to any literary work, stating what it is to contain, and how it should be executed in the most perfect manner; the other is a conclusion, shewing from various causes why the execution has not been equal to what the authour promised to himself and to the publick.'

How should puny scribblers be abashed and disappointed, when they find him displaying a perfect theory of lexicographical excellence, yet at the same time candidly and modestly allowing that he 'had not satisfied his own expectations.' Here was a fair occasion for the exercise of Johnson's modesty, when he was called upon to compare his own arduous performance, not with those of other individuals, (in which case his inflexible regard to truth would have been violated, had he affected diffidence,) but with speculative perfection; as he, who can outstrip all his competitors in the race, may yet be sensible of his deficiency when he runs against time. Well might he say, that 'the *English Dictionary* was written with little assistance of the learned,' for he told me, that the only aid which he received was a paper containing twenty etymologies, sent to him by a person then unknown,

108

who he was afterwards informed was Dr. Pearce, Bishop of Rochester. The etymologies, though they exhibit learning and judgement, are not, I think, entitled to the first praise amongst the various parts of this immense work. The definitions have always appeared to me such astonishing proofs of acuteness of intellect and precision of language, as indicate a genius of the highest rank. This it is which marks the superiour excellence of Johnson's *Dictionary* over others equally or even more voluminous, and must have made it a work of much greater mental labour than mere Lexicons, or *Wordbooks,* as the Dutch call them. They, who will make the experiment of trying how they can define a few words of whatever nature, will soon be satisfied of an unquestionable justice of this observation, which I can assure my readers is founded upon much study, and upon communication with more minds than my own.

A few of his definitions must be admitted to be erroneous. Thus, *Windward* and *Leeward,* though directly of opposite meaning, are defined identically the same way; as to which inconsiderable specks it is enough to observe, that his Preface announces that he was aware there might be many such in so immense a work; nor was he at all disconcerted when an instance was pointed out to him. A lady once asked him how he came to define *Pastern* the *knee* of a horse: instead of making an elaborate defence, as she expected, he at once answered, 'Ignorance, Madam, pure ignorance.' His definition of *Network* has been often quoted with sportive malignity, as obscuring a thing in itself very plain. But to these frivolous censures no other answer is necessary than that with which we are furnished by his own Preface.

'To explain, requires the use of terms less abstruse than that which is to be explained, and such terms cannot always be found. For as nothing can be proved but by supposing something intuitively known, and evident without proof, so nothing can be defined but by the use of words too plain to admit of definition. Sometimes easier words are changed into harder; as, *burial,* into *sepulture* or *interment; dry,* into *desiccative; dryness,* into *siccity* or *aridity; fit* into *paroxysm;* for the *easiest* word, whatever it be, can never be translated into one more easy.'

His introducing his own opinions, and even prejudices, under general definitions of words, while at the same time the original meaning of the words is not explained, as his *Tory, Whig, Pension, Oats, Excise,* and a few more, cannot be fully defended, and must be placed to the account of capricious and humourous indulgence. Talking to me upon this subject when we were at Ashbourne in 1777, he mentioned a still stronger instance of the predominance of his private feelings in the composition of this work, than any now to be found in it. 'You know, Sir, Lord Gower forsook the old Jacobite interest. When I came to the word *Renegado,* after telling that it meant "one who deserts to the enemy, a revolter," I added, *Sometimes we say a* GOWER. Thus it went to the press; but the printer had more wit than I, and struck it out.'

Let it, however, be remembered, that this indulgence does not display itself only in sarcasm towards others, but sometimes in playful allusion to the notions commonly entertained of his own laborious task. Thus: '*Grub-street,* the name of a street in London, much inhabited by writers of small histories, *dictionaries,* and temporary poems; whence any mean production is called *Grub-street.*'—'*Lexicographer,* a writer of dictionaries, a *harmless drudge.*'

At the time when he was concluding his very eloquent Preface, Johnson's mind appears to have been in such a state of depression, that we cannot contemplate without wonder the vigorous and splendid thoughts which so highly distinguish that performance. 'I (says he) may surely be contented without the praise of perfection, which if I could obtain in this gloom of solitude, what would it avail me? I have protracted my work till most of those whom I wished to please have sunk into the grave; and success and miscarriage are empty sounds. I therefore dismiss it with frigid tranquillity, having little to fear or hope from censure or from praise.' That this indifference was rather a temporary than an habitual feeling, appears, I think, from his letters to Mr. Warton; and however he may have been affected for the moment, certain it is that the honours which his great work procured him, both at home and abroad, were very grateful to him. His friend the Earl of Corke and Orrery, being at Florence, presented it to the *Academia della Crusca.* That Academy sent Johnson their *Vocabulario,* and the French Academy sent him their *Dictionnaire,* which Mr. Langton had the pleasure to convey to him.

It must undoubtedly seem strange, that the conclusion of his Preface should be expressed in terms so desponding, when it is considered that the authour was then only in his forty-sixth year. But we must ascribe its gloom to that miserable dejection of spirits to which he was constitutionally subject, and which was aggravated by the death of his wife two years before. I have heard it ingeniously observed by a lady of rank and elegance, that 'his melancholy was then at its meridian.' It pleased GOD to grant him almost thirty years of life after this time; and once, when he was in a placid frame of mind, he was obliged to own to me that he had enjoyed happier

110

days, and had had many more friends, since that gloomy hour than before.

It is a sad saying, that 'most of those whom he wished to please had sunk into the grave;' and his case at forty-five was singularly unhappy, unless the circle of his friends was very narrow. I have often thought, that as longevity is generally desired, and, I believe, generally expected, it would be wise to be continually adding to the number of our friends, that the loss of some may be supplied by others. Friendship, 'the wine of life,' should, like a well-stocked cellar, be thus continually renewed; and it is consolatory to think, that although we can seldom add what will equal the generous *first-growths* of our youth, yet friendship becomes insensibly old in much less time than is commonly imagined, and not many years are required to make it very mellow and pleasant. *Warmth* will, no doubt, make a considerable difference. Men of affectionate temper and bright fancy will coalesce a great deal sooner than those who are cold and dull.

The proposition which I have now endeavoured to illustrate was, at a subsequent period of his life, the opinion of Johnson himself. He said to Sir Joshua Reynolds, 'If a man does not make new acquaintance as he advances through life, he will soon find himself left alone. A man, Sir, should keep his friendship *in constant repair.*'

The celebrated Mr. Wilkes, whose notions and habits of life were very opposite to his, but who was ever eminent for literature and vivacity, sallied forth with a little *Jeu d'Esprit* upon the following passage in his Grammar of the English Tongue, prefixed to the *Dictionary:* 'H seldom, perhaps never, begins any but the first syllable.' In an Essay printed in *The Publick Advertiser,* this lively writer enumerated many instances in opposition to this remark; for example, 'The authour of this observation must be a man of a quick *apprehension,* and of a most *compre-hensive* genius.' The position is undoubtedly expressed with too much latitude.

This light sally, we may suppose, made no great impression on our Lexicographer; for we find that he did not alter the passage till many years afterwards. . . .

In July this year he had formed some scheme of mental improvement, the particular purpose of which does not appear. But we find in his *Prayers and Meditations*, p. 24, a prayer entitled 'On the Study of Philosophy, as an Instrument of living;' and after it follows a note, 'This study was not pursued.'

On the 13th of the same month he wrote in his *Journal* the following scheme of life, for Sunday:

'Having lived' (as he with tenderness of conscience express-

111

es himself) 'not without an habitual reverence for the Sabbath, yet without that attention to its religious duties which Christianity requires;

'1. To rise early, and in order to do it, to go to sleep early on Saturday.

'2. To use some extraordinary devotion in the morning.

'3. To examine the tenour of my life, and particularly the last week; and to mark my advances in religion, or recession from it.

'4. To read the Scripture methodically with such helps as are at hand.

'5. To go to church twice.

'6. To read books of Divinity, either speculative or practical.

'7. To instruct my family.

'8. To wear off by meditation any worldly soil contracted in the week.'

1756: ÆTAT. 47.]—IN 1756 Johnson found that the great fame of his *Dictionary* had not set him above the necessity of 'making provision for the day that was passing over him.' No royal or noble patron extended a munificent hand to give independence to the man who had conferred stability on the language of his country. We may feel indignant that there should have been such unworthy neglect; but we must, at the same time, congratulate ourselves, when we consider, that to this very neglect, operating to rouse the natural indolence of his constitution, we owe many valuable productions, which otherwise, perhaps, might never have appeared.

He had spent, during the progress of the work, the money for which he had contracted to write his *Dictionary*. We have seen that the reward of his labour was only fifteen hundred and seventy-five pounds; and when the expence of amanuenses and paper, and other articles are deducted, his clear profit was very inconsiderable. I once said to him, 'I am sorry, Sir, you did not get more for your *Dictionary*.' His answer was, 'I am sorry, too. But it was very well. The booksellers are generous, liberal-minded men.' He, upon all occasions, did ample justice to their character in this respect. He considered them as the patrons of literature; and, indeed, although they have eventually been considerable gainers by his *Dictionary*, it is to them that we owe its having been undertaken and carried through at the risk of great expence, for they were not absolutely sure of being indemnified.

On the first day of this year we find from his private devotions, that he had then recovered from sickness; and in February that his eye was restored to its use. The pious gratitude with which he acknowledges mercies upon every occasion is very edifying; as is the humble submission which he breathes, when it is the will of his heavenly Father to try him with afflictions. As such dispositions become the state of man here, and are the true effects of religious discipline, we cannot but venerate in Johnson one of the most exercised minds that our holy religion hath ever formed. If there be any thoughtless enough to suppose such exercise the weakness of a great understanding, let them look up to Johnson and be convinced that what he so earnestly practised must have a rational foundation.

His works this year were, an abstract or epitome, in octavo, of his folio *Dictionary,* and a few essays in a monthly publication, entitled, *The Universal Visiter.* Christopher Smart, with whose unhappy vacillation of mind he sincerely sympathised, was one of the stated undertakers of this miscellany; and it was to assist him that Johnson sometimes employed his pen. All the essays marked with two *asterisks* have been ascribed to him; but I am confident, from internal evidence, that of these, neither 'The Life of Chaucer,' 'Reflections on the State of Portugal,' nor an 'Essay on Architecture,' were written by him. I am equally confident, upon the same evidence, that he wrote 'Further Thoughts on Agriculture;' † being the sequel of a very inferiour essay on the same subject, and which, though carried on as if by the same hand, is both in thinking and expression so far above it, and so strikingly peculiar, as to leave no doubt of its true parent; and that he also wrote 'A Dissertation on the State of Literature and Authours,' † and 'A Dissertation on the Epitaphs written by Pope.' † The last of these, indeed, he afterwards added to his *Idler.* Why the essays truly written by him are marked in the same manner with some which he did not write, I cannot explain; but with deference to those who have ascribed to him the three essays which I have rejected, they want all the characteristical marks of Johnsonian composition.

He engaged also to superintend and contribute largely to another monthly publication, entitled *The Literary Magazine, or Universal Review;* * the first number of which came out in May this year. What were his emoluments from this undertaking, and what other writers were employed in it, I have not discovered. He continued to write in it, with intermissions, till the fifteenth number; and I think that he never gave better proofs of the force, acuteness, and vivacity of his mind, than in this miscellany, whether we consider his original essays, or his reviews of the works of others. The 'Preliminary Address' † to the Publick is a proof how this great man could embellish, with the graces of superiour composition, even so trite a thing as the plan of a magazine.

His original essays are, 'An Introduction to the Political State of Great Britain;' † 'Remarks on the Militia Bill;' † 'Observations on his Britannick Majesty's Treaties with the Empress of Russia and the Landgrave of Hesse Cassel;' † 'Observations on the Present State of Affairs;' † and 'Memoirs of Frederick III, King of Prussia.' † In all these he displays extensive political knowledge and sagacity, expressed with uncommon energy and perspicuity, without any of those words which he sometimes took a pleasure in adopting in imitation of Sir Thomas Browne; of whose *Christian Morals* he this year gave an edition, with his 'Life' † prefixed to it, which is one of Johnson's best biographical performances. In one instance only in these essays has he indulged his *Brownism*. Dr. Robertson, the historian, mentioned it to me, as having at once convinced him that Johnson was the author of the 'Memoirs of the King of Prussia.' Speaking of the pride which the old King, the father of his hero, took in being master of the tallest regiment in Europe, he says, 'To review this *towering* regiment was his daily pleasure; and to perpetuate it was so much his care, that when he met a tall woman he immediately commanded one of his *Titanian* retinue to marry her, that they might *propagate procerity*.' For this Anglo-Latian word *procerity,* Johnson had, however, the authority of Addison. . . .

His defence of tea against Mr. Jonas Hanway's violent attack upon that elegant and popular beverage, shews how very well a man of genius can write upon the slightest subject, when he writes, as the Italians say, *con amore:* I suppose no person ever enjoyed with more relish the infusion of that fragrant leaf than Johnson. The quantities which he drank of it at all hours were so great, that his nerves must have been uncommonly strong, not to have been extremely relaxed by such an intemperate use of it. He assured me, that he never felt the least inconvenience from it; which is a proof that the fault of his constitution was rather a too great tension of fibres, than the contrary. Mr. Hanway wrote an angry answer to Johnson's review of his *Essay on Tea,* and Johnson, after a full and deliberate pause, made a reply to it; the only instance, I believe, in the whole course of his life, when he condescended to oppose any thing that was written against him. . . .

Johnson's most exquisite critical essay in the *Literary Magazine,* and indeed any where, is his review of Soame Jenyns's *Inquiry into the Origin of Evil.* Jenyns was possessed of lively talents, and a style eminently pure and easy, and could very happily play with a light subject, either in prose or verse; but when he speculated on that most difficult and excruciating

114

question, the Origin of Evil, he 'ventured far beyond his depth,' and, accordingly, was exposed by Johnson, both with acute argument and brilliant wit. I remember when the late Mr. Bicknell's humourous performance, entitled *The Musical Travels of Joel Collyer,* in which a slight attempt is made to ridicule Johnson, was ascribed to Soame Jenyns, 'Ha! (said Johnson) I thought I had given *him* enough of it.' . . .

As one of the little occasional advantages which he did not disdain to take by his pen, as a man whose profession was literature, he this year accepted of a guinea from Mr. Robert Dodsley, for writing the introduction to *The London Chronicle,* an evening news-paper; and even in so slight a performance exhibited peculiar talents. This *Chronicle* still subsists, and from what I observed, when I was abroad, has a more extensive circulation upon the Continent than any of the English news-papers. It was constantly read by Johnson himself; and it is but just to observe, that it has all along been distinguished for good sense, accuracy, moderation, and delicacy.

Another instance of the same nature has been communicated to me by the Reverend Dr. Thomas Campbell, who has done himself considerable credit by his own writings.

'Sitting with Dr. Johnson one morning alone, he asked me if I had known Dr. Madden, who was authour of the premium-scheme in Ireland. On my answering in the affirmative, and also that I had for some years lived in his neighbourhood, &c., he begged of me that when I returned to Ireland, I would endeavour to procure for him a poem of Dr. Madden's called *Boulter's Monument.* The reason (said he) why I wish for it, is this: when Dr. Madden came to London, he submitted that work to my castigation; and I remember I blotted a great many lines, and might have blotted many more, without making the poem worse. However, the Doctor was very thankful, and very generous, for he gave me ten guineas, *which was to me at that time a great sum.*'

He this year resumed his scheme of giving an edition of *Shakspeare* with notes. He issued Proposals of considerable length,* in which he shewed that he perfectly well knew what a variety of research such an undertaking required; but his indolence prevented him from pursuing it with that diligence which alone can collect those scattered facts that genius, however acute, penetrating, and luminous, cannot discover by its own force. It is remarkable, that at this time his fancied activity was for the moment so vigorous, that he promised his work should be published before Christmas, 1757. Yet nine years elapsed before it saw the light. His throes in bringing it forth had been severe and remittent; and at last we may almost conclude that the Cæsarian operation was performed by the knife of Churchill, whose upbraiding satire, I dare say, made Johnson's friends urge him to dispatch.

> 'He for subscribers bates his hook,
> And takes your cash; but where's the book?
> No matter where; wise fear, you know,
> Forbids the robbing of a foe;
> But what, to serve our private ends,
> Forbids the cheating of our friends?'

About this period he was offered a living of considerable value in Lincolnshire, if he were inclined to enter into holy orders. It was a rectory in the gift of Mr. Langton, the father of his much valued friend. But he did not accept of it; partly I believe from a conscientious motive, being persuaded that his temper and habits rendered him unfit for that assiduous and familiar instruction of the vulgar and ignorant which he held to be an essential duty in a clergyman; and partly because his love of a London life was so strong, that he would have thought himself an exile in any other place, particularly if residing in the country. Whoever would wish to see his thoughts upon that subject displayed in their full force, may peruse *The Adventurer*, Number 126.

1757: ÆTAT. 48.]—IN 1757 it does not appear that he published any thing, except some of those articles in *The Literary Magazine*, which have been mentioned. That magazine, after Johnson ceased to write in it, gradually declined, though the popular epithet of *Antigallican* was added to it; and in July 1758 it expired. He probably prepared a part of his *Shakspeare* this year, and he dictated a speech on the subject of an Address to the Throne, after the expedition to Rochfort, which was delivered by one of his friends, I know not in what publick meeting. It is printed in *The Gentleman's Magazine* for October 1785 as his, and bears sufficient marks of authenticity. . . .

Dr. Burney has kindly favoured my with the following memorandum, which I take the liberty to insert in his own genuine easy style. I love to exhibit sketches of my illustrious friend by various eminent hands.

'Soon after this, Mr. Burney, during a visit to the capital, had an interview with him in Gough-square, where he dined and drank tea with him, and was introduced to the acquaintance of Mrs. Williams. After dinner, Mr. Johnson proposed to Mr. Burney to go up with him into his garret, which being accepted, he there found about five or six Greek folios, a deal writing-desk, and a chair and a half. Johnson giving to his guest the entire seat, tottered himself on one with only three legs and one arm. Here he gave Mr. Burney Mrs. Williams's history, and shewed him some volumes of his *Shakspeare* already printed, to prove that he was in earnest. Upon Mr. Burney's opening the first volume, at the *Merchant of Venice*, he observed to him, that he seemed to be more severe on Warburton than Theobald. "O poor Tib.! (said Johnson) he was ready knocked down to my hands; Warburton stands between me and him." "But, Sir, (said Mr. Burney,) you'll have Warburton upon your bones, won't you?" "No, Sir; he'll not come out: he'll only growl in his den." "But you think, Sir, that Warburton is a superiour critick to Theobald?" "O, Sir, he'd make two-and-fifty Theobalds, cut into slices! The worst of Warburton is, that he has a rage for saying something, when there's nothing to be said." Mr. Burney then asked him whether he had seen the letter which Warburton had written in answer to a pamphlet addressed "To the most impudent Man alive." He answered in the negative. Mr. Burney told him it was supposed to be written by Mallet. The controversy now raged between the friends of Pope and Bolingbroke; and Warburton and Mallet were the leaders of the several parties. Mr. Burney asked him then if he had seen Warburton's book against Bolingbroke's *Philosophy*? "No, Sir, I have never read Bolingbroke's impiety, and therefore am not interested about its confutation." '

On the fifteenth of April he began a new periodical paper, entitled *The Idler,** which came out every Saturday in a weekly news-paper, called *The Universal Chronicle, or Weekly Gazette*, published by Newbery. These essays were continued till April 5, 1760. Of one hundred and three, their total number, twelve were contributed by his friends; of which, Numbers 33, 93, and 96, were written by Mr. Thomas Warton; No. 67 by Mr. Langton; and Nos. 76, 79, and 82, by Sir Joshua Reynolds; the concluding words of No. 82, 'and pollute his canvas with deformity,' being added by Johnson, as Sir Joshua informed me.

The Idler is evidently the work of the same mind which produced *The Rambler*, but has less body and more spirit. It had more variety of real life, and greater facility of language. He describes the miseries of idleness, with the lively sensations of one who has felt them; and in his private memorandums while engaged in it, we find 'This year I hope to learn diligence.' Many of these excellent essays were written as hastily as an ordinary letter. Mr. Langton remembers Johnson, when on a visit at Oxford, asking him one evening how long it was till the post went out; and on being told about half an hour, he exclaimed, 'then we shall do very well.' He upon this instantly sat down and finished an *Idler*, which it was necessary should be in London the next day. Mr. Langton having signified a wish to read it, 'Sir, (said he) you shall not do more than I have done myself.' He then folded it up and sent it off. . . .

1759: ÆTAT. 50.]—IN 1759, in the month of January, his mother died at the great age of ninety, an event which deeply affected him; not that 'his mind had acquired no firmness by the contemplation of mortality;' but that his reverential affection for her was not abated by years, as indeed he retained all his tender feelings even to the latest period of his life. I have been told that he regretted much his not having gone to visit his mother for several years, previous to her death. But he was constantly engaged in literary labours which confined him to London; and though he had not the comfort of seeing his aged parent, he contributed liberally to her support.

Soon after this event, he wrote his *Rasselas, Prince of Abyssinia;* * concerning the publication of which Sir John Hawkins guesses vaguely and idly, instead of having taken the trouble to inform himself with authentick precision. Not to trouble my readers with a repetition of the Knight's reveries, I have to mention, that the late Mr. Strahan the printer told me, that Johnson wrote it, that with the profits he might defray the expence of his mother's funeral, and pay some little debts which she had left. He told Sir Joshua Reynolds that he composed it in the evenings of one week, sent it to the press in portions as it was written, and had never since read it over. Mr. Strahan, Mr. Johnston, and Mr. Dodsley purchased it for a hundred pounds, but afterwards paid him twenty-five pounds more, when it came to a second edition.

Considering the large sums which have been received for compilations, and works requiring not much more genius than compilations, we cannot but wonder at the very low price which he was content to receive for this admirable performance; which, though he had written nothing else, would have rendered his name immortal in the world of literature. None of his writings has been so extensively diffused over Europe; for it has been translated into most, if not all, of the modern languages. This Tale, with all the charms of oriental imagery, and all the force and beauty of which the English language is capable, leads us through the most important scenes of human life, and shews us that this stage of our being is full of 'vanity and vexation of spirit.' To those who look no further than the present life, or who maintain that human nature has not fallen from the state in which it was created, the instruction of this sublime story will be of no avail. But they who think justly, and feel with strong sensibility, will listen with eagerness and admiration to its truth and wisdom. Voltaire's *Candide,* written to refute the system of

Optimism, which it has accomplished with brilliant success, is wonderfully similar in its plan and conduct to Johnson's *Rasselas;* insomuch, that I have heard Johnson say, that if they had not been published so closely one after the other that there was not time for imitation, it would have been in vain to deny that the scheme of that which came latest was taken from the other. Though the proposition illustrated by both these works was the same, namely, that in our present state there is more evil than good, the intention of the writers was very different. Voltaire, I am afraid, meant only by wanton profaneness to obtain a sportive victory over religion, and to discredit the belief of a superintending Providence: Johnson meant, by shewing the unsatisfactory nature of things temporal, to direct the hopes of man to things eternal. *Rasselas,* as was observed to me by a very accomplished lady, may be considered as a more enlarged and more deeply philosophical discourse in prose, upon the interesting truth, which in his *Vanity of Human Wishes* he had so successfully enforced in verse.

The fund of thinking which this work contains is such, that almost every sentence of it may furnish a subject of long meditation. I am not satisfied if a year passes without my having read it through; and at every perusal, my admiration of the mind which produced it is so highly raised, that I can scarcely believe that I had the honour of enjoying the intimacy of such a man. . . .

It will be recollected, that during all this year he carried on his *Idler,* and, no doubt, was proceeding, though slowly, in his edition of *Shakspeare.* He, however, from that liberality which never failed, when called upon to assist other labourers in literature, found time to translate for Mrs. Lennox's English version of Brumoy, 'A Dissertation on the Greek Comedy,' † and The General Conclusion of the book.† . . .

He now refreshed himself by an excursion to Oxford, of which the following short characteristical notice, in his own words, is preserved:—

'* * * is now making tea for me. I have been in my gown ever since I came here. It was, at my first coming, quite new and handsome. I have swum thrice, which I had disused for many years. I have proposed to Vansittart, climbing over the wall, but he has refused me. And I have clapped my hands till they are sore, at Dr. King's speech.'

His negro servant, Francis Barber, having left him, and been some time at sea, not pressed as has been supposed, but with his own consent, it appears from a letter to John Wilkes, Esq., from Dr. Smollet, that his master kindly interested himself in procuring his release from a state of life of which

119

Johnson always expressed the utmost abhorrence. He said, 'No man will be a sailor who has contrivance enough to get himself into a jail; for being in a ship is being in a jail, with the chance of being drowned.' And at another time, 'A man in a jail has more room, better food, and commonly better company.' The letter was as follows:—

'DEAR SIR,   'Chelsea, March 16, 1759.

'I am again your petitioner, in behalf of that great CHAM of literature, Samuel Johnson. His black servant, whose name is Francis Barber, has been pressed on board the Stag Frigate, Captain Angel, and our lexicographer is in great distress. He says the boy is a sickly lad, of a delicate frame, and particularly subject to a malady in his throat, which renders him very unfit for his Majesty's service. You know what manner of animosity the said Johnson has against you; and I dare say you desire no other opportunity of resenting it than that of laying him under an obligation. He was humble enough to desire my assistance on this occasion, though he and I were never cater-cousins; and I gave him to understand that I would make application to my friend Mr. Wilkes, who, perhaps, by his interest with Dr. Hay and Mr. Elliot, might be able to procure the discharge of his lacquey. It would be superfluous to say more on the subject, which I leave to your own consideration; but I cannot let slip this opportunity of declaring that I am, with the most inviolable esteem and attachment, dear Sir, your affectionate, obliged, humble servant,   'T. SMOLLET.' . . .

1760: ÆTAT. 51.]—IN 1760 he wrote *An Address of the Painters to George III. on his Accession to the Throne of these Kingdoms*,† which no monarch ever ascended with more sincere congratulations from his people. Two generations of foreign princes had prepared their minds to rejoice in having again a King, who gloried in being 'born a Briton.' He also wrote for Mr. Baretti the Dedication† of his *Italian and English Dictionary*, to the Marquis of Abreu, then Envoy-Extraordinary from Spain at the Court of Great Britain.

Johnson was now either idle, or very busy with his *Shakspeare;* for I can find no other publick composition by him except an Introduction to the proceedings of the Committee for cloathing the French Prisoners; * one of the many proofs that he was ever awake to the calls of humanity; and an account which he gave in the *Gentleman's Magazine* of Mr. Tytler's acute and able vindication of Mary Queen of Scots.* . . .

In this year I have not discovered a single private letter written by him to any of his friends. It should seem, however, that he had at this period a floating intention of writing a history of the recent and wonderful successes of the British arms in all quarters of the globe; for among his resolutions or memorandums, September 18, there is, 'Send for books for Hist. of War.' How much is it to be regretted that this intention was not fulfilled. His majestick expression would have carried down to the latest posterity the glorious achievements of his country with the same fervent glow which they produced on the mind at the time. He would have been under no temptation to deviate in any degree from truth, which he held very sacred, or to take a licence, which a learned divine told me he once seemed, in a conversation, jocularly to allow to historians.

'There are (said he) inexcusable lies, and consecrated lies. For instance, we are told that on the arrival of the news of the unfortunate battle of Fontenoy, every heart beat, and every eye was in tears. Now we know that no man eat his dinner the worse, but there *should* have been all this concern; and to say there *was,* (smiling) may be reckoned a consecrated lie.'

This year Mr. Murphy, having thought himself ill-treated by the Reverend Dr. Francklin, who was one of the writers of *The Critical Review,* published an indignant vindication in *A Poetical Epistle to Samuel Johnson, A.M.* in which he compliments Johnson in a just and elegant manner. . . .

I take this opportunity to relate the manner in which an acquaintance first commenced between Dr. Johnson and Mr. Murphy. During the publication of *The Gray's-Inn Journal,* a periodical paper which was successfully carried on by Mr. Murphy alone, when a very young man, he happened to be in the country with Mr. Foote; and having mentioned that he was obliged to go to London in order to get ready for the press one of the numbers of that *Journal,* Foote said to him, 'You need not go on that account. Here is a French magazine, in which you will find a very pretty oriental tale; translate that, and send it to your printer.' Mr. Murphy having read the tale, was highly pleased with it, and followed Foote's advice. When he returned to town, this tale was pointed out to him in *The Rambler,* from whence it had been translated into the French magazine. Mr. Murphy then waited upon Johnson, to explain this curious incident. His talents, literature, and gentleman-like manners, were soon perceived by Johnson, and a friendship was formed which was never broken. . . .

1761: ÆTAT. 52.]—In 1761 Johnson appears to have done little. He was still, no doubt, proceeding in his edition of *Shakspeare;* but what advances he made in it cannot be ascertained. He certainly was at this time not active; for in his scrupulous examination of himself on Easter eve, he laments, in his too rigorous mode of censuring his own conduct, that his life, since the communion of the preceding Easter, had been 'dissipated and useless.' He, however, contributed this year the Preface * to Rolt's *Dictionary of Trade and Commerce,* in which he displays such a clear and comprehensive knowledge of the subject, as might lead the reader to think that its authour had devoted all his life to it. I asked him whether he knew much of Rolt, and of his work. 'Sir, (said he) I never saw the man, and never read the book. The booksellers wanted a Preface to a *Dictionary of Trade and Commerce.* I knew very well what such a Dictionary should be, and I wrote a Preface accordingly.' Rolt, who wrote a great deal for the booksellers, was, as Johnson told me, a singular character. Though not in the least acquainted with him, he used to say, 'I am just come from Sam. Johnson.' This was a sufficient specimen of his vanity and impudence. But he gave a more eminent proof of it in our sister kingdom, as Dr. Johnson informed me. When Akenside's *Pleasures of the Imagination* first came out, he did not put his name to the poem. Rolt went over to Dublin, published an edition of it, and put his own name to it. Upon the fame of this he lived for several months, being entertained at the best tables as 'the ingenious Mr. Rolt.' His conversation, indeed, did not discover much of the fire of a poet; but it was recollected, that both Addison and Thomson were equally dull till excited by wine. Akenside having been informed of this imposition, vindicated his right by publishing the poem with its real authour's name. . . .

1762: ÆTAT. 53.]—IN 1762 he wrote for the Reverend Dr. Kennedy, Rector of Bradley in Derbyshire, in a strain of very courtly elegance, a Dedication to the King * of that gentleman's work, entitled, *A complete System of Astronomical Chronology, unfolding the Scriptures.* He had certainly looked at his work before it was printed; for the concluding paragraph is undoubtedly of his composition. . . .

The accession of George the Third to the throne of these kingdoms, opened a new and brighter prospect to men of literary merit, who had been honoured with no mark of royal favour in the preceding reign. His present Majesty's education in this country, as well as his taste and benefience, prompted him to be the patron of science and the arts; and early this year Johnson, having been represented to him as a very learned and good man, without any certain provision, his Majesty was pleased to grant him a pension of three hundred pounds a year. The Earl of Bute, who was then Prime

Minister, had the honour to announce this instance of his Sovereign's bounty, concerning which many and various stories, all equally erroneous, have been propagated: maliciously representing it as a political bribe to Johnson, to desert his avowed principles, and become the tool of a government which he held to be founded in usurpation. I have taken care to have it in my power to refute them from the most authentick information. Lord Bute told me, that Mr. Wedderburne, now Lord Loughborough, was the person who first mentioned this subject to him. Lord Loughborough told me, that the pension was granted to Johnson solely as the reward of his literary merit, without any stipulation whatever, or even tacit understanding that he should write for administration. His Lordship added, that he was confident the political tracts which Johnson afterwards did write, as they were entirely consonant with his own opinions, would have been written by him though no pension had been granted to him.

Mr. Thomas Sheridan and Mr. Murphy, who then lived a good deal both with him and Mr. Wedderburne, told me, that they previously talked with Johnson upon this matter, and that it was perfectly understood by all parties that the pension was merely honorary. Sir Joshua Reynolds told me, that Johnson called on him after his Majesty's intention had been notified to him, and said he wished to consult his friends as to the propriety of his accepting this mark of the royal favour, after the definitions which he had given in his *Dictionary* of *pension* and *pensioners*. He said he would not have Sir Joshua's answer till next day, when he would call again, and desired he might think of it. Sir Joshua answered that he was clear to give his opinion then, that there could be no objection to his receiving from the King a reward for literary merit; and that certainly the definitions in his *Dictionary* were not applicable to him. Johnson, it should seem, was satisfied, for he did not call again till he had accepted the pension, and had waited on Lord Bute to thank him. He then told Sir Joshua that Lord Bute said to him expressly, 'It is not given you for anything you are to do, but for what you have done.' His Lordship, he said, behaved in the handsomest manner. He repeated the words twice, that he might be sure Johnson heard them, and thus set his mind perfectly at ease. This nobleman, who has been so virulently abused, acted with great honour in this instance, and displayed a mind truly liberal. A minister of a more narrow and selfish disposition would have availed himself of such an opportunity to fix an implied obligation on a man of Johnson's powerful talents to give him his support.

Mr. Murphy and the late Mr. Sheridan severally contended

for the distinction of having been the first who mentioned to Mr. Wedderburne that Johnson ought to have a pension. When I spoke of this to Lord Loughborough, wishing to know if he recollected the prime mover in the business, he said, 'All his friends assisted:' and when I told him that Mr. Sheridan strenuously asserted his claim to it, his Lordship said, 'He rang the bell.' And it is but just to add, that Mr. Sheridan told me, that when he communicated to Dr. Johnson that a pension was to be granted him, he replied, in a fervour of gratitude, 'The English language does not afford me terms adequate to my feelings on this occasion. I must have recourse to the French. I am *pénétré* with his Majesty's goodness.' When I repeated this to Dr. Johnson, he did not contradict it. . . .

This year his friend Sir Joshua Reynolds paid a visit of some weeks to his native county, Devonshire, in which he was accompanied by Johnson, who was much pleased with this jaunt, and declared he had derived from it a great accession of new ideas. He was entertained at the seats of several noblemen and gentlemen in the West of England; [1] but the greatest part of the time was passed at Plymouth, where the magnificence of the navy, the ship-building and all its circumstances, afforded him a grand subject of contemplation. The Commissioner of the Dock-yard paid him the compliment of ordering the yacht to convey him and his friend to the Eddystone, to which they accordingly sailed. But the weather was so tempestuous that they could not land.

Reynolds and he were at this time the guests of Dr. Mudge, the celebrated surgeon, and now physician of that place, not more distinguished for quickness of parts and variety of knowledge, than loved and esteemed for his amiable manners; and here Johnson formed an acquaintance with Dr. Mudge's father, that very eminent divine, the Reverend Zachariah Mudge, Prebendary of Exeter, who was idolised in the west, both for his excellence as a preacher and the uniform perfect propriety of his private conduct. He preached a sermon purposely that Johnson might hear him; and we shall see afterwards that Johnson honoured his memory by drawing his character. While Johnson was at Plymouth, he saw a great many of its inhabitants, and was not sparing of his very

[1] At one of these seats Dr. Amyat, Physician in London, told me he happened to meet him. In order to amuse him till dinner should be ready, he was taken out to walk in the garden. The master of the house, thinking it proper to introduce something scientifick into the conversation, addressed him thus: 'Are you a botanist, Dr. Johnson?' 'No, Sir, (answered Johnson,) I am not a botanist; and, (alluding, no doubt, to his near sightedness) should I wish to become a botanist, I must first turn myself into a reptile.'—B.

entertaining conversation. It was here that he made that frank and truly original confession, that 'ignorance, pure ignorance,' was the cause of a wrong definition in his *Dictionary* of the word *pastern*, to the no small surprise of the Lady who put the question to him; who having the most profound reverence for his character, so as almost to suppose him endowed with infallibility, expected to hear an explanation (of what, to be sure, seemed strange to a common reader,) drawn from some deep-learned source with which she was unacquainted.

Sir Joshua Reynolds, to whom I was obliged for my information concerning this excursion, mentions a very characteristical anecdote of Johnson while at Plymouth. Having observed that in consequence of the Dock-yard a new town had arisen about two miles off as a rival to the old; and knowing from his sagacity, and just observation of human nature, that it is certain if a man hates at all, he will hate his next neighbour; he concluded that this new and rising town could not but excite the envy and jealousy of the old, in which conjecture he was very soon confirmed; he therefore set himself resolutely on the side of the old town, the *established* town, in which his lot was cast, considering it as a kind of duty to *stand by* it. He accordingly entered warmly into its interests, and upon every occasion talked of the *dockers,* as the inhabitants of the new town were called, as upstarts and aliens. Plymouth is very plentifully supplied with water by a river brought into it from a great distance, which is so abundant that it runs to waste in the town. The Dock, or New-town, being totally destitute of water, petitioned Plymouth that a small portion of the conduit might be permitted to go to them, and this was now under consideration. Johnson, affecting to entertain the passions of the place, was violent in opposition; and, half-laughing at himself for his pretended zeal where he had no concern, exclaimed, 'No, no! I am against the *dockers;* I am a Plymouth man. Rogues! let them die of thirst. They shall not have a drop!' . . .

1763: ÆTAT. 54.]—IN 1763 he furnished to *The Poetical Calendar,* published by Fawkes and Woty, a character of Collins*, which he afterwards ingrafted into his entire life of that admirable poet, in the collection of lives which he wrote for the body of English poetry, formed and published by the booksellers of London. His account of the melancholy depression with which Collins was severely afflicted, and which brought him to his grave, is, I think, one of the most tender and interesting passages in the whole series of his writings. He also favoured Mr. Hoole with the Dedication of his translation of *Tasso* to the Queen*. . . .

This is to me a memorable year; for in it I had the happiness to obtain the acquaintance of that extraordinary man whose memoirs I am now writing; an acquaintance which I shall ever esteem as one of the most fortunate circumstances in my life. Though then but two-and-twenty, I had for several years read his works with delight and instruction, and had the highest reverence for their authour, which had grown up in my fancy into a kind of mysterious veneration, by figuring to myself a state of solemn elevated abstraction, in which I supposed him to live in the immense metropolis of London. Mr. Gentleman, a native of Ireland, who passed some years in Scotland as a player, and as an instructor in the English language, a man whose talents and worth were depressed by misfortunes, had given me a representation of the figure and manner of DICTIONARY JOHNSON! as he was then generally called; and during my first visit to London, which was for three months in 1760, Mr. Derrick the poet, who was Gentleman's friend and countryman, flattered me with hopes that he would introduce me to Johnson, an honour of which I was very ambitious. But he never found an opportunity; which made me doubt that he had promised to do what was not in his power; till Johnson some years afterwards told me, 'Derrick, Sir, might very well have introduced you. I had a kindness for Derrick, and am sorry he is dead.'

In the summer of 1761 Mr. Thomas Sheridan was at Edinburgh, and delivered lectures upon the English Language and Publick Speaking to large and respectable audiences. I was often in his company, and heard him frequently expatiate upon Johnson's extraordinary knowledge, talents, and virtues, repeat his pointed sayings, describe his particularities, and boast of his being his guest sometimes till two or three in the morning. At his house I hoped to have many opportunities of seeing the sage, as Mr. Sheridan obligingly assured me I should not be disappointed.

When I returned to London in the end of 1762, to my surprise and regret I found an irreconcileable difference had taken place between Johnson and Sheridan. A pension of two hundred pounds a year had been given to Sheridan. Johnson, who, as has been already mentioned, thought slightingly of Sheridan's art, upon hearing that he was also pensioned, exclaimed, 'What! have they given *him* a pension? Then it is time for me to give up mine.' Whether this proceeded from a momentary indignation, as if it were an affront to his exalted merit that a player should be rewarded in the same manner with him, or was the sudden effect of a fit of peevishness, it was unluckily said, and, indeed, cannot be justified. Mr. Sheridan's pension was granted to him not as a player, but as a sufferer in the cause of government, when he was manager of the Theatre Royal in Ireland, when parties ran high in 1753. And it must also be allowed that he was a man of literature, and had considerably improved the arts of reading and speaking with distinctness and propriety. . . .

Johnson complained that a man[1] who disliked him repeated his sarcasm to Mr. Sheridan, without telling him what followed, which was, that after a pause he added, 'However, I am glad that Mr. Sheridan has a pension, for he is a very good man.' Sheridan could never forgive this hasty contemptuous expression. It rankled in his mind; and though I informed him of all that Johnson said, and that he would be very glad to meet him amicably, he positively declined repeated offers which I made, and once went off abruptly from a house where he and I were engaged to dine, because he was told that Dr. Johnson was to be there. I have no sympathetick feeling with such persevering resentment. It is painful when there is a breach between those who have lived together socially and cordially; and I wonder that there is not, in all such cases, a mutual wish that it should be healed. I could perceive that Mr. Sheridan was by no means satisfied with Johnson's acknowledging him to be a good man. That could not sooth his injured vanity. I could not but smile, at the same time that I was offended, to observe Sheridan in *The Life of Swift,* which he afterwards published, attempting, in the writhings of his resentment, to depreciate Johnson, by characterising him as 'A writer of gigantick fame in these days of little men;' that very Johnson whom he once so highly admired and venerated.

This rupture with Sheridan deprived Johnson of one of his most agreeable resources for amusement in his lonely evenings; for Sheridan's well-informed, animated, and bustling mind never suffered conversation to stagnate; and Mrs. Sheridan was a most agreeable companion to an intellectual man. She was sensible, ingenious, unassuming, yet communicative. I recollect, with satisfaction, many pleasing hours which I passed with her under the hospitable roof of her husband, who was to me a very kind friend. Her novel, entitled *Memoirs of Miss Sydney Biddulph,* contains an excellent moral, while it inculcates a future state of retribution; and what it teaches is impressed upon the mind by a series of as deep distress as can affect humanity, in the amiable and pious heroine who goes to her grave unrelieved, but resigned, and full of hope of 'heaven's mercy.' Johnson paid her this high compliment upon it: 'I know not, Madam, that you have a right, upon moral principles, to make your readers suffer so much.'

[1] James Macpherson.

Mr. Thomas Davies the actor, who then kept a bookseller's shop in Russel-street, Covent-garden, told me that Johnson was very much his friend, and came frequently to his house, where he more than once invited me to meet him; but by some unlucky accident or other he was prevented from coming to us.

Mr. Thomas Davies was a man of good understanding and talents with the advantage of a liberal education. Though somewhat pompous, he was an entertaining companion; and his literary performances have no inconsiderable share of merit. He was a friendly and very hospitable man. Both he and his wife, (who has been celebrated for her beauty,) though upon the stage for many years, maintained an uniform decency of character; and Johnson esteemed them, and lived in as easy an intimacy with them as with any family which he used to visit. Mr. Davies recollected several of Johnson's remarkable sayings, and was one of the best of the many imitators of his voice and manner, while relating them. He increased my impatience more and more to see the extraordinary man whose works I highly valued, and whose conversation was reported to be so peculiarly excellent.

At last, on Monday the 16th of May, when I was sitting in Mr. Davies's back-parlour, after having drunk tea with him and Mrs. Davies, Johnson unexpectedly came into the shop; and Mr. Davies having perceived him through the glass-door in the room in which we were sitting, advancing towards us, —he announced his aweful approach to me, somewhat in the manner of an actor in the part of Horatio, when he addresses Hamlet on the appearance of his father's ghost, 'Look, my Lord, it comes.' I found that I had a very perfect idea of Johnson's figure, from the portrait of him painted by Sir Joshua Reynolds soon after he had published his *Dictionary*, in the attitude of sitting in his easy chair in deep meditation, which was the first picture his friend did for him, which Sir Joshua very kindly presented to me, and from which an engraving has been made for this work. Mr. Davies mentioned my name, and respectfully introduced me to him. I was much agitated; and recollecting his prejudice against the Scotch, of which I had heard much, I said to Davies, 'Don't tell where I come from.'—'From Scotland,' cried Davies roguishly. 'Mr. Johnson, (said I) I do indeed come from Scotland, but I cannot help it.' I am willing to flatter myself that I meant this as light pleasantry to sooth and conciliate him, and not as an humiliating abasement at the expence of my country. But however that might be, this speech was somewhat unlucky; for with that quickness of wit for which he was so remarkable, he seized the expression 'come from Scotland,' which I

128

used in the sense of being of that country, and, as if I had said that I had come away from it, or left it, retorted, 'That, Sir, I find, is what a very great many of your countrymen cannot help.' This stroke stunned me a good deal; and when we had sat down, I felt myself not a little embarrassed, and apprehensive of what might come next. He then addressed himself to Davies: 'What do you think of Garrick? He has refused me an order for the play for Miss Williams, because he knows the house will be full, and that an order would be worth three shillings.' Eager to take any opening to get into conversation with him, I ventured to say, 'O, Sir, I cannot think Mr. Garrick would grudge such a trifle to you.' 'Sir, (said he, with a stern look,) I have known David Garrick longer than you have done: and I know no right you have to talk to me on the subject.' Perhaps I deserved this check; for it was rather presumptuous in me, an entire stranger, to express any doubt of the justice of his animadversion upon his old acquaintance and pupil.[1] I now felt myself much mortified, and began to think that the hope which I had long indulged of obtaining his acquaintance was blasted. And, in truth, had not my ardour been uncommonly strong, and my resolution uncommonly persevering, so rough a reception might have deterred me for ever from making any further attempts. Fortunately, however, I remained upon the field not wholly discomfited; and was soon rewarded by hearing some of his conversation, of which I preserved the following short minute, without marking the questions and observations by which it was produced.

'People (he remarked) may be taken in once, who imagine that an authour is greater in private life than other men. Uncommon parts require uncommon opportunities for their exertion.'

'In barbarous society, superiority of parts is of real consequence. Great strength or great wisdom is of much value to an individual. But in more polished times there are people to do every thing for money; and then there are a number of other superiorities, such as those of birth and fortune, and rank, that dissipate men's attention, and leave no extraordinary share of respect for personal and intellectual superiority.

[1] That this was a momentary sally against Garrick there can be no doubt; for at Johnson's desire he had, some years before, given a benefit-night at his theatre to this very person, by which she had got two hundred pounds. Johnson, indeed, upon all other occasions, when I was in his company, praised the very liberal charity of Garrick. I once mentioned to him, 'It is observed, Sir, that you attack Garrick yourself, but will suffer nobody else to do it.' JOHNSON, (smiling) 'Why, Sir, that is true'—B.

This is wisely ordered by Providence, to preserve some equality among mankind.'

'Sir, this book (*The Elements of Criticism,* which he had taken up,) is a pretty essay, and deserves to be held in some estimation, though much of it is chimerical.'

Speaking of one[1] who with more than ordinary boldness attacked publick measures and the royal family, he said,

'I think he is safe from the law, but he is an abusive scoundrel; and instead of applying to my Lord Chief Justice to punish him, I would send half a dozen footmen and have him well ducked.'

'The notion of liberty amuses the people of England, and helps to keep off the *tædium vitæ.* When a butcher tells you that *his heart bleeds for his country,* he has, in fact, no uneasy feeling.'

'Sheridan will not succeed at Bath with his oratory. Ridicule has gone down before him, and, I doubt, Derrick is his enemy.' [2]

'Derrick may do very well, as long as he can outrun his character; but the moment his character gets up with him, it is all over.'

It is, however, but just to record, that some years afterwards, when I reminded him of this sarcasm, he said, 'Well, but Derrick has now got a character that he need not run away from.'

I was highly pleased with the extraordinary vigour of his conversation, and regretted that I was drawn away from it by an engagement at another place. I had, for a part of the evening, been left alone with him, and had ventured to make an observation now and then, which he received very civilly; so that I was satisfied that though there was a roughness in his manner, there was no ill-nature in his disposition. Davies followed me to the door, and when I complained to him a little of the hard blows which the great man had given me, he kindly took upon him to console me by saying, 'Don't be uneasy. I can see he likes you very well.'

A few days afterwards I called on Davies, and asked him if he thought I might take the liberty of waiting on Mr. Johnson at his Chambers in the Temple. He said I certainly might, and that Mr. Johnson would take it as a compliment. So upon Tuesday the 24th of May, after having been enlivened by the witty sallies of Messieurs Thornton, Wilkes, Churchill and Lloyd, with whom I had passed the morning, I

---

1 Wilkes.

2 Mr. Sheridan was then reading lectures upon Oratory at Bath, where Derrick was Master of the Ceremonies; or, as the phrase is, KING—B.

boldly repaired to Johnson. His Chambers were on the first floor of No. 1, Inner-Temple-lane, and I entered them with an impression given me by the Reverend Dr. Blair, of Edinburgh, who had been introduced to him not long before, and described his having 'found the Giant in his den;' an expression, which, when I came to be pretty well acquainted with Johnson, I repeated to him, and he was diverted at this picturesque account of himself. Dr. Blair had been presented to him by Dr. James Fordyce. At this time the controversy concerning the pieces published by Mr. James Macpherson, as translations of Ossian, was at its height. Johnson had all along denied their authenticity; and, what was still more provoking to their admirers, maintained that they had no merit. The subject having been introduced by Dr. Fordyce, Dr. Blair, relying on the internal evidence of their antiquity, asked Dr. Johnson whether he thought any man of a modern age could have written such poems? Johnson replied, 'Yes, Sir, many men, many women, and many children.' Johnson, at this time, did not know that Dr. Blair had just published a *Dissertation*, not only defending their authenticity, but seriously ranking them with the poems of Homer and Virgil; and when he was afterwards informed of this circumstance, he expressed some displeasure at Dr. Fordyce's having suggested the topick, and said, 'I am not sorry that they got thus much for their pains. Sir, it was like leading one to talk of a book when the authour is concealed behind the door.'

He received me very courteously; but, it must be confessed, that his apartment, and furniture, and morning dress, were sufficiently uncouth. His brown suit of cloaths looked very rusty; he had on a little old shrivelled unpowdered wig, which was too small for his head; his shirt-neck and knees of his breeches were loose; his black worsted stockings ill drawn up; and he had a pair of unbuckled shoes by way of slippers. But all these slovenly particularities were forgotten the moment that he began to talk. Some gentlemen, whom I do not recollect, were sitting with him; and when they went away, I also rose; but he said to me, 'Nay, don't go.' 'Sir, (said I,) I am afraid that I intrude upon you. It is benevolent to allow me to sit and hear you.' He seemed pleased with this compliment, which I sincerely paid him, and answered, 'Sir, I am obliged to any man who visits me.'—I have preserved the following short minute of what passed this day.

'Madness frequently discovers itself merely by unnecessary deviation from the usual modes of the world. My poor friend Smart shewed the disturbance of his mind, by falling upon his knees, and saying his prayers in the street, or in any other unusual place. Now although, rationally speaking, it is greater madness not to pray at all, than to pray as Smart did, I am afraid there are so many who do not pray, that their understanding is not called in question.'

Concerning this unfortunate poet, Christopher Smart, who was confined in a mad-house, he had, at another time, the following conversation with Dr. Burney:—BURNEY. 'How does poor Smart do, Sir; is he likely to recover?' JOHNSON. 'It seems as if his mind had ceased to struggle with the disease; for he grows fat upon it.' BURNEY. 'Perhaps, Sir, that may be from want of exercise.' JOHNSON. 'No, Sir; he has partly as much exercise as he used to have, for he digs in the garden. Indeed, before his confinement, he used for exercise to walk to the ale-house; but he was *carried* back again. I did not think he ought to be shut up. His infirmities were not noxious to society. He insisted on people praying with him; and I'd as lief pray with Kit Smart as any one else. Another charge was, that he did not love clean linen; and I have no passion for it.'—Johnson continued. 'Mankind have a great aversion to intellectual labour; but even supposing knowledge to be easily attainable, more people would be content to be ignorant than would take even a little trouble to acquire it.'

'The morality of an action depends on the motive from which we act. If I fling half a crown to a beggar with intention to break his head, and he picks it up and buys victuals with it, the physical effect is good; but, with respect to me, the action is very wrong. So, religious exercises, if not performed with an intention to please GOD, avail us nothing. As our Saviour says of those who perform them from other motives, "Verily they have their reward." '

'The Christian religion has very strong evidences. It, indeed, appears in some degree strange to reason; but in History we have undoubted facts, against which, reasoning *à priori*, we have more arguments than we have for them; but then, testimony has great weight, and casts the balance. I would recommend to every man whose faith is yet unsettled, Grotius,—Dr. Pearson,—and Dr. Clarke.'

Talking of Garrick, he said, 'He is the first man in the world for sprightly conversation.'

When I rose a second time he again pressed me to stay, which I did.

He told me, that he generally went abroad at four in the afternoon, and seldom came home till two in the morning. I took the liberty to ask if he did not think it wrong to live thus, and not make more use of his great talents. He owned it was a bad habit. On reviewing, at the distance of many years, my journal of this period, I wonder how, at my first visit, I ventured to talk to him so freely, and that he bore it with so much indulgence.

Before we parted, he was so good as to promise to favour me with his company one evening at my lodgings; and, as I took my leave, shook me cordially by the hand. It is almost needless to add, that I felt no little elation at having now so happily established an acquaintance of which I had been so long ambitious.

My readers will, I trust, excuse me for being thus minutely circumstantial, when it is considered that the acquaintance of Dr. Johnson was to me a most valuable acquisition, and laid the foundation of whatever instruction and entertainment they may receive from my collections concerning the great subject of the work which they are now perusing.

I did not visit him again till Monday, June 13, at which time I recollect no part of his conversation, except that when I told him I had been to see Johnson ride upon three horses, he said, 'Such a man, Sir, should be encouraged; for his per-formances shew the extent of the human powers in one in-stance, and thus tend to raise our opinion of the faculties of man. He shews what may be attained by persevering applica-tion; so that every man may hope, that by giving as much application, although perhaps he may never ride three horses at a time, or dance upon a wire, yet he may be equally expert in whatever profession he has chosen to pursue.'

He again shook me by the hand at parting, and asked me why I did not come oftener to him. Trusting that I was now in his good graces, I answered, that he had not given me much encouragement, and reminded him of the check I had received from him at our first interview. 'Poh, poh! (said he, with a complacent smile,) never mind these things. Come to me as often as you can. I shall be glad to see you.'

I had learnt that his place of frequent resort was the Mitre tavern in Fleet-street, where he loved to sit up late, and I begged I might be allowed to pass an evening with him there soon, which he promised I should. A few days afterwards I met him near Temple-bar, about one o'clock in the morning, and asked if he would then go to the Mitre. 'Sir, (said he) it is too late; they won't let us in. But I'll go with you another night with all my heart.'

A revolution of some importance in my plan of life had just taken place; for instead of procuring a commission in the foot-guards, which was my own inclination, I had, in compli-ance with my father's wishes, agreed to study the law; and was soon to set out for Utrecht, to hear the lectures of an excellent Civilian in that University, and then to proceed on my travels. Though very desirous of obtaining Dr. Johnson's

133

advice and instructions on the mode of pursuing my studies, I was at this time so occupied, shall I call it? or so dissipated, by the amusements of London, that our next meeting was not till Saturday, June 25, when happening to dine at Clifton's eating-house, in Butcher-row, I was surprized to perceive Johnson come in and take his seat at another table. The mode of dining, or rather being fed, at such houses in London, is well known to many to be particularly unsocial, as there is no Ordinary, or united company, but each person has his own mess, and is under no obligation to hold any intercourse with any one. A liberal and full-minded man, however, who loves to talk, will break through this churlish and unsocial restraint. Johnson and an Irish gentleman got into a dispute concerning the cause of some part of mankind being black. 'Why, Sir, (said Johnson,) it has been accounted for in three ways: either by supposing that they are the posterity of Ham, who was cursed; or that GOD at first created two kinds of men, one black and another white; or that by the heat of the sun the skin is scorched, and so acquires a sooty hue. This matter has been much canvassed among naturalists, but has never been brought to any certain issue.' What the Irishman said is totally obliterated from my mind; but I remember that he became very warm and intemperate in his expressions; upon which Johnson rose, and quietly walked away. When he had retired, his antagonist took his revenge, as he thought, by saying, 'He has a most ungainly figure, and an affectation of pomposity, unworthy of a man of genius.'

Johnson had not observed that I was in the room. I followed him, however, and he agreed to meet me in the evening at the Mitre. I called on him, and we went thither at nine. We had a good supper, and port wine, of which he then sometimes drank a bottle. The orthodox high-church sound of the MITRE,—the figure and matter of the celebrated SAMUEL JOHNSON,—the extraordinary power and precision of his conversation, and the pride arising from finding myself admitted as his companion, produced a variety of sensations, and a pleasing elevation of mind beyond what I had ever before experienced. I find in my journal the following minute of our conversation, which, though it will give but a very faint notion of what passed, is in some degree a valuable record; and it will be curious in this view, as shewing how habitual to his mind were some opinions which appear in his works.

'Colley Cibber, Sir, was by no means a blockhead; but by arrogating to himself too much, he was in danger of losing that degree of estimation to which he was entitled. His friends gave out that he *intended* his birth-day *Odes* should be bad: but that was not the case, Sir; for he kept them many months by him, and a few years before he died he shewed me one of them, with great solicitude to render it as perfect as might be, and I made some corrections, to which he was not very willing to submit. I remember the following couplet in allusion to the King and himself:

> "Perch'd on the eagle's soaring wing,
> The lowly linnet loves to sing."

Sir, he had heard something of the fabulous tale of the wren sitting upon the eagle's wing, and he had applied it to a linnet. Cibber's familiar style, however, was better than that which Whitehead has assumed. *Grand* nonsense is insupportable. Whitehead is but a little man to inscribe verses to players.'

I did not presume to controvert this censure, which was tinctured with his prejudice against players; but I could not help thinking that a dramatick poet might with propriety pay a compliment to an eminent performer, as Whitehead has very happily done in his verses to Mr. Garrick.

'Sir, I do not think Gray a first-rate poet. He has not a bold imagination, nor much command of words. The obscurity in which he has involved himself will not persuade us that he is sublime. His *Elegy in a Church-yard* has a happy selection of images, but I don't like what are called his great things. His *Ode* which begins

> "Ruin seize thee, ruthless King,
> Confusion on thy banners wait!"

has been celebrated for its abruptness, and plunging into the subject all at once. But such arts as these have no merit, unless when they are original. We admire them only once; and this abruptness has nothing new in it. We have had it often before. Nay, we have it in the old song of Johnny Armstrong:

> "Is there ever a man in all Scotland
> From the highest estate to the lowest degree," &c.

And then, Sir,

> "Yes, there is a man in Westmoreland,
> And Johnny Armstrong they do him call."

There, now, you plunge at once into the subject. You have no previous narration to lead you to it. The two next lines in that *Ode* are, I think, very good:

> "Though fanned by conquest's crimson wing,
> They mock the air with idle state."

Here let it be observed, that although his opinion of Gray's poetry was widely different from mine, and I believe from that of most men of taste, by whom it is with justice highly admired, there is certainly much absurdity in the clamour which has been raised, as if he had been culpably injurious to the merit of that bard, and had been actuated by envy. Alas! ye little short-sighted criticks, could JOHNSON be envious of the talents of any of his contemporaries? That his opinion on this subject was what in private and in publick he uniformly expressed, regardless of what others might think, we may wonder, and perhaps regret; but it is shallow and unjust to charge him with expressing what he did not think.

Finding him in a placid humour, and wishing to avail myself of the opportunity which I fortunately had of consulting a sage, to hear whose wisdom, I conceived in the ardour of youthful imagination, that men filled with a noble enthusiasm for intellectual improvement would gladly have resorted from distant lands;—I opened my mind to him ingenuously, and gave him a little sketch of my life, to which he was pleased to listen with great attention.

I acknowledged, that though educated very strictly in the principles of religion, I had for some time been misled into a certain degree of infidelity; but that I was come now to a better way of thinking, and was fully satisfied of the truth of the Christian revelation, though I was not clear as to every point considered to be orthodox. Being at all times a curious examiner of the human mind, and pleased with an undisguised display of what had passed in it, he called to me with warmth, 'Give me your hand; I have taken a liking to you.' He then began to descant upon the force of testimony, and the little we could know of final causes; so that the objections of, why was it so? or why was it not so? ought not to disturb us: adding, that he himself had at one period been guilty of a temporary neglect of religion, but that it was not the result of argument, but mere absence of thought.

After having given credit to reports of his bigotry, I was agreeably surprized when he expressed the following very liberal sentiment, which has the additional value of obviating an objection to our holy religion, founded upon the discordant tenets of Christians themselves: 'For my part, Sir, I think all Christians, whether Papists or Protestants, agree in the essential articles, and that their differences are trivial, and rather political than religious.'

We talked of belief in ghosts. He said, 'Sir, I make a distinction between what a man may experience by the mere strength of his imagination, and what imagination cannot possibly produce. Thus, suppose I should think that I saw a

136

form, and heard a voice cry "Johnson, you are a very wicked fellow, and unless you repent you will certainly be punished;" my own unworthiness is so deeply impressed upon my mind, that I might *imagine* I thus saw and heard, and therefore I should not believe that an external communication had been made to me. But if a form should appear, and a voice should tell me that a particular man had died at a particular place, and a particular hour, a fact which I had no apprehension of, nor any means of knowing, and this fact, with all its circumstances, should afterwards be unquestionably proved, I should, in that case, be persuaded that I had supernatural intelligence imparted to me.'

Here it is proper, once for all, to give a true and fair statement of Johnson's way of thinking upon the question, whether departed spirits are ever permitted to appear in this world, or in any way to operate upon human life. He has been ignorantly misrepresented as weakly credulous upon that subject; and, therefore, though I feel an inclination to disdain and treat with silent contempt so foolish a notion concerning my illustrious friend, yet as I find it has gained ground, it is necessary to refute it. The real fact then is, that Johnson had a very philosophical mind, and such a rational respect for testimony, as to make him submit his understanding to what was authentically proved, though he could not comprehend why it was so. Being thus disposed, he was willing to inquire into the truth of any relation of supernatural agency, a general belief of which has prevailed in all nations and ages. But so far was he from being the dupe of implicit faith, that he examined the matter with a jealous attention, and no man was more ready to refute its falsehood when he had discovered it. Churchill, in his poem entitled *The Ghost*, availed himself of the absurd credulity imputed to Johnson, and drew a caricature of him under the name of 'POMPOSO,' representing him as one of the believers of the story of a Ghost in Cock-lane, which, in the year 1762, had gained very general credit in London. Many of my readers, I am convinced, are to this hour under an impression that Johnson was thus foolishly deceived. It will therefore surprize them a good deal when they are informed upon undoubted authority, that Johnson was one of those by whom the imposture was detected. The story had become so popular, that he thought it should be investigated; and in this research he was assisted by the Reverend Dr. Douglas, now Bishop of Salisbury, the great detector of impostures; who informs me, that after the gentlemen who went and examined into the evidence were satisfied of its falsity, Johnson wrote in their presence an account of it, which was published in the news-papers and *Gentleman's Magazine,* and undeceived the world.

Our conversation proceeded. 'Sir, (said he) I am a friend to subordination, as most conducive to the happiness of society. There is a reciprocal pleasure in governing and being governed.'

'Dr. Goldsmith is one of the first men we now have as an authour, and he is a very worthy man too. He has been loose in his principles, but he is coming right.'

I mentioned Mallet's tragedy of *Elvira,* which had been acted the preceding winter at Drury-lane, and that the Honourable Andrew Erskine, Mr. Dempster, and myself, had joined in writing a pamphlet, entitled, *Critical Strictures,* against it. That the mildness of Dempster's disposition had, however, relented; and he had candidly said, 'We have hardly a right to abuse this tragedy: for bad as it is, how vain should either of us be to write one not near so good.' JOHNSON. 'Why no, Sir; this is not just reasoning. You *may* abuse a tragedy, though you cannot write one. You may scold a carpenter who has made you a bad table, though you cannot make a table. It is not your trade to make tables.'

When I talked to him of the paternal estate to which I was heir, he said, 'Sir, let me tell you, that to be a Scotch landlord, where you have a number of families dependent upon you, and attached to you, is, perhaps, as high a situation as humanity can arrive at. A merchant upon the 'Change of London, with a hundred thousand pounds, is nothing; an English Duke, with an immense fortune, is nothing; he has no tenants who consider themselves as under his patriarchal care, and who will follow him to the field upon any emergency.'

His notion of the dignity of a Scotch landlord had been formed upon what he had heard of the Highland Chiefs; for it is long since a lowland landlord has been so curtailed in his feudal authority, that he has little more influence over his tenants than an English landlord; and of late years most of the Highland Chiefs have destroyed, by means too well known, the princely power which they once enjoyed.

He proceeded: 'Your going abroad, Sir, and breaking off idle habits, may be of great importance to you. I would go where there are courts and learned men. There is a good deal of Spain that has not been perambulated. I would have you go thither. A man of inferiour talents to yours may furnish us with useful observations upon that country.' His supposing me, at that period of life, capable of writing an account of my travels that would deserve to be read, elated me not a little.

I appeal to every impartial reader whether this faithful detail of his frankness, complacency, and kindness to a young man, a stranger and a Scotchman, does not refute the unjust opinion of the harshness of his general demeanour. His occasional reproofs of folly, impudence, or impiety, and even the sudden sallies of his constitutional irritability of temper, which have been preserved for the poignancy of their wit, have produced that opinion among those who have not considered that such instances, though collected by Mrs. Piozzi into a small volume, and read over in a few hours, were, in fact, scattered through a long series of years; years, in which his time was chiefly spent in instructing and delighting mankind by his writings and conversation, in acts of piety to GOD, and good-will to men.

I complained to him that I had not yet acquired much knowledge, and asked his advice as to my studies. He said, 'Don't talk of study now. I will give you a plan; but it will require some time to consider of it.' 'It is very good in you (I replied,) to allow me to be with you thus. Had it been foretold to me some years ago that I should pass an evening with the authour of *The Rambler*, how should I have exulted!' What I then expressed, was sincerely from the heart. He was satisfied that it was, and cordially answered, 'Sir, I am glad we have met. I hope we shall pass many evenings and mornings too, together.' We finished a couple of bottles of port, and sat till between one and two in the morning.

He wrote this year in the *Critical Review* the account of 'Telemachus, a Mask,' by the Reverend George Graham, of Eton College. The subject of this beautiful poem was particularly interesting to Johnson, who had much experience of 'the conflict of opposite principles,' which he describes as 'The contention between pleasure and virtue, a struggle which will always be continued while the present system of nature shall subsist: nor can history or poetry exhibit more than pleasure triumphing over virtue, and virtue subjugating pleasure.'

As Dr. Oliver Goldsmith will frequently appear in this narrative, I shall endeavour to make my readers in some degree acquainted with his singular character. He was a native of Ireland, and a contemporary with Mr. Burke at Trinity College, Dublin, but did not then give much promise of future celebrity. He, however, observed to Mr. Malone, that 'though he made no great figure in mathematicks, which was a study in much repute there, he could turn an Ode of Horace into English better than any of them.' He afterwards studied physick at Edinburgh, and upon the Continent; and I have been informed, was enabled to pursue his travels on foot, partly by demanding at Universities to enter the list as a disputant, by which, according to the custom of many of them, he was entitled to the premium of a crown, when luckily for him his challenge was not accepted; so that, as I once observed to Dr. Johnson, he *disputed* his passage through Europe. He then came to England, and was employed successively in the capacities of an usher to an academy, a corrector of the press, a reviewer, and a writer for a news-paper. He had sagacity enough to cultivate assiduously the acquaintance of Johnson, and his faculties were gradually enlarged by the contemplation of such a model. To me and many others it appeared that he studiously copied the manner of Johnson, though, indeed, upon a smaller scale.

At this time I think he had published nothing with his name, though it was pretty generally known that *one Dr. Goldsmith* was the authour of *An Enquiry into the present State of polite Learning in Europe,* and of *The Citizen of the World,* a series of letters supposed to be written from London by a Chinese. No man had the art of displaying with more advantage as a writer, whatever literary acquisitions he made. *'Nihil quod tetigit non ornavit.'* [1] His mind resembled a fertile, but thin soil. There was a quick, but not a strong vegetation, of whatever chanced to be thrown upon it. No deep root could be struck. The oak of the forest did not grow here; but the elegant shrubbery and the fragrant parterre appeared in gay succession. It has been generally circulated and believed that he was a mere fool in conversation; but, in truth, this has been greatly exaggerated. He had, no doubt, a more than common share of that hurry of ideas which we often find in his countrymen, and which sometimes produces a laughable confusion in expressing them. He was very much what the French call *un étourdi,* and from vanity and an eager desire of being conspicuous wherever he was, he frequently talked carelessly without knowledge of the subject, or even without thought. His person was short, his countenance coarse and vulgar, his deportment that of a scholar aukwardly affecting the easy gentleman. Those who were in any way distinguished, excited envy in him to so ridiculous an excess, that the instances of it are hardly credible. When accompanying two beautiful young ladies with their mother on a tour in France, he was seriously angry that more attention was paid to them than to him; and once at the exhibition of the *Fantoccini* in London, when those who sat next him observed with what dexterity a puppet was made to toss a pike, he could not bear that it should have such praise, and exclaimed with some warmth, 'Pshaw! I can do it better myself.'

[1] 'He touched nothing that he did not adorn.'

He, I am afraid, had no settled system of any sort, so that his conduct must not be strictly scrutinised; but his affections were social and generous, and when he had money he gave it away very liberally. His desire of imaginary consequence predominated over his attention to truth. When he began to rise into notice, he said he had a brother who was Dean of Durham, a fiction so easily detected, that it is wonderful how he should have been so inconsiderate as to hazard it. He boasted to me at this time of the power of his pen in commanding money, which I believe was true in a certain degree, though in the instance he gave he was by no means correct. He told me that he had sold a novel for four hundred pounds. This was his *Vicar of Wakefield*. But Johnson informed me, that he had made the bargain for Goldsmith, and the price was sixty pounds. 'And, Sir, (said he,) a sufficient price too, when it was sold; for then the fame of Goldsmith had not been elevated, as it afterwards was, by his *Traveller;* and the bookseller had such faint hopes of profit by his bargain, that he kept the manuscript by him a long time, and did not publish it till after *The Traveller* had appeared. Then, to be sure, it was accidentally worth more money.'

Mrs. Piozzi and Sir John Hawkins have strangely misstated the history of Goldsmith's situation and Johnson's friendly interference, when this novel was sold. I shall give it authentically from Johnson's own exact narration:—'I received one morning a message from poor Goldsmith that he was in great distress, and, as it was not in his power to come to me, begging that I would come to him as soon as possible. I sent him a guinea, and promised to come to him directly. I accordingly went as soon as I was drest, and found that his landlady had arrested him for his rent, at which he was in a violent passion. I perceived that he had already changed my guinea, and had got a bottle of Madeira and a glass before him. I put the cork into the bottle, desired he would be calm, and began to talk to him of the means by which he might be extricated. He then told me that he had a novel ready for the press, which he produced to me. I looked into it, and saw its merit; told the landlady I should soon return, and having gone to a bookseller, sold it for sixty pounds. I brought Goldsmith the money, and he discharged his rent, not without rating his landlady in a high tone for having used him so ill.'

My next meeting with Johnson was on Friday the 1st of July, when he and I and Dr. Goldsmith supped together at the Mitre. I was before this time pretty well acquainted with Goldsmith, who was one of the brightest ornaments of the Johnsonian school. Goldsmith's respectful attachment to Johnson was then at its height; for his own literary reputation had not yet distinguished him so much as to excite a vain desire of competition with his great Master. He had increased my admiration of the goodness of Johnson's heart, by incidental remarks in the course of conversation, such as, when I mentioned Mr. Levet, whom he entertained under his roof, 'He is poor and honest, which is recommendation enough to Johnson;' and when I wondered that he was very kind to a man of whom I had heard a very bad character, 'He is now become miserable, and that insures the protection of Johnson.'

Goldsmith attempted this evening to maintain, I suppose from an affectation of paradox, 'that knowledge was not desirable on its own account, for it often was a source of unhappiness.' JOHNSON. 'Why, Sir, that knowledge may in some cases produce unhappiness, I allow. But, upon the whole, knowledge, *per se*, is certainly an object which every man would wish to attain, although, perhaps, he may not take the trouble necessary for attaining it.'

Dr. John Campbell, the celebrated political and biographical writer, being mentioned, Johnson said, 'Campbell is a man of much knowledge, and has a good share of imagination. His *Hermippus Redivivus* is very entertaining, as an account of the Hermetick philosophy, and as furnishing a curious history of the extravagancies of the human mind. If it were merely imaginary it would be nothing at all. Campbell is not always rigidly careful of truth in his conversation; but I do not believe there is any thing of this carelessness in his books. Campbell is a good man, a pious man. I am afraid he has not been in the inside of a church for many years; but he never passes a church without pulling off his hat. This shews that he has good principles. I used to go pretty often to Campbell's on a Sunday evening till I began to consider that the shoals of Scotchmen who flocked about him might probably say, when any thing of mine was well done, 'Ay, ay, he has learnt this of CAWMELL!'

He talked very contemptuously of Churchill's poetry, observing, that 'it had a temporary currency, only from its audacity of abuse, and being filled with living names, and that it would sink into oblivion.' I ventured to hint that he was not quite a fair judge, as Churchill had attacked him violently. JOHNSON. 'Nay, Sir, I am a very fair judge. He did not attack me violently till he found I did not like his poetry; and his attack on me shall not prevent me from continuing to say what I think of him, from an apprehension that it may be ascribed to resentment. No, Sir, I called the fellow a blockhead at first, and I will call him a blockhead still. However, I will acknowledge that I have a better opinion of him now,

142

than I once had; for he has shewn more fertility than I expected. To be sure, he is a tree that cannot produce good fruit: he only bears crabs. But, Sir, a tree that produces a great many crabs is better than a tree which produces only a few.'

In this depreciation of Churchill's poetry I could not agree with him. It is very true that the greatest part of it is upon the topicks of the day, on which account, as it brought him great fame and profit at the time, it must proportionally slide out of the publick attention as other occasional objects succeed. But Churchill had extraordinary vigour both of thought and expression. His portraits of the players will ever be valuable to the true lovers of the drama; and his strong caricatures of several eminent men of his age, will not be forgotten by the curious. Let me add, that there are in his works many passages which are of a general nature; and his *Prophecy of Famine* is a poem of no ordinary merit. It is, indeed, falsely injurious to Scotland, but therefore may be allowed a greater share of invention. . . .

Let me here apologize for the imperfect manner in which I am obliged to exhibit Johnson's conversation at this period. In the early part of my acquaintance with him, I was so wrapt in admiration of his extraordinary colloquial talents, and so little accustomed to his peculiar mode of expression, that I found it extremely difficult to recollect and record his conversation with its genuine vigour and vivacity. In progress of time, when my mind was, as it were, *strongly impregnated with the Johnsonian æther,* I could, with much more facility and exactness, carry in my memory and commit to paper the exuberant variety of his wisdom and wit.

At this time *Miss* Williams, as she was then called, though she did not reside with him in the Temple under his roof, but had lodgings in Bolt-court, Fleet-street, had so much of his attention, that he every night drank tea with her before he went home, however late it might be, and she always sat up for him. This, it may be fairly conjectured, was not alone a proof of his regard for *her,* but of his own unwillingness to go into solitude, before that unseasonable hour at which he had habituated himself to expect the oblivion of repose. Dr. Goldsmith, being a privileged man, went with him this night, strutting away, and calling to me with an air of superiority, like that of an esoterick over an exoterick disciple of a sage of antiquity, 'I go to Miss Williams.' I confess, I then envied him this mighty privilege, of which he seemed so proud; but it was not long before I obtained the same mark of distinction.

On Tuesday the 5th of July, I again visited Johnson. He

told me he had looked into the poems of a pretty voluminous writer, Mr. (now Dr.) John Ogilvie, one of the Presbyterian ministers of Scotland, which had lately come out, but could find no thinking in them. BOSWELL. 'Is there not imagination in them, Sir?' JOHNSON. 'Why, Sir, there is in them what *was* imagination, but it is no more imagination in *him*, than sound is sound in the echo. And his diction too is not his own. We have long ago seen *white-robed innocence*, and *flower-bespangled meads*.'

Talking of London, he observed, 'Sir, if you wish to have a just notion of the magnitude of this city, you must not be satisfied with seeing its great streets and squares, but must survey the innumerable little lanes and courts. It is not in the showy evolutions of buildings, but in the multiplicity of human habitations which are crouded together, that the wonderful immensity of London consists.' . . .

On Wednesday, July 6, he was engaged to sup with me at my lodgings in Downing-street, Westminster. But on the preceding night my landlord having behaved very rudely to me and some company who were with me, I had resolved not to remain another night in his house. I was exceedingly uneasy at the aukward appearance I supposed I should make to Johnson and the other gentlemen whom I had invited, not being able to receive them at home, and being obliged to order supper at the Mitre. I went to Johnson in the morning, and talked of it as a serious distress. He laughed, and said, 'Consider, Sir, how insignificant this will appear a twelve-month hence.'—Were this consideration to be applied to most of the little vexatious incidents of life, by which our quiet is too often disturbed, it would prevent many painful sensations. I have tried it frequently, with good effect. 'There is nothing (continued he) in this mighty misfortune; nay, we shall be better at the Mitre.' I told him that I had been at Sir John Fielding's office, complaining of my landlord, and had been informed, that though I had taken my lodgings for a year, I might, upon proof of his bad behaviour, quit them when I pleased, without being under an obligation to pay rent for any longer time than while I possessed them. The fertility of Johnson's mind could shew itself even upon so small a matter as this. 'Why, Sir, (said he,) I suppose this must be the law, since you have been told so in Bow-street. But, if your landlord could hold you to your bargain, and the lodgings should be yours for a year, you may certainly use them as you think fit. So, Sir, you may quarter two life-guardsmen upon him; or you may send the greatest scoundrel you can find into your apartments; or you may say that you want to make some experiments in natural philosophy, and may burn a large quantity of assafœtida in his house.'

I had as my guests this evening at the Mitre tavern, Dr. Johnson, Dr. Goldsmith, Mr. Thomas Davies, Mr. Eccles, an Irish gentleman, for whose agreeable company I was obliged to Mr. Davies, and the Reverend Mr. John Ogilvie,[1] who was desirous of being in company with my illustrious friend, while I, in my turn, was proud to have the honour of shewing one of my countrymen upon what easy terms Johnson permitted me to live with him.

Goldsmith, as usual, endeavoured, with too much eagerness, to *shine*, and disputed very warmly with Johnson against the well-known maxim of the British constitution, 'the King can do no wrong;' affirming, that 'what was morally false could not be politically true; and as the King might, in the exercise of his regal power, command and cause the doing of what was wrong, it certainly might be said, in sense and in reason, that he could do wrong.' JOHNSON. 'Sir, you are to consider, that in our constitution, according to its true principles, the King is the head; he is supreme; he is above every thing, and there is no power by which he can be tried. Therefore it is, Sir, that we hold the King can do no wrong; that whatever may happen to be wrong in government may not be above our reach, by being ascribed to Majesty. Redress is always to be had against oppression, by punishing the immediate agents. The King, though he should command, cannot force a Judge to condemn a man unjustly; therefore it is the Judge whom we prosecute and punish. Political institutions are formed upon the consideration of what will most frequently tend to the good of the whole, although now and then exceptions may occur. Thus it is better in general that a nation should have a supreme legislative power, although it may at times be abused. And then, Sir, there is this consideration, that *if the abuse be enormous, Nature will rise up, and claiming her original rights, overturn a corrupt political system.*' I mark this animated sentence with peculiar pleasure, as a noble instance of that truly dignified spirit of freedom which ever glowed in his heart, though he was charged with slavish tenets by superficial observers; because he was at all times indignant against that false patriotism, that pretended love of freedom, that unruly restlessness, which is inconsistent with the stable authority of any good government.

This generous sentiment, which he uttered with great fer-

[1] The northern bard mentioned page 144. When I asked Dr. Johnson's permission to introduce him, he obligingly agreed; adding, however, with a sly pleasantry, 'but he must give us none of his poetry.'—B.

vour, struck me exceedingly, and stirred my blood to that pitch of fancied resistance, the possibility of which I am glad to keep in mind, but to which I trust I never shall be forced.

'Great abilities (said he) are not requisite for an Historian; for in historical composition, all the greatest powers of the human mind are quiescent. He has facts ready to his hand; so there is no exercise of invention. Imagination is not required in any high degree; only about as much as is used in the lower kinds of poetry. Some penetration, accuracy, and colouring will fit a man for the task, if he can give the application which is necessary.'

'Bayle's *Dictionary* is a very useful work for those to consult who love the biographical part of literature, which is what I love most.'

Talking of the eminent writers in Queen Anne's reign, he observed, 'I think Dr. Arbuthnot the first man among them. He was the most universal genius, being an excellent physician, a man of deep learning, and a man of much humour. Mr. Addison was, to be sure, a great man; his learning was not profound; but his morality, his humour, and his elegance of writing, set him very high.'

Mr. Ogilvie was unlucky enough to choose for the topick of his conversation the praises of his native country. He began with saying, that there was very rich land round Edinburgh. Goldsmith, who had studied physick there, contradicted this, very untruly, with a sneering laugh. Disconcerted a little by this, Mr. Ogilvie then took new ground, where, I suppose, he thought himself perfectly safe; for he observed, that Scotland had a great many noble wild prospects. JOHNSON. 'I believe, Sir, you have a great many. Norway, too, has noble wild prospects; and Lapland is remarkable for prodigious noble wild prospects. But, Sir, let me tell you, the noblest prospect which a Scotchman ever sees, is the high road that leads him to England!' This unexpected and pointed sally produced a roar of applause. After all, however, those, who admire the rude grandeur of Nature, cannot deny it to Caledonia.

On Saturday, July 9, I found Johnson surrounded with a numerous levee, but have not preserved any part of his conversation. On the 14th we had another evening by ourselves at the Mitre. It happening to be a very rainy night, I made some common-place observations on the relaxation of nerves and depression of spirits which such weather occasioned; adding, however, that it was good for the vegetable creation. Johnson, who, as we have already seen, denied that the temperature of the air had any influence on the human frame, answered, with a smile of ridicule, 'Why yes, Sir, it is good

146

for vegetables, and for the animals who eat those vegetables, and for the animals who eat those animals.' This observation of his aptly enough introduced a good supper; and I soon forgot, in Johnson's company, the influence of a moist atmosphere.

Feeling myself now quite at ease as his companion, though I had all possible reverence for him, I expressed a regret that I could not be so easy with my father, though he was not much older than Johnson, and certainly however respectable had not more learning and greater abilities to depress me. I asked him the reason of this. JOHNSON. 'Why, Sir, I am a man of the world. I live in the world, and I take, in some degree, the colour of the world as it moves along. Your father is a Judge in a remote part of the island, and all his notions are taken from the old world. Besides, Sir, there must always be a struggle between a father and son, while one aims at power and the other at independence.' I said, I was afraid my father would force me to be a lawyer. JOHNSON. 'Sir, you need not be afraid of his forcing you to be a laborious practising lawyer; that is not in his power. For as the proverb says, "One man may lead a horse to the water, but twenty cannot make him drink." He may be displeased that you are not what he wishes you to be; but that displeasure will not go far. If he insists only on your having as much law as is necessary for a man of property, and then endeavours to get you into Parliament, he is quite in the right.'

He enlarged very convincingly upon the excellence of rhyme over blank verse in English poetry. I mentioned to him that Dr. Adam Smith, in his lectures upon composition, when I studied under him in the College of Glasgow, had maintained the same opinion strenuously, and I repeated some of his arguments. JOHNSON. 'Sir, I was once in company with Smith, and we did not take to each other; but had I known that he loved rhyme as much as you tell me he does, I should have HUGGED him.'

Talking of those who denied the truth of Christianity, he said, 'It is always easy to be on the negative side. If a man were now to deny that there is salt upon the table, you could not reduce him to an absurdity. Come, let us try this a little further. I deny that Canada is taken, and I can support my denial by pretty good arguments. The French are a much more numerous people than we; and it is not likely that they would allow us to take it. "But the ministry have assured us, in all the formality of The Gazette, that it is taken."—Very true. But the ministry have put us to an enormous expence by the war in America, and it is their interest to persuade us that

147

we have got something for our money.—"But the fact is confirmed by thousands of men who were at the taking of it."—Ay, but these men have still more interest in deceiving us. They don't want that you should think the French have beat them, but that they have beat the French. Now suppose you should go over and find that it is really taken, that would only satisfy yourself; for when you come home we will not believe you. We will say, you have been bribed.—Yet, Sir, notwithstanding all these plausible objections, we have no doubt that Canada is really ours. Such is the weight of common testimony. How much stronger are the evidences of the Christian religion!'

'Idleness is a disease which must be combated; but I would not advise a rigid adherence to a particular plan of study. I myself have never persisted in any plan for two days together. A man ought to read just as inclination leads him; for what he reads as a task will do him little good. A young man should read five hours in a day, and so may acquire a great deal of knowledge.'

To a man of vigorous intellect and ardent curiosity like his own, reading without a regular plan may be beneficial; though even such a man must submit to it, if he would attain a full understanding of any of the sciences.

To such a degree of unrestrained frankness had he now accustomed me, that in the course of this evening I talked of the numerous reflections which had been thrown out against him on account of his having accepted a pension from his present Majesty. 'Why, Sir, (said he, with a hearty laugh,) it is a mighty foolish noise that they make.[1] I have accepted of a pension as a reward which has been thought due to my literary merit; and now that I have this pension, I am the same man in every respect that I have ever been; I retain the same principles. It is true, that I cannot now curse (smiling) the House of Hanover; nor would it be decent for me to drink King James's health in the wine that King George gives me money to pay for. But, Sir, I think that the pleasure of cursing the House of Hanover, and drinking King James's health, are amply overbalanced by three hundred pounds a year.'

There was here, most certainly, an affectation of more Jacobitism than he really had; and indeed an intention of admitting, for the moment, in a much greater extent than it really existed, the charge of disaffection imputed to him by the world, merely for the purpose of shewing how dexterously he could repel an attack, even though he were placed in the

[1] When I mentioned the same idle clamour to him several years afterwards, he said, with a smile, 'I wish my pension were twice as large, that they might make twice as much noise'—B.

148

most disadvantageous position; for I have heard him declare, that if holding up his right hand would have secured victory at Culloden to Prince Charles's army, he was not sure he would have held it up; so little confidence had he in the right claimed by the house of Stuart, and so fearful was he of the consequences of another revolution on the throne of Great-Britain; and Mr. Topham Beauclerk assured me, he had heard him say this before he had his pension. At another time he said to Mr. Langton, 'Nothing has ever offered, that has made it worth my while to consider the question fully.' He, however, also said to the same gentleman, talking of King James the Second, 'It was become impossible for him to reign any longer in this country.' He no doubt had an early attachment to the House of Stuart; but his zeal had cooled as his reason strengthened. Indeed I heard him once say, that 'after the death of a violent Whig, with whom he used to contend with great eagerness, he felt his Toryism much abated.' I suppose he meant Mr. Walmsley.

Yet there is no doubt that at earlier periods he was wont often to exercise both his pleasantry and ingenuity in talking Jacobitism. My much respected friend, Dr. Douglas, now Bishop of Salisbury, has favoured me with the following admirable instance from his Lordship's own recollection. One day when dining at old Mr. Langton's, where Miss Roberts, his niece, was one of the company, Johnson, with his usual complacent attention to the fair sex, took her by the hand and said, 'My dear, I hope you are a Jacobite.' Old Mr. Langton, who, though a high and steady Tory, was attached to the present Royal Family, seemed offended, and asked Johnson, with great warmth, what he could mean by putting such a question to his niece? 'Why, Sir, (said Johnson) I meant no offence to your niece, I meant her a great compliment. A Jacobite, Sir, believes in the divine right of Kings. He that believes in the divine right of Kings believes in a Divinity. A Jacobite believes in the divine right of Bishops. He that believes in the divine right of Bishops believes in the divine authority of the Christian religion. Therefore, Sir, a Jacobite is neither an Atheist nor a Deist. That cannot be said of a Whig; for *Whiggism is a negation of all principle.*'

He advised me, when abroad, to be as much as I could with the Professors in the Universities, and with the Clergy; for from their conversation I might expect the best accounts of every thing in whatever country I should be, with the additional advantage of keeping my learning alive.

It will be observed, that when giving me advice as to my travels, Dr. Johnson did not dwell upon cities, and palaces, and pictures, and shows, and Arcadian scenes. He was of

149

Lord Essex's opinion, who advises his kinsman Roger Earl of Rutland, 'rather to go an hundred miles to speak with one wise man, than five miles to see a fair town.'

I described to him an impudent fellow[1] from Scotland, who affected to be a savage, and railed at all established systems. JOHNSON. 'There is nothing surprizing in this, Sir. He wants to make himself conspicuous. He would tumble in a hogstye, as long as you looked at him and called to him to come out. But let him alone, never mind him, and he'll soon give it over.'

I added, that the same person maintained that there was no distinction between virtue and vice. JOHNSON. 'Why, Sir, if the fellow does not think as he speaks, he is lying; and I see not what honour he can propose to himself from having the character of a lyar. But if he does really think that there is no distinction between virtue and vice, why, Sir, when he leaves our houses, let us count our spoons.' . . .

He recommended to me to keep a journal of my life, full and unreserved. He said it would be a very good exercise, and would yield me great satisfaction when the particulars were faded from my remembrance. I was uncommonly fortunate in having had a previous coincidence of opinion with him upon this subject, for I had kept such a journal for some time; and it was no small pleasure to me to have this to tell him, and to receive his approbation. He counselled me to keep it private, and said I might surely have a friend who would burn it in case of my death. From this habit I have been enabled to give the world so many anecdotes, which would otherwise have been lost to posterity. I mentioned that I was afraid I put into my journal too many little incidents. JOUNSON. 'There is nothing, Sir, too little for so little a creature as man. It is by studying little things that we attain the great art of having as little misery and as much happiness as possible.'

Next morning Mr. Dempster happened to call on me, and was so much struck even with the imperfect account which I gave him of Dr. Johnson's conversation, that to his honour be it recorded, when I complained that drinking port and sitting up late with him affected my nerves for some time after, he said, 'One had better be palsied at eighteen, than not keep company with such a man.'

On Tuesday, July 18,[2] I found tall Sir Thomas Robinson sitting with Johnson. Sir Thomas said, that the king of Prussia valued himself upon three things;—upon being a hero, a musician, and an authour. JOHNSON. 'Pretty well, Sir, for

[1] James Macpherson.
[2] Tuesday was the 19th.

one man. As to his being an authour, I have not looked at his poetry; but his prose is poor stuff. He writes just as you might suppose Voltaire's footboy to do, who has been his amanuensis. He has such parts as the valet might have, and about as much of the colouring of the style as might be got by transcribing his works.' When I was at Ferney, I repeated this to Voltaire, in order to reconcile him somewhat to Johnson, whom he, in affecting the English mode of expression, had previously characterised as 'a superstitious dog;' but after hearing such a criticism on Frederick the Great, with whom he was then on bad terms, he exclaimed, 'An honest fellow!'

But I think the criticism much too severe; for the *Memoirs of the House of Brandenburgh* are written as well as many works of that kind. His poetry, for the style of which he himself makes a frank apology, *'Jargonnaut un François barbare,'* though fraught with pernicious ravings of infidelity, has, in many places, great animation, and in some a pathetick tenderness.

Upon this contemptuous animadversion on the King of Prussia, I observed to Johnson, 'It would seem then, Sir, that much less parts are necessary to make a King, than to make an Authour; for the King of Prussia is confessedly the greatest King now in Europe, yet you think he makes a very poor figure as an Authour.'

Mr. Levet this day shewed me Dr. Johnson's library, which was contained in two garrets over his Chambers, where Lintot, son of the celebrated bookseller of that name, had formerly his warehouse. I found a number of good books, but very dusty and in great confusion. The floor was strewed with manuscript leaves, in Johnson's own handwriting, which I beheld with a degree of veneration, supposing they perhaps might contain portions of *The Rambler* or of *Rasselas*. I observed an apparatus for chymical experiments, of which Johnson was all his life very fond. The place seemed to be very favourable for retirement and meditation. Johnson told me, that he went up thither without mentioning it to his servant, when he wanted to study, secure from interruption; for he would not allow his servant to say he was not at home when he really was. 'A servant's strict regard for truth, (said he) must be weakened by such a practice. A philosopher may know that it is merely a form of denial; but few servants are such nice distinguishers. If I accustom a servant to tell a lie for *me*, have I not reason to apprehend that he will tell many lies for *himself?*' I am, however, satisfied that every servant, of any degree of intelligence, understands saying his master is not at home, not at all as the affirmation of a fact, but as custo-

151

mary words, intimating that his master wishes not to be seen; so that there can be no bad effect from it.

Mr. Temple, now vicar of St. Gluvias, Cornwall, who had been my intimate friend for many years, had at this time chambers in Farrar's-buildings, at the bottom of Inner Temple-lane, which he kindly lent me upon my quitting my lodgings, he being to return to Trinity Hall, Cambridge. I found them particularly convenient for me, as they were so near Dr. Johnson's.

On Wednesday, July 20, Dr. Johnson, Mr. Dempster, and my uncle Dr. Boswell, who happened to be now in London, supped with me at these Chambers. JOHNSON. 'Pity is not natural to man. Children are always cruel. Savages are always cruel. Pity is acquired and improved by the cultivation of reason. We may have uneasy sensations from seeing a creature in distress, without pity; for we have not pity unless we wish to relieve them. When I am on my way to dine with a friend, and finding it late, have bid the coachman make haste, if I happen to attend when he whips his horses, I may feel unpleasantly that the animals are put to pain, but I do not wish him to desist. No, Sir, I wish him to drive on.'

Mr. Alexander Donaldson, bookseller of Edinburgh, had for some time opened a shop in London, and sold his cheap editions of the most popular English books, in defiance of the supposed common-law right of *Literary Property*. Johnson, though he concurred in the opinion which was afterwards sanctioned by a judgement of the House of Lords, that there was no such right, was at this time very angry that the Booksellers of London, for whom he uniformly professed much regard, should suffer from an invasion of what they had ever considered to be secure: and he was loud and violent against Mr. Donaldson. 'He is a fellow who takes advantage of the law to injure his brethren; for, notwithstanding that the statute secures only fourteen years of exclusive right, it has always been understood by *the trade,* that he, who buys the copy-right of a book from the authour, obtains a perpetual property; and upon that belief, numberless bargains are made to transfer that property after the expiration of the statutory term. Now Donaldson, I say, takes advantage here, of people who have really an equitable title from usage; and if we consider how few of the books, of which they buy the property, succeed so well as to bring profit, we should be of opinion that the term of fourteen years is too short; it should be sixty years.' DEMPSTER. 'Donaldson, Sir, is anxious for the encouragement of literature. He reduces the price of books, so that poor students may buy them.' JOHNSON, (laughing) 'Well,

Sir, allowing that to be his motive, he is no better than Robin Hood, who robbed the rich in order to give to the poor.'

It is remarkable, that when the great question concerning Literary Property came to be ultimately tried before the supreme tribunal of this country, in consequence of the very spirited exertions of Mr. Donaldson, Dr. Johnson was zealous against a perpetuity; but he thought that the term of the exclusive right of authours should be considerably enlarged. He was then for granting a hundred years.

The conversation now turned upon Mr. David Hume's style. JOHNSON. 'Why, Sir, his style is not English; the structure of his sentences is French. Now the French structure and the English structure may, in the nature of things, be equally good. But if you allow that the English language is established, he is wrong. My name might originally have been Nicholson, as well as Johnson; but were you to call me Nicholson now, you would call me very absurdly.'

Rousseau's treatise on the inequality of mankind was at this time a fashionable topick. It gave rise to an observation by Mr. Dempster, that the advantages of fortune and rank were nothing to a wise man, who ought to value only merit. JOHNSON. 'If man were a savage, living in the woods by himself, this might be true; but in civilized society we all depend upon each other, and our happiness is very much owing to the good opinion of mankind. Now, Sir, in civilized society, external advantages make us more respected. A man with a good coat upon his back meets with a better reception than he who has a bad one. Sir, you may analyse this, and say what is there in it? But that will avail you nothing, for it is a part of a general system. Pound St. Paul's Church into atoms, and consider any single atom; it is, to be sure, good for nothing: but, put all these atoms together, and you have St. Paul's Church. So it is with human felicity, which is made up of many ingredients, each of which may be shewn to be very insignificant. In civilized society, personal merit will not serve you so much as money will. Sir, you may make the experiment. Go into the street, and give one man a lecture on morality, and another a shilling, and see which will respect you most. If you wish only to support nature, Sir William Petty fixes your allowance at three pounds a year; but as times are much altered, let us call it six pounds. This sum will fill your belly, shelter you from the weather, and even get you a strong lasting coat, supposing it to be made of good bull's hide. Now, Sir, all beyond this is artificial, and is desired in order to obtain a greater degree of respect from our fellow-creatures. And, Sir, if six hundred pounds a year procure a man more consequence, and, of course, more happiness than

153

six pounds a year, the same proportion will hold as to six thousand, and so on as far as opulence can be carried. Perhaps he who has a large fortune may not be so happy as he who has a small one; but that must proceed from other causes than from his having the large fortune: for, *cæteris paribus*, he who is rich in a civilized society, must be happier than he who is poor; as riches, if properly used, (and it is a man's own fault if they are not,) must be productive of the highest advantages. Money, to be sure, of itself is of no use; for its only use is to part with it. Rousseau, and all those who deal in paradoxes, are led away by a childish desire of novelty. When I was a boy, I used always to choose the wrong side of a debate, because most ingenious things, that is to say, most new things, could be said upon it. Sir, there is nothing for which you may not muster up more plausible arguments, than those which are urged against wealth and other external advantages. Why, now, there is stealing; why should it be thought a crime? When we consider by what unjust methods property has been often acquired, and that what was unjustly got it must be unjust to keep, where is the harm in one man's taking the property of another from him? Besides, Sir, when we consider the bad use that many people make of their property, and how much better use the thief may make of it, it may be defended as a very allowable practice. Yet, Sir, the experience of mankind has discovered stealing to be so very bad a thing, that they make no scruple to hang a man for it. When I was running about this town a very poor fellow, I was a great arguer for the advantages of poverty; but I was, at the same time, very sorry to be poor. Sir, all the arguments which are brought to represent poverty as no evil, shew it to be evidently a great evil. You never find people labouring to convince you that you may live very happily upon a plentiful fortune.—So you hear people talking how miserable a King must be; and yet they all wish to be in his place.'

It was suggested that Kings must be unhappy, because they are deprived of the greatest of all satisfactions, easy and unreserved society. JOHNSON. 'That is an ill-founded notion. Being a King does not exclude a man from such society. Great Kings have always been social. The King of Prussia, the only great King at present, is very social. Charles the Second, the last King of England who was a man of parts, was social; and our Henrys and Edwards were all social.'

Mr. Dempster having endeavoured to maintain that intrinsick merit *ought* to make the only distinction amongst mankind. JOHNSON. 'Why, Sir, mankind have found that this cannot be. How shall we determine the proportion of intrinsick merit? Were that to be the only distinction amongst mankind,

154

we should soon quarrel about the degrees of it. Were all distinctions abolished, the strongest would not long acquiesce, but would endeavour to obtain a superiority by their bodily strength. But, Sir, as subordination is very necessary for society, and contentions for superiority very dangerous, mankind, that is to say, all civilized nations, have settled it upon a plain invariable principle. A man is born to hereditary rank; or his being appointed to certain offices, gives him a certain rank. Subordination tends greatly to human happiness. Were we all upon an equality, we should have no other enjoyment than mere animal pleasure.'

I said, I considered distinction of rank to be of so much importance in civilized society, that if I were asked on the same day to dine with the first Duke in England, and with the first man in Britain for genius, I should hesitate which to prefer. JOHNSON. 'To be sure, Sir, if you were to dine only once, and it were never to be known where you dined, you would choose rather to dine with the first man for genius; but to gain most respect, you should dine with the first Duke in England. For nine people in ten that you meet with, would have a higher opinion of you for having dined with a Duke; and the great genius himself would receive you better, because you had been with the great Duke.'

He took care to guard himself against any possible suspicion that his settled principles of reverence for rank and respect for wealth were at all owing to mean or interested motives; for he asserted his own independence as a literary man. 'No man (said he) who ever lived by literature, has lived more independently than I have done.' He said he had taken longer time than he needed to have done in composing his *Dictionary*. He received our compliments upon that great work with complacency, and told us that the Academy *della Crusca* could scarcely believe that it was done by one man.

Next morning I found him alone, and have preserved the following fragments of his conversation. Of a gentleman[1] who was mentioned, he said, 'I have not met with any man for a long time who has given me such general displeasure. He is totally unfixed in his principles, and wants to puzzle other people.' I said his principles had been poisoned by a noted infidel writer,[2] but that he was, nevertheless, a benevolent good man. JOHNSON. 'We can have no dependence upon that instinctive, that constitutional goodness which is not founded upon principle. I grant you that such a man may be a very amiable member of society. I can conceive him placed in such a situation that he is not much tempted to deviate

[1] Dempster.
[2] Hume.

from what is right; and as every man prefers virtue, when there is not some strong incitement to transgress its precepts, I can conceive him doing nothing wrong. But if such a man stood in need of money, I should not like to trust him; and I should certainly not trust him with young ladies, for *there* there is always temptation. Hume, and other sceptical innovators, are vain men, and will gratify themselves at any expence. Truth will not afford sufficient food to their vanity; so they have betaken themselves to errour. Truth, Sir, is a cow which will yield such people no more milk, and so they are gone to milk the bull. If I could have allowed myself to gratify my vanity at the expence of truth, what fame might I have acquired. Every thing which Hume has advanced against Christianity had passed through my mind long before he wrote. Always remember this, that after a system is well settled upon positive evidence, a few partial objections ought not to shake it. The human mind is so limited, that it cannot take in all the parts of a subject, so that there may be objections raised against any thing. There are objections against a *plenum,* and objections against a *vacuum;* yet one of them must certainly be true.'

I mentioned Hume's argument against the belief of miracles, that it is more probable that the witnesses to the truth of them are mistaken, or speak falsely, than that the miracles should be true. JOHNSON. 'Why, Sir, the great difficulty of proving miracles should make us very cautious in believing them. But let us consider; although GOD has made Nature to operate by certain fixed laws, yet it is not unreasonable to think that he may suspend those laws, in order to establish a system highly advantageous to mankind. Now the Christian religion is a most beneficial system, as it gives us light and certainty where we were before in darkness and doubt. The miracles which prove it are attested by men who had no interest in deceiving us; but who, on the contrary, were told that they should suffer persecution, and did actually lay down their lives in confirmation of the truth of the facts which they asserted. Indeed, for some centuries the heathens did not pretend to deny the miracles; but said they were performed by the aid of evil spirits. This is a circumstance of great weight. Then, Sir, when we take the proofs derived from prophecies which have been so exactly fulfilled, we have most satisfactory evidence. Supposing a miracle possible, as to which, in my opinion, there can be no doubt, we have as strong evidence for the miracles in support of Christianity, as the nature of the thing admits.'

At night Mr. Johnson and I supped in a private room at the Turk's Head coffee-house, in the Strand. 'I encourage this house (said he;) for the mistress of it is a good civil woman, and has not much business.'

'Sir, I love the acquaintance of young people; because, in the first place, I don't like to think myself growing old. In the next place, young acquaintances must last longest, if they do last; and then, Sir, young men have more virtue than old men; they have more generous sentiments in every respect. I love the young dogs of this age: they have more wit and humour and knowledge of life than we had; but then the dogs are not so good scholars. Sir, in my early years I read very hard. It is a sad reflection, but a true one, that I knew almost as much at eighteen as I do now. My judgement, to be sure, was not so good; but I had all the facts. I remember very well, when I was at Oxford, an old gentleman said to me, "Young man, ply your book diligently now, and acquire a stock of knowledge; for when years come upon you, you will find that poring upon books will be but an irksome task." '

This account of his reading, given by himself in plain words, sufficiently confirms what I have already advanced upon the disputed question as to his application. It reconciles any seeming inconsistency in his way of talking upon it at different times; and shews that idleness and reading hard were with him relative terms, the import of which, as used by him, must be gathered from a comparison with what scholars of different degrees of ardour and assiduity have been known to do. And let it be remembered, that he was now talking spontaneously, and expressing his genuine sentiments; whereas at other times he might be induced from his spirit of contradiction, or more properly from his love of argumentative contest, to speak lightly of his own application to study. It is pleasing to consider that the old gentleman's gloomy prophecy as to the irksomeness of books to men of an advanced age, which is too often fulfilled, was so far from being verified in Johnson, that his ardour for literature never failed, and his last writings had more ease and vivacity than any of his earlier productions.

He mentioned to me now, for the first time, that he had been distrest by melancholy, and for that reason had been obliged to fly from study and meditation, to the dissipating variety of life. Against melancholy he recommended constant occupation of mind, a great deal of exercise, moderation in eating and drinking, and especially to shun drinking at night. He said melancholy people were apt to fly to intemperance for relief, but that it sunk them much deeper in misery. He observed, that labouring men who work hard, and live sparingly, are seldom or never troubled with low spirits.

He again insisted on the duty of maintaining subordination of rank. 'Sir, I would no more deprive a nobleman of his respect, than of his money. I consider myself as acting a part in the great system of society, and I do to others as I would have them to do to me. I would behave to a nobleman as I should expect he would behave to me, were I a nobleman and he Sam. Johnson. Sir, there is one Mrs. Macaulay in this town, a great republican. One day when I was at her house, I put on a very grave countenance, and said to her, "Madam, I am now become a convert to your way of thinking. I am convinced that all mankind are upon an equal footing; and to give you an unquestionable proof, Madam, that I am in earnest, here is a very sensible, civil, well-behaved fellow-citizen, your footman; I desire that he may be allowed to sit down and dine with us." I thus, Sir, shewed her the absurdity of the levelling doctrine. She has never liked me since. Sir, you levellers wish to level *down* as far as themselves; but they cannot bear levelling *up* to themselves. They would all have some people under them; why not then have some people above them?' I mentioned a certain authour[1] who disgusted me by his forwardness, and by shewing no deference to noblemen into whose company he was admitted. JOHNSON. 'Suppose a shoemaker should claim an equality with him, as he does with a Lord; how he would stare. "Why, Sir, do you stare? (says the shoemaker,) I do great service to society. 'Tis true I am paid for doing it; but so are you, Sir: and I am sorry to say it, paid better than I am, for doing something not so necessary. For mankind could do better without your books, than without my shoes." Thus, Sir, there would be a perpetual struggle for precedence, were there no fixed invariable rules for the distinction of rank, which creates no jealousy, as it is allowed to be accidental.' . . .

A writer of deserved eminence[2] being mentioned, Johnson said, 'Why, Sir, he is a man of good parts, but being originally poor, he has got a love of mean company and low jocularity; a very bad thing, Sir. To laugh is good, as to talk is good. But you ought no more to think it enough if you laugh, than you are to think it enough if you talk. You may laugh in as many ways as you talk; and surely *every* way of talking that is practised cannot be esteemed.'

I spoke of Sir James Macdonald as a young man of most distinguished merit, who united the highest reputation at Eton and Oxford, with the patriarchal spirit of a great Highland Chieftain. I mentioned that Sir James had said to me, that he had never seen Mr. Johnson, but he had a great respect for him, though at the same time it was mixed with

[1] Dr. Robertson.
[2] Thomas Warton.

some degree of terrour. JOHNSON. 'Sir, if he were to be acquainted with me, it might lessen both.'

The mention of this gentleman led us to talk of the Western Islands of Scotland, to visit which he expressed a wish that then appeared to me a very romantick fancy, which I little thought would be afterwards realized. He told me, that his father had put Martin's account of those islands into his hands when he was very young, and that he was highly pleased with it; that he was particularly struck with the St. Kilda man's notion that the high church of Glasgow had been hollowed out of a rock; a circumstance to which old Mr. Johnson had directed his attention. He said he would go to the Hebrides with me, when I returned from my travels, unless some very good companion should offer when I was absent, which he did not think probable; adding, 'There are few people to whom I take so much to as you.' And when I talked of my leaving England, he said, with a very affectionate air, 'My dear Boswell, I should be very unhappy at parting, did I think we were not to meet again.' I cannot too often remind my readers, that although such instances of his kindness are doubtless very flattering to me, yet I hope my recording them will be ascribed to a better motive than to vanity; for they afford unquestionable evidence of his tenderness and complacency, which some, while they were forced to acknowledge his great powers, have been so strenuous to deny.

He maintained that a boy at school was the happiest of human beings. I supported a different opinion, from which I have never yet varied, that a man is happier; and I enlarged upon the anxiety and sufferings which are endured at school. JOHNSON. 'Ah! Sir, a boy's being flogged is not so severe as a man's having the hiss of the world against him. Men have a solicitude about fame; and the greater share they have of it, the more afraid they are of losing it.' I silently asked myself, 'Is it possible that the great SAMUEL JOHNSON really entertains any such apprehension, and is not confident that his exalted fame is established upon a foundation never to be shaken?' . . .

On Tuesday, July 26, I found Mr. Johnson alone. It was a very wet day, and I again complained of the disagreeable effects of such weather. JOHNSON. 'Sir, this is all imagination, which physicians encourage; for man lives in air, as a fish lives in water; so that if the atmosphere press heavy from above, there is an equal resistance from below. To be sure, bad weather is hard upon people who are obliged to be abroad; and men cannot labour so well in the open air in bad weather, as in good: but, Sir, a smith or a taylor, whose work is within doors, will surely do as much in rainy weather, as in fair. Some very delicate frames, indeed, may be affected by wet weather; but not common constitutions.'

We talked of the education of children; and I asked him what he thought was best to teach them first. JOHNSON. 'Sir, it is no matter what you teach them first, any more than what leg you shall put into your breeches first. Sir, you may stand disputing which is best to put in first, but in the mean time your breech is bare. Sir, while you are considering which of two things you should teach your child first, another boy has learnt them both.'

On Thursday, July 28, we again supped in private at the Turk's Head coffee-house. JOHNSON. 'Swift has a higher reputation than he deserves. His excellence is strong sense; for his humour, though very well, is not remarkably good. I doubt whether *The Tale of a Tub* be his; for he never owned it, and it is much above his usual manner.'

'Thomson, I think, had as much of the poet about him as most writers. Every thing appeared to him through the medium of his favourite pursuit. He could not have viewed those two candles burning but with a poetical eye.'

'Has not —— a great deal of wit, Sir?' JOHNSON. 'I do not think so, Sir. He is, indeed, continually attempting wit, but he fails. And I have no more pleasure in hearing a man attempting wit and failing, than in seeing a man trying to leap over a ditch and tumbling into it.'

He laughed heartily, when I mentioned to him a saying of his concerning Mr. Thomas Sheridan, which Foote took a wicked pleasure to circulate. 'Why, Sir, Sherry is dull, naturally dull; but it must have taken him a great deal of pains to become what we now see him. Such an excess of stupidity, Sir, is not in Nature.' 'So (said he,) I allowed him all his own merit.'

He now added, 'Sheridan cannot bear me. I bring his declamation to a point. I ask him a plain question, "What do you mean to teach?" Besides, Sir, what influence can Mr. Sheridan have upon the language of this great country, by his narrow exertions? Sir, it is burning a farthing candle at Dover, to shew light at Calais.'

Talking of a young man[1] who was uneasy from thinking that he was very deficient in learning and knowledge, he said, 'A man has no reason to complain who holds a middle place, and has many below him; and perhaps he has not six of his years above him;—perhaps not one. Though he may not know any thing perfectly, the general mass of knowledge that

[1] Boswell.

160

he has acquired is considerable. Time will do for him all that is wanting.'

The conversation then took a philosophical turn. JOHNSON. 'Human experience, which is constantly contradicting theory, is the great test of truth. A system, built upon the discoveries of a great many minds, is always of more strength, than what is produced by the mere workings of any one mind, which, of itself, can do little. There is not so poor a book in the world that would not be a prodigious effort were it wrought out entirely by a single mind, without the aid of prior investigators. The French writers are superficial, because they are not scholars, and so proceed upon the mere power of their own minds; and we see how very little power they have.'

'As to the Christian religion, Sir, besides the strong evidence which we have for it, there is a balance in its favour from the number of great men who have been convinced of its truth, after a serious consideration of the question. Grotius was an acute man, a lawyer, a man accustomed to examine evidence, and he was convinced. Grotius was not a recluse, but a man of the world, who certainly had no bias to the side of religion. Sir Isaac Newton set out an infidel, and came to be a very firm believer.'

He this evening again recommended to me to perambulate Spain. I said it would amuse him to get a letter from me dated at Salamancha. JOHNSON. 'I love the University of Salamancha; for when the Spaniards were in doubt as to the lawfulness of their conquering America, the University of Salamancha gave it as their opinion that it was not lawful.' He spoke this with great emotion, and with that generous warmth which dictated the lines in his *London*, against Spanish encroachment.

I expressed my opinion of my friend Derrick as but a poor writer. JOHNSON. 'To be sure, Sir, he is; but you are to consider that his being a literary man has got for him all that he has. It has made him King of Bath. Sir, he has nothing to say for himself but that he is a writer. Had he not been a writer, he must have been sweeping the crossings in the streets, and asking halfpence from every body that past.'

In justice, however, to the memory of Mr. Derrick, who was my first tutor in the ways of London, and shewed me the town in all its variety of departments, both literary and sportive, the particulars of which Dr. Johnson advised me to put in writing, it is proper to mention what Johnson, at a subsequent period, said of him both as a writer and an editor: 'Sir, I have often said, that if Derrick's letters had been written by one of a more established name, they would have been thought very pretty letters.' And, 'I sent Derrick to Dryden's

161

relations to gather materials for his life; and I believe he got all that I myself should have got.' . . .

Johnson said once to me, 'Sir, I honour Derrick for his presence of mind. One night, when Floyd, another poor authour, was wandering about the streets in the night, he found Derrick fast asleep upon a bulk; upon being suddenly waked, Derrick started up, "My dear Floyd, I am sorry to see you in this destitute state; will you go home with me to *my lodgings?*" '

I again begged his advice as to my method of study at Utrecht. 'Come, (said he) let us make a day of it. Let us go down to Greenwich and dine, and talk of it there.' The following Saturday was fixed for this excursion.

As we walked along the Strand to-night, arm in arm, a woman of the town accosted us, in the usual enticing manner. 'No, no, my girl, (said Johnson) it won't do.' He, however, did not treat her with harshness, and we talked of the wretched life of such women; and agreed, that much more misery than happiness, upon the whole, is produced by illicit commerce between the sexes.

On Saturday, July 30, Dr. Johnson and I took a sculler at the Temple-stairs, and set out for Greenwich. I asked him if he really thought a knowledge of the Greek and Latin languages an essential requisite to a good education. JOHNSON. 'Most certainly, Sir; for those who know them have a very great advantage over those who do not. Nay, Sir, it is wonderful what a difference learning makes upon people even in the common intercourse of life, which does not appear to be much connected with it.' 'And yet, (said I) people go through the world very well, and carry on the business of life to good advantage, without learning.' JOHNSON. 'Why, Sir, that may be true in cases where learning cannot possibly be of any use; for instance, this boy rows us as well without learning, as if he could sing the song of Orpheus to the Argonauts, who were the first sailors.' He then called to the boy, 'What would you give, my lad, to know about the Argonauts?' 'Sir, (said the boy,) I would give what I have.' Johnson was much pleased with his answer, and we gave him a double fare. Dr. Johnson then turning to me, 'Sir, (said he) a desire of knowledge is the natural feeling of mankind; and every human being, whose mind is not debauched, will be willing to give all that he has to get knowledge.'

We landed at the Old Swan, and walked to Billingsgate, where we took oars, and moved smoothly along the silver Thames. It was a very fine day. We were entertained with the immense number and variety of ships that were lying at anchor, and with the beautiful country on each side of the river.

I talked of preaching, and of the great success which those called Methodists have. JOHNSON. 'Sir, it is owing to their expressing themselves in a plain and familiar manner, which is the only way to do good to the common people, and which clergymen of genius and learning ought to do from a principle of duty, when it is suited to their congregations; a practice, for which they will be praised by men of sense. To insist against drunkenness as a crime, because it debases reason, the noblest faculty of man, would be of no service to the common people: but to tell them that they may die in a fit of drunkenness, and shew them how dreadful that would be, cannot fail to make a deep impression. Sir, when your Scotch clergy give up their homely manner, religion will soon decay in that country.' Let this observation, as Johnson meant it, be ever remembered.

I was much pleased to find myself with Johnson at Greenwich, which he celebrates in his *London* as a favourite scene. I had the poem in my pocket, and read the lines aloud with enthusiasm:

> 'On Thames's banks in silent thought we stood:
> Where Greenwich smiles upon the silver flood:
> Pleas'd with the seat which gave ELIZA birth,
> We kneel, and kiss the consecrated earth.'

He remarked that the structure of Greenwich hospital was too magnificent for a place of charity, and that its parts were too much detached to make one great whole. . . .

Afterwards he entered upon the business of the day, which was to give me his advice as to a course of study. And here I am to mention with much regret, that my record of what he said is miserably scanty. I recollect with admiration an animating blaze of eloquence, which rouzed every intellectual power in me to the highest pitch, but must have dazzled me so much, that my memory could not preserve the substance of his discourse; for the note which I find of it is no more than this:—'He ran over the grand scale of human knowledge; advised me to select some particular branch to excel in, but to acquire a little of every kind.' . . .

We walked in the evening in Greenwich Park. He asked me, I suppose, by way of trying my disposition, 'Is not this very fine?' Having no exquisite relish of the beauties of Nature, and being more delighted with 'the busy hum of men,' I answered, 'Yes, Sir; but not equal to Fleet-street.' JOHNSON. 'You are right, Sir.' . . .

We staid so long at Greenwich, that our sail up the river,

163

in our return to London, was by no means so pleasant as in the morning; for the night air was so cold that it made me shiver. I was the more sensible of it from having sat up all the night before, recollecting and writing in my journal what I thought worthy of preservation; an exertion, which, during the first part of my acquaintance with Johnson, I frequently made. I remember having sat up four nights in one week, without being much incommoded in the day time.

Johnson, whose robust frame was not in the least affected by the cold, scolded me, as if my shivering had been a paltry effeminacy, saying, 'Why do you shiver?' Sir William Scott, of the Commons, told me, that when he complained of a head-ache in the post-chaise, as they were travelling together to Scotland, Johnson treated him in the same manner: 'At your age, Sir, I had no head-ache.' It is not easy to make allowance for sensations in others, which we ourselves have not at the time. We must all have experienced how very differently we are affected by the complaints of our neighbours, when we are well and when we are ill. In full health, we can scarcely believe that they suffer much; so faint is the image of pain upon our imagination: when softened by sickness, we readily sympathize with the sufferings of others.

We concluded the day at the Turk's Head coffee-house very socially. He was pleased to listen to a particular account which I gave him of my family, and of its hereditary estate, as to the extent and population of which he asked questions, and made calculations; recommending, at the same time, a liberal kindness to the tenantry, as people over whom the proprietor was placed by Providence. He took delight in hearing my description of the romantick seat of my ancestors. 'I must be there, Sir, (said he) and we will live in the old castle; and if there is not a room in it remaining, we will build one.' I was highly flattered, but could scarcely indulge a hope that Auchinleck would indeed be honoured by his presence, and celebrated by a description, as it afterwards was, in his *Journey to the Western Islands*.

After we had again talked of my setting out for Holland, he said, 'I must see thee out of England; I will accompany you to Harwich.' I could not find words to express what I felt upon this unexpected and very great mark of his affectionate regard.

Next day, Sunday, July 31, I told him I had been that morning at a meeting of the people called Quakers, where I had heard a woman preach. JOHNSON. 'Sir, a woman's preaching is like a dog's walking on his hinder legs. It is not done well; but you are surprized to find it done at all.'

On Tuesday, August 2 (the day of my departure from

London having been fixed for the 5th,) Dr. Johnson did me the honour to pass a part of the morning with me at my Chambers. He said, that 'he always felt an inclination to do nothing.' I observed, that it was strange to think that the most indolent man in Britain had written the most laborious work, *The English Dictionary*.

I mentioned an imprudent publication, by a certain friend of his, at an early period of life, and asked him if he thought it would hurt him. JOHNSON. 'No, Sir; not much. It may, perhaps, be mentioned at an election.'

I had now made good my title to be a privileged man, and was carried by him in the evening to drink tea with Miss Williams, whom, though under the misfortune of having lost her sight, I found to be agreeable in conversation; for she had a variety of literature, and expressed herself well; but her peculiar value was the intimacy in which she had long lived with Johnson, by which she was well acquainted with his habits, and knew how to lead him on to talk.

After tea he carried me to what he called his walk, which was a long narrow paved court in the neighbourhood, overshadowed by some trees. There we sauntered a considerable time; and I complained to him that my love of London and of his company was such, that I shrunk almost from the thought of going away, even to travel, which is generally so much desired by young men. He roused me by manly and spirited conversation. He advised me, when settled in any place abroad, to study with an eagerness after knowledge, and to apply to Greek an hour every day; and when I was moving about, to read diligently the great book of mankind.

On Wednesday, August 3, we had our last social evening at the Turk's Head coffee-house, before my setting out for foreign parts. I had the misfortune, before we parted, to irritate him unintentionally. I mentioned to him how common it was in the world to tell absurd stories of him, and to ascribe to him very strange sayings. JOHNSON. 'What do they make me say, Sir?' BOSWELL. 'Why, Sir, as an instance very strange indeed, (laughing heartily as I spoke,) David Hume told me, you said that you would stand before a battery of cannon, to restore the Convocation to its full powers.' Little did I apprehend that he had actually said this: but I was soon convinced of my errour; for, with a determined look, he thundered out 'And would I not, Sir? Shall the Presbyterian *Kirk* of Scotland have its General Assembly, and the Church of England be denied its Convocation?' He was walking up and down the room while I told him the anecdote; but when he uttered this explosion of high-church zeal, he had come close to my chair, and his eyes flashed with indignation. I bowed to the storm, and diverted the force of it, by leading him to expatiate on the influence which religion derived from maintaining the church with great external respectability.

I must not omit to mention that he this year wrote *The Life of Ascham* †, and the Dedication to the Earl of Shaftesbury †, prefixed to the edition of that writer's English works, published by Mr. Bennet.

On Friday, August 5, we set out early in the morning in the Harwich stage coach. A fat elderly gentlewoman, and a young Dutchman, seemed the most inclined among us to conversation. At the inn where we dined, the gentlewoman said that she had done her best to educate her children; and particularly, that she had never suffered them to be a moment idle. JOHNSON. 'I wish, madam, you would educate me too; for I have been an idle fellow all my life.' 'I am sure, Sir, (said she) you have not been idle.' JOHNSON. 'Nay, Madam, it is very true; and that gentleman there (pointing to me,) has been idle. He was idle at Edinburgh. His father sent him to Glasgow, where he continued to be idle. He then came to London, where he has been very idle; and now he is going to Utrecht, where he will be as idle as ever.' I asked him privately how he could expose me so. JOHNSON. 'Poh, poh! (said he) they knew nothing about you, and will think of it no more.' In the afternoon the gentlewoman talked violently against the Roman Catholicks, and of the horrours of the Inquisition. To the utter astonishment of all the passengers but myself, who knew that he could talk upon any side of a question, he defended the Inquisition, and maintained, that 'false doctrine should be checked on its first appearance; that the civil power should unite with the church in punishing those who dared to attack the established religion, and that such only were punished by the Inquisition.' He had in his pocket *Pomponius Mela de situ Orbis,* in which he read occasionally, and seemed very intent upon ancient geography. Though by no means niggardly, his attention to what was generally right was so minute, that having observed at one of the stages that I ostentatiously gave a shilling to the coachman, when the custom was for each passenger to give only six-pence, he took me aside and scolded me, saying that what I had done would make the coachman dissatisfied with all the rest of the passengers, who gave him no more than his due. This was a just reprimand; for in whatever way a man may indulge his generosity or his vanity in spending his money, for the sake of others he ought not to raise the price of any article for which there is a constant demand.

He talked of Mr. Blacklock's poetry, so far as it was descriptive of visible objects; and observed, that 'as its authour had the misfortune to be blind, we may be absolutely sure that such passages are combinations of what he has remembered of the works of other writers who could see. That foolish fellow, Spence, has laboured to explain philosophically how Blacklock my have done, by means of his own faculties, what it is impossible he should do. The solution, as I have given it, is plain. Suppose, I know a man to be so lame that he is absolutely incapable to move himself, and I find him in a different room from that in which I left him; shall I puzzle myself with idle conjectures, that, perhaps, his nerves have by some unknown change all at once become effective? No, Sir; it is clear how he got into a different room: he was *carried*.'

Having stopped a night at Colchester, Johnson talked of that town with veneration, for having stood a siege for Charles the First. The Dutchman alone now remained with us. He spoke English tolerably well; and thinking to recommend himself to us by expatiating on the superiority of the criminal jurisprudence of this country over that of Holland, he inveighed against the barbarity of putting an accused person to the torture, in order to force a confession. But Johnson was as ready for this, as for the Inquisition. 'Why, Sir, you do not, I find, understand the law of your own country. The torture in Holland is considered as a favour to an accused person; for no man is put to the torture there, unless there is as much evidence against him as would amount to conviction in England. An accused person among you, therefore, has one chance more to escape punishment, than those who are tried among us.'

At supper this night he talked of good eating with uncommon satisfaction. 'Some people (said he,) have a foolish way of not minding, or pretending not to mind, what they eat. For my part, I mind my belly very studiously, and very carefully; for I look upon it, that he who does not mind his belly will hardly mind anything else.' He now appeared to me *Jean Bull philosophe*, and he was, for the moment, not only serious but vehement. Yet I have heard him, upon other occasions, talk with great contempt of people who were anxious to gratify their palates; and the 206th number of his *Rambler* is a masterly essay against gulosity. His practice, indeed, I must acknowledge, may be considered as casting the balance of his different opinions upon this subject; for I never knew any man who relished good eating more than he did. When at table, he was totally absorbed in the business of the moment; his looks seemed rivetted to his plate; nor would he, unless when in very high company, say one word, or even pay the least attention to what was said by others, till he had satisfied his appetite, which was so fierce, and indulged with such intenseness, that while in the act of eating, the veins of his forehead swelled, and generally a strong perspiration was visible. To those whose sensations were delicate, this could not but be disgusting; and it was doubtless not very suitable to the character of a philosopher, who should be distinguished by self-command. But it must be owned, that Johnson, though he could be rigidly *abstemious*, was not a *temperate* man either in eating or drinking. He could refrain, but he could not use moderately. He told me, that he had fasted two days without inconvenience, and that he had never been hungry but once. They who beheld with wonder how much he eat upon all occasions when his dinner was to his taste, could not easily conceive what he must have meant by hunger; and not only was he remarkable for the extraordinary quality which he eat, but he was, or affected to be, a man of very nice discernment in the science of cookery. He used to descant critically on the dishes which had been at table where he had dined or supped, and to recollect very minutely what he had liked. I remember, when he was in Scotland, his praising 'Gordon's palates,' (a dish of palates at the Honourable Alexander Gordon's (with a warmth of expression which might have done honour to more important subjects. 'As for Maclaurin's imitation of a *made dish*, it was a wretched attempt.' He about the same time was so much displeased with the performances of a nobleman's French cook, that he exclaimed with vehemence, 'I'd throw such a rascal into the river;' and he then proceeded to alarm a lady at whose house he was to sup, by the following manifesto of his skill: 'I, Madam, who live at a variety of good tables, am a much better judge of cookery, than any person who has a very tolerable cook, but lives much at home; for his palate is gradually adapted to the taste of his cook; whereas, Madam, in trying by a wider range, I can more exquisitely judge.' When invited to dine, even with an intimate friend, he was not pleased if something better than a plain dinner was not prepared for him. I have heard him say on such an occasion, 'This was a good dinner enough, to be sure; but it was not a dinner to *ask* a man to.' On the other hand, he was wont to express, with great glee, his satisfaction when he had been entertained quite to his mind. One day when we had dined with his neighbour and landlord in Bolt-court, Mr. Allen, the printer, whose old housekeeper had studied his taste in every thing, he pronounced this eulogy: 'Sir, we could not have had a better dinner had there been a *Synod of Cooks.*'

While we were left by ourselves, after the Dutchman had gone to bed, Dr. Johnson talked of that studied behaviour which many have recommended and practised. He disapproved of it; and said, 'I never considered whether I should be a grave man, or a merry man, but just let inclination, for the time, have its course.'

He flattered me with some hopes that he would, in the course of the following summer, come over to Holland, and accompany me in a tour through the Netherlands.

I teized him with fanciful apprehensions of unhappiness. A moth having fluttered round the candle, and burnt itself, he laid hold of this little incident to admonish me; saying, with a sly look, and in a solemn but quiet tone, 'That creature was its own tormentor, and I believe its name was BOSWELL.'

Next day we got to Harwich to dinner; and my passage in the packet-boat to Helvoetsluys being secured, and my baggage put on board, we dined at our inn by ourselves. I happened to say it would be terrible if he should not find a speedy opportunity of returning to London, and be confined to so dull a place. JOHNSON. 'Don't, Sir, accustom yourself to use big words for little matters. It would *not* be *terrible*, though I *were* to be detained some time here.' The practice of using words of disproportionate magnitude, is, no doubt, too frequent every where; but I think, most remarkable among the French, of which, all who have travelled in France must have been struck with innumerable instances.

We went and looked at the church, and having gone into it and walked up to the altar, Johnson, whose piety was constant and fervent, sent me to my knees, saying, 'Now that you are going to leave your native country, recommend yourself to the protection of your CREATOR and REDEEMER.'

After we came out of the church, we stood talking for some time together of Bishop Berkeley's ingenious sophistry to prove the non-existence of matter, and that every thing in the universe is merely ideal. I observed, that though we are satisfied his doctrine is not true, it is impossible to refute it. I never shall forget the alacrity with which Johnson answered, striking his foot with mighty force against a large stone, till he rebounded from it, 'I refute it *thus*.' . . .

My revered friend walked down with me to the beach, where we embraced and parted with tenderness, and engaged to correspond by letters. I said, 'I hope, Sir, you will not forget me in my absence.' JOHNSON. 'Nay, Sir, it is more likely you should forget me, than that I should forget you.' As the vessel put out to sea, I kept my eyes upon him for a considerable time, while he remained rolling his majestick frame in his usual manner: and at last I perceived him walk back into the town, and he disappeared. . . .

1764: ÆTAT. 55.]—EARLY in 1764 Johnson paid a visit to

the Langton family, at their seat of Langton, in Lincolnshire, where he passed some time, much to his satisfaction. His friend Bennet Langton, it will not be doubted, did every thing in his power to make the place agreeable to so illustrious a guest; and the elder Mr. Langton and his lady, being fully capable of understanding his value, were not wanting in attention. He, however, told me, that old Mr. Langton, though a man of considerable learning, had so little allowance to make for his occasional 'laxity of talk,' that because in the course of discussion he sometimes mentioned what might be said in favour of the peculiar tenets of the Romish church, he went to his grave believing him to be of that communion.

Johnson, during his stay at Langton, had the advantage of a good library, and saw several gentlemen of the neighbourhood. I have obtained from Mr. Langton the following particulars of this period.

He was now fully convinced that he could not have been satisfied with a country living; for, talking of a respectable clergyman in Lincolnshire, he observed, 'This man, Sir, fills up the duties of his life well. I approve of him, but could not imitate him.'

To a lady who endeavoured to vindicate herself from blame for neglecting social attention to worthy neighbours, by saying, 'I would go to them if it would do them any good,' he said, 'What good, Madam, do you expect to have in your power to do them? It is shewing them respect, and that is doing them good.'

So socially accommodating was he, that once when Mr. Langton and he were driving together in a coach, and Mr. Langton complained of being sick, he insisted that they should go out and sit on the back of it in the open air, which they did. And being sensible how strange the appearance must be, observed, that a countryman whom they saw in a field, would probably be thinking, 'If these two madmen should come down, what would become of me?'

Soon after his return to London, which was in February, was founded that CLUB which existed long without a name, but at Mr. Garrick's funeral became distinguished by the title of THE LITERARY CLUB. Sir Joshua Reynolds had the merit of being the first proposer of it, to which Johnson acceded, and the original members were, Sir Joshua Reynolds, Dr. Johnson, Mr. Edmund Burke, Dr. Nugent, Mr. Beauclerk, Mr. Langton, Dr. Goldsmith, Mr. Chamier, and Sir John Hawkins. They met at the Turk's Head, in Gerrard-street, Soho, one evening in every week, at seven, and generally continued their conversation till a pretty late hour. This club has been gradually increased to its present number, thirty-five.

After about ten years, instead of supping weekly, it was resolved to dine together once a fortnight during the meeting of Parliament. Their original tavern having been converted into a private house, they moved first to Prince's in Sackville-street, then to Le Telier's in Dover-street, and now meet at Parsloe's, St. James's-street. . . .

In this year, except what he may have done in revising *Shakspeare*, we do not find that he laboured much in literature. He wrote a review of Grainger's *Sugar Cane, a Poem*, in the *London Chronicle*. He told me, that Dr. Percy wrote the greatest part of this review; but, I imagine, he did not recollect it distinctly, for it appears to be mostly, if not altogether, his own. He also wrote in *The Critical Review*, an account† of Goldsmith's excellent poem, *The Traveller*.

The ease and independence to which he had at last attained by royal munificence, increased his natural indolence. In his *Meditations* he thus accuses himself:—'GOOD FRIDAY, April 20, 1764.—I have made no reformation; I have lived totally useless, more sensual in thought, and more addicted to wine and meat.' And next morning he thus feelingly complains:—'My indolence, since my last reception of the sacrament, has sunk into grosser sluggishness, and my dissipation spread into wilder negligence. My thoughts have been clouded with sensuality; and, except that from the beginning of this year I have, in some measure, forborne excess of strong drink, my appetites have predominated over my reason. A kind of strange oblivion has overspread me, so that I know not what has become of the last year; and perceive that incidents and intelligence pass over me, without leaving any impression.' He then solemnly says, 'This is not the life to which heaven is promised;' and he earnestly resolves on amendment.

It was his custom to observe certain days with a pious abstraction; viz. New-year's-day, the day of his wife's death, Good Friday, Easter-day, and his own birth-day. He this year says:—'I have now spent fifty-five years in resolving; having, from the earliest time almost that I can remember, been forming schemes of a better life. I have done nothing. The need of doing, therefore, is pressing, since the time of doing is short. O GOD, grant me to resolve aright, and to keep my resolutions, for JESUS CHRIST's sake. Amen.'

Such a tenderness of conscience, such a fervent desire of improvement, will rarely be found. It is, surely, not decent in those who are hardened in indifference to spiritual improvement, to treat this pious anxiety of Johnson with contempt.

About this time he was afflicted with a very severe return of the hypochondriack disorder, which was ever lurking

171

about him. He was so ill, as, notwithstanding his remarkable love of company, to be entirely averse to society, the most fatal symptom of that malady. Dr. Adams told me, that, as an old friend, he was admitted to visit him, and that he found him in a deplorable state, sighing, groaning, talking to himself, and restlessly walking from room to room. He then used this emphatical expression of the misery which he felt: 'I would consent to have a limb amputated to recover my spirits.'

Talking to himself was, indeed, one of his singularities ever since I knew him. I was certain that he was frequently uttering pious ejaculations; for fragments of the Lord's Prayer have been distinctly overheard. His friend Mr. Thomas Davies, of whom Churchill says,

'That Davies hath a very pretty wife,'

when Dr. Johnson muttered 'lead us not into temptation,' used with waggish and gallant humour to whisper Mrs. Davies, 'You, my dear, are the cause of this.'

He had another particularity, of which none of his friends ever ventured to ask an explanation. It appeared to me some superstitious habit, which he had contracted early, and from which he had never called upon his reason to disentangle him. This was his anxious care to go out or in at a door or passage by a certain number of steps from a certain point, or at least so as that either his right or his left foot, (I am not certain which,) should constantly make the first actual movement when he came close to the door or passage. Thus I conjecture: for I have, upon innumerable occasions, observed him suddenly stop, and then seem to count his steps with a deep earnestness; and when he had neglected or gone wrong in this sort of magical movement, I have seen him go back again, put himself in a proper posture to begin the ceremony, and, having gone through it, break from his abstraction, walk briskly on, and join his companion. A strange instance of something of this nature, even when on horseback, happened when he was in the isle of Sky. Sir Joshua Reynolds has observed him to go a good way about rather than cross a particular alley in Leicester-fields; but this Sir Joshua imputed to his having had some disagreeable recollection associated with it.

That the most minute singularities which belonged to him, and made very observable parts of his appearance and manner, may not be omitted, it is requisite to mention, that while talking or even musing as he sat in his chair, he commonly held his head to one side towards his right shoulder, and shook it in a tremulous manner, moving his body backwards and forwards, and rubbing his left knee in the same direction, with the palm of his hand. In the intervals of articulating he made various sounds with his mouth, sometimes as if ruminating, or what is called chewing the cud, sometimes giving a half whistle, sometimes making his tongue play rapidly backwards from the roof of his mouth, as if clucking like a hen, and sometimes protruding it against his upper gums in front as if pronouncing quickly under his breath, *too, too, too:* all this accompanied sometimes with a thoughtful look, but more frequently with a smile. Generally when he had concluded a period, in the course of a dispute, by which time he was a good deal exhausted by violence and vociferation, he used to blow out his breath like a Whale. This I supposed was a relief to his lungs; and seemed in him to be a contemptuous mode of expression, as if he had made the arguments of his opponent fly like chaff before the wind.

I am fully aware how very obvious an occasion I here give for the sneering jocularity of such as have no relish of an exact likeness; which to render complete, he who draws it must not disdain the slightest strokes. But if witlings should be inclined to attack this account, let them have the candour to quote what I have offered in my defence. . . .

1765: ÆTAT. 56.]—EARLY in the year 1765 he paid a short visit to the University of Cambridge, with his friend Mr. Beauclerk. There is a lively picturesque account of his behaviour on this visit, in *The Gentleman's Magazine* for March 1785 being an extract of a letter from the late Dr. John Sharp. The two following sentences are very characteristical:—

'He drank his large potations of tea with me interrupted by many an indignant contradiction, and many a noble sentiment.'——'Several persons got into his company the last evening at Trinity, where, about twelve, he began to be very great; stripped poor Mrs. Macaulay to the very skin, then gave her for his toast, and drank her in two bumpers.'

The strictness of his self-examination and scrupulous Christian humility appear in his pious meditation on Easter-day this year.

'I purpose again to partake of the blessed sacrament; yet when I consider how vainly I have hitherto resolved at this annual commemoration of my Saviour's death, to regulate my life by his laws, I am almost afraid to renew my resolutions.'

The concluding words are very remarkable, and shew that he laboured under a severe depression of spirits.

'Since the last Easter I have reformed no evil habit, my

173

time has been unprofitably spent, and seems as a dream that has left nothing behind. *My memory grows confused, and I know not how the days pass over me.* Good Lord deliver me!'

No man was more gratefully sensible of any kindness done to him than Johnson. There is a little circumstance in his diary this year, which shews him in a very amiable light.

'July 2.—I paid Mr. Simpson ten guineas, which he had formerly lent me in my necessity and for which Tetty expressed her gratitude.'

'July 8.—I lent Mr. Simpson ten guineas more.'

Here he had a pleasing opportunity of doing the same kindness to an old friend, which he had formerly received from him. Indeed his liberality as to money was very remarkable. The next article in his diary is,

'July 16.—I received seventy-five pounds. Lent Mr. Davies twenty-five.'

Trinity College, Dublin, at this time surprised Johnson with a spontaneous compliment of the highest academical honours, by creating him Doctor of Laws. . . .

This unsolicited mark of distinction, conferred on so great a literary character, did much honour to the judgement and liberal spirit of that learned body. Johnson acknowledged the favour in a letter to Dr. Leland, one of their number; but I have not been able to obtain a copy of it.

He appears this year to have been seized with a temporary fit of ambition, for he had thoughts both of studying law and of engaging in politics. His 'Prayer before the Study of Law' is truly admirable:—

'Sept. 26, 1765.

'Almighty GOD, the giver of wisdom, without whose help resolutions are vain, without whose blessing study is ineffectual; enable me, if it be thy will, to attain such knowledge as may qualify me to direct the doubtful, and instruct the ignorant; to prevent wrongs and terminate contentions; and grant that I may use that knowledge which I shall attain, to thy glory and my own salvation, for JESUS CHRIST'S sake. Amen.'

His prayer in the view of becoming a politician is entitled, 'Engaging in POLITICKS with H———n,' no doubt his friend, the Right Honourable William Gerard Hamilton, for whom, during a long acquaintance, he had a great esteem, and to whose conversation he once paid this high compliment: 'I am very unwilling to be left alone, Sir, and therefore I go with my company down the first pair of stairs, in some hopes that they may, perhaps, return again. I go with you, Sir, as far as the street-door.' In what particular department he intended to

174

engage does not appear, nor can Mr. Hamilton explain. His prayer is in general terms. . . .

This year was distinguished by his being introduced into the family of Mr. Thrale, one of the most eminent brewers in England, and Member of Parliament for the borough of Southwark. Foreigners are not a little amazed when they hear of brewers, distillers, and men in similar departments of trade, held forth as persons of considerable consequence. In this great commercial country it is natural that a situation which produces much wealth should be considered as very respectable; and, no doubt, honest industry is entitled to esteem. But, perhaps, the too rapid advance of men of low extraction tends to lessen the value of that distinction by birth and gentility, which has ever been found beneficial to the grand scheme of subordination. . . .

Mr. Thrale had married Miss Hesther Lynch Salusbury, of good Welch extraction, a lady of lively talents, improved by education. That Johnson's introduction into Mr. Thrale's family, which contributed so much to the happiness of his life, was owing to her desire for his conversation, is very probable and a general supposition: but it is not the truth. Mr. Murphy, who was intimate with Mr. Thrale, having spoken very highly of Dr. Johnson, he was requested to make them acquainted. This being mentioned to Johnson, he accepted of an invitation to dinner at Thrale's, and was so much pleased with his reception, both by Mr. and Mrs. Thrale, and they so much pleased with him, that his invitations to their house were more and more frequent, till at last he became one of the family, and an apartment was appropriated to him, both in their house in Southwark, and in their villa at Streatham.

Johnson had a very sincere esteem for Mr. Thrale, as a man of excellent principles, a good scholar, well skilled in trade, of a sound understanding, and of manners such as presented the character of a plain independent English 'Squire. As this family will frequently be mentioned in the course of the following pages, and as a false notion has prevailed that Mr. Thrale was inferiour, and in some degree insignificant, compared with Mrs. Thrale, it may be proper to give a true state of the case from the authority of Johnson himself, in his own words.

'I know no man, (said he,) who is more master of his wife and family than Thrale. If he but holds up a finger, he is obeyed. It is a great mistake to suppose that she is above him in literary attainments. She is more flippant; but he has ten times her learning: he is a regular scholar; but her learning is that of a schoolboy in one of the lower forms.' My readers

175

may naturally wish for some representation of the figures of this couple. Mr. Thrale was tall, well porportioned, and stately. As for *Madam,* or *my Mistress,* by which epithets Johnson used to mention Mrs. Thrale, she was short, plump, and brisk. She has herself given us a lively view of the idea which Johnson had of her person, on her appearing before him in a dark-coloured gown; 'You little creatures should never wear those sort of clothes, however; they are unsuitable in every way. What! have not all insects gay colours?' Mr. Thrale gave his wife a liberal indulgence, both in the choice of their company, and in the mode of entertaining them. He understood and valued Johnson, without remission, from their first acquaintance to the day of his death. Mrs. Thrale was enchanted with Johnson's conversation, for its own sake, and had also a very allowable vanity in appearing to be honoured with the attention of so celebrated a man.

Nothing could be more fortunate for Johnson than this connection. He had at Mr. Thrale's all the comforts and even luxuries of life; his melancholy was diverted, and his irregular habits lessened by association with an agreeable and well-ordered family. He was treated with the utmost respect, and even affection. The vivacity of Mrs. Thrale's literary talk roused him to cheerfulness and exertion, even when they were alone. But this was not often the case; for he found here a constant succession of what gave him the highest enjoyment: the society of the learned, the witty, and the eminent in every way, who were assembled in numerous companies, called forth his wonderful powers, and gratified him with admiration, to which no man could be insensible.

In the October of this year he at length gave to the world his edition of *Shakspeare,* which, if it had no other merit but that of producing his Preface, in which the excellencies and defects of that immortal bard are displayed with a masterly hand, the nation would have had no reason to complain. A blind indiscriminate admiration of Shakspeare had exposed the British nation to the ridicule of foreigners. Johnson, by candidly admitting the faults of his poet, had the more credit in bestowing on him deserved and indisputable praise; and doubtless none of all his panegyrists have done him half so much honour. Their praise was, like that of a counsel, upon his own side of the cause: Johnson's was like the grave, well-considered, and impartial opinion of the judge, which falls from his lips with weight, and is received with reverence. What he did as a commentator has no small share of merit, though his researches were not so ample, and his investigations so acute as they might have been, which we now certainly know from the labours of other able and ingenious cricticks who have followed him. He has enriched his edition with a concise account of each play, and of its characteristick excellence. Many of his notes have illustrated obscurities in the text, and placed passages eminent for beauty in a more conspicuous light; and he has, in general, exhibited such a mode of annotation, as may be beneficial to all subsequent editors.

His *Shakspeare* was virulently attacked by Mr. William Kenrick, who obtained the degree of LL.D. from a Scotch University, and wrote for the booksellers in a great variety of branches. Though he certainly was not without considerable merit, he wrote with so little regard to decency and principles, and decorum, and in so hasty a manner, that his reputation was neither extensive nor lasting. I remember one evening when some of his works were mentioned, Dr. Goldsmith said, he had never heard of them; upon which Dr. Johnson observed, 'Sir, he is one of the many who have made themselves *publick*, without making themselves *known*.' . . .

In his Preface to *Shakspeare,* Johnson treated Voltaire very contemptuously, observing, upon some of his remarks, 'These are the petty criticisms of petty wits.' Voltaire, in revenge, made an attack upon Johnson, in one of his numerous literary sallies, which I remember to have read; but there being no general index to his voluminous works, have searched for it in vain, and therefore cannot quote it.

Voltaire was an antagonist with whom I thought Johnson should not disdain to contend. I pressed him to answer. He said, he perhaps might; but he never did. . . .

IN 1764 and 1765 it should seem that Dr. Johnson was so busily employed with his edition of Shakspeare, as to have had little leisure for any other literary exertion, or, indeed, even for private correspondence. He did not favour me with a single letter for more than two years, for which it will appear that he afterwards apologised.

He was, however, at all times ready to give assistance to his friends, and others, in revising their works, and in writing for them, or greatly improving their Dedications. In that courtly species of composition no man excelled Dr. Johnson. Though the loftiness of his mind prevented him from ever dedicating in his own person, he wrote a very great number of Dedications for others. Some of these, the persons who were favoured with them are unwilling should be mentioned, from a too anxious apprehension, as I think, that they might be suspected of having received larger assistance; and some, after all the diligence I have bestowed, have escaped my enquiries. He told me, a great many years ago, 'he believed he had dedicated to all the Royal Family round;' and it was indifferent to him what was the subject of the work dedicated, provided it were innocent. He once dedicated some Musick for the German Flute to Edward, Duke of York. In writing Dedications for others, he considered himself as by no means speaking his own sentiments.

Notwithstanding his long silence, I never omitted to write to him when I had any thing worthy of communicating. I generally kept copies of my letters to him, that I might have a full view of our correspondence, and never be at a loss to understand any reference in his letters. He kept the greater part of mine very carefully; and a short time before his death was attentive enough to seal them up in bundles, and order them to be delivered to me, which was accordingly done. Amongst them I found one, of which I had not made a copy, and which I own I read with pleasure at the distance of almost twenty years. It is dated November, 1765, at the palace of Pascal Paoli, in Corte, the capital of Corsica, and is full of generous enthusiasm. After giving a sketch of what I had seen and heard in that island, it proceeded thus: 'I dare to call this a spirited tour. I dare to challenge your approbation.' . . .

I returned to London in February, and found Dr. Johnson in a good house in Johnson's Court, Fleet-street, in which he had accommodated Miss Williams with an apartment on the ground floor, while Mr. Levett occupied his post in the garret: his faithful Francis was still attending upon him. He received me with much kindness. The fragments of our conversation, which I have preserved, are these: I told him that Voltaire, in a conversation with me, had distinguished Pope and Dryden thus:—'Pope drives a handsome chariot, with a couple of neat trim nags; Dryden a coach, and six stately horses.' JOHNSON. 'Why, Sir, the truth is, they both drive coaches and six; but Dryden's horses are either galloping or stumbling: Pope's go at a steady even trot.' He said of Goldsmith's *Traveller,* which had been published in my absence, 'There has not been so fine a poem since Pope's time.' . . .

Talking of education, 'People have now a-days, (said he,) got a strange opinion that every thing should be taught by lectures. Now, I cannot see that lectures can do so much good as reading the books from which the lectures are taken. I know nothing that can be best taught by lectures, except where experiments are to be shewn. You may teach chymistry by lectures.—You might teach making of shoes by lectures!'

At night I supped with him at the Mitre tavern, that we might renew our social intimacy at the original place of meeting. But there was now a considerable difference in his way of living. Having had an illness, in which he was advised to leave off wine, he had, from that period, continued to abstain from it, and drank only water, or lemonade.

I told him that a foreign friend[1] of his, whom I had met with abroad, was so wretchedly perverted to infidelity, that he treated the hopes of immortality with brutal levity; and said, 'As man dies like a dog, let him lie like a dog.' JOHNSON. '*If* he dies like a dog, *let* him lie like a dog.' I added, that this man said to me, 'I hate mankind, for I think myself one of the best of them, and I know how bad I am.' JOHNSON. 'Sir, he must be very singular in his opinion, if he thinks himself one of the best of men; for none of his friends think him so.' —He said, 'no honest man could be a Deist; for no man could be so after a fair examination of the proofs of Christianity.' I named Hume. JOHNSON. 'No, Sir; Hume owned to a clergyman in the bishoprick of Durham, that he had never read the New Testament with attention.' I mentioned Hume's notion, that all who are happy are equally happy; a little miss with a new gown at a dancing school ball, a general at the head of a victorious army, and an orator, after having made an eloquent speech in a great assembly. JOHNSON. 'Sir, that all who are happy, are equally happy, is not true. A peasant and a philosopher may be equally *satisfied*, but not equally *happy*. Happiness consists in the multiplicity of agreeable consciousness. A peasant has not capacity for having equal happiness with a philosopher.' I remember this very question very happily illustrated in opposition to Hume, by the Reverend Mr. Robert Brown, at Utrecht. 'A small drinking-glass and a large one, (said he,) may be equally full; but the large one holds more than the small.'

Dr. Johnson was very kind this evening, and said to me, 'You have now lived five-and-twenty years, and you have employed them well.' 'Alas, Sir, (said I,) I fear not. Do I know history? Do I know mathematicks? Do I know law?' JOHNSON. 'Why, Sir, though you may know no science so well as to be able to teach it, and no profession so well as to be able to follow it, your general mass of knowledge of books and men renders you very capable to make yourself master of any science, or fit yourself for any profession.' I mentioned that a gay friend[2] had advised me against being a lawyer, because I should be excelled by plodding block-heads. JOHNSON. 'Why, Sir, in the formulary and statutory part of law, a plodding block-head may excel; but in the ingenious and rational part of it a plodding block-head can never excel.'

I talked of the mode adopted by some to rise in the world, by courting great men, and asked him whether he had ever

1 Baretti.
2 Wilkes.

179

submitted to it. JOHNSON. 'Why, Sir, I never was near enough to great men, to court them. You may be prudently attached to great men and yet independent. You are not to do what you think wrong; and, Sir, you are to calculate, and not pay too dear for what you get. You must not give a shilling's worth of court for six-pence worth of good. But if you can get a shilling's worth of good for six-pence worth of court, you are a fool if you do not pay court.'

He said, 'If convents should be allowed at all, they should only be retreats for persons unable to serve the publick, or who have served it. It is our first duty to serve society, and, after we have done that, we may attend wholly to the salvation of our own souls. A youthful passion for abstracted devotion should not be encouraged.'

I introduced the subject of second sight, and other mysterious manifestations; the fulfilment of which, I suggested, might happen by chance. JOHNSON. 'Yes, Sir; but they have happened so often, that mankind have agreed to think them not fortuitous.'

I talked to him a great deal of what I had seen in Corsica, and of my intention to publish an account of it. He encouraged me by saying, 'You cannot go to the bottom of the subject; but all that you tell us will be new to us. Give us as many anecdotes as you can.'

Our next meeting at the Mitre was on Saturday the 15th of February, when I presented to him my old and most intimate friend, the Reverend Mr. Temple, then of Cambridge. I having mentioned that I had passed some time with Rousseau in his wild retreat, and having quoted some remark made by Mr. Wilkes, with whom I had spent many pleasant hours in Italy, Johnson said (sarcastically,) 'It seems, Sir, you have kept very good company abroad, Rousseau and Wilkes!' Thinking it enough to defend one at a time, I said nothing as to my gay friend, but answered with a smile, 'My dear Sir, you don't call Rousseau bad company. Do you really think *him* a bad man?' JOHNSON. 'Sir, if you are talking jestingly of this, I don't talk with you. If you mean to be serious, I think him one of the worst of men; a rascal who ought to be hunted out of society, as he has been. Three or four nations have expelled him; and it is a shame that he is protected in this country.' BOSWELL. 'I don't deny, Sir, but that his novel may, perhaps, do harm; but I cannot think his intention was bad.' JOHNSON. 'Sir, that will not do. We cannot prove any man's intention to be bad. You may shoot a man through the head, and say you intended to miss him; but the Judge will order you to be hanged. An alleged want of intention, when evil is committed, will not be allowed in a court of justice. Rousseau, Sir, is a very bad man. I would sooner sign a sentence for his transportation, than that of any felon who has gone from the Old Bailey these many years. Yes, I should like to have him work in the plantations.' BOSWELL. 'Sir, do you think him as bad a man as Voltaire?' JOHNSON. 'Why, Sir, it is difficult to settle the proportion of iniquity between them.' . . .

On his favourite subject of subordination, Johnson said, 'So far is it from being true that men are naturally equal, that no two people can be half an hour together, but one shall acquire an evident superiority over the other.'

I mentioned the advice given us by philosophers, to console ourselves, when distressed or embarrassed, by thinking of those who are in a worse situation than ourselves. This, I observed, could not apply to all, for there must be some who have nobody worse than they are. JOHNSON. 'Why, to be sure, Sir, there are; but they don't know it. There is no being so poor and so contemptible, who does not think there is somebody still poorer, and still more contemptible.'

As my stay in London at this time was very short, I had not many opportunities of being with Dr. Johnson; but I felt my veneration for him in no degree lessened, by my having seen *multorum hominum mores et urbes*.[1] On the contrary, by having it in my power to compare him with many of the most celebrated persons of other countries, my admiration of his extraordinary mind was increased and confirmed.

The roughness, indeed, which sometimes appeared in his manners, was more striking to me now, and from my having been accustomed to the studied smooth complying habits of the Continent; and I clearly recognised in him, not without respect for his honest conscientious zeal, the same indignant and sarcastical mode of treating every attempt to unhinge or weaken good principles.

One evening when a young gentleman[2] teized him with an account of the infidelity of his servant, who, he said, would not believe the scriptures, because he could not read them in the original tongues, and be sure that they were not invented, 'Why, foolish fellow, (said Johnson,) has he any better authority for almost every thing that he believes?' BOSWELL. 'Then the vulgar, Sir, never can know they are right, but must submit themselves to the learned.' JOHNSON. 'To be sure, Sir. The vulgar are the children of the State, and must be taught like children.' BOSWELL. 'Then, Sir, a poor Turk must be a Mahometan, just as a poor Englishman must

[1] 'The manners of many men and states.' Horace, *Art of Poetry*, l. 142.
[2] Boswell.

be a Christian?' JOHNSON. 'Why, yes, Sir; and what then? This now is such stuff as I used to talk to my mother, when I first began to think myself a clever fellow; and she ought to have whipt me for it.'

Another evening Dr. Goldsmith and I called on him, with the hope of prevailing on him to sup with us at the Mitre. We found him indisposed, and resolved not to go abroad. 'Come then, (said Goldsmith,) we will not go to the Mitre to-night, since we cannot have the big man with us.' Johnson then called for a bottle of port, of which Goldsmith and I partook, while our friend, now a water-drinker, sat by us. GOLDSMITH. 'I think, Mr. Johnson, you don't go near the theatres now. You give yourself no more concern about a new play, than if you had never had anything to do with the stage.' JOHNSON. 'Why, Sir, our tastes greatly alter. The lad does not care for the child's rattle, and the old man does not care for the young man's whore.' GOLDSMITH. 'Nay, Sir, but your Muse was not a whore.' JOHNSON. 'Sir, I do not think she was. But as we advance in the journey of life, we drop some of the things which have pleased us; whether it be that we are fatigued and don't choose to carry so many things any farther, or that we find other things which we like better.' BOSWELL. 'But, Sir, why don't you give us something in some other way?' GOLDSMITH. 'Ay, Sir, we have a claim upon you.' JOHNSON. 'No, Sir, I am not obliged to do any more. No man is obliged to do as much as he can do. A man is to have part of his life to himself. If a soldier has fought a good many campaigns, he is not to be blamed if he retires to ease and tranquillity. A physician, who has practised long in a great city, may be excused if he retires to a small town, and takes less practice. Now, Sir, the good I can do by my conversation bears the same proportion to the good I can do by my writings, that the practice of a physician, retired to a small town, does to his practice in a great city.' BOSWELL. 'But I wonder, Sir, you have not more pleasure in writing than in not writing.' JOHNSON. 'Sir, you *may* wonder.'

He talked of making verses, and observed, 'The great difficulty is to know when you have made good ones. When composing, I have generally had them in my mind, perhaps fifty at a time, walking up and down in my room; and then I have written them down, and often, from laziness, have written only half lines. I have written a hundred lines in a day. I remember I wrote a hundred lines of *The Vanity of Human Wishes* in a day. Doctor, (turning to Goldsmith,) I am not quite idle; I made one line t'other day; but I made no more.'

GOLDSMITH. 'Let us hear it; we'll put a bad one to it.'
JOHNSON. 'No, Sir, I have forgot it.'

Such specimens of the easy and playful conversation of the great Dr. Samuel Johnson are, I think, to be prized; as exhibiting the little varieties of a mind so enlarged and so powerful when objects of consequence required its exertions, and as giving us a minute knowledge of his character and modes of thinking. . . .

It appears from Johnson's diary, that he was this year at Mr. Thrale's, from before Midsummer till after Michaelmas, and that he afterwards passed a month at Oxford. He had then contracted a great intimacy with Mr. Chambers of that University, afterwards Sir Robert Chambers, one of the Judges in India. . . .

The Honourable Thomas Hervey and his lady having unhappily disagreed, and being about to separate, Johnson interfered as their friend, and wrote him a letter of expostulation, which I have not been able to find; but the substance of it is ascertained by a letter to Johnson, in answer to it, which Mr. Hervey printed. The occasion of this correspondence between Dr. Johnson and Mr. Hervey, was thus related to me by Mr. Beauclerk. 'Tom Hervey had a great liking for Johnson, and in his will had left him a legacy of fifty pounds. One day he said to me, "Johnson may want this money now, more than afterwards. I have a mind to give it him directly. Will you be so good as to carry a fifty pound note from me to him?' This I positively refused to do, as he might, perhaps, have knocked me down for insulting him, and have afterwards put the note in his pocket. But I said, if Hervey would write him a letter, and enclose a fifty pound note, I should take care to deliver it. He accordingly did write him a letter, mentioning that he was only paying a legacy a little sooner. To his letter he added, *"P.S. I am going to part with my wife."* Johnson then wrote to him, saying nothing of the note, but remonstrating with him against parting with his wife.'

When I mentioned to Johnson this story, in as delicate terms as I could, he told me that the fifty pound note was given to him by Mr. Hervey in consideration of his having written for him a pamphlet against Sir Charles Hanbury Williams, who, Mr. Hervey imagined, was the authour of an attack upon him; but that it was afterwards discovered to be the work of a garreteer who wrote *The Fool:* the pamphlet therefore against Sir Charles was not printed.

In February, 1767, there happened one of the most remarkable incidents of Johnson's life, which gratified his monarchical enthusiasm, and which he loved to relate with all its circumstances, when requested by his friends. This was his being honoured by a private conversation with his Majesty, in the library at the Queen's house. He had frequently visited those splendid rooms and noble collection of books, which he used to say was more numerous and curious than he supposed any person could have made in the time which the King had employed. Mr. Barnard, the librarian, took care that he should have every accommodation that could contribute to his ease and convenience, while indulging his literary taste in that place; so that he had here a very agreeable resource at leisure hours.

His Majesty having been informed of his occasional visits, was pleased to signify a desire that he should be told when Dr. Johnson came next to the library. Accordingly, the next time that Johnson did come, as soon as he was fairly engaged with a book, on which, while he sat by the fire, he seemed quite intent, Mr. Barnard stole round to the apartment where the King was, and, in obedience to his Majesty's commands, mentioned that Dr. Johnson was then in the library. His Majesty said he was at leisure, and would go to him; upon which Mr. Barnard took one of the candles that stood on the King's table, and lighted his Majesty through a suite of rooms, till they came to a private door into the library, of which his Majesty had the key. Being entered, Mr. Barnard stepped forward hastily to Dr. Johnson, who was still in a profound study, and whispered him, 'Sir, here is the King.' Johnson started up, and stood still. His Majesty approached him, and at once was courteously easy.

His Majesty began by observing, that he understood he came sometimes to the library; and then mentioning his having heard that the Doctor had been lately at Oxford, asked him if he was not fond of going thither. To which Johnson answered, that he was indeed fond of going to Oxford sometimes, but was likewise glad to come back again. The King then asked him what they were doing at Oxford. Johnson answered, he could not much commend their diligence, but that in some respects they were mended, for they had put their press under better regulations, and were at that time printing Polybius. He was then asked whether there were better libraries at Oxford or Cambridge. He answered, he believed the Bodleian was larger than any they had at Cambridge; at the same time adding, 'I hope, whether we have more books or not than they have at Cambridge, we shall make as good use of them as they do.' Being asked whether All-Souls or Christ-Church library was the largest, he answered, 'All-Souls library is the largest we have, except the Bodleian.' 'Aye, (said the King,) that is the publick library.'

His Majesty enquired if he was then writing any thing. He

answered, he was not, for he had pretty well told the world what he knew, and must now read to acquire more knowledge. The King, as it should seem with a view to urge him to rely on his own stores as an original writer, and to continue his labours, then said, 'I do not think you borrow much from any body.' Johnson said, he thought he had already done his part as a writer. 'I should have thought so too, (said the King,) if you had not written so well.'—Johnson observed to me, upon this, that 'No man could have paid a handsomer compliment; and it was fit for a King to pay. It was decisive.' When asked by another friend, at Sir Joshua Reynolds's, whether he made any reply to this high compliment, he answered, 'No, Sir. When the King had said it, it was to be so. It was not for me to bandy civilities with my Sovereign.' Perhaps no man who had spent his whole life in courts could have shewn a more nice and dignified sense of true politeness, than Johnson did in this instance.

His Majesty having observed to him that he supposed he must have read a great deal; Johnson answered, that he thought more than he read; that he had read a great deal in the early part of his life, but having fallen into ill health, he had not been able to read much, compared with others: for instance, he said he had not read much, compared with Dr. Warburton. Upon which the King said, that he heard Dr. Warburton was a man of such general knowledge, that you could scarce talk with him on any subject on which he was not qualified to speak; and that his learning resembled Garrick's acting, in its universality. His Majesty then talked of the controversy between Warburton and Lowth, which he seemed to have read, and asked Johnson what he thought of it. Johnson answered, 'Warburton has most general, most scholastick learning; Lowth is the more correct scholar. I do not know which of them calls names best.' The King was pleased to say he was of the same opinion; adding, 'You do not think, then, Dr. Johnson, that there was much argument in the case.' Johnson said, he did not think there was. 'Why truly, (said the King,) when once it comes to calling names, argument is pretty well at an end.'

His Majesty then asked him what he thought of Lord Lyttelton's *History*, which was then just published. Johnson said, he thought his style pretty good, but that he had blamed Henry the Second rather too much. 'Why, (said the King), they seldom do these things by halves.' 'No, Sir, (answered Johnson,) not to Kings.' But fearing to be misunderstood, he proceeded to explain himself; and immediately subjoined, 'That for those who spoke worse of Kings than they deserved, he could find no excuse; but that he could more easily

185

conceive how some might speak better of them than they deserved, without any ill intention; for, as Kings had much in their power to give, those who were favoured by them would frequently, from gratitude, exaggerate their praises; and as this proceeded from a good motive, it was certainly excusable, as far as errour could be excusable.'

The King then asked him what he thought of Dr. Hill. Johnson answered, that he was an ingenious man, but had no veracity; and immediately mentioned, as an instance of it, an assertion of that writer, that he had seen objects magnified to a much greater degree by using three or four microscopes at a time, than by using one. 'Now, (added Johnson,) every one acquainted with microscopes knows, that the more of them he looks through, the less the object will appear.' 'Why, (replied the King,) this is not only telling an untruth, but telling it clumsily; for, if that be the case, every one who can look through a microscope will be able to detect him.'

'I now, (said Johnson to his friends, when relating what had passed) began to consider that I was depreciating this man in the estimation of his Sovereign, and thought it was time for me to say something that might be more favourable.' He added, therefore, that Dr. Hill was, notwithstanding, a very curious observer; and if he would have been contented to tell the world no more than he knew, he might have been a very considerable man, and needed not to have recourse to such mean expedients to raise his reputation. . . .

His Majesty expressed a desire to have a literary biography of this country ably executed, and proposed to Dr. Johnson to undertake it. Johnson signified his readiness to comply with his Majesty's wishes.

During the whole of this interview, Johnson talked to his Majesty with profound respect, but still in his firm manly manner, with a sonorous voice, and never in that subdued tone which is commonly used at the levee and in the drawing-room. After the King withdrew, Johnson shewed himself highly pleased with his Majesty's conversation and gracious behaviour. He said to Mr. Barnard, 'Sir, they may talk of the King as they will; but he is the finest gentleman I have ever seen.' And he afterwards observed to Mr. Langton, 'Sir, his manners are those of as fine a gentleman as we may suppose Lewis the Fourteenth or Charles the Second.'

At Sir Joshua Reynolds's, where a circle of Johnson's friends was collected round him to hear his account of this memorable conversation, Dr. Joseph Warton, in his frank and lively manner, was very active in pressing him to mention the particulars. 'Come now, Sir, this is an interesting matter; do favour us with it.' Johnson, with great good humour, complied.

He told them, 'I found his Majesty wished I should talk, and I made it my business to talk. I find it does a man good to be talked to by his Sovereign. In the first place, a man cannot be in a passion—.' Here some question interrupted him, which is to be regretted, as he certainly would have pointed out and illustrated many circumstances of advantage, from being in a situation, where the powers of the mind are at once excited to vigorous exertion, and tempered by reverential awe.

During all the time in which Dr. Johnson was employed in relating to the circle at Sir Joshua Reynolds's the particulars of what passed between the King and him, Dr. Goldsmith remained unmoved upon a sopha at some distance, affecting not to join in the least in the eager curiosity of the company. He assigned as a reason for his gloom and seeming inattention, that he apprehended Johnson had relinquished his purpose of furnishing him with a Prologue to his play, with the hopes of which he had been flattered; but it was strongly suspected that he was fretting with chagrin and envy at the singular honour Dr. Johnson had lately enjoyed. At length, the frankness and simplicity of his natural character prevailed. He sprung from the sopha, advanced to Johnson, and in a kind of flutter, from imagining himself in the situation which he had just been hearing described, exclaimed, 'Well, you acquitted yourself in this conversation better than I should have done; for I should have bowed and stammered through the whole of it.'

I received no letter from Johnson this year. . . . His diary affords no light as to his employment at this time. He passed three months at Lichfield; and I cannot omit an affecting and solemn scene there, as related by himself:

'Sunday, Oct. 18, 1767. Yesterday, Oct. 17, at about ten in the morning, I took my leave for ever of my dear old friend, Catharine Chambers, who came to live with my mother about 1724, and has been but little parted from us since. She buried my father, my brother, and my mother. She is now fifty-eight years old.

'I desired all to withdraw, then told her that we were to part for ever; that as Christians, we should part with prayer; and that I would if she was willing, say a short prayer beside her. She expressed great desire to hear me; and held up her poor hands, as she lay in bed, with great fervour, while I prayed, kneeling by her. . . .

'I then kissed her. She told me, that to part was the greatest pain that she had ever felt, and that she hoped we should

187

meet again in a better place. I expressed, with swelled eyes, and great emotion of tenderness, the same hopes. We kissed, and parted. I humbly hope to meet again, and to part no more.'

By those who have been taught to look upon Johnson as a man of a harsh and stern character, let this tender and affectionate scene be candidly read; and let them then judge whether more warmth of heart, and grateful kindness, is often found in human nature.

We have the following notice in his devotional record:—'August 2, 1767. I have been disturbed and unsettled for a long time, and have been without resolution to apply to study or to business, being hindered by sudden snatches.'[1]

He, however, furnished Mr. Adams with a dedication* to the King of that ingenious gentleman's *Treatise on the Globes,* conceived and expressed in such a manner as could not fail to be very grateful to a Monarch, distinguished for his love of the sciences. . . .

1768: ÆTAT. 59.]—IT appears from his notes of the state of his mind, that he suffered great perturbation and distraction in 1768. Nothing of his writing was given to the publick this year, except the Prologue* to his friend Goldsmith's comedy of *The Good-natured Man.* The first lines of this Prologue are strongly characteristical of the dismal gloom of his mind; which in his case, as in the case of all who are distressed with the same malady of imagination, transfers to others its own feelings. Who could suppose it was to introduce a comedy, when Mr. Bensley solemnly began,

> 'Press'd with the load of life, the weary mind
> Surveys the general toil of human kind.'

But this dark ground might make Goldsmith's humour shine the more.

In the spring of this year, having published my *Account of Corsica,* with the *Journal of a Tour to that Island,* I returned to London, very desirous to see Dr. Johnson, and hear him upon the subject. I found he was at Oxford, with his friend Mr. Chambers, who was now Vinerian Professor, and lived in New Inn Hall. . . . I was impatient to be with him, and therefore followed him to Oxford, where I was entertained by Mr. Chambers, with a civility which I shall ever gratefully remember. . . . Instead of giving, with the circumstances of time and place, such fragments of his conversation as I pre-

---

[1] On Aug. 17, he recorded:—'By abstinence from wine and suppers I obtained sudden and great relief, and had freedom of mind restored to me, which I have wanted for all this year, without being able to find any means of obtaining it'—B.

served during this visit to Oxford, I shall throw them together in continuation.

I asked him whether, as a moralist, he did not think that the practice of the law, in some degree, hurt the nice feeling of honesty. JOHNSON. 'Why no, Sir, if you act properly. You are not to deceive your clients with false representations of your opinion: you are not to tell lies to a judge.' BOSWELL. 'But what do you think of supporting a cause which you know to be bad?' JOHNSON. 'Sir, you do not know it to be good or bad till the Judge determines it. I have said that you are to state facts fairly; so that your thinking, or what you call knowing, a cause to be bad, must be from reasoning, must be from your supposing your arguments to be weak and inconclusive. But, Sir, that is not enough. An argument which does not convince yourself, may convince the Judge to whom you urge it; and if it does convince him, why, then, Sir, you are wrong, and he is right. It is his business to judge; and you are not to be confident in your own opinion that a cause is bad, but to say all you can for your client, and then hear the Judge's opinion.' BOSWELL. 'But, Sir, does not affecting a warmth when you have no warmth, and appearing to be clearly of one opinion when you are in reality of another opinion, does not such dissimulation impair one's honesty? Is there not some danger that a lawyer may put on the same mask in common life, in the intercourse with his friends?' JOHNSON. 'Why no, Sir. Everybody knows you are paid for affecting warmth for your client; and it is, therefore, properly no dissimulation: the moment you come from the bar you resume your usual behaviour. Sir, a man will no more carry the artifice of the bar into the common intercourse of society, than a man who is paid for tumbling upon his hands will continue to tumble upon his hands when he should walk on his feet.'

Talking of some of the modern plays, he said *False Delicacy* was totally void of character. He praised Goldsmith's *Good-natured Man;* said, it was the best comedy that has appeared since *The Provoked Husband,* and that there had not been of late any such character exhibited on the stage as that of Croaker. I observed it was the Suspirius of his Rambler. He said, Goldsmith had owned he had borrowed it from thence. 'Sir, (continued he,) there is all the difference in the world between characters of nature and characters of manners; and *there* is the difference between the characters of Fielding and those of Richardson. Characters of manners are very entertaining; but they are to be understood by a more superficial observer than characters of nature, where a man must dive into the recesses of the human heart.'

It always appeared to me that he estimated the compositions of Richardson too highly, and that he had an unreasonable prejudice against Fielding. In comparing those two writers, he used this expression: 'that there was as great a difference between them as between a man who knew how a watch was made, and a man who could tell the hour by looking on the dial-plate.' This was a short and figurative state of his distinction between drawing characters of nature and characters only of manners. But I cannot help being of opinion, that the neat watches of Fielding are as well constructed as the large clocks of Richardson, and that his dial-plates are brighter. Fielding's characters, though they do not expand themselves so widely in dissertation, are as just pictures of human nature, and I will venture to say, have more striking features, and nicer touches of the pencil; and though Johnson used to quote with approbation a saying of Richardson's, 'that the virtues of Fielding's heroes were the vices of a truly good man,' I will venture to add, that the moral tendency of Fielding's writings, though it does not encourage a strained and rarely possible virtue, is ever favourable to honour and honesty, and cherishes the benevolent and generous affections. He who is as good as Fielding would make him, is an amiable member of society, and may be led on by more regulated instructors, to a higher state of ethical perfection.

Johnson proceeded: 'Even Sir Francis Wronghead is a character of manners, though drawn with great humour.' He then repeated, very happily, all Sir Francis's credulous account to Manly of his being with 'the great man,' and securing a place. I asked him, if *The Suspicious Husband* did not furnish a well-drawn character, that of Ranger. JOHNSON. 'No, Sir; Ranger is just a rake, a mere rake, and a lively young fellow, but no *character*.' . . .

'I have not been troubled for a long time with authours desiring my opinion of their works. I used once to be sadly plagued with a man who wrote verses, but who literally had no other notion of a verse, but that it consisted of ten syllables. *Lay your knife and your fork, across your plate,* was to him a verse:

Lay yōur knife ānd your fōrk, acrōss your plāte.

As he wrote a great number of verses, he sometimes by chance made good ones, though he did not know it.'

He renewed his promise of coming to Scotland, and going with me to the Hebrides, but said he would now content himself with seeing one or two of the most curious of them. He said, 'Macaulay, who writes the account of St. Kilda, set out with a prejudice against prejudices, and wanted to be a smart modern thinker; and yet he affirms for a truth, that when a ship arrives there, all the inhabitants are seized with a cold.'

Dr. John Campbell, the celebrated writer, took a great deal of pains to ascertain this fact, and attempted to account for it on physical principles, from the effect of effluvia from human bodies. . . .

Johnson expatiated on the advantages of Oxford for learning. 'There is here, Sir, (said he,) such a progressive emulation. The students are anxious to appear well to their tutors; the tutors are anxious to have their pupils appear well in the college; the colleges are anxious to have their students appear well in the University; and there are excellent rules of discipline in every college. That the rules are sometimes ill observed, may be true; but is nothing against the system. The members of an University may, for a season, be unmindful of their duty. I am arguing for the excellency of the institution.'

Of Guthrie, he said, 'Sir, he is a man of parts. He has no great regular fund of knowledge; but by reading so long, and writing so long, he no doubt has picked up a good deal.'

He said he had lately been a long while at Lichfield, but had grown very weary before he left it. BOSWELL. 'I wonder at that, Sir; it is your native place.' JOHNSON. 'Why, so is Scotland *your* native place.'

His prejudice against Scotland appeared remarkably strong at this time. When I talked of our advancement in literature, 'Sir, (said he,) you have learnt a little from us, and you think yourselves very great men. Hume would never have written History, had not Voltaire written it before him. He is an echo of Voltaire.' BOSWELL. 'But, Sir, we have Lord Kames.' JOHNSON. 'You *have* Lord Kames. Keep him; ha, ha, ha! We don't envy you him. Do you ever see Dr. Robertson?' BOSWELL. 'Yes, Sir.' JOHNSON. 'Does the dog talk of me?' BOSWELL. 'Indeed, Sir, he does, and loves you.' Thinking that I now had him in a corner, and being solicitous for the literary fame of my country, I pressed him for his opinion on the merit of Dr. Robertson's *History of Scotland*. But, to my surprize, he escaped.—'Sir, I love Robertson, and I won't talk of his book.'

It is but justice both to him and Dr. Robertson to add, that though he indulged himself in this sally of wit, he had too good taste not to be fully sensible of the merits of that admirable work.

An essay, written by Mr. Deane, a divine of the Church of England, maintaining the future life of brutes, by an explication of certain parts of the scriptures, was mentioned, and the doctrine insisted on by a gentleman[1] who seemed fond of curious speculation. Johnson, who did not like to hear of any thing concerning a future state which was not authorised by the regular canons of orthodoxy, discouraged this talk; and being offended at its continuation, he watched an opportunity to give the gentleman a blow of reprehension. So, when the poor speculatist, with a serious metaphysical pensive face, addressed him, 'But really, Sir, when we see a very sensible dog, we don't know what to think of him;' Johnson, rolling with joy at the thought which beamed in his eye, turned quickly round, and replied, 'True, Sir: and when we see a very foolish *fellow*, we don't know what to think of *him*.' He then rose up, strided to the fire, and stood for some time laughing and exulting.

I told him that I had several times, when in Italy, seen the experiment of placing a scorpion within a circle of burning coals; that it ran round and round in extreme pain; and finding no way to escape, retired to the centre, and like a true Stoick philosopher, darted its sting into its head, and thus at once freed itself from its woes. *'This must end 'em.'* I said, this was a curious fact, as it shewed deliberate suicide in a reptile. Johnson would not admit the fact. He said, Maupertuis was of opinion that it does not kill itself, but dies of the heat; that it gets to the centre of the circle, as the coolest place; that its turning its tail in upon its head is merely a convulsion, and that it does not sting itself. He said he would be satisfied if the great anatomist Morgagni, after dissecting a scorpion on which the experiment had been tried, should certify that its sting had penetrated into its head.

He seemed pleased to talk of natural philosophy. 'That woodcocks, (said he,) fly over to the northern countries is proved, because they have been observed at sea. Swallows certainly sleep all the winter. A number of them conglobulate together, by flying round and round, and then all in a heap throw themselves under water, and lye in the bed of a river.' He told us, one of his first essays was a Latin poem upon the glow-worm. I am sorry I did not ask where it was to be found.

Talking of the Russians and the Chinese, he advised me to read Bell's travels. I asked him whether I should read Du Halde's account of China. 'Why yes, (said he,) as one reads such a book; that is to say, consult it.'

He talked of the heinousness of the crime of adultery, by which the peace of families was destroyed. He said, 'Confusion of progeny constitutes the essence of the crime; and

[1] Boswell.

therefore a woman who breaks her marriage vows is much more criminal than a man who does it. A man, to be sure, is criminal in the sight of GOD: but he does not do his wife a very material injury, if he does not insult her; if, for instance, from mere wantonness of appetite, he steals privately to her chambermaid. Sir, a wife ought not greatly to resent this. I would not receive home a daughter who had run away from her husband on that account. A wife should study to reclaim her husband by more attention to please him. Sir, a man will not, once in a hundred instances, leave his wife and go to a harlot, if his wife has not been negligent of pleasing.'

Here he discovered that acute discrimination, that solid judgement, and that knowledge of human nature, for which he was upon all occasions remarkable. Taking care to keep in view the moral and religious duty, as understood in our nation, he shewed clearly from reason and good sense, the greater degree of culpability in the one sex deviating from it than the other; and, at the same time, inculcated a very useful lesson as to *the way to keep him*.

I asked him if it was not hard that one deviation from chastity should so absolutely ruin a young woman. JOHNSON. 'Why, no, Sir; it is the great principle which she is taught. When she has given up that principle, she has given up every notion of female honour and virtue, which are all included in chastity.'

A gentleman talked to him of a lady[1] whom he greatly admired and wished to marry, but was afraid of her superiority of talents. 'Sir, (said he,) you need not be afraid; marry her. Before a year goes about, you'll find that reason much weaker, and that wit not so bright.' Yet the gentleman may be justified in his apprehension by one of Dr. Johnson's admirable sentences in his life of Waller: 'He doubtless praised many whom he would have been afraid to marry; and, perhaps, married one whom he would have been ashamed to praise. Many qualities contribute to domestic happiness, upon which poetry has no colours to bestow; and many airs and sallies may delight imagination, which he who flatters them never can approve.'

He praised Signor Baretti. 'His account of Italy is a very entertaining book; and, Sir, I know no man who carried his head higher in conversation than Baretti. There are strong powers in his mind. He has not, indeed, many hooks; but with what hooks he has, he grapples very forcibly.'

At this time I observed upon the dial-plate of his watch a short Greek inscription, taken from the New Testament,

[1] Boswell and Isabelle de Zuylen (Zélide).

Νυξ γαρ ερχεται, being the first words of our SAVIOUR'S solemn admonition to the improvement of that time which is allowed us to prepare for eternity: 'the night cometh, when no man can work.' He sometime afterwards laid aside this dial-plate; and when I asked him the reason, he said, 'It might do very well upon a clock which a man keeps in his closet; but to have it upon his watch which he carries about with him, and which is often looked at by others, might be censured as ostentatious.' Mr. Steevens is now possessed of the dial-plate inscribed as above.

He remained at Oxford a considerable time; I was obliged to go to London. . . .

Upon his arrival in London in May, he surprized me one morning with a visit at my lodgings in Half-Moon-street, was quite satisfied with my explanation,[1] and was in the kindest and most agreeable frame of mind. As he had objected to a part of one of his letters being published, I thought it right to take this opportunity of asking him explicitly whether it would be improper to publish his letters after his death. His answer was, 'Nay, Sir, when I am dead, you may do as you will.'

He talked in his usual style with a rough contempt of popular liberty. 'They make a rout about *universal* liberty, without considering that all that is to be valued, or indeed can be enjoyed by individuals, is *private* liberty. Political liberty is good only so far as it produces private liberty. Now, Sir, there is the liberty of the press, which you know is a constant topick. Suppose you and I and two hundred more were restrained from printing our thoughts: what then? What proportion would that restraint upon us bear to the private happiness of the nation?'

This mode of representing the inconveniences of restraint as light and insignificant, was a kind of sophistry in which he delighted to indulge himself, in opposition to the extreme laxity for which it has been fashionable for too many to argue, when it is evident, upon reflection, that the very essence of government is restraint; and certain it is, that as government produces rational happiness, too much restraint is better than too little. But when restraint is unnecessary, and so close as to gall those who are subject to it, the people may and ought to remonstrate; and, if relief is not granted, to resist. Of this manly and spirited principle, no man was more convinced than Johnson himself.

About this time Dr. Kenrick attacked him, through my sides, in a pamphlet, entitled *An Epistle to James Boswell, Esq., occasioned by his having transmitted the moral Writ-*

[1] For his interest in the Corsican struggle for liberty.

ings of Dr. Samuel Johnson to Pascal Paoli, General of the Corsicans. I was at first inclined to answer this pamphlet; but Johnson, who knew that my doing so would only gratify Kenrick, by keeping alive what would soon die away of itself, would not suffer me to take any notice of it.

His sincere regard for Francis Barber, his faithful negro servant, made him so desirous of his further improvement, that he now placed him at a school at Bishop Stortford, in Hertfordshire. This humane attention does Johnson's heart much honour. Out of many letters which Mr. Barber received from his master, he has preserved three, which he kindly gave me, and which I shall insert according to their dates.

'To MR. FRANCIS BARBER

'DEAR FRANCIS.—I have been very much out of order. I am glad to hear that you are well, and design to come soon to see you. I would have you stay at Mrs. Clapp's for the present, till I can determine what we shall do. Be a good boy.

'My compliments to Mrs. Clapp and to Mr. Fowler. I am, your's affectionately,

'May 28, 1768.'   'SAM. JOHNSON.'

Soon afterwards, he supped at the Crown and Anchor tavern, in the Strand, with a company whom I collected to meet him. They were Dr. Percy, now Bishop of Dromore, Dr. Douglas, now Bishop of Salisbury, Mr. Langton, Dr. Robertson the Historian, Dr. Hugh Blair, and Mr. Thomas Davies, who wished much to be introduced to these eminent Scotch literati; but on the present occasion he had very little opportunity of hearing them talk, for with an excess of prudence, for which Johnson afterwards found fault with them, they hardly opened their lips, and that only to say something which they were certain would not expose them to the sword of Goliath; such was their anxiety for their fame when in the presence of Johnson. He was this evening in remarkable vigour of mind, and eager to exert himself in conversation, which he did with great readiness and fluency; but I am sorry to find that I have preserved but a small part of what passed.

He allowed high praise to Thomson as a poet; but when one of the company said he was also a very good man, our moralist contested this with great warmth, accusing him of gross sensuality and licentiousness of manners. I was very much afraid that in writing Thomson's *Life,* Dr. Johnson would have treated his private character with a stern severity, but I was agreeably disappointed; and I may claim a little merit in it, from my having been at pains to send him authentick accounts of the affectionate and generous conduct of that poet to his sisters, one of whom, the wife of Mr. Thomson, schoolmaster at Lanark, I knew, and was presented by her with three of his letters, one of which Dr. Johnson has inserted in his *Life*.

He was vehement against old Dr. Mounsey, of Chelsea College, as 'a fellow who swore and talked bawdy.' 'I have been often in his company, (said Dr. Percy,) and never heard him swear or talk bawdy.' Mr. Davies, who sat next to Dr. Percy, having after this had some conversation aside with him, made a discovery which, in his zeal to pay court to Dr. Johnson, he eagerly proclaimed aloud from the foot of the table: 'O, Sir, I have found out a very good reason why Dr. Percy never heard Mounsey swear or talk bawdy; for he tells me, he never saw him but at the Duke of Northumberland's table.' 'And so, Sir, (said Johnson loudly, to Dr. Percy,) you would shield this man from the charge of swearing and talking bawdy, because he did not do so at the Duke of Northumberland's table. Sir, you might as well tell us that you had seen him hold up his hand at the Old Bailey, and he neither swore nor talked bawdy; or that you had seen him in the cart at Tyburn, and he neither swore nor talked bawdy. And is it thus, Sir, that you presume to controvert what I have related?' Dr. Johnson's animadversion was uttered in such a manner, that Dr. Percy seemed to be displeased, and soon afterwards left the company, of which Johnson did not at that time take any notice.

Swift having been mentioned, Johnson, as usual, treated him with little respect as an authour. Some of us endeavoured to support the Dean of St. Patrick's by various arguments. One in particular praised his *Conduct of the Allies*. JOHNSON. 'Sir, his *Conduct of the Allies* is a performance of very little ability.' 'Surely, Sir, (said Dr. Douglas,) you must allow it has strong facts.' JOHNSON. 'Why yes, Sir; but what is that to the merit of the composition? In the Sessions-paper of the Old Bailey there are strong facts. Housebreaking is a strong fact; robbery is a strong fact; and murder is a *mighty* strong fact; but is great praise due to the historian of those strong facts? No, Sir. Swift has told what he had to tell distinctly enough, but that is all. He had to count ten, and he has counted it right.' Then recollecting that Mr. Davies, by acting as an *informer*, had been the occasion of his talking somewhat too harshly to his friend Dr. Percy, for which, probably, when the first ebullition was over, he felt some compunction, he took an opportunity to give him a hit; so added, with a preparatory laugh, 'Why, Sir, Tom Davies might have written *The Conduct of the Allies*.' Poor Tom being thus suddenly dragged into ludicrous notice in presence of the Scottish Doctors, to whom he was ambitious of appearing to advantage, was grievously mortified. Nor did his punishment rest here; for upon subsequent occasions, whenever he, 'statesman all over,'[1] assumed a strutting importance, I used to hail him—'the Authour of *The Conduct of the Allies.*'

When I called upon Dr. Johnson next morning, I found him highly satisfied with his colloquial prowess the preceding evening. 'Well, (said he,) we had good talk.' BOSWELL. 'Yes, Sir; you tossed and gored several persons.'

The late Alexander, Earl of Eglintoune, who loved wit more than wine, and men of genius more than sycophants, had a great admiration of Johnson; but from the remarkable elegance of his own manners, was, perhaps, too delicately sensible of the roughness which sometimes appeared in Johnson's behaviour. One evening about this time, when his Lordship did me the honour to sup at my lodgings with Dr. Robertson and several other men of literary distinction, he regretted that Johnson had not been educated with more refinement, and lived more in polished society. 'No, no, my Lord, (said Signor Baretti,) do with him what you would, he would always have been a bear.' 'True, (answered the Earl, with a smile,) but he would have been a *dancing* bear.'

To obviate all the reflections would have gone round the world to Johnson's prejudice, by applying to him the epithet of a *bear,* let me impress upon my readers a just and happy saying of my friend Goldsmith, who knew him well: 'Johnson, to be sure, has a roughness in his manner; but no man alive has a more tender heart. *He has nothing of the bear but his skin.*'

1769: ÆTAT. 60.]—IN 1769, so far as I can discover, the publick was favoured with nothing of Johnson's composition, either for himself or any of his friends. His *Meditations* too strongly prove that he suffered much both in body and mind; yet was he perpetually striving against *evil,* and nobly endeavouring to advance his intellectual and devotional improvement. Every generous and grateful heart must feel for the distresses of so eminent a benefactor to mankind; and now that his unhappiness is certainly known, must respect that dignity of character which prevented him from complaining.

His Majesty having the preceding year instituted the Royal Academy of Arts in London, Johnson had now the honour of being appointed Professor in Ancient Literature. In the course of the year he wrote some letters to Mrs. Thrale, passed some part of the summer at Oxford and at Lichfield, and when at Oxford wrote the following letter.[2]

[1] See the hard drawing of him in Churchill's *Rosciad*—B.
[2] To Thomas Warton, omitted here.

I came to London in the autumn, and having informed him that I was going to be married in a few months, I wished to have as much of his conversation as I could before engaging in a state of life which would probably keep me more in Scotland, and prevent my seeing him so often as when I was a single man; but I found he was at Brighthelmstone with Mr. and Mrs. Thrale. I was very sorry that I had not his company with me at the Jubilee, in honour of Shakspeare, at Stratford-upon-Avon, the great poet's native town. Johnson's connection both with Shakspeare and Garrick founded a double claim to his presence; and it would have been highly gratifying to Mr. Garrick. Upon this occasion I particularly lamented that he had not that warmth of friendship for his brilliant pupil, which we may suppose would have had a benignant effect on both. When almost every man of eminence in the literary world was happy to partake in this festival of genius, the absence of Johnson could not but be wondered at and regretted. The only trace of him there, was in the whimsical advertisement of a haberdasher, who sold *Shakspearian ribbands* of various dyes; and, by way of illustrating their appropriation to the bard, introduced a line from the celebrated Prologue at the opening of Drury-lane theatre:

'Each change of *many-colour'd* life he drew.'

. . . After his return to town, we met frequently, and I continued the practice of making notes of his conversation, though not with so much assiduity as I wish I had done. At this time, indeed, I had a sufficient excuse for not being able to appropriate so much time to my Journal; for General Paoli, after Corsica had been overpowered by the monarchy of France, was now no longer at the head of his brave countrymen, but having with difficulty escaped from his native island, had sought an asylum in Great-Britain; and it was my duty, as well as my pleasure, to attend much upon him. Such particulars of Johnson's conversation at this period as I have committed to writing, I shall here introduce, without any strict attention to methodical arrangement. Sometimes short notes of different days shall be blended together, and sometimes a day may seem important enough to be separately distinguished.

He said, he would not have Sunday kept with rigid severity and gloom, but with a gravity and simplicity of behaviour.

I told him that David Hume had made a short collection of Scotticisms.[1] 'I wonder, (said Johnson,) that *he* should find them.'

[1] The first edition of Hume's *History of England* was full of Scotticisms, many of which he corrected in subsequent editions.

He would not admit the importance of the question concerning the legality of general warrants. 'Such a power' (he observed,) 'must be vested in every government, to answer particular cases of necessity; and there can be no just complaint but when it is abused, for which those who administer government must be answerable. It is a matter of such indifference, a matter about which the people care so very little, that were a man to be sent over Britain to offer them an exemption from it at a halfpenny a piece, very few would purchase it.' This was a specimen of that laxity of talking, which I have heard him fairly acknowledge; for, surely, while the power of granting general warrants was supposed to be legal, and the apprehension of them hung over our heads, we did not possess that security of freedom, congenial to our happy constitution, and which, by the intrepid exertions of Mr. Wilkes, has been happily established.

He said, 'The duration of Parliament, whether for seven years or for the life of the King, appears to me so immaterial, that I would not give half a crown to turn the scale one way or the other. The *habeas corpus* is the single advantage which our government has over that of other countries.'

On the 30th of September we dined together at the Mitre. I attempted to argue for the superior happiness of the savage life, upon the usual fanciful topicks. JOHNSON. 'Sir, there can be nothing more false. The savages have no bodily advantages beyond those of civilised men. They have not better health; and as to care or mental uneasiness, they are not above it, but below it, like bears. No, Sir; you are not to talk such paradox: let me have no more on't. It cannot entertain, far less can it instruct. Lord Monboddo, one of your Scotch Judges, talked a great deal of such nonsense. I suffered *him;* but I will not suffer *you*.'—BOSWELL. 'But, Sir, does not Rousseau talk such nonsense?' JOHNSON. 'True, Sir; but Rousseau *knows* he is talking nonsense, and laughs at the world for staring at him.' BOSWELL. 'How so, Sir?' JOHNSON. 'Why, Sir, a man who talks nonsense so well must know that he is talking nonsense. But I am *afraid*, (chuckling and laughing,) Monboddo does *not* know that he is talking nonsense.' BOSWELL. 'Is it wrong then, Sir, to affect singularity, in order to make people stare?' JOHNSON. 'Yes, if you do it by propagating errour: and, indeed, it is wrong in any way. There is in human nature a general inclination to make people stare; and every wise man has himself to cure of it, and does cure himself. If you wish to make people stare by doing better than others, why, make them stare till they stare their eyes out. But consider how easy it is to make people stare by being absurd. I may do it by going into a drawing-room without my shoes. You remember the gentleman in *The Spectator*, who had a commission of lunacy taken out against him for his extreme singularity, such as never wearing a wig, but a night-cap. Now, Sir, abstractedly, the night-cap was best; but, relatively, the advantage was overbalanced by his making the boys run after him.'

Talking of a London life, he said, 'The happiness of London is not to be conceived but by those who have been in it. I will venture to say, there is more learning and science within the circumference of ten miles from where we now sit, than in all the rest of the kingdom.' BOSWELL. 'The only disadvantage is the great distance at which people live from one another.' JOHNSON. 'Yes, Sir; but that is occasioned by the largeness of it, which is the cause of all the other advantages.' BOSWELL. 'Sometimes I have been in the humour of wishing to retire to a desart.' JOHNSON. 'Sir, you have desart enough in Scotland.'

Although I had promised myself a great deal of instructive conversation with him on the conduct of the married state, of which I had then a near prospect, he did not say much upon that topick. Mr. Seward heard him once say, that 'a man has a very bad chance for happiness in that state, unless he marries a woman of very strong and fixed principles of religion.' He maintained to me, contrary to the common notion, that a woman would not be the worse wife for being learned; in which, from all that I have observed of *Artemisias,* I humbly differed from him. . . .

When I censured a gentleman[1] of my acquaintance for marrying a second time, as it shewed a disregard of his first wife, he said, 'Not at all, Sir. On the contrary, were he not to marry again, it might be concluded that his first wife had given him a disgust to marriage; but by taking a second wife he pays the highest compliment to the first, by shewing that she made him so happy as a married man, that he wishes to be so a second time.' So ingenious a turn did he give to this delicate question. And yet, on another occasion, he owned that he once had almost asked a promise of Mrs. Johnson that she would not marry again, but had checked himself. Indeed, I cannot help thinking, that in his case the request would have been unreasonable; for if Mrs. Johnson forgot, or thought it no injury to the memory of her first love,—the husband of her youth and the father of her children,—to make a second marriage, why should she be precluded from a third, should she be so inclined? In Johnson's persevering fond appropriation of his *Tetty,* even after her decease, he seems totally to

[1] Boswell's father.

200

have overlooked the prior claim of the honest Birmingham trader. I presume that her having been married before had, at times, given him some uneasiness; for I remember his observing upon the marriage of one of our common friends, 'He has done a very foolish thing, Sir; he has married a widow, when he might have had a maid.'

We drank tea with Mrs. Williams. I had last year the pleasure of seeing Mrs. Thrale at Dr. Johnson's one morning, and had conversation enough with her to admire her talents, and to shew her that I was as Johnsonian as herself. Dr. Johnson had probably been kind enough to speak well of me, for this evening he delivered me a very polite card from Mr. Thrale and her, inviting me to Streatham.

On the 6th of October I complied with this obliging invitation, and found, at an elegant villa, six miles from town, every circumstance that can make society pleasing. Johnson, though quite at home, was yet looked up to with an awe, tempered by affection, and seemed to be equally the care of his host and hostess. I rejoiced at seeing him so happy.

He played off his wit against Scotland with a good humoured pleasantry, which gave me, though no bigot to national prejudices, an opportunity for a little contest with him. I having said that England was obliged to us for gardeners, almost all their good gardeners being Scotchmen. JOHNSON. 'Why, Sir, that is because gardening is much more necessary amongst you than with us, which makes so many of your people learn it. It is *all* gardening with you. Things which grow wild here, must be cultivated with great care in Scotland. Pray now (throwing himself back in his chair, and laughing,) are you ever able to bring the *sloe* to perfection?'

I boasted that we had the honour of being the first to abolish the unhospitable, troublesome, and ungracious custom of giving vails to servants. JOHNSON. 'Sir, you abolished vails, because you were too poor to be able to give them.'

Mrs. Thrale disputed with him on the merit of Prior. He attacked him powerfully; said he wrote of love like a man who had never felt it: his love verses were college verses; and he repeated the song 'Alexis shunn'd his fellow swains,' &c., in so ludicrous a manner, as to make us all wonder how any one could have been pleased with such fantastical stuff. Mrs. Thrale stood to her gun with great courage, in defence of amorous ditties, which Johnson despised, till he at last silenced her by saying, 'My dear Lady, talk no more of this. Nonsense can be defended but by nonsense.'

Mrs. Thrale then praised Garrick's talent for light gay poetry; and, as a specimen, repeated his song in *Florizel and Perdita,* and dwelt with peculiar pleasure on this line:

'I'd smile with the simple, and feed with the poor.'

JOHNSON. 'Nay, my dear Lady, this will never do. Poor David! Smile with the simple! What folly is that! And who would feed with the poor that can help it? No, no; let me smile with the wise, and feed with the rich.' I repeated this sally to Garrick, and wondered to find his sensibility as a writer not a little irritated by it. To sooth him, I observed, that Johnson spared none of us; and I quoted the passage in Horace, in which he compares one who attacks his friends for the sake of a laugh, to a pushing ox, that is marked by a bunch of hay put upon his horns: *fœnum habet in cornu.*[1] 'Ay, (said Garrick vehemently,) he has a whole *mow* of it.'

Talking of history, Johnson said, 'We may know historical facts to be true, as we may know facts in common life to be true. Motives are generally unknown. We cannot trust to the characters we find in history, unless when they are drawn by those who knew the persons; as those, for instance, by Sallust and by Lord Clarendon.'

He would not allow much merit to Whitefield's oratory. 'His popularity, Sir, (said he,) is chiefly owing to the peculiarity of his manner. He would be followed by crowds were he to wear a night-cap in the pulpit, or were he to preach from a tree.'

I know not from what spirit of contradiction he burst out into a violent declamation against the Corsicans, of whose heroism I talked in high terms. 'Sir, (said he,) what is all this rout about the Corsicans? They have been at war with the Genoese for upwards of twenty years, and have never yet taken their fortified towns. They might have battered down their walls, and reduced them to powder in twenty years. They might have pulled the walls in pieces, and cracked the stones with their teeth in twenty years.' It was in vain to argue with him upon the want of artillery: he was not to be resisted for the moment.

On the evening of October 10, I presented Dr. Johnson to General Paoli. I had greatly wished that two men, for whom I had the highest esteem, should meet. They met with a manly ease, mutually conscious of their own abilities, and of the abilities of each other. The General spoke Italian, and Dr. Johson English, and understood one another very well, with a little aid of interpretation from me, in which I compared myself to an isthmus which joins two great continents. Upon Johnson's approach, the General said, 'From what I have read of your works, Sir, and from what Mr. Boswell has told me of you, I have long held you in great veneration.'

[1] 'He has hay on his horn.' Horace, *Satires*, I. iv. 34.

The General talked of languages being formed on the particular notions and manners of a people, without knowing which, we cannot know the language. We may know the direct signification of single words; but by these no beauty of expression, no sally of genius, no wit is conveyed to the mind. All this must be by allusion to other ideas. 'Sir, (said Johnson,) you talk of language, as if you had never done any thing else but study it, instead of governing a nation.' The General said, '*Questo e un troppo gran complimento;*' this is too great a compliment. Johnson answered, 'I should have thought so, Sir, if I had not heard you talk.' The General asked him, what he thought of the spirit of infidelity which was so preva` nt. JOHNSON. 'Sir, this gloom of infidelity, I hope, is only a transient cloud passing through the hemisphere, which will soon be dissipated, and the sun break forth with his usual splendour.' 'You think then, (said the General,) that they will change their principles like their clothes.' JOHNSON. 'Why, Sir, if they bestow no more thought on principles than on dress, it must be so.' The General said, that 'a great part of the fashionable infidelity was owing to a desire of shewing courage. Men who have no opportunities of shewing it as to things in this life, take death and futurity as objects on which to display it.' JOHNSON. 'That is mighty foolish affectation. Fear is one of the passions of human nature, of which it is impossible to divest it. You remember that the Emperour Charles V, when he read upon the tomb-stone of a Spanish nobleman, "Here lies one who never knew fear," wittily said, "Then he never snuffed a candle with his fingers." ' . . .

Dr. Johnson went home with me, and drank tea till late in the night. He said, 'General Paoli had the loftiest port of any man he had ever seen.' He denied that military men were always the best bred men. 'Perfect good breeding,' he observed, 'consists in having no particular mark of any profession, but a general elegance of manners; whereas, in a military man, you can commonly distinguish the *brand* of a soldier, *l'homme d'épée.*'

Dr. Johnson shunned to-night any discussion of the perplexed question of fate and free will, which I attempted to agitate. 'Sir, (said he,) we *know* our will is free, and *there's* an end on't.'

He honoured me with his company at dinner on the 16th of October, at my lodgings in Old Bond-street, with Sir Joshua Reynolds, Mr. Garrick, Dr. Goldsmith, Mr. Murphy, Mr. Bickerstaff, and Mr. Thomas Davies. Garrick played round him with a fond vivacity, taking hold of the breasts of his coat, and, looking up in his face with a lively archness, complimented him on the good health which he seemed then to enjoy; while the sage, shaking his head, beheld him with a gentle complacency. One of the company not being come at the appointed hour, I proposed, as usual upon such occasions, to order dinner to be served; adding, 'Ought six people to be kept waiting for one?' 'Why, yes, (answered Johnson, with a delicate humanity,) if the one will suffer more by your sitting down, than the six will do by waiting.' Goldsmith, to divert the tedious minutes, strutted about, bragging of his dress, and I believe was seriously vain of it, for his mind was wonderfully prone to such impressions. 'Come, come, (said Garrick,) talk no more of that. You are, perhaps, the worst—eh, eh!' —Goldsmith was eagerly attempting to interrupt him, when Garrick went on, laughing ironically, 'Nay, you will always *look* like a gentleman; but I am talking of being well or ill *drest*.' 'Well, let me tell you, (said Goldsmith,) when my tailor brought home my bloom-coloured coat, he said, "Sir, I have a favour to beg of you. When any body asks you who made your clothes, be pleased to mention John Filby, at the Harrow, in Water-lane."' JOHNSON. 'Why, Sir, that was because he knew the strange colour would attract crowds to gaze at it, and thus they might hear of him, and see how well he could make a coat even of so absurd a colour.'

After dinner our conversation first turned upon Pope. Johnson said, his characters of men were admirably drawn, those of women not so well. He repeated to us, in his forcible melodious manner, the concluding lines of the *Dunciad.* While he was talking loudly in praise of those lines, one of the company[1] ventured to say, 'Too fine for such a poem:—a poem on what?' JOHNSON, (with a disdainful look,) 'Why, on *dunces*. It was worth while being a dunce then. Ah, Sir, hadst *thou* lived in those days! It is not worth while being a dunce now, when there are no wits.' Bickerstaff observed, as a peculiar circumstance, that Pope's fame was higher when he was alive than it was then. Johnson said, his Pastorals were poor things, though the versification was fine. He told us, with high satisfaction, the anecdote of Pope's inquiring who was the authour of his *London,* and saying, he will be soon *déterré*. He observed, that in Dryden's poetry there were passages drawn from a profundity which Pope could never reach. He repeated some fine lines on love, by the former, (which I have now forgotten,) and gave great applause to the character of Zimri. Goldsmith said, that Pope's character of Addison shewed a deep knowledge of the human heart. Johnson said, that the description of the temple, in the

1 Boswell.

Mourning Bride, was the finest poetical passage he had ever read; he recollected none in Shakspeare equal to it. 'But, (said Garrick, all alarmed for 'the god of his idolatry,') we know not the extent and variety of his powers. We are to suppose there are such passages in his works. Shakspeare must not suffer from the badness of our memories.' Johnson, diverted by this enthusiastick jealousy, went on with greater ardour: 'No, Sir; Congreve has *nature*;' (smiling on the tragick eagerness of Garrick;) but composing himself, he added, 'Sir, this is not comparing Congreve on the whole, with Shakspeare on the whole; but only maintaining that Congreve has one finer passage than any that can be found in Shakspeare. Sir, a man may have no more than ten guineas in the world, but he may have those ten guineas in one piece; and so may have a finer piece than a man who has ten thousand pounds: but then he has only one ten-guinea piece. What I mean is, that you can shew me no passage where there is simply a description of material objects, without any intermixture of moral notions, which produces such an effect.' Mr. Murphy mentioned Shakspeare's description of the night before the battle of Agincourt; but it was observed, it had *men* in it. Mr. Davies suggested the speech of Juliet, in which she figures herself awaking in the tomb of her ancestors. Some one mentioned the description of Dover Cliff. JOHNSON. 'No, Sir; it should be all precipice,—all vacuum. The crows impede your fall. The diminished appearance of the boats, and other circumstances, are all very good description; but do not impress the mind at once with the horrible idea of immense height. The impression is divided; you pass on by computation, from one stage of the tremendous space to another. Had the girl in *The Mouring Bride* said, she could not cast her shoe to the top of one of the pillars in the temple, it would not have aided the idea, but weakened it.'

Talking of a Barrister who had a bad utterance, some one, (to rouse Johnson,) wickedly said, that he was unfortunate in not having been taught oratory by Sheridan. JOHNSON. 'Nay, Sir, if he had been taught by Sheridan, he would have cleared the room.' GARRICK. 'Sheridan has too much vanity to be a good man.' We shall now see Johnson's mode of *defending* a man; taking him into his own hands, and discriminating. JOHNSON. 'No, Sir. There is, to be sure, in Sheridan, something to reprehend, and every thing to laugh at; but, Sir, he is not a bad man. No, Sir; were mankind to be divided into good and bad, he would stand considerably within the ranks of good. And, Sir, it must be allowed that Sheridan excels in plain declamation, though he can exhibit no character.'

205

I should, perhaps, have suppressed this disquisition concerning a person of whose merit and worth I think with respect, had he not attacked Johnson so outrageously in his *Life of Swift*, and, at the same time, treated us, his admirers, as a set of pigmies. He who has provoked the lash of wit, cannot complain that he smarts from it.

Mrs. Montagu, a lady distinguished for having written an Essay on Shakspeare, being mentioned; REYNOLDS. 'I think that essay does her honour.' JOHNSON. 'Yes, Sir; it does *her* honour, but it would do nobody else honour. I have, indeed, not read it all. But when I take up the end of a web, and find it pack-thread, I do not expect, by looking further, to find embroidery. Sir, I will venture to say, there is not one sentence of true criticism in her book.' GARRICK. 'But, sir, surely it shews how much Voltaire has mistaken Shakspeare, which nobody else has done.' JOHNSON. 'Sir, nobody else has though it worth while. And what merit is there in that? You may as well praise a schoolmaster for whipping a boy who has construed ill. No, Sir, there is no real criticism in it: none shewing the beauty of thought, as formed on the workings of the human heart.' . . .

One day at Sir Joshua's table, when it was related that Mrs. Montagu, in an excess of compliment to the authour of a modern tragedy, had exclaimed, 'I tremble for Shakspeare;' Johnson said, 'When Shakspeare has got —— for his rival, and Mrs. Montagu for his defender, he is in a poor state indeed.'

Johnson proceeded: 'The Scotchman[1] has taken the right method in his *Elements of Criticism*. I do not mean that he has taught us any thing; but he has told us old things in a new way.' MURPHY. 'He seems to have read a great deal of French criticism, and wants to make it his own; as if he had been for years anatomising the heart of man, and peeping into every cranny of it.' GOLDSMITH. 'It is easier to write that book, than to read it.' JOHNSON. 'We have an example of true criticism in Burke's *Essay on the Sublime and Beautiful;* and, if I recollect there is also Du Bos; and Bouhours, who shews all beauty to depend on truth. There is no great merit in telling how many plays have ghosts in them, and how this Ghost is better than that. You must shew how terrour is impressed on the human heart. In the description of night in *Macbeth*, the beetle and the bat detract from the general idea of darkness,—inspissated gloom.'

Politicks being mentioned, he said, 'This petitioning is a new mode of distressing government, and a mighty easy one. I will undertake to get petitions either against quarter-guineas or half-guineas, with the help of a little hot wine. There must

[1] Lord Kames.

206

be no yielding to encourage this. The object is not important enough. We are not to blow up half a dozen palaces, because one cottage is burning.'

The conversation then took another turn. JOHNSON. 'It is amazing what ignorance of certain points one sometimes finds in men of eminence. A wit about town, who wrote Latin bawdy verses, asked me, how it happened that England and Scotland, which were once two kingdoms, were now one: —and Sir Fletcher Norton did not seem to know that there were such publications as the Reviews.'

'The ballad of Hardyknute has no great merit, if it be really ancient. People talk of nature. But mere obvious nature may be exhibited with very little power of mind.'

On Thursday, October 19, I passed the evening with him at his house. He advised me to complete a Dictionary of words peculiar to Scotland, of which I shewed him a specimen. 'Sir, (said he,) Ray has made a collection of north-country words. By collecting those of your country, you will do a useful thing towards the history of the language. He bade me also go on with collections which I was making upon the antiquities of Scotland. 'Make a large book; a folio.' BOSWELL. 'But of what use will it be, Sir?' JOHNSON. 'Never mind the use; do it.'

I complained that he had not mentioned Garrick in his Preface to Shakspeare; and asked him if he did not admire him. JOHNSON. 'Yes, as "a poor player, who frets and struts his hour upon the stage;"—as a shadow.' BOSWELL. 'But has he not brought Shakspeare into notice?' JOHN-SON. 'Sir, to allow that, would be to lampoon the age. Many of Shakspeare's plays are the worse for being acted; *Macbeth,* for instance.' BOSWELL. 'What, Sir, is nothing gained by decoration and action? Indeed, I do wish that you had mentioned Garrick.' JOHNSON. 'My dear Sir, had I mentioned him, I must have mentioned many more: Mrs. Pritchard, Mrs. Cibber,—nay, and Mr. Cibber too; he too altered Shakspeare.' BOSWELL. 'You have read his apology, Sir?' JOHNSON. 'Yes, it is very entertaining. But as for Cibber himself, taking from his conversation all that he ought not to have said, he was a poor creature. I remember when he brought me one of his Odes to have my opinion of it; I could not bear such nonsense, and would not let him read it to the end; so little respect had I for *that great man!* (laughing.) Yet I remember Richardson wondering that I could treat him with familiarity.'

I mentioned to him that I had seen the execution of several convicts at Tyburn, two days before, and that none of them seemed to be under any concern. JOHNSON. 'Most of them,

Sir, have never thought at all.' BOSWELL. 'But is not the fear of death natural to man?' JOHNSON. 'So much so, Sir, that the whole of life is but keeping away the thoughts of it.' He then, in a low and earnest tone, talked of his meditating upon the aweful hour of his own dissolution, and in what manner he should conduct himself upon that occasion: 'I know not (said he,) whether I should wish to have a friend by me, or have it all between GOD and myself.'

Talking of our feeling for the distresses of others;—JOHNSON. 'Why, Sir, there is much noise made about it, but it is greatly exaggerated. No, Sir, we have a certain degree of feeling to prompt us to do good: more than that, Providence does not intend. It would be misery to no purpose.' BOSWELL. 'But suppose now, Sir, that one of your intimate friends were apprehended for an offence for which he might be hanged.' JOHNSON. 'I should do what I could to bail him, and give him any other assistance; but if he were once fairly hanged, I should not suffer.' BOSWELL. 'Would you eat your dinner that day, Sir?' JOHNSON. 'Yes, Sir; and eat it as if he were eating it with me. Why there's Baretti, who is to be tried for his life to-morrow, friends have risen up for him on every side; yet if he should be hanged, none of them will eat a slice of plumb-pudding the less. Sir, that sympathetic feeling goes a very little way in depressing the mind.'

I told him that I had dined lately at Foote's, who shewed me a letter which he had received from Tom Davies, telling him that he had not been able to sleep from the concern which he felt on account of 'This sad affair of Baretti,' begging of him to try if he could suggest any thing that might be of service; and, at the same time, recommending to him an industrious young man who kept a pickle-shop. JOHNSON. 'Ay, Sir, here you have a specimen of human sympathy; a friend hanged, and a cucumber pickled. We know not whether Baretti or the pickle-man has kept Davies from sleep; nor does he know himself. And as to his not sleeping, Sir: Tom Davies is a very great man; Tom has been upon the stage, and knows how to do those things. I have not been upon the stage and cannot do those things.' BOSWELL. 'I have often blamed myself, Sir, for not feeling for others as sensibly as many say they do.' JOHNSON. 'Sir, don't be duped by them any more. You will find these very feeling people are not very ready to do you good. They *pay* you by *feeling*.'

BOSWELL. 'Foote has a great deal of humour?' JOHNSON. 'Yes, Sir.' BOSWELL. 'He has a singular talent of exhibiting character.' JOHNSON. 'Sir, it is not a talent; it is a vice; it is what others abstain from. It is not comedy, which exhibits the character of a species, as that of a miser gathered from many misers: it is farce, which exhibits individuals.' BOSWELL. 'Did not he think of exhibiting you, Sir?' JOHNSON. 'Sir, fear restrained him; he knew I would have broken his bones. I would have saved him the trouble of cutting off a leg; I would not have left him a leg to cut off.' BOSWELL. 'Pray, Sir, is not Foote an infidel?' JOHNSON. 'I do not know, Sir, that the fellow is an infidel; but if he be an infidel, he is an infidel as a dog is an infidel; that is to say, he has never thought upon the subject.'[1] BOSWELL. 'I suppose, Sir, he has thought superficially, and seized the first notions which occurred to his mind.' JOHNSON. 'Why then, Sir, still he is like a dog, that snatches the piece next him. Did you never observe that dogs have not the power of comparing? A dog will take a small bit of meat as readily as a large, when both are before him.' . . .

He again talked of the passage in Congreve with high commendation, and said, 'Shakspeare never has six lines together without a fault. Perhaps you may find seven, but this does not refute my general assertion. If I come to an orchard, and say there's no fruit here, and then comes a poring man, who finds two apples and three pears, and tells me. "Sir, you are mistaken, I have found both apples and pears," I should laugh at him: what would that be to the purpose?'

BOSWELL. 'What do you think of Dr. Young's *Night Thoughts,* Sir?' JOHNSON. 'Why, Sir, there are very fine things in them.' BOSWELL. 'Is there not less religion in the nation now, Sir, than there was formerly?' JOHNSON. 'I don't know, Sir, that there is.' BOSWELL. 'For instance, there used to be a chaplain in every great family, which we do not find now.' JOHNSON. 'Neither do you find many of the state servants which great families used formerly to have. There is a change of modes in the whole department[2] of life.'

Next day, October 20, he appeared, for the only time I suppose in his life, as a witness in a Court of Justice, being

---

[1] When Mr. Foote was at Edinburgh, he thought fit to entertain a numerous Scotch company, with a great deal of coarse jocularity, at the expense of Dr. Johnson, imagining it would be acceptable. I felt this as not civil to me; but sat very patiently till he had exhausted his merriment on that subject; and then observed, that surely Johnson must be allowed to have some sterling wit, and that I had heard him say a very good thing of Mr. Foote himself. 'Ah, my old friend Sam (cried Foote,) no man says better things; do let us have it.' Upon which I told the above story, which produced a very loud laugh from the company. But I never saw Foote so disconcerted. He looked grave and angry, and entered into a serious refutation of the justice of the remark. 'What, Sir, (said he,) talk thus of a man of liberal education; —a man who for years was at the University of Oxford;—a man who has added sixteen new characters to the English drama of his country!' —B.

[2] The manuscript reads 'deportment.'

called to give evidence to the chracter of Mr. Baretti, who having stabbed a man in the street, was arraigned at the Old Bailey for murder. Never did such a constellation of genius enlighten the aweful Sessions-House, emphatically called JUSTICE HALL; Mr. Burke, Mr. Garrick, Mr. Beauclerk, and Dr. Johnson: and undoubtedly their favourable testimony had due weight with the Court and Jury. Johnson gave his evidence in a slow, deliberate, and distinct manner, which was uncommonly impressive. It is well known that Mr. Baretti was acquitted.

On the 26th of October, we dined together at the Mitre tavern. I found fault with Foote for indulging his talent of ridicule at the expence of his visitors, which I colloquially termed making fools of his company. JOHNSON. 'Why, Sir, when you go to see Foote, you do not go to see a saint: you go to see a man who will be entertained at your house, and then bring you on a publick stage; who will entertain you at his house, for the very purpose of bringing you on a publick stage. Sir, he does not make fools of his company; they whom he exposes are fools already: he only brings them into action.'

Talking of trade, he observed, 'It is a mistaken notion that a vast deal of money is brought into a nation by trade. It is not so. Commodities come from commodities: but trade produces no capital accession of wealth. However, though there should be little profit in money, there is considerable profit in pleasure, as it gives to one nation the productions of another; as we have wines and fruits, and many other foreign articles, brought to us.' BOSWELL. 'Yes, Sir, and there is a profit in pleasure, by its furnishing occupation to such numbers of mankind.' JOHNSON. 'Why, Sir, you cannot call that pleasure to which all are averse, and which none begin but with the hope of leaving off; a thing which men dislike before they have tried it, and when they have tried it.' BOSWELL. 'But, Sir, the mind must be employed, and we grow weary when idle.' JOHNSON. 'That is, Sir, because, others being busy, we want company; but if we were all idle, there would be no growing weary; we should all entertain one another. There is, indeed, this in trade:—it gives men an opportunity of improving their situation. If there were no trade, many who are poor would always remain poor. But no man loves labour for itself.' BOSWELL. 'Yes, Sir, I know a person who does. He is a very laborious Judge,[1] and he loves the labour.' JOHNSON. 'Sir, that is because he loves respect and distinction. Could he have them without labour, he would like it less.' BOSWELL. 'He tells me he likes it for itself.'

[1] Lord Auchinleck.

—'Why, Sir, he fancies so, because he is not accustomed to abstract.'

We went home to his house to tea. Mrs. Williams made it with sufficent dexterity, notwithstanding her blindness, though her manner of satisfying herself that the cups were full enough appeared to me a little aukward; for I fancied she put her finger down a certain way, till she felt the tea touch it.[1] In my first elation at being allowed the privilege of attending Dr. Johnson at his late visits to this lady, which was like being *è secretioribus consiliis*,[2] I willingly drank cup after cup, as if it had been the Heliconian spring. But as the charm of novelty went off, I grew more fastidious; and besides, I discovered that she was of a peevish temper.

There was a pretty large circle this evening. Dr. Johnson was in very good humour, lively, and ready to talk upon all subjects. Mr. Fergusson, the self-taught philosopher, told him of a new-invented machine which went without horses: a man sat in it turned a handle, which worked a spring that drove it forward. 'Then, Sir, (said Johnson,) what is gained is, the man has his choice whether he will move himself alone, or himself and the machine too.' Dominicetti being mentioned, he would not allow him any merit. 'There is nothing in all this boasted system. No, Sir; medicated baths can be no better than warm water: their only effect can be that of tepid moisture.' One of the company[3] took the other side, maintaining that medicines of various sorts, and some too of most powerful effect, are introduced into the human frame by the medium of the pores; and, therefore, when warm water is impregnated with salutiferous substances, it may produce great effects as a bath. This appeared to me very satisfactory. Johnson did not answer it; but talking for victory, and determined to be master of the field, he had recourse to the device which Goldsmith imputed to him in the witty words of one of Cibber's comedies: 'There is no arguing with Johnson; for when his pistol misses fire, he knocks you down with the butt end of it.' He turned to the gentleman, 'Well, Sir, go to Dominicetti, and get thyself fumigated; but be sure that the steam be directed to thy *head*, for *that* is the *peccant part*.' This produced a triumphant roar of laughter from the motley assembly of philosophers, printers, and dependents, male and female.

[1] I have since had reason to think that I was mistaken; for I have been informed by a lady, who was long intimate with her, and likely to be a more accurate observer of such matters, that she had acquired such a niceness of touch, as to know, by the feeling on the outside of the cup, how near it was to being full—B.

[2] 'One of his inner cabinet.'

[3] Boswell.

I know not how so whimsical a thought came into my mind, but I asked, 'If, Sir, you were shut up in a castle, and a newborn child with you, what would you do?' JOHNSON. 'Why, Sir, I should not much like my company.' BOSWELL. 'But would you take the trouble of rearing it?' He seemed, as may well be supposed, unwilling to pursue the subject: but upon my persevering in my question, replied, 'Why yes, Sir, I would; but I must have all conveniencies. If I had no garden, I would make a shed on the roof, and take it there for fresh air. I should feed it, and wash it much, and with warm water to please it, not with cold water to give it pain.' BOSWELL. 'But, Sir, does not heat relax?' JOHNSON. 'Sir, you are not to imagine the water is to be very hot. I would not *coddle* the child. No, Sir, the hardy method of treating children does no good. I'll take you five children from London, who shall cuff five Highland children. Sir, a man bred in London will carry a burthen, or run, or wrestle, as well as a man brought up in the hardiest manner in the country.' BOSWELL. 'Good living, I suppose, makes the Londoners strong.' JOHNSON. 'Why, Sir, I don't know that it does. Our chairmen from Ireland, who are as strong men as any, have been brought up upon potatoes. Quantity makes up for quality.' BOSWELL. 'Would you teach this child that I have furnished you with, any thing?' JOHNSON. 'No, I should not be apt to teach it.' BOSWELL. 'Would not you have a pleasure in teaching it?' JOHNSON. 'No, Sir, I should *not* have a pleasure in teaching it.' BOSWELL. 'Have you not a pleasure in teaching men?—*There* I have you. You have the same pleasure in teaching men, that I should have in teaching children.' JOHNSON. 'Why, something about that.'

BOSWELL. 'Do you think, Sir, that what is called natural affection is born with us? It seems to me to be the effect of habit, or of gratitude for kindness. No child has it for a parent whom it has not seen.' JOHNSON. 'Why, Sir, I think there is an instinctive natural affection in parents towards their children.'

Russia being mentioned as likely to become a great empire, by the rapid increase of population:—JOHNSON. 'Why Sir, I see no prospect of their propagating more. They can have no more children than they can get. I know of no way to make them breed more than they do. It is not from reason and prudence that people marry, but from inclination. A man is poor; he thinks, "I cannot be worse, and so I'll e'en take Peggy."' BOSWELL. 'But have not nations been more populous at one period than another?' JOHNSON. 'Yes, Sir; but that has been owing to the people being less thinned at one period than another, whether by emigrations, war, or pestilence, not by their being more or less prolifick. Births at all times bear the same proportion to the same number of people.' BOSWELL. 'But, to consider the state of our own country;—does not throwing a number of farms into one hand hurt population?' JOHNSON. 'Why no, Sir; the same quantity of food being produced, will be consumed by the same number of mouths, though the people may be disposed of in different ways. We see, if corn be dear, and butchers' meat cheap, the farmers all apply themselves to the raising of corn, till it becomes plentiful and cheap, and then butchers' meat becomes dear; so that an equality is always preserved. No, Sir, let fanciful men do as they will, depend upon it, it is difficult to disturb the system of life.' BOSWELL. 'But, Sir, is it not a very bad thing for landlords to oppress their tenants, by raising their rents?' JOHNSON. 'Very bad. But, Sir, it never can have any general influence; it may distress some individuals. For, consider this: landlords cannot do without tenants. Now tenants will not give more for land, than land is worth. If they can make more of their money by keeping a shop, or any other way, they'll do it, and so oblige landlords to let land come back to a reasonable rent, in order that they may get tenants. Land, in England, is an article of commerce. A tenant who pays his landlord his rent, thinks himself no more obliged to him than you think yourself obliged to a man in whose shop you buy a piece of goods. He knows the landlord does not let him have his land for less than he can get from others, in the same manner as the shopkeeper sells his goods. No shopkeeper sells a yard of ribband for sixpence when seven-pence is the current price.' BOSWELL. 'But, Sir, is it not better that tenants should be dependant on landlords?' JOHNSON. 'Why, Sir, as there are many more tenants than landlords, perhaps, strictly speaking, we should wish not. But if you please you may let your lands cheap, and so get the value, part in money and part in homage. I should agree with you in that.' BOSWELL. 'So, Sir, you laugh at schemes of political improvement.' JOHNSON. 'Why, Sir, most schemes of political improvement are very laughable things.'

He observed, 'Providence has wisely ordered that the more numerous men are, the more difficult it is for them to agree in any thing, and so they are governed. There is no doubt, that if the poor should reason, "We'll be the poor no longer, we'll make the rich take their turn," they could easily do it, were it not that they can't agree. So the common soldiers, though so much more numerous than their officers, are governed by them for the same reason.'

He said, 'Mankind have a strong attachment to the habitations to which they have been accustomed. You see the inhabitants of Norway do not with one consent quit it, and go to some part of America, where there is a mild climate, and where they may have the same produce from land, with the tenth part of the labour. No, Sir; their affection for their old dwellings, and the terrour of general change, keep them at home. Thus, we see many of the finest spots in the world thinly inhabited, and many rugged spots well inhabited.'

The London Chronicle, which was the only news-paper he constantly took in, being brought, the office of reading it aloud was assigned to me. I was diverted by his impatience. He made me pass over so many parts of it, that my task was very easy. He would not suffer one of the petitions to the King about the Middlesex election to be read.

I had hired a Bohemian as my servant while I remained in London, and being much pleased with him, I asked Dr. Johnson whether his being a Roman Catholick should prevent my taking him with me to Scotland. JOHNSON. 'Why no, Sir, if *he* has no objection, you can have none.' BOSWELL. 'So, Sir you are no great enemy to the Roman Catholick religion.' JOHNSON. 'No more, Sir, than to the Presbyterian religion.' BOSWELL. 'You are joking.' JOHNSON. 'No, Sir, I really think so. Nay, Sir, of the two, I prefer the Popish.' BOSWELL. 'How so, Sir?' JOHNSON. 'Why, Sir, the Presbyterians have no church, no apostolical ordination.' BOSWELL. 'And do you think that absolutely essential, Sir?' JOHNSON. 'Why, Sir, as it was an apostolical institution, I think it is dangerous to be without it. And, Sir, the Presbyterians have no public worship: they have no form of prayer in which they know they are to join. They go to hear a man pray, and are to judge whether they will join with him.' BOSWELL. 'But, Sir, their doctrine is the same with that of the Church of England. Their confession of faith, and the thirty-nine articles, contain the same points, even the doctrine of predestination,' JOHNSON. 'Why yes, Sir, predestination was a part of the clamour of the times, so it is mentioned in our articles, but with as little positiveness as could be.' BOSWELL. 'Is it necessary, Sir, to believe all the thirty-nine articles?' JOHNSON. 'Why, Sir, that is a question which has been much agitated. Some have thought it necessary that they should all be believed; others have considered them to be only articles of peace, that is to say, you are not to preach against them.' BOSWELL. 'It appears to me, Sir, that predestination, or what is equivalent to it, cannot be avoided, if we hold an universal prescience in the Deity.' JOHNSON. 'Why, Sir, does not GOD every day see things going on without preventing them?' BOSWELL. 'True, Sir; but if a thing be *certainly* foreseen, it must be fixed, and cannot happen otherwise; and if we apply this consideration to the human mind, there is no free will, nor do I see how prayer can be of any avail.' He mentioned Dr. Clarke, and Bishop Bramhall on *Liberty and Necessity,* and bid me read South's *Sermons on Prayer;* but avoided the question which has excruciated philosophers and divines, beyond any other. I did not press it further, when I perceived that he was displeased, and shrunk from any abridgement of an attribute usually ascribed to the Divinity, however irreconcileable in its full extent with the grand system of moral government. His supposed orthodoxy here cramped the vigorous powers of his understanding. He was confined by a chain which early imagination and long habit made him think massy and strong, but which, had he ventured to try, he could at once have snapt asunder.

I proceeded: 'What do you think, Sir, of Purgatory, as believed by the Roman Catholicks?' JOHNSON. 'Why, Sir, it is a very harmless doctrine. They are of opinion that the generality of mankind are neither so obstinately wicked as to deserve everlasting punishment, nor so good as to merit being admitted into the society of blessed spirits; and therefore that God is graciously pleased to allow of a middle state, where they may be purified by certain degrees of suffering. You see, Sir, there is nothing unreasonable in this.' BOSWELL. 'But then, Sir, their masses for the dead?' JOHNSON. 'Why, Sir, if it be once established that there are souls in purgatory, it is as proper to pray for *them,* as for our brethren of mankind who are yet in this life.' BOSWELL. 'The idolatry of the Mass?' JOHNSON. 'Sir, there is no idolatry in the Mass. They believe GOD to be there, and they adore him.' BOSWELL. 'The worship of Saints?' JOHNSON. 'Sir, they do not worship saints; they invoke them; they only ask their prayers. I am talking all this time of the *doctrines* of the Church of Rome. I grant you that in *practice,* Purgatory is made a lucrative imposition, and that the people do become idolatrous as they recommend themselves to the tutelary protection of particular saints. I think their giving the sacrament only in one kind is criminal, because it is contrary to the express institution of CHRIST, and I wonder how the Council of Trent admitted it.' BOSWELL. 'Confession?' JOHNSON. 'Why, I don't know but that is a good thing. The scripture says, "Confess your faults one to another," and the priests confess as well as the laity. Then it must be considered that their absolution is only upon repentance, and often upon penance also. You think your sins may be forgiven without penance, upon repentance alone.'

I thus ventured to mention all the common objections against the Roman Catholick Church, that I might hear so great a man upon them. What he said is here accurately recorded. But it is not improbable that if one had taken the other side he might have reasoned differently.

I must however mention, that he had a respect for 'the old religion,' as the mild Melancthon called that of the Roman Catholick Church, even while he was exerting himself for its reformation in some particulars. Sir William Scott informs me, that he heard Johnson say, 'A man who is converted from Protestantism to Popery may be sincere: he parts with nothing: he is only superadding to what he already had. But a convert from Popery to Protestantism gives up so much of what he has held as sacred as any thing that he retains; there is so much *laceration of mind* in such a conversion, that it can hardly be sincere and lasting.' The truth of this reflection may be confirmed by many and eminent instances, some of which will occur to most of my readers.

When we were alone, I introduced the subject of death, and endeavoured to maintain that the fear of it might be got over. I told him that David Hume said to me, he was no more uneasy to think he should *not be* after this life, than that he *had not been* before he began to exist. JOHNSON. 'Sir, if he really thinks so, his perceptions are disturbed; he is mad: if he does not think so, he lies. He may tell you, he holds his finger in the flame of a candle, without feeling pain; would you believe him? When he dies, he at least gives up all he has.' BOSWELL. 'Foote, Sir, told me, that when he was very ill he was not afraid to die.' JOHNSON. 'It is not true, Sir. Hold a pistol to Foote's breast, or to Hume's breast, and threaten to kill them, and you'll see how they behave.' BOSWELL. 'But may we not fortify our minds for the approach of death?' Here I am sensible I was in the wrong, to bring before his view what he ever looked upon with horrour; for although when in a celestial frame, in his *Vanity of human Wishes*, he has supposed death to be 'kind Nature's signal for retreat,' from this state of being to 'a happier seat,' his thoughts upon this aweful change were in general full of dismal apprehensions. His mind resembled the vast amphitheatre, the Colisæum at Rome. In the centre stood his judgement, which, like a mighty gladiator, combated those apprehensions that, like the wild beasts of the *Arena,* were all around in cells, ready to be let out upon him. After a conflict, he drove them back into their dens; but not killing them, they were still assailing him. To my question, whether we might not fortify our minds for the approach of death, he answered, in a passion, 'No, Sir, let it alone. It matters not

216

how a man dies, but how he lives. The act of dying is not of importance, it lasts so short a time.' He added, (with an earnest look,) 'A man knows it must be so, and submits. It will do him no good to whine.'

I attempted to continue the conversation. He was so provoked, that he said, 'Give us no more of this;' and was thrown into such a state of agitation, that he expressed himself in a way that alarmed and distressed me; shewed an impatience that I should leave him, and when I was going away, called to me sternly, 'Don't let us meet to-morrow.'

I went home exceedingly uneasy. All the harsh observations which I had ever heard made upon his character, crowded into my mind; and I seemed to myself like the man who had put his head into the lion's mouth a great many times with perfect safety, but at last had it bit off.

Next morning I sent him a note, stating, that I might have been in the wrong, but it was not intentionally; he was therefore, I could not help thinking, too severe upon me. That notwithstanding our agreement not to meet that day, I would call on him in my way to the city, and stay five minutes by my watch. 'You are, (said I,) in my mind, since last night, surrounded with cloud and storm. Let me have a glimpse of sunshine, and go about my affairs in serenity and chearfulness.'

Upon entering his study, I was glad that he was not alone, which would have made our meeting more awkward. There were with him, Mr. Steevens and Mr. Tyers, both of whom I now saw for the first time. My note had, on his own reflection, softened him, for he received me very complacently; so that I unexpectedly found myself at ease, and joined in the conversation. . . .

Johnson spoke unfavourably of a certain pretty voluminous authour, saying, 'He used to write anonymous books, and then other books commending those books, in which there was something of rascality.'

I whispered him, 'Well, Sir, you are now in good humour.' JOHNSON. 'Yes, Sir.' I was going to leave him, and had got as far as the staircase. He stopped me, and smiling, said, 'Get you gone *in;*' a curious mode of inviting me to stay, which I accordingly did for some time longer.

This little incidental quarrel and reconciliation, which, perhaps, I may be thought to have detailed too minutely, must be esteemed as one of many proofs which his friends had, that though he might be charged with *bad humour* at times, he was always a *good-natured* man; and I have heard Sir Joshua Reynolds, a nice and delicate observer of manners, particularly remark, that when upon any occasion Johnson had been rough to any person in company, he took the first opportunity of reconciliation, by drinking to him, or addressing his discourse to him; but if he found his dignified indirect overtures sullenly neglected, he was quite indifferent, and considered himself as having done all that he ought to do, and the other as now in the wrong.

Being to set out for Scotland on the 10th of November, I wrote to him at Streatham, begging that he would meet me in town on the 9th; but if this should be very inconvenient to him, I would go thither. His answer was as follows:—

'To JAMES BOSWELL, Esq.

'DEAR SIR,—Upon balancing the inconveniencies of both parties, I find it will less incommode you to spend your night here, than me to come to town. I wish to see you, and am ordered by the lady of this house to invite you hither. Whether you can come or not, I shall not have any occasion of writing to you again before your marriage, and therefore tell you now, that with great sincerity I wish you happiness. I am, dear Sir, your most affectionate humble servant,

'Nov. 9, 1769.'   'SAM. JOHNSON.'

I was detained in town till it was too late on the ninth, so went to him early on the morning of the tenth of November. 'Now (said he,) that you are going to marry, do not expect more from life, than life will afford. You may often find yourself out of humour, and you may often think your wife not studious enough to please you; and yet you may have reason to consider yourself as upon the whole very happily married.'

Talking of marriage in general, he observed, 'Our marriage service is too refined. It is calculated only for the best kind of marriages; whereas, we should have a form for matches of convenience, of which there are many.' He agreed with me that there was no absolute necessity for having the marriage ceremony performed by a regular clergyman, for this was not commanded in scripture.

I was volatile enough to repeat to him a little epigrammatick song of mine, on matrimony, which Mr. Garrick had a few days before procured to be set to musick by the very ingenious Mr. Dibden.

'A MATRIMONIAL THOUGHT.

'IN the blithe days of honey-moon,
    With Kate's allurements smitten,
I lov'd her late, I lov'd her soon,
    And call'd her dearest kitten.

'But now my kitten's grown a cat,
    And cross like other wives,
O! by my soul, my honest Mat,
    I fear she has nine lives.'

My illustrious friend said, 'It is very well, Sir; but you should not swear.' Upon which I altered 'O! by my soul,' to 'Alas, alas!'

He was so good as to accompany me to London, and see me into the post-chaise which was to carry me on my road to Scotland. And sure I am, that, however inconsiderable many of the particulars recorded at this time may appear to some, they will be esteemed by the best part of my readers as genuine traits of his character, contributing together to give a full, fair, and distinct view of it.

1770: ÆTAT. 61.]—IN 1770 he published a political pamphlet, entitled *The False Alarm*, intended to justify the conduct of ministry and their majority in the House of Commons, for having virtually assumed it as an axiom, that the expulsion of a Member of Parliament was equivalent to exclusion, and thus having declared Colonel Lutterel to be duly elected for the county of Middlesex, notwithstanding Mr. Wilkes had a great majority of votes. This being justly considered as a gross violation of the right of election, an alarm for the constitution extended itself all over the kingdom. To prove this alarm to be false, was the purpose of Johnson's pamphlet; but even his vast powers were inadequate to cope with constitutional truth and reason, and his argument failed of effect; and the House of Commons have since expunged the offensive resolution from their Journals. That the House of Commons might have expelled Mr. Wilkes repeatedly, and as often as he should be re-chosen, was not denied; but incapacitation cannot be but by an act of the whole legislature. It was wonderful to see how a prejudice in favour of government in general, and an aversion to popular clamour, could blind and contract such an understanding as Johnson's, in this particular case; yet the wit, the sarcasm, the eloquent vivacity which this pamphlet displayed, made it be read with great avidity at the time, and it will ever be read with pleasure, for the sake of its composition. That it endeavoured to infuse a narcotick indifference, as to publick concerns, into the minds of the people, and that it broke out sometimes into an extreme coarseness of contemptuous abuse, is but too evident. . . .

The following admirable minute made by him describes so well his own state, and that of numbers to whom self-examination is habitual, that I cannot omit it:—

'June 1, 1770. Every man naturally persuades himself that he can keep his resolutions, nor is he convinced of his imbecility but by length of time and frequency of experiment. This opinion of our own constancy is so prevalent, that we always despise him who suffers his general and settled purpose to be overpowered by an occasional desire. They, therefore, whom frequent failures have made desperate, cease to form resolutions; and they who are become cunning, do not tell them. Those who do not make them are very few, but of their effect little is perceived; for scarcely any man persists in a course of life planned by choice, but as he is restrained from deviation by some external power. He who may live as he will, seldom lives long in the observation of his own rules.' . . .

During this year there was a total cessation of all correspondence between Dr. Johnson and me, without any coldness on either side, but merely from procrastination, continued from day to day; and as I was not in London, I had no opportunity of enjoying his company and recording his conversation. To supply this blank, I shall present my readers with some *Collectanea,* obligingly furnished to me by the Rev. Dr. Maxwell, of Falkland, in Ireland, some time assistant preacher at the Temple, and for many years the social friend of Johnson, who spoke of him with a very kind regard.

'My acquaintance with that great and venerable character commenced in the year 1754. I was introduced to him by Mr. Grierson, his Majesty's printer at Dublin, a gentleman of uncommon learning, and great wit and vivacity. Mr. Grierson died in Germany, at the age of twenty-seven. Dr. Johnson highly respected his abilities, and often observed that he possessed more extensive knowledge than any man of his years he had ever known. His industry was equal to his talents; and he particularly excelled in every species of philological learning, and was, perhaps, the best critick of the age he lived in.

'I must always remember with gratitude my obligation to Mr. Grierson, for the honour and happiness of Dr. Johnson's acquaintance and friendship, which continued uninterrupted and undiminished to his death: a connection, that was at once the pride and happiness of my life.

'What pity it is, that so much wit and good sense as he continually exhibited in conversation, should perish unrecorded! Few persons quitted his company without perceiving themselves wiser and better than they were before. On serious subjects he flashed the most interesting conviction upon his auditors; and upon lighter topicks, you might have supposed —*Albano musas de monte locutas.*[1]

'Though I can hope to add but little to the celebrity of so

[1] 'The Muses speaking from the Alban mount.' Horace, *Epistles,* II. i. 26.

exalted a character, by any communications I can furnish, yet out of pure respect to his memory, I will venture to transmit to you some anecdotes concerning him, which fell under my own observation. The very *minutiæ* of such a character must be interesting, and may be compared to the filings of diamonds.

'In politicks he was deemed a Tory, but certainly was not so in the obnoxious or party sense of the term; for while he asserted the legal and salutary prerogatives of the crown, he no less respected the constitutional liberties of the people. Whiggism, at the time of the Revolution, he said, was accompanied with certain principles; but latterly, as a mere party distinction under Walpole and the Pelhams, was no better than the politicks of stock-jobbers, and the religion of infidels. . . .

'The inseparable imperfection annexed to all human governments consisted, he said, in not being able to create a sufficient fund of virtue and principle to carry the laws into due and effectual execution. Wisdom might plan, but virtue alone could execute. And where could sufficient virtue be found? A variety of delegated, and often discretionary, powers must be entrusted somewhere; which, if not governed by integrity and conscience, would necessarily be abused, till at last the constable would sell his for a shilling.

'This excellent person was sometimes charged with abetting slavish and arbitrary principles of government. Nothing in my opinion could be a grosser calumny and misrepresentation; for how can it be rationally supposed, that he should adopt such pernicious and absurd opinions, who supported his philosophical character with so much dignity, was extremely jealous of his personal liberty and independence, and could not brook the smallest appearance of neglect or insult, even from the highest personages?

'But let us view him in some instances of more familiar life.

'His general mode of life, during my acquaintance, seemed to be pretty uniform. About twelve o'clock I commonly visited him, and frequently found him in bed, or declaiming over his tea, which he drank very plentifully. He generally had a levee of morning visitors, chiefly men of letters; Hawkesworth, Goldsmith, Murphy, Langton, Steevens, Beauclerk, &c. &c., and sometimes learned ladies, particularly I remember a French lady of wit and fashion doing him the honour of a visit. He seemed to me to be considered as a kind of publick oracle, whom every body thought they had a right to visit and consult; and doubtless they were well rewarded. I never could discover how he found time for his compositions.

He declaimed all the morning, then went to dinner at a tavern, where he commonly staid late, and then drank his tea at some friend's house, over which he loitered a great while, but seldom took supper. I fancy he must have read and wrote chiefly in the night, for I can scarcely recollect that he ever refused going with me to a tavern, and he often went to Ranelagh, which he deemed a place of innocent recreation.

'He frequently gave all the silver in his pocket to the poor, who watched him, between his house and the tavern where he dined. He walked the streets at all hours, and said he was never robbed, for the rogues knew he had little money, nor had the appearance of having much.

'Though the most accessible and communicative man alive, yet when he suspected he was invited to be exhibited, he constantly spurned the invitation.

'Two young women from Staffordshire visited him when I was present, to consult him on the subject of Methodism, to which they were inclined. "Come, (said he,) you pretty fools, dine with Maxwell and me at the Mitre, and we will talk over that subject;' which they did, and after dinner he took one of them upon his knee, and fondled her for half an hour together.

'Upon a vist to me at a country lodging near Twickenham, he asked what sort of society I had there. I told him, but indifferent; as they chiefly consisted of opulent traders, retired from business. He said, he never much liked that class of people; "For, Sir, (said he,) they have lost the civility of tradesmen, without acquiring the manners of gentlemen."

'Johnson was much attached to London: he observed, that a man stored his mind better there, than any where else; and that in remote situations a man's body might be feasted, but his mind was starved, and his faculties apt to degenerate, from want of exercise and competition. No place, (he said,) cured a man's vanity or arrogance so well as London; for as no man was either great or good *per se,* but as compared with others not so good or great, he was sure to find in the metropolis many his equals, and some his superiours. He observed, that a man in London was in less danger of falling in love indiscreetly, than any where else; for there the difficulty of deciding between the conflicting pretensions of a vast variety of objects, kept him safe. He told me, that he had frequently been offered country preferment, if he would consent to take orders; but he could not leave the improved society of the capital, or consent to exchange the exhilarating joys and splendid decorations of publick life, for the obscurity, insipidity, and uniformity of remote situations. . . .

'He loved, he said, the old black letter books; they were

rich in matter, though their style was inelegant; wonderfully so, considering how conversant the writers were with the best models of antiquity.

'Burton's *Anatomy of Melancholy,* he said, was the only book that ever took him out of bed two hours sooner than he wished to rise.

'He frequently exhorted me to set about writing a History of Ireland, and archly remarked, there had been some good Irish writers, and that one Irishman might at least aspire to be equal to another. He had great compassion for the miseries and distresses of the Irish nation, particularly the Papists; and severely reprobated the barbarous debilitating policy of the British government, which, he said, was the most detestable mode of persecution. To a gentleman, who hinted such policy might be necessary to support the authority of the English government, he replied by saying, "Let the authority of the English government perish, rather than be maintained by iniquity. Better would it be to restrain the turbulence of the natives by the authority of the sword, and to make them amenable to law and justice by an effectual and vigorous police, than to grind them to powder by all manner of disabilities and incapacities. Better (said he,) to hang or drown people at once, than by an unrelenting persecution to beggar and starve them." The moderation and humanity of the present times have, in some measure, justified the wisdom of his observations.

'Dr. Johnson was often accused of prejudices, nay, antipathy, with regard to the natives of Scotland. Surely, so illiberal a prejudice never entered his mind: and it is well known, many natives of that respectable country possessed a large share in his esteem; nor were any of them ever excluded from his good offices, as far as opportunity permitted. True it is, he considered the Scotch, nationally, as a crafty, designing people, eagerly attentive to their own interest, and too apt to overlook the claims and pretentions of other people. "While they confine their benevolence, in a manner, exclusively to those of their own country, they expect to share in the good offices of other people. Now (said Johnson,) this principle is either right or wrong; if right, we should do well to imitate such conduct; if wrong, we cannot too much detest it."

'Being solicited to compose a funeral sermon for the daughter of a tradesman, he naturally enquired into the character of the deceased; and being told she was remarkable for her humility and condescension to inferiours, he observed, that those were very laudable qualities, but it might not be so easy to discover who the lady's inferiours were.

'Of a certain player[1] he remarked, that his conversation usually threatened and announced more than it performed; that he fed you with a continual renovation of hope, to end in a constant succession of disappointment.

'When exasperated by contradiction, he was apt to treat his opponents with too much acrimony: as, "Sir, you don't see your way through that question:"—"Sir, you talk the language of ignorance." On my observing to him that a certain gentleman had remained silent the whole evening, in the midst of a very brilliant and learned society, "Sir, (said he,) the conversation overflowed, and drowned him."

'His philosophy, though austere and solemn, was by no means morose and cynical, and never blunted the laudable sensibilities of his character, or exempted him from the influence of the tender passions. Want of tenderness, he always alledged, was want of parts, and was no less a proof of stupidity than depravity. . . .

'Of the passion of love he remarked, that its violence and ill effects were much exaggerated; for who knows any real sufferings on that head, more than from the exorbitancy of any other passion?

'He much commended Law's *Serious Call*, which he said was the finest piece of hortatory theology in any language. "Law, (said he,) fell latterly into the reveries of Jacob Behmen, whom Law alledged to have been somewhat in the same state with St. Paul, and to have seen *unutterable things*. Were it even so, (said Johnson,) Jacob would have resembled St. Paul still more, by not attempting to utter them." . . .

'He was much affected by the death of his mother, and wrote to me to come and assist him to compose his mind, which indeed I found extremely agitated. He lamented that all serious and religious conversation was banished from the society of men, and yet great advantages might be derived from it. All acknowledged, he said, what hardly any body practised, the obligation we were under of making the concerns of eternity the governing principles of our lives. Every man, he observed, at last wishes for retreat: he sees his expectations frustrated in the world, and begins to wean himself from it, and to prepare for everlasting separation.

'He observed, that the influence of London now extended every where, and that from all manner of communication being opened, there shortly would be no remains of the ancient simplicity, or places of cheap retreat to be found.

'He was no admirer of blank-verse, and said it always failed, unless sustained by the dignity of the subject. In

[1] Thomas Sheridan.

blank-verse, he said, the language suffered more distortion, to keep it out of prose, than any inconvenience or limitation to be apprehended from the shackles and circumscription of rhyme.

'He reproved me once for saying grace without mention of the name of our LORD JESUS CHRIST, and hoped in future I would be more mindful of the apostolical injunction.

'He refused to go out of a room before me at Mr. Langton's house, saying, he hoped he knew his rank better than to presume to take place of a Doctor in Divinity. I mention such little anecdotes, merely to shew the peculiar turn and habit of his mind.

'He used frequently to observe, that there was more to be endured than enjoyed, in the general condition of human life; and frequently quoted those lines of Dryden:

"Strange cozenage! none would live past years again,
 Yet all hope pleasure from what still remain."

For his part, he said, he never passed that week in his life which he would wish to repeat, were an angel to make the proposal to him.

'He was of opinion, that the English nation cultivated both their soil and their reason better than any other people: but admitted that the French, though not the highest, perhaps, in any department of literature, yet in every department were very high. Intellectual pre-eminence, he observed, was the highest superiority; and that every nation derived their highest reputation from the splendour and dignity of their writers. Voltaire, he said, was a good narrator, and that his principal merit consisted in a happy selection and arrangement of circumstances.

'Speaking of the French novels, compared with Richardson's, he said, they might be pretty baubles, but a wren was not an eagle.

'In a Latin conversation with the Père Boscovitch, at the house of Mrs. Cholmondeley, I heard him maintain the superiority of Sir Isaac Newton over all foreign philosophers, with a dignity and eloquence that surprized that learned foreigner. It being observed to him, that a rage for every thing English prevailed much in France after Lord Chatham's glorious war, he said, he did not wonder at it, for that we had drubbed those fellows into a proper reverence for us, and that their national petulance required periodical chastisement.

'Lord Lyttleton's Dialogues he deemed a nugatory performance. "That man, (said he,) sat down to write a book, to tell the world what the world had all his life been telling him."

'Somebody observing that the Scotch Highlanders, in the year 1745, had made surprising efforts, considering their numerous wants and disadvantages: "Yes, Sir, (said he,) their wants were numerous; but you have not mentioned the greatest of them all,—the want of law."

'Speaking of the *inward light*, to which some methodists pretended, he said, it was a principle utterly incompatible with social or civil security. "If a man (said he,) pretends to a principle of action of which I can know nothing, nay, not so much as that he has it, but only that he pretends to it; how can I tell what that person may be prompted to do? When a person professes to be governed by a written ascertained law, I can then know where to find him."

'The poem of *Fingal*, he said, was a mere unconnected rhapsody, a tiresome repetition of the same images. "In vain shall we look for the *lucidus ordo*,[1] where there is neither end or object, design or moral, *nec certa recurrit imago*." [2]

'Being asked by a young nobleman, what was become of the gallantry and military spirit of the old English nobility, he replied, "Why, my Lord, I'll tell you what is become of it; it is gone into the city to look for a fortune."

'Speaking of a dull tiresome fellow, whom he chanced to meet, he said, "That fellow seems to me to possess but one idea, and that is a wrong one."

'Much enquiry having been made concerning a gentleman, who had quitted a company where Johnson was, and no information being obtained; at last Johnson observed, that "he did not care to speak ill of any man behind his back, but he believed the gentleman was an *attorney*."

'He spoke with much contempt of the notice taken of Woodhouse, the poetical shoemaker. He said, it was all vanity and childishness: and that such objects were, to those who patronised them, mere mirrours of their own superiority. "They had better (said he,) furnish the man with good implements for his trade, than raise subscriptions for his poems. He may make an excellent shoemaker, but can never make a good poet. A school-boy's exercise may be a pretty thing for a school-boy; but it is no treat for a man." . . .

'Speaking of Arthur Murphy, whom he very much loved, "I don't know (said he,) that Arthur can be classed with the very first dramatick writers; yet at present I doubt much whether we have any thing superiour to Arthur."

'Speaking of the national debt, he said, it was an idle dream to suppose that the country could sink under it. Let

[1] 'Clearness of order'. Horace, *Art of Poetry*, 1. 41.
[2] 'No definite image recurs'.

the public creditors be ever so clamorous, the interest of millions must ever prevail over that of thousands. . . .

'Johnson observed, that so many objections might be made to every thing, that nothing could overcome them but the necessity of doing something. No man would be of any profession, as simply opposed to not being of it: but every one must do something.

'He remarked, that a London parish was a very comfortless thing; for the clergyman seldom knew the face of one out of ten of his parishioners. . . .

'A gentleman who had been very unhappy in marriage, married immediately after his wife died: Johnson said, it was the triumph of hope over experience.

'He observed, that a man of sense and education should meet a suitable companion in a wife. It was a miserable thing when the conversation could only be such as, whether the mutton should be boiled or roasted, and probably a dispute about that.

'He did not approve of late marriages, observing, that more was lost in point of time, than compensated for by any possible advantages. Even ill assorted marriages were preferable to cheerless celibacy.

'Of old Sheridan he remarked, that he neither wanted parts nor literature; but that his vanity and Quixotism obscured his merits.

'He said, foppery was never cured; it was the bad stamina of the mind, which, like those of the body, were never rectified: once a coxcomb, and always a coxcomb.

'Being told that Gilbert Cowper called him the Caliban of literature; "Well, (said he,) I must dub him the Punchinello." . . .

'To find a substitution for violated morality, he said, was the leading feature in all perversions of religion. . . .

'He observed, "it was a most mortifying reflexion for any man to consider, *what he had done*, compared with what *he might have done*."

'He said few people had intellectual resources sufficient to forego the pleasures of wine. They could not otherwise contrive how to fill the interval between dinner and supper.

'He went with me, one Sunday, to hear my old Master, Gregory Sharpe, preach at the Temple. In the prefatory prayer, Sharpe ranted about *Liberty*, as a blessing most fervently to be implored, and its continuance prayed for. Johnson observed, that our *liberty* was in no sort of danger:—he would have done much better, to pray against our *licentiousness*.

'One evening at Mrs. Montagu's, where a splendid company was assembled, consisting of the most eminent literary characters, I thought he seemed highly pleased with the respect and attention that were shewn him, and asked him on our return home if he was not highly *gratified* by his visit: "No, Sir, (said he,) not highly *gratified;* yet I do not recollect to have passed many evenings *with fewer objections."*

Though of no high extraction himself, he had much respect for birth and family, especially among ladies. He said, "adventitious accomplishments may be possessed by all ranks; but one may easily distinguish the *born gentlewoman."*

'He said, "the poor in England were better provided for, than in any other country of the same extent: he did not mean little Cantons, or petty Republicks. Where a great proportion of the people (said he,) are suffered to languish in helpless misery, that country must be ill policed, and wretchedly governed: a decent provision for the poor is the true test of civilization.—Gentlemen of education, he observed, were pretty much the same in all countries; the condition of the lower orders, the poor especially, was the true mark of national discrimination."

'When the corn laws were in agitation in Ireland, by which that country has been enabled not only to feed itself, but to export corn to a large amount; Sir Thomas Robinson observed, that those laws might be prejudicial to the corn-trade of England. "Sir Thomas, (said he,) you talk the language of a savage: what, Sir? would you prevent any people from feeding themselves, if by any honest means they can do it?"

'It being mentioned, that Garrick assisted Dr. Brown, the authour of the *Estimate,* in some dramatick composition, "No, Sir, (said Johnson,) he would no more suffer Garrick to write a line in his play, than he would suffer him to mount his pulpit."

'Speaking of Burke, he said, "It was commonly observed, he spoke too often in parliament; but nobody could say he did not speak well, though too frequently and too familiarly."

'Speaking of economy, he remarked, it was hardly worth while to save anxiously twenty pounds a year. If a man could save to that degree, so as to enable him to assume a different rank in society, then indeed, it might answer some purpose.

'He observed, a principal source of erroneous judgement was, viewing things partially and only on *one side:* as for instance, *fortune-hunters,* when they contemplated the fortunes *singly* and *separately,* it was a dazzling and tempting object; but when they came to possess the wives and their fortunes *together,* they began to suspect that they had not made quite so good a bargain.

'Speaking of the late Duke of Northumberland living very magnificently when Lord Lieutenant of Ireland, somebody remarked it would be difficult to find a suitable successor to him: then exclaimed Johnson, *he is only fit to succeed him-self.*

'He advised me, if possible, to have a good orchard. He knew, he said, a clergyman of small income, who brought up a family very reputably which he chiefly fed with apple dumplins. . . .

'Speaking of a certain Prelate, who exerted himself very laudably in building churches and parsonage-houses; "however, said he, I do not find that he is esteemed a man of much professional learning, or a liberal patron of it;—yet, it is well, where a man possesses any strong positive excellence.—Few have all kinds of merit belonging to their character. We must not examine matters too deeply—No, Sir, a *fallible being will fail some-where.*"

'Talking of the Irish clergy, he said, Swift was a man of great parts, and the instrument of much good to his country. —Berkeley was a profound scholar, as well as a man of fine imagination; but Usher, he said, was the great luminary of the Irish church; and a greater, he added, no church could boast of; at least in modern times.

'We dined *tête à tête* at the Mitre, as I was preparing to return to Ireland, after an absence of many years. I regretted much leaving London, where I had formed many agreeable connexions: "Sir, (said he,) I don't wonder at it; no man, fond of letters, leaves London without regret. But remember, Sir, you have seen and enjoyed a great deal;—you have seen life in its highest decorations, and the world has nothing new to exhibit. No man is so well qualified to leave publick life as he who has long tried it and known it well. We are always hankering after untried situations, and imagining greater felicity from them than they can afford. No, Sir, knowledge and virtue may be acquired in all countries, and your local consequence will make you some amends for the intellectual gratifications you relinquish." ' . . .

1771: ÆTAT. 62.]—IN 1771 he published another political pamphlet, entitled *Thoughts on the late Transactions respecting Falkland's Islands,* in which, upon materials furnished to him by ministry, and upon general topicks expanded in his richest style, he successfully endeavoured to persuade the nation that it was wise and laudable to suffer the question of right to remain undecided, rather than involve our country in another war. It has been suggested by some, with what truth I shall not take upon me to decide, that he rated the consequence of those islands to Great-Britain too low. But however this may be, every humane mind must surely applaud the earnestness with which he averted the calamity of war; a calamity so dreadful, that it is astonishing how civilised, nay, Christian nations, can deliberately continue to renew it. His description of its miseries in this pamphlet, is one of the finest pieces of eloquence in the English language. Upon this occasion, too, we find Johnson lashing the party in opposition with unbounded severity, and making the fullest use of what he ever reckoned a most effectual argumentative instrument, —contempt. His character of their very able mysterious champion, JUNIUS, is executed with all the force of his genius, and finished with the highest care. He seems to have exulted in sallying forth to single combat against the boasted and formidable hero, who bade defiance to 'principalities and powers, and the rulers of this world.' . . .

Mr. Strahan, the printer, who had been long in intimacy with Johnson, in the course of his literary labours, who was at once his friendly agent in receiving his pension for him, and his banker in supplying him with money when he wanted it; who was himself now a Member of Parliament, and who loved much to be employed in political negociation; thought he should do eminent service both to government and Johnson, if he could be the means of his getting a seat in the House of Commons. With this view, he wrote a letter to one of the Secretaries of the Treasury.[1]

This recommendation, we know, was not effectual; but how, or for what reason, can only be conjectured. It is not to be believed that Mr. Strahan would have applied, unless Johnson had approved of it. I never heard him mention the subject; but at a later period of his life, when Sir Joshua Reynolds told him that Mr. Edmund Burke had said, that if he had come early into parliament, he certainly would have been the greatest speaker that ever was there, Johnson exclaimed, 'I should like to try my hand now.'

It has been much agitated among his friends and others, whether he would have been a powerful speaker in Parliament, had he been brought in when advanced in life. I am inclined to think that his extensive knowledge, his quickness and force of mind, his vivacity and richness of expression, his wit and humour, and above all his poignancy of sarcasm, would have had great effect in a popular assembly; and that the magnitude of his figure, and striking peculiarity of his manner, would have aided the effect. But I remember it was observed by Mr. Flood, that Johnson, having been long used to sententious brevity and the short flights of conversation, might have failed in that continued and expanded kind of argument, which is requisite in stating complicated matters in publick speaking; and as a proof of this he mentioned the supposed speeches in Parliament written by him for the magazine, none of which, in his opinion, were at all like real de-

[1] Omitted here.

bates. The opinion of one who was himself so eminent an orator, must be allowed to have great weight. It was confirmed by Sir William Scott, who mentioned that Johnson had told him that he had several times tried to speak in the Society of Arts and Sciences, but 'had found he could not get on.' From Mr. William Gerrard Hamilton I have heard that Johnson, when observing to him that it was prudent for a man who had not been accustomed to speak in publick, to begin his speech in as simple a manner as possible, acknowledged that he rose in that society to deliver a speech which he had prepared; 'but (said he,) all my flowers of oratory forsook me.' I however cannot help wishing, that he *had* 'tried his hand' in Parliament; and I wonder that ministry did not make the experiment. . . .

In his religious record of this year, we observe that he was better than usual, both in body and mind, and better satisfied with the regularity of his conduct. But he is still 'trying his ways' too rigorously. He charges himself with not rising early enough; yet he mentions what was surely a sufficient excuse for this, supposing it to be a duty seriously required, as he all his life appears to have thought it. 'One great hindrance is want of rest; my nocturnal complaints grow less troublesome towards morning; and I am tempted to repair the deficiencies of the night.' Alas! how hard would it be if this indulgence were to be imputed to a sick man as a crime. In his retrospect on the following Easter-Eve, he says, 'When I review the last year, I am able to recollect so little done, that shame and sorrow, though perhaps too weakly, come upon me.' Had he been judging of any one else in the same circumstances, how clear would he have been on the favourable side. How very difficult, and in my opinion almost constitutionally impossible it was for him to be raised early, even by the strongest resolutions, appears from a note in one of his little paper-books, (containing words arranged for his *Dictionary*,) written, I suppose, about 1753: 'I do not remember that since I left Oxford I ever rose early by mere choice, but once or twice at Edial, and two or three times for the *Rambler*.' I think he had fair ground enough to have quieted his mind on this subject, by concluding that he was physically incapable of what is at best but a commodious regulation.

In 1772 he was altogether quiescent as an authour; but it will be found, from the various evidences which I shall bring together, that his mind was acute, lively, and vigorous. . . .

On the 21st of March, I was happy to find myself again in my friend's study, and was glad to see my old acquaintance, Mr. Francis Barber, who was now returned home. Dr. Johnson received me with a hearty welcome; saying, 'I am glad you are come, and glad you are come upon such an errand:' (alluding to the cause of the schoolmaster.)[1] BOSWELL. 'I hope, Sir, he will be in no danger. It is a very delicate matter to interfere between a master and his scholars: nor do I see how you can fix the degree of severity that a master may use.' JOHNSON. 'Why, Sir, till you can fix the degree of obstinacy and negligence of the scholars, you cannot fix the degree of severity of the master. Severity must be continued until obstinacy be subdued, and negligence be cured.' He mentioned the severity of Hunter, his own Master. 'Sir, (said I,) Hunter is a Scotch name: so it should seem this schoolmaster who beat you so severely was a Scotchman. I can now account for your prejudice against the Scotch.' JOHNSON. 'Sir, he was not Scotch; and abating his brutality, he was a very good master.'

We talked of his two political pamphlets, *The False Alarm*, and *Thoughts concerning Falkland's Islands*. JOHNSON. 'Well, Sir, which of them did you think the best?' BOSWELL. 'I liked the second best.' JOHNSON. 'Why, Sir, I liked the first best; and Beattie liked the first best. Sir, there is a subtlety of disquisition in the first, that is worth all the fire of the second.' BOSWELL. Pray, Sir, is it true that Lord North paid you a visit, and that you got two hundred a year in addition to your pension?' JOHNSON. 'No, Sir. Except what I had from the bookseller, I did not get a farthing by them. And, between you and me, I believe Lord North is no friend to me.' BOSWELL. 'How so, Sir?' JOHNSON. 'Why, Sir you cannot account for the fancies of men. Well, how does Lord Elibank? and how does Lord Monboddo?' BOSWELL. 'Very well, Sir. Lord Monboddo still maintains the superiority of the savage life.' JOHNSON. 'What strange narrowness of mind now is that, to think the things we have not known, are better than the things which we have known.' BOSWELL. 'Why, Sir, that is a common prejudice.' JOHNSON. 'Yes, Sir; but a common prejudice should not be found in one whose trade it is to rectify errour.'

A gentleman having come in who was to go as a mate in the ship along with Mr. Banks and Dr. Solander, Dr. Johnson asked what were the names of the ships destined for the expedition. The gentleman answered, they were once to be called the Drake and the Ralegh, but now they were to be called the Resolution and the Adventure. JOHNSON. 'Much better; for had the Ralegh returned without going round the world, it would have been ridiculous. To give them the names of the Drake and the Ralegh was laying a trap for satire.' BOSWELL. 'Had not you some desire to go upon this expe-

[1] Whom Boswell was representing in an appeal to the House of Lords.

'dition, Sir?' JOHNSON. 'Why yes, but I soon laid it aside. Sir, there is very little of intellectual, in the course. Besides, I see but at a small distance. So it was not worth my while to go to see birds fly, which I should not have seen fly; and fishes swim, which I should not have seen swim.'

The gentleman being gone, and Dr. Johnson having left the room for some time, a debate arose between the Reverend Mr. Stockdale and Mrs. Desmoulins, whether Mr. Banks and Dr. Solander were entitled to any share of glory from their expedition. When Dr. Johnson returned to us, I told him the subject of their dispute. JOHNSON. 'Why, Sir, it was properly for botany that they went out: I believe they thought only of culling of simples.'

I thanked him for showing civilities to Beattie. 'Sir, (said he,) I should thank *you*. We all love Beattie. Mrs. Thrale says, if ever she has another husband, she'll have Beattie. He sunk upon us that he was married; else we should have shewn his lady more civilities. She is a very fine woman. But how can you shew civilities to a nonentity? I did not think he had been married. Nay, I did not think about it one way or other; but he did not tell us of his lady till late.'

He then spoke of St. Kilda, the most remote of the Hebrides. I told him, I thought of buying it. JOHNSON. 'Pray do, Sir. We will go and pass a winter amid the blasts there. We shall have fine fish, and we will take some dried tongues with us, and some books. We will have a strong built vessel, and some Orkney men to navigate her. We must build a tolerable house: but we may carry with us a wooden house ready made, and requiring nothing but to be put up. Consider, Sir, by buying St. Kilda, you may keep the people from falling into worse hands. We must give them a clergyman, and he shall be one of Beattie's choosing. He shall be educated at Marischal College. I'll be your Lord Chancellor, or what you please.' BOSWELL. 'Are you serious, Sir, in advising me to buy St. Kilda? for if you should advise me to go to Japan, I believe I should do it.' JOHNSON. 'Why yes, Sir, I am serious.' BOSWELL. 'Why then, I'll see what can be done.' . . .

He was engaged to dine abroad, and asked me to return to him in the evening, at nine, which I accordingly did.

We drank tea with Mrs. Williams, who told us a story of second sight, which happened in Wales where she was born. He listened to it very attentively, and said he should be glad to have some instances of that faculty well authenticated. His elevated wish for more and more evidence for spirit, in opposition to the groveling belief of materialism, led him to a love of such mysterious disquisitions. He again justly observed, that we could have no certainty of the truth of supernatural appearances, unless something was told us which we could not know by ordinary means, or something done which could not be done but by supernatural power; that Pharaoh in reason and justice required such evidence from Moses; nay, that our Saviour said, 'If I had not done among them the works which none other man did, they had not had sin.' He had said in the morning, that Macaulay's *History of St. Kilda* was very well written, except some foppery about liberty and slavery. I mentioned to him that Macaulay told me, he was advised to leave out of his book the wonderful story that upon the approach of a stranger all the inhabitants catch cold; but that it had been so well authenticated, he determined to retain it. JOHNSON. 'Sir, to leave things out of a book, merely because people tell you they will not be believed, is meanness. Macaulay acted with more magnanimity.'

We talked of the Roman Catholick religion, and how little difference there was in essential matters between ours and it. JOHNSON. 'True, Sir; all denominations of Christians have really little difference in point of doctrine, though they may differ widely in external forms. There is a prodigious difference between the external form of one of your Presbyterian churches in Scotland, and a church in Italy; yet the doctrine taught is essentially the same.'

I mentioned the petition to Parliament for removing the subscription to the Thirty-nine Articles. JOHNSON. 'It was soon thrown out. Sir, they talk of not making boys at the University subscribe to what they do not understand; but they ought to consider, that our Universities were founded to bring up members for the Church of England, and we must not supply our enemies with arms from our arsenal. No, Sir, the meaning of subscribing is, not that they fully understand all the articles, but that they will adhere to the Church of England. Now take it in this way, and suppose that they should only subscribe their adherence to the Church of England, there would be still the same difficulty; for still the young men would be subscribing to what they do not understand. For if you should ask them, what do you mean by the Church of England? Do you know in what it differs from the Presbyterian Church? from the Romish Church? from the Greek Church? from the Coptic Church? they could not tell you. So, Sir, it comes to the same thing.' BOSWELL. 'But, Sir, would it not be sufficient to subscribe the Bible?' JOHNSON. 'Why no, Sir; for all sects will subscribe the Bible; nay, the Mahometans will subscribe the Bible; for the Mahometans acknowledge JESUS CHRIST, as well as Moses, but maintain that GOD sent Mahomet as a still greater prophet than either.'

I mentioned the motion which had been made in the House of Commons, to abolish the fast of the 30th of January. JOHNSON. 'Why, Sir, I could have wished that it had been a temporary act, perhaps, to have expired with the century. I am against abolishing it; because that would be declaring it was wrong to establish it; but I should have no objection to make an act, continuing it for another century, and then letting it expire.'

He disapproved of the Royal Marriage Bill; 'Because (said he) I would not have the people think that the validity of marriage depends on the will of man, or that the right of a King depends on the will of man. I should not have been against making the marriage of any of the royal family, without the approbation of King and Parliament, highly criminal.'

In the morning we had talked of old families, and the respect due to them. JOHNSON. 'Sir, you have a right to that kind of respect, and are arguing for yourself. I am for supporting the principle, and am disinterested in doing it, as I have no such right.' BOSWELL. 'Why, Sir, it is one more incitement to a man to do well.' JOHNSON. 'Yes, Sir, and it is a matter of opinon, very necessary to keep society together. What is it but opinion, by which we have a respect for authority, that prevents us, who are the rabble, from rising up and pulling down you who are gentlemen from your places, and saying, "We will be gentlemen in our turn?" Now, Sir, that respect for authority is much more easily granted to a man whose father has had it, than to an upstart, and so Society is more easily supported.' BOSWELL. 'Perhaps, Sir, it might be done by the respect belonging to office, as among the Romans, where the dress, the *toga*, inspired reverence. JOHNSON. 'Why, Sir, we know very little about the Romans. But, surely, it is much easier to respect a man who has always had respect, than to respect a man who we know was last year no better than ourselves, and will be no better next year. In republicks there is not a respect for authority, but a fear of power.' BOSWELL. 'At present, Sir, I think riches seem to gain most respect.' JOHNSON. 'No, Sir, riches do not gain hearty respect; they only procure external attention. A very rich man, from low beginnings, may buy his election in a borough; but, *cæteris paribus,* a man of family will be preferred. People will prefer a man for whose father their fathers have voted, though they should get no more money, or even less. That shows that the respect for family is not merely fanciful, but has an actual operation. If gentlemen of family would allow the rich upstarts to spend their money profusely, which they are ready enough to do, and not vie with them in expence, the upstarts would soon be at an end, and the gentlemen would remain: but if the gentlemen will vie in expence with the upstarts, which is very foolish, they must be ruined.'

I gave him an account of the excellent mimickry of a friend of mine in Scotland; observing, at the same time, that some people thought it a very mean thing. JOHNSON. 'Why, Sir, it is making a very mean use of a man's powers. But to be a good mimick, requires great powers, great acuteness of observation, great retention of what is observed, and great pliancy of organs, to represent what is observed. I remember a lady of quality in this town, Lady ——, who was a wonderful mimick, and used to make me laugh immoderately. I have heard she is now gone mad.' BOSWELL. 'It is amazing how a mimick can not only give you the gestures and voice of a person whom he represents; but even what a person would say on any particular subject.' JOHNSON. 'Why, Sir, you are to consider that the manner and some particular phrases of a person do much to impress you with an idea of him, and you are not sure that he would say what the mimick says in his character.' BOSWELL. 'I don't think Foote a good mimick, Sir.' JOHNSON. 'No, Sir; his imitations are not like. He gives you something different from himself, but not the character which he means to assume. He goes out of himself, without going into other people. He cannot take off any person unless he is strongly marked, such as George Faulkner. He is like a painter, who can draw the portrait of a man who has a wen upon his face, and who, therefore, is easily known. If a man hops upon one leg, Foote can hop upon one leg. But he has not that nice discrimination which your friend seems to possess. Foote is, however, very entertaining, with a kind of conversation between wit and buffoonery.'

On Monday, March 23, I found him busy, preparing a fourth edition of his folio Dictionary. Mr. Peyton, one of his original amanuenses, was writing for him. I put him in mind of a meaning of the word *side*, which he had omitted, viz. relationship; as father's side, mother's side. He inserted it. I asked him if *humiliating* was a good word. He said, he had seen it frequently used, but he did not know it to be legitimate English. He would not admit *civilization*, but only *civility*. With great deference to him, I thought *civilization*, from *to civilize* better in the sense opposed to *barbarity*, than *civility;* as it is better to have a distinct word for each sense, than one word with two senses, which *civility* is, in his way of using it.

He seemed also to be intent on some sort of chymical operation. I was entertained by observing how he contrived to send Mr. Peyton on an errand, without seeming to degrade him. 'Mr. Peyton,—Mr. Peyton, will you be so good as to take a walk to Temple-Bar? You will there see a chymist's shop; at which you will be pleased to buy for me an ounce of oil of vitroil; not spirit of vitriol, but oil of vitriol. It will cost three half-pence.' Peyton immediately went, and and returned with it, and told him it cost but a penny.

I then reminded him of the schoolmaster's cause, and proposed to read to him the printed papers concerning it. 'No, Sir, (said he,) I can read quicker than I can hear.' So he read them to himself.

After he had read for some time, we were interrupted by the entrance of Mr. Kristrom, a Swede, who was tutor to some young gentlemen in the city. He told me, that there was a very good History of Sweden, by Daline. Having at that time an intention of writing the history of that country, I asked Dr. Johnson whether one might write a history of Sweden, without going thither. 'Yes, Sir, (said he,) one for common use.'

We talked of languages. Johnson observed, that Leibnitz had made some progress in a work, tracing all languages up to the Hebrew. 'Why, Sir, (said he,) you would not imagine that the French *jour*, day, is derived from the Latin *dies*, and yet nothing is more certain; and the intermediate steps are very clear. From *dies*, comes *diurnus. Diu* is, by inaccurate ears, or inaccurate pronunciation, easily confounded with *giu;* then the Italians form a substantive of the ablative of an adjective, and thence *giurno*, or, as they make it, *giorno;* which is readily contracted into *giour*, or *jour.*' He observed, that the Bohemian language was true Sclavonick. The Swede said, it had some similarity with the German. JOHNSON. 'Why, Sir, to be sure, such parts of Sclavonia as confine with Germany, will borrow German words; and such parts as confine with Tartary will borrow Tartar words.'

He said, he never had it properly ascertained that the Scotch Highlanders and the Irish understood each other. I told him that my cousin Colonel Graham, of the Royal Highlanders, whom I met at Drogheda, told me they did. JOHNSON. 'Sir, if the Highlanders understood Irish, why translate the New Testament into Erse, as was done lately at Edinburgh, when there is an Irish translation?' BOSWELL. 'Although the Erse and Irish are both dialects of the same language, there may be a good deal of diversity between them, as between the different dialects in Italy.'—The Swede went away, and Mr. Johnson continued his reading of the papers. I said, 'I am afraid, Sir, it is troublesome to you.' 'Why, Sir, (said he,) I do not take much delight in it; but I'll go through it.' . . .

On Saturday, March 27,[1] I introduced to him Sir Alexander Macdonald, with whom he had expressed a wish to be acquainted. He received him very courteously.

[1] Actually, 28.

Sir Alexander observed, that the Chancellors in England are chosen from views much inferiour to the office, being chosen from temporary political views. JOHNSON. 'Why, Sir, in such a government as ours, no man is appointed to an office because he is the fittest for it, nor hardly in any other government; because there are so many connections and dependencies to be studied. A despotick prince may choose a man to an office, merely because he is the fittest for it. The King of Prussia may do it.' SIR A. 'I think, Sir, almost all great lawyers, such at least as have written upon law, have known only law, and nothing else.' JOHNSON. 'Why no, Sir; Judge Hale was a great lawyer, and wrote upon law; and yet he knew a great many other things, and has written upon other things. Selden too.' SIR A. 'Very true, Sir; and Lord Bacon. But was not Lord Coke a mere lawyer?' JOHNSON. 'Why, I am afraid he was; but he would have taken it very ill if you had told him so. He would have prosecuted you for scandal.' BOSWELL. 'Lord Mansfield is not a mere lawyer.' JOHNSON. 'No, Sir. I never was in Lord Mansfield's company; but, Lord Mansfield was distinguished at the University. Lord Mansfield, when he first came to town, "drank champagne with the wits," as Prior says. He was the friend of Pope.' SIR A. 'Barristers, I believe, are not so abusive now as they were formerly. I fancy they had less law long ago, and so were obliged to take to abuse, to fill up the time. Now they have such a number of precedents, they have no occasion for abuse.' JOHNSON. 'Nay, Sir, they had more law long ago than they have now. As to precedents, to be sure they will increase in course of time; but the more precedents there are, the less occasion is there for law; that is to say, the less occasion is there for investigating principles.' SIR A. 'I have been correcting several Scotch accents in my friend Boswell. I doubt, Sir, if any Scotchman ever attains to a perfect English pronunciation.' JOHNSON. 'Why, Sir, few of them do, because they do not persevere after acquiring a certain degree of it. But, Sir, there can be no doubt that they may attain to a perfect English pronunciation, if they will. We find how near they come to it; and certainly, a man who conquers nineteen parts of the Scottish accent, may conquer the twentieth. But, Sir, when a man has got the better of nine tenths, he grows weary, he relaxes his diligence, he finds he has corrected his accent so far as not to be disagreeable, and he no longer desires his friends to tell him when he is wrong; nor does he choose to be told. Sir, when people watch me narrowly, and I do not watch myself, they will find me out to be of a particular county. In the same manner, Dunning may be found out to be a Devonshire man. So most Scotchmen may be found out. But, Sir, little aberrations are of no disadvantage. I never catched Mallet in a Scotch accent; and yet Mallet, I suppose, was past five-and-twenty before he came to London.'

Upon another occasion I talked to him on this subject, having myself taken some pains to improve my pronunciation, by the aid of the late Mr. Love, of Drury-lane theatre, when he was a player at Edinburgh, and also of old Mr. Sheridan. Johnson said to me, 'Sir, your pronunciation is not offensive.' . . .

Boswell. 'It may be of use, Sir, to have a Dictionary to ascertain the pronunciation.' Johnson. 'Why, Sir, my Dictionary shows you the accents of words, if you can but remember then.' Boswell. 'But, Sir, we want marks to ascertain the pronunciation of the vowels. Sheridan, I believe, has finished such a work.' Johnson. 'Why, Sir, consider how much easier it is to learn a language by the ear, than by any marks. Sheridan's Dictionary may do very well; but you cannot always carry it about with you: and, when you want the word, you have not the Dictionary. It is like a man who has a sword that will not draw. It is an admirable sword, to be sure: but while your enemy is cutting your throat, you are unable to use it. Besides, Sir, what entitles Sheridan to fix the pronunciation of English? He has, in the first place, the disadvantage of being an Irishman: and if he says he will fix it after the example of the best company, why they differ among themselves. I remember an instance: when I published the Plan for my Dictionary, Lord Chesterfield told me that the word *great* should be pronounced so as to rhyme to *state;* and Sir William Yonge sent me word that it should be pronounced so as to rhyme to *seat,* and that none but an Irishman would pronounce it *grait.* Now here were two men of the highest rank, the one, the best speaker in the House of Lords, the other, the best speaker in the House of Commons, differing entirely.'

I again visited him at night. Finding him in a very good humour, I ventured to lead him to the subject of our situation in a future state, having much curiosity to know his notions on that point. Johnson. 'Why, Sir, the happiness of an unembodied spirit will consist in a consciousness of the favour of God, in the contemplation of truth, and in the possession of felicitating ideas.' Boswell. 'But, Sir, is there any harm in our forming to ourselves conjectures as to the particulars of our happiness, though the scripture has said but very little on the subject? "We know not what we shall be." ' Johnson. 'Sir, there is no harm. What philosophy suggests to us on this topick is probable: what scripture tells us is certain. Dr. Henry More has carried it as far as philosophy can. You may buy both this theological and philosophical works in two volumes folio, for about eight shillings.' BOSWELL. 'One of the most pleasing thoughts is, that we shall see our friends again. JOHNSON. 'Yes, Sir; but you must consider, that when we are become purely rational, many of our friendships will be cut off. Many friendships are formed by a community of sensual pleasures: all these will be cut off. We form many friendships with bad men, because they have agreeable qualities, and they can be useful to us; but, after death, they can no longer be of use to us. We form many friendships by mistake, imagining people to be different from what they really are. After death, we shall see every one in a true light. Then, Sir, they talk of our meeting our relations: but then all relationship is dissolved; and we shall have no regard for one person more than another, but for their real value. However, we shall either have the satisfaction of meeting our friends, or be satisfied without meeting them.' BOSWELL. 'Yet, Sir, we see in scripture, that Dives still retained an anxious concern about his brethren. JOHNSON. 'Why, Sir, we must either suppose that passage to be metaphorical, or hold with many divines, and all the Purgatorians, that departed souls do not all at once arrive at the utmost perfection of which they are capable.' BOSWELL. 'I think, Sir, that is a very rational supposition.' JOHNSON. 'Why, yes, Sir; but we do not know it is a true one. There is no harm in believing it: but you must not compel others to make it an article of faith; for it is not revealed. BOSWELL. 'Do you think, Sir, it is wrong in a man who holds the doctrine of purgatory, to pray for the souls of his deceased friends?' JOHNSON. 'Why, no, Sir.' BOSWELL. 'I have been told, that in the Liturgy of the Episcopal Church of Scotland, there was a form of prayer for the dead. JOHNSON. 'Sir, it is not in the Liturgy which Laud framed for the Episcopal Church of Scotland: if there is a liturgy older than that, I should be glad to see it.' BOSWELL. 'As to our employment in the future state, the sacred writings say little. The Revelation, however, of St. John gives us many ideas, and particularly mentions musick.' JOHNSON. 'Why, Sir, ideas must be given you by means of something which you know: and as to musick, there are some philosophers and divines who have maintained that we shall not be spiritualized to such a degree, but that something of matter, very much refined, will remain. In that case, musick may make a part of our future felicity.'

BOSWELL. 'I do not know whether there are any well-attested stories of the appearance of ghosts. You know there is a famous story of the appearance of Mrs. Veal, prefixed to *Drelincourt on Death.*' JOHNSON. 'I believe, sir, that is given up. I believe the woman declared upon her death-bed that it was a lie.' BOSWELL. 'This objection is made against the truth of ghosts appearing: that if they are in a state of happiness, it would be a punishment to them to return to this world; and if they are in a state of misery, it would be giving them a respite.' JOHNSON. 'Why, Sir, as the happiness or misery of unembodied spirits does not depend upon place, but is intellectual, we cannot say that they are less happy or less miserable by appearing upon earth.'

We went down between twelve and one to Mrs. Williams's room, and drank tea. I mentioned that we were to have the remains of Mr. Gray, in prose and verse, published by Mr. Mason. JOHNSON. 'I think we have had enough of Gray. I see they have published a splendid edition of Akenside's works. One bad ode may be suffered; but a number of them together makes one sick.' BOSWELL. 'Akenside's distinguished poem is his *Pleasures of Imagination:* but, for my part, I never could admire it so much as most people do.' JOHNSON. 'Sir, I could not read it through.' BOSWELL. 'I have read it through; but I did not find any great power in it.'

I mentioned Elwal, the heretick, whose trial Sir John Pringle had given me to read. JOHNSON. 'Sir, Mr. Elwal was, I think, an ironmonger at Wolverhampton; and he had a mind to make himself famous, by being the founder of a new sect, which he wished much should be called *Elwallians.* He held, that every thing in the Old Testament that was not typical, was to be of perpetual observance; and so he wore a ribband in the plaits of his coat, and he also wore a beard. I remember I had the honour of dining in company with Mr. Elwal. There was one Barter, a miller, who wrote against him; and so you had the controversy between Mr. ELWAL and Mr. BARTER. To try to make himself distinguished, he wrote a letter to King George the Second, challenging him to dispute with him, in which he said, "George, if you be afraid to come by yourself, to dispute with a poor old man, you may bring a thousand of your *black*-guards with you; and if you should still be afraid, you may bring a thousand of your *red*-guards." The letter had something of the impudence of Junius to our present King. But the men of Wolverhampton were not so inflammable as the Common-Council of London; so Mr. Elwal failed in his scheme of making himself a man of great consequence.'

On Tuesday, March 31, he and I dined at General Paoli's. A question was started, whether the state of marriage was natural to man. JOHNSON. 'Sir, it is so far from being nat-

241

ural for a man and woman to live in a state of marriage, that we find all the motives which they have for remaining in that connection, and the restraints which civilized society imposes to prevent separation, are hardly sufficient to keep them together.' The General said, that in a state of nature a man and woman uniting together would form a strong and constant affection, by the mutual pleasure each would receive; and that the same causes of dissention would not arise between them, as occur between husband and wife in a civilized state. JOHNSON. 'Sir, they would have dissentions enough, though of another kind. One would choose to go a hunting in this wood, the other in that; one would choose to go a fishing in this lake, the other in that; or, perhaps, one would choose to go a hunting, when the other would choose to go a fishing; and so they would part. Besides, Sir, a savage man and a savage woman meet by chance; and when the man sees another woman that pleases him better, he will leave the first.'

We then fell into a disquisition whether there is any beauty independent of utility. The General maintained there was not. Dr. Johnson maintained that there was; and he instanced a coffee-cup which he held in his hand, the painting of which was of no real use, as the cup would hold the coffee equally well if plain; yet the painting was beautiful.

We talked of the strange custom of swearing in conversation. The General said, that all barbarous nations swore from a certain violence of temper, that could not be confined to earth, but was always reaching at the powers above. He said, too, that there was greater variety of swearing, in proportion as there was a greater variety of religious ceremonies.

Dr. Johnson went home with me to my lodgings in Conduit-street and drank tea, previous to our going to the Pantheon, which neither of us had seen before.

He said, 'Goldsmith's *Life of Parnell* is poor; not that it is poorly written, but that he had poor materials; for nobody can write the life of a man, but those who have eat and drunk and lived in social intercourse with him.'

I said, that if it was not troublesome and presuming too much, I would request him to tell me all the little circumstances of his life; what schools he attended, when he came to Oxford, when he came to London, &c. &c. He did not disapprove of my curiosity as to these particulars; but said, 'They'll come out by degrees as we talk together.'

He censured Ruffhead's *Life of Pope;* and said, 'he knew nothing of Pope, and nothing of poetry.' He praised Dr. Joseph Warton's *Essay on Pope;* but said, he supposed we should have no more of it, as the authour had not been able to persuade the world to think of Pope as he did.

BOSWELL. 'Why, Sir, should that prevent him from continuing his work? He is an ingenious Counsel, who has made the most of his cause: he is not obliged to gain it.' JOHNSON. 'But, Sir, there is a difference when the cause is of a man's own making.'

We talked of the proper use of riches. JOHNSON. 'If I were a man of a great estate, I would drive all the rascals whom I did not like out of the county at an election.'

I asked him how far he thought wealth should be employed in hospitality. JOHNSON. 'You are to consider that ancient hospitality, of which we hear so much, was in an uncommercial country, when men being idle, were glad to be entertained at rich men's tables. But in a commercial country, a busy country, time becomes precious, and therefore hospitality is not so much valued. No doubt there is still room for a certain degree of it; and a man has a satisfaction in seeing his friends eating and drinking around him. But promiscuous hospitality is not the way to gain real influence. You must help some people at table before others; you must ask some people how they like their wine oftener than others. You therefore offend more people than you please. You are like the French statesman, who said, when he granted a favour, *"J'ai fait dix mécontents et un ingrat."* Besides, Sir, being entertained ever so well at a man's table, impresses no lasting regard or esteem. No, Sir, the way to make sure of power and influence is, by lending money confidentially to your neighbours at a small interest, or, perhaps, at no interest at all, and having their bonds in your possession.' BOSWELL. 'May not a man, Sir, employ his riches to advantage in educating young men of merit?' JOHNSON. 'Yes, Sir, if they fall in your way; but if it is understood that you patronize young men of merit, you will be harassed with solicitations. You will have numbers forced upon you who have no merit; some will force them upon you from mistaken partiality; and some from downright interested motives, without scruple; and you will be disgraced.'

'Were I a rich man, I would propagate all kinds of trees that will grow in the open air. A greenhouse is childish. I would introduce foreign animals into the country; for instance, the rein-deer.' . . .

We then walked to the Pantheon. The first view of it did not strike us so much as Ranelagh, of which he said, the *'coup d'œil* was the finest thing he had ever seen.' The truth is, Ranelagh is of a more beautiful form; more of it, or rather indeed the whole *rotunda,* appears at once, and it is better lighted. However, as Johnson observed, we saw the Pantheon in time of mourning, when there was a dull uniformity; whereas we had seen Ranelagh when the view was enlivened with a gay profusion of colours. Mrs. Bosville, of Gunthwait, in Yorkshire, joined us, and entered into conversation with us. Johnson said to me afterwards, 'Sir, this is a mighty intelligent lady.'

I said there was not half a guinea's worth of pleasure in seeing this place. JOHNSON. 'But, Sir, there is a half a guinea's worth of inferiority to other people in not having seen it.' BOSWELL. 'I doubt, Sir whether there are many happy people here.' JOHNSON. 'Yes, Sir, there are many happy people here. There are many people here who are watching hundreds, and who think hundreds are watching them.'

Happening to meet Sir Adam Fergusson, I presented him to Dr. Johnson. Sir Adam expressed some apprehension that the Pantheon would encourage luxury. 'Sir, (said Johnson,) I am a great friend to publick amusements; for they keep people from vice. You now (addressing himself to me,) would have been with a wench, had you not been here.—O! I forgot you were married.'

Sir Adam suggested, that luxury corrupts a people, and destroys the spirit of liberty. JOHNSON. 'Sir, that is all visionary. I would not give half a guinea to live under one form of government rather than another. It is of no moment to the happiness of an individual. Sir, the danger of the abuse of power is nothing to a private man. What Frenchman is prevented from passing his life as he pleases? SIR ADAM. 'But, Sir, in the British constitution it is surely of importance to keep up a spirit in the people, so as to preserve a balance against the crown.' JOHNSON. 'Sir, I perceive you are a vile Whig. Why all this childish jealousy of the power of the crown? The crown has not power enough. When I say that all governments are alike, I consider that in no government power can be abused long. Mankind will not bear it. If a sovereign oppresses his people to a great degree, they will rise and cut off his head. There is a remedy in human nature against tyranny, that will keep us safe under every form of government. Had not the people of France thought themselves honoured as sharing in the brilliant actions of Lewis XIV, they would not have endured him; and we may say the same of the King of Prussia's people.' Sir Adam introduced the ancient Greeks and Romans. JOHNSON. 'Sir, the mass of both of them were barbarians. The mass of every people must be barbarous where there is no printing, and consequently knowledge is not generally diffused. Knowledge is diffused among our people by the news-papers.' Sir Adam mentioned the orators, poets, and artists of Greece. JOHNSON. 'Sir, I am talking of the mass of the people. We see even what the boasted Athenians were. The little effect which Demos-

244

thenes's orations had upon them, shews that they were barbarians.'

Sir Adam was unlucky in his topicks; for he suggested a doubt of the propriety of Bishops having seats in the House of Lords. JOHNSON. 'How so, Sir? Who is more proper for having the dignity of a peer, than a Bishop, provided a Bishop be what he ought to be; and if improper Bishops be made, that is not the fault of the Bishops, but of those who make them.'

On Sunday, April 5, after attending divine service at St. Paul's church, I found him alone. Of a schoolmaster of his acquaintance, a native of Scotland, he said, 'He has a great deal of good about him; but he is also very defective in some respects. His inner part is good, but his outer part is mighty aukward. You in Scotland do not attain that nice critical skill in languages, which we get in our schools in England. I would not put a boy to him, whom I intended for a man of learning. But for the sons of citizens, who are to learn a little, get good morals, and then go to trade, he may do very well.'

I mentioned a cause in which I had appeared as counsel at the bar of the General Assembly of the Church of Scotland, where a *Probationer,* (as one licensed to preach, but not yet ordained, is called,) was opposed in his application to be inducted, because it was alledged that he had been guilty of fornication five years before. JOHNSON. 'Why, Sir, if he has repented, it is not a sufficient objection. A man who is good enough to go to heaven, is good enough to be a clergyman.' . . . I told him, that by the rules of the Church of Scotland, in their *Book of Discipline,* if a *scandal,* as it is called, is not prosecuted for five years, it cannot afterwards be proceeded upon, 'unless it be *of a heinous nature,* or again become flagrant;' and that hence a question arose, whether fornication was a sin of a heinous nature; and that I had maintained, that it did not deserve that epithet, in as much as it was not one of those sins which argue very great depravity of heart: in short, was not, in the general acceptation of mankind, a heinous sin. JOHNSON. 'No, Sir, it is not a heinous sin. A heinous sin is that for which a man is punished with death or banishment.' BOSWELL. 'But, Sir, after I had argued that it was not a heinous sin, an old clergyman rose up, and repeating the text of scripture denouncing judgement against whoremongers, asked, whether, considering this, there could be any doubt of fornication being a heinous sin.' JOHNSON. 'Why, Sir, observe the word *whoremonger.* Every sin, if persisted in, will become heinous. Whoremonger is a dealer in whores, as ironmonger is a dealer in iron. But as you don't call a man an ironmonger for buying and selling a penknife; so you don't call a man a whoremonger for getting one wench with child.'

I spoke of the inequality of the livings of the clergy in England, and the scanty provisions of some of the Curates. JOHNSON. 'Why yes, Sir; but it cannot be helped. You must consider, that the revenues of the clergy are not at the disposal of the state, like the pay of the army. Different men have founded different churches; and some are better endowed, some worse. The State cannot interfere and make an equal division of what has been particularly appropriated. Now when a clergyman has but a small living, or even two small livings, he can afford very little to a curate.'

He said, he went more frequently to church when there were prayers only, than when there was also a sermon, as the people required more an example for the one than the other; it being much easier for them to hear a sermon, than to fix their minds on prayer.

On Monday, April 6, I dined with him at Sir Alexander Macdonald's, where was a young officer in the regimentals of the Scots Royal, who talked with a vivacity, fluency, and precision so uncommon, that he attracted particular attention. He proved to be the Honourable Thomas Erskine, youngest brother to the Earl of Buchan, who has since risen into such brilliant reputation at the bar in Westminster-hall.

Fielding being mentioned, Johnson exclaimed, 'he was a blockhead;' and upon my expressing my astonishment at so strange an assertion, he said, 'What I mean by his being a blockhead is that he was a barren rascal.' BOSWELL. 'Will you not allow, Sir, that he draws very natural pictures of human life?' JOHNSON. 'Why, Sir, it is of very low life. Richardson used to say, that had he not known who Fielding was, he should have believed he was an ostler. Sir, there is more knowledge of the heart in one letter of Richardson's, than in all *Tom Jones*. I, indeed, never read *Joseph Andrews*.' ERSKINE. 'Surely, Sir, Richardson is very tedious.' JOHNSON. 'Why, Sir, if you were to read Richardson for the story, your impatience would be so much fretted that you would hang yourself. But you must read him for the sentiment, and consider the story as only giving occasion to the sentiment.' —I have already given my opinion of Fielding; but I cannot refrain from repeating here my wonder at Johnson's excessive and unaccountable depreciation of one of the best writers that England has produced. *Tom Jones* has stood the test of publick opinion with such success, as to have established its great merit, both for the story, the sentiments, and the manners, and also the varieties of diction, so as to leave no doubt of its having an animated truth of execution throughout.

A book of travels, lately published under the title of *Coriat Junior,* and written by Mr. Paterson, was mentioned. Johnson said, this book was an imitation of Sterne, and not of Coriat, whose name Paterson had chosen as a whimsical one. 'Tom Coriat, (said he) was a humorist about the court of James the First. He had a mixture of learning, of wit, and of buffoonery. He first travelled through Europe, and published his travels. He afterwards travelled on foot through Asia, and had made many remarks; but he died at Mandoa, and his remarks were lost.'

We talked of gaming, and animadverted on it with severity. JOHNSON. 'Nay, gentlemen, let us not aggravate the matter. It is not roguery to play with a man who is ignorant of the game, while you are master of it, and so win his money; for he thinks he can play better than you, as you think you can play better than he; and the superiour skill carries it.' ERSKINE. 'He is a fool, but you are not a rogue.' JOHNSON. 'That's much about the truth, Sir. It must be considered, that a man who only does what every one of the society to which he belongs would do, is not a dishonest man. In the republick of Sparta, it was agreed, that stealing was not dishonourable, if not discovered. I do not commend a society where there is an agreement that what would not otherwise be fair, shall be fair; but I maintain, that an individual of any society, who practises what is allowed, is not a dishonest man.' BOSWELL. 'So then, Sir, you do not think ill of a man who wins perhaps forty thousand pounds in a winter?' JOHNSON. 'Sir, I do not call a gamester a dishonest man; but I call him an unsocial man, an unprofitable man. Gaming is a mode of transferring property without producing any intermediate good. Trade gives employment to numbers, and so produces intermediate good.'

Mr. Erskine told us, that when he was in the island of Minorca, he not only read prayers, but preached two sermons to the regiment. He seemed to object to the passage in scripture where we are told that the angel of the Lord smote in one night forty thousand Assyrians. 'Sir, (said Johnson,) you should recollect that there was a supernatural interposition; they were destroyed by pestilence. You are not to suppose that the angel of the LORD went about and stabbed each of them with a dagger, or knocked them on the head, man by man.'

After Mr. Erskine was gone, a discussion took place, whether the present Earl of Buchan, when Lord Cardross, did right to refuse to go Secretary of the Embassy to Spain, when Sir

James Gray, a man of inferiour rank, went Ambassadour. Dr. Johnson said, that perhaps in point of interest he did wrong; but in point of dignity he did well. Sir Alexander insisted that he was wrong; and said that Mr. Pitt intended it as an advantageous thing for him. 'Why, Sir, (said Johnson,) Mr. Pitt might think it an advantageous thing for him to make him a vintner, and get him all the Portugal trade; but he would have demeaned himself strangely had he accepted of such a situation. Sir, had he gone Secretary while his inferiour was Ambassadour, he would have been a traitor to his rank and family.'

I talked of the little attachment which subsisted between near relations in London. 'Sir, (said Johnson,) in a country so commercial as ours, where every man can do for himself, there is not so much occasion for that attachment. No man is thought the worse of here, whose brother was hanged. In uncommercial countries, many of the branches of a family must depend on the stock; so, in order to make the head of the family take care of them, they are represented as connected with his reputation, that, self-love being interested, he may exert himself to promote their interest. You have first large circles, or clans; as commerce increases, the connection is confined to families. By degrees, that too goes off, as having become unnecessary, and there being few opportunities of intercourse. One brother is a merchant in the city, and another is an officer in the guards. How little intercourse can these two have!'

I argued warmly for the old feudal system. Sir Alexander opposed it, and talked of the pleasure of seeing all men free and independent. JOHNSON. 'I agree with Mr. Boswell that there must be a high satisfaction in being a feudal Lord; but we are to consider, that we ought not to wish to have a number of men unhappy for the satisfaction of one.'—I maintained that numbers, namely, the vassals or followers, were not unhappy; for that there was a reciprocal satisfaction between the Lord and them: he being kind in his authority over them; they being respectful and faithful to him.

On Thursday, April 9, I called on him to beg he would go and dine with me at the Mitre tavern. He had resolved not to dine at all this day, I know not for what reason; and I was so unwilling to be deprived of his company, that I was content to submit to suffer a want, which was at first somewhat painful, but he soon made me forget it; and a man is always pleased with himself when he finds his intellectual inclinations predominate.

He observed, that to reason too philosophically on the nature of prayer, was very unprofitable.

248

Talking of ghosts, he said, he knew one friend, who was an honest man and a sensible man, who told him he had seen a ghost, old Mr. Edward Cave, the printer at St. John's Gate. He said, Mr. Cave did not like to talk of it, and seemed to be in great horrour whenever it was mentioned. BOSWELL. 'Pray, Sir, what did he say was the appearance?' JOHNSON. 'Why, Sir, something of a shadowy being.'

I mentioned witches, and asked him what they properly meant. JOHNSON. 'Why, Sir, they properly mean those who make use of the aid of evil spirits.' BOSWELL. 'There is no doubt, Sir, a general report and belief of their having existed.' JOHNSON. 'Sir, you have not only the general report and belief, but you have many voluntary solemn confessions.' He did not affirm anything positively upon a subject which it is the fashion of the times to laugh at as a matter of absurd credulity. He only seemed willing, as a candid enquirer after truth, however strange and inexplicable, to shew that he understood what might be urged for it.

On Friday, April 10, I dined with him at General Oglethorpe's, where we found Dr. Goldsmith.

Armorial bearings having been mentioned, Johnson said, they were as ancient as the siege of Thebes, which he proved by a passage in one of the tragedies of Euripides.

I started the question whether duelling was consistent with moral duty. The brave old General fired at this, and said, with a lofty air, 'Undoubtedly a man has a right to defend his honour.' GOLDSMITH. (turning to me,) 'I ask you first, Sir, what would you do if you were affronted?' I answered I should think it necessary to fight. 'Why then, (replied Goldsmith,) that solves the question.' JOHNSON. 'No, Sir, it does not solve the question. It does not follow that what a man would do is therefore right.' I said, I wished to have it settled, whether duelling was contrary to the laws of Christianity. Johnson immediately entered on the subject, and treated it in a masterly manner; and so far as I have been able to recollect, his thoughts were these: 'Sir, as men become in a high degree refined, various causes of offence arise; which are considered to be of such importance, that life must be staked to atone for them, though in reality they are not so. A body that has received a very fine polish may be easily hurt. Before men arrive at this artificial refinement, if one tells his neighbour he lies, his neighbour tells him he lies; if one gives his neighbour a blow, his neighbour gives him a blow: but in a state of highly polished society, an affront is held to be a serious injury. It must, therefore, be resented, or rather a duel must be fought upon it; as men have agreed to banish from their society one who puts up with an affront without fighting a duel. Now, Sir, it is never unlawful to fight in self-defence. He, then, who fights a duel, does not fight from passion against his antagonist, but out of self-defence; to avert the stigma of the world, and to prevent himself from being driven out of society. I could wish there was not that superfluity of refinement; but while such notions prevail, no doubt a man may lawfully fight a duel.'

Let it be remembered, that this justification is applicable only to the person who *receives* an affront. All mankind must condemn the aggressor.

The General told us, that when he was a very young man, I think only fifteen, serving under Prince Eugene of Savoy, he was sitting in a company at table with a Prince of Wirtemberg. The Prince took up a glass of wine, and, by a fillip, made some of it fly in Oglethorpe's face. Here was a nice dilemma. To have challenged him instantly, might have fixed a quarrelsome character upon the young soldier: to have taken no notice of it might have been considered as cowardice. Oglethorpe, therefore, keeping his eye upon the Prince, and smiling all the time, as if he took what his Highness had done in jest, said 'Mon Prince,—' (I forget the French words he used, the purport however was,) 'That's a good joke; but we do it much better in England;' and threw a whole glass of wine in the Prince's face. An old General who sat by, said, '*Il a bien fait, mon Prince, vous l'avez commencé:*' and thus all ended in good humour.

Dr. Johnson said, 'Pray, General, give us an account of the siege of Belgrade.' Upon which the General, pouring a little wine upon the table, described every thing with a wet finger: 'Here we were, here were the Turks,' &c. &c. Johnson listened with the closest attention.

A question was started, how far people who disagree in any capital point can live in friendship together. Johnson said they might. Goldsmith said they could not, as they had not the *idem velle atque idem nolle*—the same likings and the same aversions. JOHNSON. 'Why, Sir, you must shun the subject as to which you disagree. For instance, I can live very well with Burke: I love his knowledge, his genius, his diffusion, and affluence of conversation; but I would not talk to him of the Rockingham party.' GOLDSMITH. 'But, Sir, when people live together who have something as to which they disagree, and which they want to shun, they will be in the situation mentioned in the story of Bluebeard: "You may look into all the chambers but one." But we should have the greatest inclination to look into that chamber, to talk of that subject.' JOHNSON. (with a loud voice,) 'Sir, I am not saying that *you* could live in friendship with a man from whom you differ as to some point: I am only saying that *I* could do it. You put me in mind of Sappho in Ovid.'

Goldsmith told us, that he was now busy in writing a natural history, and, that he might have full leisure for it, he had taken lodgings, at a farmer's house, near to the six milestone, on the Edgeware road, and had carried down his books in two returned post-chaises. He said, he believed the farmer's family thought him an odd character, similar to that in which the *Spectator* appeared to his landlady and her children: he was *The Gentleman*. Mr. Mickle, the translator of *The Lusiad*, and I went to visit him at this place a few days afterwards. He was not at home; but having a curiosity to see his apartment, we went in and found curious scraps of descriptions of animals, scrawled upon the walls with a black lead pencil.

The subject of ghosts being introduced, Johnson repeated what he had told me of a friend of his, an honest man and a man of sense, having asserted to him, that he had seen an apparitition. Goldsmith told us, he was assured by his brother, the Reverend Mr. Goldsmith, that he also had seen one. General Oglethorpe told us, that Prendergast, an officer in the Duke of Marlborough's army, had mentioned to many of his friends, that he should die on a particular day. That upon that day a battle took place with the French; that after it was over, and Prendergast was still alive, his brother officers, while they were yet in the field, jestingly asked him, where was his prophecy now. Prendergast gravely answered, 'I shall die, notwithstanding what you see.' Soon afterwards, there came a shot from a French battery, to which the orders for a cessation of arms had not yet reached, and he was killed upon the spot. . . .

On Saturday, April 11, he appointed me to come to him in the evening, when he should be at leisure to give me some assistance for the defence of Hastie, the schoolmaster of Campbelltown, for whom I was to appear in the House of Lords. When I came, I found him unwilling to exert himself. I pressed him to write down his thoughts upon the subject. He said, 'There's no occasion for my writing. I'll talk to you.' He was, however, at last prevailed on to dictate to me, while I wrote as follows.[1]

Of our friend, Goldsmith, he said, 'Sir, he is so much afraid of being unnoticed, that he often talks merely lest you should forget that he is in the company.' BOSWELL. 'Yes, he stands forward.' JOHNSON. 'True, Sir; but if a man is to stand forward, he should wish to do it not in an awkward

[1] Johnson's disquisition is omitted here.

posture, not in rags, not so as that he shall only be exposed to ridicule.' BOSWELL. 'For my part, I like very well to hear honest Goldsmith talk away carelessly.' JOHNSON. 'Why yes, Sir; but he should not like to hear himself.'

On Tuesday, April 14, the decree of the Court of Session in the schoolmaster's cause was reversed in the House of Lords, after a very eloquent speech by Lord Mansfield, who shewed himself an adept in school discipline, but I thought was too rigorous towards my client. On the evening of the next day I supped with Dr. Johnson, at the Crown and Anchor tavern, in the Strand, in company with Mr. Langton and his brother-in-law, Lord Binning. I repeated a sentence of Lord Mansfield's speech, of which, by the aid of Mr. Longlands, the solicitor on the other side, who obligingly allowed me to compare his note with my own, I have a full copy: 'My Lords, severity is not the way to govern either boys or men.' 'Nay, (said Johnson,) it is the way to *govern* them. I know not whether it be the way to *mend* them.'

I talked of the recent expulsion of six students from the University of Oxford, who were methodists, and would not desist from publickly praying and exhorting. JOHNSON. 'Sir, that expulsion was extremely just and proper. What have they to do at an University who are not willing to be taught, but will presume to teach? Where is religion to be learnt but at an University? Sir, they were examined, and found to be mighty ignorant fellows.' BOSWELL. 'But, was it not hard, Sir, to expel them, for I am told they were good beings?' JOHNSON. 'Sir, I believe they might be good beings; but they were not fit to be in the University of Oxford. A cow is a very good animal in the field; but we turn her out of a garden.' Lord Elibank used to repeat this as an illustration uncommonly happy.

Desirous of calling Johnson forth to talk, and exercise his wit, though I should myself be the object of it, I resolutely ventured to undertake the defence of convivial indulgence in wine, though he was not to-night in the most genial humour. After urging the common plausible topicks, I at last had recourse to the maxim, *in vino veritas;* a man who is well warmed with wine will speak truth. JOHNSON. 'Why, Sir, that may be an argument for drinking, if you suppose men in general to be liars. But Sir, I would not keep company with a fellow, who lyes as long as he is sober, and whom you must make drunk before you can get a word of truth out of him.'

Mr. Langton told us he was about to establish a school upon his estate, but it had been suggested to him, that it might have a tendency to make the people less industrious. JOHNSON. 'No, Sir. While learning to read and write is a distinction, the few who have that distinction may be the less inclined to work; but when every body learns to read and write, it is no longer a distinction. A man who has a laced waistcoat is too fine a man to work; but if every body had laced waistcoats, we should have people working in laced waistcoats. There are no people whatever more industrious, none who work more, than our manufacturers; yet they have all learnt to read and write. Sir, you must not neglect doing a thing immediately good, from fear of remote evil;—from fear of its being abused. A man who has candles may sit up too late, which he would not do if he had not candles; but nobody will deny that the art of making candles, by which light is continued to us beyond the time that the sun gives us light, is a valuable art, and ought to be preserved.' BOSWELL. 'But, Sir, would it not be better to follow Nature; and go to bed and rise just as nature gives us light or with-holds it?' JOHNSON. 'No, Sir; for then we should have no kind of equality in the partition of our time between sleeping and waking. It would be very different in different seasons and in different places. In some of the northern parts of Scotland how little light is there in the depth of winter!'

We talked of Tacitus, and I hazarded an opinion, that with all his merit for penetration, shrewdness of judgement, and terseness of expression, he was too compact, too much broken into hints, as it were, and therefore too difficult to be understood. To my great satisfaction, Dr. Johnson sanctioned this opinion. 'Tacitus, Sir, seems to me rather to have made notes for an historical work, than to have written a history.'

At this time it appears from his *Prayers and Meditations,* that he had been more than commonly diligent in religious duties, particularly in reading the Holy Scriptures. It was Passion Week, that solemn season which the Christian world has appropriated to the commemoration of the mysteries of our redemption, and during which, whatever embers of religion are in our breasts, will be kindled into pious warmth.

I paid him short visits both on Friday and Saturday, and seeing his large folio Greek Testament before him, beheld him with a reverential awe, and would not intrude upon his time. While he was thus employed to such good purpose, and while his friends in their intercourse with him constantly found a vigorous intellect and a lively imagination, it is melancholy to read in his private register, 'My mind is unsettled and my memory confused. I have of late turned my thoughts with a very useless earnestness upon past incidents. I have yet got no command over my thoughts; an unpleasing incident is almost certain to hinder my rest.' What philosophick heroism was it in him to appear with such manly fortitude to the world, while he was inwardly so distressed! We may surely believe that the mysterious principle of being 'made perfect through suffering' was to be strongly exemplified in him.

On Sunday, April 19, being Easter-day, General Paoli and I paid him a visit before dinner. We talked of the notion that blind persons can distinguish colours by the touch. Johnson said, that Professor Sanderson mentions his having attempted to do it, but that he found he was aiming at an impossibility; that to be sure a difference in the surface makes the difference of colours; but that difference is so fine, that it is not sensible to the touch. The General mentioned jugglers and fraudulent gamesters, who could know cards by the touch. Dr. Johnson said, 'the cards used by such persons must be less polished than ours commonly are.'

We talked of sounds. The General said, there was no beauty in a simple sound, but only in an harmonious composition of sounds. I presumed to differ from this opinion, and mentioned the soft and sweet sound of a fine woman's voice. JOHNSON. 'No, Sir, if a serpent or a toad uttered it, you would think it ugly.' BOSWELL. 'So you would think, Sir, were a beautiful tune to be uttered by one of those animals.' JOHNSON. 'No, Sir, it would be admired. We have seen fine fiddlers whom we liked as little as toads,' (laughing).

Talking on the subject of taste in the arts, he said, that difference of taste was, in truth, difference of skill. BOSWELL. 'But, Sir, is there not a quality called taste, which consists merely in perception or in liking? For instance, we find people differ much as to what is the best style of English composition. Some think Swift's the best; others prefer a fuller and grander way of writing.' JOHNSON. 'Sir, you must first define what you mean by style, before you can judge who has a good taste in style, and who has a bad. The two classes of persons whom you have mentioned don't differ as to good and bad. They both agree that Swift has a good neat style; but one loves a neat style, another loves a style of more splendour. In like manner, one loves a plain coat, another loves a laced coat; but neither will deny that each is good in its kind.'

While I remained in London this spring, I was with him at several other times, both by himself and in company. I dined with him one day at the Crown and Anchor tavern, in the Strand, with Lord Elibank, Mr. Langton, and Dr. Vansittart of Oxford. Without specifying each particular day, I have preserved the following memorable things.

I regretted the reflection in his Preface to Shakspeare against Garrick, to whom we cannot but apply the following passage: 'I collated such copies as I could procure, and wished for more, but have not found the collectors of these

254

rarities very communicative.' I told him, that Garrick had complained to me of it, and had vindicated himself by assuring me, that Johnson was made welcome to the full use of his collection, and that he left the key of it with a servant, with orders to have a fire and every convenience for him. I found Johnson's notion was, that Garrick wanted to be courted for them, and that, on the contrary, Garrick should have courted him, and sent him the plays of his own accord. But, indeed, considering the slovenly and careless manner in which books were treated by Johnson, it could not be expected that scarce and valuable editions should have been lent to him.

A gentleman[1] having to some of the usual arguments for drinking added this: 'You know, Sir, drinking drives away care, and makes us forget whatever is disagreeable. Would not you allow a man to drink for that reason?' JOHNSON. 'Yes, Sir, if he sat next *you*.'

I expressed a liking for Mr. Francis Osborne's works, and asked him what he thought of that writer. He answered, 'A conceited fellow. Were a man to write so now, the boys would throw stones at him.' He, however, did not alter my opinion of a favourite authour, to whom I was first directed by his being quoted in *The Spectator,* and in whom I have found much shrewd and lively sense, expressed indeed in a style somewhat quaint, which, however, I do not dislike. His book has an air of originality. We figure to ourselves an ancient gentleman talking to us.

When one of his friends endeavoured to maintain that a country gentleman might contrive to pass his life very agreeably, 'Sir, (said he,) you cannot give me an instance of any man who is permitted to lay out his own time, contriving not to have tedious hours.' This observation, however, is equally applicable to gentlemen who live in cities, and are of no profession.

He said, 'there is no permanent national character; it varies according to circumstances. Alexander the Great swept India: now the Turks sweep Greece.'

A learned gentleman who in the course of conversation wished to inform us of this simple fact, that the Counsel upon the circuit at Shrewsbury were much bitten by fleas, took, I suppose, seven or eight minutes in relating it circumstantially. He in a plenitude of phrase told us, that large bales of woollen cloth were lodged in the town-hall;—that by reason of this, fleas nestled there in prodigious numbers; that the lodgings of the counsel were near to the town-hall;—and that those little animals moved from place to place with wonderful agility. Johnson sat in great impatience till the gentleman

[1] Boswell.

had finished his tedious narrative and then burst out (playfully however,) 'It is a pity, Sir, that you have not seen a lion; for a flea has taken you such a time, that a lion must have served you a twelve-month.'

He would not allow Scotland to derive any credit from Lord Mansfield; for he was educated in England. 'Much (said he,) may be made of a Scotchman, if he be *caught* young.'

Talking of a modern historian and a modern moralist,[1] he said, 'There is more thought in the moralist than in the historian. There is but a shallow stream of thought in history.' BOSWELL. 'But surely, Sir, an historian has reflection.' JOHNSON. 'Why yes, Sir; and so has a cat when she catches a mouse for her kitten. But she cannot write like *******; neither can *********.'

He said, 'I am very unwilling to read the manuscripts of authours, and give them my opinion. If the authours who apply to me have money, I bid them boldly print without a name; if they have written in order to get money, I tell them to go to the booksellers, and make the best bargain they can.' BOSWELL. 'But, Sir, if a bookseller should bring you a manuscript to look at?' JOHNSON. 'Why, Sir, I would desire the bookseller to take it away.'

I mentioned a friend of mine who had resided long in Spain, and was unwilling to return to Britain. JOHNSON. 'Sir, he is attached to some woman.' BOSWELL. 'I rather believe, Sir, it is the fine climate which keeps him there.' JOHNSON. 'Nay, Sir, how can you talk so? What is *climate* to happiness? Place me in the heart of Asia, should I not be exiled? What proportion does climate bear to the complex system of human life? You may advise me to go to live at Bologna to eat sausages. The sausages there are the best in the world; they lose much by being carried.'

On Saturday, May 9, Mr. Dempster and I had agreed to dine by ourselves at the British Coffee-house. Johnson, on whom I happened to call in the morning, said he would join us, which he did, and we spent a very agreeable day, though I recollect but little of what passed.

He said, 'Walpole was a minister given by the King to the people: Pitt was a minister given by the people to the King, —as an adjunct.'

'The misfortune of Goldsmith in conversation is this: he goes on without knowing how he is to get off. His genius is great, but his knowledge is small. As they say of a generous man, it is a pity he is not rich, we may say of Goldsmith, it is a pity he is not knowing. He would not keep his knowledge to himself.' . . .

[1] Robertson and Beattie.

1773: ÆTAT. 64.]—IN 1773 his only publication was an edition of his folio *Dictionary*, with additions and corrections; nor did he, so far as is known, furnish any productions of his fertile pen to any of his numerous friends or dependants, except the Preface to his old amanuensis Macbean's *Dictionary of Ancient Geography*. His *Shakspeare*, indeed, which had been received with high approbation by the publick, and gone through several editions, was this year re-published by George Steevens, Esq., a gentleman not only deeply skilled in ancient learning, and of very extensive reading in English literature, especially the early writers, but at the same time of acute discernment and elegant taste. It is almost unnecessary to say, that by his great and valuable additions to Dr. Johnson's work, he justly obtained considerable reputation. . . .

On Saturday, April 3, the day after my arrival in London this year, I went to his house late in the evening, and sat with Mrs. Williams till he came home. I found in the *London Chronicle,* Dr. Goldsmith's apology to the publick for beating Evans, a bookseller, on account of a paragraph in a newspaper published by him, which Goldsmith thought impertinent to him and to a lady of his acquaintance. The apology was written so much in Dr. Johnson's manner, that both Mrs. Williams and I supposed it to be his; but when he came home, he soon undeceived us. When he said to Mrs. Williams, 'Well, Dr. Goldsmith's *manifesto* has got into your paper;' I asked him if Dr. Goldsmith had written it, with an air that made him see I suspected it was his, though subscribed by Goldsmith. JOHNSON. 'Sir, Dr. Goldsmith would no more have asked me to write such a thing as that for him, than he would have asked me to feed him with a spoon, or to do anything else that denoted his imbecility. I as much believe that he wrote it, as if I had seen him do it. Sir, had he shewn it to any one friend, he would not have been allowed to publish it. He has indeed, done it very well; but it is a foolish thing well done. I suppose he has been so much elated with the success of his new comedy, that he has thought every thing that concerned him must be of importance to the publick.' BOSWELL. 'I fancy, Sir, this is the first time that he has been engaged in such an adventure.' JOHNSON. 'Why, Sir, I believe it is the first time he has *beat;* he may have *been beaten* before. This, Sir, is a new plume to him.'

I mentioned Sir John Dalrymple's *Memoirs of Great-Britain and Ireland,* and his discoveries to the prejudice of Lord Russel and Algernon Sydney. JOHNSON. 'Why, Sir, every body who had just notions of government thought them rascals before. It is well that all mankind now see them to be rascals.' BOSWELL. 'But, Sir, may not those discoveries be true without their being rascals?' JOHNSON. 'Consider, Sir; would any of them have been willing to have had it known that they intrigued with France? Depend upon it, Sir, he who does what he is afraid should be known, has something rotten about him. This Dalrymple seems to be an honest fellow; for he tells equally what makes against both sides. But nothing can be poorer than his mode of writing: it is the mere bouncing of a school-boy. Great He! but greater She! and such stuff.'

I could not agree with him in this criticism; for though Sir John Dalrymple's style is not regularly formed in any respect, and one cannot help smiling sometimes at his affected *grandiloquence*, there is in his writing a pointed vivacity, and much of a gentlemanly spirit.

At Mr. Thrale's, in the evening, he repeated his usual paradoxical declamation against action in publick speaking. 'Action can have no effect upon reasonable minds. It may augment noise, but it never can enforce argument. If you speak to a dog, you use action; you hold up your hand thus, because he is a brute; and in proportion as men are removed from brutes, action will have the less influence upon them.' MRS. THRALE. 'What then, Sir, becomes of Demosthenes's saying? "Action, action, action!"' JOHNSON. 'Demosthenes, Madam, spoke to an assembly of brutes; to a barbarous people.'

I thought it extraordinary, that he should deny the power of rhetorical action upon human nature, when it is proved by innumerable facts in all stages of society. Reasonable beings are not solely reasonable. They have fancies which may be pleased, passions which may be roused.

Lord Chesterfield being mentioned, Johnson remarked, that almost all of that celebrated nobleman's witty sayings were puns. He, however, allowed the merit of good wit to his Lordship's saying of Lord Tyrawley and himself, when both very old and infirm: 'Tyrawley and I have been dead these two years; but we don't choose to have it known.'

He talked with approbation of an intended edition of *The Spectator*, with notes; two volumes of which had been prepared by a gentleman eminent in the literary world, and the materials which he had collected for the remainder had been transferred to another hand. He observed, that all works which describe manners, require notes in sixty or seventy years, or less; and told us, he had communicated all he knew that could throw light upon *The Spectator*. He said, 'Addison had made his Sir Andrew Freeport a true Whig, arguing against giving charity to beggars, and throwing out other such ungracious sentiments; but that he had thought better, and

258

made amends by making him found an hospital for decayed farmers. He called for the volume of *The Spectator,* in which that account is contained, and read it aloud to us. He read so well, that every thing acquired additional weight and grace from his utterance. . . .

On Thursday, April 8, I sat a good part of the evening with him, but he was very silent. He said, 'Burnet's *History of his own Times* is very entertaining. The style, indeed, is mere chit-chat. I do not believe that Burnet intentionally lyed; but he was so much prejudiced, that he took no pains to find out the truth. He was like a man who resolves to regulate his time by a certain watch; but will not inquire whether the watch is right or not.'

Though he was not disposed to talk, he was unwilling that I should leave him; and when I looked at my watch, and told him it was twelve o'clock, he cried, 'What's that to you and me?' and ordered Frank to tell Mrs. Williams that we were coming to drink tea with her, which we did. It was settled that we should go to church together next day.

On the 9th of April, being Good Friday, I breakfasted with him on tea and cross-buns; *Doctor* Levet, as Frank called him, making the tea. He carried me with him to the church of St. Clement Danes, where he had his seat; and his behaviour was, as I had imaged to myself, solemnly devout. I never shall forget the tremulous earnestness with which he pronounced the awful petition in the Litany: 'In the hour of death, and at the day of judgement, good LORD deliver us.'

We went to church both in the morning and evening. In the interval between the two services we did not dine; but he read in the Greek New Testament, and I turned over several of his books.

In Archbisop Laud's Diary, I found the following passage, which I read to Dr. Johnson:—

'1623. February 1, Sunday. I stood by the most illustrious Prince Charles, at dinner. He was then very merry, and talked occasionally of many things with his attendants. Among other things, he said, that if he were necessitated to take any particular profession of life, he could not be a lawyer, adding his reasons: "I cannot (saith he,) defend a bad, nor yield in a good cause." '

JOHNSON. 'Sir, this is false reasoning; because every cause has a bad side: and a lawyer is not overcome, though the cause which he has endeavoured to support be determined against him.'

I told him that Goldsmith had said to me a few days before, 'As I take my shoes from the shoemaker, and my coat from the taylor, so I take my religion from the priest.' I regretted this loose way of talking. JOHNSON. 'Sir, he knows nothing; he has made up his mind about nothing.'

To my great surprize he asked me to dine with him on Easter-day. I never supposed that he had a dinner at his house; for I had not then heard of any one of his friends having been entertained at his table. He told me, 'I generally have a meat pye on Sunday: it is baked at a publick oven, which is very properly allowed, because one man can attend it; and thus the advantage is obtained of not keeping servants from church to dress dinners.'

April 11, being Easter-Sunday, after having attended Divine Service at St. Paul's, I repaired to Dr. Johnson's. I had gratified my curiosity much in dining with JEAN JACQUES ROUSSEAU, while he lived in the wilds of Neufchatel: I had as great a curiosity to dine with DR. SAMUEL JOHNSON, in the dusky recess of a court in Fleet-street. I supposed we should scarcely have knives and forks, and only some strange, uncouth, ill-drest dish: but I found every thing in very good order. We had no other company but Mrs. Williams and a young woman whom I did not know. As a dinner here was considered as a singular phænomenon, and as I was frequently interrogated on the subject, my readers may perhaps be desirous to know our bill of fare. Foote, I remember, in allusion to Francis, the *negro,* was willing to suppose that our repast was *black broth.* But the fact was, that we had a very good soup, a boiled leg of lamb and spinach, a veal pye, and a rice pudding.

Of Dr. John Campbell, the authour, he said, 'He is a very inquisitive and a very able man, and a man of good religious principles, though I am afraid he has been deficient in practice. Campbell is radically right; and we may hope, that in time there will be good practice.'

He owned that he thought Hawkesworth was one of his imitators, but he did not think Goldsmith was. Goldsmith, he said, had great merit. BOSWELL. 'But, Sir, he is much indebted to you for his getting so high in the publick estimation.' JOHNSON. 'Why, Sir, he has perhaps got *sooner* to it by his intimacy with me.'

Goldsmith, though his vanity often excited him to occasional competition, had a very high regard for Johnson, which he at this time expressed in the strongest manner in the Dedication of his comedy, entitled, *She Stoops to Conquer.* . . .

I put a question to him upon a fact in common life, which he could not answer, nor have I found any one else who could. What is the reason that women servants, though obliged to be at the expense of purchasing their own clothes, have much lower wages than men servants, to whom a great proportion of that article is furnished, and when in fact our female house servants work much harder than the male?

He told me, that he had twelve or fourteen times attempted to keep a journal of his life, but never could persevere. He advised me to do it. 'The great thing to be recorded, (said he,) is the state of your own mind; and you should write down every thing that you remember, for you cannot judge at first what is good or bad; and write immediately while the impression is fresh, for it will not be the same a week afterwards.'

I again solicited him to communicate to me the particulars of his early life. He said, 'You shall have them all for two-pence. I hope you shall know a great deal more of me before you write my Life.' He mentioned to me this day many circumstances, which I wrote down when I went home, and have interwoven in the former part of this narrative.

On Tuesday, April 13, he and Dr. Goldsmith and I dined at General Oglethorpe's. Goldsmith expatiated on the common topick, that the race of our people was degenerated, and that this was owing to luxury. JOHNSON. 'Sir, in the first place, I doubt the fact. I believe there are as many tall men in England now, as ever there were. But, secondly, supposing the stature of our people to be diminished, that is not owing to luxury; for, Sir, consider to how very small a proportion of our people luxury can reach. Our soldiery, surely, are not luxurious, who live on six-pence a day; and the same remark will apply to almost all the other classes. Luxury, so far as it reaches the poor, will do good to the race of people; it will strengthen, and multiply them. Sir, no nation was ever hurt by luxury; for, as I said before, it can reach but to a very few. I admit that the great increase of commerce and manufactures hurts the military spirit of a people; because it produces a competition for something else than martial honours,—a competition for riches. It also hurts the bodies of the people; for you will observe, there is no man who works at any particular trade, but you may know him from his appearance to do so. One part or other of his body being more used than the rest, he is in some degree deformed: but, Sir, that is not luxury. A tailor sits cross-legged; but that is not luxury.' GOLDSMITH. 'Come, you're just going to the same place by another road.' JOHNSON. 'Nay, Sir, I say that is not *luxury*. Let us take a walk from Charing-cross to Whitechapel, through, I suppose, the greatest series of shops in the world; what is there in any of these shops (if you except gin-shops,) that can do any human being any harm?' GOLDSMITH. 'Well, Sir, I'll accept your challenge. The very next shop to Northumberland-house is a pickle-shop.'

JOHNSON. 'Well, Sir: do we not know that a maid can in one afternoon make pickles sufficient to serve a whole family for a year? nay, that five pickle-shops can serve all the kingdom? Besides, Sir, there is no harm done to any body by the making of pickles, or the eating of pickles.'

We drank tea with the ladies; and Goldsmith sung Tony Lumpkin's song in his comedy, *She Stoops to Conquer,* and a very pretty one, to an Irish tune, which he had designed for Miss Hardcastle; but as Mrs. Bulkeley, who played the part, could not sing, it was left out. He afterwards wrote it down for me, by which means it was preserved, and now appears amongst his poems. Dr. Johnson, in his way home, stopped at my lodgings in Piccadilly, and sat with me, drinking tea a second time, till a late hour.

I told him that Mrs. Macaulay said, she wondered how he could reconcile his political principles with his moral; his notions of inequality and subordination with wishing well to the happiness of all mankind, who might live so agreeably, had they all their portions of land, and none to domineer over another. JOHNSON. 'Why, Sir, I reconcile my principles very well, because mankind are happier in a state of inequality and subordination. Were they to be in this pretty state of equality, they would soon degenerate into brutes;—they would become Monboddo's nation;—their tails would grow. Sir, all would be losers were all to work for all:—they would have no intellectual improvement. All intellectual improvement arises from leisure; all leisure arises from one working for another.'

Talking of the family of Stuart, he said, 'It should seem that the family at present on the throne has now established as good a right as the former family, by the long consent of the people; and that to disturb this right might be considered as culpable. At the same time I own, that it is a very difficult question, when considered with respect to the house of Stuart. To oblige people to take oaths as to the disputed right, is wrong. I know not whether I could take them: but I do not blame those who do.' So conscientious and so delicate was he upon this subject, which has occasioned so much clamour against him. . . .

On Thursday, April 15, I dined with him and Dr. Goldsmith at General Paoli's. We found here Signor Martinelli, of Florence, authour of a *History of England,* in Italian, printed at London.

I spoke of Allan Ramsay's *Gentle Shepherd,* in the Scottish dialect, as the best pastoral that had ever been written; not only abounding with beautiful rural imagery, and just and pleasing sentiments, but being a real picture of manners; and

I offered to teach Dr. Johnson to understand it. 'No, Sir, (said he,) I won't learn it. You shall retain your superiority by my not knowing it.'

This brought on a question whether one man is lessened by another's acquiring an equal degree of knowledge with him. Johnson asserted the affirmative. I maintained that the position might be true in those kinds of knowledge which produce wisdom, power, and force, so as to enable one man to have the government of others; but that a man is not in any degree lessened by others knowing as well as he what ends in mere pleasure:—eating fine fruits, drinking delicious wines, reading exquisite poetry.

The General observed, that Martinelli was a Whig. JOHNSON. 'I am sorry for it. It shows the spirit of the times: he is obliged to temporise.' BOSWELL. 'I rather think, Sir, that Toryism prevails in this reign.' JOHNSON. 'I know not why you should think so, Sir. You see your friend Lord Lyttelton, a nobleman, is obliged in his *History* to write the most vulgar Whiggism.'

An animated debate took place whether Martinelli should continue his *History of England* to the present day. GOLDSMITH. 'To be sure he should.' JOHNSON. 'No, Sir; he would give great offence. He would have to tell of almost all the living great what they do not wish told.' GOLDSMITH. 'It may, perhaps, be necessary for a native to be more cautious; but a foreigner who comes among us without prejudice, may be considered as holding the place of a Judge, and may speak his mind freely.' JOHNSON. 'Sir, a foreigner, when he sends a work from the press, ought to be on his guard against catching the errour and mistaken enthusiasm of the people among whom he happens to be.' GOLDSMITH. 'Sir, he wants only to sell his history, and to tell truth; one an honest, the other a laudable motive.' JOHNSON. 'Sir, they are both of laudable motives. It is laudable in a man to wish to live by his labours; but he should write so as he may *live* by them, not so as he may be knocked on the head. I would advise him to be at Calais before he publishes his history of the present age. A foreigner who attaches himself to a political party in this country, is in the worst state that can be imagined: he is looked upon as a mere intermeddler. A native may do it from interest.' BOSWELL. 'Or principle.' GOLDSMITH. There are people who tell a hundred political lies every day, and are not hurt by it. Surely, then, one may tell truth with safety.' JOHNSON. 'Why, Sir, in the first place, he who tells a hundred lies has disarmed the force of his lies. But besides; a man had rather have a hundred lies told of him, than one truth which he does not

263

wish should be told.' GOLDSMITH. 'For my part, I'd tell truth, and shame the devil.' JOHNSON. 'Yes, Sir; but the devil will be angry. I wish to shame the devil as much as you do, but I should choose to be out of the reach of his claws.' GOLDSMITH. 'His claws can do you no harm, when you have the shield of truth.'

It having been observed that there was little hospitality in London;—JOHNSON. 'Nay, Sir, any man who has a name, or who has the power of pleasing, will be very generally invited in London. The man, Sterne, I have been told, has had engagements for three months.' GOLDSMITH. 'And a very dull fellow.' JOHNSON. 'Why no, Sir.'

Martinelli told us, that for several years he lived much with Charles Townshend, and that he ventured to tell him he was a bad joker. JOHNSON. 'Why, Sir, thus much I can say upon the subject. One day he and a few more agreed to go and dine in the country, and each of them was to bring a friend in his carriage with him. Charles Townshend asked Fitzherbert to go with him, but told him, "You must find somebody to bring you back: I can only carry you there." Fitzherbert did not much like this arrangement. He however consented, observing sarcastically, "It will do very well; for then the same jokes will serve you in returning as in going." '

An eminent publick character[1] being mentioned;—JOHNSON. 'I remember being present when he shewed himself to be so corrupted, or at least something so different from what I think right, as to maintain, that a member of parliament should go along with his party right or wrong. Now, Sir, this is so remote from native virtue, from scholastick virtue, that a good man must have undergone a great change before he can reconcile himself to such a doctrine. It is maintaining that you may lie to the publick; for you lie when you call that right which you think wrong, or the reverse. A friend of ours,[2] who is too much an echo of that gentleman, observed, that a man who does not stick uniformly to a party, is only waiting to be bought. Why then, said I, he is only waiting to be what that gentleman is already.'

We talked of the King's coming to see Goldsmith's new play.—'I wish he would,' said Goldsmith; adding, however, with an affected indifference, 'Not that it would do me the least good.' JOHNSON. 'Well then, Sir, let us say it would do *him* good, (laughing.) No, Sir, this affectation will not pass;—it is mighty idle. In such a state as ours, who would

[1] Burke.
[2] Reynolds.

not wish to please the Chief Magistrate?' GOLDSMITH. 'I *do* wish to please him. I remember a line in Dryden,—

> "And every poet is the monarch's friend."

It ought to be reversed.' JOHNSON. 'Nay, there are finer lines in Dryden on this subject:—

> "For colleges on bounteous Kings depend,
> And never rebel was to arts a friend." '

General Paoli observed, that 'successful rebels might.' MARTINELLI. 'Happy rebellions.' GOLDSMITH. 'We have no such phrase.' GENERAL PAOLI. 'But have you not the *thing?*' GOLDSMITH. 'Yes; all our *happy* revolutions. They have hurt our constitution, and will hurt it, till we mend it by another HAPPY REVOLUTION.' I never before discovered that my friend Goldsmith had so much of the old prejudice in him. . . .

A person was mentioned, who it was said could take down in short hand the speeches in parliament with perfect exactness. JOHNSON. 'Sir, it is impossible. I remember one Angel, who came to me to write for him a Preface or Dedication to a book upon short hand, and he professed to write as fast as a man could speak. In order to try him, I took down a book, and read while he wrote; and I favoured him, for I read more deliberately than usual. I had proceeded but a very little way, when he begged I would desist, for he could not follow me.' Hearing now for the first time of this Preface or Dedication, I said, 'What an expense, Sir, do you put us to in buying books, to which you have written Prefaces or Dedications.' JOHNSON. 'Why, I have dedicated to the Royal family all round; that is to say, to the last generation of the Royal Family.' GOLDSMITH. 'And perhaps, Sir, not one sentence of wit in a whole Dedication.' JOHNSON. 'Perhaps not, Sir.' BOSWELL. 'What then is the reason for applying to a particular person to do that which any one may do as well?' JOHNSON. 'Why, Sir, one man has greater readiness at doing it than another.'

I spoke of Mr. Harris, of Salisbury, as being a very learned man, and in particular an eminent Grecian. JOHNSON. 'I am not sure of that. His friends give him out as such, but I know not who of his friends are able to judge of it.' GOLDSMITH. 'He is what is much better: he is a worthy humane man.' JOHNSON. 'Nay, Sir, that is not to the purpose of our argument: that will as much prove that he can play upon the fiddle as well as Giardini, as that he is an eminent Grecian.' GOLDSMITH. 'The greatest musical performers have but small emoluments. Giardini, I am told, does not get above seven hundred a year.' JOHNSON. 'That is, indeed, but little for a man to get, who does best that which so many endeavour to do. There is nothing, I think, in which the power of art is shown so much as in playing on the fiddle. In all other things we can do something at first. Any man will forge a bar of iron, if you give him a hammer; not so well as a smith, but tolerably. A man will saw a piece of wood, and make a box, though a clumsy one; but give him a fiddle and a fiddle-stick, and he can do nothing.'

On Monday, April 19, he called on me with Mrs. Williams, in Mr. Strahan's coach, and carried me out to dine with Mr. Elphinston, at his academy at Kensington. A printer having acquired a fortune sufficient to keep his coach, was a good topick for the credit of literature. Mrs. Williams said, that another printer, Mr. Hamilton, had not waited so long as Mr. Strahan, but had kept his coach several years sooner. JOHNSON. 'He was in the right. Life is short. The sooner that a man begins to enjoy his wealth the better.'

Mr. Elphinston talked of a new book that was much admired, and asked Dr. Johnson if he had read it. JOHNSON. 'I have looked into it.' 'What, (said Elphinston,) have you not read it through?' Johnson, offended at being thus pressed, and so obliged to own his cursory mode of reading, answered tartly, 'No, Sir, do *you* read books *through?*'

He this day again defended duelling, and put his argument upon what I have ever thought the most solid basis; that if publick war be allowed to be consistent with morality, private war must be equally so. Indeed we may observe what strained arguments are used, to reconcile war with the Christian religion. But, in my opinion, it is exceedingly clear that duelling, having better reasons for its barbarous violence, is more justifiable than war, in which thousands go forth without any cause of personal quarrel, and massacre each other.

On Wednesday, April 21, I dined with him at Mr. Thrale's. A gentleman[1] attacked Garrick for being vain. JOHNSON. 'No wonder, Sir, that he is vain; a man who is perpetually flattered in every mode that can be conceived. So many bellows have blown the fire, that one wonders he is not by this time become a cinder.' BOSWELL. 'And such bellows too. Lord Mansfield with his cheeks like to burst: Lord Chatham like an Æolus. I have read such notes from them to him, as were enough to turn his head.' JOHNSON. 'True. When he whom every body else flatters, flatters me, I then am truly happy.' MRS. THRALE. 'The sentiment is in Congreve, I think.' JOHNSON. 'Yes, Madam, in *The Way of the World:*

"If there's delight in love, 'tis when I see

1 Murphy.

266

That heart which others bleed for, bleed for me."

. . . The modes of living in different countries, and the various views with which men travel in quest of new scenes, having been talked of, a learned gentleman who holds a considerable office in the law, expatiated on the happiness of a savage life; and mentioned an instance of an officer who had actually lived for some time in the wilds of America, of whom, when in that state, he quoted this reflection with an air of admiration, as if it had been deeply philosophical: 'Here am I, free and unrestrained, amidst the rude magnificence of Nature, with this Indian woman by my side, and this gun with which I can procure food when I want it: what more can be desired for human happiness?' It did not require much sagacity to foresee that such a sentiment would not be permitted to pass without due animadversion. JOHNSON. 'Do not allow yourself, Sir, to be imposed upon by such gross absurdity. It is sad stuff; it is brutish. If a bull could speak, he might as well exclaim,—Here am I with this cow and this grass; what being can enjoy greater felicity?'

We talked of the melancholy end of a gentleman[1] who had destroyed himself. JOHNSON. 'It was owing to imaginary difficulties in his affairs, which, had he talked with any friend, would soon have vanished.' BOSWELL. 'Do you think, Sir, that all who commit suicide are mad?' JOHNSON. 'Sir, they are often not universally disordered in their intellects, but one passion presses so upon them, that they yield to it, and commit suicide, as a passionate man will stab another.' He added, 'I have often thought, that after a man has taken the resolution to kill himself, it is not courage in him to do any thing, however desperate, because he has nothing to fear.' GOLDSMITH. 'I don't see that.' JOHNSON. 'Nay but, my dear Sir, why should not you see what every one else sees?' GOLDSMITH. 'It is for fear of something that he has resolved to kill himself; and will not that timid disposition restrain him?' JOHNSON. 'It does not signify that the fear of something made him resolve; it is upon the state of his mind, after the resolution is taken, that I argue. Suppose a man, either from fear, or pride, or conscience, or whatever motive, has resolved to kill himself; when once the resolution is taken, he has nothing to fear. He may then go and take the King of Prussia by the nose, at the head of his army. He cannot fear the rack, who is resolved to kill himself. When Eustace Budgel was walking down to the Thames, determined to drown himself, he might, if he

[1] William Fitzherbert.

pleased, without any apprehension of danger, have turned aside, and first set fire to St. James's palace.'

On Tuesday, April 27, Mr. Beauclerk and I called on him in the morning. As we walked up Johnson's-court, I said, 'I have a veneration for this court;' and was glad to find that Beauclerk had the same reverential enthusiasm. . . .

He said, 'Goldsmith should not be for ever attempting to shine in conversation: he has not temper for it, he is so much mortified when he fails. Sir, a game of jokes is composed partly of skill, partly of chance. A man may be beat at times by one who has not the tenth part of his wit. Now Goldsmith's putting himself against another, is like a man laying a hundred to one who cannot spare the hundred. It is not worth a man's while. A man should not lay a hundred to one, unless he can easily spare it, though he has a hundred chances for him: he can get but a guinea, and he may lose a hundred. Goldsmith is in this state. When he contends, if he gets the better, it is a very little addition to a man of his literary reputation: if he does not get the better, he is miserably vexed.'

Johnson's own superlative power of wit set him above any risk of such uneasiness. Garrick had remarked to me of him, a few days before, 'Rabelais and all other wits are nothing compared with him. You may be diverted by them; but Johnson gives you a forcible hug, and shakes laughter out of you, whether you will or no.'

Goldsmith, however, was often very fortunate in his witty contests, even when he entered the lists with Johnson himself. Sir Joshua Reynolds was in company with them one day, when Goldsmith said, that he thought he could write a good fable, mentioned the simplicity which that kind of composition requires, and observed, that in most fables the animals introduced seldom talk in character. 'For instance, (said he,) the fable of the little fishes, who saw birds fly over their heads, and envying them, petitioned Jupiter to be changed into birds. The skill (continued he,) consists in making them talk like little fishes.' While he indulged himself in this fanciful reverie, he observed Johnson shaking his sides and laughing. Upon which he smartly proceeded, 'Why, Dr. Johnson, this is not so easy as you seem to think; for if you were to make little fishes talk, they would talk like WHALES.'

Johnson, though remarkable for his great variety of composition, never exercised his talents in fable, except we allow his beautiful tale published in Mrs. Williams's *Miscellanies* to be of that species. I have, however, found among his manuscript collections the following sketch of one:—

'Glow-worm lying in the garden saw a candle in a neighbouring palace,—and complained of the littleness of his own light;—another observed—wait a little;—soon dark;—have outlasted πολλ [*many*] of these glaring lights which are only brighter as they haste to nothing.'

On Thursday, April 29, I dined with him at General Oglethorpe's, where were Sir Joshua Reynolds, Mr. Langton, Dr. Goldsmith, and Mr. Thrale. I was very desirous to get Dr. Johnson absolutely fixed in his resolution to go with me to the Hebrides this year; and I told him that I had received a letter from Dr. Robertson the historian, upon the subject, with which he was much pleased; and now talked in such a manner of his long-intended tour, that I was satisfied he meant to fulfil his engagement.

The custom of eating dogs at Otaheite being mentioned, Goldsmith observed, that this was also a custom in China; that a dog-butcher is as common there as any other butcher; and that when he walks abroad all the dogs fall on him. JOHNSON. 'That is not owing to his killing dogs, Sir. I remember a butcher at Lichfield, whom a dog that was in the house where I lived, always attacked. It is the smell of carnage which provokes this, let the animals he has killed be what they may.' GOLDSMITH. 'Yes, there is a general abhorrence in animals at the signs of massacre. If you put a tub full of blood into a stable, the horses are like to go mad.' JOHNSON. 'I doubt that.' GOLDSMITH. 'Nay, Sir, it is a fact well authenticated.' THRALE. 'You had better prove it before you put it into your book on natural history. You may do it in my stable if you will.' JOHNSON. 'Nay, Sir, I would not have him prove it. If he is content to take his information from others, he may get through his book with little trouble, and without much endangering his reputation. But if he makes experiments for so comprehensive a book as his, there would be no end to them; his erroneous assertions would then fall upon himself, and he might be blamed for not having made experiments as to every particular.'

The character of Mallet having been introduced, and spoken of slightingly by Goldsmith; JOHNSON. 'Why, Sir, Mallet had talents enough to keep his literary reputation alive as long as he himself lived; and that, let me tell you, is a good deal.' GOLDSMITH. 'But I cannot agree that it was so. His literary reputation was dead long before his natural death. I consider an authour's literary reputation to be alive only while his name will ensure a good price for his copy from the booksellers. I will get you (to Johnson,) a hundred guineas for any thing whatever that you shall write, if you put your name to it.'

Dr. Goldsmith's new play, *She Stoops to Conquer*, being mentioned; JOHNSON. 'I know of no comedy for many years that has so much exhilarated an audience, that has answered so much the great end of comedy—making an audience merry.'

Goldsmith having said, that Garrick's compliment to the Queen, which he introduced into the play of *The Chances,* which he had altered and revised this year, was mean and gross flattery; JOHNSON. 'Why, Sir, I would not *write,* I would not give solemnly under my hand, a character beyond what I thought really true; but a speech on the stage, let it flatter ever so extravagantly, is formular. It has always been formular to flatter Kings and Queens; so much so, that even in our church-service we have "our most religious King," used indiscriminately, whoever is King. Nay, they even flatter themselves;—"we have been graciously pleased to grant." No modern flattery, however, is so gross as that of the Augustan age, where the Emperour was deified. *"Præsens Divus habebitur Augustus."*[1] And as to meanness, (rising into warmth,) how is it mean in a player,—a showman,—a fellow who exhibits himself for a shilling, to flatter his Queen? The attempt, indeed, was dangerous; for if it had missed, what became of Garrick, and what became of the Queen? As Sir William Temple says of a great General, it is necessary not only that his designs should be formed in a masterly manner, but that they should be attended with success. Sir, it is right, at a time when the Royal Family is not generally liked, to let it be seen that the people like at least one of them.' SIR JOSHUA REYNOLDS. 'I do not perceive why the profession of a player should be despised; for the great and ultimate end of all the employments of mankind is to produce amusement. Garrick produces more amusement than any body.' BOSWELL. 'You say, Dr. Johnson, that Garrick exhibits himself for a shilling. In this respect he is only on a footing with a lawyer who exhibits himself for his fee, and even will maintain any nonsense or absurdity, if the case requires it. Garrick refuses a play or a part which he does not like; a lawyer never refuses.' JOHNSON. 'Why, Sir, what does this prove? only that a lawyer is worse. Boswell is now like Jack in *The Tale of a Tub,* who, when he is puzzled by an argument, hangs himself. He thinks I shall cut him down, but I'll let him hang,' (laughing vociferously.) SIR JOSHUA REYNOLDS. 'Mr. Boswell thinks that the profession of a lawyer being unquestionably honourable, if he can show the profession of a player to be more honourable, he proves his argument.'

[1] 'Augustus shall be esteemed a God on earth.' Horace, *Odes,* III. v. 2-3.

On Friday, April 30, I dined with him at Mr. Beauclerk's, where were Lord Charlemont, Sir Joshua Reynolds, and some more members of the LITERARY CLUB, whom he had obligingly invited to meet me, as I was this evening to be balloted for as candidate for admission into that distinguished society. Johnson had done me the honour to propose me, and Beauclerk was very zealous for me.

Goldsmith being mentioned; JOHNSON. 'It is amazing how little Goldsmith knows. He seldom comes where he is not more ignorant than any one else.' SIR JOSHUA REYNOLDS. 'Yet there is no man whose company is more liked.' JOHNSON. 'To be sure, Sir. When people find a man of the most distinguished abilities as a writer, their inferiour while he is with them, it must be highly gratifying to them. What Goldsmith comically says of himself is very true,—he always gets the better when he argues alone; meaning, that he is master of a subject in his study, and can write well upon it; but when he comes into company, grows confused, and unable to talk. Take him as a poet, his *Traveller* is a very fine performance; ay, and so is his *Deserted Village,* were it not sometimes too much the echo of his *Traveller*. Whether, indeed, we take him as a poet,—as a comick writer,—or as an historian, he stands in the first class.' BOSWELL. 'An historian! My dear Sir, you surely will not rank his compilation of the Roman History with the works of other historians of this age?' JOHNSON. 'Why, who are before him?' BOSWELL 'Hume,—Robertson,—Lord Lyttelton.' JOHNSON (his antipathy to the Scotch beginning to rise). 'I have not read Hume; but, doubtless, Goldsmith's *History* is better than the *verbiage* of Robertson, or the fo₋pery of Dalrymple.' BOSWELL. 'Will you not admit the superiority of Robertson, in whose *History* we find such penetration—such painting?' JOHNSON. 'Sir, you must consider how that penetration and that painting are employed. It is not history, it is imagination. He who describes what he never saw, draws from fancy. Robertson paints minds as Sir Joshua paints faces in a history-piece: he imagines an heroic countenance. You must look upon Robertson's work as romance, and try it by that standard. History it is not. Besides, Sir, it is the great excellence of a writer to put into his book as much as his book will hold. Goldsmith has done this in his *History*. Now Robertson might have put twice as much into his book. Robertson is like a man who has packed gold in wool: the wool takes up more room than the gold. No, Sir; I always thought Robertson would be crushed by his own weight,—would be buried under his own ornaments. Goldsmith tells you shortly all you want to know: Robertson detains you a great deal too

271

long. No man will read Robertson's cumbrous detail a second time; but Goldsmith's plain narrative will please again and again. I would say to Robertson what an old tutor of a college said to one of his pupils: "Read over your compositions, and where ever you meet with a passage which you think is particularly fine, strike it out." Goldsmith's abridgement is better than that of Lucius Florus or Eutropius; and I will venture to say, that if you compare him with Vertot, in the same places of the Roman History, you will find that he excels Vertot. Sir, he has the art of compiling, and of saying every thing he has to say in a pleasing manner. He is now writing a Natural History and will make it as entertaining as a Persian Tale.'

I cannot dismiss the present topick without observing, that it is probable that Dr. Johnson, who owned that he often 'talked for victory,' rather urged plausible objections to Dr. Robertson's excellent historical works, in the ardour of contest, than expressed his real and decided opinion; for it is not easy to suppose, that he should so widely differ from the rest of the literary world.

JOHNSON. 'I remember once being with Goldsmith in Westminster-abbey. While we surveyed the Poets' Corner, I said to him,

"Forsitan et nostrum nomen miscebitur istis."[1]

When we got to Temple-bar he stopped me, pointed to the heads upon it, and slily whispered me,

"Forsitan et nostrum nomen miscebitur ISTIS."[2]

Johnson praised John Bunyan highly. 'His *Pilgrim's Progress* has great merit, both for invention, imagination, and the conduct of the story; and it has had the best evidence of its merit, the general and continued approbation of mankind. Few books, I believe, have had a more extensive sale. It is remarkable, that it begins very much like the poem of Dante; yet there was no translation of Dante when Bunyan wrote. There is reason to think that he had read Spenser.'

A proposition which had been agitated, that monuments to eminent persons should, for the time to come, be erected in St. Paul's church as well as in Westminster-abbey, was mentioned; and it was asked, who should be honoured by having his monument first erected there. Somebody suggested Pope.

[1] 'Perhaps our names will mingle with these.' Ovid, *Art of Love*, iii. 339.

[2] In allusion to Dr. Johnson's supposed political principles, and perhaps his own—B.

JOHNSON. 'Why, Sir, as Pope was a Roman Catholick, I would not have his to be first. I think Milton's rather should have the precedence. I think more highly of him now than I did at twenty. There is more thinking in him and in Butler, than in any of our poets.'

Some of the company expressed a wonder why the authour of so excellent a book as *The Whole Duty of Man* should conceal himself. JOHNSON. 'There may be different reasons assigned for this, any one of which would be very sufficient. He may have been a clergyman, and may have thought that his religious counsels would have less weight when known to come from a man whose profession was Theology. He may have been a man whose practice was not suitable to his principles, so that his character might injure the effect of his book, which he had written in a season of penitence. Or he may have been a man of rigid self-denial, so that he would have no reward for his pious labours while in this world, but refer it all to a future state.'

The gentlemen went away to their club, and I was left at Beauclerk's till the fate of my election should be announced to me. I sat in a state of anxiety which even the charming conversation of Lady Di Beauclerk could not entirely dissipate. In a short time I received the agreeable intelligence that I was chosen. I hastened to the place of meeting, and was introduced to such a society as can seldom be found. Mr. Edmund Burke, whom I then saw for the first time, and whose splendid talents had long made me ardently wish for his acquaintance; Dr. Nugent, Mr. Garrick, Dr. Goldsmith, Mr. (afterwards Sir William) Jones, and the company with whom I had dined. Upon my entrance, Johnson placed himself behind a chair, on which he leaned as on a desk or pulpit, and with humorous formality gave me a *Charge,* pointing out the conduct expected from me as a good member of this club.

Goldsmith produced some very absurd verses which had been publickly recited to an audience for money. JOHNSON. 'I can match this nonsense. There was a poem called *Eugenio,* which came out some years ago, and concludes thus:

> "And now, ye trifling, self-assuming elves,
> Brimful of pride, of nothing, of yourselves,
> Survey Eugenio, view him o'er and o'er,
> Then sink into yourselves, and be no more."

Nay, Dryden in his poem on the Royal Society, has these lines:

> "Then we upon our globe's last verge shall go,
> And see the ocean leaning on the sky;

> From thence our rolling neighbours we shall know,
> And on the lunar world securely pry." '

. . . Much pleasant conversation passed, which Johnson relished with great good humour. But his conversation alone, or what led to it, or was interwoven with it, is the business of this work.

On Saturday, May 1, we dined by ourselves at our old rendezvous, the Mitre tavern. He was placid, but not much disposed to talk. He observed that 'The Irish mix better with the English than the Scotch do; their language is nearer to English; as a proof of which, they succeed very well as players, which Scotchmen do not. Then, Sir, they have not that extreme nationality which we find in the Scotch. I will do you, Boswell, the justice to say, that you are the most *unscottified* of your countrymen. You are almost the only instance of a Scotchman that I have known, who did not at every other sentence bring in some other Scotchman.' . . .

On Friday, May 7, I breakfasted with him at Mr. Thrale's in the Borough. While we were alone, I endeavoured as well as I could to apologise for a lady[1] who had been divorced from her husband by act of Parliament. I said, that he had used her very ill, had behaved brutally to her, and that she could not continue to live with him without having her delicacy contaminated; that all affection for him was thus destroyed; that the essence of conjugal union being gone, there remained only a cold form, a mere civil obligation; that she was in the prime of life, with qualities to produce happiness; that these ought not to be lost; and, that the gentleman[2] on whose account she was divorced had gained her heart while thus unhappily situated. Seduced, perhaps, by the charms of the lady in question, I thus attempted to palliate what I was sensible could not be justified; for, when I had finished my harangue, my venerable friend gave me a proper check: 'My dear Sir, never accustom your mind to mingle virtue and vice. The woman's a whore, and there's an end on't.'

He described the father[3] of one of his friends thus: 'Sir, he was so exuberant a talker at publick meetings, that the gentlemen of his county were afraid of him. No business could be done for his declamation.'

He did not give me full credit when I mentioned that I had carried on a short conversation by signs with some Esquimaux who were then in London, particularly with one of them who was a priest. He thought I could not make them

---

1 Lady Diana Beauclerk.
2 Topham Beauclerk.
3 Old Mr. Langton.

understand me. No man was more incredulous as to particular facts, which were at all extraordinary; and therefore no man was more scrupulously inquisitive, in order to discover the truth.

I dined with him this day at the house of my friends, Messieurs Edward and Charles Dilly, booksellers in the Poultry: there were present, their elder brother Mr. Dilly of Bedfordshire, Dr. Goldsmith, Mr. Langton, Mr. Claxton, Reverend Dr. Mayo a dissenting minister, the Reverend Mr. Toplady, and my friend the Reverend Mr. Temple.

Hawkesworth's compilation of the voyages to the South Sea being mentioned; JOHNSON. 'Sir, if you talk of it as a subject of commerce, it will be gainful; if as a book that is to increase human knowledge, I believe there will not be much of that. Hawkesworth can tell only what the voyagers have told him; and they have found very little, only one new animal, I think.' BOSWELL. 'But many insects, Sir. JOHNSON. 'Why, Sir, as to insects, Ray reckons of British insects twenty thousand species. They might have staid at home and discovered enough in that way.'

Talking of birds, I mentioned Mr. Daines Barrington's ingenious Essay against the received notion of their migration. JOHNSON. 'I think we have as good evidence for the migration of woodcocks as can be desired. We find they disappear at a certain time of the year, and appear again at a certain time of the year; and some of them, when weary in their flight, have been known to alight on the rigging of ships far out at sea.' One of the company observed, that there had been instances of some of them found in summer in Essex. JOHNSON. 'Sir, that strengthens our argument. *Exceptio probat regulam*.[1] Some being found shews, that, if all remained, many would be found. A few sick or lame ones may be found.' GOLDSMITH. 'There is a partial migration of the swallows; the stronger ones migrate, the others do not.'

BOSWELL. 'I am well assured that the people of Otaheite who have the bread tree, the fruit of which serves them for bread, laughed heartily when they were informed of the tedious process necessary with us to have bread;—plowing, sowing, harrowing, reaping, threshing, grinding, baking.' JOHNSON. 'Why, Sir, all ignorant savages will laugh when they are told of the advantages of civilized life. Were you to tell men who live without houses, how we pile brick upon brick, and rafter upon rafter, and that after a house is raised to a certain height, a man tumbles off a scaffold, and breaks his neck, he would laugh heartily at our folly in building;

[1] 'The exception proves the rule.'

but it does not follow that men are better without houses. No, Sir, (holding up a slice of a good loaf,) this is better than the bread tree.'

He repeated an argument, which is to be found in his *Rambler*, against the notion that the brute creation is endowed with the faculty of reason: 'birds build by instinct; they never improve; they build their first nest as well as any one that they ever build.' GOLDSMITH. 'Yet we see if you take away a bird's nest with the eggs in it, she will make a slighter nest and lay again.' JOHNSON. 'Sir, that is because at first she has full time and makes her nest deliberately. In the case you mention she is pressed to lay, and must therefore make her nest quickly, and consequently it will be slight.' GOLDSMITH. 'The nidification of birds is what is least known in natural history, though one of the most curious things in it.'

I introduced the subject of toleration. JOHNSON. 'Every society has a right to preserve publick peace and order, and therefore has a good right to prohibit the propagation of opinions which have a dangerous tendency. To say the *magistrate* has this right, is using an inadequate word: it is the *society* for which the magistrate is agent. He may be morally or theologically wrong in restraining the propagation of opinions which he thinks dangerous, but he is politically right.' MAYO. 'I am of opinion, Sir, that every man is entitled to liberty of conscience in religion; and that the magistrate cannot restrain that right.' JOHNSON. 'Sir, I agree with you. Every man has a right to liberty of conscience, and with that the magistrate cannot interfere. People confound liberty of thinking with liberty of talking; nay, with liberty of preaching. Every man has a physical right to think as he pleases; for it cannot be discovered how he thinks. He has not a moral right; for he ought to inform himself, and think justly. But, Sir, no member of a society has a right to *teach* any doctrine contrary to what that society holds to be true. The magistrate, I say, may be wrong in what he thinks: but while he thinks himself right, he may and ought to enforce what he thinks.' MAYO. 'Then, Sir, we are to remain always in errour, and truth never can prevail; and the magistrate was right in persecuting the first Christians.' JOHNSON. 'Sir, the only method by which religious truth can be established is by martyrdom. The magistrate has a right to enforce what he thinks; and he who is conscious of the truth has a right to suffer. I am afraid there is no other way of ascertaining the truth, but by persecution on the one hand and enduring it on the other.' GOLDSMITH. 'But how is a man to act, Sir? Though firmly convinced of the truth of his doctrine, may he not think it wrong to expose himself to persecution? Has he a right to do so? Is it not, as it were, committing voluntary suicide?' JOHNSON. 'Sir, as to voluntary suicide, as you call it, there are twenty thousand men in an army who will go without scruple to be shot at, and mount a breach for five-pence a day.' GOLDSMITH. 'But have they a moral right to do this?' JOHNSON. 'Nay, Sir, if you will not take the universal opinion of mankind, I have nothing to say. If mankind cannot defend their own way of thinking, I cannot defend it. Sir, if a man is in doubt whether it would be better for him to expose himself to martyrdom or not, he should not do it. He must be convinced that he has a delegation from heaven.' GOLDSMITH. 'I would consider whether there is the greater chance of good or evil upon the whole. If I see a man who had fallen into a well, I would wish to help him out; but if there is a greater probability that he shall pull me in, than that I shall pull him out, I would not attempt it. So were I to go to Turkey, I might wish to convert the Grand Signor to the Christian faith; but when I considered that I should probably be put to death without effectuating my purpose in any degree, I should keep myself quiet.' JOHNSON. 'Sir, you must consider that we have perfect and imperfect obligations. Perfect obligations, which are generally not to do something, are clear and positive; as, "thou shalt not kill". But charity, for instance, is not definable by limits. It is a duty to give to the poor; but no man can say how much another should give to the poor, or when a man has given too little to save his soul. In the same manner, it is a duty to instruct the ignorant, and of consequence to convert infidels to Christianity; but no man in the common course of things is obliged to carry this to such a degree as to incur the danger of martyrdom, as no man is obliged to strip himself to the shirt in order to give charity. I have said, that a man must be persuaded that he has a particular delegation from heaven.' GOLDSMITH. 'How is this to be known? Our first reformers, who were burnt for not believing bread and wine to be CHRIST'—JOHNSON. (interrupting him,) 'Sir, they were not burnt for not believing bread and wine to be CHRIST, but for insulting those who did believe it. And, Sir, when the first reformers began, they did not intend to be martyred: as many of them ran away as could.' BOSWELL. 'But, Sir, there was your countryman, Elwal, who you told me challenged King George with his black-guards, and his red-guards.' JOHNSON. 'My countryman, Elwal, Sir, should have been put in the stocks; a proper pulpit for him; and he'd have had a numerous audience. A man who preaches in the stocks will always have hearers enough.' BOSWELL. 'But Elwal thought himself in the right.' JOHNSON. 'We are not providing for mad people; there are places for them in the neighbourhood,' (meaning Moorfields.) MAYO. 'But, Sir, is it not very hard that I should not be allowed to teach my children what I really believe to be the truth?' JOHNSON. 'Why, Sir, you might contrive to teach your children *extrà scandalum;* [1] but, Sir, the magistrate, if he knows it, has a right to restrain you. Suppose you teach your children to be thieves?' MAYO. 'This is making a joke of the subject.' JOHNSON. 'Nay, Sir, take it thus:—that you teach them the community of goods; for which there are as many plausible arguments as for most erroneous doctrines. You teach them that all things at first were in common, and that no man had a right to any thing but as he laid his hands upon it, and that this still is, or ought to be, the rule amongst mankind. Here, Sir, you sap a great principle in society,—property. And don't you think the magistrate would have a right to prevent you? Or, suppose you should teach your children the notions of the Adamites, and they should run naked into the streets, would not the magistrate have a right to flog 'em into their doublets?' MAYO. 'I think the magistrate has no right to interfere till there is some overt act.' BOSWELL. 'So, Sir, though he sees an enemy to the state charging a blunderbuss, he is not to interfere till it is fired off?' MAYO. 'He must be sure of its direction against the state.' JOHNSON. 'The magistrate is to judge of that.—He has no right to restrain your thinking, because the evil centers in yourself. If a man were sitting at this table, and chopping off his fingers, the magistrate, as guardian of the community, has no authority to restrain him, however he might do it from kindness as a parent.—Though, indeed, upon more consideration, I think he may; as it is probable, that he who is chopping off his own fingers, may soon proceed to chop off those of other people. If I think it right to steal Mr. Dilly's plate, I am a bad man; but he can say nothing to me. If I make an open declaration that I think so, he will keep me out of his house. If I put forth my hand, I shall be sent to Newgate. This is the gradation of thinking, preaching, and acting: if a man thinks erroneously, he may keep his thoughts to himself, and nobody will trouble him; if he preaches erroneous doctrine, society may expel him; if he acts in consequence of it, the law takes place, and he is hanged.' MAYO. 'But, Sir, ought not Christians to have liberty of conscience?' JOHNSON. 'I have already told you so, Sir. You are coming back to where you were.' BOSWELL. 'Dr. Mayo is always taking a return post-chaise, and going the stage over again. He has it at half price.' JOHNSON. 'Dr. Mayo, like other cham-

[1] 'Without offence.'

pions for unlimited toleration, has got a set of words.[1] Sir, it is no matter, politically, whether the magistrate be right or wrong. Suppose a club were to be formed, to drink confusion to King George the Third, and a happy restoration to Charles the Third, this would be very bad with respect to the State; but every member of that club must either conform to its rules, or be turned out of it. Old Baxter, I remember, maintains, that the magistrate should "tolerate all things that are tolerable." This is no good definition of toleration upon any principle; but it shews that he thought some things were not tolerable.' TOPLADY. 'Sir, you have untwisted this difficult subject with great dexterity.'

During this argument, Goldsmith sat in restless agitation, from a wish to get in and *shine*. Finding himself excluded, he had taken his hat to go away, but remained for some time with it in his hand, like a gamester, who at the close of a long night, lingers for a little while, to see if he can have a favourable opening to finish with success. Once when he was beginning to speak, he found himself overpowered by the loud voice of Johnson, who was at the opposite end of the table, and did not perceive Goldsmith's attempt. Thus disappointed of his wish to obtain the attention of the company, Goldsmith in a passion threw down his hat, looking angrily at Johnson, and exclaiming in a bitter tone, '*Take it.*' When Toplady was going to speak, Johnson uttered some sound, which led Goldsmith to think that he was beginning again, and taking the words from Toplady. Upon which, he seized this opportunity of venting his own envy and spleen, under the pretext of supporting another person: 'Sir, (said he to Johnson,) the gentleman has heard you patiently for an hour; pray allow us now to hear him.' JOHNSON. (sternly,) 'Sir, I was not interrupting the gentleman. I was only giving him a signal of my attention. Sir, you are impertinent.' Goldsmith made no reply, but continued in the company for some time.

A gentleman present[2] ventured to ask Dr. Johnson if there was not a material difference as to toleration of opinions which lead to action, and opinions merely speculative; for instance, would it be wrong in the magistrate to tolerate those who preach against the doctrine of the TRINITY? Johnson was highly offended, and said, 'I wonder, Sir, how a gentleman of

[1] Dr. Mayo's calm temper and steady perseverance rendered him an admirable subject for the exercise of Dr. Johnson's powerful abilities. He never flinched; but, after reiterated blows, remained seemingly unmoved as at the first. The scintillations of Johnson's genius flashed every time he was struck, without his receiving any injury. Hence he obtained the epithet of THE LITERARY ANVIL—B.

[2] Langton.

your piety can introduce this subject in a mixed company.' He told me afterwards, that the impropriety was, that perhaps some of the company might have talked on the subject in such terms as would have shocked him; or he might have been forced to appear in their eyes a narrow-minded man. The gentleman, with submissive deference, said, he had only hinted at the question from a desire to hear Dr. Johnson's opinion upon it. JOHNSON. 'Why then, Sir, I think that permitting men to preach any opinion contrary to the doctrine of the established church tends, in a certain degree, to lessen the authority of the church, and, consequently, to lessen the influence of religion.' 'It may be considered, (said the gentleman,) whether it would not be politick to tolerate in such a case.' JOHNSON. 'Sir, we have been talking of *right*: this is another question. *I* think it is *not* politick to tolerate in such a case.' . . .

BOSWELL. 'Pray, Mr. Dilly, how does Dr. Leland's *History of Ireland* sell?' JOHNSON. (bursting forth with a generous indignation,) 'The Irish are in a most unnatural state; for we see there the minority prevailing over the majority. There is no instance, even in the ten persecutions, of such severity as that which the Protestants of Ireland have exercised against the Catholicks. Did we tell them we have conquered them, it would be above board: to punish them by confiscation and other penalties, as rebels, was monstrous injustice. King William was not their lawful sovereign: he had not been acknowledged by the Parliament of Ireland, when they appeared in arms against him.'

I here suggested something favourable of the Roman Catholicks. TOPLADY. 'Does not their invocation of saints suppose omnipresence in the saints?' JOHNSON. 'No, Sir, it supposes only pluri-presence; and when spirits are divested of matter, it seems probable that they should see with more extent than when in an embodied state. There is, therefore, no approach to an invasion of any of the divine attributes, in the invocation of saints. But I think it is will-worship, and presumption. I see no command for it, and therefore think it is safer not to practise it.'

He and Mr. Langton and I went together to THE CLUB, where we found Mr. Burke, Mr. Garrick, and some other members, and amongst them our friend Goldsmith, who sat silently brooding over Johnson's reprimand to him after dinner. Johnson perceived this, and said aside to some of us, 'I'll make Goldsmith forgive me;' and then called to him in a loud voice, 'Dr. Goldsmith,—something passed to-day where you and I dined; I ask your pardon.' Goldsmith answered placidly, 'It must be much from you, Sir, that I take ill.' And so at once the difference was over, and they were on as easy terms as ever, and Goldsmith rattled away as usual.

In our way to the club to-night, when I regretted that Goldsmith would, upon every occasion, endeavour to shine, by which he often exposed himself, Mr. Langton observed, that he was not like Addison, who was content with the fame of his writings, and did not aim also at excellency in conversation, for which he found himself unfit; and that he said to a lady, who complained of his having talked little in company, 'Madam, I have but nine-pence in ready money, but I can draw for a thousand pounds.' I observed, that Goldsmith had a great deal of gold in his cabinet, but, not content with that, was always taking out his purse. JOHNSON. 'Yes, Sir, and that so often an empty purse!'

Goldsmith's incessant desire of being conspicuous in company, was the occasion of his sometimes appearing to such disadvantage as one should hardly have supposed possible in a man of his genius. When his literary reputation had risen deservedly high, and his society was much courted, he became very jealous of the extraordinary attention which was every where paid to Johnson. One evening, in a circle of wits, he found fault with me for talking of Johnson as entitled to the honour of unquestionable superiority. 'Sir, (said he,) you are for making a monarchy of what should be a republick.'

He was still more mortified, when talking in a company with fluent vivacity, and, as he flattered himself, to the admiration of all who were present; a German who sat next him, and perceived Johnson rolling himself, as if about to speak, suddenly stopped him, saying, 'Stay, stay,—Toctor Shonson is going to say something.' This was, no doubt, very provoking, especially to one so irritable as Goldsmith, who frequently mentioned it with strong expressions of indignation.

It may also be observed, that Goldsmith was sometimes content to be treated with an easy familiarity, but, upon occasions, would be consequential and important. An instance of this occurred in a small particular. Johnson had a way of contracting the names of his friends; as Beauclerk, Beau; Boswell, Bozzy; Langton, Lanky; Murphy, Mur; Sheridan, Sherry. I remember one day, when Tom Davies was telling that Dr. Johnson said, 'We are all in labour for a name to Goldy's play,' Goldsmith seemed displeased that such a liberty should be taken with his name, and said, 'I have often desired him not to call me Goldy.' Tom was remarkably attentive to the most minute circumstance about Johnson. I recollect his telling me once, on my arrival in London, 'Sir, our great friend has made an improvement on his appellation of old Mr. Sheridan. He calls him now Sherry derry.' . . .

On Sunday, May 8,[1] I dined with Johnson at Mr. Langton's with Dr. Beattie and some other company. He descanted on the subject of Literary Property. 'There seems (said he,) to be in authours a stronger right of property than that by occupancy; a metaphysical right, a right, as it were, of creation, which should from its nature be perpetual; but the consent of nations is against it, and indeed reason and the interests of learning are against it; for were it to be perpetual, no book, however useful, could be universally diffused amongst mankind, should the proprietor take it into his head to restrain its circulation. No book could have the advantage of being edited with notes, however necessary to its elucidation, should the proprietor perversely oppose it. For the general good of the world, therefore, whatever valuable work has once been created by an authour, and issued out by him, should be understood as no longer in his power, but as belonging to the publick; at the same time the authour is entitled to an adequate reward. This he should have by an exclusive right to his work for a considerable number of years.'

He attacked Lord Monboddo's strange speculation on the primitive state of human nature; observing, 'Sir, it is all conjecture about a thing useless, even were it known to be true. Knowledge of all kinds is good. Conjecture, as to things useful, is good; but conjecture as to what it would be useless to know, such as whether men went upon all four, is very idle.'

On Monday, May 9,[2] as I was to set out on my return to Scotland next morning, I was desirous to see as much of Dr. Johnson as I could. But I first called on Goldsmith to take leave of him. The jealousy and envy which, though possessed of many most amiable qualities, he frankly avowed, broke out violently at this interview. Upon another occasion, when Goldsmith confessed himself to be of an envious disposition, I contended with Johnson that we ought not to be angry with him, he was so candid in owning it. 'Nay, Sir, (said Johnson,) we must be angry that a man has such a superabundance of an odious quality, that he cannot keep it within his own breast, but it boils over.' In my opinion, however, Goldsmith had not more of it than other people have, but only talked of it freely.

He now seemed very angry that Johnson was going to be a traveller; said, 'he would be a dead weight for me to carry, and that I should never be able to lug him along through the Highlands and Hebrides.' Nor would he patiently allow me to enlarge upon Johnson's wonderful abilities; but exclaimed, 'Is

[1] Actually, May 9.
[2] Actually, May 10.

he like Burke, who winds into a subject like a serpent?' 'But, (said I,) Johnson is the Hercules who strangled serpents in his cradle.'

I dined with Dr. Johnson at General Paoli's. He was obliged, by indisposition, to leave the company early; he appointed me, however, to meet him in the evening at Mr. (now Sir Robert) Chambers's in the Temple, where he accordingly came, though he continued to be very ill. Chambers, as is common on such occasions, prescribed various remedies to him. JOHNSON. (fretted by pain,) 'Pr'ythee don't tease me. Stay till I am well, and then you shall tell me how to cure myself.' He grew better, and talked with a noble enthusiasm of keeping up the representation of respectable families. His zeal on this subject was a circumstance in his character exceedingly remarkable, when it is considered that he himself had no pretensions to blood. I heard him once say, 'I have great merit in being zealous for subordination and the honours of birth; for I can hardly tell who was my grandfather.' He maintained the dignity and propriety of male succession, in opposition to the opinion of one of our friends,[1] who had that day employed Mr. Chambers to draw his will, devising his estate to his three sisters, in preference to a remote heir male. Johnson called them 'three *dowdies,*' and said, with as high a spirit as the boldest Baron in the most perfect days of the feudal system, 'An ancient estate should always go to males. It is mighty foolish to let a stranger have it because he marries your daughter, and takes your name. As for an estate newly acquired by trade, you may give it, if you will, to the dog *Towser,* and let him keep his *own* name.'

I have known him at times exceedingly diverted at what seemed to others a very small sport. He now laughed immoderately, without any reason that we could perceive, at our friend's making his will; called him the *testator,* and added, 'I dare say, he thinks he has done a mighty thing. He won't stay till he gets home to his seat in the country, to produce this wonderful deed: he'll call up the landlord of the first inn on the road; and, after a suitable preface upon mortality and the uncertainty of life, will tell him that he should not delay making his will; and here, Sir, will he say, is my will, which I have just made, with the assistance of one of the ablest lawyers in the kingdom; and he will read it to him (laughing all the time). He believes he has made this will; but he did not make it: you, Chambers, made it for him. I trust you have had more conscience than to make him say, "being of sound understanding;" ha, ha, ha! I hope he has

[1] Langton.

left me a legacy. I'd have his will turned into verse, like a ballad.'

In this playful manner did he run on, exulting in his own pleasantry, which certainly was not such as might be expected from the authour of *The Rambler,* but which is here preserved, that my readers may be acquainted even with the slightest occasional characteristicks of so eminent a man.

Mr. Chambers did not by any means relish this jocularity upon a matter of which *pars magna fuit,*[1] and seemed impatient till he got rid of us. Johnson could not stop his merriment, but continued it all the way till we got without the Temple-gate. He then burst into such a fit of laughter, that he appeared to be almost in a convulsion; and, in order to support himself, laid hold of one of the posts at the side of the foot pavement, and sent forth peals so loud, that in the silence of the night his voice seemed to resound from Temple-bar to Fleet-ditch.

This most ludicrous exhibition of the aweful, melancholy, and venerable Johnson, happened well to counteract the feelings of sadness which I used to experience when parting with him for a considerable time. I accompanied him to his door, where he gave me his blessing. . . .

In a letter from Edinburgh, dated the 29th of May, I pressed him to persevere in his resolution to make this year the projected visit to the Hebrides, of which he and I had talked for many years, and which I was confident would afford us much entertainment. . . .

His stay in Scotland was from the 18th of August, on which day he arrived, till the 22nd of November, when he set out on his return to London; and I believe ninety-four days were never passed by any man in a more vigorous exertion.

He came by the way of Berwick upon Tweed to Edinburgh, where he remained a few days, and then went by St. Andrew's, Aberdeen, Inverness, and Fort Augustus, to the Hebrides, to visit which was the principal object he had in view. He visited the isles of Sky, Rasay, Col, Mull, Inchkenneth, and Icolmkill. He travelled through Argyleshire by Inverary, and from thence by Lochlomond and Dunbarton to Glasgow, then by Loudon to Auchinleck in Ayrshire, the seat of my family, and then by Hamilton, back to Edinburgh, where he again spent some time. He thus saw the four Universities of Scotland, its three principal cities, and as much of the Highland and insular life as was sufficient for his philosophical contemplation. I had the pleasure of accompanying him during the whole of this journey. He was respectfully en-

[1] 'He was a great part.' See *Aeneid,* ii. 6.

tertained by the great, the learned, and the elegant, wherever he went; nor was he less delighted with the hospitality which he experienced in humbler life.

His various adventures, and the force and vivacity of his mind, as exercised during this peregrination, upon innumerable topicks, have been faithfully, and to the best of my abilities, displayed in my *Journal of a Tour to the Hebrides*, to which, as the publick has been pleased to honour it by a very extensive circulation, I beg leave to refer, as to a separate and remarkable portion of his life, which may be there seen in detail, and which exhibits as striking a view of his powers in conversation, as his works do of his excellence in writing. . . .

His humane forgiving disposition was put to a pretty strong test on his return to London, by a liberty which Mr. Thomas Davies had taken with him in his absence, which was, to publish two volumes, entitled, *Miscellaneous and fugitive Pieces,* which he advertised in the newspapers, 'By the Authour of the Rambler.' In this collection, several of Dr. Johnson's acknowledged writings, several of his anonymous performances, and some which he had written for others, were inserted; but there were also some in which he had no concern whatever. He was at first very angry, as he had good reason to be. But, upon consideration of his poor friend's narrow circumstances, and that he had only a little profit in view, and meant no harm, he soon relented, and continued his kindness to him as formerly.

In the course of his self-examination with retrospect to this year, he seems to have been much dejected; for he says, January 1, 1774, 'This year has passed with so little improvement, that I doubt whether I have not rather impaired than increased my learning'; and yet we have seen how he *read,* and we know how he *talked* during that period.

He was now seriously engaged in writing an account of our travels in the Hebrides, in consequence of which I had the pleasure of a more frequent correspondence with him.[1]

This tour to Wales, which was made in company with Mr. and Mrs. Thrale, though it no doubt contributed to his health and amusement, did not give occasion to such a discursive exercise of his mind as our tour to the Hebrides. I do not find that he kept any journal or notes of what he saw there. All that I heard him say of it was, that 'instead of bleak and barren mountains, there were green and fertile ones; and that one of the castles in Wales would contain all the castles that he had seen in Scotland.'

[1] This correspondence, in which Johnson speaks of touring Wales, is omitted.

Parliament having been dissolved, and his friend Mr. Thrale, who was a steady supporter of government, having again to encounter the storm of a contested election, he wrote a short political pamphlet, entitled *The Patriot,** addressed to the electors of Great-Britain; a title which, to factious men, who consider a patriot only as an opposer of the measures of government, will appear strangely misapplied. It was, however, written with energetick vivacity; and, except those passages in which it endeavours to vindicate the glaring outrage of the House of Commons in the case of the Middlesex election, and to justify the attempt to reduce our fellow-subjects in America to unconditional submission, it contained an admirable display of the properties of a real patriot, in the original and genuine sense;—a sincere, steady, rational, and unbiassed friend to the interests and prosperity of his King and country. It must be acknowledged, however, that both in this and his two former pamphlets, there was, amidst many powerful arguments, not only a considerable portion of sophistry, but a contemptuous ridicule of his opponents, which was very provoking. . . .

In his manuscript diary of this year, there is the following entry:—

'Nov. 27. Advent Sunday. I considered that this day, being the beginning of the ecclesiastical year, was a proper time for a new course of life. I began to read the Greek Testament regularly at 160 verses every Sunday. This day I began the Acts.

'In this week I read Virgil's *Pastorals*. I learned to repeat the *Pollio* and *Gallus*. I read carelessly the first *Georgick*.'

Such evidences of his unceasing ardour, both for 'divine and human lore,' when advanced into his sixty-fifth year, and notwithstanding his many disturbances from disease, must make us at once honour his spirit, and lament that it should be so grievously clogged by its material tegument. It is remarkable, that he was very fond of the precision which calculation produces. Thus we find in one of his manuscript diaries, '12 pages in 4to. Gr. Test. and 30 pages in Beza's folio, comprize the whole in 40 days.' . . .

'*To* JAMES BOSWELL, ESQ.[1]

'MY DEAR BOSWELL,—I am surprized that, knowing as you do the disposition of your countrymen to tell lies in favour of each other, you can be at all affected by any reports

---

[1] Johnson had recently published his *Journey to the Western Islands of Scotland,* in which he attacked the authenticity of Macpherson's Ossian.

that circulate among them. Macpherson never in his life offered me the sight of any original or of any evidence of any kind; but thought only of intimidating me by noise and threats, till my last answer,—that I would not be deterred from detecting what I thought a cheat, by the menaces of a ruffian—put an end to our correspondence.

'The state of the question is this. He, and Dr. Blair, whom I consider as deceived, say, that he copied the poem from old manuscripts. His copies, if he had them, and I believe him to have none, are nothing. Where are the manuscripts? They can be shewn if they exist, but they were never shewn. *De non existentibus et non apparentibus*, says our law, *eadem est ratio*.[1] No man has a claim to credit upon his own word, when better evidence, if he had it, may be easily produced. But, so far as we can find, the Erse language was never written till very lately for the purposes of religion. A nation that cannot write, or a language that was never written, has no manuscripts.

'But whatever he has, he never offered to show. If old manuscripts should now be mentioned, I should, unless there were more evidence than can be easily had, suppose them another proof of Scotch conspiracy in national falsehood.

'Do not censure the expression; you know it to be true. . . .
'February 7, 1775.'   'SAM. JOHNSON.'

What words were used by Mr. Macpherson in his letter to the venerable Sage, I have never heard; but they are generally said to have been of a nature very different from the language of literary contest. Dr. Johnson's answer appeared in the newspapers of the day, and has since been frequently republished; but not with perfect accuracy. I give it as dictated to me by himself, written down in his presence, and authenticated by a note in his own hand-writing, *This, I think, is a true copy.*

'MR. JAMES MACPHERSON,—I received your foolish and impudent letter. Any violence offered me I shall do my best to repel; and what I cannot do for myself, the law shall do for me. I hope I shall never be deterred from detecting what I think a cheat, by the menaces of a ruffian.

'What would you have me retract? I thought your book an imposture; I think it an imposture still. For this opinion I have given my reasons to the publick, which I here dare you to refute. Your rage I defy. Your abilities, since your Homer, are not so formidable; and what I hear of your morals, in-

---

[1] 'It is assumed that what does not appear does not exist.'

clines me to pay regard not to what you shall say, but to what you shall prove. You may print this if you will.

'SAM. JOHNSON.'

Mr. Macpherson little knew the character of Dr. Johnson, if he supposed that he could be easily intimidated; for no man was ever more remarkable for personal courage. He had, indeed, an aweful dread of death, or rather, 'of something after death;' and what rational man, who seriously thinks of quitting all that he has ever known, and going into a new and unknown state of being, can be without that dread? But his fear was from reflection; his courage natural. His fear, in that one instance, was the result of philosophical and religious consideration. He feared death, but he feared nothing else, not even what might occasion death. Many instances of his resolution may be mentioned. One day, at Mr. Beauclerk's house in the country, when two large dogs were fighting, he went up to them, and beat them till they separated; and at another time, when told of the danger there was that a gun might burst if charged with many balls, he put in six or seven, and fired it off against a wall. Mr. Langton told me, that when they were swimming together near Oxford, he cautioned Dr. Johnson against a pool, which was reckoned particularly dangerous; upon which Johnson directly swam into it. He told me himself that one night he was attacked in the street by four men, to whom he would not yield, but kept them all at bay, till the watch came up, and carried both him and them to the roundhouse. In the playhouse at Lichfield, as Mr. Garrick informed me, Johnson having for a moment quitted a chair which was placed for him between the side-scenes, a gentleman took possession of it, and when Johnson on his return civilly demanded his seat, rudely refused to give it up; upon which Johnson laid hold of it, and tossed him and the chair into the pit. Foote, who so successfully revived the old comedy, by exhibiting living characters, had resolved to imitate Johnson on the stage, expecting great profits from his ridicule of so celebrated a man. Johnson being informed of his intention, and being at dinner at Mr. Thomas Davies's the bookseller, from whom I had the story, he asked Mr. Davies 'what was the common price of an oak stick;' and being answered six-pence, 'Why then, Sir, (said he,) give me leave to send your servant to purchase me a shilling one. I'll have a double quantity; for I am told Foote means to *take me off,* as he calls it, and I am determined the fellow shall not do it with impunity.' Davies took care to acquaint Foote of this, which effectually checked the wantonness of the mimick. Mr. Macpherson's menaces made Johnson provide himself with the same implement of defence; and had he been attacked, I have no doubt that, old as he was, he would have made his corporal prowess be felt as much as his intellectual.

His *Journey to the Western Islands of Scotland* * is a most valuable performance. It abounds in extensive philosophical views of society, and in ingenious sentiments and lively description. A considerable part of it, indeed, consists of speculations, which many years before he saw the wild regions which we visited together, probably had employed his attention, though the actual sight of those scenes undoubtedly quickened and augmented them. Mr. Orme, the very able historian, agreed with me in this opinion, which he thus strongly expressed:—'There are in that book thoughts, which, by long revolution in the great mind of Johnson, have been formed and polished like pebbles rolled in the ocean!'

That he was to some degree of excess a *true-born Englishman*, so as to have ever entertained an undue prejudice against both the country and the people of Scotland, must be allowed. But it was a prejudice of the head, and not of the heart. He had no ill-will to the Scotch; for, if he had been conscious of that, he would never have thrown himself into the bosom of their country, and trusted to the protection of its remote inhabitants with a fearless confidence. His remark upon the nakedness of the country, from its being denuded of trees, was made after having travelled two hundred miles along the eastern coast, where certainly trees are not to be found near the road; and he said it was 'a map of the road' which he gave. His disbelief of the authenticity of the poems ascribed to Ossian, a Highland bard, was confirmed in the course of his journey, by a very strict examination of the evidence offered for it; and although their authenticity was made too much a national point by the Scotch, there were many respectable persons in that country, who did not concur in this; so that his judgement upon the question ought not to be decried, even by those who differ from him. As to myself, I can only say, upon a subject now become very uninteresting, that when the fragments of Highland poetry first came out, I was much pleased with their wild peculiarity, and was one of those who subscribed to enable their editor, Mr. Macpherson, then a young man, to make a search in the Highlands and Hebrides for a long poem in the Erse language, which was reported to be preserved somewhere in those regions. But when there came forth an Epick Poem in six books, with all the common circumstances of former compositions of that nature; and when, upon an attentive examination of it, there was found a perpetual recurrence of the same images which appear in the fragments; and when no ancient manuscript, to authenticate the work, was deposited in any publick library, though that was insisted on as a reasonable proof, *who* could forbear to doubt?

Johnson's grateful acknowledgements of kindnesses received in the course of this tour, completely refute the brutal reflections which have been thrown out against him, as if he had made an ungrateful return; and his delicacy in sparing in his book those who we find from his letters to Mrs. Thrale were just objects of censure, is much to be admired. His candour and amiable disposition is conspicuous from his conduct, when informed by Mr. Macleod, of Rasay, that he had committed a mistake, which gave that gentleman some uneasiness. He wrote him a courteous and kind letter, and inserted in the news-papers an advertisement, correcting the mistake. . . .

It is painful to recollect with what rancour he was assailed by numbers of shallow irritable North Britons, on account of his supposed injurious treatment of their country and countrymen, in his *Journey*. . . . Johnson treated Scotland no worse than he did even his best friends, whose characters he used to give as they appeared to him, both in light and shade. Some people, who had not exercised their minds sufficiently, condemned him for censuring his friends. But Sir Joshua Reynolds, whose philosophical penetration and justness of thinking were not less known to those who lived with him, than his genius in his art is admired by the world, explained his conduct thus: 'He was fond of discrimination, which he could not shew without pointing out the bad as well as the good in every character; and as his friends were those whose characters he knew best, they afforded him the best opportunity for showing the acuteness of his judgement.'

He expressed to his friend Mr. Windham of Norfolk, his wonder at the extreme jealousy of the Scotch, and their resentment at having their country described by him as it really was; when, to say that it was a country as good as England, would have been a gross falsehood. 'None of us, (said he,) would be offended if a foreigner who has travelled here should say, that vines and olives don't grow in England.' And as to his prejudice against the Scotch, which I always ascribed to that nationality which he observed in *them*, he said to the same gentleman, 'When I find a Scotchman, to whom an Englishman is as a Scotchman, that Scotchman shall be as an Englishman to me.' His intimacy with many gentlemen of Scotland, and his employing so many natives of that country as his amanuenses, prove that his prejudice was not virulent; and I have deposited in the British Museum, amongst other pieces of his writing, the following note in answer to one from me, asking if he would meet me at dinner at the Mitre, though a friend of mine, a Scotchman, was to be there:——

'Mr. Johnson does not see why Mr. Boswell should suppose a Scotchman less acceptable than any other man. He will be at the Mitre.'

My much-valued friend Dr. Barnard, now Bishop of Killaloe, having once expressed to him an apprehension, that if he should visit Ireland he might treat the people of that country more unfavourably than he had done the Scotch, he answered, with strong pointed double-edged wit, 'Sir, you have no reason to be afraid of me. The Irish are not in a conspiracy to cheat the world by false representations of the merits of their countrymen. No, Sir; the Irish are a FAIR PEOPLE;—they never speak well of one another.' . . .

On Tuesday, March 21,[1] I arrived in London; and on repairing to Dr. Johnson's before dinner, found him in his study, sitting with Mr. Peter Garrick, the elder brother of David, strongly resembling him in countenance and voice, but of more sedate and placid manners. Johnson informed me, that 'though Mr. Beauclerk was in great pain, it was hoped he was not in danger, and that he now wished to consult Dr. Heberden to try the effect of a *new understanding*.' Both at this interview, and in the evening at Mr. Thrale's, where he and Mr. Peter Garrick and I met again, he was vehement on the subject of the Ossian controversy; observing, 'We do not know that there are any ancient Erse manuscripts; and we have no other reason to disbelieve that there are men with three heads, but that we do not know that there are any such men.' He also was outrageous, upon his supposition that my countrymen 'loved Scotland better than truth,' saying, 'All of them,—nay not all,—but *droves* of them, would come up, and attest any thing for the honour of Scotland.' He also persevered in his wild allegation, that he questioned if there was a tree between Edinburgh and the English border older than himself. I assured him he was mistaken, and suggested that the proper punishment would be that he should receive a stripe at every tree above a hundred years old, that was found within that space. He laughed, and said, 'I believe I might submit to it for a *baubee!*'

The doubts which, in my correspondence with him, I had ventured to state as to the justice and wisdom of the conduct of Great-Britain towards the American colonies, while I at the same time requested that he would enable me to inform myself upon that momentous subject, he had altogether disregarded; and had recently published a pamphlet, entitled, *Tax-*

[1] 1775.

ation no Tyranny; an answer to the Resolutions and Address of the American Congress. *

He had long before indulged most unfavourable sentiments of our fellow-subjects in America. For, as early as 1769, I was told by Dr. John Campbell, that he had said of them, 'Sir, they are a race of convicts, and ought to be thankful for any thing we allow them short of hanging.'

Of this performance I avoided to talk with him; for I had now formed a clear and settled opinion, that the people of America were well warranted to resist a claim that their fellow-subjects in the mother-country should have the entire command of their fortunes, by taxing them without their own consent; and the extreme violence which it breathed, appeared to me so unsuitable to the mildness of a Christian philosopher, and so directly opposite to the principles of peace which he had so beautifully recommended in his pamphlet respecting Falkland's Islands, that I was sorry to see him appear in so unfavourable a light. Besides, I could not perceive in it that ability of argument, or that felicity of expression, for which he was, upon other occasions, so eminent. Positive assertion, sarcastical severity, and extravagant ridicule, which he himself reprobated as a test of truth, were united in this rhapsody. . . .

He complained to a Right Honourable friend[1] of distinguished talents and very elegant manners, with whom he maintained a long intimacy, and whose generosity towards him will afterwards appear, that his pension having been given to him as a literary character, he had been applied to by administration to write political pamphlets; and he was even so much irritated, that he declared his resolution to resign his pension. His friend shewed him the impropriety of such a measure, and he afterwards expressed his gratitude, and said he had received good advice. To that friend he once signified a wish to have his pension secured to him for his life; but he neither asked nor received from government any reward whatsoever for his political labours.

On Friday, March 24, I met him at the LITERARY CLUB, where were Mr. Beauclerk, Mr. Langton, Mr. Colman, Dr. Percy, Mr. Vesey, Sir Charles Bunbury, Dr. George Fordyce, Mr. Steevens, and Mr. Charles Fox. Before he came in, we talked of his *Journey to the Western Islands,* and of his coming away 'willing to believe the second sight,' which seemed to excite some ridicule. I was then so impressed with the truth of many of the stories of it which I had been told, that I avowed my conviction, saying, 'He is only *willing* to be-

[1] William Gerard Hamilton.

lieve: I *do* believe. The evidence is enough for me, though not for his great mind. What will not fill a quart bottle will fill a pint bottle. I am filled with belief.' 'Are you? (said Colman,) then cork it up.'

I found his *Journey* the common topick of conversation in London at this time, wherever I happened to be. At one of Lord Mansfield's formal Sunday evening conversations, strangely called *Levées,* his Lordship addressed me, 'We have all been reading your travels, Mr. Boswell.' I answered, 'I was but the humble attendant of Dr. Johnson.' The Chief Justice replied, with that air and manner which none, who ever saw and heard him, can forget, 'He speaks ill of nobody but Ossian.'

Johnson was in high spirits this evening at the club, and talked with great animation and success. He attacked Swift, as he used to do upon all occasions. 'The *Tale of a Tub* is so much superiour to his other writings, that one can hardly believe he was the authour of it. There is in it such a vigour of mind, such a swarm of thoughts, so much of nature, and art, and life.' I wondered to hear him say of *Gulliver's Travels,* 'When once you have thought of big men and little men, it is very easy to do all the rest.' I endeavoured to make a stand for Swift, and tried to rouse those who were much more able to defend him; but in vain. Johnson at last, of his own accord, allowed very great merit to the inventory of articles found in the pockets of *the Man Mountain,* particularly the description of his watch, which it was conjectured was his GOD, as he consulted it upon all occasions. He observed, that 'Swift put his name to but two things, (after he had a name to put,) *The Plan for the Improvement of the English Language,* and the last *Drapier's Letter.*'

From Swift, there was an easy transition to Mr. Thomas Sheridan.—JOHNSON. 'Sheridan is a wonderful admirer of the tragedy of *Douglas,* and presented its authour with a gold medal. Some years ago, at a coffee-house in Oxford, I called to him, "Mr. Sheridan, Mr. Sheridan, how came you to give a gold medal to Home, for writing that foolish play?" This, you see, was wanton and insolent; but I *meant* to be wanton and insolent. A medal has no value but as a stamp of merit. And was Sheridan to assume to himself the right of giving that stamp? If Sheridan was magnificent enough to bestow a gold medal as an honorary reward of dramatick excellence, he should have requested one of the Universities to choose the person on whom it should be conferred. Sheridan had no right to give a stamp of merit: it was counterfeiting Apollo's coin.'

On Monday, March 27, I breakfasted with him at Mr.

Strahan's. He told us, that he was engaged to go that evening to Mrs. Abington's benefit. 'She was visiting some ladies whom I was visiting, and begged that I would come to her benefit. I told her I could not hear: but she insisted so much on my coming, that it would have been brutal to have refused her.' This was a speech quite characteristical. He loved to bring forward his having been in the gay circles of life; and he was, perhaps, a little vain of the solicitations of this elegant and fashionable actress. He told us, the play was to be *The Hypocrite,* altered from Cibber's *Nonjuror,* so as to satirize the Methodists. 'I do not think (said he,) the character of *The Hypocrite* justly applicable to the Methodists, but it was very applicable to the Nonjurors. I once said to Dr. Madan, a clergyman of Ireland, who was a great Whig, that perhaps a Nonjuror would have been less criminal in taking the oaths imposed by the ruling power, than refusing them; because refusing them, necessarily laid him under almost an irresistible temptation to be more criminal; for, a man *must* live, and if he precludes himself from the support furnished by the establishment, will probably be reduced to very wicked shifts to maintain himself.' BOSWELL. 'I should think, Sir, that a man who took the oaths contrary to his principles, was a determined wicked man, because he was sure he was committing perjury; where as a Nonjuror might be insensibly led to do what was wrong, without being so directly conscious of it.' JOHNSON. 'Why, Sir, a man who goes to bed to his patron's wife is pretty sure that he is committing wickedness.' BOSWELL. 'Did the nonjurying clergyman do so, Sir?' JOHNSON. 'I am afraid many of them did.'

I was startled at his argument, and could by no means think it convincing. Had not his own father complied with the requisition of government, (as to which he once observed to me, when I pressed him upon it, *'That,* Sir, he was to settle with himself,')' he would probably have thought more unfavourably of a Jacobite who took the oaths:

> '———— had he not resembled
> My father as he *swore*————.'

Mr. Strahan talked of launching into the great ocean of London, in order to have a chance for rising into eminence; and, observing that many men were kept back from trying their fortunes there, because they were born to a competency, said, 'Small certainties are the bane of men of talents;' which Johnson confirmed. Mr. Strahan put Johnson in mind of a remark which he had made to him; 'There are few ways in which a man can be more innocently employed than in getting money.' 'The more one thinks of this, (said Strahan,) the juster it will appear.'

Mr. Strahan had taken a poor boy from the country as an apprentice, upon Johnson's recommendation. Johnson having enquired after him, said, 'Mr. Strahan, let me have five guineas on account, and I'll give this boy one. Nay, if a man recommends a boy, and does nothing for him, it is sad work. Call him down.'

I followed him into the court-yard, behind Mr. Strahan's house; and there I had a proof of what I had heard him profess, that he talked alike to all. 'Some people (said he), tell you that they let themselves down to the capacity of their hearers. I never do that. I speak uniformly, in as intelligible a manner as I can.'

'Well, my boy, how do you go on?'—'Pretty well, Sir; but they are afraid I an't strong enough for some parts of the business.' JOHNSON. 'Why, I shall be sorry for it; for when you consider with how little mental power and corporeal labour a printer can get a guinea a week, it is a very desirable occupation for you. Do you hear,—take all the pains you can; and if this does not do, we must think of some other way of life for you. There's a guinea.'

Here was one of the many, many instances of his active benevolence. At the same time, the slow and sonorous solemnity with which, while he bent himself down, he addressed a little thick short-legged boy, contrasted with the boy's awkwardness and awe, could not but excite some ludicrous emotions.

I met him at Drury-lane play-house in the evening. Sir Joshua Reynolds, at Mrs. Abington's request, had promised to bring a body of wits to her benefit; and having secured forty places in the front boxes, had done me the honour to put me in the group. Johnson sat on the seat directly behind me; and as he could neither see nor hear at such a distance from the stage, he was wrapped up in grave abstraction, and seemed quite a cloud, amidst all the sunshine of glitter and gaiety. I wondered at his patience in sitting out a play of five acts, and a farce of two. He said very little; but after the prologue to *Bon Ton* had been spoken, which he could hear pretty well from the more slow and distinct utterance, he talked of prologue-writing, and observed, 'Dryden has written prologues superiour to any that David Garrick has written; but David Garrick has written more good prologues than Dryden has done. It is wonderful that he has been able to write such a variety of them.'

At Mr. Beauclerk's, where I supped, was Mr. Garrick, whom I made happy with Johnson's praise of his prologues;

and I suppose, in gratitude to him, he took up one of his favourite topicks, the nationality of the Scotch, which he maintained in his pleasant manner, with the aid of a little poetical fiction. 'Come, come, don't deny it: they are really national. Why, now, the Adams are as liberal-minded men as any in the world: but, I don't know how it is, all their workmen are Scotch. You are, to be sure, wonderfully free from that nationality: but so it happens, that you employ the only Scotch shoe-black in London.' He imitated the manner of his old master with ludicrous exaggeration; repeating, with pauses and half-whistlings interjected,

> 'Os homini sublime dedit,—cælumque tueri
> Jussit,—et erectos ad sidera—tollere vultus;[1]

looking downwards all the time, and, while pronouncing the four last words, absolutely touching the ground with a kind of contorted gesticulation.

Garrick, however, when he pleased, could imitate Johnson very exactly; for that great actor, with his distinguished powers of expression which were so universally admired, possessed also an admirable talent of mimickry. He was always jealous that Johnson spoke lightly of him. I recollect his exhibiting him to me one day, as if saying, 'Davy has some convivial pleasantry about him, but 'tis a futile fellow;' which he uttered perfectly with the tone and air of Johnson.

I cannot too frequently request of my readers, while they peruse my account of Johnson's conversation, to endeavour to keep in mind his deliberate and strong utterance. His mode of speaking was indeed very impressive;[2] and I wish it could be preserved as musick is written, according to the very ingenious method of Mr. Steele, who has shewn how the recitation of Mr. Garrick, and other eminent speakers, might be transmitted to posterity in score.

Next day I dined with Johnson at Mr. Thrale's. He attacked Gray, calling him a 'dull fellow.' BOSWELL. 'I understand he was reserved, and might appear dull in company; but surely he was not dull in poetry.' JOHNSON. 'Sir, he was dull in company, dull in his closet, dull every where. He was dull in a new way, and that made many people think him GREAT. He was a mechanical poet.' He then repeated some ludicrous lines, which have escaped my memory, and said, 'Is

---

1   'Man looks aloft, and with erected eyes
        Beholds his own hereditary skies.'
                   Ovid, *Metamorphoses*, i. 85-86. (Dryden.)

2 My noble friend Lord Pembroke said once to me at Wilton, with a happy pleasantry and some truth, that 'Dr. Johnson's sayings would not appear so extraordinary, were it not for his *bow-wow way*.'—B.

not that GREAT, like his Odes?' Mrs. Thrale maintained that his Odes were melodious; upon which he exclaimed,

'Weave the warp, and weave the woof;'—

I added, in a solemn tone,

'The winding-sheet of Edward's race.'

'*There* is a good line.' 'Ay, (said he,) and the next line is a good one,' (pronouncing it contemptuously;)

'Give ample verge and room enough.'—

'No, Sir, there are but two good stanzas in Gray's poetry, which are in his *Elegy in a Country Church-yard.*' He then repeated the stanza,

'For who to dumb forgetfulness a prey,' &c.

mistaking one word; for instead of *precincts* he said *confines.* He added, 'The other stanza I forget.'

A young lady who had married a man much her inferiour in rank being mentioned, a question arose how a woman's relations should behave to her in such a situation; and, while I recapitulate the debate, and recollect what has since happened, I cannot but be struck in a manner that delicacy forbids me to express. While I contended that she ought to be treated with an inflexible steadiness of displeasure, Mrs. Thrale was all for mildness and forgiveness, and, according to the vulgar phrase, 'making the best of a bad bargain.' JOHNSON. 'Madam, we must distinguish. Were I a man of rank, I would not let a daughter starve who had made a mean marriage; but having voluntarily degraded herself from the station which she was originally entitled to hold, I would support her only in that which she herself had chosen; and would not put her on a level with my other daughters. You are to consider, Madam, that it is our duty to maintain the subordination of civilized society; and when there is a gross and shameful deviation from rank, it should be punished so as to deter others from the same perversion.' . . .

Lord Chesterfield's *Letters* being mentioned, Johnson said, 'It was not to be wondered at that they had so great a sale, considering that they were the letters of a statesman, a wit, one who had been so much in the mouths of mankind, one long accustomed *virûm volitare per ora.'* [1]

On Friday, March 31, I supped with him and some friends at a tavern. One of the company [2] attempted, with too much forwardness, to rally him on his late appearance at the thea-

[1] 'To fly through the mouths of men.' Virgil, *Georgics,* iii. 9.
[2] Boswell.

tre; but had reason to repent of his temerity. 'Why, Sir, did you go to Mrs. Abington's benefit? Did you see?' JOHNSON. 'No, Sir.' 'Did you hear?' JOHNSON. 'No, Sir.' 'Why then, Sir, did you go?' JOHNSON. 'Because, Sir, she is a favourite of the publick; and when the publick cares the thousandth part for you that it does for her, I will go to your benefit too.'

Next morning I won a small bet from Lady Diana Beauclerk, by asking him as to one of his particularities, which her Ladyship laid I durst not do. It seems he had been frequently observed at the Club to put into his pocket the Seville oranges, after he had squeezed the juice of them into the drink which he made for himself. Beauclerk and Garrick talked of it to me, and seemed to think that he had a strange unwillingness to be discovered. We could not divine what he did with them; and this was the bold question to be put. I saw on his table the spoils of the preceding night, some fresh peels nicely scraped and cut into pieces. 'O, Sir, (said I,) I now partly see what you do with the squeezed oranges which you put into your pocket at the Club.' JOHNSON. 'I have a great love for them.' BOSWELL. 'And pray, Sir, what do you do with them? You scrape them, it seems, very neatly, and what next?' JOHNSON. 'I let them dry, Sir.' BOSWELL. 'And what next?' JOHNSON. 'Nay, Sir, you shall know their fate no further.' BOSWELL. 'Then the world must be left in the dark. It must be said (assuming a mock solemnity,) he scraped them, and let them dry, but what he did with them next, he never could be prevailed upon to tell.' JOHNSON. 'Nay, Sir, you should say it more emphatically:—he could not be prevailed upon, even by his dearest friends, to tell.'

He had this morning received his Diploma as Doctor of Laws from the University of Oxford. He did not vaunt of his new dignity, but I understood he was highly pleased with it. . . .

He revised some sheets of Lord Hailes's *Annals of Scotland*, and wrote a few notes on the margin with red ink, which he bade me tell his Lordship did not sink into the paper, and might be wiped off with a wet sponge, so that he did not spoil his manuscript. I observed to him that there were very few of his friends so accurate as that I could venture to put down in writing what they told me as his sayings. JOHNSON. 'Why should you write down *my* sayings?' BOSWELL. 'I write them when they are good.' JOHNSON. 'Nay, you may as well write down the sayings of any one else that are good.' But *where*, I might with great propriety have added, can I find such?

I visited him by appointment in the evening, and we drank tea with Mrs. Williams. He told me that he had been in the company of a gentleman [1] whose extraordinary travels had been much the subject of conversation. But I found that he had not listened to him with that full confidence, without which there is little satisfaction in the society of travellers. I was curious to hear what opinion so able a judge as Johnson had formed of his abilities, and I asked if he was not a man of sense. JOHNSON. 'Why, Sir, he is not a distinct relater; and I should say, he is neither abounding nor deficient in sense. I did not perceive any superiority of understanding.' BOSWELL. 'But will you not allow him a nobleness of resolution, in penetrating into distant regions?' JOHNSON. 'That, Sir, is not to the present purpose. We are talking of his sense. A fighting cock has a nobleness of resolution.'

Next day, Sunday, April 2, I dined with him at Mr. Hoole's. We talked of Pope. JOHNSON. 'He wrote his *Dunciad* for fame. That was his primary motive. Had it not been for that, the dunces might have railed against him till they were weary, without his troubling himself about them. He delighted to vex them, no doubt; but he had more delight in seeing how well he could vex them.'

The *Odes to Obscurity and Oblivion*, in ridicule of 'cool Mason and warm Gray,' being mentioned, Johnson said, 'They are Colman's best things.' Upon its being observed that it was believed these Odes were made by Colman and Lloyd jointly;—JOHNSON. 'Nay, Sir, how can two people make an Ode? Perhaps one made one of them, and one the other.' I observed that two people had made a play, and quoted the anecdote of Beaumont and Fletcher, who were brought under suspicion of treason, because while concerting the plan of a tragedy when sitting together at a tavern, one of them was overheard saying to the other, 'I'll kill the King.' JOHNSON. 'The first of these Odes is the best: but they are both good. They exposed a very bad kind of writing.' BOSWELL. 'Surely, Sir, Mr. Mason's *Elfrida* is a fine poem: at least you will allow there are some good passages in it.' JOHNSON. 'There are now and then some good imitations of Milton's bad manner.' . . .

His *Taxation no Tyranny* being mentioned, he said, 'I think I have not been attacked enough for it. Attack is the re-action; I never think I have hit hard, unless it rebounds.' BOSWELL. 'I don't know, Sir, what you would be at. Five or six shots of small arms in every newspaper, and repeated cannonading in pamphlets, might, I think, satisfy you. But, Sir,

[1] James Bruce.

you'll never make out this match, of which we have talked, with a certain political lady,[1] since you are so severe against her principles.' JOHNSON. 'Nay, Sir, I have the better chance for that. She is like the Amazons of old; she must be courted by the sword. But I have not been severe upon her.' BOSWELL. 'Yes, Sir, you have made her ridiculous.' JOHNSON. 'That was already done, Sir. To endeavour to make *her* ridiculous, is like blacking the chimney.'

I put him in mind that the landlord at Ellon in Scotland said, that he heard he was the greatest man in England,—next to Lord Mansfield. 'Ay, Sir, (said he,) the exception defined the idea. A Scotchman could go no farther:

> "The force of Nature could no farther go." '

Lady Miller's collection of verses by fashionable people, which were put into her Vase at Batheaston villa, near Bath, in competition for honorary prizes, being mentioned, he held them very cheap: *'Bouts rimés* (said he,) is a mere conceit, and an *old* conceit *now;* I wonder how people were persuaded to write in that manner for this lady.' I named a gentleman of his acquaintance who wrote for the Vase. JOHNSON. 'He was a blockhead for his pains.' BOSWELL. 'The Duchess of Northumberland wrote.' JOHNSON. 'Sir, the Duchess of Northumberland may do what she pleases: nobody will say anything to a lady of her high rank. But I should be apt to throw ******'s verses in his face.'

I talked of the cheerfulness of Fleet-street, owing to the constant quick succession of people which we perceive passing through it. JOHNSON. 'Why, Sir, Fleet-street has a very animated appearance; but I think the full tide of human existence is at Charing-cross.'

He made the common remark on the unhappiness which men who have led a busy life experience, when they retire in expectation of enjoying themselves at ease, and that they generally languish for want of their habitual occupation, and wish to return to it. He mentioned as strong an instance of this as can well be imagined. 'An eminent tallow-chandler in London, who had acquired a considerable fortune, gave up the trade in favour of his foreman, and went to live at a country-house near town. He soon grew weary, and paid frequent visits to his old shop, where he desired they might let him know their *melting-days,* and he would come and assist them; which he accordingly did. Here, Sir, was a man, to whom the most disgusting circumstance in the business to which he had been used was a relief from idleness.'

---

[1] Mrs. Macaulay.

On Wednesday, April 5, I dined with him at Messieurs Dilly's, with Mr. John Scott of Amwell, the Quaker, Mr. Langton, Mr. Miller, (now Sir John,) and Dr. Thomas Campbell, an Irish clergyman, whom I took the liberty of inviting to Mr. Dilly's table, having seen him at Mr. Thrale's, and been told that he had come to England chiefly with a view to see Dr. Johnson, for whom he entertained the highest veneration. . . .

We talked of publick speaking.—JOHNSON. 'We must not estimate a man's powers by his being able or not able to deliver his sentiments in publick. Isaac Hawkins Browne, one of the first wits of this country, got into Parliament, and never opened his mouth. For my own part, I think it is more disgraceful never to try to speak, than to try it and fail; as it is more disgraceful not to fight, than to fight and be beaten.' This argument appeared to me fallacious; for if a man has not spoken, it may be said that he would have done very well if he had tried; whereas, if he has tried and failed, there is nothing to be said for him. 'Why then, (I asked,) is it thought disgraceful for a man not to fight, and not disgraceful not to speak in publick?' JOHNSON. 'Because there may be other reasons for a man's not speaking in publick than want of resolution: he may have nothing to say, (laughing.) Whereas, Sir, you know courage is reckoned the greatest of all virtues; because, unless a man has that virtue, he has no security for preserving any other.'

He observed, that 'the statutes against bribery were intended to prevent upstarts with money from getting into Parliament;' adding, that 'if he were a gentleman of landed property, he would turn out all his tenants who did not vote for the candidate whom he supported.' LANGTON. 'Would not that, Sir, be checking the freedom of election?' JOHNSON. 'Sir, the law does not mean that the privilege of voting should be independent of old family interest; of the permanent property of the country.'

On Thursday, April 6, I dined with him at Mr. Thomas Davies's, with Mr. Hicky, the painter, and my old acquaintance Mr. Moody, the player.

Dr. Johnson, as usual, spoke contemptuously of Colley Cibber. 'It is wonderful that a man, who for forty years had lived with the great and the witty, should have acquired so ill the talents of conversation: and he had but half to furnish; for one half of what he said was oaths.' He, however, allowed considerable merit to some of his comedies, and said there was no reason to believe that the *Careless Husband* was not written by himself. Davies said, he was the first dramatick writer who introduced genteel ladies upon the stage. Johnson refuted this observation by instancing several such characters in comedies before his time. DAVIES. (trying to defend himself from a charge of ignorance,) 'I mean genteel moral characters.' 'I think (said Hicky,) gentility and morality are inseparable.' BOSWELL. 'By no means, Sir. The genteelest characters are often the most immoral. Does not Lord Chesterfield give precepts for uniting wickedness and the graces? A man, indeed, is not genteel when he gets drunk; but most vices may be committed very genteelly: a man may debauch his friend's wife genteelly: he may cheat at cards genteelly.' HICKY. 'I do not think *that* is genteel.' BOSWELL. 'Sir, it may not be like a gentleman, but it may be genteel.' JOHNSON. 'You are meaning two different things. One means exteriour grace; the other honour. It is certain that a man may be very immoral with exteriour grace. Lovelace, in *Clarissa*, is a very genteel and a very wicked character. Tom Hervey, who died t'other day, though a vicious man, was one of the genteelest men that ever lived.' Tom Davies instanced Charles the Second. JOHNSON. (taking fire at any attack upon that Prince, for whom he had an extraordinary partiality,) 'Charles the Second was licentious in his practice; but he always had a reverence for what was good. Charles the Second knew his people, and rewarded merit. The Church was at no time better filled than in his reign. He was the best King we have had from his time till the reign of his present Majesty, except James the Second, who was a very good King, but unhappily believed that it was necessary for the salvation of his subjects that they should be Roman Catholicks. *He* had the merit of endeavouring to do what he thought was for the salvation of the souls of his subjects, till he lost a great Empire. *We,* who thought that we should *not* be saved if we were Roman Catholicks, had the merit of maintaining our religion, at the expence of submitting ourselves to the government of King William, (for it could not be done otherwise,)—to the government of one of the most worthless scoundrels that ever existed. No; Charles the Second was not such a man as ——, (naming another King[1]). He did not destroy his father's will. He took money, indeed, from France: but he did not betray those over whom he ruled: he did not let the French fleet pass ours. George the First knew nothing, and desired to know nothing; did nothing and desired to do nothing: and the only good thing that is told of him is, that he wished to restore the crown to its hereditary successor.' He roared with prodigious violence against George the Second. When he ceased, Moody interjected, in an Irish tone, and with a comick look, 'Ah! poor George the Second.'

[1] George II.

I mentioned that Dr. Thomas Campbell had come from Ireland to London, principally to see Dr. Johnson. He seemed angry at this observation. DAVIES. 'Why, you know, Sir, there came a man from Spain to see Livy; and Corelli came to England to see Purcell, and when he heard he was dead, went directly back again to Italy.' JOHNSON. 'I should not have wished to be dead to disappoint Campbell, had he been so foolish as you represent him; but I should have wished to have been a hundred miles off.' This was apparently perverse; and I do believe it was not his real way of thinking: he could not but like a man who came so far to see him. He laughed with some complacency when I told him Campbell's odd expression to me concerning him: 'That having seen such a man, was a thing to talk of a century hence,'—as if he could live so long.

We got into an argument whether the Judges who went to India might with propriety engage in trade. Johnson warmly maintained that they might. 'For why (he urged,) should not Judges get riches, as well as those who deserve them less?' I said, they should have sufficient salaries, and have nothing to take off their attention from the affairs of the publick. JOHNSON. 'No Judge, Sir, can give his whole attention to his office; and it is very proper that he should employ what time he has to himself, for his own advantage, in the most profitable manner.' 'Then, Sir, (said Davies, who enlivened the dispute by making it somewhat dramatick,) he may become an insurer; and when he is going to the bench, he may be stopped,— "Your Lordship cannot go yet: here is a bunch of invoices: several ships are about to sail." ' JOHNSON. 'Sir, you may as well say a Judge should not have a house; for they may come and tell him, "Your Lordship's house is on fire;" and so, instead of minding the business of his Court, he is to be occupied in getting the engine with the greatest speed. There is no end of this. Every Judge who has land, trades to a certain extent in corn or in cattle; and in the land itself, undoubtedly. His steward acts for him, and so do clerks for a great merchant. A Judge may be a farmer; but he is not to geld his own pigs. A Judge may play a little at cards for his amusement; but he is not to play at marbles, or at chuck-farthing in the Piazza. No, Sir; there is no profession to which a man gives a very great proportion of this time. It is wonderful, when a calculation is made, how little the mind is actually employed in the discharge of any profession. No man would be a Judge, upon the condition of being obliged to be totally a Judge. The best employed lawyer has his mind at work but for a small proportion of his time: a great deal of his occupation is merely mechanical. I once wrote for a magazine: I made a calculation, that if I should write but a page a day, at the same rate, I should, in ten years, write nine volumes in folio, of an ordinary size and print.' BOSWELL. 'Such as Carte's *History?*' JOHNSON. 'Yes, Sir. When a man writes from his own mind, he writes very rapidly. The greatest part of a writer's time is spent in reading, in order to write: a man will turn over half a library to make one book.'

I argued warmly against the Judges trading, and mentioned Hale as an instance of a perfect Judge, who devoted himself entirely to his office. JOHNSON. 'Hale, Sir, attended to other things besides law: he left a great estate.' BOSWELL. 'That was, because what he got, accumulated without any exertion and anxiety on his part.'

While the dispute went on, Moody once tried to say something upon our side. Tom Davies clapped him on the back, to encourage him. Beauclerk, to whom I mentioned this circumstance, said, 'that he could not conceive a more humiliating situation than to be clapped on the back by Tom Davies.'

We spoke of Rolt, to whose *Dictionary of Commerce* Dr. Johnson wrote the Preface. JOHNSON. 'Old Gardner the bookseller employed Rolt and Smart to write a monthly miscellany, called *The Universal Visitor*. There was a formal written contract, which Allen the printer saw. Gardner thought as you do of the Judge. They were bound to write nothing else; they were to have, I think, a third of the profits of this sixpenny pamphlet; and the contract was for ninety-nine years. I wish I had thought of giving this to Thurlow, in the cause about Literary Property. What an excellent instance would it have been of the oppression of booksellers towards poor authours! (smiling.) Davies, zealous for the honour of *the Trade,* said, Gardner was not properly a bookseller. JOHNSON. 'Nay, Sir; he certainly was a bookseller. He had served his time regularly, was a member of the Stationers' company, kept a shop in the face of mankind, purchased copyright, and was a *bibliopole*, Sir, in every sense. I wrote for some months in *The Universal Visitor,* for poor Smart, while he was mad, not then knowing the terms on which he was engaged to write, and thinking I was doing him good. I hoped his wits would soon return to him. Mine returned to me, and I wrote in *The Universal Visitor* no longer.'

Friday, April 7, I dined with him at a tavern, with a numerous company. JOHNSON. 'I have been reading Twiss's *Travels in Spain,* which are just come out. They are as good as the first book of travels that you will take up. They are as good as those of Keysler or Blainville; nay, as Addison's, if you except the learning. They are not so good as Brydone's, but they are better than Pococke's. I have not, indeed, cut the leaves yet; but I have read in them where the pages are open, and I do not suppose that what is in the pages which are closed is worse than what is in the open pages. It would seem (he added,) that Addison had not acquired much Italian learning, for we do not find it introduced into his writings. The only instance that I recollect, is his quoting *"Stavo bene; per star meglio, sto qui."* '[1]

I mentioned Addison's having borrowed many of his classical remarks from Leandro Alberti. Mr. Beauclerk said, 'It was alledged that he had borrowed also from another Italian authour.' JOHNSON. 'Why, Sir, all who go to look for what the Classicks have said of Italy, must find the same passages; and I should think it would be one of the first things the Italians would do on the revival of learning, to collect all that the Roman authours have said of their country.'

Ossian being mentioned;—JOHNSON. 'Supposing the Irish and Erse languages to be the same, which I do not believe, yet as there is no reason to suppose that the inhabitants of the Highlands and Hebrides ever wrote their native language, it is not to be credited that a long poem was preserved among them. If we had no evidence of the art of writing being practised in one of the counties of England, we should not believe that a long poem was preserved *there,* though in the neighbouring counties, where the same language was spoken, the inhabitants could write. BEAUCLERK. 'The ballad of *Lilliburlero* was once in the mouths of all the people of this country, and is said to have had a great effect in bringing about the Revolution. Yet I question whether any body can repeat it now; which shews how improbable it is that much poetry should be preserved by tradition.'

One of the company[2] suggested an internal objection to the antiquity of the poetry said to be Ossian's, that we do not find the wolf in it, which must have been the case had it been of that age.

The mention of the wolf had led Johnson to think of other wild beasts; and while Sir Joshua Reynolds and Mr. Langton were carrying on a dialogue about something which engaged them earnestly, he, in the midst of it, broke out, 'Pennant tells of Bears—' [what he added, I have forgotten.] They went on, which he being dull of hearing, did not perceive, or, if he did, was not willing to break off his talk; so he continued to vociferate his remarks, and *Bear* ('like a word in a catch' as Beauclerk said,) was repeatedly heard at intervals, which coming from him who, by those who did not know

[1] 'I was well; I would be better; here I am.' (An epitaph.)
[2] Percy.

him, had been so often assimilated to that ferocious animal, while we who were sitting around could hardly stifle laughter, produced a very ludicrous effect. Silence having ensued, he proceeded: 'We are told, that the black bear is innocent; but I should not like to trust myself with him.' Mr. Gibbon muttered, in a low tone of voice, 'I should not like to trust myself with *you*.' This piece of sarcastick pleasantry was a prudent resolution, if applied to a competition of abilities.

Patriotism having become one of our topicks, Johnson suddenly uttered, in a strong determined tone, an apophthegm, at which many will start: 'Patriotism is the last refuge of a scoundrel.' But let it be considered, that he did not mean a real and generous love of our country, but that pretended patriotism which so many, in all ages and countries, have made a cloak for self-interest. I maintained, that certainly all patriots were not scoundrels. Being urged, (not by Johnson,) to name one exception, I mentioned an eminent person,[1] whom we all greatly admired. JOHNSON. 'Sir, I do not say that he is *not* honest; but we have no reason to conclude from his political conduct that he *is* honest. Were he to accept of a place from this ministry, he would lose that character of firmness which he has, and might be turned out of his place in a year. This ministry is neither stable, nor grateful to their friends, as Sir Robert Walpole was, so that he may think it more for his interest to take his chance of his party coming in.'

Mrs. Pritchard being mentioned, he said, 'Her playing was quite mechanical. It is wonderful how little mind she had. Sir, she had never read the tragedy of *Macbeth* all through. She no more thought of the play out of which her part was taken, than a shoemaker thinks of the skin, out of which the piece of leather, of which he is making a pair of shoes, is cut.'

On Saturday, May 8,[2] I dined with him at Mr. Thrale's, where we met the Irish Dr. Campbell. Johnson had supped the night before at Mrs. Abington's, with some fashionable people whom he named; and he seemed much pleased with having made one in so elegant a circle. Nor did he omit to pique his *mistress* a little with jealousy of her housewifery; for he said, (with a smile,) 'Mrs. Abington's jelly, my dear lady, was better than yours.'

Mrs. Thrale, who frequently practised a coarse mode of flattery, by repeating his *bon-mots* in his hearing, told us that he had said, a certain celebrated actor[3] was just fit to stand

---

[1] Burke.
[2] Actually, April 8.
[3] Barry.

306

at the door of an auction-room with a long pole, and cry 'Pray gentlemen, walk in;' and that a certain authour,[1] upon hearing this, had said, that another still more celebrated actor[2] was fit for nothing better than that, and would pick your pocket after you came out. JOHNSON. 'Nay, my dear lady, there is no wit in what our friend added; there is only abuse. You may as well say of any man that he will pick a pocket. Besides, the man who is stationed at the door does not pick people's pockets; that is done within, by the auctioneer.'

Mrs. Thrale told us, that Tom Davies repeated, in a very bald manner, the story of Dr. Johnson's first repartee to me, which I have related exactly. He made me say, 'I *was born* in Scotland,' instead of 'I *come from* Scotland;' so that Johnson saying, 'That, Sir, is what a great many of your countrymen cannot help,' had no point, or even meaning: and that upon this being mentioned to Mr. Fitzherbert, he observed, 'It is not every man that can *carry* a *bon mot*.'

On Monday, April 10, I dined with him at General Oglethorpe's, with Mr. Langton and the Irish Dr. Campbell, whom the General had obligingly given me leave to bring with me. This learned gentleman was thus gratified with a very high intellectual feast, by not only being in company with Dr. Johnson, but with General Oglethorpe, who had been so long a celebrated name both at home and abroad.

I must, again and again, intreat of my readers not to suppose that my imperfect record of conversation contains the whole of what was said by Johnson, or other eminent persons who lived with him. What I have preserved, however, has the value of the most perfect authenticity.

He this day enlarged upon Pope's melancholy remark,

'Man never *is,* but always *to be* blest.'

He asserted, that *the present* was never a happy state to any human being; but that, as every part of life, of which we are conscious, was at some point of time a period yet to come, in which felicity was expected, there was some happiness produced by hope. Being pressed upon this subject, and asked if he really was of opinion, that though, in general, happiness was very rare in human life, a man was not sometimes happy in the moment that was present, he answered, 'Never, but when he is drunk.'

He urged General Oglethorpe to give the world his Life. He said, 'I know no man whose Life would be more interest-

[1] Murphy.
[2] Garrick.

307

ing. If I were furnished with materials, I should be very glad to write it.'

Mr. Scott of Amwell's *Elegies* were lying in the room. Dr. Johnson observed, 'They are very well; but such as twenty people might write.' Upon this I took occasion to controvert Horace's maxim,

'————— *mediocribus esse poetis*
Non Di, non homines, non concessêre columnæ.'[1]

For here, (I observed,) was a very middle-rate poet, who pleased many readers, and therefore poetry of a middle sort was entitled to some esteem; nor could I see why poetry should not, like every thing else, have different gradations of excellence, and consequently of value. Johnson repeated the common remark, that, 'as there is no necessity for our having poetry at all, it being merely a luxury, an instrument of pleasure, it can have no value, unless when exquisite in its kind.' I declared myself not satisfied. 'Why then, Sir, (said he,) Horace and you must settle it.' He was not much in the humour of talking.

No more of his conversation for some days appears in my journal, except that when a gentleman[2] told him he had bought a suit of laces for his lady, he said, 'Well, Sir, you have done a good thing and a wise thing.' 'I have done a good thing, (said the gentleman,) but I do not know that I have done a wise thing.' JOHNSON. 'Yes, Sir; no money is better spent than what is laid out for domestick satisfaction. A man is pleased that his wife is drest as well as other people; and a wife is please that she is drest.'

On Friday, April 14, being Good-Friday, I repaired to him in the morning, according to my usual custom on that day, and breakfasted with him. I observed that he fasted so very strictly, that he did not even taste bread, and took no milk with his tea; I suppose because it is a kind of animal food.

He entered upon the state of the nation, and thus discoursed: 'Sir, the great misfortune now is, that government has too little power. All that it has to bestow, must of necessity be given to support itself; so that it cannot reward merit. No man, for instance, can now be made a Bishop for his learning and piety; his only chance for promotion is his being connected with somebody who has parliamentary interest. Our several ministries in this reign have outbid each other in concessions to the people. Lord Bute, though a very honourable man,—a man who meant well,—a man who had his

---

[1] 'To be a mediocre poet neither gods nor men nor booksellers have allowed.' Horace, *Art of Poetry*, ll. 372-73.

[2] Boswell.

blood full of prerogative,—was a theoretical statesman,—a book-minister,—and thought this country could be governed by the influence of the Crown alone. Then, Sir, he gave up a great deal. He advised the King to agree that the Judges should hold their places for life, instead of losing them at the accession of a new King. Lord Bute, I suppose, thought to make the King popular by this concession; but the people never minded it; and it was a most impolitick measure. There is no reason why a Judge should hold his office for life, more than any other person in publick trust. A Judge may be partial otherwise than to the Crown: we have seen Judges partial to the populace. A Judge may become corrupt, and yet there may not be legal evidence against him. A Judge may become froward from age. A Judge may grow unfit for his office in many ways. It was desirable that there should be a possibility of being delivered from him by a new King. That is now gone by an act of Parliament *ex gratiâ* of the Crown. Lord Bute advised the King to give up a very large sum of money, for which nobody thanked him. It was of consequence to the King, but nothing to the publick, among whom it was divided. When I say Lord Bute advised, I mean, that such acts were done when he was minister, and we are to suppose that he advised them.—Lord Bute shewed an undue partiality to Scotchmen. He turned out Dr. Nichols, a very eminent man, from being physician to the King, to make room for one of his countrymen, a man very low in his profession. He had *********** and ****¹ to go on errands for him. He had occasion for people to go on errands for him; but he should not have had Scotchmen; and, certainly, he should not have suffered them to have access to him before the first people in England.'

I told him, that the admission of one of them before the first people in England, which had given the greatest offence, was no more than what happens at every minister's levee, where those who attend are admitted in the order that they have come, which is better than admitting them according to their rank; for if that were to be the rule, a man who has waited all the morning might have the mortification to see a peer, newly come, go in before him, and keep him waiting still. JOHNSON. 'True, Sir; but **** should not have come to the levee, to be in the way of people of consequence. He saw Lord Bute at all times; and could have said what he had to say at any time, as well as at the levee. There is now no Prime Minister: there is only an agent for government in the House of Commons. We are governed by the Cabinet: but

¹ Wedderburne and Home.

309

there is no one head there, as in Sir Robert Walpole's time.' BOSWELL. 'What then, Sir, is the use of Parliament?' JOHNSON. 'Why, Sir, Parliament is a larger council to the King; and the advantage of such a council is, having a great number of men of property concerned in the legislature, who, for their own interest, will not consent to bad laws. And you must have observed, Sir, that administration is feeble and timid, and cannot act with that authority and resolution which is necessary. Were I in power, I would turn out every man who dared to oppose me. Government has the distribution of offices, that it may be enabled to maintain its authority.'

'Lord Bute (he added,) took down too fast, without building up something new.' BOSWELL. 'Because, Sir, he found a rotten building. The political coach was drawn by a set of bad horses: it was necessary to change them.' JOHNSON. 'But he should have changed them one by one.'

I told him that I had been informed by Mr. Orme, that many parts of the East-Indies were better mapped than the Highlands of Scotland. JOHNSON. 'That a country may be mapped, it must be travelled over.' 'Nay, (said I, meaning to laugh with him at one of his prejudices,) can't you say, it is not *worth* mapping?'

As we walked to St. Clement's church, and saw several shops open upon this most solemn fast-day of the Christian world, I remarked, that one disadvantage arising from the immensity of London, was, that nobody was heeded by his neighbour; there was no fear of censure for not observing Good-Friday, as it ought to be kept, and as it is kept in country-towns. He said, it was, upon the whole, very well observed even in London. He, however, owned, that London was too large; but added, 'It is nonsense to say the head is too big for the body. It would be as much too big, though the body were ever so large; that is to say, though the country were ever so extensive. It has no similarity to a head connected with a body.'

Dr. Wetherell, Master of University College, Oxford, accompanied us home from church; and after he was gone, there came two other gentlemen, one of whom uttered the commonplace complaints, that by the increase of taxes, labour would be dear, other nations would undersell us, and our commerce would be ruined. JOHNSON. (smiling,) 'Never fear, Sir. Our commerce is in a very good state; and suppose we had no commerce at all, we could live very well on the produce of our own country.' I cannot omit to mention, that I never knew any man who was less disposed to be querulous than Johnson. Whether the subject was his own situation, or the state of the publick, or the state of human nature in general, though he saw the evils, his mind was turned to resolution, and never to whining or complaint.

We went again to St. Clement's in the afternoon. He had found fault with the preacher in the morning for not choosing a text adapted to the day. The preacher in the afternoon had chosen one extremely proper: 'It is finished.'

After the evening service, he said, 'Come, you shall go home with me, and sit just an hour.' But he was better than his word; for after we had drunk tea with Mrs. Williams, he asked me to go up to his study with him, where we sat a long while together in a serene undisturbed frame of mind, sometimes in silence, and sometimes conversing, as we felt ourselves inclined, or more properly speaking, as *he* was inclined; for during all the course of my long intimacy with him, my respectful attention never abated, and my wish to hear him was such, that I constantly watched every dawning of communication from that great and illuminated mind.

He observed, 'All knowledge is of itself of some value. There is nothing so minute or inconsiderable, that I would not rather know it than not. In the same manner, all power, of whatever sort, is of itself desirable. A man would not submit to learn to hem a ruffle, of his wife, or his wife's maid; but if a mere wish could attain it, he would rather wish to be able to hem a ruffle.'

He again advised me to keep a journal fully and minutely, but not to mention such trifles as, that meat was too much or too little done, or that the weather was fair or rainy. He had, till very near his death, a contempt for the notion that the weather affects the human frame.

I told him that our friend Goldsmith had said to me, that he had come too late into the world, for that Pope and other poets had taken up the places in the Temple of Fame; so that, as but a few at any period can possess poetical reputation, a man of genius can now hardly acquire it. JOHNSON. 'That is one of the most sensible things I have ever heard of Goldsmith. It is difficult to get literary fame, and it is every day growing more difficult. Ah, Sir, that should make a man think of securing happiness in another world, which all who try sincerely for it may attain. In comparison of that, how little are all other things! The belief of immortality is impressed upon all men, and all men act under an impression of it, however they may talk, and though, perhaps, they may be scarcely sensible of it.' I said, it appeared to me that some people had not the least notion of immortality; and I men-

311

tioned a distinguished gentleman of our acquaintance.[1] JOHN-
SON. 'Sir, if it were not for the notion of immortality, he
would cut a throat to fill his pockets.' When I quoted this to
Beauclerk, who knew much more of the gentleman than we
did, he said, in his acid manner, 'He would cut a throat to
fill his pockets, if it were not for fear of being hanged.'

Dr. Johnson proceeded: 'Sir, there is a great cry about infidelity; but there are, in reality, very few infidels. I have
heard a person, originally a Quaker, but now, I am afraid, a
Deist,[2] say, that he did not believe there were, in all England,
above two hundred infidels.'

He was pleased to say, 'If you come to settle here, we will
have one day in the week on which we will meet by ourselves. That is the happiest conversation where there is no
competition, no vanity, but a calm quiet interchange of sentiments.' In his private register this evening is thus marked,
'Boswell sat with me till night; we had some serious talk.' It
also appears from the same record, that after I left him he was
occupied in religious duties, in 'giving Francis, his servant,
some directions for preparation to communicate; in reviewing
his life, and resolving on better conduct.' The humility and
piety which he discovers on such occasions, is truely edifying.
No saint, however, in the course of his religious warfare, was
more sensible of the unhappy failure of pious resolves, than
Johnson. He said one day, talking to an acquaintance on this
subject, 'Sir, Hell is paved with good intentions.'

On Sunday, April 16, being Easter Day, after having
attended the solemn service at St. Paul's, I dined with Dr.
Johnson and Mrs. Williams. I maintained that Horace was
wrong in placing happiness in *Nil admirari*,[3] for that I
thought admiration one of the most agreeable of all our
feelings; and I regretted that I had lost much of my disposition to admire, which people generally do as they advance in life. JOHNSON. 'Sir, as a man advances in life, he
gets what is better than admiration—judgement, to estimate
things at their true value.' I still insisted that admiration was
more pleasing than judgement, as love is more pleasing than
friendship. The feeling of friendship is like that of being
comfortably filled with roast beef; love, like being enlivened
with champagne. JOHNSON. 'No, Sir; admiration and love are
like being intoxicated with champagne; judgement and friendship like being enlivened. Waller has hit upon the same
thought with you: but I don't believe you have borrowed

[1] Fox.
[2] Dr. Brocklesby.
[3] 'To admire nothing.' Horace, *Epistles,* I. vi. 1.

from Waller. I wish you would enable yourself to borrow more.'

He then took occasion to enlarge on the advantages of reading, and combated the idle superficial notion, that knowledge enough may be acquired in conversation. 'The foundation (said he,) must be laid by reading. General principles must be had from books, which, however, must be brought to the test of real life. In conversation you never get a system. What is said upon a subject is to be gathered from a hundred people. The parts of a truth, which a man gets thus, are at such a distance from each other that he never attains to a full view.' . . .

On Tuesday, April 18, he and I were engaged to go with Sir Joshua Reynolds to dine with Mr. Cambridge, at his beautiful villa on the banks of the Thames, near Twickenham. Dr. Johnson's tardiness was such, that Sir Joshua, who had an appointment at Richmond, early in the day, was obliged to go by himself on horseback, leaving his coach to Johnson and me. Johnson was in such good spirits, that every thing seemed to please him as we drove along.

Our conversation turned on a variety of subjects. He thought portrait-painting an improper employment for a woman. 'Publick practice of any art, (he observed,) and staring in men's faces, is very indelicate in a female.' I happened to start a question of propriety, whether, when a man knows that some of his intimate friends are invited to the house of another friend, with whom they are all equally intimate, he may join them without an invitation. JOHNSON. 'No, Sir; he is not to go when he is not invited. They may be invited on purpose to abuse him,' (smiling).

As a curious instance how little a man knows, or wishes to know, his own character in the world, or, rather, as a convincing proof that Johnson's roughness was only external, and did not proceed from his heart, I insert the following dialogue. JOHNSON. 'It is wonderful, Sir, how rare a quality good humour is in life. We meet with very few good humoured men.' I mentioned four of our friends,[1] none of whom he would allow to be good humoured. One was *acid*, another was *muddy*, and to the others he had objections which have escaped me. Then, shaking his head and stretching himself at his ease in the coach, and smiling with much complacency, he turned to me and said, 'I look upon *myself* as a good humoured fellow.' The epithet *fellow*, applied to the great Lexicographer, the stately Moralist, the masterly Critick, as if he had been *Sam* Johnson, a mere pleasant companion, was high-

---

[1] Reynolds, Burke, Beauclerk (acid), Langton (muddy).

ly diverting; and this light notion of himself struck me with wonder. I answered, also smiling, 'No, no, Sir; that will *not* do. You are good natured, but not good humoured: you are irascible. You have not patience with folly and absurdity. I believe you would pardon them, if there were time to deprecate your vengeance; but punishment follows so quick after sentence, that they cannot escape.'

I had brought with me a great bundle of Scotch magazines and news-papers, in which his *Journey to the Western Islands* was attacked in every mode; and I read a great part of them to him, knowing they would afford him entertainment. I wish the writers of them had been present: they would have been sufficiently vexed. One ludicrous imitation of his style, by Mr. Maclaurin, now one of the Scotch Judges, with the title of Lord Dreghorn, was distinguished by him from the rude mass. 'This (said he,) is the best. But I could caricature my own style much better myself.' He defended his remark upon the general insufficiency of education in Scotland; and confirmed to me the authenticity of his witty saying on the learning of the Scotch;—'Their learning is like bread in a besieged town: every man gets a little, but no man gets a full meal.' 'There is (said he,) in Scotland, a diffusion of learning, a certain portion of it widely and thinly spread. A merchant there has as much learning as one of their clergy.'

He talked of Isaac Walton's *Lives,* which was one of his most favourite books. Dr. Donne's *Life,* he said, was the most perfect of them. He observed, that 'it was wonderful that Walton, who was in a very low situation in life, should have been familiarly received by so many great men, and that at a time when the ranks of society were kept more separate than they are now.' He supposed that Walton had then given up his business as a linendraper and sempster, and was only an authour; and added, 'that he was a great panegyrist.' Boswell. 'No quality will get a man more friends than a disposition to admire the qualities of others. I do not mean flattery, but a sincere admiration.' Johnson. 'Nay, Sir, flattery pleases very generally. In the first place, the flatterer may think what he says to be true: but, in the second place, whether he thinks so or not, he certainly thinks those whom he flatters of consequence enough to be flattered.'

No sooner had we made our bow to Mr. Cambridge, in his library, than Johnson ran eagerly to one side of the room, intent on poring over the backs of the books. Sir Joshua observed, (aside,) 'He runs to the books, as I do to the pictures: but I have the advantage. I can see much more of the pictures than he can of the books.' Mr. Cambridge, upon this, politely said, 'Dr. Johnson, I am going, with your pardon, to

314

accuse myself, for I have the same custom which I perceive you have. But it seems odd that one should have such a desire to look at the backs of books.' Johnson, ever ready for contest, instantly started from his reverie, wheeled about, and answered, 'Sir, the reason is very plain. Knowledge is of two kinds. We know a subject ourselves, or we know where we can find information upon it. When we enquire into any subject, the first thing we have to do is to know what books have treated of it. This leads us to look at catalogues, and at the backs of books in libraries.' Sir Joshua observed to me the extraordinary promptitude with which Johnson flew upon an argument. 'Yes, (said I,) he has no formal preparation, no flourishing with his sword; he is through your body in an instant.'

Johnson was here solaced with an elegant entertainment, a very accomplished family, and much good company; among whom was Mr. Harris of Salisbury, who paid him many compliments on his *Journey to the Western Islands*.

The common remark as to the utility of reading history being made;—JOHNSON. 'We must consider how very little history there is; I mean real authentick history. That certain Kings reigned, and certain battles were fought, we can depend upon as true; but all the colouring, all the philosophy, of history is conjecture.' BOSWELL. 'Then, Sir, you would reduce all history to no better than an almanack, a mere chronological series of remarkable events.' Mr. Gibbon, who must at that time have been employed upon his *History*, of which he published the first volume in the following year, was present; but did not step forth in defence of that species of writing. He probably did not like to *trust* himself with JOHNSON!

Johnson observed, that the force of our early habits was so great, that though reason approved, nay, though our senses relished a different course, almost every man returned to them. I do not believe there is any observation upon human nature better founded than this; and, in many cases, it is a very painful truth; for where early habits have been mean and wretched, the joy and elevation resulting from better modes of life must be damped by the gloomy consciousness of being under an almost inevitable doom to sink back into a situation which we recollect with disgust. It surely may be prevented, by constant attention and unremitting exertion to establish contrary habits of superiour efficacy.

The Beggar's Opera, and the common question, whether it was pernicious in its effects, having been introduced;—JOHNSON. 'As to this matter, which has been very much contested, I myself am of opinion, that more influence has been ascribed to *The Beggar's Opera*, than it in reality ever had; for

I do not believe that any man was ever made a rogue by being present at its representation. At the same time I do not deny that it may have some influence, by making the character of a rogue familiar, and in some degree pleasing.' Then collecting himself as it were, to give a heavy stroke: 'There is in it such a *labefactation* of all principles, as may be injurious to morality.'

While he pronounced this response, we sat in a comical sort of restraint, smothering a laugh, which we were afraid might burst out. In his *Life of Gay,* he has been still more decisive as to the inefficiency of *The Beggar's Opera* in corrupting society. But I have ever thought somewhat differently; for, indeed, not only are the gaiety and heroism of a highwayman very captivating to a youthful imagination, but the arguments for adventurous depredation are so plausible, the allusions so lively, and the contrasts with the ordinary and more painful modes of acquiring property are so artfully displayed, that it requires a cool and strong judgement to resist so imposing an aggregate: yet, I own, I should be very sorry to have *The Beggar's Opera* suppressed; for there is in it so much of real London life, so much brilliant wit, and such a variety of airs, which, from early association of ideas, engage, soothe, and enliven the mind, that no performance which the theatre exhibits, delights me more. . . .

We talked of a young gentleman's marriage with an eminent singer,[1] and his determination that she should no longer sing in publick, though his father was very earnest she should, because her talents would be liberally rewarded, so as to make her a good fortune. It was questioned whether the young gentleman, who had not a shilling in the world, but was blest with very uncommon talents, was not foolishly delicate, or foolishly proud, and his father truely rational without being mean. Johnson, with all the high spirit of a Roman senator, exclaimed, 'He resolved wisely and nobly to be sure. He is a brave man. Would not a gentleman be disgraced by having his wife singing publickly for hire? No, Sir, there can be no doubt here. I know not if I should not *prepare* myself for a publick singer, as readily as let my wife be one.'

Johnson arraigned the modern politicks of this country, as entirely devoid of all principle of whatever kind. 'Politicks (said he,) are now nothing more than means of rising in the world. With this sole view do men engage in politicks, and their whole conduct proceeds upon it. How different in that respect is the state of the nation now from what it was in the time of Charles the First, during the Usurpation, and

---

[1] R. B. Sheridan and Elizabeth Linley.

after the Restoration, in the time of Charles the Second. *Hudibras* affords a strong proof how much hold political principles had then upon the minds of men. There is in *Hudibras* a great deal of bullion which will always last. But to be sure the brightest strokes of his wit owed their force to the impression of the characters, which was upon men's minds at the time; to their knowing them, at table and in the street; in short, being familiar with them; and above all, to his satire being directed against those whom a little while before they had hated and feared. The nation in general has ever been loyal, has been at all times attached to the monarch, though a few daring rebels have been wonderfully powerful for a time. The murder of Charles the First was undoubtedly not committed with the approbation or consent of the people. Had that been the case, Parliament would not have ventured to consign the regicides to their deserved punishment. And we know what exuberance of joy there was when Charles the Second was restored. If Charles the Second had bent all his mind to it, had made it his sole object, he might have been as absolute as Louis the Fourteenth.' A gentleman[1] observed he would have done no harm if he had. JOHNSON. 'Why, Sir, absolute princes seldom do any harm. But they who are governed by them are governed by chance. There is no security for good government.' CAMBRIDGE. 'There have been many sad victims to absolute power.' JOHNSON. 'So, Sir, have there been to popular factions.' BOSWELL. 'The question is, which is worst, one wild beast or many?'

Johnson praised *The Spectator,* particularly the character of Sir Roger de Coverley. He said, 'Sir Roger did not die a violent death, as has been generally fancied. He was not killed; he died only because others were to die, and because his death afforded an opportunity to Addison for some very fine writing. We have the example of Cervantes making Don Quixote die.—I never could see why Sir Roger is represented as a little cracked. It appears to me that the story of the widow was intended to have something superinduced upon it: but the superstructure did not come.'

Somebody[2] found fault with writing verses in a dead language, maintaining that they were merely arrangements of so many words, and laughed at the Universities of Oxford and Cambridge, for sending forth collections of them not only in Greek and Latin, but even in Syriac, Arabick, and other more unknown tongues. JOHNSON. 'I would have as many of these as possible; I would have verses in every language that

[1] Boswell.
[2] Reynolds.

there are the means of acquiring. Nobody imagines that an University is to have at once two hundred poets; but it should be able to show two hundred scholars. Pieresc's death was lamented, I think, in forty languages. And I would have at every coronation, and every death of a King, every *Gaudium*, and every *Luctus*, University verses, in as many languages as can be acquired. I would have the world to be thus told, "Here is a school where every thing may be learnt." '

Having set out next day on a visit to the Earl of Pembroke, at Wilton, and to my friend, Mr. Temple, at Mamhead, in Devonshire, and not having returned to town till the second of May, I did not see Dr. Johnson for a considerable time, and during the remaining part of my stay in London, kept very imperfect notes of his conversation, which had I according to my usual custom written out at large soon after the time, much might have been preserved, which is now irretrievably lost. I can now only record some particular scenes, and a few fragments of his *memorabilia*.

On Monday, May 8, we went together and visited the mansions of Bedlam. I had been informed that he had once been there before with Mr. Wedderburne, (now Lord Loughborough,) Mr. Murphy, and Mr. Foote; and I had heard Foote give a very entertaining account of Johnson's happening to have his attention arrested by a man who was very furious, and who, while beating his straw, supposed it to be William Duke of Cumberland, whom he was punishing for his cruelties in Scotland, in 1746. There was nothing peculiarly remarkable this day; but the general contemplation of insanity was very affecting. I accompanied him home, and dined and drank tea with him.

Talking of an acquaintance of ours, distinguished for knowing an uncommon variety of miscellaneous articles both in antiquities and polite literature, he observed, 'You know, Sir, he runs about with little weight upon his mind.' And talking of another very ingenious gentleman,[1] who from the warmth of his temper was at variance with many of his acquaintance, and wished to avoid them, he said, 'Sir, he leads the life of an outlaw.'

On Friday, May 12, as he had been so good as to assign me a room in his house, where I might sleep occasionally, when I happened to sit with him to a late hour, I took possession of it this night, found every thing in excellent order, and was attended by honest Francis with a most civil assiduity. I asked Johnson whether I might go to a consultation with another lawyer upon Sunday, as that appeared to me to be

[1] Steevens.

doing work as much in my way, as if an artisan should work on the day appropriated for religious rest. JOHNSON. 'Why, Sir, when you are of consequence enough to oppose the practice of consulting upon Sunday, you should do it: but you may go now. It is not criminal, though it is not what one should do, who is anxious for the preservation and increase of piety, to which a peculiar observance of Sunday is a great help. The distinction is clear between what is of moral and what is of ritual obligation.'

On Saturday, May 13, I breakfasted with him by invitation, accompanied by Mr. Andrew Crosbie, a Scotch Advocate, whom he had seen at Edinburgh, and the Hon. Colonel (now General) Edward Stopford, brother to Lord Courtown, who was desirous of being introduced to him. His tea and rolls and butter, and whole breakfast apparatus were all in such decorum, and his behaviour was so courteous, that Colonel Stopford was quite surprized, and wondered at his having heard so much said of Johnson's slovenliness and roughness. I have preserved nothing of what passed, except that Crosbie pleased him much by talking learnedly of alchymy, as to which Johnson was not a positive unbeliever, but rather delighted in considering what progress had actually been made in the transmutation of metals, what near approaches there had been to the making of gold; and told us that it was affirmed, that a person in the Russian dominions had discovered the secret, but died without revealing it, as imagining it would be prejudicial to society. He added, that it was not impossible but it might in time be generally known.

It being asked whether it was reasonable for a man to be angry at another whom a woman had preferred to him;— JOHNSON. 'I do not see, Sir, that it is reasonable for a man to be angry at another, whom a woman has preferred to him: but angry he is, no doubt; and he is loath to be angry at himself.'

Before setting out for Scotland on the 23rd, I was frequently in his company at different places, but during this period have recorded only two remarks: one concerning Garrick: 'He has not Latin enough. He finds out the Latin by the meaning, rather than the meaning by the Latin.' And another concerning writers of travels, who, he observed, 'were more defective than any other writers.'

I passed many hours with him on the 17th, of which I find all my memorial is, 'much laughing.' It should seem he had that day been in a humour for jocularity and merriment, and upon such occasions I never knew a man laugh more heartily. We may suppose, that the high relish of a state so different from his habitual gloom, produced more than ordi-

319

nary exertions of that distinguishing faculty of man, which has puzzled philosophers so much to explain. Johnson's laugh was as remarkable as any circumstance in his manner. It was a kind of good humoured growl. Tom Davies described it drolly enough: 'He laughs like a rhinoceros.' . . .

'To JAMES BOSWELL, ESQ.

'MY DEAR SIR,—I now write to you, lest in some of your freaks and humours you should fancy yourself neglected. Such fancies I must entreat you never to admit, at least never to indulge: for my regard for you is so radicated and fixed, that it is become part of my mind, and cannot be effaced but by some cause uncommonly violent; therefore, whether I write or not, set your thoughts at rest. I now write to tell you that I shall not very soon write again, for I am to set out to-morrow on another journey. . . .

'Your friends are all well at Streatham, and in Leicester-fields.[1] Make my compliments to Mrs. Boswell, if she is in good humour with me. I am, Sir, &c.

'September 14, 1775.'   'SAM. JOHNSON.'

What he mentions in such light terms as, 'I am to set out to-morrow on another journey,' I soon afterwards discovered was no less than a tour to France with Mr. and Mrs. Thrale. This was the only time in his life that he went upon the Continent. . . .

It is to be regretted that he did not write an account of his travels in France; for as he is reported to have once said, that 'he could write the Life of a Broomstick,' so, notwithstanding so many former travellers have exhausted almost every subject for remark in that great kingdom, his very accurate observation, and peculiar vigour of thought and illustration, would have produced a valuable work. During his visit to it, which lasted but about two months, he wrote notes or minutes of what he saw. He promised to show me them, but I neglected to put him in mind of it; and the greatest part of them has been lost, or perhaps, destroyed in a precipitate burning of his papers a few days before his death, which must ever be lamented. One small paperbook, however, entitled 'FRANCE II,' has been preserved, and is in my possession. It is a diurnal register of his life and observations, from the 10th of October to the 4th of November, inclusive, being twenty-six days, and shews an extraordinary attention to various minute particulars. Being the only memorial of this tour that remains, my readers, I am confident, will peruse it with pleas-

1 Where Sir Joshua Reynolds lived—B.

ure, though his notes are very short, and evidently written only to assist his own recollection.[1] . . .

'Oct. 15. Sunday. At Choisi, a royal palace on the banks of the Seine, about 7 m. from Paris.—The terrace noble along the river.—The rooms numerous and grand, but not discriminated from other palaces.—The chapel beautiful, but small.—China globes.—Inlaid table.—Labyrinth.—Sinking table.—Toilet tables.

'Oct. 16. Monday. The Palais Royal very grand, large and lofty.—A very great collection of pictures.—Three of Raphael.—Two Holy Family.—One small piece of M. Angelo.—One room of Rubens—I thought the pictures of Raphael fine. . . .

'Austin Nuns.—Grate.—Mrs. Fermor, Abbess.—She knew Pope, and thought him disagreeable.—Mrs. —— has many books;—has seen life.—Their frontlet disagreeable.—Their hood.—Their life easy.—Rise about five; hour and half in chapel.—Dine at ten.—Another hour and half at chapel; half an hour about three, and half an hour more at seven:—four hours in chapel.—A large garden.—Thirteen pensioners.—Teacher complained. . . .

'Nov. 5. Sunday. We saw the cathedral.[2]—It is very beautiful, with chapels on each side.—The choir splendid.—The balustrade in one part brass.—The Neff very high and grand.—The altar silver as far as it is seen.—The vestments very splendid.——At the Benedictines church————'

Here his Journal ends abruptly. Whether he wrote any more after this time, I know not; but probably not much, as he arrived in England about the 12th of November. These short notes of his tour, though they may seem minute taken singly, make together a considerable mass of information, and exhibit such an ardour of enquiry and acuteness of examination, as, I believe, are found in but few travellers, especially at an advanced age. They completely refute the idle notion which has been propagated, *that he could not see;* and, if he had taken the trouble to revise and digest them, he undoubtedly could have expanded them into a very entertaining narrative.

When I met him in London the following year, the account which he gave me of his French tour, was, 'Sir, I have seen all the visibilities of Paris, and around it; but to have formed an acquaintance with the people there, would have required more time than I could stay. I was just beginning to creep into acquaintance by means of Colonel Drumgold, a very

---

[1] Only a sample of Johnson's entries is given in this edition.
[2] At Cambrai.

high man, Sir, head of *L'Ecole Militaire*, a most complete character, for he had first been a professor of rhetorick, and then became a soldier. And, Sir, I was very kindly treated by the English Benedictines, and have a cell appropriated to me in their convent.'

He observed, 'The great in France live very magnificently, but the rest very miserably. There is no happy middle state as in England. The shops of Paris are mean; the meat in the markets is such as would be sent to a gaol in England: and Mr. Thrale justly observed, that the cookery of the French was forced upon them by necessity; for they could not eat their meat, unless they added some taste to it. The French are an indelicate people; they will spit upon any place. At Madame ———'s, a literary lady of rank, the footman took the sugar in his fingers, and threw it into my coffee. I was going to put it aside; but hearing it was made on purpose for me, I e'en tasted Tom's fingers. The same lady would needs make tea *á l'Angloise*. The spout of the tea-pot did not pour freely; she bad the footman blow into it. France is worse than Scotland in every thing but climate. Nature has done more for the French; but they have done less for themselves than the Scotch have done.'

It happened that Foote was at Paris at the same time with Dr. Johnson, and his description of my friend while there, was abundantly ludicrous. He told me, that the French were quite astonished at his figure and manner, and at his dress, which he obstinately continued exactly as in London;—his brown clothes, black stockings, and plain shirt. He mentioned, that an Irish gentleman said to Johnson, 'Sir, you have not seen the best French players.' JOHNSON. 'Players, Sir! I look on them as no better than creatures set upon tables and joint-stools to make faces and produce laughter, like dancing dogs.'—'But, Sir, you will allow that some players are better than others?' JOHNSON. 'Yes, Sir, as some dogs dance better than others.'

While Johnson was in France, he was generally very resolute in speaking Latin. It was a maxim with him that a man should not let himself down, by speaking a language which he speaks imperfectly. Indeed, we must have often observed how inferiour, how much like a child a man appears, who speaks a broken tongue. When Sir Joshua Reynolds, at one of the dinners of the Royal Academy, presented him to a Frenchman of great distinction, he would not deign to speak French, but talked Latin, though his Excellency did not understand it, owing, perhaps, to Johnson's English pronunciation: yet upon another occasion he was observed to speak French to a Frenchman of high rank, who spoke English;

322

and being asked the reason, with some expression of surprise, —he answered, 'because I think my French is as good as his English.' Though Johnson understood French perfectly, he could not speak it readily. . . .

Here let me not forget a curious anecdote, as related to me by Mr. Beauclerk, which I shall endeavour to exhibit as well as I can in that gentleman's lively manner; and in justice to him it is proper to add, that Dr. Johnson told me I might rely both on the correctness of his memory, and the fidelity of his narrative. 'When Madame de Boufflers was first in England, (said Beauclerk,) she was desirous to see Johnson. I accordingly went with her to his chambers in the Temple, where she was entertained with his conversation for some time. When our visit was over, she and I left him, and were got into Inner Temple-lane, when all at once I heard a noise like thunder. This was occasioned by Johnson, who it seems, upon a little recollection, had taken it into his head that he ought to have done the honours of his literary residence to a foreign lady of quality, and eager to show himself a man of gallantry, was hurrying down the stair-case in violent agitation. He overtook us before we reached the Temple-gate, and brushing in between me and Madame de Boufflers, seized her hand, and conducted her to her coach. His dress was a rusty brown morning suit, a pair of old shoes by way of slippers, a little shrivelled wig sticking on the top of his head, and the sleeves of his shirt and the knees of his breeches hanging loose. A considerable crowd of people gathered round, and were not a little struck by this singular appearance.'

He spoke Latin with wonderful fluency and elegance. When Pere Boscovich was in England, Johnson dined in company with him at Sir Joshua Reynolds's, and at Dr. Douglas's, now Bishop of Salisbury. Upon both occasions that celebrated foreigner expressed his astonishment at Johnson's Latin conversation. When at Paris, Johnson thus characterised Voltaire to Freron the Journalist: *Vir est acerrimi ingenii et paucarum literarum.*[1] . . .

In the course of this year Dr. Burney informs me, that 'he very frequently met Dr. Johnson at Mr. Thrale's, at Streatham, where they had many long conversations, often sitting up as long as the fire and candles lasted, and much longer than the patience of the servants subsisted.'

A few of Johnson's sayings, which that gentleman recollects, shall here be inserted.

'I never take a nap after dinner but when I have had a bad night, and then the nap takes me.'

[1] 'A man of very acute intellect and little literature.'

'The writer of an epitaph should not be considered as saying nothing but what is strictly true. Allowance must be made for some degree of exaggerated praise. In lapidary inscriptions a man is not upon oath.'

'There is now less flogging in our great schools than formerly, but then less is learned there; so that what the boys get at one end, they lose at the other.'

'More is learned in publick than in private schools, from emulation; there is the collision of mind with mind, or the radiation of many minds pointing to one centre. Though few boys make their own exercises, yet if a good exercise is given up, out of a great number of boys, it is made by somebody.'

'I hate by-roads in education. Education is as well known, and has long been as well known, as ever it can be. Endeavouring to make children prematurely wise is useless labour. Suppose they have more knowledge at five or six years old than other children, what use can be made of it? It will be lost before it is wanted, and the waste of so much time and labour of the teacher can never be repaid. Too much is expected from precocity, and too little performed. Miss —— was an instance of early cultivation, but in what did it terminate? In marrying a little Presbyterian parson, who keeps an infant boarding-school, so that all her employment now is,

"To suckle fools, and chronicle small-beer."

She tells the children, "This is a cat, and that is a dog, with four legs and a tail; see there! you are much better than a cat or a dog, for you can speak." If I had bestowed such an education on a daughter, and had discovered that she thought of marrying such a fellow, I would have sent her to the *Congress*.'

'After having talked slightingly of musick, he was observed to listen very attentively while Miss Thrale played on the harpsichord and with eagerness he called to her, "Why don't you dash away like Burney?" Dr. Burney upon this said to him, "I believe, Sir, we shall make a musician of you at last." Johnson with candid complacency replied, "Sir, I shall be glad to have a new sense given to me." '

'He had come down one morning to the breakfast-room, and been a considerable time by himself before any body appeared. When, on a subsequent day, he was twitted by Mrs. Thrale for being very late, which he generally was, he defended himself by alluding to the extraordinary morning, when he had been too early, "Madam, I do not like to come down to *vacuity*." '

'Dr. Burney having remarked that Mr. Garrick was beginning to look old, he said, "Why, Sir, you are not to wonder at that; no man's face has had more wear and tear."' . . .

1776: ÆTAT. 67.]—IN 1776, Johnson wrote, so far as I can discover, nothing for the publick: but that his mind was still ardent, and fraught with generous wishes to attain to still higher degrees of literary excellence, is proved by his private notes of this year, which I shall insert in their proper place. . . .

Having arrived in London late on Friday, the 15th of March, I hastened next morning to wait on Dr. Johnson, at his house; but found he was removed from Johnson's-court, No. 7, to Bolt-court, No. 8, still keeping to his favourite Fleet-street. My reflection at the time upon this change as marked in my Journal, is as follows: 'I felt a foolish regret that he had left a court which bore his name,[1] but it was not foolish to be affected with some tenderness of regard for a place in which I had seen him a great deal, from whence I had often issued a better and a happier man than when I went in, and which had often appeared to my imagination while I trod its pavement, in the solemn darkness of the night, to be sacred to wisdom and piety.' Being informed that he was at Mr. Thrale's, in the Borough, I hastened thither, and found Mrs. Thrale and him at breakfast. I was kindly welcomed. In a moment he was in a full glow of conversation, and I felt myself elevated as if brought into another state of being. Mrs. Thrale and I looked to each other while he talked, and our looks expressed our congenial admiration and affection for him. I shall ever recollect this scene with great pleasure. I exclaimed to her, 'I am now, intellectually, *Hermippus redivivus,*[2] I am quite restored by him, by transfusion of *mind.*' 'There are many (she replied) who admire and respect Mr. Johnson; but you and I *love* him.'

He seemed very happy in the near prospect of going to Italy with Mr. and Mrs. Thrale. 'But, (said he,) before leaving England I am to take a jaunt to Oxford, Birmingham, my native city Lichfield, and my old friend, Dr. Taylor's, at Ashbourn, in Derbyshire. I shall go in a few days, and you, Boswell, shall go with me.' I was ready to accompany him; being willing even to leave London to have the pleasure of his conversation.

I mentioned with much regret the extravagance of the representative[3] of a great family in Scotland, by which there was danger of its being ruined; and as Johnson respected it

[1] He said, when in Scotland, that he was *Johnson of that Ilk*—B.
[2] Hermes reborn.
[3] Norman Macleod, 20th Chief of Macleod.

for its antiquity, he joined with me in thinking it would be happy if this person should die. Mrs. Thrale seemed shocked at this, as feudal barbarity; and said, 'I do not understand this preference of the estate to its owner; of the land to the man who walks upon that land.' JOHNSON. 'Nay, Madam, it is not a preference of the land to its owner, it is the preference of a family to an individual. Here is an establishment in a country, which is of importance for ages, not only to the chief but to his people; an establishment which extends upwards and downwards; that this should be destroyed by one idle fellow is a sad thing.' . . .

I mentioned Dr. Adam Smith's book on *The Wealth of Nations,* which was just published, and that Sir John Pringle had observed to me, that Dr. Smith, who had never been in trade, could not be expected to write well on that subject any more than a lawyer upon physick. JOHNSON. 'He is mistaken, Sir: a man who has never been engaged in trade himself may undoubtedly write well upon trade, and there is nothing which requires more to be illustrated by philosophy than trade does. As to mere wealth, that is to say, money, it is clear that one nation or one individual cannot increase its store but by making another poorer: but trade procures what is more valuable, the reciprocation of the peculiar advantages of different countries. A merchant seldom thinks but of his own particular trade. To write a good book upon it, a man must have extensive views. It is not necessary to have practised, to write well upon a subject.' I mentioned law as a subject on which no man could write well without practice. JOHNSON. 'Why, Sir, in England, where so much money is to be got by the practice of the law, most of our writers upon it have been in practice; though Blackstone had not been much in practice when he published his *Commentaries.* But upon the Continent, the great writers on law have not all been in practice: Grotius, indeed, was; but Puffendorf was not, Burlamaqui was not.'

When we had talked of the great consequence which a man acquired by being employed in his profession, I suggested a doubt of the justice of the general opinion, that it is improper in a lawyer to solicit employment; for why, I urged, should it not be equally allowable to solicit that as the means of consequence, as it is to solicit votes to be elected a member of Parliament? Mr. Strahan had told me that a countryman of his and mine, who had risen to eminence in the law, had, when first making his way, solicited him to get him employed in city causes. JOHNSON. 'Sir, it is wrong to stir up law-suits; but when once it is certain that a law-suit is to go on, there is nothing wrong in a lawyer's endeavouring that he shall have the benefit, rather than another.' BOSWELL. 'You would not solicit employment, Sir, if you were a lawyer.' JOHNSON. 'No, Sir, but not because I should think it wrong, but because I should disdain it.' This was a good distinction, which will be felt by men of just pride. He proceeded: 'However, I would not have a lawyer to be wanting to himself in using fair means. I would have him to inject a little hint now and then, to prevent his being overlooked.'

Lord Mountstuart's bill for a Scotch Militia, in supporting which his Lordship had made an able speech in the House of Commons, was now a pretty general topick of conversation. JOHNSON. 'As Scotland contributes so little land-tax towards the general support of the nation, it ought not to have a militia paid out of the general fund, unless it should be thought for the general interest, that Scotland should be protected from an invasion, which no man can think will happen; for what enemy would invade Scotland, where there is nothing to be got? No, Sir; now that the Scotch have not the pay of English soldiers spent among them, as so many troops are sent abroad, they are trying to get money another way, by having a militia paid. If they are afraid, and seriously desire to have an armed force to defend them, they should pay for it. Your scheme is to retain a part of your little land-tax, by making us pay and clothe your militia.' BOSWELL. 'You should not talk of *we* and *you*, Sir: there is now an *Union*.' JOHNSON. 'There must be a distinction of interest, while the proportions of land-tax are so unequal. If Yorkshire should say, "Instead of paying our land-tax, we will keep a greater number of militia," it would be unreasonable.' In this argument my friend was certainly in the wrong. The land-tax is as unequally proportioned between different parts of England, as between England and Scotland; nay, it is considerably unequal in Scotland itself. But the land-tax is but a small part of the numerous branches of publick revenue, all of which Scotland pays precisely as England does. A French invasion made in Scotland would soon penetrate into England.

He thus discoursed upon supposed obligations in settling estates:—'Where a man gets the unlimited property of an estate, there is no obligation upon him in *justice* to leave it to one person rather than to another. There is a motive of preference from *kindness*, and this kindness is generally entertained for the nearest relation. If I *owe* a particular man a sum of money, I am obliged to let that man have the next money I get, and cannot in justice let another have it: but if I owe money to no man, I may dispose of what I get as I please. There is not a *debitum justitiæ*[1] to a man's next heir; there is only a *debitum caritatis*.[2] It is plain, then, that I have morally a choice, according to my liking. If I have a brother in want, he has a claim from affection to my assistance; but if I have also a brother in want, whom I like better, he has a preferable claim. The right of an heir at law is only this, that he is to have the succession to an estate, in case no other person is appointed to it by the owner. His right is merely preferable to that of the King.'

We got into a boat to cross over to Black-friars; and as we moved along the Thames, I talked to him of a little volume, which, altogether unknown to him, was advertised to be published in a few days, under the title of *Johnsoniana, or Bon-Mots of Dr. Johnson*. JOHNSON. 'Sir, it is a mighty impudent thing.' BOSWELL. 'Pray, Sir, could you have no redress if you were to prosecute a publisher for bringing out, under your name, what you never said, and ascribing to you dull stupid nonsense, or making you swear profanely, as many ignorant relaters of your *bon-mots* do?' JOHNSON. 'No, Sir; there will always be some truth mixed with the falsehood, and how can it be ascertained how much is true and how much is false? Besides, Sir, what damages would a jury give me for having been represented as swearing?' BOSWELL. 'I think, Sir, you should at least disavow such a publication, because the world and posterity might with much plausible foundation say, "Here is a volume which was publickly advertised and came out in Dr. Johnson's own time, and, by his silence, was admitted by him to be genuine." ' JOHNSON. 'I shall give myself no trouble about the matter.' . . .

He said, 'The value of every story depends on its being true. A story is a picture either of an individual or of human nature in general: if it be false, it is a picture of nothing. For instance: suppose a man should tell that Johnson, before setting out for Italy, as he had to cross the Alps, sat down to make himself wings. This many people would believe; but it would be a picture of nothing. ********[3] (naming a worthy friend of ours,) used to think a story, a story, till I shewed him that truth was essential to it.' I observed, that Foote entertained us with stories which were not true; but that, indeed, it was properly not as narratives that Foote's stories pleased us, but as collections of ludicrous images. JOHNSON. 'Foote is quite impartial, for he tells lies of every body.'

The importance of strict and scrupulous veracity cannot be

---

[1] 'A debt in law.'
[2] 'A debt of kindness.'
[3] Langton.

too often inculcated. Johnson was known to be so rigidly attentive to it, that even in his common conversation the slightest circumstance was mentioned with exact precision. The knowledge of his having such a principle and habit made his friends have a perfect reliance on the truth of every thing that he told, however it might have been doubted if told by many others. As an instance of this, I may mention an odd incident which he related as having happened to him one night in Fleet-street. 'A gentlewoman (said he) begged I would give her my arm to assist her in crossing the street, which I accordingly did; upon which she offered me a shilling, supposing me to be the watchman. I perceived that she was somewhat in liquor.' This, if told by most people, would have been thought an invention; when told by Johnson, it was believed by his friends as much as if they had seen what passed.

We landed at the Temple-stairs, where we parted.

I found him in the evening in Mrs. Williams's room. We talked of religious orders. He said, 'It is as unreasonable for a man to go into a Carthusian convent for fear of being immortal, as for a man to cut off his hands for fear he should steal. There is, indeed, great resolution in the immediate act of dismembering himself; but when that is once done, he has no longer any merit: for though it is out of his power to steal, yet he may all his life be a thief in his heart. So when a man has once become a Carthusian, he is obliged to continue so, whether he chooses it or not. Their silence, too, is absurd. We read in the Gospel of the apostles being sent to preach, but not to hold their tongues. All severity that does not tend to increase good, or prevent evil, is idle. I said to the Lady Abbess of a convent, "Madam, you are here, not for the love of virtue, but the fear of vice." She said, "She should remember this as long as she lived." ' I thought it hard to give her this view of her situation, when she could not help it; and, indeed, I wondered at the whole of what he now said; because, both in his *Rambler* and *Idler*, he treats religious austerities with much solemnity and respect.

Finding him still persevering in his abstinence from wine, I ventured to speak to him of it.—JOHNSON. 'Sir, I have no objection to a man's drinking wine, if he can do it in moderation. I found myself apt to go to excess in it, and therefore, after having been for some time without it, on account of illness, I thought it better not to return to it. Every man is to judge for himself, according to the effects which he experiences. One of the fathers tells us, he found fasting made him so peevish that he did not practise it.'

Though he often enlarged upon the evil of intoxication, he

was by no means harsh and unforgiving to those who indulged in occasional excess in wine. One of his friends,[1] I well remember, came to sup at a tavern with him and some other gentlemen, and too plainly discovered that he had drunk too much at dinner. When one who loved mischief,[2] thinking to produce a severe censure, asked Johnson, a few days afterwards, 'Well, Sir, what did your friend say to you, as an apology for being in such a situation?' Johnson answered, 'Sir, he said all that a man *should* say: he said he was sorry for it.'

I heard him once give a very judicious practical advice upon this subject: 'A man, who has been drinking wine at all freely, should never go into a new company. With those who have partaken of wine with him, he may be pretty well in unison; but he will probably be offensive, or appear ridiculous, to other people.'

He allowed very great influence to education. 'I do not deny, Sir, but there is some original difference in minds; but it is nothing in comparison of what is formed by education. We may instance the science of *numbers*, which all minds are equally capable of attaining; yet we find a prodigious difference in the powers of different men, in that respect, after they are grown up, because their minds have been more or less exercised in it: and I think the same cause will explain the difference of excellence in other things, gradations admitting always some difference in the first principles.'

This is a difficult subject; but it is best to hope that diligence may do a great deal. We are *sure* of what it can do, in increasing our mechanical force and dexterity.

I again visited him on Monday. He took occasion to enlarge, as he often did, upon the wretchedness of a sea-life. 'A ship is worse than a gaol. There is, in a gaol, better air, better company, better conveniency of every kind; and a ship has the additional disadvantage of being in danger. When men come to like a sea-life, they are not fit to live on land.'— 'Then (said I) it would be cruel in a father to breed his son to the sea.' JOHNSON. 'It would be cruel in a father who thinks as I do. Men go to sea, before they know the unhappiness of that way of life; and when they have come to know it, they cannot escape from it, because it is then too late to choose another profession; as indeed is generally the case with men, when they have once engaged in any particular way of life.'

On Tuesday, March 19, which was fixed for our proposed jaunt, we met in the morning at the Somerset coffee-house in

---

[1] Boswell.
[2] Colman.

the Strand, where we were taken up by the Oxford coach. He was accompanied by Mr. Gwyn, the architect; and a gentleman of Merton College, whom we did not know, had the fourth seat. We soon got into conversation; for it was very remarkable of Johnson, that the presence of a stranger was no restraint upon his talk. I observed that Garrick, who was about to quit the stage, would soon have an easier life. JOHNSON. 'I doubt that, Sir.' BOSWELL. 'Why, Sir, he will be Atlas with the burthen off his back.' JOHNSON. 'But I know not, Sir, if he will be so steady without his load. However, he should never play any more, but be entirely the gentleman, and not partly the player: he should no longer subject himself to be hissed by a mob, or to be insolently treated by performers, whom he used to rule with a high hand, and who would gladly retaliate.' BOSWELL. 'I think he should play once a year for the benefit of decayed actors, as it has been said he means to do.' JOHNSON. 'Alas, Sir! he will soon be a decayed actor himself.'

Johnson expressed his disapprobation of ornamental architecture, such as magnificent columns supporting a portico, or expensive pilasters supporting merely their own capitals, 'because it consumes labour disproportionate to its utility.' For the same reason he satyrised statuary. 'Painting (said he) consumes labour not disproportionate to its effect; but a fellow will hack half a year at a block of marble to make something in stone that hardly resembles a man. The value of statuary is owing to its difficulty. You would not value the finest head cut upon a carrot.' Here he seemed to me to be strangely deficient in taste; for surely statuary is a noble art of imitation, and preserves a wonderful expression of the varieties of the human frame; and although it must be allowed that the circumstances of difficulty enhance the value of a marble head, we should consider, that if it requires a long time in the performance, it has a proportionate value in durability.

Gwyn was a fine lively rattling fellow. Dr. Johnson kept him in subjection, but with a kindly authority. The spirit of the artist, however, rose against what he thought a Gothick attack, and he made a brisk defence. 'What, Sir, will you allow no value to beauty in architecture or in statuary? Why should we allow it then in writing? Why do you take the trouble to give us so many fine allusions, and bright images, and elegant phrases? You might convey all your instruction without these ornaments.' Johnson smiled with complacency; but said, 'Why, Sir, all these ornaments are useful, because they obtain an easier reception for truth; but a building is not at all more convenient for being decorated with superfluous carved work.' . . .

Upon our arrival at Oxford, Dr. Johnson and I went directly to University College, but were disappointed on finding that one of the fellows, his friend Mr. Scott, who accompanied him from Newcastle to Edinburgh, was gone to the country. We put up at the Angel inn, and passed the evening by ourselves in easy and familiar conversation. Talking of constitutional melancholy, he observed, 'A man so afflicted, Sir, must divert distressing thoughts, and not combat with them.' BOSWELL. 'May not he think them down, Sir?' JOHNSON. 'No, Sir. To attempt to *think them down* is madness. He should have a lamp constantly burning in his bed-chamber during the night, and if wakefully disturbed, take a book, and read, and compose himself to rest. To have the management of the mind is a great art, and it may be attained in a considerable degree by experience and habitual exercise.' BOSWELL. 'Should not he provide amusements for himself? Would it not, for instance, be right for him to take a course of chymistry?' JOHNSON. 'Let him take a course of chymistry, or a course of rope-dancing, or a course of any thing to which he is inclined at the time. Let him contrive to have as many retreats for his mind as he can, as many things to which it can fly from itself. Burton's *Anatomy of Melancholy* is a valuable work. It is, perhaps, overloaded with quotation. But there is great spirit and great power in what Burton says, when he writes from his own mind.'

Next morning we visited Dr. Wetherell, Master of University College, with whom Dr. Johnson conferred on the most advantageous mode of disposing of the books printed at the Clarendon press, on which subject his letter has been inserted in a former page.[1] I often had occasion to remark, Johnson loved business, loved to have his wisdom actually operate on real life. Dr. Wetherell and I talked of him without reserve in his own presence. WETHERELL. 'I would have given him a hundred guineas if he would have written a preface to his *Political Tracts*, by way of a Discourse on the British Constitution.' BOSWELL. 'Dr. Johnson, though in his writings, and upon all occasions a great friend to the constitution both in church and state, has never written expressly in support of either. There is really a claim upon him for both. I am sure he could give a volume of no great bulk upon each, which would comprise all the substance, and with his spirit would effectually maintain them. He should erect a fort on the confines of each.' I could perceive that he was displeased with this dialogue. He burst out, 'Why should *I* be always writing?' I hoped he was conscious that the debt was just, and meant to discharge it, though he disliked being dunned.

[1] Omitted here.

332

We then went to Pembroke College, and waited on his old friend Dr. Adams, the master of it, whom I found to be a most polite, pleasing, communicative man. . . .

Dr. Adams had distinguished himself by an able answer to David Hume's *Essay on Miracles*. He told me he had once dined in company with Hume in London; that Hume shook hands with him, and said, 'You have treated me much better than I deserve;' and that they exchanged visits. I took the liberty to object to treating an infidel writer with smooth civility. Where there is a controversy concerning a passage in a classick authour, or concerning a question in antiquities, or any other subject in which human happiness is not deeply interested, a man may treat his antagonist with politeness and even respect. But where the controversy is concerning the truth of religion, it is of such vast importance to him who maintains it, to obtain the victory, that the person of an opponent ought not to be spared. If a man firmly believes that religion is an invaluable treasure, he will consider a writer who endeavours to deprive mankind of it as a *robber;* he will look upon him as *odious,* though the infidel might think himself in the right. A robber who reasons as the gang do in the *Beggar's Opera,* who call themselves *practical* philosophers, and may have as much sincerity as pernicious *speculative* philosophers, is not the less an object of just indignation. An abandoned profligate may think that it is not wrong to debauch my wife, but shall I, therefore, not detest him? And if I catch him in making an attempt, shall I treat him with politeness? No, I will kick him down stairs, or run him through the body; that is, if I really love my wife, or have a true rational notion of honour. An Infidel then shall not be treated handsomely by a Christian, merely because he endeavours to rob with ingenuity. I do declare, however, that I am exceedingly unwilling to be provoked to anger, and could I be persuaded that truth would not suffer from a cool moderation in its defenders, I should wish to preserve good humor, at least, in every controversy; nor, indeed, do I see why a man should lose his temper while he does all he can to refute an opponent. I think ridicule may be fairly used against an infidel; for instance, if he be an ugly fellow, and yet absurdly vain of his person, we may contrast his appearance with Cicero's beautiful image of Virtue, could she be seen. Johnson coincided with me and said, 'When a man voluntarily engages in an important controversy, he is to do all he can to lessen his antagonist, because authority from personal respect has much weight with most people, and often more than reasoning. If my antagonist writes bad language, though that may not be essential to the question, I will attack him for his bad language.' ADAMS. 'You would not jostle a chimney-sweeper.' JOHNSON. 'Yes, Sir, if it were necessary to jostle him *down*.'

Dr. Adams told us, that in some of the Colleges at Oxford, the fellows had excluded the students from social intercourse with them in the common room. JOHNSON. 'They are in the right, Sir, for there can be no real conversation, no fair exertion of mind amongst them, if the young men are by; for a man who has a character does not choose to stake it in their presence.' BOSWELL. 'But, Sir, may there not be very good conversation without a contest for superiority?' JOHNSON. 'No animated conversation, Sir, for it cannot be but one or other will come off superior. I do not mean that the victor must have the better of the argument, for he may take the weak side; but his superiority of parts and knowledge will necessarily appear: and he to whom he thus shews himself superiour is lessened in the eyes of the young men. You know it was said, *"Mallem cum Scaligero errare quam cum Clavio rectè sapere."*[1] In the same manner take Bentley's and Jason de Nores' Comments upon Horace, you will admire Bentley more when wrong, than Jason when right.'

We walked with Dr. Adams into the master's garden, and into the common room. JOHNSON. (after a reverie of meditation,) 'Ay! Here I used to play at draughts with Phil. Jones and Fludyer. Jones loved beer, and did not get very forward in the church. Fludyer turned out a scoundrel, a Whig, and said he was ashamed of having been bred at Oxford. He had a living at Putney, and got under the eye of some retainers to the court at that time, and so became a violent Whig: but he had been a scoundrel all along, to be sure.' BOSWELL. 'Was he a scoundrel, Sir, in any other way than that of being a political scoundrel? Did he cheat at draughts?' JOHNSON. 'Sir, we never played for *money*.'

He then carried me to visit Dr. Bentham, Canon of Christ-Church, and Divinity Professor, with whose learned and lively conversation we were much pleased. He gave us an invitation to dinner, which Dr. Johnson told me was a high honour. 'Sir, it is a great thing to dine with the Canons of Christ-Church.' We could not accept his invitation, as we were engaged to dine at University College. We had an excellent dinner there, with the Master and Fellows, it being St. Cuthbert's day, which is kept by them as a festival, as he was a saint of Durham, with which this college is much connected.

We drank tea with Dr. Horne, late President of Magdalen College, and Bishop of Norwich, of whose abilities, in dif-

[1] 'Better to err with Scaliger than to be right with Clavius.'

ferent respects, the publick has had eminent proofs, and the esteem annexed to whose character was increased by knowing him personally. He had talked of publishing an edition of Walton's *Lives,* but had laid aside that design, upon Dr. Johnson's telling him, from mistake, that Lord Hailes intended to do it. I had wished to negociate between Lord Hailes and him, that one or other should perform so good a work. JOHNSON. 'In order to do it well, it will be necessary to collect all the editions of Walton's *Lives.* By way of adapting the book to the taste of the present age, they have, in a later edition, left out a vision which he relates Dr. Donne had, but it should be restored; and there should be a critical catalogue given of the works of the different persons whose lives were written by Walton, and therefore their works must be carefully read by the editor.'

We then went to Trinity College, where he introduced me to Mr. Thomas Warton, with whom we passed a part of the evening. We talked of biography.—JOHNSON. 'It is rarely well executed. They only who live with a man can write his life with any genuine exactness and discrimination; and few people who have lived with a man know what to remark about him. The chaplain of a late Bishop, whom I was to assist in writing some memoirs of his Lordship, could tell me scarcely any thing.'

I said, Mr. Robert Dodsley's life should be written, as he had been so much connected with the wits of his time, and by his literary merit had raised himself from the station of a footman. Mr. Warton said, he had published a little volume under the title of *The Muse in Livery.* JOHNSON. 'I doubt whether Dodsley's brother would thank a man who should write his life: yet Dodsley himself was not unwilling that his original low condition should be recollected. When Lord Lyttelton's *Dialogues of the Dead* came out, one of which is between Apicius, an ancient epicure, and Dartineuf, a modern epicure, Dodsley said to me, "I knew Dartineuf well, for I was once his footman." '

Biography led us to speak of Dr. John Campbell, who had written a considerable part of the *Biographia Britannica.* Johnson, though he valued him highly, was of opinion that there was not so much in his great work, *A Political Survey of Great Britain,* as the world had been taught to expect; and had said to me, that he believed Campbell's disappointment, on account of the bad success of that work, had killed him. He this evening observed of it, 'That work was his death.' Mr. Warton, not adverting to his meaning, answered, 'I believe so; from the great attention he bestowed on it.'

JOHNSON. 'Nay, Sir, he died of *want* of attention, if he died at all by that book.'

We talked of a work much in vogue at that time, written in a very mellifluous style, but which, under pretext of another subject, contained much artful infidelity. I said it was not fair to attack us thus unexpectedly; he should have warned us of our danger, before we entered his garden of flowery eloquence, by advertising, 'Spring-guns and men-traps set here.' The authour[1] had been an Oxonian, and was remembered there for having 'turned Papist'. I observed, that as he had changed several times—from the Church of England to the Church of Rome,—from the Church of Rome to infidelity, —I did not despair yet of seeing him a methodist preacher. JOHNSON. (laughing,) 'It is said, that his range has been more extensive, and that he has once been Mahometan. However, now that he has published his infidelity, he will probably persist in it.' BOSWELL. 'I am not quite sure of that, Sir.'

I mentioned Sir Richard Steele having published his *Christian Hero*, with the avowed purpose of obliging himself to lead a religious life; yet, that his conduct was by no means strictly suitable. JOHNSON. 'Steele, I believe, practised the lighter vices.'

Mr. Warton, being engaged, could not sup with us at our inn; we had therefore another evening by ourselves. I asked Johnson, whether a man's[2] being forward in making himself known to eminent people, and seeing as much of life, and getting as much information as he could in every way, was not yet lessening himself by his forwardness. JOHNSON. 'No, Sir; a man always makes himself greater as he increases his knowledge.'

I censured some ludicrous fantastick dialogues between two coach-horses, and other such stuff, which Baretti had lately published. He joined with me, and said, 'Nothing odd will do long. *Tristram Shandy* did not last.' I expressed a desire to be acquainted with a lady who had been much talked of,[3] and universally celebrated for extraordinary address and insinuation. JOHNSON. 'Never believe extraordinary characters which you hear of people. Depend upon it, Sir, they are exaggerated. You do not see one man shoot a great deal higher than another.' I mentioned Mr. Burke. JOHNSON. 'Yes; Burke *is* an extraordinary man. His stream of mind is perpetual.' It is very pleasing to me to record, that Johnson's high estimation of the talents of this gentleman was uniform from their early

[1] Gibbon.
[2] Boswell.
[3] Margaret Caroline Rudd, later Boswell's mistress.

acquaintance. Sir Joshua Reynolds informs me, that when Mr. Burke was first elected a member of Parliament, and Sir John Hawkins expressed a wonder at his attaining a seat, Johnson said, 'Now we who know Burke know, that he will be one of the first men in this country.' And once, when Johnson was ill, and unable to exert himself as much as usual without fatigue, Mr. Burke having been mentioned, he said, 'That fellow calls forth all my powers. Were I to see Burke now, it would kill me.' So much was he accustomed to consider conversation as a contest, and such was his notion of Burke as an opponent.

Next morning, Thursday, March 21, we set out in a post-chaise to pursue our ramble. It was a delightful day, and we drove through Blenheim park. When I looked at the magnificent bridge built by John Duke of Marlborough, over a small rivulet, and recollected the Epigram made upon it—

> 'The lofty arch his high ambition shows,
> The stream, an emblem of his bounty flows:'

and saw that now, by the genius of Brown, a magnificent body of water was collected, I said, 'They have *drowned* the Epigram.' I observed to him, while in the midst of the noble scene around us, 'You and I, Sir, have, I think, seen together the extremes of what can be seen in Britain:—the wild rough island of Mull, and Blenheim Park.'

We dined at an excellent inn at Chapel-house, where he expatiated on the felicity of England in its taverns and inns, and triumphed over the French for not having, in any perfection, the tavern life. 'There is no private house, (said he,) in which people can enjoy themselves so well, as at a capital tavern. Let there be ever so great plenty of good things, ever so much grandeur, ever so much elegance, ever so much desire that every body should be easy; in the nature of things it cannot be: there must always be some degree of care and anxiety. The master of the house is anxious to entertain his guests; the guests are anxious to be agreeable to him: and no man, but a very impudent dog indeed, can as freely command what is in another man's house, as if it were his own. Whereas, at a tavern, there is a general freedom from anxiety. You are sure you are welcome: and the more noise you make, the more trouble you give, the more good things you call for, the welcomer you are. No servants will attend you with the alacrity which waiters do, who are incited by the prospect of an immediate reward in proportion as they please. No, Sir; there is nothing which has yet been contrived by man, by which so much happiness is produced as by a good tavern or inn.'¹ He then repeated, with great emotion, Shenstone's lines:—

> 'Whoe'er has travell'd life's dull round,
> Where'er his stages may have been,
> May sigh to think he still has found
> The warmest welcome at an inn.'²

. . . In the afternoon, as we were driven rapidly along in the post-chaise, he said to me 'Life has not many things better than this.'

We stopped at Stratford-upon-Avon, and drank tea and coffee; and it pleased me to be with him upon the classick ground of Shakspeare's native place.

He spoke slightingly of Dyer's *Fleece*.—'The subject, Sir, cannot be made poetical. How can a man write poetically of serges and druggets? Yet you will hear many people talk to you gravely of that *excellent* poem, *The Fleece*.' Having talked of Grainger's *Sugar-Cane*, I mentioned to him Mr. Langton's having told me, that this poem, when read in manuscript at Sir Joshua Reynolds's, had made all the assembled wits burst into a laugh, when, after much blank-verse pomp, the poet began a new paragraph thus:—

> 'Now, Muse, let's sing of *rats*.'

And what increased the ridicule was, that one of the company, who slily overlooked the reader, perceived that the word had been originally *mice*, and had been altered to *rats*, as more dignified.

This passage does not appear in the printed work. Dr. Grainger, or some of his friends, it should seem, having become sensible that introducing even *Rats* in a grave poem, might be liable to banter. He, however, could not bring himself to relinquish the idea; for they are thus, in a still more ludicrous manner, periphrastically exhibited in his poem as it now stands:

> 'Nor with less waste the whisker'd vermin race
> A countless clan despoil the lowland cane.'

Johnson said, that Dr. Grainger was an agreeable man; a man who would do any good that was in his power. His trans-

---

¹ Sir John Hawkins has preserved very few *Memorabilia* of Johnson. There is, however, to be found, in his bulky tome, a very excellent one upon this subject:—'In contradiction to those, who, having a wife and children, prefer domestick enjoyments to those which a tavern affords, I have heard him assert, *that a tavern chair was the throne of human felicity*—B.

² We happened to lie this night at the inn at Henley, where Shenstone wrote these lines—B.

lation of *Tibullus,* he thought, was very well done; but *The Sugar-Cane,* a poem, did not please him; for, he exclaimed, 'What could he make of a sugar-cane? One might as well write the "Parsley-bed, a Poem;" or "The Cabbage-garden, a Poem."' BOSWELL. 'You must then *pickle* your cabbage with the *sal atticum.*'[1] JOHNSON. 'You know there is already *The Hop-Garden,* a Poem: and, I think, one could say a great deal about cabbage. The poem might begin with the advantages of civilized society over a rude state, exemplified by the Scotch, who had no cabbages till Oliver Cromwell's soldiers introduced them, and one might thus shew how arts are propagated by conquest, as they were by the Roman arms.' He seemed to be much diverted with the fertility of his own fancy.

I told him, that I heard Dr. Percy was writing the history of the wolf in Great-Britain. JOHNSON. 'The wolf, Sir! why the wolf? Why does he not write of the bear, which we had formerly? Nay, it is said we had the beaver. Or why does he not write of the grey rat, the Hanover rat, as it is called, because it is said to have come into this country about the time that the family of Hanover came? I should like to see *The History of the Grey Rat, by Thomas Percy, D.D., Chaplain in Ordinary to His Majesty,*' (laughing immoderately). BOSWELL. 'I am afraid a court chaplain could not decently write of the grey rat.' JOHNSON. 'Sir, he need not give it the name of the Hanover rat.' Thus could he indulge a luxuriant sportive imagination, when talking of a friend whom he loved and esteemed. . . .

On Friday, March 22, having set out early from Henley, where we had lain the preceding night, we arrived at Birmingham about nine o'clock, and, after breakfast, went to call on his old schoolfellow Mr. Hector. A very stupid maid, who opened the door, told us, that 'her master was gone out; he was gone to the country; she could not tell when he would return.' In short, she gave us a miserable reception; and Johnson observed, 'She would have behaved no better to people who wanted him in the way of his profession.' He said to her, 'My name is Johnson; tell him I called. Will you remember the name?' She answered with rustick simplicity, in the Warwickshire pronunciation, 'I don't understand you, Sir.'— 'Blockhead, (said he,) I'll write.' I never heard the word *blockhead* applied to a woman before, though I do not see why it should not, when there is evident occasion for it. He, however, made another attempt to make her understand him,

[1] 'Attic salt,' i.e., wit.

and roared loud in her ear, 'Johnson,' and then she catched the sound.

We next called on Mr. Lloyd, one of the people called Quakers. He too was not at home; but Mrs. Lloyd was, and received us courteously, and asked us to dinner. Johnson said to me, 'After the uncertainty of all human things at Hector's, this invitation came very well.' We walked about the town, and he was pleased to see it increasing.

I talked of legitimation by subsequent marriage, which obtained in the Roman law, and still obtains in the law of Scotland. JOHNSON. 'I think it a bad thing; because the chastity of women being of the utmost importance, as all property depends upon it, they who forfeit it should not have any possibility of being restored to good character; nor should the children, by an illicit connection, attain the full rights of lawful children, by the posteriour consent of the offending parties.' . . .

Mr. Lloyd joined us in the street; and in a little while we met *Friend Hector,* as Mr. Lloyd called him. It gave me pleasure to observe the joy which Johnson and he expressed on seeing each other again. Mr. Lloyd and I left them together, while he obligingly shewed me some of the manufactures of this very curious assemblage of artificers. We all met at dinner at Mr. Lloyd's, where we were entertained with great hospitality. Mr. and Mrs. Lloyd had been married the same year with their Majesties, and, like them, had been blessed with a numerous family of fine children, their numbers being exactly the same. Johnson said, 'Marriage is the best state for man in general; and every man is a worse man, in proportion as he is unfit for the married state.'

I have always loved the simplicity of manners, and the spiritual-mindedness of the Quakers; and talking with Mr. Lloyd, I observed, that the essential part of religion was piety, a devout intercourse with the Divinity; and that many a man was a Quaker without knowing it.

As Dr. Johnson had said to me in the morning, while we walked together, that he liked individuals among the Quakers, but not the sect; when we were at Mr. Lloyd's, I kept clear of introducing any question concerning the peculiarities of their faith. But I having asked to look at Baskerville's edition of *Barclay's Apology,* Johnson laid hold of it; and the chapter on baptism happening to open, Johnson remarked, 'He says there is neither precept nor practice for baptism, in the scriptures; that is false.' Here he was the aggressor, by no means in a gentle manner; and the good Quakers had the advantage of him; for he had read negligently, and had not observed that Barclay speaks of *infant* baptism; which they calmly made him perceive. Mr. Lloyd, however, was in as great a mistake; for when insisting that the rite of baptism by water was to cease, when the *spiritual* administration of CHRIST began, he maintained, that John the Baptist said, '*My baptism* shall decrease, but *his* shall increase.' Whereas the words are, '*He* must increase, but *I* must decrease.'

One of them having objected to the 'observance of days, and months, and years,' Johnson answered, 'The Church does not superstitiously observe days, merely as days, but as memorials of important facts. Christmas might be kept as well upon one day of the year as another; but there should be a stated day for commemorating the birth of our Saviour, because there is danger that what may be done on any day, will be neglected.' . . .

Mr. Hector was so good as to accompany me to see the great works of Mr. Bolton, at a place which he has called Soho, about two miles from Birmingham, which the very ingenious proprietor shewed me himself to the best advantage. I wish that Johnson had been with us: for it was a scene which I should have been glad to contemplate by his light. The vastness and the contrivance of some of the machinery would have 'matched his mighty mind'. I shall never forget Mr. Bolton's expression to me: 'I sell here, Sir, what all the world desires to have—POWER.' He had about seven hundred people at work. I contemplated him as an *iron chieftain,* and he seemed to be a father to his tribe. One of them came to him, complaining grievously of his landlord for having distrained his goods. 'Your landlord is in the right, Smith, (said Bolton). But I'll tell you what: find you a friend who will lay down one half of your rent, and I'll lay down the other half; and you shall have your goods again.' . . .

Dr. Johnson said to me in the morning, 'You will see, Sir, at Mr. Hector's, his sister, Mrs. Careless, a clergyman's widow. She was the first woman with whom I was in love. It dropt out of my head imperceptibly; but she and I shall always have a kindness for each other.' He laughed at the notion that a man never can be really in love but once, and considered it as a mere romantick fancy.

On our return from Mr. Bolton's, Mr. Hector took me to his house, where we found Johnson sitting placidly at tea, with his *first love;* who, though now advanced in years, was a genteel woman, very agreeable, and well-bred.

Johnson lamented to Mr. Hector the state of one of their school-fellows, Mr. Charles Congreve, a clergyman, which he thus described: 'He obtained, I believe, considerable preferment in Ireland, but now lives in London, quite as a valetudinarian, afraid to go into any house but his own. He takes a short airing in his post-chaise every day. He has an elderly woman, whom he calls cousin, who lives with him, and jogs his elbow when his glass has stood too long empty, and encourages him in drinking, in which he is very willing to be encouraged; not that he gets drunk, for he is a very pious man, but he is always muddy. He confesses to one bottle of port every day, and he probably drinks more. He is quite unsocial; his conversation is monosyllabical: and when, at my last visit, I asked him what a clock it was? that signal of my departure had so pleasing an effect on him, that he sprung up to look at his watch, like a greyhound bounding at a hare.' When Johnson took leave of Mr. Hector, he said, 'Don't grow like Congreve; nor let me grow like him, when you are near me.'

When he again talked of Mrs. Careless to-night, he seemed to have had his affection revived; for he said, 'If I had married her, it might have been as happy for me.' BOSWELL. Pray, Sir, do you not suppose that there are fifty women in the world, with any one of whom a man may be as happy, as with any one woman in particular?' JOHNSON. 'Ay, Sir, fifty thousand.' BOSWELL. 'Then, Sir, you are not of opinion with some who imagine that certain men and certain women are made for each other; and that they cannot be happy if they miss their counterparts?' JOHNSON. 'To be sure not, Sir. I believe marriages would in general be as happy, and often more so, if they were all made by the Lord Chancellor, upon a due consideration of characters and circumstances, without the parties having any choice in the matter.'

I wished to have staid at Birmingham to-night, to have talked more with Mr. Hector; but my friend was impatient to reach his native city; so we drove on that stage in the dark, and were long pensive and silent. When we came within the focus of the Lichfield lamps, 'Now (said he,) we are getting out of a state of death.' We put up at the Three Crowns, not one of the great inns, but a good old fashioned one, which was kept by Mr. Wilkins, and was the very next house to that in which Johnson was born and brought up, and which was still his own property. We had a comfortable supper, and got into high spirits. I felt all my Toryism glow in this old capital of Staffordshire. I could have offered incense *genio loci*;[1] and I indulged in libations of that ale, which Boniface, in *The Beaux Stratagem*, recommends with such an eloquent jollity.

Next morning he introduced me to Mrs. Lucy Porter, his step-daughter. She was now an old maid, with much simplicity of manner. She had never been in London. Her brother, a

---

[1] 'To the genius of the place.'

Captain in the navy, had left her a fortune of ten thousand pounds; about a third of which she had laid out in building a stately house, and making a handsome garden, in an elevated situation in Lichfield. Johnson, when here by himself, used to live at her house. She reverenced him, and he had a parental tenderness for her.

We then visited Mr. Peter Garrick, who had that morning received a letter from his brother David, announcing our coming to Lichfield. He was engaged to dinner, but asked us to tea, and to sleep at his house. Johnson, however, would not quit his old acquaintance Wilkins, of the Three Crowns. The family likeness of the Garricks was very striking; and Johnson thought that David's vivacity was not so peculiar to himself as was supposed. 'Sir, (said he,) I don't know but if Peter had cultivated all the arts of gaiety as much as David has done, he might have been as brisk and lively. Depend upon it, Sir, vivacity is much an art, and depends greatly on habit.' . . .

We dined at our inn, and had with us a Mr. Jackson, one of Johnson's schoolfellows, whom he treated with much kindness, though he seemed to be a low man, dull and untaught. He had a coarse grey coat, black waistcoat, greasy leather breeches, and a yellow uncurled wig; and his countenance had the ruddiness which betokens one who is in no haste to 'leave his can.' He drank only ale. He had tried to be a cutler at Birmingham, but had not succeeded; and now he lived poorly at home, and had some scheme of dressing leather in a better manner than common; to his indistinct account of which, Dr. Johnson listened with patient attention, that he might assist him with his advice. Here was an instance of genuine humanity and real kindness in this great man, who has been most unjustly represented as altogether harsh and destitute of tenderness. A thousand such instances might have been recorded in the course of his long life; though, that his temper was warm and hasty, and his manner often rough, cannot be denied.

I saw here, for the first time, *oat ale;* and oat cakes not hard as in Scotland, but soft like a Yorkshire cake, were served at breakfast. It was pleasant to me to find, that *Oats,* the *food of horses,* were so much used as the *food of the people* in Dr. Johnson's own town. He expatiated in praise of Lichfield and its inhabitants, who, he said, were 'the most sober, decent people in England, the genteelest in proportion to their wealth, and spoke the purest English.' I doubted as to the last article of this eulogy: for they had several provincial sounds; as, *there,* pronounced like *fear,* instead of like *fair;* *once* pronounced *woonse,* instead of *wunse,* or *wonse.* Johnson himself never got entirely free of those provincial accents. Garrick sometimes used to take him off, squeezing a lemon into a punch-bowl, with uncouth gesticulations, looking round the company, and calling out, 'Who's for *poonsh?*'

Very little business appeared to be going forward in Lichfield. I found however two strange manufactures for so inland a place, sail-cloth and streamers for ships; and I observed them making some saddle-cloths, and dressing sheepskins: but upon the whole, the busy hand of industry seemed to be quite slackened. 'Surely, Sir, (said I,) you are an idle set of people.' 'Sir, (said Johnson,) we are a city of philosophers: we work with our heads, and make the boobies of Birmingham work for us with their hands.'

There was at this time a company of players performing at Lichfield. The manager, Mr. Stanton, sent his compliments, and begged leave to wait on Dr. Johnson. Johnson received him very courteously, and he drank a glass of wine with us. He was a plain decent well-behaved man, and expressed his gratitude to Dr. Johnson for having once got him permission from Dr. Taylor at Ashbourne to play there upon moderate terms. Garrick's name was soon introduced. JOHNSON. 'Garrick's conversation is gay and grotesque. It is a dish of all sorts, but all good things. There is no solid meat in it: there is a want of sentiment in it. Not but that he has sentiment sometimes, and sentiment, too, very powerful and very pleasing: but it has not its full proportion in his conversation.'

When we were by ourselves he told me, 'Forty years ago, Sir, I was in love with an actress here, Mrs. Emmet, who acted Flora, in *Hob in the Well.*' What merit this lady had as an actress, or what was her figure, or her manner, I have not been informed: but, if we may believe Mr. Garrick, his old master's taste in theatrical merit was by no means refined; he was not an *elegans formarum spectator.*[1] Garrick used to tell, that Johnson said of an actor, who played Sir Harry Wildair at Lichfield, 'There is a courtly vivacity about the fellow;' when in fact, according to Garrick's account, 'he was the most vulgar ruffian that ever went upon *boards.*'

We had promised Mr. Stanton to be at his theatre on Monday. Dr. Johnson jocularly proposed me to write a Prologue for the occasion: 'A Prologue, by James Boswell, Esq. from the Hebrides.' I was really inclined to take the hint. Methought, 'Prologue, spoken before Dr. Samuel Johnson, at Lichfield, 1776;' would have sounded as well as, 'Prologue, spoken before the Duke of York, at Oxford,' in Charles the

---

[1] 'A nice observer of the female form.' Terence, *Eunuchus*, iii, 5.

Second's time. Much might have been said of what Lichfield had done for Shakspeare, by producing Johnson and Garrick. But I found he was averse to it.

We went and viewed the museum of Mr. Richard Green, apothecary here, who told me he was proud of being a relation of Dr. Johnson's. It was, truely, a wonderful collection, both of antiquities and natural curiosities, and ingenious works of art. He had all the articles accurately arranged, with their names upon labels, printed at his own little press; and on the staircase leading to it was a board, with the names of contributors marked in gold letters. A printed catalogue of the collection was to be had at a bookseller's. Johnson expressed his admiration of the activity and diligence and good fortune of Mr. Green, in getting together, in his situation, so great a variety of things; and Mr. Green told me that Johnson once said to him, 'Sir, I should as soon have thought of building a man of war, as of collecting such a museum.' Mr. Green's obliging alacrity in shewing it was very pleasing. His engraved portrait, with which he has favoured me, has a motto truely characteristical of his disposition, *'Nemo sibi vivat.'*[1]

A physician[2] being mentioned who had lost his practice, because his whimsically changing his religion had made people distrustful of him, I maintained that this was unreasonable, as religion is unconnected with medical skill. JOHNSON. 'Sir, it is not unreasonable; for when people see a man absurd in what they understand, they may conclude the same of him in what they do not understand. If a physician were to take to eating of horse-flesh, nobody would employ him; though one may eat horse-flesh, and be a very skilful physician. If a man were educated in an absurd religion, his continuing to profess it would not hurt him, though his changing to it would.'

We drank tea and coffee at Mr. Peter Garrick's, where was Mrs. Aston, one of the maiden sisters of Mrs. Walmsley, wife of Johnson's first friend, and sister also of the lady of whom Johnson used to speak with the warmest admiration, by the name of Molly Aston, who was afterwards married to Captain Brodie of the navy.

On Sunday, March 24, we breakfasted with Mrs. Cobb, a widow lady, who lived in an agreeable sequestered place close by the town, called the Friary, it having been formerly a religious house. She and her niece, Miss Adey, were great admirers of Dr. Johnson; and he behaved to them with a kindness

---

[1] 'Let no man live for himself.'

[2] Boswell's uncle, Dr. John Boswell.

and easy pleasantry, such as we see between old and intimate acquaintance. He accompanied Mrs. Cobb to St. Mary's church, and I went to the cathedral, where I was very much delighted with the musick, finding it to be peculiarly solemn and accordant with the words of the service.

We dined at Mr. Peter Garrick's, who was in a very lively humour, and verified Johnson's saying, that if he had cultivated gaiety as much as his brother David, he might have equally excelled in it. He was to-day quite a London narrator, telling us a variety of anecdotes with that earnestness and attempt at mimicry which we usually find in the wits of the metropolis. Dr. Johnson went with me to the cathedral in the afternoon. It was grand and pleasing to contemplate this illustrious writer, now full of fame, worshipping in 'the 'solemn temple' of his native city.

I returned to tea and coffee at Mr. Peter Garrick's, and then found Dr. Johnson at the Reverend Mr. Seward's, Canon Residentiary, who inhabited the Bishop's palace, in which Mr. Walmsley lived, and which had been the scene of many happy hours in Johnson's early life. Mr. Seward had, with ecclesiastical hospitality and politeness, asked me in the morning, merely as a stranger, to dine with him; and in the afternoon, when I was introduced to him, he asked Dr. Johnson and me to spend the evening and sup with him. He was a genteel well-bred dignified clergyman, had travelled with Lord Charles Fitzroy, uncle of the present Duke of Grafton, who died when abroad, and he had lived much in the great world. He was an ingenious and literary man, had published an edition of Beaumont and Fletcher, and written verses in Dodsley's collection. His lady was the daughter of Mr. Hunter, Johnson's first schoolmaster. And now, for the first time, I had the pleasure of seeing his celebrated daughter, Miss Anna Seward, to whom I have since been indebted for many civilities, as well as some obliging communications concerning Johnson.

Mr. Seward mentioned to us the observations which he had made upon the strata of earth in volcanos, from which it appeared, that they were so very different in depth at different periods, that no calculation whatever could be made as to the time required for their formation. This fully refuted an anti-mosaical remark introduced into Captain Brydone's entertaining tour, I hope heedlessly, from a kind of vanity which is too common in those who have not sufficiently studied the most important of all subjects. Dr. Johnson, indeed, had said before, independent of this observation, 'Shall all the accumulated evidence of the history of the world;—shall the authority of what is unquestionably the most ancient writing, be overturned by an uncertain remark such as this?'

On Monday, March 25, we breakfasted at Mrs. Lucy Porter's. Johnson had sent an express to Dr. Taylor's, acquainting him of our being at Lichfield, and Taylor had returned an answer that his postchaise should come for us this day. While we sat at breakfast, Dr. Johnson received a letter by the post, which seemed to agitate him very much. When he had read it, he exclaimed, 'One of the most dreadful things that has happened in my time.' The phrase *my time*, like the word *age*, is usually understood to refer to an event of a publick or general nature. I imagined something like an assassination of the King—like a gunpowder plot carried into execution—or like another fire of London. When asked, 'What is it, Sir?' he answered, 'Mr. Thrale has lost his only son!' This was, no doubt, a very great affliction to Mr. and Mrs. Thrale, which their friends would consider accordingly; but from the manner in which the intelligence of it was communicated by Johnson, it appeared for the moment to be comparatively small. I, however, soon felt a sincere concern, and was curious to observe, how Dr. Johnson would be affected. He said, 'This is a total extinction to their family, as much as if they were sold into captivity.' Upon my mentioning that Mr. Thrale had daughters, who might inherit his wealth;— 'Daughters, (said Johnson, warmly,) he'll no more value his daughters than—' I was going to speak.—'Sir, (said he,) don't you know how you yourself think? Sir, he wishes to propagate his name.' In short, I saw male succession strong in his mind, even where there was no name, no family of any long standing. I said, it was lucky he was not present when this misfortune happened. JOHNSON. 'It is lucky for *me*. People in distress never think that you feel enough.' BOSWELL. 'And Sir, they will have the hope of seeing you, which will be a relief in the mean time; and when you get to them, the pain will be so far abated, that they will be capable of being consoled by you, which, in the first violence of it, I believe, would not be the case.' JOHNSON. 'No, Sir; violent pain of mind, like violent pain of body, *must* be severely felt.' BOSWELL. 'I own, Sir, I have not so much feeling for the distress of others, as some people have, or pretend to have: but I know this, that I would do all in my power to relieve them.' JOHNSON. 'Sir, it is affectation to pretend to feel the distress of others, as much as they do themselves. It is equally so, as if one should pretend to feel as much pain while a friend's leg is cutting off, as he does. No, Sir; you have expressed the rational and just nature of sympathy. I would have gone to the extremity of the earth to have preserved this boy.'

He was soon quite calm. The letter was from Mr. Thrale's clerk, and concluded, 'I need not say how much they wish to see you in London.' He said, 'We shall hasten back from Taylor's.'

Mrs. Lucy Porter and some other ladies of the place talked a great deal of him when he was out of the room, not only with veneration but affection. It pleased me to find that he was so much *beloved* in his native city.

Mrs. Aston, whom I had seen the preceding night, and her sister, Mrs. Gastrel, a widow lady, had each a house and garden, and pleasure-ground, prettily situated upon Stowhill, a gentle eminence adjoining to Lichfield. Johnson walked away to dinner there, leaving me by myself without any apology; I wondered at this want of that facility of manners, from which a man has no difficulty in carrying a friend to a house where he is intimate; I felt it very unpleasant to be thus left in solitude in a country town, where I was an entire stranger, and began to think myself unkindly deserted: but I was soon relieved, and convinced that my friend, instead of being deficient in delicacy, had conducted the matter with perfect propriety, for I received the following note in his handwriting: 'Mrs. Gastrel, at the lower house on Stowhill, desires Mr. Boswell's company to dinner at two.' I accepted of the invitation and had here another proof how amiable his character was in the opinion of those who knew him best. I was not informed, till afterwards, that Mrs. Gastrel's husband was the clergyman who, while he lived at Stratford upon Avon, where he was proprietor of Shakspeare's garden, with Gothick barbarity cut down his mulberry-tree, and, as Dr. Johnson told me, did it to vex his neighbours. His lady, I have reason to believe, on the same authority, participated in the guilt of what the enthusiasts for our immortal bard deem almost a species of sacrilege.

After dinner Dr. Johnson wrote a letter to Mrs. Thrale on the death of her son. I said it would be very distressing to Thrale, but she would soon forget it, as she had so many things to think of. JOHNSON. 'No, Sir, Thrale will forget it first. *She* has many things that she *may* think of. *He* has many things that he *must* think of.' This was a very just remark upon the different effect of those light pursuits which occupy a vacant and easy mind, and those serious engagements which arrest attention, and keep us from brooding over grief.

He observed of Lord Bute, 'It was said of Augustus, that it would have been better for Rome that he had never been born, or had never died. So it would have been better for this nation if Lord Bute had never been minister, or had never resigned.'

In the evening we went to the Town-hall, which was converted into a temporary theatre, and saw *Theodosius,* with *The Stratford Jubilee.* I was happy to see Dr. Johnson sitting in a conspicuous part of the pit, and receiving affectionate homage from all his acquaintance. We were quite gay and merry. I afterwards mentioned to him that I condemned myself for being so, when poor Mr. and Mrs. Thrale were in such distress. JOHNSON. 'You are wrong, Sir; twenty years hence Mr. and Mrs. Thrale will not suffer much pain from the death of their son. Now, Sir, you are to consider, that distance of place, as well as distance of time, operates upon the human feelings. I would not have you be gay in the presence of the distressed, because it would shock them; but you may be gay at a distance. Pain for the loss of a friend, or of a relation whom we love, is occasioned by the want which we feel. In time the vacuity is filled with something else; or, sometimes the vacuity closes up of itself.'

Mr. Seward and Mr. Pearson, another clergyman here, supt with us at our inn, and after they left us, we sat up late as we used to do in London.

Here I shall record some fragments of my friend's conversation during this jaunt.

'Marriage, Sir, is much more necessary to a man than to a woman; for he is much less able to supply himself with domestick comforts. You will recollect my saying to some ladies the other day, that I had often wondered why young women should marry, as they have so much more freedom, and so much more attention paid to them while unmarried, than when married. I indeed did not mention the *strong* reason for their marrying—the *mechanical* reason.' BOSWELL. 'Why, that *is* a strong one. But does not imagination make it seem much more important than it is in reality? Is it not, to a certain degree, a delusion in us as well as in women?' JOHNSON. 'Why yes, Sir; but it is a delusion that is always beginning again.' BOSWELL. 'I don't know but there is upon the whole more misery than happiness produced by that passion.' JOHNSON. 'I don't think so, Sir.'

'Never speak of a man in his own presence. It is always indelicate, and may be offensive.'

'Questioning is not the mode of conversation among gentlemen. It is assuming a superiority, and it is particularly wrong to question a man concerning himself. There may be parts of his former life which he may not wish to be made known to other persons, or even brought to his own recollection.'

'A man should be careful never to tell tales of himself to his own disadvantage. People may be amused and laugh at the time, but they will be remembered, and brought out against him upon some subsequent occasion.'

'Much may be done if a man puts his whole mind to a particular object. By doing so, Norton[1] has made himself the great lawyer that he is allowed to be.'

I mentioned an acquaintance of mine,[2] a sectary, who was a very religious man, who not only attended regularly on publick worship with those of his communion, but made a particular study of the Scriptures, and even wrote a commentary on some parts of them, yet was known to be very licentious in indulging himself with women; maintaining that men are to be saved by faith alone, and that the Christian religion had not prescribed any fixed rule for the intercourse between the sexes. JOHNSON. 'Sir, there is no trusting to that crazy piety.'

I observed that it was strange how well Scotchmen were known to one another in their own country, though born in very distant counties; for we do not find that the gentlemen of neighbouring counties in England are mutually known to each other. Johnson, with his usual acuteness, at once saw and explained the reason of this; 'Why, Sir, you have Edinburgh, where the gentlemen from all your counties meet, and which is not so large but that they are all known. There is no such common place of collection in England, except London, where from its great size and diffusion, many of those who reside in contiguous counties of England, may long remain unknown to each other.'

On Tuesday, March 26, there came for us an equipage properly suited to a wealthy well-beneficed clergyman;—Dr. Taylor's large roomy post-chaise, drawn by four stout plump horses, and driven by two steady jolly postillions, which conveyed us to Ashbourne; where I found my friend's schoolfellow living upon an establishment perfectly corresponding with his substantial creditable equipage: his house, garden, pleasure-grounds, table, in short every thing good, and no scantiness appearing. Every man should form such a plan of living as he can execute completely. Let him not draw an outline wider than he can fill up. I have seen many skeletons of shew and magnificence which excite at once ridicule and pity. Dr. Taylor had a good estate of his own, and good preferment in the church, being a prebendary of Westminster,

---

[1] Sir Fletcher Norton, afterwards Speaker of the House of Commons, and in 1782 created Baron Grantley.

[2] Dr. John Boswell.

and rector of Bosworth. He was a diligent justice of the peace, and presided over the town of Ashbourne, to the inhabitants of which I was told he was very liberal; and as a proof of this it was mentioned to me, he had the preceding winter distributed two hundred pounds among such of them as stood in need of his assistance. He had consequently a considerable political interest in the county of Derby, which he employed to support the Devonshire family; for though the schoolfellow and friend of Johnson, he was a Whig. I could not perceive in his character much congeniality of any sort with that of Johnson, who, however, said to me, 'Sir, he has a very strong understanding.' His size, and figure, and countenance, and manner, were that of a hearty English 'Squire, with the parson superinduced: and I took particular notice of his upper servant, Mr. Peters, a decent grave man, in purple clothes, and a large white wig, like the butler or *major domo* of a Bishop.

Dr. Johnson and Dr. Taylor met with great cordiality; and Johnson soon gave him the same sad account of their schoolfellow, Congreve, that he had given to Mr. Hector; adding a remark of such moment to the rational conduct of a man in the decline of life, that it deserves to be imprinted upon every mind: 'There is nothing against which an old man should be so much upon his guard as putting himself to nurse.' Innumerable have been the melancholy instances of men once distinguished for firmness, resolution, and spirit, who in their latter days have been governed like children, by interested female artifice.

Dr. Taylor commended a physician[1] who was known to him and Dr. Johnson, and said, 'I fight many battles for him, as many people in the country dislike him.' JOHNSON. 'But you should consider, Sir, that by every one of your victories he is a loser; for, every man of whom you get the better, will be very angry, and will resolve not to employ him; whereas if people get the better of you in argument about him, they'll think, "We'll send for Dr. ****** nevertheless."' This was an observation deep and sure in human nature.

Next day we talked of a book in which an eminent judge[2] was arraigned before the bar of the publick, as having pronounced an unjust decision in a great cause. Dr. Johnson maintained that this publication would not give any uneasiness to the judge. 'For (said he,) either he acted honestly, or he meant to do injustice. If he acted honestly, his own consciousness will protect him; if he meant to do injustice, he

[1] Dr. Butter.
[2] Lord Mansfield.

351

will be glad to see the man who attacks him, so much vexed.'

Next day, as Dr. Johnson had acquainted Dr. Taylor of the reason for his returning speedily to London, it was resolved that we should set out after dinner. A few of Dr. Taylor's neighbours were his guests that day.

Dr. Johnson talked with approbation of one who had attained to the state of the philosophical wise man, that is, to have no want of any thing. 'Then, Sir, (said I,) the savage is a wise man.' 'Sir, (said he,) I do not mean simply being without,—but not having a want.' I maintained, against this proposition, that it was better to have fine clothes, for instance, than not to feel the want of them. JOHNSON. 'No, Sir; fine clothes are good only as they supply the want of other means of procuring respect. Was Charles the Twelfth, think you, less respected for his coarse blue coat and black stock? And you find the King of Prussia dresses plain, because the dignity of his character is sufficient.' I here brought myself into a scrape, for I heedlessly said, 'Would not *you*, Sir, be the better for velvet and embroidery?' JOHNSON. 'Sir, you put an end to all argument when you introduce your opponent himself. Have you no better manners? There is *your want*.' I apologised by saying, I had mentioned him as an instance of one who wanted as little as any man in the world, and yet, perhaps, might receive some additional lustre from dress.

Having left Ashbourne in the evening, we stopped to change horses at Derby, and availed ourselves of a moment to enjoy the conversation of my countryman, Dr. Butter, then physician there. He was in great indignation because Lord Mountstuart's bill for a Scotch militia had been lost. Dr. Johnson was as violent against it. 'I am glad, (said he,) that Parliament has had the spirit to throw it out. You wanted to take advantage of the timidity of our scoundrels;' (meaning, I suppose, the ministry). It may be observed, that he used the epithet scoundrel very commonly, not quite in the sense in which it is generally understood, but as a strong term of disapprobation; as when he abruptly answered Mrs. Thrale, who had asked him how he did, 'Ready to become a scoundrel, Madam; with a little more spoiling you will, I think, make me a complete rascal:' he meant, easy to become a capricious and self-indulgent valetudinarian; a character for which I have heard him express great disgust.

Johnson had with him upon this jaunt, *Il Palmerino d'Inghilterra*, a romance praised by Cervantes; but did not like it much. He said, he read it for the language, by way of preparation for his Italian expedition.—We lay this night at Loughborough.

On Thursday, March 28, we pursued our journey. I mentioned that old Mr. Sheridan complained of the ingratitude of Mr. Wedderburne and General Fraser, who had been much obliged to him when they were young Scotchmen entering upon life in England. JOHNSON. 'Why, Sir, a man is very apt to complain of the ingratitude of those who have risen far above him. A man when he gets into a higher sphere, into other habits of life, cannot keep up all his former connections. Then, Sir, those who knew him formerly upon a level with themselves, may think that they ought still to be treated as on a level, which cannot be; and an acquaintance in a former situation may bring out things which it would be very disagreeable to have mentioned before higher company, though, perhaps, every body knows of them.' . . .

He said, 'It is commonly a weak man who marries for love.' We then talked of marrying women of fortune; and I mentioned a common remark, that a man may be, upon the whole, richer by marrying a woman with a very small portion, because a woman of fortune will be proportionally expensive; whereas a woman who brings none will be very moderate in expenses. JOHNSON. 'Depend upon it, Sir, this is not true. A woman of fortune being used to the handling of money, spends it judiciously; but a woman who gets the command of money for the first time upon her marriage, has such a gust in spending it, that she throws it away with great profusion.'

He praised the ladies of the present age, insisting that they were more faithful to their husbands, and more virtuous in every respect, than in former times, because their understandings were better cultivated. It was an undoubted proof of his good sense and good disposition, that he was never querulous, never prone to inveigh against the present times, as is so common when superficial minds are on the fret. On the contrary, he was willing to speak favourably of his own age; and, indeed, maintained its superiority in every respect, except in its reverence for government; the relaxation of which he imputed, as its grand cause, to the shock which our monarchy received at the Revolution, though necessary; and secondly, to the timid concessions made to faction by successive administrations in the reign of his present Majesty. I am happy to think, that he lived to see the Crown at last recover its just influence.

At Leicester we read in the newspapers that Dr. James was dead. I thought that the death of an old school-fellow, and one with whom he had lived a good deal in London, would have affected my fellow-traveller much: but he only said, 'Ah! poor Jamy.' Afterwards, however, when we were in the chaise, he said, with more tenderness. 'Since I set out on this jaunt, I have lost an old friend and a young one;—Dr. James, and poor Harry,' (meaning Mr. Thrale's son.)

Having lain at St. Alban's on Thursday, March 28, we breakfasted the next morning at Barnet. I expressed to him a weakness of mind which I could not help; an uneasy apprehension that my wife and children, who were at a great distance from me, might, perhaps, be ill. 'Sir, (said he,) consider how foolish you would think it in *them* to be apprehensive that *you* are ill.' This sudden turn relieved me for the moment; but I afterwards perceived it to be an ingenious fallacy. I might, to be sure, be satisfied that they had no reason to be apprehensive about me, because I *knew* that I myself was well: but we might have a mutual anxiety, without the charge of folly; because each was, in some degree, uncertain as to the condition of the other.

I enjoyed the luxury of our approach to London, that metropolis which we both loved so much, for the high and varied intellectual pleasure which it furnishes. I experienced immediate happiness while whirled along with such a companion, and said to him, 'Sir, you observed one day at General Oglethorpe's, that a man is never happy for the present, but when he is drunk. Will you not add,—or when driving rapidly in a post-chaise?' JOHNSON. 'No, Sir, you are driving rapidly *from* something, or *to* something.'

Talking of melancholy, he said, 'Some men, and very thinking men too, have not those vexing thoughts. Sir Joshua Reynolds is the same all the year round. Beauclerk, except when ill and in pain, is the same. But I believe most men have them in the degree in which they are capable of having them. If I were in the country, and were distressed by that malady, I would force myself to take a book; and every time I did it I should find it the easier. Melancholy, indeed, should be diverted by every means but drinking.'

We stopped at Messieurs Dillys, booksellers in the Poultry; from whence he hurried away, in a hackney coach, to Mr. Thrale's, in the Borough. I called at his house in the evening, having promised to acquaint Mrs. Williams of his safe return; when, to my surprize, I found him sitting with her at tea, and, as I thought, not in a very good humour: for, it seems, when he had got to Mr. Thrale's, he found the coach was at the door waiting to carry Mrs. and Miss Thrale, and Signor Baretti, their Italian master, to Bath. This was not shewing the attention which might have been expected to the 'Guide, Philosopher, and Friend,' the *Imlac* who had hastened from the country to console a distressed mother, who he understood was very anxious for his return. They had, I found, without ceremony, proceeded on their intended journey. I was glad to understand from him that it was still resolved that his tour to Italy with Mr. and Mrs. Thrale should take place, of which he had entertained some doubt, on account of the loss which they had suffered; and his doubts afterwards proved to be well-founded. He observed, indeed very justly, that 'their loss was an additional reason for their going abroad; and if it had not been fixed that he should have been one of the party, he would force them out; but he would not advise them unless his advice was asked, lest they might suspect that he recommended what he wished on his own account.' I was not pleased that his intimacy with Mr. Thrale's family, though it no doubt contributed much to his comfort and enjoyment, was not without some degree of restraint. Not, as has been grossly suggested, that it was required of him as a task to talk for the entertainment of them and their company; but that he was not quite at his ease; which, however, might partly be owing to his own honest pride—that dignity of mind which is always jealous of appearing too compliant.

On Sunday, March 31, I called on him, and shewed him as a curiosity which I had discovered, his *Translation of Lobo's Account of Abyssinia*, which Sir John Pringle had lent me, it being then little known as one of his works. He said, 'Take no notice of it,' or 'don't talk of it.' He seemed to think it beneath him, though done at six-and-twenty. I said to him, 'Your style, Sir, is much improved since you translated this.' He answered with a sort of triumphant smile, 'Sir, I hope it is.'

On Wednesday, April 3, in the morning I found him very busy putting his books in order, and as they were generally very old ones, clouds of dust were flying around him. He had on a pair of large gloves, such as hedgers use. His present appearance put me in mind of my uncle, Dr. Boswell's description of him, 'A robust genius, born to grapple with whole libraries.'

I gave him an account of a conversation which had passed between me and Captain Cook, the day before, at dinner at Sir John Pringle's; and he was much pleased with the conscientious accuracy of that celebrated circumnavigator, who set me right as to many of the exaggerated accounts given by Dr. Hawkesworth of his Voyages. I told him that while I was with the Captain, I catched the enthusiasm of curiosity and adventure, and felt a strong inclination to go with him on his next voyage. JOHNSON. 'Why, Sir, a man *does* feel so, till he considers how very little he can learn from such voyages.' BOSWELL. 'But one is carried away with the general grand and indistinct notion of A VOYAGE ROUND THE WORLD.' JOHNSON. 'Yes, Sir, but a man is to guard himself against taking a thing in general.' I said I was certain that a great part of what we are told by the travellers to the South Sea must be conjecture, because they had not enough of the language of those countries to understand so much as they have related. Objects falling under the observation of the senses might be clearly known; but every thing intellectual, every thing abstract—politicks, morals, and religion, must be darkly guessed. Dr. Johnson was of the same opinion. He upon another occasion, when a friend mentioned to him several extraordinary facts, as communicated to him by the circumnavigators, slily observed, 'Sir, I never before knew how much I was respected by these gentlemen; they told *me* none of these things.'

He had been in company with Omai, a native of one of the South Sea Islands, after he had been some time in this country. He was struck with the elegance of his behaviour, and accounted for it thus: 'Sir, he had passed his time, while in England, only in the best company; so that all that he had acquired of our manners was genteel. As a proof of this, Sir, Lord Mulgrave and he dined one day at Streatham; they sat with their backs to the light fronting me, so that I could not see distinctly; and there was so little of the savage in Omai, that I was afraid to speak to either, lest I should mistake one for the other.'

We agreed to dine to-day at the Mitre-tavern, after the rising of the House of Lords, where a branch of the litigation concerning the Douglas Estate, in which I was one of the counsel, was to come on. I brought with me Mr. Murray, Solicitor-General of Scotland, now one of the Judges of the Court of Session, with the title of Lord Henderland. I mentioned Mr. Solicitor's relation, Lord Charles Hay, with whom I knew Dr. Johnson had been acquainted. JOHNSON. 'I wrote something for Lord Charles; and I thought he had nothing to fear from a court-martial. I suffered a great loss when he died; he was a mighty pleasing man in conversation, and a reading man. The character of a soldier is high. They who stand forth the foremost in danger, for the community, have the respect of mankind. An officer is much more respected than any other man who has as little money. In a commercial country, money will always purchase respect. But you find, an officer, who has, properly speaking, no money, is every where well received and treated with attention. The character of a soldier always stands him in stead.' BOSWELL. 'Yet, Sir, I think that common soldiers are worse thought of than other men in the same rank of life; such as labourers.' JOHNSON. 'Why, Sir, a common soldier is usually a very gross man, and any quality which procures respect may be overwhelmed by

356

grossness. A man of learning may be so vicious or so ridiculous that you cannot respect him. A common soldier too, generally eats more than he can pay for. But when a common soldier is civil in his quarters, his red coat procures him a degree of respect.' The peculiar respect paid to the military character in France was mentioned. BOSWELL. 'I should think that where military men are so numerous, they would be less valued as not being rare.' JOHNSON. 'Nay, Sir, wherever a particular character or profession is high in the estimation of a people, those who are of it will be valued above other men. We value an Englishman highly in this country, and yet Englishmen are not rare in it.'

Mr. Murray praised the ancient philosophers for the candour and good humour with which those of different sects disputed with each other. JOHNSON. 'Sir, they disputed with good humour, because they were not in earnest as to religion. Had the ancients been serious in their belief, we should not have had their Gods exhibited in the manner we find them represented in the Poets. The people would not have suffered it. They disputed with good humour upon their fanciful theories, because they were not interested in the truth of them: when a man has nothing to lose, he may be in good humour with his opponent. Accordingly you see in Lucian, the Epicurean, who argues only negatively, keeps his temper; the Stoick, who has something positive to preserve, grows angry. Being angry with one who controverts an opinion which you value, is a necessary consequence of the uneasiness which you feel. Every man who attacks my belief, diminishes in some degree my confidence in it, and therefore makes me uneasy; and I am angry with him who makes me uneasy. Those only who believed in revelation have been angry at having their faith called in question; because they only had something upon which they could rest as matter of fact. MURRAY. 'It seems to me that we are not angry at a man for controverting an opinion which we believe and value; we rather pity him.' JOHNSON. 'Why, Sir; to be sure when you wish a man to have that belief which you think is of infinite advantage, you wish well to him; but your primary consideration is your own quiet. If a madman were to come into this room with a stick in his hand, no doubt we should pity the state of his mind; but our primary consideration would be to take care of ourselves. We should knock him down first, and pity him afterwards. No, Sir; every man will dispute with great good humour upon a subject in which he is not interested. I will dispute very calmly upon the probability of another man's son being hanged; but if a man zealously enforces the probability that my own son will be hanged, I shall certainly not be in a very good humour with him.' I added this illustration, 'If a man endeavours to convince me that my wife, whom I love very much, and in whom I place great confidence, is a disagreeable woman, and is even unfaithful to me, I shall be very angry, for he is putting me in fear of being unhappy.' MURRAY. 'But, Sir, truth will always bear an examination.' JOHNSON. 'Yes, Sir, but it is painful to be forced to defend it. Consider, Sir, how should you like, though conscious of your innocence, to be tried before a jury for a capital crime, once a week.' . . .

I introduced the topick, which is often ignorantly urged, that the Universities of England are too rich; so that learning does not flourish in them as it would do, if those who teach had smaller salaries, and depended on their assiduity for a great part of their income. JOHNSON. 'Sir, the very reverse of this is the truth; the English Universities are not rich enough. Our fellowships are only sufficient to support a man during his studies to fit him for the world, and accordingly in general they are held no longer than till an opportunity offers of getting away. Now and then, perhaps, there is a fellow who grows old in his college; but this is against his will, unless he be a man very indolent indeed. A hundred a year is reckoned a good fellowship, and that is no more than is necessary to keep a man decently as a scholar. We do not allow our fellows to marry, because we consider academical institutions as preparatory to a settlement in the world. It is only by being employed as a tutor, that a fellow can obtain any thing more than a livelihood. To be sure a man, who has enough without teaching, will probably not teach; for we would all be idle if we could. In the same manner, a man who is to get nothing by teaching, will not exert himself. Gresham College was intended as a place of instruction for London; able professors were to read lectures gratis, they contrived to have no scholars; whereas, if they had been allowed to receive but sixpence a lecture from each scholar, they would have been emulous to have had many scholars. Every body will agree that it should be the interest of those who teach to have scholars; and this is the case in our Universities. That they are too rich is certainly not true; for they have nothing good enough to keep a man of eminent learning with them for his life. In the foreign Universities a professorship is a high thing. It is as much almost as a man can make by his learning; and therefore we find the most learned men abroad are in the Universities. It is not so with us. Our Universities are impoverished of learning, by the penury of their provisions. I wish there were many places of a thousand a-year at Oxford, to keep first-rate men of learning from quitting the University.' . . .

I mentioned Mr. Maclaurin's uneasiness on account of a degree of ridicule carelessly thrown on his deceased father, in Goldsmith's *History of Animated Nature,* in which that celebrated mathematician is represented as being subject to fits of yawning so violent as to render him incapable of proceeding in his lecture; a story altogether unfounded, but for the publication of which the law would give no reparation. This led us to agitate the question, whether legal redress could be obtained, even when a man's deceased relation was calumniated in a publication. Mr. Murray maintained there should be reparation, unless the authour could justify himself by proving the fact. JOHNSON. 'Sir, it is of so much more consequence that truth should be told, than that individuals should not be made uneasy, that it is much better that the law does not restrain writing freely concerning the characters of the dead. Damages will be given to a man who is calumniated in his life-time, because he may be hurt in his worldly interest, or at least hurt in his mind: but the law does not regard that uneasiness which a man feels on having his ancestor calumniated. That is too nice. Let him deny what is said, and let the matter have a fair chance by discussion. But, if a man could say nothing against a character but what he can prove, history could not be written; for a great deal is known of men of which proof cannot be brought. A minister may be notoriously known to take bribes, and yet you may not be able to prove it.' Mr. Murray suggested, that the authour should be obliged to shew some sort of evidence, though he would not require a strict legal proof: but Johnson firmly and resolutely opposed any restraint whatever, as adverse to a free investigation of the characters of mankind.

On Thursday, April 4, having called on Dr. Johnson, I said, it was a pity that truth was not so firm as to bid defiance to all attacks, so that it might be shot at as much as people chose to attempt, and yet remain unhurt. JOHNSON. 'Then, Sir, it would not be shot at. Nobody attempts to dispute that two and two make four: but with contests concerning moral truth, human passions are generally mixed, and therefore it must ever be liable to assault and misrepresentation.'

On Friday, April 5, being Good Friday, after having attended the morning service at St. Clement's Church. I walked home with Johnson. We talked of the Roman Catholick religion. JOHNSON. 'In the barbarous ages, Sir, priests and people were equally deceived; but afterwards there were gross corruptions introduced by the clergy, such as indulgencies to priests to have concubines, and the worship of images, not, indeed, inculcated, but knowingly permitted.' He strongly censured the licensed stews at Rome. BOSWELL. 'So then, Sir, you would allow of no irregular intercourse whatever between the sexes?' JOHNSON. 'To be sure I would not, Sir. I would punish it much more than is done, and so restrain it. In all countries there has been fornication, as in all countries there has been theft; but there may be more or less of the one, as well as of the other, in proportion to the force of law. All men will naturally commit fornication, as all men will naturally steal. And, Sir, it is very absurd to argue, as has been often done, that prostitutes are necessary to prevent the violent effects of appetite from violating the decent order of life; nay, should be permitted, in order to preserve the chastity of our wives and daughters. Depend upon it, Sir, severe laws, steadily enforced, would be sufficient against those evils, and would promote marriage.'

I stated to him this case:—'Suppose a man has a daughter, who he knows has been seduced, but her misfortune is concealed from the world: should he keep her in his house? Would he not, by doing so, be accessary to imposition? And, perhaps, a worthy, unsuspecting man might come and marry this woman, unless the father inform him of the truth.' JOHNSON. 'Sir, he is accessary to no imposition. His daughter is in his house; and if a man courts her, he takes his chance. If a friend, or, indeed, if any man asks his opinion whether he should marry her, he ought to advise him against it, without telling why, because his real opinion is then required. Or, if he has other daughters who know of her frailty, he ought not to keep her in his house. You are to consider the state of life is this; we are to judge of one another's characters as well as we can; and a man is not bound, in honesty or honour, to tell us the faults of his daughter or of himself. A man who has debauched his friend's daughter is not obliged to say to every body—"Take care of me; don't let me into your houses without suspicion. I once debauched a friend's daughter: I may debauch yours." '

Mr. Thrale called upon him, and appeared to bear the loss of his son with a manly composure. There was no affectation about him; and he talked, as usual, upon indifferent subjects. He seemed to me to hesitate as to the intended Italian tour, on which, I flattered myself, he and Mrs. Thrale and Dr. Johnson were soon to set out; and, therefore, I pressed it as much as I could. I mentioned, that Mr. Beauclerk had said, that Baretti, whom they were to carry with them, would keep them so long in the little towns of his own district, that they would not have time to see Rome. I mentioned this, to put them on their guard. JOHNSON. 'Sir, we do not thank Mr. Beauclerk for supposing that we are to be directed by Baretti.

No, Sir; Mr. Thrale is to go, by my advice, to Mr. Jackson, (the all-knowing) and get from him a plan for seeing the most that can be seen in the time that we have to travel. We must, to be sure, see Rome, Naples, Florence, and Venice, and as much more as we can.' (Speaking with a tone of animation.)

When I expressed an earnest wish for his remarks on Italy, he said, 'I do not see that I could make a book upon Italy; yet I should be glad to get two hundred pounds, or five hundred pounds, by such a work.' This shewed both that a journal of his Tour upon the Continent was not wholly out of his contemplation, and that he uniformly adhered to that strange opinion, which his indolent disposition made him utter: 'No man but a blockhead ever wrote, except for money.' Numerous instances to refute this will occur to all who are versed in the history of literature.

He gave us one of the many sketches of character which were treasured in his mind, and which he was wont to produce quite unexpectedly in a very entertaining manner. 'I lately, (said he,) received a letter from the East Indies, from a gentleman whom I formerly knew very well; he had returned from that country with a handsome fortune, as it was reckoned, before means were found to acquire those immense sums which have been brought from thence of late; he was a scholar, and an agreeable man, and lived very prettily in London, till his wife died. After her death, he took to dissipation and gaming, and lost all he had. One evening he lost a thousand pounds to a gentleman whose name I am sorry I have forgotten. Next morning he sent the gentleman five hundred pounds, with an apology that it was all he had in the world. The gentleman sent the money back to him, declaring he would not accept of it; and adding, that if Mr. ——— had occasion for five hundred pounds more, he would lend it to him. He resolved to go out again to the East Indies, and make his fortune anew. He got a considerable appointment, and I had some intention of accompanying him. Had I thought then as I do now, I should have gone: but, at that time, I had objections to quitting England.'

It was a very remarkable circumstance about Johnson, whom shallow observers have supposed to have been ignorant of the world, that very few men had seen greater variety of characters; and none could observe them better, as was evident from the strong, yet nice portraits which he often drew. I have frequently thought that if he had made out what the French call *une catalogue raisonnée* of all the people who had passed under his observation, it would have afforded a very rich fund of instruction and entertainment. The suddenness with which his accounts of some of them started out in conversation, was not less pleasing than surprising. I remember he once observed to me, 'It is wonderful, Sir, what is to be found in London. The most literary conversation that I ever enjoyed, was at the table of Jack Ellis, a money-scrivener behind the Royal Exchange, with whom I at one period used to dine generally once a week.'

Volumes would be required to contain a list of his numerous and various acquaintance, none of whom he ever forgot; and could describe and discriminate them all with precision and vivacity. He associated with persons the most widely different in manners, abilities, rank, and accomplishments. He was at once the companion of the brilliant Colonel Forrester of the Guards, who wrote *The Polite Philosopher*, and of the aukward and uncouth Robert Levet; of Lord Thurlow, and Mr. Sastres, the Italian master; and has dined one day with the beautiful, gay, and fascinating Lady Craven, and the next with good Mrs. Gardiner the tallow chandler, on Snow-hill.

On my expressing my wonder at his discovering so much of the knowledge peculiar to different professions, he told me, 'I learnt what I know of law, chiefly from Mr. Ballow, a very able man. I learnt some, too, from Chambers; but was not so teachable then. One is not willing to be taught by a young man.' When I expressed a wish to know more about Mr. Ballow, Johnson said, 'Sir, I have seen him but once these twenty years. The tide of life has driven us different ways.' I was sorry at the time to hear this; but whoever quits the creeks of private connections, and fairly gets into the great ocean of London, will, by imperceptible degrees, unavoidably experience such cessations of acquaintance.

'My knowledge of physick, (he added,) I learnt from Dr. James, whom I helped in writing the proposals for his *Dictionary* and also a little in the *Dictionary* itself. I also learnt some from Dr. Lawrence, but was then grown more stubborn.'

A curious incident happened to-day, while Mr. Thrale and I sat with him. Francis announced that a large packet was brought to him from the post-office, said to have come from Lisbon, and it was charged *seven pounds ten shillings*. He would not receive it, supposing it to be some trick, nor did he even look at it. But upon enquiry afterwards he found that it was a real packet for him, from that very friend in the East Indies of whom he had been speaking; and the ship which carried it having come to Portugal, this packet, with others, had been put into the post-office at Lisbon.

I mentioned a new gaming-club, of which Mr. Beauclerk had given me an account, where the members played to a desperate extent. JOHNSON. 'Depend upon it, Sir, this is mere talk. *Who* is ruined by gaming? You will not find six instances in an age. There is a strange rout made about deep play: whereas you have many more people ruined by adventurous trade, and yet we do not hear such an outcry against it.' THRALE. 'There may be few people absolutely ruined by deep play; but very many are much hurt in their circumstances by it.' JOHNSON. 'Yes, Sir, and so are very many by other kinds of expence.' I had heard him talk once before in the same manner; and at Oxford he said, 'he wished he had learnt to play at cards.' The truth, however, is, that he loved to display his ingenuity in argument; and therefore would sometimes in conversation maintain opinions which he was sensible were wrong, but in supporting which, his reasoning and wit would be most conspicuous. He would begin thus: 'Why, Sir, as to the good or evil of card-playing—' 'Now, (said Garrick,) he is thinking which side he shall take.' He appeared to have a pleasure in contradiction, especially when any opinion whatever was delivered with an air of confidence; so that there was hardly any topick, if not one of the great truths of Religion and Morality, that he might not have been incited to argue, either for or against it. Lord Elibank had the highest admiration of his powers. He once observed to me, 'Whatever opinion Johnson maintains, I will not say that he convinces me; but he never fails to shew me, that he has good reasons for it.' I have heard Johnson pay his Lordship this high compliment: 'I never was in Lord Elibank's company without learning something.'

We sat together till it was too late for the afternoon service. Thrale said he had come with intention to go to church with us. We went at seven to evening prayers at St. Clement's church, after having drank coffee; an indulgence, which I understood Johnson yielded to on this occasion, in compliment to Thrale.

On Sunday, April 7, Easter-day, after having been at St. Paul's cathedral, I came to Dr. Johnson, according to my usual custom. It seemed to me, that there was always something peculiarly mild and placid in his manner upon this holy festival, the commemoration of the most joyful event in the history of our world, the resurrection of our LORD and SAVIOUR, who, having triumphed over death and the grave, proclaimed immortality to mankind.

I repeated to him an argument of a lady of my acquaintance, who maintained, that her husband's having been guilty of numberless infidelities, released her from conjugal obligations, because they were reciprocal. JOHNSON. 'This is miserable stuff, Sir. To the contract of marriage, besides the man and wife, there is a third party—Society; and, if it be considered as a vow—GOD: and, therefore, it cannot be dissolved by their consent alone. Laws are not made for particular cases, but for men in general. A woman may be unhappy with her husband; but she cannot be freed from him without the approbation of the civil and ecclesiastical power. A man may be unhappy, because he is not so rich as another; but he is not to seize upon another's property with his own hand.' BOSWELL. 'But, Sir, this lady does not want that the contract should be dissolved; she only argues that she may indulge herself in gallantries with equal freedom as her husband does, provided she takes care not to introduce a spurious issue into his family. You know, Sir, what Macrobius has told us of Julia.'[1] JOHNSON. 'This lady of yours, Sir, I think, is very fit for a brothel.'

Mr. Macbean, authour of the *Dictionary of ancient Geography*, came in. He mentioned, that he had been forty years absent from Scotland. 'Ah, Boswell! (said Johnson, smiling,) what would you give to be forty years from Scotland?' I said, 'I should not like to be so long absent from the seat of my ancestors.' This gentleman, Mrs. Williams, and Mr. Levett, dined with us.

Dr. Johnson made a remark, which both Mr. Macbean and I thought new. It was this: that 'the law against usury is for the protection of creditors as well as of debtors; for if there were no such check, people would be apt, from the temptation of great interest, to lend to desperate persons, by whom they would lose their money. Accordingly there are instances of ladies being ruined, by having injudiciously sunk their fortunes for high annuities, which, after a few years, ceased to be paid, in consequence of the ruined circumstances of the borrower.'

Mrs. Williams was very peevish; and I wondered at Johnson's patience with her now, as I had often done on similar occasions. The truth is, that his humane consideration of the forlorn and indigent state in which this lady was left by her father, induced him to treat her with the utmost tenderness, and even to be desirous of procuring her amusement, so as sometimes to incommode many of his friends, by carrying her with him to their houses, where, from her manner of eating, in consequence of her blindness, she could not but offend the delicacy of persons of nice sensations.

After coffee, we went to afternoon service in St. Clement's church. Observing some beggars in the street as we walked along, I said to him I supposed there was no civilised country

---

[1] 'I never take on a passenger but when the ship is full.' Boswell provides only the Latin, here omitted.

in the world, where the misery of want in the lowest classes of the people was prevented. JOHNSON. 'I believe, Sir, there is not; but it is better that some should be unhappy, than that none should be happy, which would be the case in a general state of equality.'

When the service was ended, I went home with him, and we sat quietly by ourselves. He recommended Dr. Cheyne's books. I said, I thought Cheyne had been reckoned whimsical. 'So he was, (said he,) in some things; but there is no end of objections. There are few books to which some objection or other may not be made.' He added, 'I would not have you read anything else of Cheyne, but his book on Health, and his *English Malady*.'

Upon the question whether a man who had been guilty of vicious actions would do well to force himself into solitude and sadness; JOHNSON. 'No, Sir, unless it prevent him from being vicious again. With some people, gloomy penitence is only madness turned upside down. A man may be gloomy, till, in order to be relieved from gloom, he has recourse again to criminal indulgencies.'

On Wednesday, April 10, I dined with him at Mr. Thrale's, where were Mr. Murphy and some other company. Before dinner, Dr. Johnson and I passed some time by ourselves. I was sorry to find it was now resolved that the proposed journey to Italy should not take place this year. He said, 'I am disappointed, to be sure; but it is not a great disappointment.' I wondered to see him bear, with a philosophical calmness, what would have made most people peevish and fretful. I perceived, however, that he had so warmly cherished the hope of enjoying classical scenes, that he could not easily part with the scheme; for he said, 'I shall probably contrive to get to Italy some other way. But I won't mention it to Mr. and Mrs. Thrale, as it might vex them.' I suggested, that going to Italy might have done Mr. and Mrs. Thrale good. JOHNSON. 'I rather believe not, Sir. While grief is fresh, every attempt to divert only irritates. You must wait till grief be *digested,* and then amusement will dissipate the remains of it.' . . . .

I said, I disliked the custom which some people had of bringing their children into company, because it in a manner forced us to pay foolish compliments to please their parents. JOHNSON. 'You are right, Sir. We may be excused for not caring much about other people's children, for there are many who care very little about their own children. It may be observed, that men, who from being engaged in business, or from their course of life in whatever way, seldom see their children, do not care much about them. I myself should not have had much fondness for a child of my own.' MRS.

THRALE. 'Nay, Sir, how can you talk so?' JOHNSON. 'At least, I never wished to have a child.' . . .

We talked of Flatman's Poems; and Mrs. Thrale observed, that Pope had partly borrowed from him *The dying Christian to his Soul*. Johnson repeated Rochester's verses upon Flatman, which, I think, by much too severe:

> 'Nor that slow drudge in swift Pindarick strains,
> Flatman, who Cowley imitates with pains,
> And rides a jaded Muse, whipt with lose reins.'

I like to recollect all the passages that I heard Johnson repeat: it stamps a value on them. . . .

Mr. Murphy said, that 'The *Memoirs of Gray's Life* set him much higher in his estimation than his poems did; for you there saw a man constantly at work in literature.' Johnson acquiesced in this; but depreciated the book, I thought, very unreasonably. For he said, 'I forced myself to read it, only because it was a common topick of conversation. I found it mighty dull; and, as to the style, it is fit for the second table.' Why he thought so, I was at a loss to conceive. He now gave it as his opinion, that 'Akenside was a superiour poet both to Gray and Mason.'

Talking of the Reviews, Johnson said, 'I think them very impartial: I do not know an instance of partiality.' He mentioned what had passed upon the subject of the *Monthly* and *Critical Reviews*, in the conversation with which his Majesty had honoured him. He expatiated a little more on them this evening. 'The Monthly Reviewers (said he,) are not Deists; but they are Christians with as little christianity as may be; and are for pulling down all establishments. The Critical Reviewers are for supporting the constitution, both in church and state. The Critical Reviewers, I believe, often review without reading the books through; but lay hold of a topick, and write chiefly from their own minds. The Monthly Reviewers are duller men, and are glad to read the books through.'

He talked of Lord Lyttelton's extreme anxiety as an authour; observing, that 'he was thirty years in preparing his *History*, and that he employed a man to point it for him; as if (laughing) another man could point his sense better than himself.' Mr. Murphy said, he understood, his history was kept back several years for fear of Smollet. JOHNSON. 'This seems strange to Murphy and me, who never felt that anxiety, but sent what we wrote to the press, and let it take its chance.' MRS. THRALE. 'The time has been, Sir, when you felt it.' JOHNSON. 'Why really, Madam, I do not recollect a time when that was the case.'

Talking of *The Spectator,* he said, 'It is wonderful that there is such a proportion of bad papers, in the half of the work which was not written by Addison; for there was all the world to write that half, yet not a half of that half is good. One of the finest pieces in the English language is the paper on Novelty, yet we do not hear it talked of. It was written by Grove, a dissenting *teacher.*' He would not, I perceived, call him a *clergyman,* though he was candid enough to allow very great merit to his composition. Mr. Murphy said, he remembered when there were several people alive in London, who enjoyed a considerable reputation merely from having written a paper in *The Spectator.* He mentioned particularly Mr. Ince, who used to frequent Tom's coffee-house. 'But (said Johnson,) you must consider how highly Steele speaks of Mr. Ince.' He would not allow that the paper on carrying a boy to travel, signed *Philip Homebred,* which was reported to be written by the Lord Chancellor Hardwicke, had merit. He said, 'it was quite vulgar, and had nothing luminous.'

Johnson mentioned Dr. Barry's System of Physick. 'He was a man (said he,) who had acquired a high reputation in Dublin, came over to England, and brought his reputation with him, but had not great success. His notion was, that pulsation occasions death by attrition; and that, therefore, the way to preserve life is to retard pulsation. But we know that pulsation is strongest in infants, and that we increase in growth while it operates in its regular course; so it cannot be the cause of destruction.' Soon after this, he said something very flattering to Mrs. Thrale, which I do not recollect; but it concluded with wishing her long life. 'Sir, (said I,) if Dr. Barry's system be true, you have now shortened Mrs. Thrale's life, perhaps, some minutes, by accelerating her pulsation.'

On Thursday, April 11, I dined with him at General Paoli's, in whose house I now resided, and where I had ever afterwards the honour of being entertained with the kindest attention as his constant guest, while I was in London, till I had a house of my own there. I mentioned my having that morning introduced to Mr. Garrick, Count Neni, a Flemish Nobleman of great rank and fortune, to whom Garrick talked of Abel Drugger as *a small part;* and related, with pleasant vanity, that a Frenchman who had seen him in one of his low characters, exclaimed, *'Comment! je ne le crois pas. Ce n'est pas Monsieur Garrick, ce Grand Homme!'* Garrick added, with an appearance of grave recollection, 'If I were to begin life again, I think I should not play those low characters.' Upon which I observed, 'Sir, you would be in the wrong; for your great excellence is your variety of playing, your representing so well, characters so very different.' JOHNSON. 'Garrick, Sir, was not in earnest in what he said; for, to be sure, his peculiar excellence is his variety: and, perhaps, there is not any one character which has not been as well acted by somebody else, as he could do it.' BOSWELL. 'Why then, Sir, did he talk so?' JOHNSON. 'Why, Sir, to make you answer as you did.' BOSWELL. 'I don't know, Sir; he seemed to dip deep into his mind for the reflection.' JOHNSON. He had not far to dip, Sir: he said the same thing, probably, twenty times before.'

Of a nobleman[1] raised at a very early period to high office, he said, 'His parts, Sir, are pretty well for a Lord; but would not be distinguished in a man who had nothing else but his parts.'

A journey to Italy was still in his thoughts. He said, 'A man who has not been in Italy, is always conscious of an inferiority, from his not having seen what it is expected a man should see. The grand object of travelling is to see the shores of the Mediterranean. On those shores were the four great Empires of the world; the Assyrian, the Persian, the Grecian, and the Roman.—All our religion, almost all our law, almost all our arts, almost all that sets us above savages, has come to us from the shores of the Mediterranean.' The General observed, that 'THE MEDITERRANEAN would be a noble subject for a poem.'

We talked of translation. I said, I could not define it, nor could I think of a similitude to illustrate it: but that it appeared to me the translation of poetry could be only imitation. JOHNSON. 'You may translate books of science exactly. You may also translate history, in so far as it is not embellished with oratory, which is poetical. Poetry, indeed, cannot be translated; and, therefore, it is the poets that preserve languages; for we would not be at the trouble to learn a language, if we could have all that is written in it just as well in a translation. But as the beauties of poetry cannot be preserved in any language except that in which it was originally written, we learn the language.'

A gentleman[2] maintained that the art of printing had hurt real learning, by disseminating idle writings.—JOHNSON. 'Sir, if it had not been for the art of printing, we should now have no learning at all; for books would have perished faster than they could have been transcribed.' This observation seems not just, considering for how many ages books were preserved by writing alone.

[1] Lord Shelburne.
[2] Paoli.

The same gentleman maintained, that a general diffusion of knowledge among a people was a disadvantage; for it made the vulgar rise above their humble sphere. JOHNSON. 'Sir, while knowledge is a distinction, those who are possessed of it will naturally rise above those who are not. Merely to read and write was a distinction at first; but we see when reading and writing have become general, the common people keep their stations. And so, were higher attainments to become general the effect would be the same.'

'Goldsmith (he said,) referred every thing to vanity; his virtues, and his vices too, were from that motive. He was not a social man. He never exchanged mind with you.'

We spent the evening at Mr. Hoole's. Mr. Mickle, the excellent translator of *The Lusiad*, was there. I have preserved little of the conversation of this evening. Dr. Johnson said, 'Thomson had a true poetical genius, the power of viewing every thing in a poetical light. His fault is such a cloud of words sometimes, that the sense can hardly peep through. Shiels, who compiled *Cibber's Lives of the Poets*, was one day sitting with me. I took down Thomson, and read aloud a large portion of him, and then asked,—Is not this fine? Shiels having expressed the highest admiration. Well, Sir, (said I,) I have omitted every other line.'

I related a dispute between Goldsmith and Mr. Robert Dodsley, one day when they and I were dining at Tom Davies's, in 1762. Goldsmith asserted, that there was no poetry produced in this age. Dodsley appealed to his own *Collection*, and maintained, that though you could not find a palace like Dryden's *Ode on St. Cecilia's Day*, you had villages composed of very pretty houses; and he mentioned particularly *The Spleen*. JOHNSON. 'I think Dodsley gave up the question. He and Goldsmith said the same thing; only he said it in a softer manner than Goldsmith did; for he acknowledged that there was no poetry, nothing that towered above the common mark. You may find wit and humour in verse, and yet no poetry. *Hudibras* has a profusion of these; yet it is not to be reckoned a poem. *The Spleen*, in Dodsley's *Collection*, on which you say he chiefly rested, is not poetry.' BOSWELL. 'Does not Gray's poetry, Sir, tower above the common mark?' JOHNSON. 'Yes, Sir; but we must attend to the difference between what men in general cannot do if they would, and what every man may do if he would. Sixteen-string Jack[1] towered above the common mark.' BOSWELL. 'Then,

---

[1] A noted highwayman, who after having been several times tried and acquitted, was at last hanged. He was remarkable for foppery in his dress, and particularly for wearing a bunch of sixteen strings at the knees of his breeches—B.

Sir, what is poetry?' JOHNSON. 'Why, Sir, it is much easier to say what it is not. We all *know* what light is; but it is not easy to *tell* what it is.'

On Friday, April 12, I dined with him at our friend Tom Davies's, where we met Mr. Cradock, of Leicestershire, authour of *Zobeide,* a tragedy; a very pleasing gentleman, to whom my friend Dr. Farmer's very excellent *Essay on the Learning of Shakspeare* is addressed; and Dr. Harwood, who has written and published various works; particularly a fantastical translation of the New Testament, in modern phrase, and with a Socinian twist.

I introduced Aristotle's doctrine in his *Art of Poetry,* of . . . 'the purging of the passions,' as the purpose of tragedy. 'But how are the passions to be purged by terrour and pity?' (said I, with an assumed air of ignorance, to incite him to talk, for which it was often necessary to employ some address.) JOHNSON. 'Why, Sir, you are to consider what is the meaning of purging in the original sense. It is to expel impurities from the human body. The mind is subject to the same imperfection. The passions are the great movers of human actions; but they are mixed with such impurities, that it is necessary they should be purged or refined by means of terrour and pity. For instance, ambition is a noble passion; but by seeing upon the stage, that a man who is so excessively ambitious as to raise himself by injustice, is punished, we are terrified at the fatal consequences of such a passion. In the same manner a certain degree of resentment is necessary; but if we see that a man carries it too far, we pity the object of it, and are taught to moderate that passion.' My record upon this occasion does great injustice to Johnson's expression, which was so forcible and brilliant, that Mr. Cradock whispered me, 'O that his words were written in a book!'

I observed the great defect of the tragedy of *Othello* was, that it had not a moral; for that no man could resist the circumstances of suspicion which were artfully suggested to Othello's mind. JOHNSON. 'In the first place, Sir, we learn from *Othello* this very useful moral, not to make an unequal match; in the second place, we learn not to yield too readily to suspicion. The handkerchief is merely a trick, though a very pretty trick; but there are no other circumstances of reasonable suspicion, except what is related by Iago of Cassio's warm expressions concerning Desdemona in his sleep; and that depended entirely upon the assertion of one man. No, Sir, I think *Othello* has more moral than almost any play.'

Talking of a penurious gentleman of our acquaintance, Johnson said, 'Sir, he is narrow, not so much from avarice, as from impotence to spend his money. He cannot find in his heart to pour out a bottle of wine; but he would not much care if it should sour.'

Davies said of a well-known dramatick authour,[1] that 'he lived upon *potted stories,* and that he made his way as Hannibal did, by vinegar; having begun by attacking people; particularly the players.'

He reminded Dr. Johnson of Mr. Murphy's having paid him the highest compliment that ever was paid to a layman, by asking his pardon for repeating some oaths in the course of telling a story.

Johnson and I supt this evening at the Crown and Anchor tavern, in company with Sir Joshua Reynolds, Mr. Langton, Mr. Nairne, now one of the Scotch Judges, with the title of Lord Dunsinan, and my very worthy friend, Sir William Forbes, of Pitsligo.

We discussed the question whether drinking improved conversation and benevolence. Sir Joshua maintained it did. JOHNSON. 'No, Sir: before dinner men meet with great inequality of understanding; and those who are conscious of their inferiority, have the modesty not to talk. When they have drunk wine, every man feels himself happy, and loses that modesty, and grows impudent and vociferous: but he is not improved; he is only not sensible of his defects.' Sir Joshua said the Doctor was talking of the effects of excess in wine; but that a moderate glass enlivened the mind, by giving a proper circulation to the blood. 'I am (said he,) in very good spirits when I get up in the morning. By dinnertime I am exhausted; wine puts me in the same state as when I got up; and I am sure that moderate drinking makes people talk better.' JOHNSON. 'No, Sir; wine gives not light, gay, ideal hilarity; but tumultuous, noisy, clamorous merriment. I have heard none of those drunken,—nay, drunken is a coarse word,—none of those *vinous* flights.' SIR JOSHUA. 'Because you have sat by, quite sober, and felt an envy of the happiness of those who were drinking.' JOHNSON. 'Perhaps, contempt.—And, Sir, it is not necessary to be drunk one's self, to relish the wit of drunkenness. Do we not judge of the drunken wit of the dialogue between Iago and Cassio, the most excellent in its kind, when we are quite sober? Wit is wit, by whatever means it is produced; and, if good, will appear so at all times. I admit that the spirits are raised by drinking, as by the common participation of any pleasure: cock-fighting, or bear-baiting, will raise the spirits of a company, as drinking does, though surely they will not improve conversation. I also admit, that there are some sluggish men who are improved

[1] Murphy.

by drinking; as there are fruits which are not good till they are rotten. There are such men, but they are medlars. I indeed allow that there have been a very few men of talents who were improved by drinking; but I maintain that I am right as to the effects of drinking in general: and let it be considered, that there is no position, however false in its universality, which is not true of some particular man.' Sir William Forbes said, 'Might not a man warmed with wine be like a bottle of beer, which is made brisker by being set before the fire?'—'Nay, (said Johnson, laughing,) I cannot answer that: that is too much for me.'

I observed, that wine did some people harm, by inflaming, confusing, and irritating their minds; but that the experience of mankind had declared in favour of moderate drinking. JOHNSON. 'Sir, I do not say it is wrong to produce self-complacency by drinking; I only deny that it improves the mind. When I drank wine, I scorned to drink it when in company. I have drunk many a bottle by myself; in the first place, because I had need of it to raise my spirits; in the second place, because I would have nobody to witness its effects upon me.'

He told us, 'almost all his *Ramblers* were written just as they were wanted for the press; that he sent a certain portion of the copy of an essay, and wrote the remainder, while the former part of it was printing. When it was wanted, and he had fairly sat down to it, he was sure it would be done.'

He said, that for general improvement, a man should read whatever his immediate inclination prompts him to; though, to be sure, if a man has a science to learn, he must regularly and resolutely advance. He added, 'what we read with inclination makes a much stronger impression. If we read without inclination, half the mind is employed in fixing the attention; so there is but one half to be employed on what we read.' He told us, he read Fielding's *Amelia* through without stopping. He said, 'if a man begins to read in the middle of a book, and feels an inclination to go on, let him not quit it, to go to the beginning. He may, perhaps, not feel again the inclination.' . . .

We talked of the Reviews, and Dr. Johnson spoke of them as he did at Thrale's. Sir Joshua said, what I have often thought, that he wondered to find so much good writing employed in them, when the authours were to remain unknown, and so could not have the motive of fame. JOHNSON. 'Nay, Sir, those who write in them, write well, in order to be paid well.'

Soon after this day, he went to Bath with Mr. and Mrs. Thrale. I had never seen that beautiful city, and wished to take the opportunity of visiting it, while Johnson was there.

Having written to him, I received the following answer.[1]

On the 26th of April, I went to Bath; and on my arrival at the Pelican inn, found lying for me an obliging invitation from Mr. and Mrs. Thrale, by whom I was agreeably entertained almost constantly during my stay. They were gone to the rooms; but there was a kind note from Dr. Johnson, that he should sit at home all the evening. I went to him directly, and before Mr. and Mrs. Thrale returned, we had by ourselves some hours of tea-drinking and talk.

I shall group together such of his sayings as I preserved during the few days that I was at Bath.

Of a person[2] who differed from him in politicks, he said, 'In private life he is a very honest gentleman; but I will not allow him to be so in publick life. People *may* be honest, though they are doing wrong: that is between their Maker and them. But *we*, who are suffering by their pernicious conduct, are to destroy them. We are sure that ———— acts from interest. We know what his genuine principles were. They who allow their passions to confound the distinctions between right and wrong, are criminal. They may be convinced; but they have not come honestly by their conviction.'

It having been mentioned, I know not with what truth, that, a certain female political writer,[3] whose doctrines he disliked, had of late become very fond of dress, sat hours together at her toilet, and even put on rouge:—JOHNSON. 'She is better employed at her toilet, than using her pen. It is better she should be reddening her own cheeks, than blackening other people's characters.' . . .

'The mode of government by one may be ill adapted to a small society, but is best for a great nation. The characteristic of our own government at present is imbecility. The magistrate dare not call the guards for fear of being hanged. The guards will not come, for fear of being given up to the blind rage of popular juries.'

Of the father[4] of one of our friends, he observed, 'He never clarified his notions, by filtrating them through other minds. He had a canal upon his estate, where at one place the bank was too low.—I dug the canal deeper, said he.' . . .

A literary lady of large fortune was mentioned, as one who did good to many, but by no means 'by stealth,' and instead of 'blushing to find it fame,' acted evidently from vanity. JOHNSON. 'I have seen no beings who do as much good from

[1] In his answer, omitted here, Johnson invites Boswell to Bath.
[2] Burke.
[3] Mrs. Macaulay.
[4] Old Mr. Langton.

benevolence, as she does, from whatever motive. If there are such under the earth, or in the clouds, I wish they would come up, or come down. What Soame Jenyns says upon this subject is not to be minded; he is a wit. No, Sir; to act from pure benevolence is not possible for finite beings. Human benevolence is mingled with vanity, interest, or some other motive.'

He would not allow me to praise a lady then at Bath; observing, 'She does not gain upon me, Sir; I think her empty-headed.' He was, indeed, a stern critick upon characters and manners. Even Mrs. Thrale did not escape his friendly animadversion at times. When he and I were one day endeavouring to ascertain, article by article, how one of our friends[1] could possibly spend as much money in his family as he told us he did, she interrupted us by a lively extravagant sally, on the expense of clothing his children, describing it in a very ludicrous and fanciful manner. Johnson looked a little angry, and said, 'Nay, Madam, when you are declaiming, declaim; and when you are calculating, calculate.' At another time, when she said, perhaps affectedly, 'I don't like to fly.' JOHNSON. 'With *your* wings, Madam, you *must* fly: but have a care, there are *clippers* abroad.' How very well was this said, and how fully has experience proved the truth of it! But have they not *clipped* rather *rudely,* and gone a great deal *closer* than was necessary?

A gentleman[2] expressed a wish to go and live three years at Otaheité, or New-Zealand, in order to obtain a full acquaintance with people, so totally different from all that we have ever known, and be satisfied what pure nature can do for man. JOHNSON. 'What could you learn, Sir? What can savages tell, but what they themselves have seen? Of the past, or the invisible, they can tell nothing. The inhabitants of Otaheité and New-Zealand are not in a state of pure nature; for it is plain they broke off from some other people. Had they grown out of the ground, you might have judged of a state of pure nature. Fanciful people may talk of a mythology being amongst them; but it must be invention. They have once had religion, which has been gradually debased. And what account of their religion can you suppose to be learnt from savages? Only consider, Sir, our own state: our religion is in a book; we have an order of men whose duty it is to teach it; we have one day in the week set apart for it, and this is in general pretty well observed: yet ask the first ten

[1] Langton.
[2] Boswell.

gross men you meet, and hear what they can tell of their religion.'

On Monday, April 29, he and I made an excursion to Bristol, where I was entertained with seeing him enquire upon the spot, into the authenticity of 'Rowley's Poetry,' as I had seen him enquire upon the spot into the authenticity of 'Ossian's Poetry.' George Catcot, the pewterer, who was as zealous for Rowley, as Dr. Hugh Blair was for Ossian, (I trust my Reverend friend will excuse the comparison,) attended us at our inn, and with a triumphant air of lively simplicity called out, 'I'll make Dr. Johnson a convert.' Dr. Johnson, at his desire, read aloud some of Chatterton's fabricated verses, while Catcot stood at the back of his chair, moving himself like a pendulum, and beating time with his feet, and now and then looking into Dr. Johnson's face, wondering that he was not yet convinced. We called on Mr. Barret, the surgeon, and saw some of the *originals* as they were called, which were executed very artificially; but from a careful inspection of them, and a consideration of the circumstances with which they were attended, we were quite satisfied of the imposture, which, indeed, has been clearly demonstrated from internal evidence, by several able criticks.

Honest Catcot seemed to pay no attention whatever to any objections, but insisted, as an end of all controversy, that we should go with him to the tower of the church of St. Mary, Redcliff, and *view with our own eyes* the ancient chest in which the manuscripts were found. To this, Dr. Johnson good-naturedly agreed; and though troubled with a shortness of breathing, laboured up a long flight of steps, till we came to the place where the wonderous chest stood. 'There, (said Catcot, with a bouncing confident credulity,) *there* is the very chest itself.' After this *ocular demonstration*, there was no more to be said. He brought to my recollection a Scotch Highlander, a man of learning too, and who had seen the world, attesting, and at the same time giving his reasons for the authenticity of Fingal:—'I have heard all that poem when I was young.'—'Have you, Sir? Pray what have you heard?'—'I have heard Ossian, Oscar, and *every one of them.*'

Johnson said of Chatterton, 'This is the most extraordinary young man that has encountered my knowledge. It is wonderful how the whelp has written such things.'

We were by no means pleased with our inn at Bristol. 'Let us see now, (said I,) how we should describe it.' Johnson was ready with his raillery. 'Describe it, Sir?—Why, it was so bad that Boswell wished to be in Scotland!'

After Dr. Johnson's return to London, I was several times

with him at his house, where I occasionally slept, in the room that had been assigned to me. I dined with him at Dr. Taylor's, at General Oglethorpe's, and at General Paoli's. To avoid a tedious minuteness, I shall group together what I have preserved of his conversation during this period also, without specifying each scene where it passed, except one, which will be found so remarkable as certainly to deserve a very particular relation. Where the place or the persons do not contribute to the zest of the conversation, it is unnecessary to encumber my page with mentioning them. To know of what vintage our wine is, enables us to judge of its value, and to drink it with more relish: but to have the produce of each vine of one vineyard, in the same year, kept separate, would serve no purpose. To know that our wine, (to use an advertising phrase,) is 'of the stock of an Ambassadour lately deceased,' heightens its flavour: but it signifies nothing to know the bin where each bottle was once deposited.

'Garrick (he observed,) does not play the part of Archer in *The Beaux Stratagem* well. The gentleman should break out through the footman, which is not the case as he does it.'

'Where there is no education, as in savage countries, men will have the upper hand of women. Bodily strength, no doubt, contributes to this; but it would be so, exclusive of that; for it is mind that always governs. When it comes to dry understanding, man has the better.' . . .

'There is much talk of the misery which we cause to the brute creation; but they are recompensed by existence. If they were not useful to man, and therefore protected by him, they would not be nearly so numerous.' . . . .

'That man is never happy for the present is so true, that all his relief from unhappiness is only forgetting himself for a little while. Life is a progress from want to want, not from enjoyment to enjoyment.'

'Though many men are nominally entrusted with the administration of hospitals and other publick institutions, almost all the good is done by one man, by whom the rest are driven on; owing to confidence in him, and indolence in them.'

'Lord Chesterfield's *Letters to his Son,* I think, might be made a very pretty book. Take out the immorality, and it should be put into the hands of every young gentleman. An elegant manner and easiness of behaviour are acquired gradually and imperceptibly. No man can say "I'll be genteel." There are ten genteel women for one genteel man, because they are more restrained. A man without some degree of restraint is insufferable; but we are all less restrained than women. Were a woman sitting in company to put out her legs before her as most men do, we should be tempted to kick them in.'

No man was a more attentive and nice observer of behaviour in those in whose company he happened to be, than Johnson; or, however strange it may seem to many, had a higher estimation of its refinements. Lord Eliot informs me, that one day when Johnson and he were at dinner at a gentleman's house in London, upon Lord Chesterfield's *Letters* being mentioned, Johnson surprized the company by this sentence: 'Every man of any education would rather be called a rascal, than accused of deficiency in *the graces*.' Mr. Gibbon, who was present, turned to a lady who knew Johnson well, and lived much with him, and in his quaint manner, tapping his box, addressed her thus: 'Don't you think, Madam, (looking towards Johnson,) that among *all* your acquaintance, you could find *one* exception?' The lady smiled, and seemed to acquiesce. . . .

'Mrs. Williams was angry that Thrale's family did not send regularly to her every time they heard from me while I was in the Hebrides. Little people are apt to be jealous: but they should not be jealous; for they ought to consider, that superiour attention will necessarily be paid to superiour fortune or rank. Two persons may have equal merit, and on that account may have an equal claim to attention; but one of them may have also fortune and rank, and so may have a double claim.' . . .

A gentleman,[1] whom I found sitting with him one morning, said, that in his opinion the character of an infidel was more detestable than that of a man notoriously guilty of an atrocious crime. I differed from him, because we are surer of the odiousness of the one, than of the errour of the other. JOHNSON. 'Sir, I agree with him; for the infidel would be guilty of any crime if he were inclined to it.'

'Many things which are false are transmitted from book to book, and gain credit in the world. One of these is the cry against the evil of luxury. Now the truth is, that luxury produces much good. Take the luxury of building in London. Does it not produce real advantage in the conveniency and elegance of accommodation, and this all from the exertion of industry? People will tell you, with a melancholy face, how many builders are in gaol. It is plain they are in gaol, not for building; for rents are not fallen.—A man gives half a guinea for a dish of green peas. How much gardening does this occasion? how many labourers must the competition to have such things early in the market, keep in employment? You

[1] Steevens.

will hear it said, very gravely, "Why was not the half-guinea, thus spent in luxury, given to the poor? To how many might it have afforded a good meal?" Alas! has it not gone to the *industrious* poor, whom it is better to support than the *idle* poor? You are much surer that you are doing good when you *pay* money to those who work, as the recompence of their labour, than when you *give* money merely in charity. Suppose the ancient luxury of a dish of peacock's brains were to be revived, how many carcases would be left to the poor at a cheap rate? And as to the rout that is made about people who are ruined by extravagance, it is no matter to the nation that some individuals suffer. When so much general productive exertion is the consequence of luxury, the nation does not care though there are debtors in gaol; nay, they would not care though their creditors were there too.'

The uncommon vivacity of General Oglethorpe's mind, and variety of knowledge, having sometimes made his conversation seem too desultory, Johnson observed, 'Oglethorpe, Sir, never *completes* what he has to say.'

He on the same account made a similar remark on Patrick Lord Elibank: 'Sir, there is nothing *conclusive* in his talk.'

When I complained of having dined at a splendid table[1] without hearing one sentence of conversation worthy of being remembered, he said, 'Sir, there seldom is any such conversation.' BOSWELL. 'Why then meet at table?' JOHNSON. 'Why, to eat and drink together, and to promote kindness; and, Sir, this is better done when there is no solid conversation; for when there is, people differ in opinion, and get into bad humour, or some of the company who are not capable of such conversation, are left out, and feel themselves uneasy. It was for this reason, Sir Robert Walpole said, he always talked bawdy at his table, because in that all could join.'

Being irritated by hearing a gentleman[2] ask Mr. Levett a variety of questions concerning him, when he was sitting by, he broke out, 'Sir, you have but two topicks, yourself and me. I am sick of both.' 'A man, (said he,) should not talk of himself, nor much of any particular person. He should take care not to be made a proverb; and, therefore, should avoid having any one topick of which people can say, "We shall hear him upon it." There was a Dr. Oldfield, who was always talking of the Duke of Marlborough. He came into a coffee-house one day, and told that his Grace had spoken in the House of Lords for half an hour. "Did he indeed speak for half an hour?" (said Belchier, the surgeon,)—"Yes."—"And

1 The Earl of Pembroke's at Wilton.
2 Boswell.

what did he say of Dr. Oldfield?"—"Nothing."—"Why then, Sir, he was very ungrateful; for Dr. Oldfield could not have spoken for a quarter of an hour, without saying something of him."'

'Every man is to take existence on the terms on which it is given to him. To some men it is given on condition of not taking liberties, which other men may take without much harm. One man may drink wine, and be nothing the worse for it; on another, wine may have effects so inflammatory as to injure him both in body and mind, and perhaps, make him commit something for which he may deserve to be hanged.' . . .

I am now to record a very curious incident in Dr. Johnson's Life, which fell under my own observation; of which *pars magna fui*,[1] and which I am persuaded will, with the liberal-minded, be much to his credit.

My desire of being acquainted with celebrated men of every description, had made me, much about the same time, obtain an introduction to Dr. Samuel Johnson and to John Wilkes, Esq. Two men more different could perhaps not be selected out of all mankind. They had even attacked one another with some asperity in their writings; yet I lived in habits of friendship with both. I could fully relish the excellence of each; for I have ever delighted in that intellectual chymistry, which can separate good qualities from evil in the same person.

Sir John Pringle, 'mine own friend and my Father's friend,' between whom and Dr. Johnson I in vain wished to establish an acquaintance, as I respected and lived in intimacy with both of them, observed to me once, very ingeniously, 'It is not in friendship as in mathematicks, where two things, each equal to a third, are equal between themselves. You agree with Johnson as a middle quality, and you agree with me as a middle quality; but Johnson and I should not agree.' Sir John was not sufficiently flexible; so I desisted; knowing, indeed, that the repulsion was equally strong on the part of Johnson; who, I know not from what cause, unless his being a Scotchman, had formed a very erroneous opinion of Sir John. But I conceived an irresistible wish, if possible, to bring Dr. Johnson and Mr. Wilkes together. How to manage it, was a nice and difficult matter.

My worthy booksellers and friends, Messieurs Dilly in the Poultry, at whose hospitable and well-covered table I have seen a greater number of literary men, than at any other, except that of Sir Joshua Reynolds, had invited me to meet Mr.

[1] 'I was no small part.' *Aeneid*, ii. 5.

Wilkes and some more gentlemen on Wednesday, May 15. 'Pray (said I), let us have Dr. Johnson.'—'What, with Mr. Wilkes? not for the world, (said Mr. Edward Dilly:) Dr. Johnson would never forgive me.'—'Come, (said I,) if you'll let me negociate for you, I will be answerable that all shall go well.' DILLY. 'Nay, if you will take it upon you, I am sure I shall be very happy to see them both here.'

Notwithstanding the high veneration which I entertained for Dr. Johnson, I was sensible that he was sometimes a little actuated by the spirit of contradiction, and by means of that I hoped I should gain my point. I was persuaded that if I had come upon him with a direct proposal, 'Sir, will you dine in company with Jack Wilkes?' he would have flown into a passion, and would probably have answered, 'Dine with Jack Wilkes, Sir! I'd as soon dine with Jack Ketch.' I therefore, while we were sitting quietly by ourselves at his house in an evening, took occasion to open my plan thus:—'Mr. Dilly, Sir, sends his respectful compliments to you, and would be happy if you would do him the honour to dine with him on Wednesday next along with me, as I must soon go to Scotland.' JOHNSON. 'Sir, I am obliged to Mr. Dilly. I will wait upon him—' BOSWELL. 'Provided, Sir, I suppose, that the company which he is to have, is agreeable to you.' JOHNSON. 'What do you mean, Sir? What do you take me for? Do you think I am so ignorant of the world, as to imagine that I am to prescribe to a gentleman what company he is to have at his table?' BOSWELL. 'I beg your pardon, Sir, for wishing to prevent you from meeting people whom you might not like. Perhaps he may have some of what he calls his patriotick friends with him.' JOHNSON. 'Well, Sir, and what then? What care I for his *patriotick friends*? Poh!' BOSWELL. 'I should not be surprized to find Jack Wilkes there.' JOHNSON. 'And if Jack Wilkes *should* be there, what is that to *me*, Sir? My dear friend, let us have no more of this. I am sorry to be angry with you; but really it is treating me strangely to talk to me as if I could not meet any company whatever, occasionally.' BOSWELL. 'Pray forgive me, Sir: I meant well. But you shall meet whoever comes, for me.' Thus I secured him, and told Dilly that he would find him very well pleased to be one of his guests on the day appointed.

Upon the much-expected Wednesday, I called on him about half an hour before dinner, as I often did when we were to dine out together, to see that he was ready in time, and to accompany him. I found him buffeting his books, as upon a former occasion, covered with dust, and making no preparation for going abroad. 'How is this, Sir? (said I.) Don't you recollect that you are to dine at Mr. Dilly's?'

JOHNSON. 'Sir, I did not think of going to Dilly's: it went out of my head. I have ordered dinner at home with Mrs. Williams.' BOSWELL. 'But, my dear Sir, you know you were engaged to Mr. Dilly, and I told him so. He will expect you, and will be much disappointed if you don't come.' JOHNSON. 'You must talk to Mrs. Williams about this.'

Here was a sad dilemma. I feared that what I was so confident I had secured would yet be frustrated. He had accustomed himself to shew Mrs. Williams such a degree of humane attention, as frequently imposed some restraint upon him; and I knew that if she should be obstinate, he would not stir. I hastened down stairs to the blind lady's room, and told her I was in great uneasiness, for Dr. Johnson had engaged to me to dine this day at Mr. Dilly's, but that he had told me he had forgotten his engagement, and had ordered dinner at home. 'Yes, Sir, (said she, pretty peevishly,) Dr. Johnson is to dine at home.'—'Madam, (said I,) his respect for you is such, that I know he will not leave you unless you absolutely desire it. But as you have so much of his company, I hope you will be good enough to forego it for a day; as Mr. Dilly is a very worthy man, has frequently had agreeable parties at his house for Dr. Johnson, and will be vexed if the Doctor neglects him to-day. And then, Madam, be pleased to consider my situation; I carried the message, and I assured Mr. Dilly that Dr. Johnson was to come, and no doubt he has made a dinner, and invited a company, and boasted of the honour he expected to have. I shall be quite disgraced if the Doctor is not there.' She gradually softened to my solicitations, which were certainly as earnest as most entreaties to ladies upon any occasion, and was graciously pleased to empower me to tell Dr. Johnson, 'That all things considered, she thought he should certainly go.' I flew back to him, still in dust, and careless of what should be the event, 'indifferent in his choice to go or stay;' but as soon as I had announced to him Mrs. Williams's consent, he roared, 'Frank, a clean shirt,' and was very soon drest. When I had him fairly seated in a hackney-coach with me, I exulted as much as a fortune-hunter who has got an heiress into a post-chaise with him to set out for Gretna-Green.

When we entered Mr. Dilly's drawing room, he found himself in the midst of a company he did not know. I kept myself snug and silent, watching how he would conduct himself. I observed him whispering to Mr. Dilly, 'Who is that gentleman, Sir?'—'Mr. Arthur Lee.'—JOHNSON. 'Too, too, too,' (under his breath,) which was one of his habitual mutterings. Mr. Arthur Lee could not but be very obnoxious to Johnson, for he was not only a *patriot* but an *American*. He was afterwards minister from the United States at the court of Madrid. 'And who is the gentleman in lace?'—'Mr. Wilkes, Sir.' This information confounded him still more; he had some difficulty to restrain himself, and taking up a book, sat down upon a window-seat and read, or at least kept his eye upon it intently for some time, till he composed himself. His feelings, I dare say, were aukward enough. But he no doubt recollected his having rated me for supposing that he could be at all disconcerted by any company, and he, therefore, resolutely set himself to behave quite as an easy man of the world, who could adapt himself at once to the disposition and manners of those whom he might chance to meet.

The cheering sound of 'Dinner is upon the table,' dissolved his reverie, and we *all* sat down without any symptom of ill humour. There were present, besides Mr. Wilkes, and Mr. Arthur Lee, who was an old companion of mine when he studied physick at Edinburgh, Mr. (now Sir John) Miller, Dr. Lettsom, and Mr. Slater the druggist. Mr. Wilkes placed himself next to Dr. Johnson, and behaved to him with so much attention and politeness, that he gained upon him insensibly. No man eat more heartily than Johnson, or loved better what was nice and delicate. Mr. Wilkes was very assiduous in helping him to some fine veal. 'Pray give me leave, Sir:—It is better here—A little of the brown—Some fat, Sir —A little of the stuffing—Some gravy—Let me have the pleasure of giving you some butter—Allow me to recommend a squeeze of this orange;—or the lemon, perhaps, may have more zest.'—'Sir, Sir, I am obliged to you, Sir,' cried Johnson, bowing, and turning his head to him with a look for some time of 'surly virtue,' but, in a short while, of complacency.

Foote being mentioned, Johnson said, 'He is not a good mimick.' One of the company[1] added, 'A merry Andrew, a buffoon.' JOHNSON. 'But he has wit too, and is not deficient in ideas, or in fertility and variety of imagery, and not empty of reading; he has knowledge enough to fill up his part. One species of wit he has in an eminent degree, that of escape. You drive him into a corner with both hands; but he's gone, Sir, when you think you have got him—like an animal that jumps over your head. Then he has a great range for his wit; he never lets truth stand between him and a jest, and he is sometimes mighty coarse. Garrick is under many restraints from which Foote is free.' WILKES. 'Garrick's wit is more like Lord Chesterfield's.' JOHNSON. 'The first time I was in company with Foote was at Fitzherbert's. Having no good opinion of the fellow, I was resolved not to be pleased; and it

1 Edward Dilly.

is very difficult to please a man against his will. I went on eating my dinner pretty sullenly, affecting not to mind him. But the dog was so very comical, that I was obliged to lay down my knife and fork, throw myself back upon my chair, and fairly laugh it out. No, Sir, he was irresistible.[1] He upon one occasion experienced, in an extraordinary degree, the efficacy of his powers of entertaining. Amongst the many and various modes which he tried of getting money, he became a partner with a small-beer brewer, and he was to have a share of the profits for procuring customers amongst his numerous acquaintance. Fitzherbert was one who took his small-beer; but it was so bad that the servants resolved not to drink it. They were at some loss how to notify their resolution, being afraid of offending their master, who they knew liked Foote much as a companion. At last they fixed upon a little black boy, who was rather a favourite, to be their deputy, and deliver their remonstrance; and having invested him with the whole authority of the kitchen, he was to inform Mr. Fitzherbert, in all their names, upon a certain day, that they would drink Foote's small-beer no longer. On that day Foote happened to dine at Fitzherbert's, and this boy served at table; he was so delighted with Foote's stories, and merriment, and grimace, that when he went down stairs, he told them, "This is the finest man I have ever seen. I will not deliver your message. I will drink his small-beer." '

Somebody observed that Garrick could not have done this. WILKES. 'Garrick would have made the small-beer still smaller. He is now leaving the stage; but he will play *Scrub* all his life.' I knew that Johnson would let nobody attack Garrick but himself, as Garrick once said to me, and I had heard him praise his liberality; so to bring out his commendation of his celebrated pupil, I said, loudly, 'I have heard Garrick is liberal.' JOHNSON. 'Yes, Sir, I know that Garrick has given away more money than any man in England that I am acquainted with, and that not from ostentatious views. Garrick was very poor when he began life; so when he came to have money, he probably was very unskilful in giving away, and saved when he should not. But Garrick began to be liberal as soon as he could; and I am of opinion, the reputation of avarice which he has had, has been very lucky for him, and prevented his having many enemies. You despise a man for avarice, but do not hate him. Garrick might have been much better attacked for living with more splendour than is suitable to a player: if they had had the wit to have

---

[1] Foote told me that Johnson said of him, 'For loud obstreperous broadfaced mirth, I know not his equal'—B.

assaulted him in that quarter, they might have galled him more. But they have kept clamouring about his avarice, which has rescued him from much obloquy and envy.'

Talking of the great difficulty of obtaining authentick information for biography, Johnson told us, 'When I was a young fellow I wanted to write the *Life of Dryden,* and in order to get materials, I applied to the only two persons then alive who had seen him; these were old Swinney, and old Cibber. Swinney's information was no more than this, "That at Will's coffee-house Dryden had a particular chair for himself, which was set by the fire in winter, and was then called his winter-chair; and that it was carried out for him to the balcony in summer, and was then called his summer-chair." Cibber could tell no more but "That he remembered him a decent old man, arbiter of critical disputes at Will's." You are to consider that Cibber was then at a great distance from Dryden, had perhaps one leg only in the room, and durst not draw in the other.' BOSWELL. 'Yet Cibber was a man of observation?' JOHNSON. 'I think not.' BOSWELL. 'You will allow his *Apology* to be well done.' JOHNSON. 'Very well done, to be sure, Sir. That book is a striking proof of the justice of Pope's remark:

> "Each might his several province well command,
>   Would all but stoop to what they understand." '

BOSWELL. 'And his plays are good.' JOHNSON. 'Yes; but that was his trade; *l'esprit du corps*: he had been all his life among players and play-writers. I wondered that he had so little to say in conversation, for he had kept the best company, and learnt all that can be got by the ear. He abused Pindar to me, and then shewed me an Ode of his own, with an absurd couplet, making a linnet soar on an eagle's wing. I told him that when the ancients made a simile, they always made it like something real.'

Mr. Wilkes remarked, that 'among all the bold flights of Shakspeare's imagination, the boldest was making Birnamwood march to Dunsinane; creating a wood where there never was a shrub; a wood in Scotland! ha! ha! ha!' And he also observed, that 'the clannish slavery of the Highlands of Scotland was the single exception to Milton's remark of "The Mountain Nymph, sweet Liberty," being worshipped in all hilly countries.'—'When I was at Inverary (said he,) on a visit to my old friend, Archibald, Duke of Argyle, his dependents congratulated me on being such a favourite of his Grace. I said, "It is then, gentlemen, truely lucky for me; for if I had displeased the Duke, and he had wished it, there is

384

not a Campbell among you but would have been ready to bring John Wilkes's head to him in a charger. It would have been only

"Off with his head! So much for Aylesbury."

I was then member for Aylesbury.'

Dr. Johnson and Mr. Wilkes talked of the contested passage in Horace's *Art of Poetry*, '*Difficile est propriè communia dicere.*' Mr. Wilkes according to my note, gave the interpretation thus; 'It is difficult to speak with propriety of common things; as, if a poet had to speak of Queen Caroline drinking tea, he must endeavour to avoid the vulgarity of cups and saucers.' But upon reading my note, he tells me that he meant to say, that 'the word *communia*, being a Roman law term, signifies here things *communis juris,* that is to say, what have never yet been treated by any body; and this appears clearly from what followed,

"——*Tuque*
Rectiùs Iliacum carmen deducis in actus,
Quàm si proferres ignota indictaque primus."

You will easier make a tragedy out of the *Iliad* than on any subject not handled before.' JOHNSON. 'He means that it is difficult to appropriate to particular persons qualities which are common to all mankind, as Homer has done.'

WILKES. 'We have no City-Poet now: that is an office which has gone into disuse. The last was Elkanah Settle. There is something in *names* which one cannot help feeling. Now *Elkanah Settle* sounds so *queer,* who can expect much from that name? We should have no hesitation to give it for John Dryden, in preference to Elkanah Settle, from the names only, without knowing their different merits.' JOHNSON. 'I suppose, Sir, Settle did as well for Aldermen in his time, as John Home could do now. Where did Beckford and Trecothick learn English?'

Mr. Arthur Lee mentioned some Scotch who had taken possession of a barren part of America, and wondered why they should choose it. JOHNSON. 'Why, Sir, all barrenness is comparative. The *Scotch* would not know it to be barren.' BOSWELL. 'Come, come, he is flattering the English. You have now been in Scotland, Sir, and say if you did not see meat and drink enough there.' JOHNSON. 'Why yes, Sir; meat and drink enough to give the inhabitants sufficient strength to run away from home.' All these quick and lively sallies were said sportively, quite in jest, and with a smile, which showed that he meant only wit. Upon this topick he and Mr. Wilkes could perfectly assimilate; here was a bond

385

of union between them, and I was conscious that as both of them had visited Caledonia, both were fully satisfied of the strange narrow ignorance of those who imagine that it is a land of famine. But they amused themselves with persevering in the old jokes. When I claimed a superiority for Scotland over England in one respect, that no man can be arrested there for a debt merely because another swears it against him; but there must first be the judgement of a court of law ascertaining its justice; and that a seizure of the person, before judgement is obtained, can take place only, if his creditor should swear that he is about to fly from the country, or, as it is technically expressed, is *in meditatione fugæ*:[1] WILKES. 'That, I should think, may be safely sworn of all the Scotch nation.' JOHNSON. (to Mr. Wilkes,) 'You must know, Sir, I lately took my friend Boswell and shewed him genuine civilised life in an English provincial town. I turned him loose at Lichfield, my native city, that he might see for once real civility: for you know he lives among savages in Scotland, and among rakes in London.' WILKES. 'Except when he is with grave, sober, decent people like you and me.' JOHNSON. (smiling,) 'And we ashamed of him.'

They were quite frank and easy. Johnson told the story of his asking Mrs. Macaulay to allow her footman to sit down with them, to prove the ridiculousness of the argument for the equality of mankind; and he said to me afterwards, with a nod of satisfaction, 'You saw Mr. Wilkes acquiesced.' Wilkes talked with all imaginable freedom of the ludicrous title given to the Attorney-General, *Diabolus Regis;*[2] adding, 'I have reason to know something about that officer; for I was prosecuted for a libel.' Johnson, who many people would have supposed must have been furiously angry at hearing this talked of so lightly, said not a word. He was now, *indeed,* 'A good-humoured fellow.'

After dinner we had an accession of Mrs. Knowles, the Quaker lady, well known for her various talents, and of Mr. Alderman Lee. Amidst some patriotick groans, somebody (I think the Alderman) said, 'Poor old England is lost.' JOHNSON. 'Sir, it is not so much to be lamented that Old England is lost, as that the Scotch have found it.' WILKES. 'Had Lord Bute governed Scotland only, I should not have taken the trouble to write his eulogy, and dedicate *Mortimer* to him.'

Mr. Wilkes held a candle to shew a fine print of a beautiful female figure which hung in the room, and pointed out

[1] 'meditating flight.'
[2] 'The King's Devil.'

the elegant contour of the bosom with the finger of an arch connoisseur. He afterwards, in a conversation with me, waggishly insisted, that all the time Johnson shewed visible signs of a fervent admiration of the corresponding charms of the fair Quaker.

This record, though by no means so perfect as I could wish, will serve to give a notion of a very curious interview, which was not only pleasing at the time, but had the agreeable and benignant effect of reconciling any animosity, and sweetening any acidity, which in the various bustle of political contest, had been produced in the minds of two men, who though widely different, had so many things in common—classical learning, modern literature, wit, and humour, and ready repartee—that it would have been much to be regretted if they had been for ever at a distance from each other.

Mr. Burke gave me much credit for this successful *negociation;* and pleasantly said, that 'there was nothing to equal it in the whole history of the *Corps Diplomatique.*'

I attended Dr. Johnson home, and had the satisfaction to hear him tell Mrs. Williams how much he had been pleased with Mr. Wilkes's company, and what an agreeable day he had passed.

I talked a good deal to him of the celebrated Margaret Caroline Rudd, whom I had visited, induced by the fame of her talents, address, and irresistible power of fascination. To a lady who disapproved of my visiting her, he said on a former occasion, 'Nay, Madam, Boswell is in the right; I should have visited her myself, were it not that they have now a trick of putting every thing into the news-papers.' This evening he exclaimed, 'I envy him his acquaintance with Mrs. Rudd.'

I mentioned a scheme which I had of making a tour to the Isle of Man, and giving a full account of it; and that Mr. Burke had playfully suggested as a motto,

'The proper study of mankind is MAN.'

JOHNSON. 'Sir, you will get more by the book than the jaunt will cost you; so you will have your diversion for nothing, and add to your reputation.'

On the evening of the next day I took leave of him, being to set out for Scotland. I thanked him with great warmth for all his kindness. 'Sir, (said he,) you are very welcome. Nobody repays it with more.'

How very false is the notion which has gone round the world of the rough, and passionate, and harsh manners of this great and good man. That he had occasional sallies of heat of temper, and that he was sometimes, perhaps, too 'easily provoked' by absurdity and folly, and sometimes too desirous of triumph in colloquial contest, must be allowed. The quickness both of his perception and sensibility disposed him to sudden explosions of satire; to which his extraordinary readiness of wit was a strong and almost irresistible incitement. To adopt one of the finest images in Mr. Home's *Douglas*,

> 'On each glance of thought
> Decision followed, as the thunderbolt
> Pursues the flash!'

I admit that the beadle within him was often so eager to apply the lash, that the Judge had not time to consider the case with sufficient deliberation.

That he was occasionally remarkable for violence of temper may be granted: but let us ascertain the degree, and not let it be supposed that he was in a perpetual rage, and never without a club in his hand, to knock down every one who approached him. On the contrary, the truth is, that by much the greatest part of his time he was civil, obliging, nay, polite in the true sense of the word; so much so, that many gentlemen, who were long acquainted with him, never received, or even heard a strong expression from him. . . .

It was, I think, after I had left London this year, that this Epitaph gave occasion to a *Remonstrance* to the MONARCH OF LITERATURE, for an account of which I am indebted to Sir William Forbes, of Pitsligo. . . .

Sir William Forbes writes to me thus:—

'I enclose the *Round Robin*. This *jeu d'esprit* took its rise one day at dinner at our friend Sir Joshua Reynolds's. All the company present, except myself, were friends and acquaintance of Dr. Goldsmith. The Epitaph, written for him by Dr. Johnson, became the subject of conversation, and various emendations were suggested, which it was agreed should be submitted to the Doctor's consideration. But the question was, who should have the courage to propose them to him? At last it was hinted, that there could be no way so good as that of a *Round Robin*, as the sailors call it, which they make use of when they enter into a conspiracy, so as not to let it be known who puts his name first or last to the paper. This proposition was instantly assented to; and Dr. Barnard, Dean of Derry, now Bishop of Killaloe, drew up an address to Dr. Johnson on the occasion, replete with wit and humour, but which it was feared the Doctor might think treated the subject with too much levity. Mr. Burke then proposed the address as it stands in the paper in writing, to which I had the honour to officiate as clerk.

'Sir Joshua agreed to carry it to Dr. Johnson, who received it with much good humour,[1] and desired Sir Joshua to tell the gentlemen, that he would alter the Epitaph in any manner they pleased, as to the sense of it; but *he would never consent to disgrace the walls of Westminster Abbey with an English inscription.*

'I consider this *Round Robin* as a species of literary curiosity worth preserving, as it marks, in a certain degree, Dr. Johnson's character.' . . .

Sir William Forbes's observation is very just. The anecdote now related proves, in the strongest manner, the reverence and awe with which Johnson was regarded, by some of the most eminent men of his time, in various departments, and even by such of them as lived most with him; while it also confirms what I have again and again inculcated, that he was by no means of that ferocious and irascible character which has been ignorantly imagined. . . .

1777: ÆTAT. 68.]—IN 1777, it appears from his *Prayers and Meditations,* that Johnson suffered much from a state of mind 'unsettled and perplexed,' and from that constitutional gloom, which, together with his extreme humility and anxiety with regard to his religious state, made him contemplate himself through too dark and unfavourable a medium. It may be said of him, that he 'saw GOD in clouds.' Certain we may be of his injustice to himself in the following lamentable paragraph, which it is painful to think came from the contrite heart of this great man, to whose labours the world is so much indebted: 'When I survey my past life, I discover nothing but a barren waste of time, with some disorders of body, and disturbances of the mind, very near to madness, which I hope He that made me will suffer to extenuate many faults, and excuse many deficiencies.' But we find his devotions in this year eminently fervent; and we are comforted by observing intervals of quiet, composure, and gladness. . . .

To those who delight in tracing the progress of works of literature, it will be an entertainment to compare the limited design with the ample execution of that admirable performance, *The Lives of the English Poets,* which is the richest,

[1] He, however, upon seeing Dr. Warton's name to the suggestion, that the Epitaph should be in English, observed to Sir Joshua, 'I wonder that Joe Warton, a scholar by profession, should be such a fool.' He said too, 'I should have thought Mund Burke would have had more sense.' Mr. Langton, who was one of the company at Sir Joshua's, like a sturdy scholar, resolutely refused to sign the *Round Robin.* The Epitaph is engraved upon Dr. Goldsmith's monument without any alteration.—B.

most beautiful, and indeed most perfect production of Johnson's pen. His notion of it at this time appears in the preceding letter.[1] He has a memorandum in this year, '29 May, Easter Eve, I treated with booksellers on a bargain, but the time was not long.' The bargain was concerning that undertaking; but his tender conscience seems alarmed lest it should have intruded too much on his devout preparation for the solemnity of the ensuing day. But, indeed, very little time was necessary for Johnson's concluding a treaty with the booksellers; as he had, I believe, less attention to profit from his labours than any man to whom literature has been a profession. . . .

On Sunday evening, September 14, I arrived at Ashbourne, and drove directly up to Dr. Taylor's door.[2] Dr. Johnson and he appeared before I had got out of the post-chaise, and welcomed me cordially.

I told them that I had travelled all the preceding night, and gone to bed at Leek, in Staffordshire; and that when I rose to go to church in the afternoon, I was informed there had been an earthquake, of which, it seems, the shock had been felt, in some degree, at Ashbourne. JOHNSON. 'Sir, it will be much exaggerated in popular talk: for, in the first place, the common people do not accurately adapt their thoughts to the objects; nor, secondly, do they accurately adapt their words to their thoughts: they do not mean to lie; but, taking no pains to be exact, they give you very false accounts. A great part of their language is proverbial. If anything rocks at all, they say *it rocks like a cradle;* and in this way they go on.'

The subject of grief for the loss of relations and friends being introduced, I observed that it was strange to consider how soon it in general wears away. Dr. Taylor mentioned a gentleman of the neighbourhood as the only instance he had ever known of a person who had endeavoured to *retain* grief. He told Dr. Taylor, that after his Lady's death, which affected him deeply, he *resolved* that the grief, which he cherished with a kind of sacred fondness, should be lasting; but that he found he could not keep it long. JOHNSON. 'All grief for what cannot in the course of nature be helped, soon wears away; in some sooner, indeed, in some later; but it never continues very long, unless where there is madness, such as will make a man have pride so fixed in his mind, as to imagine himself a King; or any other passion in an unrea-

[1] To Boswell. Johnson says, 'I am engaged to write little Lives, and little Prefaces, to a little edition of *The English Poets.*'

[2] Unable to meet Johnson in London the preceding spring, Boswell had arranged to meet him at Dr. Taylor's in Derbyshire.

sonable way: for all unnecessary grief is unwise, and there-fore will not be long retained by a sound mind. If, indeed, the cause of our grief is occasioned by our own misconduct, if grief is mingled with remorse of conscience, it should be lasting.' BOSWELL. 'But, Sir, we do not approve of a man who very soon forgets the loss of a wife or a friend.' JOHNSON. 'Sir, we disapprove of him, not because he soon forgets his grief, for the sooner it is forgotten the better, but because we suppose, that if he forgets his wife or his friend soon, he has not had much affection for them.'

I was somewhat disappointed in finding that the edition of *The English Poets,* for which he was to write Prefaces and Lives, was not an undertaking directed by him: but that he was to furnish a Preface and Life to any poet the booksellers pleased. I asked him if he would do this to any dunce's works, if they should ask him. JOHNSON. 'Yes, Sir, and *say* he was a dunce.' My friend seemed now not much to rel-ish talking of this edition.

On Monday, September 15, Dr. Johnson observed, that every body commended such parts of his *Journey to the Western Islands,* as were in their own way. 'For instance, (said he,) Mr. Jackson (the all-knowing) told me there was more good sense upon trade in it, than he should hear in the House of Commons in a year, except from Burke. Jones commended the part which treats of language; Burke that which describes the inhabitants of mountainous countries.'

After breakfast, Johnson carried me to see the garden be-longing to the school of Ashbourne, which is very prettily formed upon a bank, rising gradually behind the house. The Reverend Mr. Langley, the head-master, accompanied us.

While we sat basking in the sun upon a seat here, I intro-duced a common subject of complaint, the very small salaries which many curates have, and I maintained, 'that no man should be invested with the character of a clergyman, unless he has a security for such an income as will enable him to appear respectable; that, therefore, a clergyman should not be allowed to have a curate, unless he gives him a hundred pounds a year; if he cannot do that, let him perform the duty himself.' JOHNSON. 'To be sure, Sir, it is wrong that any clergyman should be without a reasonable income; but as the church revenues were sadly diminished at the Reformation, the clergy who have livings cannot afford, in many instances, to give good salaries to curates, without leaving themselves too little; and, if no curate were to be permitted unless he had a hundred pounds a year, their number would be very small, which would be a disadvantage, as then there would not be such choice in the nursery for the church, curates being candidates for the higher ecclesiastical offices, according to their merit and good behaviour.' He explained the system of the English Hierarchy exceedingly well. 'It is not thought fit (said he,) to trust a man with the care of a parish till he has given proof as a curate that he shall deserve such a trust.' This is an excellent *theory;* and if the *practice* were according to it, the Church of England would be admirable indeed. However, as I have heard Dr. Johnson observe as to the Universities, bad practice does not infer that the *constitution* is bad.

We had with us at dinner several of Dr. Taylor's neighbours, good civil gentlemen, who seemed to understand Dr. Johnson very well, and not to consider him in the light that a certain person did, who being struck, or rather stunned by his voice and manner, when he was afterwards asked what he thought of him, answered, 'He's a tremendous companion.'

Johnson told me, that 'Taylor was a very sensible acute man, and had a strong mind; that he had great activity in some respects, and yet such a sort of indolence, that if you should put a pebble upon his chimney-piece, you would find it there, in the same state, a year afterwards.'

And here is the proper place to give an account of Johnson's humane and zealous interference in behalf of the Reverend Dr. William Dodd, formerly Prebendary of Brecon, and chaplain in ordinary to his Majesty; celebrated as a very popular preacher, an encourager of charitable institutions, and author of a variety of works, chiefly theological. Having unhappily contracted expensive habits of living, partly occasioned by licentiousness of manners, he in an evil hour, when pressed by want of money, and dreading an exposure of his circumstances, forged a bond of which he attempted to avail himself to support his credit, flattering himself with hopes that he might be able to repay its amount without being detected. The person, whose name he thus rashly and criminally presumed to falsify, was the Earl of Chesterfield, to whom he had been tutor, and who, he perhaps, in the warmth of his feelings, flattered himself would have generously paid the money in case of an alarm being taken, rather than suffer him to fall a victim to the dreadful consequences of violating the law against forgery, the most dangerous crime in a commercial country; but the unfortunate divine had the mortification to find that he was mistaken. His noble pupil appeared against him, and he was capitally convicted.

Johnson told me that Dr. Dodd was very little acquainted with him, having been but once in his company, many years previous to this period (which was precisely the state of my own acquaintance with Dodd); but in his distress he bethought himself of Johnson's persuasive power of writing, if haply it might avail to obtain for him the Royal Mercy. He did not apply to him directly, but, extraordinary as it may seem, through the late Countess of Harrington, who wrote a letter to Johnson, asking him to employ his pen in favour of Dodd. Mr. Allen, the printer, who was Johnson's landlord and next neighbour in Bolt-court, and for whom he had much kindness, was one of Dodd's friends, of whom, to the credit of humanity be it recorded, that he had many who did not desert him, even after his infringement of the law had reduced him to the state of a man under sentence of death. Mr. Allen told me that he carried Lady Harrington's letter to Johnson, that Johnson read it walking up and down his chamber, and seemed much agitated, after which he said, 'I will do what I can;'—and certainly he did make extraordinary exertions.

He this evening, as he had obligingly promised in one of his letters, put into my hands the whole series of his writings upon this melancholy occasion, and I shall present my readers with the abstract which I made from the collection; in doing which I studied to avoid copying what had appeared in print, and now make part of the edition of *Johnson's Works*, published by the Booksellers of London, but taking care to mark Johnson's variations in some of the pieces there exhibited.

Dr. Johnson wrote in the first place, Dr. Dodd's *Speech to the Recorder of London*, at the Old-Bailey, when sentence of death was about to be pronounced upon him.

He wrote also *The Convict's Address to his unhappy Brethren*, a sermon delivered by Dr. Dodd, in the chapel of Newgate. . . . The other pieces written by Johnson in the above-mentioned collection, are two letters, one to the Lord Chancellor Bathurst, (not Lord North, as is erroneously supposed,) and one to Lord Mansfield;—A Petition from Dr. Dodd to the King;—A Petition from Mrs. Dodd to the Queen;—Observations of some length inserted in the newspapers, on occasion of Earl Percy's having presented to his Majesty a petition for mercy to Dodd, signed by twenty thousand people, but all in vain. He told me that he had also written a petition from the city of London; 'but (said he, with a significant smile) they *mended* it.'

The last of these articles which Johnson wrote is *Dr. Dodd's last solemn Declaration*, which he left with the sheriff at the place of execution. Here also my friend marked the variations on a copy of that piece now in my possession. Dodd inserted, 'I never knew or attended to the calls of frugality, or the needful minuteness of painful œconomy;' and in the next sentence he introduced the words which I distinguish by *Italicks;* 'My life for some *few unhappy* years past has been *dreadfully erroneous.*' Johnson's expression was *hypocritical;* but his remark on the margin is 'With this he said he could not charge himself.' . . .

All applications for the Royal Mercy having failed, Dr. Dodd prepared himself for death; and, with a warmth of gratitude, wrote to Dr. Johnson as follows:—

'June 25, *Midnight.*

'Accept, thou *great* and *good* heart, my earnest and fervent thanks and prayers for all thy benevolent and kind efforts in my behalf.—Oh! Dr. Johnson! as I sought your knowledge at an early hour in life, would to heaven I had cultivated the love and acquaintance of so excellent a man!—I pray GOD most sincerely to bless you with the highest transports—the infelt satisfaction of *humane* and benevolent exertions!—And admitted, as I trust I shall be, to the realms of bliss before you, I shall hail *your* arrival there with transport, and rejoice to acknowledge that you was my Comforter, my Advocate, and my *Friend!* GOD *be ever* with *you!*'

Dr. Johnson lastly wrote to Dr. Dodd this solemn and soothing letter:—

'*To* THE REVEREND DR. DODD

'DEAR SIR,—That which is appointed to all men is now coming upon you. Outward circumstances, the eyes and the thoughts of men, are below the notice of an immortal being about to stand the trial for eternity, before the Supreme Judge of heaven and earth. Be comforted: your crime, morally or religiously considered, has no very deep dye of turpitude. It corrupted no man's principles; it attacked no man's life. It involved only a temporary and reparable injury. Of this, and of all other sins, you are earnestly to repent; and may GOD, who knoweth our frailty, and desireth not our death, accept your repentance, for the sake of his Son JESUS CHRIST our Lord.

'In requital of those well-intended offices which you are pleased so emphatically to acknowledge, let me beg that you make in your devotions one petition for my eternal welfare. I am, dear Sir, your affectionate servant,

'June 26, 1777.'   'SAM. JOHNSON.'

Under the copy of this letter I found written, in Johnson's own hand, 'Next day, June 27, he was executed.' . . .

Johnson gave us this evening, in his happy discriminative

394

manner, a portrait of the late Mr. Fitzherbert, of Derbyshire. 'There was (said he,) no sparkle, no brilliancy in Fitzherbert; but I never knew a man who was so generally acceptable. He made every body quite easy, overpowered nobody by the superiority of his talents, made no man think worse of himself by being his rival, seemed always to listen, did not oblige you to hear much from him, and did not oppose what you said. Every body liked him; but he had no friend, as I understand the word, nobody with whom he exchanged intimate thoughts. People were willing to think well of every thing about him. A gentleman was making an affected rant, as many people do, of great feelings about "his dear son," who was at school near London; how anxious he was lest he might be ill, and what he would give to see him. "Can't you (said Fitzherbert), take a post-chaise and go to him." This, to be sure, *finished* the affected man, but there was not much in it. However, this was circulated as wit for a whole winter, and I believe part of a summer too; a proof that he was no very witty man. He was an instance of the truth of the observation, that a man will please more upon the whole by negative qualities than by positive; by never offending, than by giving a great deal of delight. In the first place, men hate more steadily than they love; and if I have said something to hurt a man once, I shall not get the better of this by saying many things to please him.'

Tuesday, September 16, Dr. Johnson having mentioned to me the extraordinary size and price of some cattle reared by Dr. Taylor, I rode out with our host, surveyed his farm, and was shown one cow which he had sold for a hundred and twenty guineas, and another for which he had been offered a hundred and thirty. Taylor thus described to me his old schoolfellow and friend, Johnson: 'He is a man of a very clear head, great power of words, and a very gay imagination; but there is no disputing with him. He will not hear you, and having a louder voice than you, must roar you down.'

In the afternoon I tried to get Dr. Johnson to like the Poems of Mr. Hamilton of Bangour, which I had brought with me: I had been much pleased with them at a very early age; the impression still remained on my mind; it was confirmed by the opinion of my friend the Honourable Andrew Erskine, himself both a good poet and a good critick, who thought Hamilton as true a poet as ever wrote, and that his not having fame was unaccountable. Johnson, upon repeated occasions, while I was at Ashbourne, talked slightingly of Hamilton. He said there was no power of thinking in his verses, nothing that strikes one, nothing better than what you generally find in magazines; and that the highest praise they deserved was, that they were very well for a gentleman to hand about among his friends. He said the imitation of *Ne sit ancillæ tibi amor, &c.*[1] was too solemn; he read part of it at the beginning. He read the beautiful pathetick song, *Ah the poor shepherd's mournful fate,* and did not seem to give attention to what I had been used to think tender elegant strains, but laughed at the rhyme, in Scotch pronunciation, *wishes* and *blushes,* reading *wushes*—and there he stopped. He owned that the epitaph on Lord Newhall was pretty well done. He read the *Inscription in a Summer-house,* and a little of the imitations of Horace's *Epistles;* but said, he found nothing to make him desire to read on. When I urged that there were some good poetical passages in the book, 'Where (said he,) will you find so large a collection without some?' I thought the description of Winter might obtain his approbation:

> 'See Winter, from the frozen north
> Drives his iron chariot forth!
> His grisly hand in icy chains
> Fair Tweeda's silver flood constrains,' &c.

He asked why an '*iron* chariot'? and said 'icy chains' was an old image. I was struck with the uncertainty of taste, and somewhat sorry that a poet whom I had long read with fondness, was not approved by Dr. Johnson. I comforted myself with thinking that the beauties were too delicate for his robust perceptions. Garrick maintained that he had not a taste for the finest productions of genius: but I was sensible, that when he took the trouble to analyse critically, he generally convinced us that he was right.

In the evening, the Reverend Mr. Seward, of Lichfield, who was passing through Ashbourne in his way home, drank tea with us. Johnson described him thus:—'Sir, his ambition is to be a fine talker; so he goes to Buxton, and such places, where he may find companies to listen to him. And, Sir, he is a valetudinarian, one of those who are always mending themselves. I do not know a more disagreeable character than a valetudinarian, who thinks he may do any thing that is for his ease, and indulges himself in the grossest freedoms: Sir, he brings himself to the state of a hog in a stye.'

Dr. Taylor's nose happening to bleed, he said, it was because he had omitted to have himself blooded four days after a quarter of a year's interval. Dr. Johnson, who was a great dabbler in physick, disapproved much of periodical bleeding.

[1] 'Your love for your maidservant need not make you blush.' Horace, *Odes,* II. iv. 1.

'For (said he,) you accustom yourself to an evacuation which Nature cannot perform of herself, and therefore she cannot help you, should you, from forgetfulness or any other cause, omit it; so you may be suddenly suffocated. You may accustom yourself to other periodical evacuations, because should you omit them, Nature can supply the omission; but Nature cannot open a vein to blood you.'—'I do not like to take an emetick, (said Taylor,) for fear of breaking some small vessels.'—'Poh! (said Johnson,) if you have so many things that will break, you had better break your neck at once, and there's an end on't. You will break no small vessels:' (blowing with high derision.)

I mentioned to Dr. Johnson, that David Hume's persisting in his infidelity, when he was dying, shocked me much. JOHNSON. 'Why should it shock you, Sir? Hume owned he had never read the New Testament with attention. Here then was a man, who had been at no pains to inquire into the truth of religion, and had continually turned his mind the other way. It was not to be expected that the prospect of death would alter his way of thinking, unless GOD should send an angel to set him right.' I said, I had reason to believe that the thought of annihilation gave Hume no pain. JOHNSON. 'It was not so, Sir. He had a vanity in being thought easy. It is more probable that he should assume an appearance of ease, than that so very improbable a thing should be, as a man not afraid of going (as, in spite of his delusive theory, he cannot be sure but he may go,) into an unknown state, and not being uneasy at leaving all he knew. And you are to consider, that upon his own principle of annihilation he had no motive to speak the truth.' The horrour of death which I had always observed in Dr. Johnson, appeared strong to-night. I ventured to tell him, that I had been, for moments in my life, not afraid of death; therefore I could suppose another man in that state of mind for a considerable space of time. He said, 'he never had a moment in which death was not terrible to him.' He added, that it had been observed, that scarce any man dies in publick, but with apparent resolution; from that desire of praise which never quits us. I said, Dr. Dodd seemed to be willing to die, and full of hopes of happiness. 'Sir, (said he,) Dr. Dodd would have given both his hands and both his legs to have lived. The better a man is, the more afraid he is of death, having a clearer view of infinite purity.' He owned, that our being in an unhappy uncertainty as to our salvation, was mysterious; and said, 'Ah! we must wait till we are in another state of being, to have many things explained to us.' Even the powerful mind of Johnson seemed foiled by futurity. But I thought, that the gloom of uncertainty in solemn religious speculation, being mingled with hope, was yet more consolatory than the emptiness of infidelity. A man can live in thick air, but perishes in an exhausted receiver.

Dr. Johnson was much pleased with a remark which I told him was made to me by General Paoli:—'That it is impossible not to be afraid of death; and that those who at the time of dying are not afraid, are not thinking of death, but of applause, or something else, which keeps death out of their sight: so that all men are equally afraid of death when they see it; only some have a power of turning their sight away from it better than others.'

On Wednesday, September 17, Dr. Butter, physician at Derby, drank tea with us; and it was settled that Dr. Johnson and I should go on Friday and dine with him. Johnson said, 'I'm glad of this.' He seemed weary of the uniformity of life at Dr. Taylor's.

Talking of biography, I said, in writing a life, a man's peculiarities should be mentioned, because they mark his character. JOHNSON. 'Sir, there is no doubt as to peculiarities: the question is, whether a man's vices should be mentioned; for instance, whether it should be mentioned that Addison and Parnell drank too freely: for people will probably more easily indulge in drinking from knowing this; so that more ill may be done by the example than good by telling the whole truth.' Here was an instance of his varying from himself in talk; for when Lord Hailes and he sat one morning calmly conversing in my house at Edinburgh, I well remember that Dr. Johnson maintained, that 'If a man is to write *A Panegyrick,* he may keep vices out of sight; but if he professes to write *A Life,* he must represent it really as it was:' and when I objected to the danger of telling that Parnell drank to excess, he said, that 'it would produce an instructive caution to avoid drinking, when it was seen, that even the learning and genius of Parnell could be debased by it.' And in the Hebrides he maintained, as appears from my *Journal,* that a man's intimate friend should mention his faults, if he writes his life.

He had this evening, partly, I suppose, from the spirit of contradiction to his Whig friend, a violent argument with Dr. Taylor, as to the inclinations of the people of England at this time towards the Royal Family of Stuart. He grew so outrageous as to say, 'that, if England were fairly polled, the present King would be sent away to-night, and his adherents hanged tomorrow.' Taylor, who was as violent a Whig as Johnson was a Tory, was roused by this to a pitch of bellowing. He denied, loudly, what Johnson said; and maintained, that there was an abhorrence against the Stuart family, though he admitted that the people were not much attached to the present King. JOHNSON. 'Sir, the state of the country is this: the people knowing it to be agreed on all hands that this King has not the hereditary right to the crown, and there being no hope that he who has it can be restored, have grown cold and indifferent upon the subject of loyalty, and have no warm attachment to any King. They would not, therefore, risk any thing to restore the exiled family. They would not give twenty shillings a piece to bring it about. But, if a mere vote could do it, there would be twenty to one; at least, there would be a very great majority of voices for it. For, Sir, you are to consider, that all those who think a King has a right to his crown, as a man has to his estate, which is the just opinion, would be for restoring the King who certainly has the hereditary right, could he be trusted with it; in which there would be no danger now, when laws and every thing else are so much advanced: and every King will govern by the laws. And you must also consider, Sir, that there is nothing on the other side to oppose to this; for it is not alledged by any one that the present family has any inherent right: so that the Whigs could not have a contest between two rights.'

Dr. Taylor admitted, that if the question as to hereditary right were to be tried by a poll of the people of England, to be sure the abstract doctrine would be given in favour of the family of Stuart; but he said, the conduct of that family, which occasioned their expulsion, was so fresh in the minds of the people, that they would not vote for a restoration. Dr. Johnson, I think, was contented with the admission as to the hereditary right, leaving the original point in dispute, *viz.* what the people upon the whole would do, taking in right and affection; for he said, people were afraid of a change, even though they think it right. Dr. Taylor said something of the slight foundation of the hereditary right of the house of Stuart. 'Sir, (said Johnson,) the house of Stuart succeeded to the full right of both the houses of York and Lancaster, whose common source had the undisputed right. A right to a throne is like a right to any thing else. Possession is sufficient, where no better right can be shown. This was the case with the Royal Family of England, as it is now with the King of France: for as to the first beginning of the right, we are in the dark.'

Thursday, September 18. Last night Dr. Johnson had proposed that the crystal lustre, or chandelier, in Dr. Taylor's large room, should be lighted up some time or other. Taylor said, it should be lighted up next night. 'That will do very well, (said I,) for it is Dr. Johnson's birth-day.' When we were in the Isle of Sky, Johnson had desired me not to mention his birth-day. He did not seem pleased at this time that I mentioned it, and said (somewhat sternly,) 'he would *not* have the lustre lighted the next day.'

Some ladies, who had been present yesterday when I mentioned his birth-day, came to dinner to-day, and plagued him unintentionally, by wishing him joy. I know not why he disliked having his birth-day mentioned, unless it were that it reminded him of his approaching nearer to death, of which he had a constant dread.

I mentioned to him a friend of mine[1] who was formerly gloomy from low spirits, and much distressed by the fear of death, but was now uniformly placid, and contemplated his dissolution without any perturbation. 'Sir, (said Johnson,) this is only a disordered imagination taking a different turn.'

We talked of a collection being made of all the English Poets who had published a volume of poems. Johnson told me 'that a Mr. Coxeter, whom he knew, had gone the greatest length towards this; having collected, I think, about five hundred volumes of poets whose works were little known; but that upon his death Tom Osborne bought them, and they were dispersed, which he thought a pity, as it was curious to see any series complete; and in every volume of poems something good may be found.'

He observed, that a gentleman of eminence in literature[2] had got into a bad style of poetry of late. 'He puts (said he,) a very common thing in a strange dress till he does not know it himself, and thinks other people do not know it.' BOSWELL. 'That is owing to his being so much versant in old English poetry.' JOHNSON. 'What is that to the purpose, Sir? If I say a man is drunk, and you tell me it is owing to his taking much drink, the matter is not mended. No, Sir, ———— has taken to an odd mode. For example, he'd write thus:

> "Hermit hoar, in solemn cell,
>   Wearing out life's evening gray."

Gray evening is common enough; but *evening gray* he'd think fine.—Stay;—we'll make out the stanza:

> "Hermit hoar, in solemn cell,
>   Wearing out life's evening gray;
> Smite thy bosom, sage, and tell,
>   What is bliss? and which the way?"'

1 George Dempster.
2 Tom Warton.

BOSWELL. 'But why smite his bosom, Sir?' JOHNSON. 'Why, to shew he was in earnest,' (smiling.)—He at an after period added the following stanza:

> 'Thus I spoke; and speaking sigh'd;
> —Scarce repress'd the starting tear;—
> When the smiling sage reply'd—
> —Come, my lad, and drink some beer.'

I cannot help thinking the first stanza very good solemn poetry, as also the three first lines of the second. Its last line is an excellent burlesque surprise on gloomy sentimental enquirers. And, perhaps, the advice is as good as can be given to a low-spirited dissatisfied being:—'Don't trouble your head with sickly thinking: take a cup, and be merry.'

Friday, September 19, after breakfast Dr. Johnson and I set out in Dr. Taylor's chaise to go to Derby. The day was fine, and we resolved to go by Keddlestone, the seat of Lord Scarsdale, that I might see his Lordship's fine house. I was struck with the magnificence of the building; and the extensive park, with the finest verdure, covered with deer, and cattle, and sheep, delighted me. The number of old oaks, of an immense size, filled me with a sort of respectful admiration: for one of them sixty pounds was offered. The excellent smooth gravel roads; the large piece of water formed by his Lordship from some small brooks, with a handsome barge upon it; the venerable Gothick church, now the family chapel, just by the house; in short, the grand group of objects agitated and distended my mind in a most agreeable manner. 'One should think (said I,) that the proprietor of all this *must* be happy.'—'Nay, Sir, (said Johnson,) all this excludes but one evil—poverty.'

Our names were sent up, and a well-drest elderly housekeeper, a most distinct articulator, shewed us the house; which I need not describe, as there is an account of it published in *Adam's Works in Architecture*. Dr. Johnson thought better of it to-day than when he saw it before; for he had lately attacked it violently, saying, 'It would do excellently for a town-hall. The large room with the pillars (said he,) would do for the Judges to sit in at the assizes; the circular room for a jury-chamber; and the rooms above for prisoners.' Still he thought the large room ill lighted, and of no use but for dancing in; and the bed-chambers but indifferent rooms; and that the immense sum which it cost was injudiciously laid out. Dr. Taylor had put him in mind of his *appearing* pleased with the house. 'But (said he,) that was when Lord Scarsdale was present. Politeness obliges us to appear pleased with a man's works when he is present. No man will be so ill bred

401

as to question you. You may therefore pay compliments without saying what is not true. I should say to Lord Scarsdale of his large room, "My Lord, this is the most *costly* room that I ever saw;" which is true.'

Dr. Manningham, physician in London, who was visiting at Lord Scarsdale's, accompanyed us through many of the rooms, and soon afterwards my Lord himself, to whom Dr. Johnson was known, appeared, and did the honours of the house. We talked of Mr. Langton. Johnson, with a warm vehemence of affectionate regard, exclaimed, 'The earth does not bear a worthier man than Bennet Langton.' We saw a good many fine pictures, which I think are described in one of *Young's Tours*. There is a printed catalogue of them which the housekeeper put into my hand; I should like to view them at leisure. I was much struck with Daniel interpreting Nebuchadnezzar's dream by Rembrandt. We were shown a pretty large library. In his Lordship's dressing-room lay Johnson's small *Dictionary:* he shewed it to me, with some eagerness, saying, 'Look'ye! *Quæ terra nostri non plena laboris.*'[1] He observed, also, Goldsmith's *Animated Nature;* and said, 'Here's our friend! The poor Doctor would have been happy to hear of this.'

In our way, Johnson strongly expressed his love of driving fast in a post-chaise. 'If (said he,) I had no duties, and no reference to futurity, I would spend my life in driving briskly in a post-chaise with a pretty woman; but she should be one who could understand me, and would add something to the conversation.' I observed, that we were this day to stop just where the Highland army did in 1745. JOHNSON. 'It was a noble attempt.' BOSWELL. 'I wish we could have an authentick history of it. JOHNSON. 'If you were not an idle dog you might write it, by collecting from every body what they can tell, and putting down your authorities.' BOSWELL. 'But I could not have the advantage of it in my life-time.' JOHNSON. 'You might have the satisfaction of its fame, by printing it in Holland; and as to profit, consider how long it was before writing came to be considered in a pecuniary view. Baretti says, he is the first man that ever received copy-money in Italy.' I said that I would endeavour to do what Dr. Johnson suggested; and I thought that I might write so as to venture to publish my *History of the Civil War in Great-Britain in 1745 and 1746,* without being obliged to go to a foreign press.

When we arrived at Derby, Dr. Butter accompanied us to

[1] 'What place does not know our work.' Adapted from Virgil, *Aeneid,* i. 460.

see the manufactory of china there. I admired the ingenuity and delicate art with which a man fashioned clay into a cup, a saucer, or a tea-pot, while a boy turned round a wheel to give the mass rotundity. I thought this as excellent in its species of power, as making good verses in *its* species. Yet I had no respect for this potter. Neither, indeed, has a man of any extent of thinking for a mere verse-maker, in whose numbers, however perfect, there is no poetry, no mind. The china was beautiful, but Dr. Johnson justly observed it was too dear; for that he could have vessels of silver, of the same size, as cheap as what were here made of porcelain.

I felt a pleasure in walking about Derby such as I always have in walking about any town to which I am not accustomed. There is an immediate sensation of novelty; and one speculates on the way in which life is passed in it, which, although there is a sameness every where upon the whole, is yet minutely diversified. The minute diversities in every thing are wonderful. Talking of shaving the other night at Dr. Taylor's, Dr. Johnson said, 'Sir, of a thousand shavers, two do not shave so much alike as not to be distinguished.' I thought this not possible, till he specified so many of the varieties in shaving;—holding the razor more or less perpendicular;—drawing long or short strokes;—beginning at the upper part of the face, or the under;—at the right side or the left side. Indeed, when one considers what variety of sounds can be uttered by the windpipe, in the compass of a very small aperture, we may be convinced how many degrees of difference there may be in the application of a razor.

We dined with Dr. Butter, whose lady is daughter of my cousin, Sir John Douglas, whose grandson is now presumptive heir of the noble family of Queensberry. Johnson and he had a good deal of medical conversation. Johnson said, he had somewhere or other given an account of Dr. Nichols's discourse *De Animâ Medicâ*. He told us 'that whatever a man's distemper was, Dr. Nichols would not attend him as a physician, if his mind was not at ease; for he believed that no medicines would have any influence. He once attended a man in trade, upon whom he found none of the medicines he prescribed had any effect: he asked the man's wife privately whether his affairs were not in a bad way? She said no. He continued his attendance some time, still without success. At length the man's wife told him, she had discovered that her husband's affairs *were* in a bad way. When Goldsmith was dying, Dr. Turton said to him, "Your pulse is in greater disorder than it should be, from the degree of fever which you have: is your mind at ease?" Goldsmith answered it was not.'

After dinner, Mrs. Butter went with me to see the silk-mill

which Mr. John Lombe had had a patent for, having brought away the contrivance from Italy. I am not very conversant with mechanicks; but the simplicity of this machine, and its multiplied operations, struck me with an agreeable surprize. I had learnt from Dr. Johnson, during this interview, not to think with a dejected indifference of the works of art, and the pleasures of life, because life is uncertain and short; but to consider such indifference as a failure of reason, a morbidness of mind; for happiness should be cultivated as much as we can, and the objects which are instrumental to it should be steadily considered as of importance, with a reference not only to ourselves, but to multitudes in successive ages. . . .

Dr. Johnson told us at tea, that when some of Dr. Dodd's pious friends were trying to console him by saying that he was going to leave 'a wretched world,' he had honesty enough not to join in the cant:—'No, no, (said he,) it has been a very agreeable world to me.' Johnson added, 'I respect Dodd for thus speaking the truth; for, to be sure, he had for several years enjoyed a life of great voluptuousness.'

He told us, that Dodd's city friends stood by him so, that a thousand pounds were ready to be given to the gaoler, if he would let him escape. He added, that he knew a friend of Dodd's, who walked about Newgate for some time on the evening before the day of his execution, with five hundred pounds in his pocket, ready to be paid to any of the turnkeys who could get him out: but it was too late; for he was watched with much circumspection. He said, Dodd's friends had an image of him made of wax, which was to have been left in his place; and he believed it was carried into the prison.

Johnson disapproved of Dr. Dodd's leaving the world persuaded that *The Convict's Address to his unhappy Brethren* was of his own writing. 'But, Sir, (said I,) you contributed to the deception; for when Mr. Seward expressed a doubt to you that it was not Dodd's own, because it had a great deal more force of mind in it than any thing known to be his, you answered,—"Why should you think so? Depend upon it, Sir, when a man knows he is to be hanged in a fortnight, it concentrates his mind wonderfully."' JOHNSON. 'Sir, as Dodd got it from me to pass as his own, while that could do him any good, there was an *implied promise* that I should not own it. To own it, therefore, would have been telling a lie, with the addition of breach of promise, which was worse than simply telling a lie to make it be believed it was Dodd's. Besides, Sir, I did not *directly* tell a lie: I left the matter uncertain. Perhaps I thought that Seward would not believe it the less to be mine for what I said; but I would not put it in his power to say I had owned it.' . . .

He said, 'Goldsmith was a plant that flowered late. There appeared nothing remarkable about him when he was young; though when he had got high in fame, one of his friends[1] began to recollect something of his being distinguished at College. Goldsmith in the same manner recollected more of that friend's early years, as he grew a greater man.'

I mentioned that Lord Monboddo told me, he awaked every morning at four, and then for his health got up and walked in his room naked, with the window open, which he called taking *an air bath;* after which he went to bed again, and slept two hours more. Johnson, who was always ready to beat down any thing that seemed to be exhibited with disproportionate importance, thus observed: 'I suppose, Sir, there is no more in it than this, he awakes at four, and cannot sleep till he chills himself, and makes the warmth of the bed a grateful sensation.'

I talked of the difficulty of rising in the morning. Dr. Johnson told me, 'that the learned Mrs. Carter, at that period when she was eager in study, did not awake as early as she wished, and she therefore had a contrivance, that, at a certain hour, her chamber-light should burn a string to which a heavy weight was suspended, which then fell with a strong sudden noise: this roused her from sleep, and then she had no difficulty in getting up.' But I said *that* was my difficulty; and wished there could be some medicine invented which would make one rise without pain, which I never did, unless after lying in bed a very long time. Perhaps there may be something in the stores of Nature which could do this. I have thought of a pulley to raise me gradually; but that would give me pain, as it would counteract my internal inclination. I would have something that can dissipate the *vis inertiæ*[2] and give elasticity to the muscles. As I imagine that the human body may be put, by the operation of other substances, into any state in which it has ever been; and as I have experienced a state in which rising from bed was not disagreeable, but easy, nay, sometimes agreeable; I suppose that this state may be produced, if we knew by what. We can heat the body, we can cool it; we can give it tension or relaxation; and surely it is possible to bring it into a state in which rising from bed will not be a pain.

Johnson observed, that 'a man should take a sufficient quantity of sleep, which Dr. Mead says is between seven and

1 Burke.
2 'The power of inertness.'

nine hours.' I told him, that Dr. Cullen said to me, that a man should not take more sleep than he can take at once. JOHNSON. 'This rule, Sir, cannot hold in all cases; for many people have their sleep broken by sickness; and surely, Cullen would not have a man to get up, after having slept but an hour. Such a regimen would soon end in a *long sleep*.' Dr. Taylor remarked, I think very justly, that 'a man who does not feel an inclination to sleep at the ordinary time, instead of being stronger than other people, must not be well; for a man in health has all the natural inclinations to eat, drink, and sleep, in a strong degree.'

Johnson advised me to-night not to *refine* in the education of my children. 'Life (said he,) will not bear refinement: you must do as other people do.'

As we drove back to Ashbourne, Dr. Johnson recommended to me, as he had often done, to drink water only: 'For (said he,) you are then sure not to get drunk; whereas if you drink wine you are never sure.' I said, drinking wine was a pleasure which I was unwilling to give up. 'Why, Sir, (said he,) there is no doubt that not to drink wine is a great deduction from life; but it may be necessary.' He however owned, that in his opinion a free use of wine did not shorten life; and said, he would not give less for the life of a certain Scotch Lord (whom he named)[1] celebrated for hard drinking, than for that of a sober man. 'But stay, (said he, with his usual intelligence, and accuracy of enquiry,) does it take much wine to make him drunk?' I answered, 'a great deal either of wine or strong punch.'—'Then (said he,) that is the worse.' I presume to illustrate my friend's observation thus: 'A fortress which soon surrenders has its walls less shattered than when a long and obstinate resistance is made.'

I ventured to mention a person[2] who was as violent a Scotsman as he was an Englishman; and literally had the same contempt for an Englishman compared with a Scotsman, that he had for a Scotsman compared with an Englishman; and that he would say of Dr. Johnson, 'Damned rascal! to talk as he does of the Scotch.' This seemed, for a moment, 'to give him pause.' It, perhaps, presented his extreme prejudice against the Scotch in a point of view somewhat new to him, by the effect of *contrast*.

By the time when we returned to Ashbourne, Dr. Taylor was gone to bed. Johnson and I sat up a long time by ourselves.

He was much diverted with an article which I shewed him

[1] Archibald, 11th Earl of Eglinton.
[2] Archibald, 11th Earl of Eglinton.

in the *Critical Review* of this year, giving an account of a curious publication, entitled, *A Spiritual Diary and Soliloquies,* by John Rutty, M.D. Dr. Rutty was one of the people called Quakers, a physician of some eminence in Dublin, and authour of several works. This Diary, which was kept from 1753 to 1775, the year in which he died, and was now published in two volumes octavo, exhibited, in the simplicity of his heart, a minute and honest register of the state of his mind; which, though frequently laughable enough, was not more so than the history of many men would be, if recorded with equal fairness.

The following specimens were extracted by the Reviewers:—
'Tenth month, 1753.

23. Indulgence in bed an hour too long.

Twelfth month, 17. An hypochondriack obnubilation from wind and indigestion.

Ninth month, 28. An over-dose of whisky.

29. A dull, cross, cholerick day.

First month, 1757—22. A little swinish at dinner and repast.

31. Dogged on provocation.

Second month, 5. Very dogged or snappish.

14. Snappish on fasting.

26. Cursed snappishness to those under me, on a bodily indisposition.

Third month, 11. On a provocation, exercised a dumb resentment for two days, instead of scolding.

22. Scolded too vehemently.

23. Dogged again.

Fourth month, 29. Mechanically and sinfully dogged.'

Johnson laughed heartily at this good Quietist's self-condemning minutes; particularly at his mentioning, with such a serious regret, occasional instances of *'swinishness* in eating, and *doggedness of temper.'* . . .

I mentioned to him that Dr. Hugh Blair, in his lectures on Rhetorick and Belles Lettres, which I heard him deliver at Edinburgh, had animadverted on the Johnsonian style as too pompous; and attempted to imitate it, by giving a sentence of Addison in *The Spectator,* No. 411, in the manner of Johnson. When treating of the utility of the pleasures of imagination in preserving us from vice, it is observed of those 'who know not how to be idle and innocent,' that 'their very first step out of business is into vice or folly;' which Dr. Blair supposed wou'd have been expressed in *The Rambler* thus: 'Their very first step out of the regions of business is into the perturbation of vice, or the vacuity of folly.' JOHNSON. 'Sir, these are not the words I should have used. No, Sir; the imitators of my style have not hit it. Miss Aikin has done it the best; for she has imitated the sentiment as well as the diction.' . . .

In Baretti's Review, which he published in Italy, under the title of *Frusta Letteraria,* it is observed, that Dr. Robertson the historian had formed his style upon that of *Il celebre Samuele Johnson.* My friend himself was of that opinion; for he once said to me, in a pleasant humour, 'Sir, if Robertson's style be faulty, he owes it to me; that is, having too many words, and those too big ones.'

I read to him a letter which Lord Monboddo had written to me, containing some critical remarks upon the style of his *Journey to the Western Islands of Scotland.* His Lordship praised the very fine passage upon landing at Icolmkill; but his own style being exceedingly dry and hard, he disapproved of the richness of Johnson's language, and of his frequent use of metaphorical expressions. JOHNSON. 'Why, Sir, this criticism would be just, if in my style, superfluous words, or words too big for the thoughts, could be pointed out; but this I do not believe can be done. For instance; in the passage which Lord Monboddo admires, 'We were now treading that illustrious region,' the word *illustrious,* contributes nothing to the mere narration; for the fact might be told without it: but it is not, therefore, superfluous; for it wakes the mind to peculiar attention, where something of more than usual importance is to be presented. "Illustrious!" for what? and then the sentence proceeds to expand the circumstances connected with Iona. And, Sir, as to metaphorical expression, that is a great excellence in style, when it is used with propriety, for it gives you two ideas for one;—conveys the meaning more luminously, and generally with a perception of delight.' . . .

On Saturday, September 20, after breakfast, when Taylor was gone out to his farm, Dr. Johnson and I had a serious conversation by ourselves on melancholy and madness; which he was, I always thought, erroneously inclined to confound together. Melancholy, like 'great wit,' may be 'near allied to madness;' but there is, in my opinion, a distinct separation between them. When he talked of madness, he was to be understood as speaking of those who were in any great degree disturbed, or as it is commonly expressed, 'troubled in mind.' Some of the ancient philosophers held, that all deviations from right reason were madness; and whoever wishes to see the opinions both of ancients and moderns upon this subject, collected and illustrated with a variety of curious facts, may read Dr. Arnold's very entertaining work.

Johnson said, 'A madman loves to be with people whom he fears; not as a dog fears the lash; but of whom he stands in awe.' I was struck with the justice of this observation. To be with those of whom a person, whose mind is wavering and dejected, stands in awe, represses and composes an uneasy tumult of spirits, and consoles him with the contemplation of something steady, and at least comparatively great.

He added, 'Madmen are all sensual in the lower stages of the distemper. They are eager for gratifications to sooth their minds, and divert their attention from the misery which they suffer: but when they grow very ill, pleasure is too weak for them, and they seek for pain. Employment, Sir, and hardships, prevent melancholy. I suppose in all our army in America there was not one man who went mad.'

We entered seriously upon a question of much importance to me, which Johnson was pleased to consider with friendly attention. I had long complained to him that I felt myself discontented in Scotland, as too narrow a sphere, and that I wished to make my chief residence in London, the great scene of ambition, instruction, and amusement: a scene, which was to me, comparatively speaking, a heaven upon earth. JOHNSON. 'Why, Sir, I never knew any one who had such a *gust* for London as you have: and I cannot blame you for your wish to live there: yet, Sir, were I in your father's place, I should not consent to your settling there; for I have the old feudal notions, and I should be afraid that Auchinleck would be deserted, as you would soon find it more desirable to have a country-seat in a better climate. I own, however, that to consider it as a *duty* to reside on a family estate is a prejudice; for we must consider, that working-people get employment equally, and the produce of land is sold equally, whether a great family resides at home or not; and if the rents of an estate be carried to London, they return again in the circulation of commerce; nay, Sir, we must perhaps allow, that carrying the rents to a distance is a good, because it contributes to that circulation. We must, however, allow, that a well-regulated great family may improve a neighbourhood in civility and elegance, and give an example of good order, virtue, and piety; and so its residence at home may be of much advantage. But if a great family be disorderly and vicious, its residence at home is very pernicious to a neighbourhood. There is not now the same inducement to live in the country as formerly; the pleasures of social life are much better enjoyed in town; and there is no longer in the country that power and influence in proprietors of land which they had in old times, and which made the country so agreeable to them. The Laird of Auchinleck now is not near so great a man as the Laird of Auchinleck was a hundred years ago.'

I told him, that one of my ancestors never went from home without being attended by thirty men on horseback. Johnson's shrewdness and spirit of enquiry were exerted upon every occasion. 'Pray (said he,) how did your ancestor support his thirty men and thirty horses, when he went at a distance from home, in an age when there was hardly any money in circulation?' I suggested the same difficulty to a friend, who mentioned Douglas's going to the Holy Land with a numerous train of followers. Douglas could, no doubt, maintain followers enough while living upon his own lands, the produce of which supplied them with food; but he could not carry that food to the Holy Land; and as there was no commerce by which he could be supplied with money, how could he maintain them in foreign countries?

I suggested a doubt, that if I were to reside in London, the exquisite zest with which I relished it in occasional visits might go off, and I might grow tired of it. JOHNSON. 'Why, Sir, you find no man, at all intellectual, who is willing to leave London. No, Sir, when a man is tired of London, he is tired of life; for there is in London all that life can afford.'

To obviate his apprehension, that by settling in London I might desert the seat of my ancestors, I assured him, that I had old feudal principles to a degree of enthusiasm; and that I felt all the *dulcedo* of the *natale solum*.[1] I reminded him, that the Laird of Auchinleck had an elegant house, in front of which he could ride ten miles forward upon his own territories, upon which he had upwards of six hundred people attached to him; that the family seat was rich in natural romantick beauties of rock, wood, and water; and that in my 'morn of life.' I had appropriated the finest descriptions in the ancient Classicks to certain scenes there, which were thus associated in my mind. That when all this was considered, I should certainly pass a part of the year at home, and enjoy it the more from variety, and from bringing with me a share of the intellectual stores of the metropolis. He listened to all this, and kindly 'hoped it might be as I now supposed.'

He said, 'A country gentleman should bring his lady to visit London as soon as he can, that they may have agreeable topicks for conversation when they are by themselves.'

As I meditated trying my fortune in Westminster Hall, our conversation turned upon the profession of the law in England. JOHNSON. 'You must not indulge too sanguine hopes, should you be called to our bar. I was told, by a very

[1] 'Charm of the native soil.' Ovid, *Epistles from the Pontus*, I. iii. 35.

sensible lawyer, that there are a great many chances against any man's success in the profession of the law; the candidates are so numerous, and those who get large practice so few. He said, it was by no means true that a man of good parts and application is sure of having business, though he, indeed, allowed that if such a man could but appear in a few causes, his merit would be known, and he would get forward; but that the great risk was, that a man might pass half a life-time in the Courts, and never have an opportunity of shewing his abilities.'

We talked of employment being absolutely necessary to preserve the mind from wearying and growing fretful, especially in those who have a tendency to melancholy; and I mentioned to him a saying which somebody had related of an American savage, who, when an European was expatiating on all the advantages of money, put this question: 'Will it purchase *occupation?*' JOHNSON. 'Depend upon it, Sir, this saying is too refined for a savage. And, Sir, money *will* purchase occupation; it will purchase all the conveniencies of life; it will purchase variety of company; it will purchase all sorts of entertainment.'

I talked to him of Forster's *Voyage to the South Seas,* which pleased me; but I found he did not like it. 'Sir, (said he,) there is a great affectation of fine writing in it.' BOSWELL. 'But he carries you along with him.' JOHNSON. 'No, Sir; he does not carry *me* along with him: he leaves me behind him: or rather, indeed, he sets me before him; for he makes me turn over many leaves at a time.'

On Sunday, September 21, we went to the church of Ashbourne, which is one of the largest and most luminous that I have seen in any town of the same size. I felt great satisfaction in considering that I was supported in my fondness for solemn publick worship by the general concurrence and munificence of mankind.

Johnson and Taylor were so different from each other, that I wondered at their preserving such an intimacy. Their having been at school and college together, might, in some degree, account for this; but Sir Joshua Reynolds has furnished me with a stronger reason; for Johnson mentioned to him, that he had been told by Taylor he was to be his heir. I shall not take upon me to animadvert upon this; but certain it is, that Johnson paid great attention to Taylor. He now, however, said to me, 'Sir, I love him; but I do not love him more; my regard for him does not increase. As it is said in the Apocrypha, "his talk is of bullocks:" I do not suppose he is very fond of my company. His habits are by no means sufficiently clerical: this he knows that I see; and no man likes to live under the eye of perpetual disapprobation.'

I have no doubt that a good many sermons were composed for Taylor by Johnson. At this time I found, upon his table, a part of one which he had newly begun to write: and *Concio pro Tayloro*[1] appears in one of his diaries. When to these circumstances we add the internal evidence from the power of thinking and style, in the collection which the Reverend Mr. Hayes has published, with the *significant* title of 'Sermons *left for publication* by the Reverend John Taylor, LL.D.,' our conviction will be complete.

I, however, would not have it thought, that Dr. Taylor, though he could not write like Johnson, (as, indeed, who could?) did not sometimes compose sermons as good as those which we generally have from very respectable divines. He shewed me one with notes on the margin in Johnson's handwriting; and I was present when he read another to Johnson, that he might have his opinion of it, and Johnson said it was 'very well.' These, we may be sure, were not Johnson's; for he was above little arts, or tricks of deception.

Johnson was by no means of opinion, that every man of a learned profession should consider it as incumbent upon him, or as necessary to his credit, to appear as an authour. When in the ardour of ambition for literary fame, I regretted to him one day that an eminent Judge had nothing of it, and therefore would leave no perpetual monument of himself to posterity. 'Alas, Sir, (said Johnson,) what a mass of confusion should we have, if every Bishop, and every Judge, every Lawyer, Physician, and Divine, were to write books.'

I mentioned to Johnson a respectable person[2] of a very strong mind, who had little of that tenderness which is common to human nature; as an instance of which, when I suggested to him that he should invite his son,[3] who had been settled ten years in foreign parts, to come home and pay him a visit, his answer was, 'No, no, let him mind his business.' JOHNSON. 'I do not agree with him, Sir, in this. Getting money is not all a man's business: to cultivate kindness is a valuable part of the business of life.'

In the evening, Johnson, being in very good spirits, entertained us with several characteristical portraits. I regret that any of them escaped my retention and diligence. I found, from experience, that to collect my friend's conversation so as to exhibit it with any degree of its original flavour, it was

[1] 'A sermon for Taylor.'
[2] Lord Auchinleck.
[3] Boswell's brother, David.

necessary to write it down without delay. To record his sayings, after some distance of time, was like preserving or pickling long-kept and faded fruits, or other vegetables, which, when in that state, have little or nothing of their taste when fresh.

I shall present my readers with a series of what I gathered this evening from the Johnsonian garden.

'My friend, the late Earl of Corke, had a great desire to maintain the literary character of his family: he was a genteel man, but did not keep up the dignity of his rank. He was so generally civil, that nobody thanked him for it.'

'Did we not hear so much said of Jack Wilkes, we should think more highly of his conversation. Jack has great variety of talk, Jack is a scholar, and Jack has the manners of a gentleman. But after hearing his name sounded from pole to pole, as the phœnix of convivial felicity, we are disappointed in his company. He has always been *at me:* but I would do Jack a kindness, rather than not. The contest is now over.'

'Garrick's gaiety of conversation has delicacy and elegance: Foote makes you laugh more; but Foote has the air of a buffoon paid for entertaining the company. He, indeed, well deserves his hire.'

'Colley Cibber once consulted me as to one of his birth-day Odes, a long time before it was wanted. I objected very freely to several passages. Cibber lost patience, and would not read his Ode to an end. When we had done with criticism, we walked over to Richardson's, the authour of *Clarissa,* and I wondered to find Richardson displeased that I "did not treat Cibber with more *respect.*" Now, Sir, to talk of *respect* for a *player!*' (smiling disdainfully.) BOSWELL. 'There, Sir, you are always heretical: you never will allow merit to a player.' JOHNSON. 'Merit, Sir! what merit? Do you respect a rope-dancer, or a ballad-singer?' BOSWELL. 'No, Sir: but we respect a great player, as a man who can conceive lofty sentiments, and can express them gracefully.' JOHNSON. 'What, Sir, a fellow who claps a hump on his back, and a lump on his leg, and cries *"I am Richard the Third"*? Nay, Sir, a ballad-singer is a higher man, for he does two things; he repeats and he sings: there is both recitation and musick in his performance: the player only recites.' BOSWELL. 'My dear Sir! you may turn anything into ridicule. I allow, that a player of farce is not entitled to respect; he does a little thing: but he who can represent exalted characters, and touch the noblest passions, has very respectable powers; and mankind have agreed in admiring great talents for the stage. We must consider, too, that a great player does what very few are capable to do: his art is a very rare faculty. *Who* can repeat Hamlet's

413

soliloquy, "To be, or not to be," as Garrick does it?' JOHNSON. 'Any body may. Jemmy, there (a boy about eight years old, who was in the room,) will do it as well in a week.' BOSWELL. 'No, no, Sir: and as a proof of the merit of great acting, and of the value which mankind set upon it, Garrick has got a hundred thousand pounds.' JOHNSON. 'Is getting a hundred thousand pounds a proof of excellence? That has been done by a scoundrel commissary.'

This was most fallacious reasoning. I was *sure*, for once, that I had the best side of the argument. I boldly maintained the just distinction between a tragedian and a mere theatrical droll; between those who rouse our terrour and pity, and those who only make us laugh. 'If (said I,) Betterton and Foote were to walk into this room, you would respect Betterton much more than Foote.' JOHNSON. 'If Betterton were to walk into this room with Foote, Foote would soon drive him out of it. Foote, Sir, *quatenùs* Foote, has powers superiour to them all.'

On Monday, September 22, when at breakfast, I unguardedly said to Dr. Johnson, 'I wish I saw you and Mrs. Macaulay together.' He grew very angry; and, after a pause, while a cloud gathered on his brow, he burst out, 'No, Sir; you would not see us quarrel, to make you sport. Don't you know that it is very uncivil to *pit* two people against one another?' Then, checking himself, and wishing to be more gentle, he added, 'I do not say you should be hanged or drowned for this; but it *is* very uncivil.' Dr. Taylor thought him in the wrong, and spoke to him privately of it; but I afterwards acknowledged to Johnson that I was to blame, for I candidly owned, that I meant to express a desire to see a contest between Mrs. Macaulay and him; but then I knew how the contest would end; so that I was to see him triumph. JOHNSON. 'Sir, you cannot be sure how a contest will end; and no man has a right to engage two people in a dispute by which their passions may be inflamed, and they may part with bitter resentment against each other. I would sooner keep company with a man from whom I must guard my pockets, than with a man who contrives to bring me into a dispute with somebody that he may hear it. This is the great fault of ———, (naming one of our friends,) endeavouring to introduce a subject upon which he knows two people in the company differ.' BOSWELL. 'But he told me, Sir, he does it for instruction.' JOHNSON. 'Whatever the motive be, Sir, the man who does so, does very wrong. He has no more right to instruct himself at such a risk, than he has to make two people fight a duel, that he may learn how to defend himself.'

414

He found great fault with a gentleman[1] of our acquaintance for keeping a bad table. 'Sir, (said he,) when a man is invited to dinner, he is disappointed if he does not get something good. I advised Mrs. Thrale, who has no card-parties at her house, to give sweet-meats, and such good things, in an evening, as are not commonly given, and she would find company enough come to her; for every body loves to have things which please the palate put in their way, without trouble or preparation.' Such was his attention to the *minutiæ* of life and manners.

He thus characterised the Duke of Devonshire, grandfather of the present representative of that very respectable family: 'He was not a man of superiour abilities, but he was a man strictly faithful to his word. If, for instance, he had promised you an acorn, and none had grown that year in his woods, he would not have contented himself with that excuse; he would have sent to Denmark for it. So unconditional was he in keeping his word; so high as to the point of honour.' This was a liberal testimony from the Tory Johnson to the virtue of a great Whig nobleman.

Mr. Burke's *Letter to the Sheriffs of Bristol, on the affairs of America,* being mentioned, Johnson censured the composition much, and he ridiculed the definition of a free government, *viz.* 'For any practical purpose, it is what the people think so.'—'I will let the King of France govern me on those conditions, (said he,) for it is to be governed just as I please.' And when Dr. Taylor talked of a girl being sent to a parish workhouse, and asked how much she could be obliged to work, 'Why, (said Johnson,) as much as is reasonable: and what is that? as much as *she thinks* reasonable.'

Dr. Johnson obligingly proposed to carry me to see Islam, a romantick scene, now belonging to a family of the name of Port, but formerly the seat of the Congreves. I suppose it is well described in some of the Tours. Johnson described it distinctly and vividly, at which I could not but express to him my wonder; because, though my eyes, as he observed, were better than his, I could not by any means equal him in representing visible objects. I said, the difference between us in this respect was as that between a man who has a bad instrument, but plays well on it, and a man who has a good instrument, on which he can play very imperfectly.

I recollect a very fine amphitheatre, surrounded with hills covered with wood, and walks neatly formed along the side of a rocky steep, on the quarter next the house, with recesses under projections of rock, overshadowed with trees; in one of

---

[1] Langton, who is also referred to in the previous paragraph.

which recesses, we were told, Congreve wrote his *Old Bachelor*. We viewed a remarkable natural curiosity at Islam; two rivers bursting near each other from the rock, not from immediate springs, but after having run for many miles under ground. Plott, in his *History of Staffordshire*, gives an account of this curiosity; but Johnson would not believe it, though we had the attestation of the gardener, who said, he had put in corks, where the river *Manyfold* sinks into the ground, and had catched them in a net, placed before one of the openings where the water bursts out. Indeed, such subterraneous courses of water are found in various parts of our globe.

Talking of Dr. Johnson's unwillingness to believe extraordinary things, I ventured to say, 'Sir, you come near Hume's argument against miracles, "That it is more probable witnesses should lie, or be mistaken, than that they should happen." ' JOHNSON. 'Why, Sir, Hume, taking the proposition simply, is right. But the Christian revelation is not proved by the miracles alone, but as connected with prophecies, and with the doctrines in confirmation of which the miracles were wrought.'

He repeated his observation, that the differences among Christians are really of no consequence. 'For instance (said he,) if a Protestant objects to a Papist, "You worship images;" the Papist can answer, "I do not insist on *your* doing it; you may be a very good Papist without it: I do it only as a help to my devotion." ' I said, the great article of Christianity is the revelation of immortality. Johnson admitted it was.

In the evening, a gentleman-farmer, who was on a visit at Dr. Taylor's, attempted to dispute with Johnson in favour of Mungo Campbell, who shot Alexander, Earl of Eglintoune, upon his having fallen, when retreating from his Lordship, who he believed was about to seize his gun, as he had threatened to do. He said, he should have done just as Campbell did. JOHNSON. 'Whoever would do as Campbell did, deserves to be hanged; not that I could, as a juryman, have found him legally guilty of murder; but I am glad they found means to convict him.' The gentleman-farmer said, 'A poor man has as much honour as a rich man; and Campbell had *that* to defend.' Johnson exclaimed, 'A poor man has no honour.' The English yeoman, not dismayed, proceeded: 'Lord Eglintoune was a damned fool to run on upon Campbell, after being warned that Campbell would shoot him if he did.' Johnson, who could not bear any thing like swearing, angrily replied, 'He was *not* a *damned* fool: he only thought too well of Campbell. He did not believe Campbell would be such a *damned* scoundrel, as to do so *damned* a thing.' His emphasis on *damned,* accompanied with his frowning looks, reproved his opponent's want of decorum in *his* presence.

Talking of the danger of being mortified by rejection, when making approaches to the acquaintance of the great, I observed: 'I am, however, generally for trying, "Nothing venture, nothing have."' JOHNSON. 'Very true, Sir; but I have always been more afraid of failing, than hopeful of success.' And, indeed, though he had all just respect for rank, no man ever less courted the favour of the great.

During this interview at Ashbourne, Johnson seemed to be more uniformly social, cheerful, and alert, than I had almost ever seen him. He was prompt on great occasions and on small. Taylor, who praised every thing of his own to excess; in short, 'whose geese were all swans,' as the proverb says, expatiated on the excellence of his bull-dog, which, he told us, was 'perfectly well shaped.' Johnson, after examining the animal attentively, thus repressed the vain-glory of our host: —'No, Sir, he is *not* well shaped; for there is not the quick transition from the thickness of the fore-part, to the *tenuity* —the thin part—behind, which a bull-dog ought to have.' This *tenuity* was the only *hard word* that I heard him use during this interview, and it will be observed, he instantly put another expression in its place. Taylor said, a small bull-dog was as good as a large one. JOHNSON. 'No, Sir; for, in proportion to his size, he has strength: and your argument would prove, that a good bull-dog may be as small as a mouse.' It was amazing how he entered with perspicuity and keenness upon every thing that occurred in conversation. Most men, whom I know, would no more think of discussing a question about a bull-dog, than of attacking a bull.

I cannot allow any fragment whatever that floats in my memory concerning the great subject of this work to be lost. Though a small particular may appear trifling to some, it will be relished by others; while every little spark adds something to the general blaze: and to please the true, candid, warm admirers of Johnson, and in any degree increase the splendour of his reputation, I bid defiance to the shafts of ridicule, or even of malignity. Showers of them have been discharged at my *Journal of a Tour to the Hebrides;* yet it still sails unhurt along the stream of time, and, as an attendant upon Johnson,

'Pursues the triumph, and partakes the gale.'

One morning after breakfast, when the sun shone bright, we walked out together, and 'pored' for some time with placid indolence upon an artificial water-fall, which Dr. Taylor had made by building a strong dyke of stone across the river behind his garden. It was now somewhat obstructed by

417

branches of trees and other rubbish, which had come down the river, and settled close to it. Johnson, partly from a desire to see it play more freely, and partly from that inclination to activity which will animate, at times, the most inert and sluggish mortal, took a long pole which was lying on the bank, and pushed down several parcels of this wreck with painful assiduity, while I stood quietly by, wondering to behold the sage thus curiously employed, and smiling with an humorous satisfaction each time when he carried his point. He worked till he was quite out of breath; and having found a large dead cat so heavy that he could not move it after several efforts, 'Come,' said he, (throwing down the pole,) '*you* shall take it now;' which I accordingly did, and being a fresh man, soon made the cat tumble over the cascade. This may be laughed at as too trifling to record; but it is a small characteristick trait in the Flemish picture which I give of my friend, and in which, therefore I mark the most minute particulars. And let it be remembered, that *Æsop at play* is one of the instructive apologues of antiquity.

I mentioned an old gentleman[1] of our acquaintance whose memory was beginning to fail. JOHNSON. 'There must be a diseased mind, where there is a failure of memory at seventy. A man's head, Sir, must be morbid, if he fails so soon.' My friend, being now himself sixty-eight, might think thus: but I imagine, that *threescore and ten*, the Psalmist's period of sound human life, in later ages may have a failure, though there be no disease in the constitution.

Talking of Rochester's Poems, he said, he had given them to Mr. Steevens to castrate for the edition of the poets, to which he was to write Prefaces. Dr. Taylor (the only time I ever heard him say any thing witty) observed, that 'if Rochester had been castrated himself, his exceptionable poems would not have been written.' I asked if Burnet had not given a good Life of Rochester. JOHNSON. 'We have a good *Death*: there is not much *Life*.' I asked whether Prior's Poems were to be printed entire: Johnson said they were. I mentioned Lord Hailes's censure of Prior, in his Preface to a collection of *Sacred Poems,* by various hands, published by him at Edinburgh a great many years ago, where he mentions, 'those impure tales which will be the eternal opprobrium of their ingenious authour.' JOHNSON. 'Sir, Lord Hailes has forgot. There is nothing in Prior that will excite to lewdness. If Lord Hailes thinks there is, he must be more combustible than other people.' I instanced the tale of *Paulo Purganti and his Wife*. JOHNSON. 'Sir, there is nothing there, but that his wife

[1] Lord Auchinleck.

418

wanted to be kissed when poor Paulo was out of pocket. No, Sir, Prior is a lady's book. No lady is ashamed to have it standing in her library.'

The hypochondriack disorder being mentioned, Dr. Johnson did not think it so common as I supposed. 'Dr. Taylor (said he,) is the same one day as another. Burke and Reynolds are the same. Beauclerk, except when in pain, is the same. I am not so myself; but this I do not mention commonly.'

I complained of a wretched changefulness, so that I could not preserve, for any long continuance, the same views of any thing. It was most comfortable to me to experience, in Dr. Johnson's company, a relief from this uneasiness. His steady vigorous mind held firm before me those objects which my own feeble and tremulous imagination frequently presented, in such a wavering state, that my reason could not judge well of them.

Dr. Johnson advised me to-day, to have as many books about me as I could; that I might read upon any subject upon which I had a desire for instruction at the time. 'What you read *then* (said he,) you will remember; but if you have not a book immediately ready, and the subject moulds in your mind, it is a chance if you again have a desire to study it.' He added, 'If a man never has an eager desire for instruction, he should prescribe a task for himself. But it is better when a man reads from immediate inclination.'

He repeated a good many lines of Horace's *Odes*, while we were in the chaise. I remember particularly the Ode *Eheu fugaces*.[1]

He said, the dispute as to the comparative excellence of Homer or Virgil[2] was inaccurate. 'We must consider (said he,) whether Homer was not the greatest poet, though Virgil may have produced the finest poem. Virgil was indebted to Homer for the whole invention of the structure of an epick poem, and for many of his beauties.'

He told me that Bacon was a favourite authour with him; but he had never read his works till he was compiling the *English Dictionary*, in which, he said, I might see Bacon very often quoted. Mr. Seward recollects his having mentioned, that a Dictionary of the English Language might be compiled

[1] II. xiv.

[2] I am informed by Mr. Langton, that a great many years ago he was present when this question was agitated between Dr. Johnson and Mr. Burke; and, to use Johnson's phrase, they 'talked their best;' Johnson for Homer, Burke for Virgil. It may well be supposed to have been one of the ablest and most brilliant contests that ever was exhibited. How much must we regret that it has not been preserved—B.

from Bacon's writings alone, and that he had once an intention of giving an edition of Bacon, at least of his English works, and writing the Life of that great man. Had he executed this intention, there can be no doubt that he would have done it in a most masterly manner. Mallet's *Life of Bacon* has no inconsiderable merit as an acute and elegant dissertation relative to its subject; but Mallet's mind was not comprehensive enough to embrace the vast extent of Lord Verulam's genius and research. Dr. Warburton therefore observed, with witty justness, 'that Mallet, in his *Life of Bacon,* had forgotten that he was a philosopher; and if he should write the Life of the Duke of Marlborough, which he had undertaken to do, he would probably forget that he was a general.'

Wishing to be satisfied what degree of truth there was in a story which a friend[1] of Johnson's and mine had told me to his disadvantage, I mentioned it to him in direct terms; and it was to this effect: that a gentleman[2] who had lived in great intimacy with him, shewn him much kindness, and even relieved him from a spunging-house, having afterwards fallen into bad circumstances, was one day, when Johnson was at dinner with him, seized for debt, and carried to prison; that Johnson sat still undisturbed, and went on eating and drinking; upon which the gentleman's sister, who was present, could not suppress her indignation: 'What, Sir, (said she,) are you so unfeeling, as not even to offer to go to my brother in his distress; you who have been so much obliged to him?' And that Johnson answered, 'Madam, I owe him no obligation; what he did for me he would have done for a dog.'

Johnson assured me, that the story was absolutely false: but like a man conscious of being in the right, and desirous of completely vindicating himself from such a charge, he did not arrogantly rest on a mere denial, and on his general character, but proceeded thus:—'Sir, I was very intimate with that gentleman, and was once relieved by him from an arrest; but I never was present when he was arrested, never knew that he was arrested, and I believe he never was in difficulties after the time when he relieved me. I loved him much; yet, in talking of his general character, I may have said, though I do not remember that I ever did say so, that as his generosity proceeded from no principle, but was a part of his profusion, he would do for a dog what he would do for a friend: but I never applied this remark to any particular instance, and certainly not to his kindness to me. If a profuse man, who does not value his money, and gives a large sum to a whore, gives

1 Beauclerk.
2 The Hon. Henry Hervey.

half as much, or an equally large sum to relieve a friend, it cannot be esteemed as virtue. This was all that I could say of that gentleman; and, if said at all, it must have been said after his death. Sir, I would have gone to the world's end to relieve him. The remark about the dog, if made by me, was such a sally as might escape one when painting a man highly.'

On Tuesday, September 23, Johnson was remarkably cordial to me. It being necessary for me to return to Scotland soon, I had fixed on the next day for my setting out, and I felt a tender concern at the thought of parting with him. He had, at this time, frankly communicated to me many particulars, which are inserted in this work in their proper places; and once, when I happened to mention that the expence of my jaunt would come to much more than I had computed, he said, 'Why, Sir, if the expence were to be an inconvenience, you would have reason to regret it: but, if you have had the money to spend, I know not that you could have purchased as much pleasure with it in any other way.'

During this interview at Ashbourne, Johnson and I frequently talked with wonderful pleasure of mere trifles which had occurred in our tour to the Hebrides; for it had left a most agreeable and lasting impression upon his mind.

He found fault with me for using the phrase to *make* money. 'Don't you see (said he,) the impropriety of it? To *make* money is to *coin* it: you should say *get* money.' The phrase, however, is, I think, pretty current. But Johnson was at all times jealous of infractions upon the genuine English language, and prompt to repress colloquial barbarisms; such as, *pledging myself*, for *undertaking; line*, for *department* or *branch*, as, the *civil line*, the *banking line*. He was particularly indignant against the almost universal use of the word *idea* in the sense of *notion* or *opinion*, when it is clear that *idea* can only signify something of which an image can be formed in the mind. We may have an *idea* or *image* of a mountain, a tree, a building; but we cannot surely have an *idea* or *image* of an *argument* or *proposition*. Yet we hear the sages of the law 'delivering their *ideas* upon the question under consideration;' and the first speakers in parliament 'entirely coinciding in the *idea* which has been ably stated by an honourable member;'—or 'reprobating an *idea* unconstitutional, and fraught with the most dangerous consequences to a great and free country.' Johnson called this 'modern cant.'

I perceived that he pronounced the word *heard*, as if spelt with a double e, *heerd*, instead of sounding it *herd*, as is most usually done. He said, his reason was, that if it were pronounced *herd*, there would be a single exception from the

English pronunciation of the syllable *ear,* and he thought it better not to have that exception. . . .

In the evening our gentleman-farmer, and two others, entertained themselves and the company with a great number of tunes on the fiddle. Johnson desired to have 'Let ambition fire thy mind,' played over again, and appeared to give a patient attention to it; though he owned to me that he was very insensible to the power of musick. I told him, that it affected me to such a degree, as often to agitate my nerves painfully, producing in my mind alternate sensations of pathetick dejection, so that I was ready to shed tears; and of daring resolution, so that I was inclined to rush into the thickest part of the battle. 'Sir, (said he,) I should never hear it, if it made me such a fool.'

Much of the effect of musick, I am satisfied, is owing to the association of ideas. That air, which instantly and irresistibly excites in the Swiss, when in a foreign land, the *maladie du pais,* has, I am told, no intrinsick power of sound. And I know from my own experience, that Scotch reels, though brisk, make me melancholy, because I used to hear them in my early years, at a time when Mr. Pitt called for soldiers 'from the mountains of the north,' and numbers of brave Highlanders were going abroad, never to return. Whereas the airs in *The Beggar's Opera,* many of which are very soft, never fail to render me gay, because they are associated with the warm sensations and high spirits of London. This evening, while some of the tunes of ordinary composition were played with no great skill, my frame was agitated, and I was conscious of a generous attachment to Johnson, as my preceptor and friend, mixed with an affectionate regret that he was an old man, whom I should probably lose in a short time. I thought I could defend him at the point of my sword. My reverence and affection for him were in full glow. I said to him, 'My dear Sir, we must meet every year, if you don't quarrel with me.' JOHNSON. 'Nay, Sir, you are more likely to quarrel with me, than I with you. My regard for you is greater almost than I have words to express; but I do not choose to be always repeating it; write it down in the first leaf of your pocket-book, and never doubt of it again.'

I talked to him of misery being 'the doom of man' in this life, as displayed in his *Vanity of Human Wishes.* Yet I observed that things were done upon the supposition of happiness; grand houses were built, fine gardens were made, splendid places of publick amusement were contrived, and crowded with company. JOHNSON. 'Alas, Sir, these are all only struggles for happiness. When I first entered Ranelagh, it gave an expansion and gay sensation to my mind, such as I never experienced any where else. But, as Xerxes wept when he viewed his immense army, and considered that not one of that great multitude would be alive a hundred years afterwards, so it went to my heart to consider that there was not one in all that brilliant circle, that was not afraid to go home and think; but that the thoughts of each individual there, would be distressing when alone.' This reflection was experimentally just. The feeling of languor, which succeeds the animation of gaiety, is itself a very severe pain; and when the mind is then vacant, a thousand disappointments and vexations rush in and excruciate. Will not many even of my fairest readers allow this to be true?

I suggested, that being in love, and flattered with hopes of success; or having some favourite scheme in view for the next day, might prevent that wretchedness of which we had been talking. JOHNSON. 'Why, Sir, it may sometimes be so as you suppose; but my conclusion is in general but too true.'

While Johnson and I stood in calm conference by ourselves in Dr. Taylor's garden, at a pretty late hour in a serene autumn night, looking up to the heavens, I directed the discourse to the subject of a future state. My friend was in a placid and most benignant frame. 'Sir, (said he,) I do not imagine that all things will be made clear to us immediately after death, but that the ways of Providence will be explained to us very gradually.' I ventured to ask him whether, although the words of some texts of Scripture seemed strong in support of the dreadful doctrine of an eternity of punishment, we might not hope that the denunciation was figurative, and would not literally be executed. JOHNSON. 'Sir, you are to consider the intention of punishment in a future state. We have no reason to be sure that we shall then be no longer liable to offend against GOD. We do not know that even the angels are quite in a state of security; nay we know that some of them have fallen. It may, therefore, perhaps be necessary, in order to preserve both men and angels in a state of rectitude, that they should have continually before them the punishment of those who have deviated from it; but we may hope that by some other means a fall from rectitude may be prevented. Some of the texts of Scripture upon this subject are, as you observe, indeed strong; but they may admit of a mitigated interpretation.' He talked to me upon this aweful and delicate question in a gentle tone, and as if afraid to be decisive.

After supper I accompanied him to his apartment, and at my request he dictated to me an argument in favour of the negro who was then claiming his liberty, in an action in the Court of Session in Scotland. He had always been very zealous against slavery in every form, in which I, with all deference, thought that he discovered 'a zeal without knowledge.' Upon one occasion, when in company with some very grave men at Oxford, his toast was, 'Here's to the next insurrection of the negroes in the West Indies.' His violent prejudice against our West Indian and American settlers appeared whenever there was an opportunity. Towards the conclusion of his *Taxation no Tyranny*, he says, 'how is it that we hear the loudest *yelps* for liberty among the drivers of negroes?' . . .

When I said now to Johnson, that I was afraid I kept him too late up. 'No, Sir, (said he,) I don't care though I sit all night with you.' This was an animated speech from a man in his sixty-ninth year.

Had I been as attentive not to displease him as I ought to have been, I know not but this vigil might have been fulfilled; but I unluckily entered upon the controversy concerning the right of Great-Britain to tax America, and attempted to argue in favour of our fellow-subjects on the other side of the Atlantick. I insisted that America might be very well governed, and made to yield sufficient revenue by the means of *influence*, as exemplified in Ireland, while the people might be pleased with the imagination of their participating of the British constitution, by having a body of representatives, without whose consent money could not be exacted from them. Johnson could not bear my thus opposing his avowed opinion, which he had exerted himself with an extreme degree of heat to enforce; and the violent agitation into which he was thrown, while answering, or rather reprimanding me, alarmed me so, that I heartily repented of my having unthinkingly introduced the subject. I myself, however, grew warm, and the change was great, from the calm state of philosophical discussion in which we had a little before been pleasingly employed.

I talked of the corruption of the British Parliament, in which I alledged that any question, however unreasonable or unjust, might be carried by a venal majority; and I spoke with high admiration of the Roman Senate, as if composed of men sincerely desirous to resolve what they should think best for their country. My friend would allow no such character to the Roman Senate; and he maintained that the British Parliament was not corrupt, and that there was no occasion to corrupt its members; asserting, that there was hardly ever any question of great importance before Parliament, any question in which a man might not very well vote either upon one side or the other. He said there had been none in his time except that respecting America.

We were fatigued by the contest, which was produced by

my want of caution; and he was not then in the humour to slide into easy and cheerful talk. It therefore so happened, that we were after an hour or two very willing to separate and go to bed.

On Wednesday, September 24, I went into Dr. Johnson's room before he got up, and finding that the storm of the preceding night was quite laid, I sat down upon his bed-side, and he talked with as much readiness and good-humour as ever. He recommended to me to plant a considerable part of a large moorish farm which I had purchased, and he made several calculations of the expence and profit: for he delighted in exercising his mind on the science of numbers. He pressed upon me the importance of planting at the first in a very sufficient manner, quoting the saying *'In bello non licet bis errare:'*[1] and adding, 'this is equally true in planting.'

I spoke with gratitude of Dr. Taylor's hospitality; and, as evidence that it was not on account of his good table alone that Johnson visited him often, I mentioned a little anecdote which had escaped my friend's recollection, and at hearing which repeated, he smiled. One evening, when I was sitting with him, Frank delivered this message: 'Sir, Dr. Taylor sends his compliments to you, and begs you will dine with him to-morrow. He has got a hare.'—'My compliments (said Johnson,) and I'll dine with him—hare or rabbit.' . . .

From this meeting at Ashbourne I derived a considerable accession to my Johnsonian store. I communicated my original Journal to Sir William Forbes, in whom I have always placed deserved confidence; and what he wrote to me concerning it is so much to my credit as the biographer of Johnson, that my readers will, I hope, grant me their indulgence for here inserting it: 'It is not once or twice going over it (says Sir William,) that will satisfy me; for I find in it a high degree of instruction as well as entertainment; and I derive more benefit from Dr. Johnson's admirable discussions than I should be able to draw from his personal conversation; for, I suppose there is not a man in the world to whom he discloses his sentiments so freely as to yourself.'

I cannot omit a curious circumstance which occurred at Edensor-inn, close by Chatsworth, to survey the magnificence of which I had gone a considerable way out of my road to Scotland. The inn was then kept by a very jolly landlord, whose name, I think, was Malton. He happened to mention that 'the celebrated Dr. Johnson had been in his house.' I inquired *who* this Dr. Johnson was, that I might hear mine host's notion of him. 'Sir, (said he,) Johnson, the

[1] 'One cannot make a mistake twice in war.'

great writer; *Oddity,* as they call him. He's the greatest writer in England; he writes for the ministry; he has a correspondence abroad, and lets them know what's going on.'

My friend, who had a thorough dependance upon the authenticity of my relation without any *embellishment,* as *falsehood* or *fiction* is too gently called, laughed a good deal at this representation of himself. . . .

On Wednesday, March 18,[1] I arrived in London, and was informed by good Mr. Francis that his master was better, and was gone to Mr. Thrale's at Streatham, to which place I wrote to him, begging to know when he would be in town. He was not expected for some time; but next day having called on Dr. Taylor, in Dean's-yard, Westminster, I found him there, and was told he had come to town for a few hours. He met me with his usual kindness, but instantly returned to the writing of something on which he was employed when I came in, and on which he seemed much intent. Finding him thus engaged, I made my visit very short, and had no more of his conversation, except his expressing a serious regret that a friend of ours[2] was living at too much expence, considering how poor an appearance he made: 'If (said he,) a man has splendour from his expence, if he spends his money in pride or in pleasure, he has value: but if he lets others spend it for him, which is most commonly the case, he has no advantage from it.'

On Friday, March 20, I found him at his own house, sitting with Mrs. Williams, and was informed that the room formerly allotted to me was now appropriated to a charitable purpose; Mrs. Desmoulins, and I think her daughter, and a Miss Carmichael, being all lodged in it. Such was his humanity, and such his generosity, that Mrs. Desmoulins herself told me, he allowed her half-a-guinea a week. Let it be remembered, that this was above a twelfth part of his pension.

His liberality, indeed, was at all periods of his life very remarkable. Mr. Howard, of Lichfield, at whose father's house Johnson had in his early years been kindly received, told me, that when he was a boy at the Charter-House, his father wrote to him to go and pay a visit to Mr. Samuel Johnson, which he accordingly did, and found him in an upper room, of poor appearance. Johnson received him with much courteousness, and talked a great deal to him, as to a school-boy, of the course of his education, and other particulars. When he afterwards came to know and understand the high character of this great man, he recollected his condescension with won-

1 1778. Actually, Boswell arrived on the 17th.
2 Langton.

426

der. He added, that when he was going away, Mr. Johnson presented him with half-a-guinea; and this, said Mr. Howard, was at a time when he probably had not another.

We retired from Mrs. Williams to another room. Tom Davies soon after joined us. He had now unfortunately failed in his circumstances, and was much indebted to Dr. Johnson's kindness for obtaining for him many alleviations of his distress. After he went away, Johnson blamed his folly in quitting the stage, by which he and his wife got five hundred pounds a year. I said, I believed it was owing to Churchill's attack upon him,

'He mouths a sentence, as curs mouth a bone.'

JOHNSON. 'I believe so too, Sir. But what a man is he, who is to be driven from the stage by a line? Another line would have driven him from his shop.'

I told him, that I was engaged as Counsel at the bar of the House of Commons to oppose a road-bill in the county of Stirling, and asked him what mode he would advise me to follow in addressing such an audience. JOHNSON. 'Why, Sir, you must provide yourself with a good deal of extraneous matter, which you are to produce occasionally, so as to fill up the time; for you must consider, that they do not listen much. If you begin with the strength of your cause, it may be lost before they begin to listen. When you catch a moment of attention, press the merits of the question upon them.' He said, as to one point of the merits, that he thought 'it would be a wrong thing to deprive the small landholders of the privilege of assessing themselves for making and repairing the high roads; *it was destroying a certain portion of liberty, without a good reason, which was always a bad thing.*' When I mentioned this observation next day to Mr. Wilkes, he pleasantly said, 'What! does *he* talk of liberty? *Liberty* is as ridiculous in *his* mouth as *Religion* in *mine.*' Mr. Wilkes's advice, as to the best mode of speaking at the bar of the House of Commons, was not more respectful towards the senate, than that of Dr. Johnson. 'Be as impudent as you can, as merry as you can, and say whatever comes uppermost. Jack Lee is the best heard there of any Counsel; and he is the most impudent dog, and always abusing us.'

In my interview with Dr. Johnson this evening, I was quite easy, quite as his companion; upon which I find in my Journal the following reflection: 'So ready is my mind to suggest matter for dissatisfaction, that I felt a sort of regret that I was so easy. I missed that aweful reverence with which I used to contemplate MR. SAMUEL JOHNSON, in the complex magnitude of his literary, moral, and religious character. I have a wonderful superstitious love of *mystery;* when, perhaps, the truth is, that it is owing to the cloudy darkness of my own mind. I should be glad that I am more advanced in my progress of being, so that I can view Dr. Johnson with a steadier and clearer eye. My dissatisfaction to-night was foolish. Would it not be foolish to regret that we shall have less mystery in a future state? That we "now see in a glass darkly," but shall "then see face to face"? ' This reflection, which I thus freely communicate, will be valued by the thinking part of my readers, who may have themselves experienced a similar state of mind.

He returned next day to Streatham, to Mr. Thrale's; where, as Mr. Strahan once complained to me, 'he was in a great measure absorbed from the society of his old friends.' I was kept in London by business, and wrote to him on the 27th, that a separation from him for a week, when we were so near, was equal to a separation for a year, when we were at four hundred miles distance. I went to Streatham on Monday, March 30. Before he appeared, Mrs. Thrale made a very characteristical remark:—'I do not know for certain what will please Dr. Johnson: but I know for certain that it will displease him to praise any thing, even what he likes, extravagantly.'

At dinner he laughed at querulous declamations against the age, on account of luxury,—increase of London,—scarcity of provisions,—and other such topicks. 'Houses (said he,) will be built till rents fall: and corn is more plentiful now than ever it was.'. . .

Thomas à Kempis (he observed,) must be a good book, as the world has opened its arms to receive it. It is said to have been printed, in one language or other, as many times as there have been months since it first came out. I always was struck with this sentence in it: 'Be not angry that you cannot make others as you wish them to be, since you cannot make yourself as you wish to be.'. . .

When we were at tea and coffee, there came in Lord Trimlestown, in whose family was an ancient Irish peerage, but it suffered by taking the generous side in the troubles of the last century. He was a man of pleasing conversation, and was accompanied by a young gentleman, his son.

I mentioned that I had in my possession the Life of Sir Robert Sibbald, the celebrated Scottish antiquary, and founder of the Royal College of Physicians at Edinburgh, in the original manuscript in his own handwriting; and that it was I believed the most natural and candid account of himself that ever was given by any man. As an instance, he tells that the Duke of Perth, then Chancellor of Scotland, pressed him very much to come over to the Roman Catholic faith: that he resisted all his Grace's arguments for a considerable time, till one day he felt himself, as it were, instantaneously convinced, and with tears in his eyes ran into the Duke's arms, and embraced the ancient religion; that he continued very steady in it for some time, and accompanied his Grace to London one winter, and lived in his household; that there he found the rigid fasting prescribed by the church very severe upon him; that this disposed him to reconsider the controversy, and having then seen that he was in the wrong, he returned to Protestantism. I talked of some time or other publishing this curious life. MRS. THRALE. 'I think you had as well let alone that publication. To discover such weakness, exposes a man when he is gone.' JOHNSON. 'Nay, it is an honest picture of human nature. How often are the primary motives of our greatest actions as small as Sibbald's, for his reconversion.' MRS. THRALE. 'But may they not as well be forgotten?' JOHNSON. 'No, Madam, a man loves to review his own mind. That is the use of a diary, or journal.' LORD TRIMLESTOWN. 'True, Sir. As the ladies love to see themselves in a glass; so a man likes to see himself in his journal.' BOSWELL. 'A very pretty allusion.' JOHNSON. 'Yes, indeed.' BOSWELL. 'And as a lady adjusts her dress before a mirror, a man adjusts his character by looking at his journal.' . . .

Next morning, while we were at breakfast, Johnson gave a very earnest recommendation of what he himself practised with the utmost conscientiousness: I mean a strict attention to truth, even in the most minute particulars. 'Accustom your children (said he,) constantly to this; if a thing happened at one window, and they, when relating it, say that it happened at another, do not let it pass, but instantly check them; you do not know where deviation from truth will end.' BOSWELL. 'It may come to the door: and when once an account is at all varied in one circumstance, it may by degrees be varied so as to be totally different from what really happened.' Our lively hostess, whose fancy was impatient of the rein, fidgeted at this, and ventured to say, 'Nay, this is too much. If Mr. Johnson should forbid me to drink tea, I would comply, as I should feel the restraint only twice a day; but little variations in narrative must happen a thousand times a day, if one is not perpetually watching.' JOHNSON. 'Well, Madam, and you *ought* to be perpetually watching. It is more from carelessness about truth than from intentional lying, that there is so much falsehood in the world.' . . .

He was indeed so much impressed with the prevalence of falsehood, voluntary or unintentional, that I never knew any person who upon hearing an extraordinary circumstance told, discovered more of the *incredulus odi*.[1] He would say, with a significant look and decisive tone, 'It is not so. Do not tell this again.' He inculcated upon all his friends the importance of perpetual vigilance against the slightest degrees of falsehood; the effect of which, as Sir Joshua Reynolds observed to me, has been, that all who were of his *school* are distinguished for a love of truth and accuracy, which they would not have possessed in the same degree, if they had not been acquainted with Johnson.

Talking of ghosts, he said, 'It is wonderful that five thousand years have now elapsed since the creation of the world, and still it is undecided whether or not there has ever been an instance of the spirit of any person appearing after death. All argument is against it; but all belief is for it.'

He said, 'John Wesley's conversation is good, but he is never at leisure. He is always obliged to go at a certain hour. This is very disagreeable to a man who loves to fold his legs and have out his talk, as I do.'

On Friday, April 3, I dined with him in London, in a company where were present several eminent men, whom I shall not name, but distinguish their parts in the conversation by different letters.[2]

F. 'I have been looking at this famous antique marble dog of Mr. Jennings, valued at a thousand guineas, said to be Alcibiades's dog.' JOHNSON. 'His tail then must be docked. That was the mark of Alcibiades's dog.' E. 'A thousand guineas! The representation of no animal whatever is worth so much. At this rate a dead dog would indeed be better than a living lion.' JOHNSON. 'Sir, it is not the worth of the thing, but of the skill in forming it which is so highly estimated. Every thing that enlarges the sphere of human powers, that shows man he can do what he thought he could not do, is valuable. The first man who balanced a straw upon his nose; Johnson, who rode upon three horses at a time; in short, all such men deserved the applause of mankind, not on account of the use of what they did, but of the dexterity which they exhibited.' BOSWELL. 'Yet a misapplication of time and assiduity is not to be encouraged. Addison, in one of his *Spectators*, commends the judgement of a King, who, as a suitable reward to a man that by long perseverance had attained to the art of throwing a barley-corn through the eye of a needle, gave him a bushel of barley.' JOHNSON. 'He must have been a King of Scotland, where barley is scarce.' F. 'One of the most re-

---

[1] 'I hate the incredible.' Horace, *Art of Poetry*, l. 188.

[2] C=Chemist (Fordyce), E=Edmund (Burke), F=Fitzpatrick (Lord Upper Ossory), I or J=Infidel (Gibbon), P=Painter (Reynolds), R=R. B. Sheridan.

markable antique figures of an animal is the boar at Florence.' JOHNSON. 'The first boar that is well made in marble should be preserved as a wonder. When men arrive at a facility of making boars well, then the workmanship is not of such value, but they should however be preserved as examples, and as a greater security for the restoration of the art, should it be lost.'

E. 'We hear prodigious complaints at present of emigration. I am convinced that emigration makes a country more populous.' J. 'That sounds very much like a paradox.' E. 'Exportation of men, like exportation of all other commodities, makes more be produced.' JOHNSON. 'But there would be more people were there not emigration, provided there were food for more.' E. 'No; leave a few breeders, and you'll have more people than if there were no emigration.' 'JOHNSON. 'Nay, Sir, it is plain there will be more people, if there are more breeders. Thirty cows in good pasture will produce more calves than ten cows, provided they have good bulls.' E. 'There are bulls enough in Ireland.' JOHNSON. (smiling,) 'So, Sir, I should think from your argument.' BOSWELL. 'You said, exportation of men, like exportation of other commodities, makes more be produced. But a bounty is given to encourage the exportation of corn, and no bounty is given for the exportation of men; though, indeed, those who go, gain by it.' R. 'But the bounty on the exportation of corn is paid at home.' E. 'That's the same thing.' JOHNSON. 'No, Sir.' R. 'A man who stays at home, gains nothing by his neighbours emigrating.' BOSWELL. 'I can understand that emigration may be the cause that more people may be produced in a country; but the country will not therefore be the more populous; for the people issue from it. It can only be said that there is a flow of people. It is an encouragement to have children, to know that they can get a living by emigration.' R. 'Yes, if there were an emigration of children under six years of age. But they don't emigrate till they could earn their livelihood in some way at home.' C. 'It is remarkable that the most unhealthy countries, where there are the most destructive diseases, such as Egypt and Bengal, are the most populous.' JOHNSON. 'Countries which are the most populous have the most destructive diseases. *That* is the true state of the proposition.' C. 'Holland is very unhealthy, yet it is exceedingly populous.' JOHNSON. 'I know not that Holland is unhealthy. But its populousness is owing to an influx of people from all other countries. Disease cannot be the cause of populousness, for it not only carries off a great proportion of the people, but those who are left are weakened and unfit for the purposes of increase.'

R. 'Mr. E., I don't mean to flatter, but when posterity reads one of your speeches in Parliament, it will be difficult to believe that you took so much pains, knowing with certainty that it could produce no effect, that not one vote would be gained by it.' E. 'Waiving your compliment to me, I shall say in general, that it is very well worth while for a man to take pains to speak well in Parliament. A man, who has vanity, speaks to display his talents; and if a man speaks well, he gradually establishes a certain reputation and consequence in the general opinion, which sooner or later will have its political reward. Besides, though not one vote is gained, a good speech has its effect. Though an act which has been ably opposed passes into a law, yet in its progress it is modelled, it is softened in such a manner, that we see plainly the Minister has been told, that the Members attached to him are so sensible of its injustice or absurdity from what they have heard, that it must be altered.' JOHNSON. 'And, Sir, there is a gratification of pride. Though we cannot out-vote them we will out-argue them. They shall not do wrong without its being shown both to themselves and to the world.' E. 'The House of Commons is a mixed body. (I except the Minority, which I hold to be pure, [smiling,] but I take the whole House.) It is a mass by no means pure; but neither is it wholly corrupt, though there is a large proportion of corruption in it. There are many members who generally go with the Minister, who will not go all lengths. There are many honest well-meaning country gentlemen who are in parliament only to keep up the consequence of their families. Upon most of these a good speech will have influence.' JOHNSON. 'We are all more or less governed by interest. But interest will not make us do every thing. In a case which admits of doubt, we try to think on the side which is for our interest, and generally bring ourselves to act accordingly. But the subject must admit of diversity of colouring; it must receive a colour on that side. In the House of Commons there are members enough who will not vote what is grossly unjust or absurd. No, Sir, there must always be right enough, or appearance of right, to keep wrong in countenance. BOSWELL. 'There is surely always a majority in parliament who have places, or who want to have them, and who therefore will be generally ready to support government without requiring any pretext.' E. 'True, Sir; that majority will always follow.

"Quo clamor vocat et turba faventium." ' [1]

BOSWELL. 'Well now, let us take the common phrase, Place-

[1] 'Where the shouting calls and the crowd of applauders.' Horace, *Odes,* III. xxiv. 46.

432

hunters. I thought they had hunted without regard to any thing, just as their huntsmen, the Minister, leads, looking only to the prey.' J. 'But taking your metaphor, you know that in hunting there are few so desperately keen as to follow without reserve. Some do not choose to leap ditches and hedges and risk their necks, or gallop over steeps, or even to dirty themselves in bogs and mire.' BOSWELL. 'I am glad there are some good, quiet, moderate political hunters.' E. 'I believe, in any body of men in England, I should have been in the Minority; I have always been in the Minority.' P. 'The House of Commons resembles a private company. How seldom is any man convinced by another's argument; passion and pride rise against it.' R. 'What would be the consequence, if a Minister, sure of a majority in the House of Commons, should resolve that there should be no speaking at all upon his side.' E. 'He must soon go out. That has been tried; but it was found it would not do.'

E. 'The Irish language is not primitive; it is Teutonick, a mixture of the northern tongues: it has much English in it.' JOHNSON. 'It may have been radically Teutonick; but English and High Dutch have no similarity to the eye, though radically the same. Once, when looking into Low Dutch, I found, in a whole page, only one word similar to English; *stroem*, like *stream*, and it signified *tide*.' E. 'I remember having seen a Dutch Sonnet, in which I found this word, *roesnopies*. Nobody would at first think that this could be English; but, when we enquire, we find *roes*, rose, and *nopie*, knob; so we have *rosebuds*.'

JOHNSON. 'I have been reading Thicknesse's *Travels*, which I think are entertaining.' BOSWELL. 'What, Sir, a good book?' JOHNSON. 'Yes, Sir, to read once; I do not say you are to make a study of it, and digest it; and I believe it to be a true book in his intention. All travellers generally mean to tell truth; though Thicknesse observes, upon Smollet's account of his alarming a whole town in France by firing a blunderbuss, and frightening a French nobleman till he made him tie on his portmanteau, that he would be loth to say Smollet had told two lies in one page, but he had found the only town in France where these things could have happened. Travellers must often be mistaken. In every thing, except where mensuration can be applied, they may honestly differ. There has been, of late, a strange turn in travellers to be displeased.'

E. 'From the experience which I have had,—and I have had a great deal,—I have learnt to think *better* of mankind.' JOHNSON. 'From my experience I have found them worse in commercial dealings, more disposed to cheat, than I had any notion of; but more disposed to do one another good than I had conceived.' J. 'Less just and more beneficent.' JOHNSON. 'And really it is wonderful, considering how much attention is necessary for men to take care of themselves, and ward off immediate evils which press upon them, it is wonderful how much they do for others. As it is said of the greatest liar, that he tells more truth than falsehood; so it may be said of the worst man, that he does more good than evil.' BOSWELL. 'Perhaps from experience men may be found *happier* than we suppose.' JOHNSON. 'No, Sir; the more we enquire, we shall find men the less happy.' P. 'As to thinking better or worse of mankind from experience, some cunning people will not be satisfied unless they have put men to the test, as they think. There is a very good story told of Sir Godfrey Kneller, in his character of a Justice of the peace. A gentleman brought his servant before him, upon an accusation of having stolen some money from him; but it having come out that he had laid it purposely in the servant's way, in order to try his honesty, Sir Godfrey sent the master to prison.' JOHNSON. 'To resist temptation once, is not a sufficient proof of honesty. If a servant, indeed, were to resist the continued temptation of silver lying in a window, as some people let it lye, when he is sure his master does not know how much there is of it, he would give a strong proof of honesty. But this is a proof to which you have no right to put a man. You know, humanly speaking, there is a certain degree of temptation which will overcome any virtue. Now, in so far as you approach temptation to a man, you do him an injury; and, if he is overcome, you share his guilt.' P. 'And, when once overcome, it is easier for him to be got the better of again.' BOSWELL. 'Yes, you are his seducer; you have debauched him. I have known a man resolve to put friendship to the test, by asking a friend to lend him money merely with that view, when he did not want it.' JOHNSON. 'That is very wrong, Sir. Your friend may be a narrow man, and yet have many good qualities: narrowness may be his only fault. Now your are trying his general character as a friend, by one particular singly, in which he happens to be defective, when, in truth, his character is composed of many particulars.'

E. 'I understand the hogshead of claret, which this society was favoured with by our friend the Dean, is nearly out; I think he should be written to, to send another of the same kind. Let the request be made with a happy ambiguity of expression, so that we may have the chance of his sending *it* also as a present.' JOHNSON. 'I am willing to offer my services as secretary on this occasion.' P. 'As many as are for Dr. Johnson being secretary hold up your hands.—Carried unanimously.' BOSWELL. 'He will be our Dictator.' JOHNSON. 'No, the company is to dictate to me. I am only to write for wine; and I am quite disinterested, as I drink none; I shall not be suspected of having forged the application. I am no more than humble *scribe*.' E. 'Then you shall *pre*scribe.' BOSWELL. 'Very well. The first play of words to-day.' J. 'No, no; the *bulls* in Ireland.' JOHNSON. 'Were I your Dictator you should have no wine. It would be my business *cavere ne quid detrimenti Respublica caperet*,[1] and wine is dangerous. Rome was ruined by luxury,' (smiling.) E. 'If you allow no wine as Dictator, you shall not have me for your master of horse.'

On Saturday, April 4, I drank tea with Johnson at Dr. Taylor's, where he had dined. He entertained us with an account of a tragedy written by a Dr. Kennedy, (not the Lisbon physician.) The catastrophe of it (said he,) was, that a King, who was jealous of his Queen with his prime-minister, castrated himself. This tragedy was actually shewn about in manuscript to several people, and, amongst others, to Mr. Fitzherbert, who repeated to me two lines of the Prologue:

> "Our hero's fate we have but gently touch'd;
> The fair might blame us, if it were less couch'd."

It is hardly to be believed what absurd and indecent images men will introduce into their writings, without being sensible of the absurdity and indecency. I remember Lord Orrery told me, that there was a pamphlet written against Sir Robert Walpole, the whole of which was an allegory on the PHALLIC OBSCENITY. The Duchess of Buckingham asked Lord Orrery *who* this person was? He answered, he did not know. She said, she would send to Mr. Pulteney, who, she supposed, could inform her. So then, to prevent her from making herself ridiculous, Lord Orrery sent her Grace a note, in which he gave her to understand what was meant.'

He was very silent this evening; and read in a variety of books: suddenly throwing down one, and taking up another.

He talked of going to Streatham that night. TAYLOR. 'You'll be robbed if you do: or you must shoot a highwayman. Now I would rather be robbed than do that; I would not shoot a highwayman.' JOHNSON. 'But I would rather shoot him in the instant when he is attempting to rob me, than afterwards swear against him at the Old-Bailey, to take away his life, after he has robbed me. I am surer I am right in the one case than in the other. I may be mistaken as to the man, when I swear: I cannot be mistaken, if I shoot him in the act. Besides, we feel less reluctance to take away a man's life, when we are heated by the injury, than to do it at a distance of time by an oath, after we have cooled.' Bos-

---

[1] 'To take care that the State suffer no harm.'

WELL. 'So, Sir, you would rather act from the motive of private passion, than that of publick advantage.' JOHNSON. 'Nay, Sir, when I shoot the highwayman I act from both.' BOSWELL. 'Very well, very well.—There is no catching him.' JOHNSON. 'At the same time one does not know what to say. For perhaps one may, a year after, hang himself from uneasiness for having shot a man. Few minds are fit to be trusted with so great a thing.' BOSWELL. 'Then, Sir, you would not shoot him?' JOHNSON. 'But I might be vexed afterwards for that too.'

Thrale's carriage not having come for him, as he expected, I accompanied him some part of the way home to his own house. I told him, that I had talked of him to Mr. Dunning a few days before, and had said, that in his company we did not so much interchange conversation, as listen to him; and that Dunning observed, upon this, 'One is always willing to listen to Dr. Johnson:' to which I answered, 'That is a great deal from you, Sir.'—'Yes, Sir, (said Johnson,) a great deal indeed. Here is a man willing to listen, to whom the world is listening all the rest of the year.' BOSWELL. 'I think, Sir, it is right to tell one man of such a handsome thing, which has been said of him by another. It tends to increase benevolence.' JOHNSON. 'Undoubtedly it is right, Sir.'

On Tuesday, April 7, I breakfasted with him at his house. He said, 'nobody was content.' I mentioned to him a respectable person[1] in Scotland whom he knew; and I asserted, that I really believed he was always content. JOHNSON. 'No, Sir, he is not content with the present; he has always some new scheme, some new plantation, something which is future. You know he was not content as a widower; for he married again.' BOSWELL. 'But he is not restless.' JOHNSON. 'Sir, he is only locally at rest. A chymist is locally at rest; but his mind is hard at work. This gentleman has done with external exertions. It is too late for him to engage in distant projects.' BOSWELL. He seems to amuse himself quite well; to have his attention fixed, and his tranquillity preserved by very small matters. I have tried this; but it would not do with me. 'JOHNSON. (laughing,) 'No, Sir; it must be born with a man to be contented to take up with little things. Women have a great advantage that they may take up with little things, without disgracing themselves: a man cannot, except with fiddling. Had I learnt to fiddle, I should have done nothing else.' BOSWELL. 'Pray, Sir, did you ever play on any musical instrument?' JOHNSON. 'No, Sir. I once bought me a flagelet; but I never made out a tune.' BOSWELL. 'A flagelet, Sir!—so small

[1] Lord Auchinleck.

an instrument? I should have liked to hear you play on the violoncello. *That* should have been *your* instrument.' JOHNSON. 'Sir, I might as well have played on the violoncello as another; but I should have done nothing else. No, Sir; a man would never undertake great things, could he be amused with small. I once tried knotting. Dempster's sister undertook to teach me; but I could not learn it.' BOSWELL. 'So, Sir; it will be related in pompous narrative, "Once for his amusement he tried knotting; nor did this Hercules disdain the distaff."' JOHNSON. 'Knitting of stockings is a good amusement. As a freeman of Aberdeen I should be a knitter of stockings.' He asked me to go down with him and dine at Mr. Thrale's at Streatham, to which I agreed. I had lent him *An Account of Scotland, in 1702*, written by a man of various enquiry, an English chaplain to a regiment stationed there. JOHNSON. 'It is sad stuff, Sir, miserably written, as books in general then were. There is now an elegance of style universally diffused. No man now writes so ill as Martin's *Account of the Hebrides* is written. A man could not write so ill, if he should try. Set a merchant's clerk now to write, and he'll do better.'

He talked to me with serious concern of a certain female friend's[1] laxity of narration, and inattention to truth.' —'I am as much vexed (said he,) at the ease with which she hears it mentioned to her, as at the thing itself. I told her, "Madam, you are contented to hear every day said to you, what the highest of mankind have died for, rather than bear." —You know, Sir, the highest of mankind have died rather than bear to be told they had uttered a falsehood. Do talk to her of it: I am weary.'

BOSWELL. 'Was not Dr. John Campbell a very inaccurate man in his narrative, Sir? He once told me, that he drank thirteen bottles of port at a sitting.' JOHNSON. 'Why, Sir, I do not know that Campbell ever lied with pen and ink; but you could not entirely depend on any thing he told you in conversation, if there was fact mixed with it. However, I loved Campbell: he was a solid orthodox man: he had a reverence for religion. Though defective in practice, he was religious in principle; and he did nothing grossly wrong that I have heard.'

I told him, that I had been present the day before, when Mrs. Montagu, the literary lady, sat to Miss Reynolds for her picture; and that she said, 'she had bound up Mr. Gibbon's *History* without the last two offensive chapters; for that she thought the book so far good, as it gave, in an elegant manner, the substance of the bad writers *medii ævi*, which the

[1] Mrs. Thrale.

late Lord Lyttelton advised her to read.' JOHNSON. 'Sir, she has not read them: she shews none of this impetuosity to me: she does not know Greek, and, I fancy, knows little Latin. She is willing you should think she knows them; but she does not say she does.' BOSWELL. 'Mr. Harris, who was present, agreed with her.' JOHNSON. 'Harris was laughing at her, Sir. Harris is a sound sullen scholar; he does not like interlopers. Harris, however, is a prig, and a bad prig. I looked into his book, and thought he did not understand his own system.' BOSWELL. 'He says plain things in a formal and abstract way, to be sure: but this method is good: for to have clear notions upon any subject, we must have recourse to analytick arrangement.' JOHNSON. 'Sir, it is what every body does, whether they will or no. But sometimes things may be made darker by definition. I see a *cow*, I define her, *Animal quadrupes ruminans cornutum*.[1] But a goat ruminates, and a cow may have no horns. *Cow* is plainer.' BOSWELL. 'I think Dr. Franklin's definition of *Man* a good one—"A tool-making animal."' JOHNSON. 'But many a man never made a tool; and suppose a man without arms, he could not make a tool.'

Talking of drinking wine, he said. 'I did not leave off wine because I could not bear it; I have drunk three bottles of port without being the worse for it. University College has witnessed this.' BOSWELL. 'Why then, Sir, did you leave it off?' JOHNSON. 'Why, Sir, because it is so much better for a man to be sure that he is never to be intoxicated, never to lose the power over himself. I shall not begin to drink wine again, till I grow old, and want it.' BOSWELL. 'I think, Sir, you once said to me, that not to drink wine was a great deduction from life.' JOHNSON. 'It is a diminution of pleasure, to be sure; but I do not say a diminution of happiness. There is more happiness in being rational.' BOSWELL. 'But if we could have pleasure always, should not we be happy? The greatest part of men would compound for pleasure.' JOHNSON. 'Supposing we could have pleasure always, an intellectual man would not compound for it. The greatest part of men would compound, because the greatest part of men are gross.' BOSWELL. 'I allow there may be greater pleasure than from wine. I have had more pleasure from your conversation, I have indeed; I assure you I have.' JOHNSON. 'When we talk of pleasure, we mean sensual pleasure. When a man says, he had pleasure with a woman, he does not mean conversation, but something of a very different nature. Philosophers tell you, that pleasure is *contrary* to happiness. Gross men prefer animal pleasure. So there are men who have preferred living among savages.

[1] 'A quadruped which chews the cud and has horns.'

Now what a wretch must he be, who is content with such conversation as can be had among savages! You may remember an officer at Fort Augustus, who had served in America, told us of a woman whom they were obliged to *bind*, in order to get her back from savage life.' BOSWELL. 'She must have been an animal, a beast.' JOHNSON. 'Sir, she was a speaking cat.'

I mentioned to him that I had become very weary in a company where I heard not a single intellectual sentence, except that 'a man who had been settled ten years in Minorca was become a much inferiour man to what he was in London, because a man's mind grows narrow in a narrow place.' JOHNSON. 'A man's mind grows narrow in a narrow place, whose mind is enlarged only because he has lived in a large place: but what is got by books and thinking is preserved in a narrow place as well as in a large place. A man cannot know modes of life as well in Minorca as in London; but he may study mathematicks as well in Minorca.' BOSWELL. 'I don't know, Sir: if you had remained ten years in the Isle of Col, you would not have been the man that you now are.' JOHNSON. 'Yes, Sir, if I had been there from fifteen to twenty-five; but not if from twenty-five to thirty-five.' BOSWELL. 'I own, Sir, the spirits which I have in London make me do every thing with more readiness and vigour. I can talk twice as much in London as any where else.'

Of Goldsmith he said, 'He was not an agreeable companion, for he talked always for fame. A man who does so never can be pleasing. The man who talks to unburthen his mind is the man to delight you. An eminent friend of ours[1] is not so agreeable as the variety of his knowledge would otherwise make him, because he talks partly from ostentation.'

Soon after our arrival at Thrale's, I heard one of the maids calling eagerly on another, to go to Dr. Johnson. I wondered what this could mean. I afterwards learnt, that it was to give her a Bible, which he had brought from London as a present to her.

He was for a considerable time occupied in reading *Mémoires de Fontenelle*, leaning and swinging upon the low gate into the court, without his hat.

I looked into Lord Kames's *Sketches of the History of Man;* and mentioned to Dr. Johnson his censure of Charles the Fifth, for celebrating his funeral obsequies in his lifetime, which, I told him, I had been used to think a solemn and affecting act. JOHNSON. 'Why, Sir, a man may dispose his mind to think so of that act of Charles; but it is so liable to

1 Burke.

ridicule, that if one man out of ten thousand laughs at it, he'll make the other nine thousand nine hundred and ninety-nine laugh too.' I could not agree with him in this. . . .

At dinner, Mrs. Thrale expressed a wish to go and see Scotland. JOHNSON. 'Seeing Scotland, Madam, is only seeing a worse England. It is seeing the flower gradually fade away to the naked stalk. Seeing the Hebrides, indeed, is seeing quite a different scene.'

Our poor friend, Mr. Thomas Davies, was soon to have a benefit at Drury-lane theatre, as some relief to his unfortunate circumstances. We were all warmly interested for his success, and had contributed to it. However, we thought there was no harm in having our joke, when he could not be hurt by it. I proposed that he should be brought on to speak a Prologue upon the occasion; and I began to mutter fragments of what it might be: as, that when now grown *old*, he was obliged to cry, 'Poor Tom's *a-cold*;'—that he owned he had been driven from the stage by a Churchill, but that this was no disgrace, for a Churchill had beat the French;—that he had been satyrised as 'mouthing a sentence as curs mouth a bone,' but he was now glad of a bone to pick.—'Nay, (said Johnson,) I would have him to say,

"Mad Tom is come to see the world again." '

He and I returned to town in the evening. Upon the road, I endeavoured to maintain, in argument, that a landed gentleman is not under any obligation to reside upon his estate; and that by living in London he does no injury to his country. JOHNSON. 'Why, Sir, he does no injury to his country in general, because the money which he draws from it gets back again in circulation; but to his particular district, his particular parish, he does an injury. All that he has to give away is not given to those who have the first claim to it. And though I have said that the money circulates back, it is a long time before that happens. Then, Sir, a man of family and estate ought to consider himself as having the charge of a district, over which he is to diffuse civility and happiness.'

Next day I found him at home in the morning. He praised Delany's *Observations on Swift;* said that his book and Lord Orrery's might both be true, though one viewed Swift more, and the other less favourably; and that, between both, we might have a complete notion of Swift.

Talking of a man's resolving to deny himself the use of wine, from moral and religious considerations, he said, 'He must not doubt about it. When one doubts as to pleasure, we know what will be the conclusion. I now no more think of drinking wine, than a horse does. The wine upon the table is no more for me, than for the dog that is under the table.'

On Thursday, April 9, I dined with him at Sir Joshua Reynolds's, with the Bishop of St. Asaph, (Dr. Shipley,) Mr. Allan Ramsay, Mr. Gibbon, Mr. Cambridge, and Mr. Langton. Mr. Ramsay had lately returned from Italy, and entertained us with his observations upon Horace's villa, which he had examined with great care. I relished this much, as it brought fresh into my mind what I had viewed with great pleasure thirteen years before. The Bishop, Dr. Johnson, and Mr. Cambridge, joined with Mr. Ramsay, in recollecting the various lines in Horace relating to the subject.

Horace's journey to Brundusium being mentioned, Johnson observed, that the brook which he describes is to be seen now, exactly as at that time, and that he had often wondered how it happened, that small brooks, such as this, kept the same situation for ages, notwithstanding earthquakes, by which even mountains have been changed, and agriculture, which produces such a variation upon the surface of the earth. . . .

The Bishop said, it appeared from Horace's writings that he was a cheerful contented man. JOHNSON. 'We have no reason to believe that, my Lord. Are we to think Pope was happy, because he says so in his writings? We see in his writings what he wished the state of his mind to appear. Dr. Young, who pined for preferment, talks with contempt of it in his writings, and affects to despise every thing that he did not despise.' BISHOP OF ST. ASAPH. 'He was like other chaplains, looking for vacancies: but that is not peculiar to the clergy. I remember when I was with the army, after the battle of Lafeldt, the officers seriously grumbled that no general was killed.' CAMBRIDGE. 'We may believe Horace more when he says,

"Romæ Tibur amem, ventosus Tibure Romam;"[1]

than when he boasts of his consistency.' BOSWELL. 'How hard is it that man can never be at rest.' RAMSAY. 'It is not in his nature to be at rest. When he is at rest, he is in the worst state that he can be in; for he has nothing to agitate him. He is then like the man in the Irish song,

"There liv'd a young man in Ballinacrazy.
Who wanted a wife for to make him un*aisy*." '

Goldsmith being mentioned, Johnson observed, that it was

[1] 'At Rome I love Tibur: then, inconstant as the wind at Tibur, Rome.' Horace, *Epistles*, I. viii. 12.

441

long before his merit came to be acknowledged. That he once complained to him, in ludicrous terms of distress, 'Whenever I write any thing, the publick *make a point* to know nothing about it:' but that his *Traveller* brought him into high reputation. LANGTON. 'There is not one bad line in that poem; not one of Dryden's careless verses.' SIR JOSHUA. 'I was glad to hear Charles Fox say, it was one of the finest poems in the English language.' LANGTON. 'Why was you glad? You surely had no doubt of this before.' JOHNSON. 'No; the merit of *The Traveller* is so well established, that Mr. Fox's praise cannot augment it, nor censure diminish it.' SIR JOSHUA. 'But his friends may suspect they had too great a partiality for him.' JOHNSON. 'Nay, Sir, the partiality of his friends was all against him. It was with difficulty we could give him a hearing. Goldsmith had no settled notions upon any subject; so he talked always at random. It seemed to be his intention to blurt out whatever was in his mind, and see what would become of it. He was angry too, when catched in an absurdity; but it did not prevent him from falling into another the next minute. I remember Chamier, after talking with him for some time, said, "Well, I do believe he wrote this poem himself: and, let me tell you, that is believing a great deal." Chamier once asked him, what he meant by *slow,* the last word in the first line of *The Traveller,*

"Remote, unfriended, melancholy, slow."

Did he mean tardiness of locomotion? Goldsmith, who would say something without consideration, answered, "Yes." I was sitting by, and said, "No, Sir; you do not mean tardiness of locomotion; you mean, that sluggishness of mind which comes upon a man in solitude." Chamier believed then that I had written the line as much as if he had seen me write it. Goldsmith, however, was a man, who, whatever he wrote, did it better than any other man could do. He deserved a place in Westminster-Abbey, and every year he lived, would have deserved it better. He had, indeed, been at no pains to fill his mind with knowledge. He transplanted it from one place to another; and it did not settle in his mind; so he could not tell what was in his own books.'

We talked of living in the country. JOHNSON. 'No wise man will go to live in the country, unless he has something to do which can be better done in the country. For instance: if he is to shut himself up for a year to study a science, it is better to look out to the fields, than to an opposite wall. Then, if a man walks out in the country, there is nobody to keep him from walking in again: but if a man walks out in London, he is not sure when he shall walk in again. A great city is, to be sure, the school for studying life; and "The proper study of mankind is man," as Pope observes.' BOSWELL. 'I fancy London is the best place in the world for society; though I have heard that the very first society of Paris is still beyond any thing that we have here.' JOHNSON. 'Sir, I question if in Paris such a company as is sitting round this table could be got together in less than half a year. They talk in France of the felicity of men and women living together: the truth is, that there the men are not higher than the women, they know no more than the women do, and they are not held down in their conversation by the presence of women.' RAMSAY. 'Literature is upon the growth, it is in its spring in France. Here it is rather *passée*.' JOHNSON. 'Literature was in France long before we had it. Paris was the second city for the revival of letters: Italy had it first, to be sure. What have we done for literature, equal to what was done by the Stephani and others in France? Our literature came to us through France. Caxton printed only two books, Chaucer and Gower, that were not translations from the French; and Chaucer, we know, took much from the Italians. No, Sir, if literature be in its spring in France, it is a second spring; it is after a winter. We are now before the French in literature; but we had it long after them. In England, any man who wears a sword and a powdered wig is ashamed to be illiterate. I believe it is not so in France. Yet there is, probably, a great deal of learning in France, because they have such a number of religious establishments; so many men who have nothing else to do but to study. I do not know this; but I take it upon the common principles of chance. Where there are many shooters, some will hit.'

We talked of old age. Johnson (now in his seventieth year,) said, 'It is a man's own fault, it is from want of use, if his mind grows torpid in old age.' The Bishop asked, if an old man does not lose faster than he gets. JOHNSON. 'I think not, my Lord, if he exerts himself.' One of the company[1] rashly observed, that he thought it was happy for an old man that insensibility comes upon him. JOHNSON. (with a noble elevation and disdain,) 'No, Sir, I should never be happy by being less rational.' . . .

His Lordship mentioned a charitable establishment in Wales, where people were maintained, and supplied with every thing, upon the condition of their contributing the weekly produce of their labour; and he said, they grew quite torpid for want of property. JOHNSON. They have no object

[1] Cambridge.

443

for hope. Their condition cannot be better. It is rowing without a port.' . . .

This season there was a whimsical fashion in the newspapers of applying Shakspeare's words to describe living persons well known in the world; which was done under the title of *Modern Characters from Shakspeare;* many of which were admirably adapted. The fancy took so much, that they were afterwards collected into a pamphlet. Somebody said to Johnson, across the table, that he had not been in those characters. 'Yes (said he,) I have. I should have been sorry to be left out.' He then repeated what had been applied to him,

'I must borrow GARAGANTUA's mouth.'

Miss Reynolds not perceiving at once the meaning of this, he was obliged to explain it to her, which had something of an aukward and ludicrous effect. 'Why, Madam, it has a reference to me, as using big words, which require the mouth of a giant to pronounce them. Garagantua is the name of a giant in Rabelais.' BOSWELL. 'But, Sir, there is another amongst them for you:

"He would not flatter Neptune for his trident,
    Or Jove for his power to thunder." '

JOHNSON. 'There is nothing marked in that. No, Sir, Garagantua is the best.' Notwithstanding this ease and good humour, when I, a little while afterwards, repeated his sarcasm on Kenrick, which was received with applause, he asked, '*Who* said that?' and on my suddenly answering, *Garagantua,* he looked serious, which was a sufficient indication that he did not wish it to be kept up.

When we went to the drawing-room there was a rich assemblage. Besides the company who had been at dinner, there were Mr. Garrick, Mr. Harris of Salisbury, Dr. Percy, Dr. Burney, Honourable Mrs. Cholmondeley, Miss Hannah More, &c. &c.

After wandering about in a kind of pleasing distraction for some time, I got into a corner, with Johnson, Garrick, and Harris. GARRICK. (to Harris,) 'Pray, Sir, have you read Potter's *Æschylus?*' 'HARRIS. 'Yes; and think it pretty.' GARRICK. (to Johnson,) 'And what think you, Sir, of it?' JOHNSON. 'I thought what I read of it *verbiage:* but upon Mr. Harris's recommendation, I will read a play. (To Mr. Harris,) Don't prescribe two.' Mr. Harris suggested one, I do not remember which. JOHNSON. 'We must try its effect as an English poem; that is the way to judge of the merit of a translation. Translations are, in general, for people who cannot read the original.' I mentioned the vulgar saying, that Pope's

Homer was not a good representation of the original. JOHNSON. 'Sir, it is the greatest work of the kind that has ever been produced.' BOSWELL. 'The truth is, it is impossible perfectly to translate poetry. In a different language it may be the same tune, but it has not the same tone. Homer plays it on a bassoon; Pope on a flagelet.' HARRIS. 'I think Heroick poetry is best in blank verse; yet it appears that rhyme is essential to English poetry, from our deficiency in metrical quantities. In my opinion, the chief excellence of our language is numerous prose.' JOHNSON. 'Sir William Temple was the first writer who gave cadence to English prose. Before his time they were careless of arrangement, and did not mind whether a sentence ended with an important word or an insignificant word, or with what part of speech it was concluded.' Mr. Langton, who now had joined us, commended Clarendon. JOHNSON. 'He is objected to for his parentheses, his involved clauses, and his want of harmony. But he is supported by his matter. It is, indeed, owing to a plethora of matter that his style is so faulty. Every *substance,* (smiling to Mr. Harris,) has so many *accidents.*—To be distinct, we must talk *analytically.* If we analyse language, we must speak of it grammatically; if we analyse argument, we must speak of it logically.' GARRICK. 'Of all the translations that ever were attempted, I think Elphinston's *Martial* the most extraordinary. He consulted me upon it, who am a little of an epigrammatist myself, you know. I told him freely, "You don't seem to have that turn." I asked him if he was serious; and finding he was, I advised him against publishing. Why, his translation is more difficult to understand than the original. I thought him a man of some talents; but he seems crazy in this.' JOHNSON. 'Sir, you have done what I had not courage to do. But he did not ask my advice, and I did not force it upon him, to make him angry with me.' GARRICK. 'But as a friend, Sir—.' JOHNSON. 'Why, such a friend as I am with him—no.' GARRICK. 'But if you see a friend going to tumble over a precipice?' JOHNSON. 'That is an extravagant case, Sir. You are sure a friend will thank you for hindering him from tumbling over a precipice; but, in the other case, I should hurt his vanity, and do him no good. He would not take my advice. His brother-in-law, Strahan, sent him a subscription of fifty pounds, and said he would send him fifty more, if he would not publish.' GARRICK. 'What! eh! is Strahan a good judge of an Epigram? Is not he rather an *obtuse* man, eh?' JOHNSON. 'Why, Sir, he may not be a judge of an Epigram: but you see he is a judge of what is *not* an Epigram.' BOSWELL. 'It is easy for you, Mr. Garrick, to talk to an authour as you talked to Elphinston; you, who have been so long the manager of a theatre, rejecting the plays of poor authours. You are an old Judge, who have often pronounced sentence of death. You are a practiced surgeon, who have often amputated limbs; and though this may have been for the good of your patients, they cannot like you. Those who have undergone a dreadful operation are not very fond of seeing the operator again.' GARRICK. 'Yes, I know enough of that. There was a reverend gentleman, (Mr. Hawkins,) who wrote a tragedy, the SIEGE of something, which I refused.' HARRIS. 'So, the siege was raised.' JOHNSON. 'Ay, he came to me and complained; and told me, that Garrick said his play was wrong in the *concoction*. Now, what is the concoction of a play?' (Here Garrick started, and twisted himself, and seemed sorely vexed; for Johnson told me, he believed the story was true.) GARRICK. 'I—I—I— said *first* concoction.' JOHNSON. (smiling,) 'Well, he left out *first*. And Rich, he said, refused him *in false English;* he could shew it under his hand.' GARRICK. 'He wrote to me in violent wrath, for having refused his play: "Sir, this is growing a very serious and terrible affair. I am resolved to publish my play. I will appeal to the world; and how will your judgement appear?" I answered, "Sir, notwithstanding all the seriousness, and all the terrours, I have no objection to your publishing your play; and as you live at a great distance, (Devonshire, I believe,) if you will send it to me, I will convey it to the press." I never heard more of it, ha! ha! ha!'

On Friday, April 10, I found Johnson at home in the morning. We resumed the conversation of yesterday. He put me in mind of some of it which had escaped my memory, and enabled me to record it more perfectly than I otherwise could have done. He was much pleased with my paying so great attention to his recommendation in 1763, the period when our acquaintance began, that I should keep a journal; and I could perceive he was secretly pleased to find so much of the fruit of his mind preserved; and as he had been used to imagine and say that he always laboured when he said a good thing—it delighted him, on a review, to find that his conversation teemed with point and imagery.

I said to him, 'You were yesterday, Sir, in remarkably good humour: but there was nothing to offend you, nothing to produce irritation or violence. There was no bold offender. There was not one capital conviction. It was a maiden assize. You had on your white gloves.'

He found fault with our friend Langton for having been too silent. 'Sir, (said I,) you will recollect, that he very properly took up Sir Joshua for being glad that Charles Fox had praised Goldsmith's *Traveller,* and you joined him.' JOHNSON. 'Yes, Sir, I knocked Fox on the head, without ceremony.

Reynolds is too much under Fox and Burke at present. He is under the *Fox star* and the *Irish constellation*. He is always under some planet.' BOSWELL. 'There is no Fox star.' JOHNSON. 'But there is a dog star.' BOSWELL. 'They say, indeed, a fox and a dog are the same animal.'

I reminded him of a gentleman,[1] who, Mrs. Cholmondeley said, was first talkative from affectation, and then silent from the same cause; that he first thought, 'I shall be celebrated as the liveliest man in every company;' and then, all at once, 'O! it is much more respectable to be grave and look wise.' 'He has reversed the Pythagorean discipline, by being first talkative, and then silent. He reverses the course of Nature too: he was first the gay butterfly, and then the creeping worm.' Johnson laughed loud and long at this expansion and illustration of what he himself had told me.

We dined together with Mr. Scott (now Sir William Scott, his Majesty's Advocate General,) at his chambers in the Temple, nobody else there. The company being small, Johnson was not in such spirits as he had been the preceding day, and for a considerable time little was said. At last he burst forth, 'Subordination is sadly broken down in this age. No man, now, has the same authority which his father had,—except a gaoler. No master has it over his servants: it is diminished in our colleges; nay, in our grammar-schools.' BOSWELL. 'What is the cause of this, Sir?' JOHNSON. 'Why, the coming in of the Scotch,' (laughing sarcastically.) BOSWELL. 'That is to say, things have been turned topsy turvey.—But your serious cause.' JOHNSON. 'Why, Sir, there are many causes, the chief of which is, I think, the great increase of money. No man now depends upon the Lord of a Manour, when he can send to another country, and fetch provisions. The shoe-black at the entry of my court does not depend on me. I can deprive him but of a penny a day, which he hopes somebody else will bring him; and that penny I must carry to another shoe-black, so the trade suffers nothing. I have explained, in my *Journey to the Hebrides*, how gold and silver destroy feudal subordination. But, besides, there is a general relaxation of reverence. No son now depends upon his father as in former times. Paternity used to be considered as of itself a great thing, which had a right to many claims. That is, in general, reduced to very small bounds. My hope is, that as anarchy produces tyranny, this extreme relaxation will produce *freni strictio*.'[2]

Talking of fame, for which there is so great a desire, I ob-

[1] Langton.

[2] 'A tight rein'.

447

served how little there is of it in reality, compared with the other objects of human attention. 'Let every man recollect, and he will be sensible how small a part of his time is employed in talking or thinking of Shakspeare, Voltaire, or any of the most celebrated men that have ever lived, or are now supposed to occupy the attention and admiration of the world. Let this be extracted and compressed; into what a narrow space will it go!' I then slily introduced Mr. Garrick's fame, and his assuming the airs of a great man. JOHNSON. 'Sir, it is wonderful how *little* Garrick assumes. No, Sir, Garrick *fortunam reverenter habet.*[1] Consider, Sir: celebrated men, such as you have mentioned, have had their applause at a distance; but Garrick had it dashed in his face, sounded in his ears, and went home every night with the plaudits of a thousand in his *cranium.* Then, Sir, Garrick did not *find,* but *made* his way to the tables, the levees, and almost the bedchambers of the great. Then, Sir, Garrick had under him a numerous body of people; who, from fear of his power, and hopes of his favour, and admiration of his talents, were constantly submissive to him. And here is a man who has advanced the dignity of his profession. Garrick has made a player a higher character.' SCOTT. 'And he is a very sprightly writer too.' JOHNSON. 'Yes, Sir; and all this supported by great wealth of his own acquisition. If all this had happened to me, I should have had a couple of fellows with long poles walking before me, to knock down every body that stood in the way. Consider, if all this had happened to Cibber or Quin, they'd have jumped over the moon.—Yet Garrick speaks to *us.* (smiling.) BOSWELL. 'And Garrick is a very good man, a charitable man.' JOHNSON. 'Sir, a liberal man. He has given away more money than any man in England. There may be a little vanity mixed; but he has shewn, that money is not his first object.' BOSWELL. 'Yet Foote used to say of him, that he walked out with an intention to do a generous action; but, turning the corner of a street, he met with the ghost of a half-penny, which frightened him.' JOHNSON. 'Why, Sir, that is very true, too; for I never knew a man of whom it could be said with less certainty to-day, what he will do to-morrow, than Garrick; it depends so much on his humour at the time.' SCOTT. 'I am glad to hear of his liberality. He has been represented as very saving.' JOHNSON. 'With his domestick saving we have nothing to do. I remember drinking tea with him long ago, when Peg Woffington made it, and he grumbled at

---

[1] 'Respects his good fortune.' Ausonius, *Epigrams,* ii. 7.

her for making it too strong.[1] He had then begun to feel money in his purse, and did not know when he should have enough of it.'

On the subject of wealth, the proper use of it, and the effects of that art which is called œconomy, he observed, 'It is wonderful to think how men of very large estates not only spend their yearly income, but are often actually in want of money. It is clear, they have not value for what they spend. Lord Shelburne told me, that a man of high rank, who looks into his own affairs, may have all that he ought to have, all that can be of any use, or appear with any advantage, for five thousand pounds a year. Therefore, a great proportion must go in waste; and, indeed, that is the case with most people, whatever their fortune is.' BOSWELL. 'I have no doubt, Sir, of this. But how is it? What is waste?' JOHNSON. 'Why, Sir, breaking bottles, and a thousand other things. Waste cannot be accurately told, though we are sensible how destructive it is. Œconomy on the one hand, by which a certain income is made to maintain a man genteelly, and waste on the other, by which, on the same income, another man lives shabbily, cannot be defined. It is a very nice thing: as one man wears his coat out much sooner than another, we cannot tell how.'

We talked of war. 'JOHNSON. 'Every man thinks meanly of himself for not having been a soldier, or not having been at sea.' BOSWELL. 'Lord Mansfield does not.' JOHNSON. 'Sir, if Lord Mansfield were in a company of General Officers and Admirals who have been in service, he would shrink; he'd wish to creep under the table.' BOSWELL. 'No; he'd think he could *try* them all.' JOHNSON. 'Yes, if he could catch them: but they'd try him much sooner. No, Sir; were Socrates and Charles the Twelfth of Sweden both present in any company, and Socrates to say, "Follow me, and hear a lecture on philosophy;" and Charles, laying his hand on his sword, to say, "Follow me, and dethrone the Czar;" a man would be ashamed to follow Socrates. Sir, the impression is universal; yet it is strange. As to the sailor, when you look down from the quarter deck to the space below, you see the utmost extremity of human misery; such crouding, such filth, such stench!' BOSWELL. 'Yet sailors are happy.' JOHNSON. 'They are happy as brutes are happy, with a piece of fresh meat,— with the grossest sensuality. But, Sir, the profession of soldiers and sailors has the dignity of danger. Mankind reverence those who have got over fear, which is so general a

[1] When Johnson told this little anecdote to Sir Joshua Reynolds, he mentioned a circumstance which he omitted to-day:—'Why (said Garrick) it is as red as blood'—B.

weakness.' SCOTT. 'But is not courage mechanical, and to be acquired?' JOHNSON. 'Why yes, Sir, in a collective sense. Soldiers consider themselves only as parts of a great machine.' SCOTT. 'We find people fond of being sailors.' JOHNSON. 'I cannot account for that, any more than I can account for other strange perversions of imagination.'

His abhorrence of the profession of a sailor was uniformly violent; but in conversation he always exalted the profession of a soldier. And yet I have, in my large and various collection of his writings, a letter to an eminent friend, in which he expresses himself thus: 'My god-son called on me lately. He is weary, and rationally weary, of a military life. If you can place him in some other state, I think you may increase his happiness, and secure his virtue. A soldier's time is passed in distress and danger, or in idleness and corruption.' Such was his cool reflection in his study, but whenever he was warmed and animated by the presence of company, he, like other philosophers, whose minds are impregnated with poetical fancy, caught the common enthusiasm for splendid renown.

He talked of Mr. Charles Fox, of whose abilities he thought highly, but observed, that he did not talk much at our CLUB. I have heard Mr. Gibbon remark, 'that Mr. Fox could not be afraid of Dr. Johnson; yet he certainly was very shy of saying any thing in Dr. Johnson's presence.' . . .

He told us, that he had given Mrs. Montagu a catalogue of all Daniel Defoe's works of imagination; most, if not all of which, as well as of his other works, he now enumerated, allowing a considerable share of merit to a man, who, bred a tradesman, had written so variously and so well. Indeed, his *Robinson Crusoe* is enough of itself to establish his reputation.

He expressed great indignation at the imposture of the Cock-lane Ghost, and related, with much satisfaction, how he had assisted in detecting the cheat, and had published an account of it in the news-papers. Upon this subject I incautiously offended him, by pressing him with too many questions, and he shewed his displeasure. I apologised, saying that 'I asked questions in order to be instructed and entertained; I repaired eagerly to the fountain; but that the moment he gave me a hint, the moment he put a lock upon the well, I desisted.'—'But, Sir, (said he,) that is forcing one to do a disagreeable thing:' and he continued to rate me. 'Nay, Sir, (said I,) when you have put a lock upon the well, so that I can no longer drink, do not make the fountain of your wit play upon me and wet me.'

He sometimes could not bear being teazed with questions.

I was once present when a gentleman[1] asked so many as, 'What did you do, Sir?' 'What did you say, Sir?' that he at last grew enraged, and said, 'I will not be put to the *question*. Don't you consider, Sir, that these are not the manners of a gentleman? I will not be baited with *what*, and *why*; what is this? what is that? why is a cow's tail long? why is a fox's tail bushy?' The gentleman, who was a good deal out of countenance, said, 'Why, Sir, you are so good, that I venture to trouble you.' JOHNSON. 'Sir, my being so *good* is no reason why you should be so *ill*.'

Talking of the Justitia hulk at Woolwich, in which criminals were punished, by being confined to labour, he said, 'I do not see that they are punished by this: they must have worked equally had they never been guilty of stealing. They now only work; so, after all, they have gained; what they stole is clear gain to them; the confinement is nothing. Every man who works is confined: the smith to his shop, the tailor to his garret.' BOSWELL. 'And Lord Mansfield to his Court.' JOHNSON. 'Yes, Sir, you know the notion of confinement may be extended, as in the song, "Every island is a prison." There is, in Dodsley's *Collection,* a copy of verses to the authour of that song.' . . .

He talked with an uncommon animation of travelling into distant countries; that the mind was enlarged by it, and that an acquisition of dignity of character was derived from it. He expressed a particular enthusiasm with respect to visiting the wall of China. I catched it for the moment, and said I really believed I should go and see the wall of China had I not children, of whom it was my duty to take care. 'Sir, (said he,) by doing so, you would do what would be of importance in raising your children to eminence. There would be a lustre reflected upon them from your spirit and curiosity. They would be at all times regarded as the children of a man who had gone to view the wall of China. I am serious, Sir.'

When we had left Mr. Scott's, he said, 'Will you go home with me?' 'Sir, (said I,) it is late; but I'll go with you for three minutes.' JOHNSON. 'Or *four*.' We went to Mrs. Williams's room, where we found Mr. Allen the printer, who was the landlord of his house in Bolt-court, a worthy obliging man, and his very old acquaintance; and what was exceedingly amusing, though he was of a very diminutive size, he used, even in Johnson's presence, to imitate the stately periods and slow and solemn utterance of the great man.—I this evening boasted, that although I did not write what is called stenography, or short-hand, in appropriated characters devised for

[1] Boswell.

the purpose, I had a method of my own of writing half words, and leaving out some altogether, so as yet to keep the substance and language of any discourse which I had heard so much in view, that I could give it very completely soon after I had taken it down. He defied me, as he once defied an actual short-hand writer, and he made the experiment by reading slowly and distinctly a part of Robertson's *History of America*, while I endeavoured to write it in my way of taking notes. It was found that I had it very imperfectly; the conclusion from which was, that its excellence was principally owing to a studied arrangement of words, which could not be varied or abridged without an essential injury.

On Sunday, April 12, I found him at home before dinner; Dr. Dodd's poem entitled *Thoughts in Prison* was lying upon his table. This appearing to me an extraordinary effort by a man who was in Newgate for a capital crime, I was desirous to hear Johnson's opinion of it: to my surprize, he told me he had not read a line of it. I took up the book and read a passage to him. JOHNSON. 'Pretty well, if you are previously disposed to like them.' I read another passage, with which he was better pleased. He then took the book into his own hands, and having looked at the prayer at the end of it, he said, 'What *evidence* is there that this was composed the night before he suffered? *I* do not believe it.' He then read aloud where he prays for the King, &c. and observed, 'Sir, do you think that a man the night before he is to be hanged cares for the succession of a royal family?— Though, he *may* have composed this prayer, then. A man who has been canting all his life, may cant to the last.—And yet a man who has been refused a pardon after so much petitioning, would hardly be praying thus fervently for the King.'

He and I, and Mrs. Williams, went to dine with the Reverend Dr. Percy. Talking of Goldsmith, Johnson said, he was very envious. I defended him, by observing that he owned it frankly upon all occasions. JOHNSON. 'Sir, you are enforcing the charge. He had so much envy, that he could not conceal it. He was so full of it that he overflowed. He talked of it to be sure often enough. Now, Sir, what a man avows, he is not ashamed to think; though many a man thinks, what he is ashamed to avow. We are all envious naturally; but by checking envy, we get the better of it. So we are all thieves naturally; a child always tries to get at what it wants, the nearest way; by good instruction and good habits this is cured, till a man has not even an inclination to seize what is another's; has no struggle with himself about it.'

And here I shall record a scene of too much heat between Dr. Johnson and Dr. Percy, which I should have suppressed were it not that it gave occasion to display the truely tender and benevolent heart of Johnson, who, as soon as he found a friend was at all hurt by any thing which he had 'said in his wrath,' was not only prompt and desirous to be reconciled, but exerted himself to make ample reparation.

Books of Travels having been mentioned, Johnson praised Pennant very highly, as he did at Dunvegan, in the Isle of Sky. Dr. Percy, knowing himself to be the heir male of the ancient Percies, and having the warmest and most dutiful attachment to the noble House of Northumberland, could not sit quietly and hear a man praised, who had spoken disrespectfully of Alnwick-Castle and the Duke's pleasure grounds, especially as he thought meanly of his travels. He therefore opposed Johnson eagerly. JOHNSON. 'Pennant in what he has said of Alnwick, has done what he intended; he has made you very angry.' PERCY. 'He has said the garden is *trim*, which is representing it like a citizen's parterre, when the truth is, there is a very large extent of fine turf and gravel walks.' JOHNSON. 'According to your own account, Sir, Pennant is right. It *is* trim. Here is grass cut close, and gravel rolled smooth. Is not that trim? The extent is nothing against that; a mile may be as trim as a square yard. Your extent puts me in mind of the citizen's enlarged dinner, two pieces of roast-beef, and two puddings. There is no variety, no mind exerted in laying out the ground, no trees.' PERCY. 'He pretends to give the natural history of Northumberland, and yet takes no notice of the immense number of trees planted there of late.' JOHNSON. 'That, Sir, has nothing to do with the *natural* history; that is *civil* history. A man who gives the natural history of the oak, is not to tell how many oaks have been planted in this place or that. A man who gives the natural history of the cow, is not to tell how many cows are milked at Islington. The animal is the same, whether milked in the Park or at Islington.' PERCY. 'Pennant does not describe well; a carrier who goes along the side of Loch-lomond would describe it better.' JOHNSON. 'I think he describes very well.' PERCY. 'I travelled after him.' JOHNSON. 'And *I* travelled after him.' PERCY. 'But, my good friend, you are short-sighted, and do not see so well as I do.' I wondered at Dr. Percy's venturing thus. Dr. Johnson said nothing at the time; but inflammable particles were collecting for a cloud to burst. In a little while Dr. Percy said something more in disparagement of Pennant. JOHNSON. (pointedly,) 'This is the resentment of a narrow mind, because he did not find every thing in Northumberland.' PERCY. (feeling the stroke,) 'Sir, you may be as rude as you please.' JOHNSON. 'Hold, Sir! Don't talk of rudeness; remember, Sir, you told me (puffing hard with passion struggling for a vent,) I was short-sighted. We have done with civility. We are to be as rude as we please.' PERCY. 'Upon my honour, Sir, I did not mean to be uncivil.' JOHNSON. 'I cannot say so, Sir; for I *did* mean to be uncivil, thinking *you* had been uncivil.' Dr. Percy rose, ran up to him, and taking him by the hand, assured him affectionately that his meaning had been misunderstood; upon which a reconciliation instantly took place. JOHNSON. 'My dear Sir, I am willing you shall *hang* Pennant.' PERCY. (resuming the former subject,) 'Pennant complains that the helmet is not hung out to invite to the hall of hospitality. Now I never heard that it was a custom to hang out a *helmet.*' 'JOHNSON. 'Hang him up, hang him up.' BOSWELL. (humouring the joke,) 'Hang out his skull instead of a helmet, and you may drink ale out of it in your hall of Odin, as he is your enemy; that will be truly ancient. *There* will be *Northern Antiquities.*'[1] JOHNSON. 'He's a *Whig*, Sir; a *sad dog.* (smiling at his own violent expressions, merely for *political* difference of opinion.) But he's the best traveller I ever read; he observes more things than any one else does.' . . .

We had a calm after the storm, staid the evening and supped, and were pleasant and gay. But Dr. Percy told me he was very uneasy at what had passed; for there was a gentleman there who was acquainted with the Northumberland family, to whom he hoped to have appeared more respectable, by shewing how intimate he was with Dr. Johnson, and who might now, on the contrary, go away with an opinion to his disadvantage. He begged I would mention this to Dr. Johnson, which I afterwards did. His observation upon it was, 'This comes of *stratagem;* had he told me that he wished to appear to advantage before that gentleman, he should have been at the top of the house, all the time.' He spoke of Dr. Percy in the handsomest terms. 'Then, Sir, (said I,) may I be allowed to suggest a mode by which you may effectually counteract any unfavourable report of what passed. I will write a letter to you upon the subject of the unlucky contest of that day, and you will be kind enough to put in writing as an answer to that letter, what you have now said, and as Lord Percy is to dine with us at General Paoli's soon, I will take an opportunity to read the correspondence in his Lordship's presence.' This friendly scheme was accordingly carried into execution without Dr. Percy's knowledge. Johnson's letter placed Dr. Percy's unquestionable merit in the fairest point of view; and I contrived that Lord Percy should hear the correspondence, by introducing it at General Paoli's, as an

---

[1] The title of a book translated by Dr. Percy—B.

instance of Dr. Johnson's kind disposition towards one in whom his Lordship was interested. Thus every unfavourable impression was obviated that could possibly have been made on those by whom he wished most to be regarded. I breakfasted the day after with him, and informed him of my scheme, and its happy completion, for which he thanked me in the warmest terms, and was highly delighted with Dr. Johnson's letter in his praise, of which I gave him a copy. He said, 'I would rather have this than degrees from all the Universities in Europe. It will be for me, and my children and grand-children.' Dr. Johnson having afterwards asked me if I had given him a copy of it, and being told I had, was offended, and insisted that I should get it back, which I did. . . .

On Monday, April 13, I dined with Johnson at Mr. Langton's, where were Dr. Porteus, then Bishop of Chester, now of London, and Dr. Stinton. He was at first in a very silent mood. Before dinner he said nothing but 'Pretty baby,' to one of the children. Langton said very well to me afterwards, that he could repeat Johnson's conversation before dinner, as Johnson had said that he could repeat a complete chapter of *The Natural History of Iceland*, from the Danish of *Horrebow*, the whole of which was exactly thus:—

'CHAP. LXXII. *Concerning snakes.*
'There are no snakes to be met with throughout the whole island.'

. . . We talked of the styles of different painters, and how certainly a connoisseur could distinguish them; I asked, if there was as clear a difference of styles in language as in painting, or even as in hand-writing, so that the composition of every individual may be distinguished? JOHNSON. 'Yes. Those who have a style of eminent excellence, such as Dryden and Milton, can always be distinguished.' I had no doubt of this, but what I wanted to know was, whether there was really a peculiar style to every man whatever, as there is certainly a peculiar hand-writing, a peculiar countenance, not widely different in many, yet always enough to be distinctive.' . . . The Bishop thought not; and said, he supposed that many pieces in Dodsley's collection of poems, though all very pretty, had nothing appropriated in their style, and in that particular could not be at all distinguished. JOHNSON. 'Why, Sir, I think every man whatever has a peculiar style, which may be discovered by nice examination and comparison with others: but a man must write a great deal to make his style obviously discernible. As logicians say, this appropriation of style is infinite *in potestate*, limited *in actu*.'[1]

1 'Potentially . . . actually.'

Mr. Topham Beauclerk came in the evening, and he and Dr. Johnson and I staid to supper. It was mentioned that Dr. Dodd had once wished to be a member of THE LITERARY CLUB. JOHNSON. 'I should be sorry if any of our Club were hanged. I will not say but some of them deserve it.' Beauclerk (supposing this to be aimed at persons for whom he had at that time a wonderful fancy, which, however, did not last long,) was irritated, and eagerly said, 'You, Sir, have a friend, (naming him)[1] who deserves to be hanged; for he speaks behind their backs against those with whom he lives on the best terms, and attacks them in the news-papers. *He* certainly ought to be *kicked*.' JOHNSON. 'Sir, we all do this in some degree. *"Veniam petimus damusque vicissim."*[2] To be sure it may be done so much, that a man may deserve to be kicked.' BEAUCLERK. 'He is very malignant.' JOHNSON. 'No, Sir; he is not malignant. He is mischievous, if you will. He would do no man an essential injury; he may, indeed, love to make sport of people by vexing their vanity. I, however, once knew an old gentleman who was absolutely malignant. He really wished evil to others, and rejoiced at it.' BOSWELL. 'The gentleman, Mr. Beauclerk, against whom you are so violent, is, I know, a man of good principles.' BEAUCLERK. 'Then he does not wear them out in practice.'

Dr. Johnson, who, as I have observed before, delighted in discrimination of character, and having a masterly knowledge of human nature, was willing to take men as they are, imperfect and with a mixture of good and bad qualities, I suppose thought he had said enough in defence of his friend, of whose merits, notwithstanding his exceptional points, he had a just value; and added no more on the subject.

On Tuesday, April 14, I dined with him at General Oglethorpe's, with General Paoli and Mr. Langton. General Oglethorpe declaimed against luxury. JOHNSON. 'Depend upon it, Sir, every state of society is as luxurious as it can be. Men always take the best they can get.' OGLETHORPE. 'But the best depends much upon ourselves; and if we can be as well satisfied with plain things, we are in the wrong to accustom our palates to what is high-seasoned and expensive. What says Addison in his *Cato,* speaking of the Numidian?

> "Coarse are his meals, the fortune of the chace,
> Amid the running stream he slakes his thirst,
> Toils all the day, and at the approach of night,
> On the first friendly bank he throws him down,

---

[1] Steevens.

[2] 'This privilege we demand and allow reciprocally.' Horace, *Art of Poetry*, l. 11.

> Or rests his head upon a rock till morn;
> And if the following day he chance to find
> A new repast, or an untasted spring,
> Blesses his stars, and thinks it luxury."

Let us have *that* kind of luxury, Sir, if you will.' JOHNSON. 'But hold, Sir; to be merely satisfied is not enough. It is in refinement and elegance that the civilized man differs from the savage. A great part of our industry, and all our ingenuity is exercised in procuring pleasure; and, Sir, a hungry man has not the same pleasure in eating a plain dinner, that a hungry man has in eating a luxurious dinner. You see I put the case fairly. A hungry man may have as much, nay, more pleasure in eating a plain dinner, than a man grown fastidious has in eating a luxurious dinner. But I suppose the man who decides between the two dinners, to be equally a hungry man.'

Talking of different governments,—JOHNSON. 'The more contracted that power is, the more easily it is destroyed. A country governed by a despot is an inverted cone. Government there cannot be so firm, as when it rests upon a broad basis gradually contracted, as the government of Great Britain, which is founded on the parliament, then is in the privy council, then in the King.' BOSWELL. 'Power, when contracted into the person of a despot, may be easily destroyed, as the prince may be cut off. So Caligula wished that the people of Rome had but one neck, that he might cut them off at a blow.' OGLETHORPE. 'It was of the Senate he wished that. The Senate by its usurpation controuled both the Emperour and the people. And don't you think that we see too much of that in our own Parliament?' . . .

On Wednesday, April 15, I dined with Dr. Johnson at Mr. Dilly's, and was in high spirits, for I had been a good part of the morning with Mr. Orme, the able and eloquent historian of Hindostan, who expressed a great admiration of Johnson. 'I do not care (said he,) on what subject Johnson talks; but I love better to hear him talk than any body. He either gives you new thoughts, or a new colouring. It is a shame to the nation that he has not been more liberally rewarded. Had I been George the Third, and thought as he did about America, I would have given Johnson three hundred a year for his *Taxation no Tyranny* alone.' I repeated this, and Johnson was much pleased with such praise from such a man as Orme.

At Mr. Dilly's to-day were Mrs. Knowles, the ingenious Quaker lady, Miss Seward, the poetess of Lichfield, the Reverend Dr. Mayo, and the Rev. Mr. Beresford, Tutor to the Duke of Bedford. Before dinner Dr. Johnson seized upon Mr. Charles Sheridan's *Account of the late Revolution in Sweden,* and seemed to read it ravenously, as if he devoured

457

it, which was to all appearance his method of studying. 'He knows how to read better than any one (said Mrs. Knowles;) he gets at the substance of a book directly; he tears out the heart of it.' He kept it wrapt up in the table-cloth in his lap during the time of dinner, from an avidity to have one entertainment in readiness when he should have finished another; resembling (if I may use so coarse a simile) a dog who holds a bone in his paws in reserve, while he eats something else which has been thrown to him.

The subject of cookery having been very naturally introduced at a table where Johnson, who boasted of the niceness of his palate, owned that 'he always found a good dinner,' he said, 'I could write a better book of cookery than has ever yet been written; it should be a book upon philosophical principles. Pharmacy is now made much more simple. Cookery may be made so too. A prescription which is now compounded of five ingredients, had formerly fifty in it. So in cookery, if the nature of the ingredients be well known, much fewer will do. Then as you cannot make bad meat good, I would tell what is the best butcher's meat, the best beef, the best pieces; how to choose young fowls; the proper seasons of different vegetables; and then how to roast and boil, and compound.' DILLY. 'Mrs. Glasse's *Cookery*, which is the best, was written by Dr. Hill. Half the *trade*[1] know this.' JOHNSON. 'Well, Sir. This shews how much better the subject of cookery may be treated by a philosopher. I doubt if the book be written by Dr. Hill; for, in Mrs. Glasse's *Cookery*, which I have looked into, salt-petre and sal-prunella are spoken of as different substances, whereas sal-prunella is only salt-petre burnt on charcoal; and Hill could not be ignorant of this. However, as the greatest part of such a book is made by transcription, this mistake may have been carelessly adopted. But you shall see what a Book of Cookery I shall make! I shall agree with Mr. Dilly for the copy-right' MISS SEWARD. 'That would be Hercules with the distaff indeed.' JOHNSON. 'No, Madam. Women can spin very well; but they cannot make a good book of Cookery.'

JOHNSON. 'O! Mr. Dilly—you must know that an English Benedictine Monk at Paris has translated *The Duke of Berwick's Memoirs*, from the original French, and has sent them to me to sell. I offered them to Strahan, who sent them back with this answer:—"That the first book he had published was the *Duke of Berwick's Life*, by which he had lost: and he

---

[1] As Physicians are called *the Faculty*, and Counsellors at Law *the Profession*; the Booksellers of London are denominated *the Trade*. Johnson disapproved of these denominations—B.

hated the name."——Now I honestly tell you, that Strahan has refused them; but I also honestly tell you, that he did it upon no principle, for he never looked into them.' DILLY. 'Are they well translated, Sir?' JOHNSON. 'Why, Sir, very well——in a style very current and very clear. I have written to the Benedictine to give me an answer upon two points——what evidence is there that the letters are authentick? (for if they are not authentick they are nothing;)——And how long will it be before the original French is published? For if the French edition is not to appear for a considerable time, the translation will be almost as valuable as an original book. They will make two volumes in octavo; and I have undertaken to correct every sheet as it comes from the press.' Mr. Dilly desired to see them, and said he would send for them. He asked Dr. Johnson if he would write a Preface to them. JOHNSON. 'No, Sir. The Benedictines were very kind to me, and I'll do what I undertook to do; but I will not mingle my name with them. I am to gain nothing by them. I'll turn them loose upon the world, and let them take their chance.' . . .

Mrs. Knowles affected to complain that men had much more liberty allowed them than women. JOHNSON. 'Why, Madam, women have all the liberty they should wish to have. We have all the labour and the danger, and the women all the advantage. We go to sea, we build houses, we do everything, in short, to pay our court to the women.' MRS. KNOWLES. 'The Doctor reasons very wittily, but not convincingly. Now, take the instance of building; the mason's wife, if she is ever seen in liquor, is ruined; the mason may get himself drunk as often as he pleases, with little loss of character; nay, may let his wife and children starve.' JOHNSON. 'Madam, you must consider, if the mason does get himself drunk, and let his wife and children starve, the parish will oblige him to find security for their maintenance. We have different modes of restraining evil. Stocks for the men, a ducking-stool for women, and a pound for beasts. If we require more perfection from women than from ourselves, it is doing them honour. And women have not the same temptations that we have: they may always live in virtuous company; men must mix in the world indiscriminately. If a woman has no inclination to do what is wrong, being secured from it is no restraint to her. I am at liberty to walk into the Thames; but if I were to try it, my friends would restrain me in Bedlam, and I should be obliged to them.' MRS. KNOWLES. 'Still, Doctor, I cannot help thinking it a hardship that more indulgence is allowed to men than to women. It gives a superiority to men, to which I do not see how they are entitled.' JOHNSON. 'It is plain, Madam, one or other must have the superiority. As

Shakspeare says, "If two men ride on a horse, one must ride behind." ' DILLY. 'I suppose, Sir, Mrs. Knowles would have them to ride in panniers, one on each side.' JOHNSON. 'Then, Sir, the horse would throw them both.' MRS. KNOWLES. 'Well, I hope that in another world the sexes will be equal.' BOSWELL. 'That is being too ambitious, Madam. We might as well desire to be equal with the angels. We shall all, I hope, be happy in a future state, but we must not expect to be all happy in the same degree. It is enough if we be happy according to our several capacities. A worthy carman will get to heaven as well as Sir Isaac Newton. Yet, though equally good, they will not have the same degrees of happiness.' JOHNSON. 'Probably not.'

Upon this subject I had once before sounded him, by mentioning the late Reverend Mr. Brown, of Utrecht's, image; that a great and small glass, though equally full, did not hold an equal quantity; which he threw out to refute David Hume's saying, that a little miss, going to dance at a ball, in a fine new dress, was as happy as a great oratour, after having made an eloquent and applauded speech. After some thought, Johnson said, 'I come over to the parson.' . . .

Dr. Mayo having asked Johnson's opinion of Soame Jenyns's *View of the Internal Evidence of the Christian Religion;* —JOHNSON. 'I think it a pretty book; not very theological indeed; and there seems to be an affectation of ease and carelessness, as if it were not suitable to his character to be very serious about the matter.' BOSWELL. 'He may have intended this to introduce his book the better among genteel people, who might be unwilling to read too grave a treatise. There is a general levity in the age. We have physicians now with bag-wigs; may we not have airy divines, at least somewhat less solemn in their appearance than they used to be?' JOHNSON. 'Jenyns might mean as you say.' BOSWELL. '*You* should like his book, Mrs. Knowles, as it maintains, as you *friends* do, that courage is not a Christian virtue.' MRS. KNOWLES. 'Yes, indeed, I like him there; but I cannot agree with him, that friendship is not a Christian virtue.' JOHNSON. 'Why, Madam, strictly speaking, he is right. All friendship is preferring the interest of a friend, to the neglect, or, perhaps, against the interest of others; so that an old Greek said, "He that has *friends* has *no friend*." Now Christianity recommends universal benevolence, to consider all men as our brethren, which is contrary to the virtue of friendship, as described by the ancient philosophers. Surely, Madam, your sect must approve of this; for, you call all men *friends*.' MRS. KNOWLES. 'We are commanded to do good to all men, "but especially to them who are of the household of Faith." '

JOHNSON. 'Well, Madam. The household of Faith is wide enough.' MRS. KNOWLES. 'But Doctor, our Saviour had twelve Apostles, yet there was *one* whom he *loved*. John was called "the disciple whom JESUS loved." ' JOHNSON. (with eyes sparkling benignantly,) 'Very well, indeed, Madam. You have said very well.' BOSWELL. 'A fine application. Pray, Sir, had you ever thought of it?' JOHNSON. 'I had not, Sir.'

From this pleasing subject, he, I know not how or why, made a sudden transition to one upon which he was a violent aggressor; for he said, 'I am willing to love all mankind, *except an American:*' and his inflammable corruption bursting into horrid fire, he 'breathed out threatenings and slaughter;' calling them, 'Rascals—Robbers—Pirates;' and exclaiming, he'd 'burn and destroy them.' Miss Seward, looking to him with mild but steady astonishment, said, 'Sir, this is an instance that we are always most violent against those whom we have injured.'—He was irritated still more by this delicate and keen reproach; and roared out another tremendous volley, which one might fancy could be heard across the Atlantick. During this tempest I sat in great uneasiness, lamenting his heat of temper; till, by degrees, I diverted his attention to other topicks.

DR. MAYO. (to Dr. Johnson,) 'Pray, Sir, have you read *Edwards, of New England, on Grace?*' JOHNSON. 'No, Sir.' BOSWELL. 'It puzzled me so much as to the freedom of the human will, by stating, with wonderful acute ingenuity, our being actuated by a series of motives which we cannot resist, that the only relief I had was to forget it.' MAYO. 'But he makes the proper distinction between moral and physical necessity.' BOSWELL. 'Alas, Sir, they come both to the same thing. You may be bound as hard by chains when covered by leather, as when the iron appears. The argument for the moral necessity of human actions is always, I observe, fortified by supposing universal prescience to be one of the attributes of the Deity.' JOHNSON. 'You are surer that you are free, than you are of prescience; you are surer that you can lift up your finger or not as you please, than you are of any conclusion from a deduction of reasoning. But let us consider a little the objection from prescience. It is certain I am either to go home to-night or not; that does not prevent my freedom.' BOSWELL. 'That it is certain you are *either* to go home or not, does not prevent your freedom; because the liberty of choice between the two is compatible with that certainty. But if *one* of these events be certain *now,* you have no *future* power of volition. If it be certain you are to go home to-night, you *must* go home.' JOHNSON. 'If I am well acquainted with a man, I can judge with great probability how he will

461

act in any case, without his being restrained by my judging. GOD may have this probability increased to certainty.' BOSWELL. 'When it is increased to *certainty,* freedom ceases, because that cannot be certainly foreknown, which is not certain at the time; but if it be certain at the time, it is a contradiction in terms to maintain that there can be afterwards any *contingency* dependent upon the exercise of will or any thing else.' JOHNSON. 'All theory is against the freedom of the will; all experience for it.'—I did not push the subject any farther. I was glad to find him so mild in discussing a question of the most abstract nature, involved with theological tenets, which he generally would not suffer to be in any degree opposed.

He as usual defended luxury; 'You cannot spend money in luxury without doing good to the poor. Nay, you do more good to them by spending it in luxury, than by giving it: for by spending it in luxury, you make them exert industry, whereas by giving it, you keep them idle. I own, indeed, there may be more virtue in giving it immediately in charity than in spending it in luxury; though there may be a pride in that too.' Miss Seward asked, if this was not Mandeville's doctrine of 'private vices publick benefits.' JOHNSON. 'The fallacy of that book is, that Mandeville defines neither vices nor benefits. He reckons among vices everything that gives pleasure. He takes the narrowest system of morality, monastick morality, which holds pleasure itself to be a vice, such as eating salt with our fish, because it makes it taste better; and he reckons wealth as a publick benefit, which is by no means always true. Pleasure of itself is not a vice. Having a garden, which we all know to be perfectly innocent, is a great pleasure. At the same time, in this state of being there are many pleasures vices, which however are so immediately agreeable that we can hardly abstain from them. The happiness of Heaven will be, that pleasure and virtue will be perfectly consistent. Mandeville puts the case of a man who gets drunk in an alehouse; and says it is a publick benefit, because so much money is got by it to the publick. But it must be considered, that all the good gained by this, through the gradation of alehouse-keeper, brewer, maltster, and farmer, is overbalanced by the evil caused to the man and his family by his getting drunk. This is the way to try what is vicious, by ascertaining whether more evil than good is produced by it upon the whole, which is the case in all vice. It may happen that good is produced by vice; but not as vice; for instance, a robber may take money from its owner, and give it to one who will make a better use of it. Here is good produced; but not by the robbery as robbery, but as translation of property. I read Mandeville forty, or, I believe, fifty years ago. He did not puzzle me; he opened my views into real life very much. No, it is clear that the happiness of society depends on virtue. In Sparta, theft was allowed by general consent: theft, therefore, was *there* not a crime, but then there was no security; and what a life must they have had, when there was no security. Without truth there must be a dissolution of society. As it is, there is so little truth, that we are almost afraid to trust our ears; but how should we be, if falsehood were multiplied ten times? Society is held together by communication and information; and I remember this remark of Sir Thomas Brown's, 'Do the devils lie? No; for then Hell could not subsist.' '

Talking of Miss ———,[1] a literary lady, he said, 'I was obliged to speak to Miss Reynolds, to let her know that I desired she would not flatter me so much.' Somebody now observed, 'She flatters Garrick.' JOHNSON. 'She is in the right to flatter Garrick. She is in the right for two reasons; first, because she has the world with her, who have been praising Garrick these thirty years; and secondly, because she is rewarded for it by Garrick. Why should she flatter *me?* I can do nothing for her. Let her carry her praise to a better market. (Then turning to Mrs. Knowles.) You, Madam, have been flattering me all the evening; I wish you would give Boswell a little now. If you knew his merit as well as I do, you would say a great deal; he is the best travelling companion in the world.'

Somebody mentioned the Reverend Mr. Mason's prosecution of Mr. Murray, the bookseller, for having inserted in a collection of *Gray's Poems,* only fifty lines, of which Mr. Mason had still the exclusive property, under the statute of Queen Anne; and that Mr. Mason had persevered, notwithstanding his being requested to name his own terms of compensation. Johnson signified his displeasure at Mr. Mason's conduct very strongly; but added, by way of shewing that he was not surprized at it, 'Mason's a Whig.' MRS. KNOWLES. (not hearing distinctly,) 'What! a Prig, Sir?' JOHNSON. 'Worse, Madam; a Whig! But he is both.'

I expressed a horrour at the thought of death. MRS. KNOWLES. 'Nay, thou should'st not have a horrour for what is the gate of life.' JOHNSON. (standing upon the hearth rolling about, with a serious, solemn, and somewhat gloomy air,) 'No rational man can die without uneasy apprehension.' MRS. KNOWLES. 'The Scriptures tell us, "The righteous shall have *hope* in his death." ' JOHNSON. 'Yes, Madam; that is, he shall not have despair. But, consider, his hope of salvation must be founded on the terms on which it is promised that the media-

[1] Hannah More.

463

tion of our SAVIOUR shall be applied to us,—namely, obedience; and where obedience has failed, then, as suppletory to it, repentance. But what man can say that his obedience has been such, as he would approve of in another, or even in himself upon close examination, or that his repentance has not been such as to require being repented of? No man can be sure that his obedience and repentance will obtain salvation.' MRS. KNOWLES. 'But divine intimation of acceptance may be made to the soul.' JOHNSON. 'Madam, it may; but I should not think the better of a man who should tell me on his death-bed he was sure of salvation. A man cannot be sure himself that he has divine intimation of acceptance; much less can he make others sure that he has it.' BOSWELL. 'Then, Sir, we must be contented to acknowledge that death is a terrible thing.' JOHNSON. 'Yes, Sir. I have made no approaches to a state which can look on it as not terrible.' MRS. KNOWLES. (seeming to enjoy a pleasing serenity in the persuasion of benignant divine light,) 'Does not St. Paul say, "I have fought the good fight of faith, I have finished my course; henceforth is laid up for me a crown of life?"' JOHNSON. 'Yes, Madam; but here was a man inspired, a man who had been converted by supernatural interposition.' BOSWELL. 'In prospect death is dreadful; but in fact we find that people die easy.' JOHNSON. 'Why, Sir, most people have not *thought* much of the matter, so cannot *say* much, and it is supposed they die easy. Few believe it certain they are then to die; and those who do, set themselves to behave with resolution, as a man does who is going to be hanged. He is not the less unwilling to be hanged.' MISS SEWARD. 'There is one mode of the fear of death, which is certainly absurd; and that is the dread of annihilation, which is only a pleasing sleep without a dream.' JOHNSON. 'It is neither pleasing, nor sleep; it is nothing. Now mere existence is so much better than nothing, that one would rather exist even in pain, than not exist.' BOSWELL. 'If annihilation be nothing, then existing in pain is not a comparative state, but is a positive evil, which I cannot think we should choose. I must be allowed to differ here; and it would lessen the hope of a future state founded on the argument, that the Supreme Being, who is good as he is great, will hereafter compensate for our present sufferings in this life. For if existence, such as we have it here, be comparatively a good, we have no reason to complain, though no more of it should be given to us. But if our only state of existence were in this world, then we might with some reason complain that we are so dissatisfied with our enjoyments compared with our desires.' JOHNSON. 'The lady confounds annihilation, which is nothing, with the apprehension of it, which is dreadful. It is in the apprehension of it that the horrour of annihilation consists.'

Of John Wesley, he said, 'He can talk well on any subject.' BOSWELL. 'Pray, Sir, what has he made of his story of a ghost?' JOHNSON. 'Why, Sir, he believes it; but not on sufficient authority. He did not take time enough to examine the girl. It was at Newcastle, where the ghost was said to have appeared to a young woman several times, mentioning something about the right to an old house, advising application to be made to an attorney, which was done; and, at the same time, saying the attorney would do nothing, which proved to be the fact. "This (says John,) is a proof that a ghost knows our thoughts." Now (laughing,) it is not necessary to know our thoughts, to tell that an attorney will sometimes do nothing. Charles Wesley, who is a more stationary man, does not believe the story. I am sorry that John did not take more pains to inquire into the evidence for it.' MISS SEWARD. (with an incredulous smile,) 'What, Sir! about a ghost?' JOHNSON. (with solemn vehemence,) 'Yes, Madam: this is a question which, after five thousand years, is yet undecided; a question, whether in theology or philosophy, one of the most important that can come before the human understanding.'

Mrs. Knowles mentioned, as a proselyte to Quakerism, Miss ————, a young lady well known to Dr. Johnson, for whom he had shewn much affection; while she ever had, and still retained, a great respect for him. Mrs. Knowles at the same time took an opportunity of letting him know 'that the amiable young creature was sorry at finding that he was offended at her leaving the Church of England and embracing a simpler faith;' and, in the gentlest and most persuasive manner, solicited his kind indulgence for what was sincerely a matter of conscience. JOHNSON. (frowning very angrily,) 'Madam, she is an odious wench. She could not have any proper conviction that it was her duty to change her religion, which is the most important of all subjects, and should be studied with all care, and with all the helps we can get. She knew no more of the Church which she left, and that which she embraced, than she did of the difference between the Copernican and Ptolemaick systems.' MRS. KNOWLES. 'She had the New Testament before her.' JOHNSON. 'Madam, she could not understand the New Testament, the most difficult book in the world, for which the study of a life is required.' MRS. KNOWLES. 'It is clear as to essentials.' JOHNSON. 'But not as to controversial points. The heathens were easily converted, because they had nothing to give up; but we ought not, without very strong conviction indeed, to desert the religion in which we have been educated. That is the religion given you, the religion in which it may be said Providence has placed you. If you live conscientiously in that religion, you may be safe. But errour is dangerous indeed, if you err when you choose a religion for yourself.' MRS. KNOWLES. 'Must we then go by implicit faith?' JOHNSON. 'Why, Madam, the greatest part of our knowledge is implicit faith; and as to religion, have we heard all that a disciple of Confucius, all that a Mahometan, can say for himself?' He then rose again into passion, and attacked the young proselyte in the severest terms of reproach, so that both the ladies seemed to be much shocked.

We remained together till it was pretty late. Notwithstanding occasional explosions of violence, we were all delighted upon the whole with Johnson. I compared him at this time to a warm West-Indian climate, where you have a bright sun, quick vegetation, luxuriant foliage, luscious fruits; but where the same heat sometimes produces thunder, lightning, earthquakes, in a terrible degree.

April 17, being Good Friday, I waited on Johnson, as usual. I observed at breakfast that although it was a part of his abstemious discipline on this most solemn fast, to take no milk in his tea, yet when Mrs. Desmoulins inadvertently poured it in, he did not reject it. I talked of the strange indecision of mind, and imbecility in the common occurrences of life, which we may observe in some people. JOHNSON. 'Why, Sir, I am in the habit of getting others to do things for me.' BOSWELL. 'What, Sir! have you that weakness?' JOHNSON. 'Yes, Sir. But I always think afterwards I should have done better for myself.'

I told him that at a gentleman's[1] house where there was thought to be such extravagance or bad management, that he was living much beyond his income, his lady had objected to the cutting of a pickled mango, and that I had taken an opportunity to ask the price of it, and found it was only two shillings; so here was a very poor saving. JOHNSON. 'Sir, that is the blundering œconomy of a narrow understanding. It is stopping one hole in a sieve.'

I expressed some inclination to publish an account of my *Travels* upon the continent of Europe, for which I had a variety of materials collected. JOHNSON. 'I do not say, Sir, you may not publish your travels; but I give you my opinion, that you would lessen yourself by it. What can you tell of countries so well known as those upon the continent of Europe, which you have visited?' BOSWELL. 'But I can give an enter-

[1] Langton's.

taining narrative, with many incidents, anecdotes, *jeux d'esprit,* and remarks, so as to make very pleasant reading.' JOHNSON. 'Why, Sir, most modern travellers in Europe who have published their travels, have been laughed at: I would not have you added to the number. The world is now not contented to be merely entertained by a traveller's narrative; they want to learn something. Now some of my friends asked me, why I did not give some account of my travels in France. The reason is plain; intelligent readers had seen more of France than I had. *You* might have liked my travels in France, and THE CLUB might have liked them; but upon the whole, there would have been more ridicule than good produced by them.' BOSWELL. 'I cannot agree with you, Sir. People would like to read what you say of any thing. Suppose a face has been painted by fifty painters before; still we love to see it done by Sir Joshua.' JOHNSON. 'True, Sir, but Sir Joshua cannot paint a face when he has not time to look on it.' BOSWELL. 'Sir, a sketch of any sort by him is valuable. And, Sir, to talk to you in your own style (raising my voice, and shaking my head,) you *should* have given us your travels in France. I am *sure* I am right, and *there's an end on't.*'

I said to him that it was certainly true, as my friend Dempster had observed in his letter to me upon the subject, that a great part of what was in his *Journey to the Western Islands of Scotland* had been in his mind before he left London. JOHNSON. 'Why yes, Sir, the topicks were; and books of travels will be good in proportion to what a man has previously in his mind; his knowing what to observe; his power of contrasting one mode of life with another. As the Spanish proverb says, "He, who would bring home the wealth of the Indies, must carry the wealth of the Indies with him." So it is in travelling; a man must carry knowledge with him, if he would bring home knowledge.' BOSWELL. 'The proverb, I suppose, Sir, means, he must carry a large stock with him to trade with.' JOHNSON. 'Yes, Sir.'

It was a delightful day; as we walked to St. Clement's church, I again remarked that Fleet-street was the most cheerful scene in the world. 'Fleet-street (said I,) is in my mind more delightful than Tempé.' JOHNSON. 'Ay, Sir; but let it be compared with Mull.'

There were a very numerous congregation to-day at St. Clement's church, which Dr. Johnson said he observed with pleasure.

And now I am to give a pretty full account of one of the most curious incidents in Johnson's life, of which he himself has made the following minute on this day: 'In my return from church, I was accosted by Edwards, an old fellow-collegian, who had not seen me since 1729. He knew me, and asked if I remembered one Edwards; I did not at first recollect the name, but gradually as we walked along, recovered it, and told him a conversation that had passed at an ale-house between us. My purpose is to continue our acquaintance.'

It was in Butcher-row that this meeting happened. Mr. Edwards, who was a decent-looking elderly man in grey clothes, and a wig of many curls, accosted Johnson with familiar confidence, knowing who he was, while Johnson returned his salutation with a courteous formality, as to a stranger. But as soon as Edwards had brought to his recollection their having been at Pembroke-College together nine-and-forty years ago, he seemed much pleased, asked where he lived, and said he should be glad to see him in Bolt-court. EDWARDS. 'Ah, Sir! we are old men now.' JOHNSON. (who never liked to think of being old,) 'Don't let us discourage one another.' EDWARDS. 'Why, Doctor, you look stout and hearty, I am happy to see you so; for the news-papers told us you were very ill.' JOHNSON. 'Ay, Sir, they are always telling lies of *us old fellows.*'

Wishing to be present at more of so singular a conversation as that between two fellow-collegians, who had lived forty years in London without ever having chanced to meet, I whispered to Mr. Edwards that Dr. Johnson was going home, and that he had better accompany him now. So Edwards walked along with us, I eagerly assisting to keep up the conversation. Mr. Edwards informed Dr. Johnson that he had practised long as a solicitor in Chancery, but that he now lived in the country upon a little farm, about sixty acres, just by Stevenage in Hertfordshire, and that he came to London (to Barnard's Inn, No. 6), generally twice a week. Johnson appearing to be in a reverie, Mr. Edwards addressed himself to me, and expatiated on the pleasure of living in the country. BOSWELL. 'I have no notion of this, Sir. What you have to entertain you, is, I think, exhausted in half an hour.' EDWARDS. 'What? don't you love to have hope realized? I see my grass, and my corn, and my trees growing. Now, for instance, I am curious to see if this frost has not nipped my fruit-trees.' JOHNSON. (who we did not imagine was attending,) 'You find, Sir, you have fears as well as hopes.'—So well did he see the whole, when another saw but the half of a subject.

When we got to Dr. Johnson's house, and were seated in his library, the dialogue went on admirably. EDWARDS. 'Sir, I remember you would not let us say *prodigious* at College. For even then, Sir, (turning to me,) he was delicate in language, and we all feared him.[1] JOHNSON. (to Edwards,) 'From your having practised the law long, Sir, I presume you must be rich.' EDWARDS. 'No, Sir; I got a good deal of money; but I had a number of poor relations to whom I gave a great part of it.' JOHNSON. 'Sir, you have been rich in the most valuable sense of the word.' EDWARDS. 'But I shall not die rich.' JOHNSON. 'Nay, sure, Sir, it is better to *live* rich than to *die* rich.' EDWARDS. 'I wish I had continued at College.' JOHNSON. 'Why do you wish that, Sir?' EDWARDS. 'Because I think I should have had a much easier life than mine has been. I should have been a parson, and had a good living, like Bloxam and several others, and lived comfortably.' JOHNSON. 'Sir, the life of a parson, of a conscientious clergyman, is not easy. I have always considered a clergyman as the father of a larger family than he is able to maintain. I would rather have Chancery suits upon my hands than the cure of souls. No, Sir, I do not envy a clergyman's life as an easy life, nor do I envy the clergyman who makes it an easy life.' Here taking himself up all of a sudden, he exclaimed, 'O! Mr. Edwards! I'll convince you that I recollect you. Do you remember our drinking together at an alehouse near Pembroke gate? At that time, you told me of the Eton boy, who, when verses on our SAVIOUR's turning water into wine were prescribed as an exercise, brought up a single line, which was highly admired,—

"Vidit et erubuit lympha pudica DEUM"[2]

and I told you of another fine line in Camden's *Remains,* an eulogy upon one of our Kings, who was succeeded by his son, a prince of equal merit:—

"Mira cano, Sol occubuit, nox nulla secuta est." [3]

EDWARDS. 'You are a philosopher, Dr. Johnson. I have tried too in my time to be a philosopher; but, I don't know how, cheerfulness was always breaking in.'—Mr. Burke, Sir Joshua Reynolds, Mr. Courtenay, Mr. Malone, and, indeed, all the eminent men to whom I have mentioned this, have thought it an exquisite trait of character. The truth is, that philosophy, like religion, is too generally supposed to be hard and severe, at least so grave as to exclude all gaiety.

EDWARDS. 'I have been twice married, Doctor. You, I suppose, have never known what it was to have a wife.' JOHN-

---

[1] Johnson said to me afterwards, 'Sir, they respected me for my literature; and yet it was not great but by comparison. Sir, it is amazing how little literature there is in the world'—B.

[2] 'The modest nymph saw her God and blushed.'

[3] 'I sing a marvel: the sun set, but no night followed.'

SON. 'Sir, I have known what it was to have a wife, and (in a solemn, tender, faultering tone) I have known what it was to *lose a wife.*—It had almost broke my heart.'

EDWARDS. 'How do you live, Sir? For my part, I must have my regular meals, and a glass of good wine. I find I require it.' JOHNSON. 'I now drink no wine, Sir. Early in life I drank wine: for many years I drank none. I then for some years drank a great deal.' EDWARDS. 'Some hogsheads, I warrant you.' JOHNSON. 'I then had a severe illness, and left it off, and I have never begun it again. I never felt any difference upon myself from eating one thing rather than another, nor from one kind of weather rather than another. There are people, I believe, who feel a difference; but I am not one of them. And as to regular meals, I have fasted from the Sunday's dinner to the Tuesday's dinner, without any inconvenience. I believe it is best to eat just as one is hungry: but a man who is in business, or a man who has a family, must have stated meals. I am a straggler. I may leave this town and go to Grand Cairo, without being missed here or observed there.' EDWARDS. 'Don't you eat supper, Sir?' JOHNSON. 'No, Sir.' EDWARDS. 'For my part, now, I consider supper as a turnpike through which one must pass, in order to get to bed.'[1]

JOHNSON. 'You are a lawyer, Mr. Edwards. Lawyers know life practically. A bookish man should always have them to converse with. They have what he wants.' EDWARDS. 'I am grown old: I am sixty-five.' JOHNSON. 'I shall be sixty-eight next birth-day. Come, Sir, drink water, and put in for a hundred.'

Mr. Edwards mentioned a gentleman who had left his whole fortune to Pembroke College. JOHNSON. 'Whether to leave one's whole fortune to a College be right, must depend upon circumstances. I would leave the interest of the fortune I bequeathed to a College to my relations or my friends, for their lives. It is the same thing to a College, which is a permanent society, whether it gets the money now or twenty years hence; and I would wish to make my relations or friends feel the benefit of it.'

This interview confirmed my opinion of Johnson's most humane and benevolent heart. His cordial and placid behaviour to an old fellow-collegian, a man so different from himself; and his telling him that he would go down to his farm and visit him, showed a kindliness of disposition very rare at an advanced age. He observed, 'how wonderful it was that they had both been in London forty years, without having

[1] I am not absolutely sure but this was my own suggestion, though it is truly in the character of Edwards—B.

ever once met, and both walkers in the street too!' Mr. Edwards, when going away, again recurred to his consciousness of senility, and looking full in Johnson's face, said to him, 'You'll find in Dr. Young,

"O my coevals! remnants of yourselves!" '

Johnson did not relish this at all; but shook his head with impatience. Edwards walked off, seemingly highly pleased with the honour of having been thus noticed by Dr. Johnson. When he was gone, I said to Johnson, I thought him but a weak man. JOHNSON. 'Why, yes, Sir. Here is a man who has passed through life without experience: yet I would rather have him with me than a more sensible man who will not talk readily. This man is always willing to say what he has to say.' Yet Dr. Johnson had himself by no means that willingness which he praised so much, and I think so justly; for who has not felt the painful effect of the dreary void, when there is a total silence in a company, for any length of time; or, which is a bad, or perhaps worse, when the conversation is with difficulty kept up by a perpetual effort?

Johnson once observed to me, 'Tom Tyers described me the best: "Sir, (said he,) you are like a ghost: you never speak till you are spoken to." ' . . .

Mr. Edwards had said to me aside, that Dr. Johnson should have been of a profession. I repeated the remark to Johnson that I might have his own thoughts on the subject. JOHNSON. 'Sir, it *would* have been better that I had been of a profession. I ought to have been a lawyer.' BOSWELL. 'I do not think, Sir, it would have been better, for we should not have had the *English Dictionary*.' JOHNSON. 'But you would have had *Reports*.' BOSWELL. 'Ay; but there would not have been another, who could have written the *Dictionary*. There have been many very good Judges. Suppose you had been Lord Chancellor; you would have delivered opinions with more extent of mind, and in a more ornamented manner, than perhaps any Chancellor ever did, or ever will do. But, I believe, causes have been as judiciously decided as you could have done.' JOHNSON. 'Yes, Sir. Property has been as well settled.'

Johnson, however, had a noble ambition floating in his mind, and had, undoubtedly, often speculated on the possibility of his supereminent powers being rewarded in this great and liberal country by the highest honours of the state. Sir William Scott informs me, that upon the death of the late Lord Lichfield, who was Chancellor of the University of Oxford, he said to Johnson, 'What a pity it is, Sir, that you did not follow the profession of the law. You might have been Lord Chancellor of Great Britain, and attained to the dignity of the peerage; and now that the title of Lichfield, your native city, is extinct, you might have had it.' Johnson, upon this, seemed much agitated; and, in an angry tone, exclaimed, 'Why will you vex me by suggesting this, when it is too late?'

But he did not repine at the prosperity of others. The late Dr. Thomas Leland told Mr. Courtenay, that when Mr. Edmund Burke shewed Johnson his fine house and lands near Beaconsfield, Johnson coolly said, *Non equidem invideo; miror magis.*[1]

Yet no man had a higher notion of the dignity of literature than Johnson, or was more determined in maintaining the respect which he justly considered as due to it. Of this, besides the general tenor of his conduct in society, some characteristical instances may be mentioned.

He told Sir Joshua Reynolds, that once when he dined in a numerous company of booksellers, where the room being small, the head of the table, at which he sat, was almost close to the fire, he persevered in suffering a great deal of inconvenience from the heat, rather than quit his place, and let one of them sit above him.

Goldsmith, in his diverting simplicity, complained one day, in a mixed company, of Lord Camden. 'I met him (said he,) at Lord Clare's house in the country, and he took no more notice of me than if I had been an ordinary man.' The company having laughed heartily, Johnson stood forth in defence of his friend. 'Nay, Gentlemen, (said he,) Dr. Goldsmith is in the right. A nobleman ought to have made up to such a man as Goldsmith; and I think it is much against Lord Camden that he neglected him.'

Nor could he patiently endure to hear that such respect as he thought due only to higher intellectual qualities, should be bestowed on men of slighter, though perhaps more amusing talents. I told him, that one morning, when I went to breakfast with Garrick, who was very vain of his intimacy with Lord Camden, he accosted me thus:—'Pray now, did you—did you meet a little lawyer turning the corner, eh?'—'No, Sir, (said I.) Pray what do you mean by the question?'—'Why, (replied Garrick, with an affected indifference, yet as if standing on tiptoe,) Lord Camden has this moment left me. We have had a long walk together.' JOHNSON. 'Well, Sir,

---

[1] 'I grudge thee not—rather I marvel.' Virgil, *Eclogues,* i. 11. I am not entirely without suspicion that Johnson may have felt a little momentary envy; for no man loved the good things of this life better than he did; and he could not but be conscious that he deserved a much larger share of them, than he ever had—B.

Garrick talked very properly. Lord Camden *was* a *little lawyer* to be associating so familiarly with a player.'

Sir Joshua Reynolds observed, with great truth, that Johnson considered Garrick to be as it were his *property*. He would allow no man either to blame or to praise Garrick in his presence, without contradicting him.

Having fallen into a very serious frame of mind, in which mutual expressions of kindness passed between us, such as would be thought too vain in me to repeat, I talked with regret of the sad inevitable certainty that one of us must survive the other. JOHNSON. 'Yes, Sir, that is an affecting consideration. I remember Swift, in one of his letters to Pope, says, "I intend to come over, that we may meet once more; and when we must part, it is what happens to all human beings."' BOSWELL. 'The hope that we shall see our departed friends again must support the mind.' JOHNSON. 'Why yes, Sir.' BOSWELL. 'There is a strange unwillingness to part with life, independent of serious fears as to futurity. A reverend friend[1] of ours (naming him) tells me, that he feels an uneasiness at the thoughts of leaving his house, his study, his books.' JOHNSON. 'This is foolish in *****. A man need not be uneasy on these grounds; for, as he will retain his consciousness, he may say with the philosopher, *Omnia mea mecum porto.*'[2] BOSWELL. 'True, Sir: we may carry our books in our heads; but still there is something painful in the thought of leaving for ever what has given us pleasure. I remember, many years ago, when my imagination was warm, and I happened to be in a melancholy mood, it distressed me to think of going into a state of being in which Shakspeare's poetry did not exist. A lady whom I then much admired, a very amiable woman, humoured my fancy, and relieved me by saying, "The first thing you will meet in the other world, will be an elegant copy of Shakspeare's works presented to you."' Dr. Johnson smiled benignantly at this, and did not appear to disapprove of the notion.

We went to St. Clement's church again in the afternoon, and then returned and drank tea and coffee in Mrs. Williams's room; Mrs. Desmoulins doing the honours of the tea-table. I observed that he would not even look at a proof-sheet of his *Life of Waller* on Good-Friday.

Mr. Allen, the printer, brought a book on agriculture, which was printed, and was soon to be published. It was a very strange performance, the authour having mixed in it his own thoughts upon various topicks, along with his remarks

[1] Dr. Blair.
[2] 'All that is mine I carry with me.' Cicero, *Paradoxes of Stoicism*, i.

on ploughing, sowing, and other farming operations. He seemed to be an absurd profane fellow, and had introduced in his book many sneers at religion, with equal ignorance and conceit. Dr. Johnson permitted me to read some passages aloud. One was, that he resolved to work on Sunday, and did work, but he owned he felt *some* weak compunction; and he had this very curious reflection:—'I was born in the wilds of Christianity, and the briars and thorns still hang about me.' Dr. Johnson could not help laughing at this ridiculous image, yet was very angry at the fellow's impiety. 'However, (said he,) the Reviewers will make him hang himself.' He, however, observed, 'that formerly there might have been a dispensation obtained for working on Sunday in the time of harvest.' Indeed in ritual observances, were all the ministers of religion what they should be, and what many of them are, such a power might be wisely and safely lodged with the Church.

On Saturday, April 14,[1] I drank tea with him. He praised the late Mr. Duncombe, of Canterbury, as a pleasing man. 'He used to come to me: I did not seek much after *him*. Indeed I never sought much after any body.' BOSWELL. 'Lord Orrery, I suppose.' JOHNSON. 'No, Sir; I never went to him but when he sent for me.' BOSWELL. 'Richardson?' JOHNSON. 'Yes, Sir. But I sought after George Psalmanazar the most. I used to go and sit with him at an alehouse in the city.'

I am happy to mention another instance which I discovered of his *seeking after* a man of merit. Soon after the Honourable Daines Barrington had published his excellent *Observations on the Statutes,* Johnson waited on that worthy and learned gentleman; and, having told him his name, courteously said, 'I have read your book, Sir, with great pleasure, and wish to be better known to you.' Thus began an acquaintance, which was continued with mutual regard as long as Johnson lived.

Talking of a recent seditious delinquent, he said, 'They should set him in the pillory, that he may be punished in a way that would disgrace him.' I observed, that the pillory does not always disgrace. And I mentioned an instance of a gentleman who I thought was not dishonoured by it. JOHNSON. 'Ay, but he was, Sir. He could not mouth and strut as he used to do, after having been there. People are not very willing to ask a man to their tables who has stood in the pillory.'

The Gentleman who had dined with us at Dr. Percy's came in. Johnson attacked the Americans with intemperate vehemence of abuse. I said something in their favour; and

[1] April 18.

added, that I was always sorry when he talked on that subject. This, it seems, exasperated him; though he said nothing at the time. The cloud was charged with sulphureous vapour, which was afterwards to burst in thunder.—We talked of a gentleman[1] who was running out his fortune in London; and I said, 'We must get him out of it. All his friends must quarrel with him, and that will soon drive him away.' JOHNSON. 'Nay, Sir; we'll send *you* to him. If your company does not drive a man out of his house, nothing will.' This was a horrible shock, for which there was no visible cause. I afterwards asked him why he had said so harsh a thing. JOHNSON. 'Because, Sir, you made me angry about the Americans.' BOSWELL. 'But why did you not take your revenge directly?' JOHNSON. (smiling,) 'Because, Sir, I had nothing ready. A man cannot strike till he has his weapons.' This was a candid and pleasant confession.

He shewed me to-night his drawing-room, very genteelly fitted up; and said, 'Mrs. Thrale sneered when I talked of my having asked you and your lady to live at my house. I was obliged to tell her, that you would be in as respectable a situation in my house as in hers. Sir, the insolence of wealth will creep out.' BOSWELL. 'She has a little both of the insolence of wealth, and the conceit of parts.' JOHNSON. 'The insolence of wealth is a wretched thing; but the conceit of parts has some foundation. To be sure it should not be. But who is without it?' BOSWELL. 'Yourself, Sir.' JOHNSON. 'Why, I play no tricks: I lay no traps.' BOSWELL. 'No, Sir. You are six feet high, and you only do not stoop.'

We talked of the numbers of people that sometimes have composed the household of great families. I mentioned that there were a hundred in the family of the present Earl of Eglintoune's father. Dr. Johnson seeming to doubt it, I began to enumerate. 'Let us see: my Lord and my Lady two.' JOHNSON. 'Nay, Sir, if you are to count by twos, you may be long enough.' BOSWELL. 'Well, but now I add two sons and seven daughters, and a servant for each, that will make twenty; so we have the fifth party already.' JOHNSON. 'Very true. You get at twenty pretty readily; but you will not so easily get further on. We grow to five feet pretty readily; but it is not so easy to grow to seven.'

On Sunday, April 19, being Easter-day, after the solemnities of the festival in St. Paul's Church, I visited him, but could not stay to dinner. I expressed a wish to have the arguments for Christianity always in readiness, that my religious faith might be as firm and clear as any proposition whatever,

[1] Langton.

so that I need not be under the least uneasiness, when it should be attacked. JOHNSON. 'Sir, you cannot answer all objections. You have demonstration for a First Cause: you see he must be good as well as powerful, because there is nothing to make him otherwise, and goodness of itself is preferable. Yet you have against this, what is very certain, the unhappiness of human life. This, however, gives us reason to hope for a future state of compensation, that there may be a perfect system. But of that we were not sure, till we had a positive revelation.' I told him, that his *Rasselas* had often made me unhappy; for it represented the misery of human life so well, and so convincingly to a thinking mind, that if at any time the impression wore off, and I felt myself easy, I began to suspect some delusion.

On Monday, April 20, I found him at home in the morning. We talked of a gentleman who we apprehended was gradually involving his circumstances by bad management. JOHNSON. 'Wasting a fortune is evaporation by a thousand imperceptible means. If it were a stream, they'd stop it. You must speak to him. It is really miserable. Were he a gamester, it could be said he had hopes of winning. Were he a bankrupt in trade, he might have grown rich; but he has neither spirit to spend nor resolution to spare. He does not spend fast enough to have pleasure from it. He has the crime of prodigality, and the wretchedness of parsimony. If a man is killed in a duel, he is killed as many a one has been killed; but it is a sad thing for a man to lie down and die; to bleed to death, because he has not fortitude enough to sear the wound, or even to stitch it up.' I cannot but pause a moment to admire the fecundity of fancy, and choice of language, which in this instance, and, indeed, on almost all occasions, he displayed. It was well observed by Dr. Percy, now Bishop of Dromore, 'The conversation of Johnson is strong and clear, and may be compared to an antique statue, where every vein and muscle is distinct and bold. Ordinary conversation resembles an inferiour cast.'

On Saturday, April 25, I dined with him at Sir Joshua Reynolds's, with the learned Dr. Musgrave, Counsellor Leland of Ireland, son to the historian, Mrs. Cholmondeley, and some more ladies. *The Project,* a new poem, was read to the company by Dr. Musgrave. JOHNSON. 'Sir, it has no power. Were it not for the well-known names with which it is filled, it would be nothing: the names carry the poet, not the poet the names.' MUSGRAVE. 'A temporary poem always entertains us.' JOHNSON. 'So does an account of the criminals hanged yesterday entertain us.'

He proceeded:—'Demosthenes Taylor, as he was called,

(that is, the Editor of Demosthenes) was the most silent man, the merest statue of a man that I have ever seen. I once dined in company with him, and all he said during the whole time was no more than *Richard.* How a man should say only Richard, it is not easy to imagine. But it was thus: Dr. Douglas was talking of Dr. Zachary Grey, and ascribing to him something that was written by Dr. Richard Grey. So, to correct him, Taylor said, (imitating his affected sententious emphasis and nod,) *"Richard." '*

Mrs. Cholmondeley, in a high flow of spirits, exhibited some lively sallies of hyperbolical compliment to Johnson, with whom she had been long acquainted, and was very easy. He was quick in catching the *manner* of the moment, and answered her somewhat in the style of the hero of a romance, 'Madam, you crown me with unfading laurels.'

I happened, I know not how, to say that a pamphlet meant a prose piece. JOHNSON. 'No, Sir. A few sheets of poetry unbound are a pamphlet, as much as a few sheets of prose.' MUSGRAVE. 'A pamphlet may be understood to mean a poetical piece in Westminster-Hall, that is, in formal language; but in common language it is understood to mean prose.' JOHNSON. (and here was one of the many instances of his knowing clearly and telling exactly how a thing is,) 'A pamphlet is understood in common language to mean prose, only from this, that there is so much more prose written than poetry; as when we say a *book,* prose is understood for the same reason, though a book may as well be in poetry as in prose. We understand what is most general, and we name what is less frequent.'

We talked of a lady's verses on Ireland. MISS REYNOLDS. 'Have you seen them, Sir?' JOHNSON. 'No, Madam. I have seen a translation from Horace, by one of her daughters. She shewed it me.' MISS REYNOLDS. 'And how was it, Sir?' JOHNSON. 'Why, very well for a young Miss's verses;—that is to say, compared with excellence, nothing; but, very well, for the person who wrote them. I am vexed at being shewn verses in that manner.' MISS REYNOLDS. 'But if they should be good, why not give them hearty praise?' JOHNSON. 'Why, Madam, because I have not then got the better of my bad humour from having been shewn them. You must consider, Madam; beforehand they may be bad, as well as good. Nobody has a right to put another under such a difficulty, that he must either hurt the person by telling the truth, or hurt himself by telling what is not true.' BOSWELL. 'A man often shews his writings to people of eminence, to obtain from them, either from their good-nature, or from their not being able to tell the truth firmly, a commendation, of which he may afterwards avail himself.' JOHNSON. 'Very true, Sir. Therefore a man, who is asked by an authour, what he thinks of his work, is put to the torture, and is not obliged to speak the truth; so that what he says is not considered as his opinion; yet he has said it, and cannot retract it; and this authour, when mankind are hunting him with a cannister at his tail, can say, "I would not have published, had not Johnson, or Reynolds, or Musgrave, or some other good judge commended the work." Yet I consider it as a very difficult question in conscience, whether one should advise a man not to publish a work, if profit be his object; for the man may say, "Had it not been for you, I should have had the money." Now you cannot be sure; for you have only your own opinion, and the publick may think very differently.' SIR JOSHUA REYNOLDS. 'You must upon such an occasion have two judgements; one as to the real value of the work, the other as to what may please the general taste at the time.' JOHNSON. 'But you can be *sure* of neither; and therefore I should scruple much to give a suppressive vote. Both Goldsmith's comedies were once refused; his first by Garrick, his second by Colman, who was prevailed on at last by much solicitation, nay, a kind of force, to bring it on. His *Vicar of Wakefield* I myself did not think would have had much success. It was written and sold to a bookseller before his *Traveller;* but published after; so little expectation had the bookseller from it. Had it been sold after *The Traveller,* he might have had twice as much money for it, though sixty guineas was no mean price. The bookseller had the advantage of Goldsmith's reputation from *The Traveller* in the sale, though Goldsmith had it not in selling the copy.' SIR JOSHUA REYNOLDS. '*The Beggar's Opera* affords a proof how strangely people will differ in opinion about a literary performance. Burke thinks it has no merit.' JOHNSON. 'It was refused by one of the houses; but I should have thought it would succeed, not from any great excellence in the writing, but from the novelty, and the general spirit and gaiety of the piece, which keeps the audience always attentive, and dismisses them in good humour.'

We went to the drawing-room, where was a considerable increase of company. Several of us got round Dr. Johnson, and complained that he would not give us an exact catalogue of his works, that there might be a complete edition. He smiled, and evaded our entreaties. That he intended to do it, I have no doubt, because I have heard him say so; and I have in my possession an imperfect list, fairly written out, which he entitles *Historia Studiorum.* I once got from one of his

478

friends[1] a list, which there was pretty good reason to suppose was accurate, for it was written down in his presence by this friend, who enumerated each article aloud, and had some of them mentioned to him by Mr. Levett, in concert with whom it was made out; and Johnson, who heard all this, did not contradict it. But when I shewed a copy of this list to him, and mentioned the evidence for its exactness, he laughed, and said, 'I was willing to let them go on as they pleased, and never interfered.' Upon which I read it to him, article by article, and got him positively to own or refuse; and then, having obtained certainty so far, I got some other articles confirmed by him directly; and afterwards, from time to time, made additions under his sanction.

His friend Edward Cave having been mentioned, he told us, 'Cave used to sell ten thousand of *The Gentleman's Magazine;* yet such was then his minute attention and anxiety that the sale should not suffer the smallest decrease, that he would name a particular person who he heard had talked of leaving off the *Magazine,* and would say, "Let us have something good next month." '

It was observed, that avarice was inherent in some dispositions. JOHNSON. 'No man was born a miser, because no man was born to possession. Every man is born *cupidus*—desirous of getting; but not *avarus,*—desirous of keeping.' BOSWELL. 'I have heard old Mr. Sheridan maintain, with much ingenuity, that a complete miser is a happy man; a miser who gives himself wholly to the one passion of saving.' JOHNSON. 'That is flying in the face of all the world, who have called an avaricious man a *miser,* because he is miserable. No, Sir; a man who both spends and saves money is the happiest man, because he has both enjoyments.' . . .

He observed, 'A man cannot with propriety speak of himself, except he relates simple facts; as, "I was at Richmond:" or what depends on mensuration; as, "I am six feet high." He is sure he has been at Richmond; he is sure he is six feet high: but he cannot be sure he is wise, or that he has any other excellence. Then, all censure of a man's self is oblique praise. It is in order to shew how much he can spare. It has all the invidiousness of self-praise, and all the reproach of falsehood.' BOSWELL. 'Sometimes it may proceed from a man's strong consciousness of his faults being observed. He knows that others would throw him down, and therefore he had better lye down softly of his own accord.'

On Tuesday, April 28, he was engaged to dine at General Paoli's, where, as I have already observed, I was still enter-

[1] Percy.

tained in elegant hospitality, and with all the ease and comfort of a home. I called on him, and accompanied him in a hackney-coach. We stopped first at the bottom of Hedge-lane, into which he went to leave a letter, 'with good news for a poor man in distress', as he told me. I did not question him particularly as to this. He himself often resembled Lady Bolingbroke's lively description of Pope; that 'he was *un politique aux choux et aux raves.*' He would say, 'I dine to-day in Grosvenor-square;' this might be with a Duke: or, perhaps, 'I dine to-day at the other end of the town:' or, 'A gentleman of great eminence called on me yesterday.' He loved thus to keep things floating in conjecture: *Omne ignotum pro magnifico est.*[1] I believe I ventured to dissipate the cloud, to unveil the mystery, more freely and frequently than any of his friends. We stopped again at Wirgman's, the well-known *toyshop,* in St. James's-street, at the corner of St. James's-place, to which he had been directed, but not clearly, for he searched about some time, and could not find it at first; and said, 'To direct one only to a corner shop is *toying* with one.' I suppose he meant this as a play upon the word *toy:* it was the first time that I knew him stoop to such sport. After he had been some time in the shop, he sent for me to come out of the coach, and help him to choose a pair of silver buckles, as those he had were too small. Probably this alteration in dress had been suggested by Mrs. Thrale, by associating with whom, his external appearance was much improved. He got better cloaths; and the dark colour, from which he never deviated, was enlivened by metal buttons. His wigs, too, were much better; and during their travels in France, he was furnished with a Paris-made wig, of handsome construction. This choosing of silver buckles was a negociation: 'Sir, (said he,) I will not have the ridiculous large ones now in fashion; and I will give no more than a guinea for a pair.' Such were the *principles* of the business; and, after some examination, he was fitted. As we drove along, I found him in a talking humour, of which I availed myself. BOSWELL. 'I was this morning in Ridley's shop, Sir; and was told, that the collection called *Johnsoniana* has sold very much.' JOHNSON. 'Yet the *Journey to the Hebrides* has not had a great sale.' BOSWELL. 'That is strange.' JOHNSON. 'Yes, Sir; for in that book I have told the world a great deal that they did not know before.'

BOSWELL. 'I drank chocolate, Sir, this morning with Mr. Eld; and, to my no small surprize, found him to be a

---

[1] 'The unknown always passes for something great.' Tacitus, *Agricola*, ch. xxx.

Staffordshire Whig, a being which I did not believe had existed.' JOHNSON. 'Sir, there are rascals in all countries.' BOSWELL. 'Eld said, a Tory was a creature generated between a non-juring parson and one's grandmother.' JOHNSON. 'And I have always said, the first Whig was the Devil.' BOSWELL. 'He certainly was, Sir. The Devil was impatient of subordination; he was the first who resisted power:—

> "Better to reign in Hell, than serve in Heaven." '

At General Paoli's were Sir Joshua Reynolds, Mr. Langton, Marchese Gherardi of Lombardy, and Mr. John Spottiswoode the younger, of Spottiswoode, the solicitor. At this time fears of an invasion were circulated; to obviate which, Mr. Spottiswoode observed, that Mr. Fraser the engineer, who had lately come from Dunkirk, said, that the French had the same fears of us. JOHNSON. 'It is thus that mutual cowardice keeps us in peace. Were one half of mankind brave, and one half cowards, the brave would be always beating the cowards. Were all brave, they would lead a very uneasy life; all would be continually fighting: but being all cowards, we go on very well.'

We talked of drinking wine. JOHNSON. 'I require wine, only when I am alone. I have then often wished for it, and often taken it.' SPOTTISWOODE. 'What, by way of a companion, Sir?' JOHNSON. 'To get rid of myself, to send myself away. Wine gives great pleasure; and every pleasure is of itself a good. It is a good, unless counterbalanced by evil. A man may have a strong reason not to drink wine; and that may be greater than the pleasure. Wine makes a man better pleased with himself. I do not say that it makes him more pleasing to others. Sometimes it does. But the danger is, that while a man grows better pleased with himself, he may be growing less pleasing to others. Wine gives a man nothing. It neither gives him knowledge nor wit; it only animates a man, and enables him to bring out what a dread of the company has repressed. It only puts in motion what has been locked up in frost. But this may be good, or it may be bad.' SPOTTISWOODE. 'So, Sir, wine is a key which opens a box; but this box may be either full or empty.' JOHNSON. 'Nay, Sir, conversation is the key: wine is a pick-lock, which forces open the box and injures it. A man should cultivate his mind so as to have that confidence and readiness without wine, which wine gives.' BOSWELL. 'The great difficulty of resisting wine is from benevolence. For instance, a good worthy man asks you to taste his wine, which he has had twenty years in his cellar.' JOHNSON. 'Sir, all this notion about benevolence arises from a man's imagining himself to be of more importance to others,

481

than he really is. They don't care a farthing whether he drinks wine or not.' SIR JOSHUA REYNOLDS. 'Yes, they do for the time.' JOHNSON. 'For the time!—If they care this minute, they forget it the next. And as for the good worthy man; how do you know he is good and worthy? No good and worthy man will insist upon another man's drinking wine. As to the wine twenty years in the cellar,—of ten men, three say this, merely because they must say something;—three are telling a lie, when they say they have had the wine twenty years;—three would rather save the wine;—one, perhaps, cares. I allow it is something to please one's company: and people are always pleased with those who partake pleasure with them. But after a man has brought himself to relinquish the great personal pleasure which arises from drinking wine, any other consideration is a trifle. To please others by drinking wine, is something, only if there be nothing against it. I should, however, be sorry to offend worthy men:—

> "Curst be the verse, how well so e'er it flow,
> That tends to make one worthy man my foe." '

BOSWELL. 'Curst be the *spring*, the *water*.' JOHNSON. 'But let us consider what a sad thing it would be, if we were obliged to drink or do any thing else that may happen to be agreeable to the company where we are.' LANGTON. 'By the same rule you must join with a gang of cut-purses.' JOHNSON. 'Yes, Sir: but yet we must do justice to wine; we must allow it the power it possesses. To make a man pleased with himself, let me tell you, is doing a very great thing;

"Si patriæ volumus, si Nobis vivere cari." '[1]

I was at this time myself a water-drinker, upon trial, by Johnson's recommendation. JOHNSON. 'Boswell is a bolder combatant than Sir Joshua: he argues for wine without the help of wine; but Sir Joshua with it.' SIR JOSHUA REYNOLDS. 'But to please one's company is a strong motive.' JOHNSON. (who, from drinking only water, supposed every body who drank wine to be elevated,) 'I won't argue any more with you, Sir. You are too far gone.' SIR JOSHUA. 'I should have thought so indeed, Sir, had I made such a speech as you have now done.' JOHNSON. (drawing himself in, and, I really thought blushing,) 'Nay, don't be angry. I did not mean to offend you.' SIR JOSHUA. 'At first the taste of wine was disagreeable to me; but I brought myself to drink it, that I might be like other people. The pleasure of drinking wine is so con-

[1] 'If we wish to make our life of value to our country *and to ourselves.*' Horace, *Epistles*, i. 3.29.

nected with pleasing your company, that altogether there is something of social goodness in it.' JOHNSON. 'Sir, this is only saying the same thing over again.' SIR JOSHUA. 'No, this is new.' JOHNSON. 'You put it in new words, but it is an old thought. This is one of the disadvantages of wine. It makes a man mistake words for thoughts.' BOSWELL. 'I think it is a new thought; at least, it is in a new *attitude*.' JOHNSON. 'Nay, Sir, it is only in a new coat; or an old coat with a new facing. (Then laughing heartily,) It is the old dog in a new doublet. —An extraordinary instance however may occur where a man's patron will do nothing for him, unless he will drink: *there* may be a good reason for drinking.'

I mentioned a nobleman,[1] who I believed was really uneasy if his company would not drink hard. JOHNSON. 'That is from having had people about him whom he has been accustomed to command.' BOSWELL. 'Supposing I should be *tête-à-tête* with him at table.' JOHNSON. 'Sir, there is no more reason for your drinking with *him*, than his being sober with *you*.' BOSWELL. 'Why, that is true; for it would do him less hurt to be sober, than it would do me to get drunk.' JOHNSON. 'Yes, Sir; and from what I have heard of him, one would not wish to sacrifice himself to such a man. If he must always have somebody to drink with him, he should buy a slave, and then he would be sure to have it. They who submit to drink as another pleases, make themselves his slaves.' BOSWELL. 'But, Sir, you will surely make allowance for the duty of hospitality. A gentleman who loves drinking, comes to visit me.' JOHNSON. 'Sir, a man knows whom he visits; he comes to the table of a sober man.' BOSWELL. 'But, Sir, you and I should not have been so well received in the Highlands and Hebrides, if I had not drunk with our worthy friends. Had I drunk water only as you did, they would not have been so cordial.' JOHNSON. 'Sir William Temple mentions that in his travels through the Netherlands he had two or three gentlemen with him; and when a bumper was necessary, he put it on *them*. Were I to travel again through the islands, I would have Sir Joshua with me to take the bumpers.' BOSWELL. 'But, Sir, let me put a case. Suppose Sir Joshua should take a jaunt into Scotland; he does me the honour to pay me a visit at my house in the country; I am overjoyed at seeing him; we are quite by ourselves, shall I unsociably and churlishly let him sit drinking by himself? No, no, my dear Sir Joshua, you shall not be treated so, I *will* take a bottle with you.'

The celebrated Mrs. Rudd being mentioned. JOHNSON. 'Fifteen years ago I should have gone to see her.' SPOTTISWOODE.

---

[1] Archibald, 11th Earl of Eglinton.

'Because she was fifteen years younger?' JOHNSON. 'No, Sir; but now they have a trick of putting every thing into the newspapers.' . . .

On Wednesday, April 29, I dined with him at Mr. Allan Ramsay's, where were Lord Binning, Dr. Robertson the historian, Sir Joshua Reynolds, and the Honourable Mrs. Boscawen, widow of the Admiral, and mother of the present Viscount Falmouth; of whom, if it be not presumptuous in me to praise her, I would say, that her manners are the most agreeable, and her conversation the best, of any lady with whom I ever had the happiness to be acquainted. Before Johnson came we talked a good deal of him; Ramsay said he had always found him a very polite man, and that he treated him with great respect, which he did very sincerely. I said I worshipped him. ROBERTSON. 'But some of you spoil him; you should not worship him; you should worship no man.' BOSWELL. 'I cannot help worshipping him, he is so much superiour to other men.' ROBERTSON. 'In criticism, and in wit in conversation, he is no doubt very excellent; but in other respects he is not above other men; he will believe any thing, and will strenuously defend the most minute circumstance connected with the Church of England.' BOSWELL. 'Believe me, Doctor, you are much mistaken as to this; for when you talk with him calmly in private, he is very liberal in his way of thinking.' ROBERTSON. 'He and I have been always very gracious; the first time I met him was one evening at Strahan's, when he had just had an unlucky altercation with Adam Smith, to whom he had been so rough, that Strahan, after Smith was gone, had remonstrated with him, and told him that I was coming soon, and that he was uneasy to think that he might behave in the same manner to me. "No, no, Sir, (said Johnson,) I warrant you Robertson and I shall do very well." Accordingly he was gentle and good-humoured, and courteous with me the whole evening; and he has been so upon every occasion that we have met since. I have often said (laughing,) that I have been in a great measure indebted to Smith for my good reception.' BOSWELL. 'His power of reasoning is very strong, and he has a peculiar art of drawing characters, which is as rare as good portrait painting.' SIR JOSHUA REYNOLDS. 'He is undoubtedly admirable in this; but, in order to mark the characters which he draws, he overcharges them, and gives people more than they really have, whether of good or bad.'

No sooner did he, of whom we had been thus talking so easily, arrive, than we were all as quiet as a school upon the entrance of the head-master; and were very soon set down to a table covered with such variety of good things, as contributed not a little to dispose him to be pleased.

RAMSAY. 'I am old enough to have been a contemporary of Pope. His poetry was highly admired in his life-time, more a great deal than after his death.' JOHNSON. 'Sir, it has not been less admired since his death; no authours ever had so much fame in their own life-time as Pope and Voltaire; and Pope's poetry has been as much admired since his death as during his life; it has only not been as much talked of, but that is owing to its being now more distant, and people having other writings to talk of. Virgil is less talked of than Pope, and Homer is less talked of than Virgil; but they are not less admired. We must read what the world reads at the moment. It has been maintained that this superfœtation, this teeming of the press in modern times, is prejudicial to good literature, because it obliges us to read so much of what is of inferiour value, in order to be in the fashion; so that better works are neglected for want of time, because a man will have more gratification of his vanity in conversation, from having read modern books, than from having read the best works of antiquity. But it must be considered, that we have now more knowledge generally diffused; all our ladies read now, which is a great extension. Modern writers are the moons of literature; they shine with reflected light, with light borrowed from the ancients. Greece appears to me to be the fountain of knowledge; Rome of elegance.' RAMSAY. 'I suppose Homer's *Iliad* to be a collection of pieces which had been written before his time. I should like to see a translation of it in poetical prose like the book of Ruth or Job.' ROBERTSON. 'Would you, Dr. Johnson, who are master of the English language, but try your hand upon a part of it.' JOHNSON. 'Sir, you could not read it without the pleasure of verse.'

We talked of antiquarian researches. JOHNSON. 'All that is really *known* of the ancient state of Britain is contained in a few pages. We *can* know no more than what the old writers have told us; yet what large books have we upon it, the whole of which, excepting such parts as are taken from those old writers, is all a dream, such as Whitaker's *Manchester*. I have heard Henry's *History of Britain* well spoken of: I am told it is carried on in separate divisions, as the civil, the military, the religious history: I wish much to have one branch well done, and that is the history of manners, of common life.' ROBERTSON. 'Henry should have applied his attention to that alone, which is enough for any man; and he might have found a great deal scattered in various books, had he read solely with that view. Henry erred in not selling his first volume at a moderate price to the booksellers, that they might

485

have pushed him on till he had got reputation. I sold my *History of Scotland* at a moderate price, as a work by which the booksellers might either gain or not; and Cadell has told me that Millar and he have got six thousand pounds by it. I afterwards received a much higher price for my writings. An authour should sell his first work for what the booksellers will give, till it shall appear whether he is an authour of merit, or, which is the same thing as to purchase-money, an authour who pleases the publick.'

Dr. Robertson expatiated on the character of a certain nobleman;[1] that he was one of the strongest-minded men that ever lived; that he would sit in company quite sluggish, while there was nothing to call forth his intellectual vigour; but the moment that any important subject was started, for instance, how this country is to be defended against a French invasion, he would rouse himself, and shew his extraordinary talents with the most powerful ability and animation. JOHNSON. 'Yet this man cut his own throat. The true strong and sound mind is the mind that can embrace equally great things and small. Now I am told the King of Prussia will say to a servant, "Bring me a bottle of such a wine, which came in such a year; it lies in such a corner of the cellars." I would have a man great in great things, and elegant in little things.' He said to me afterwards, when we were by ourselves, 'Robertson was in a mighty romantick humour, he talked of one whom he did not know; but I *downed* him with the King of Prussia.' 'Yes, Sir, (said I,) you threw a *bottle* at his head.'

An ingenious gentleman[2] was mentioned, concerning whom both Robertson and Ramsay agreed that he had a constant firmness of mind; for after a laborious day, and amidst a multiplicity of cares and anxieties, he would sit down with his sisters and be quite cheerful and good-humoured. Such a disposition, it was observed, was a happy gift of nature. JOHNSON. 'I do not think so; a man has from nature a certain portion of mind; the use he makes of it depends upon his own free will. That a man has always the same firmness of mind I do not say; because every man feels his mind less firm at one time than at another; but I think a man's being in a good or bad humour depends upon his will.' I, however, could not help thinking that a man's humour is often uncontroulable by his will.

Johnson harangued against drinking wine. 'A man (said he,) may choose whether he will have abstemiousness and knowledge, or claret and ignorance.' Dr. Robertson, (who is

[1] Lord Clive.
[2] Robert Adam.

very companionable,) was beginning to dissent as to the proscription of claret. JOHNSON. (with a placid smile), 'Nay, Sir, you shall not differ with me; as I have said that the man is most perfect who takes in the most things, I am for knowledge and claret.' ROBERTSON. (holding a glass of generous claret in his hand,) 'Sir, I can only drink your health.' JOHNSON. 'Sir, I should be sorry if *you* should be ever in such a state as to be able to do nothing more.' ROBERTSON. 'Dr. Johnson, allow me to say, that in one respect I have the advantage of you; when you were in Scotland you would not come to hear any of our preachers, whereas, when I am here, I attend your publick worship without scruple, and indeed, with great satisfaction.' JOHNSON. 'Why, Sir, that is not so extraordinary: the King of Siam sent ambassadors to Louis the Fourteenth; but Louis the Fourteenth sent none to the King of Siam.'

Here my friend for once discovered a want of knowledge or forgetfulness; for Louis the Fourteenth did send an embassy to the King of Siam, and the Abbé Choisi, who was employed in it, published an account of it in two volumes.

Next day, Thursday, April 30, I found him at home by himself. JOHNSON. 'Well, Sir, Ramsay gave us a splendid dinner. I love Ramsay. You will not find a man in whose conversation there is more instruction, more information, and more elegance, than in Ramsay's.' BOSWELL. 'What I admire in Ramsay, is his continuing to be so young.' JOHNSON. 'Why, yes, Sir, it is to be admired. I value myself upon this, that there is nothing of the old man in my conversation. I am now sixty-eight, and I have no more of it than at twenty-eight.' BOSWELL. 'But, Sir, would not you wish to know old age? He who is never an old man, does not know the whole of human life; for old age is one of the divisions of it.' JOHNSON. 'Nay Sir, what talk is this?' BOSWELL. 'I mean, Sir, the Sphinx's description of it;—morning, noon, and night. I would know night, as well as morning and noon.' JOHNSON. 'What, Sir, would you know what it is to feel the evils of old age? Would you have the gout? Would you have decreptitude?'—Seeing him heated, I would not argue any farther; but I was confident that I was in the right. I would, in due time, be a Nestor, an elder of the people; and there *should* be some difference between the conversation of twenty-eight and sixty-eight. A grave picture should not be gay. There is a serene, solemn, placid old age. JOHNSON. 'Mrs. Thrale's mother said of me what flattered me much. A clergyman was complaining of want of society in the country where he lived; and said, "They talk of *runts;*" (that is, young cows). "Sir, (said Mrs. Salusbury,) Mr. Johnson would learn to talk of runts:"

meaning that I was a man who would make the most of my situation, whatever it was.' He added, 'I think myself a very polite man.'

On Saturday, May 2, I dined with him at Sir Joshua Reynolds's, where there was a very large company, and a great deal of conversation; but owing to some circumstance which I cannot now recollect, I have no record of any part of it, except that there were several people there by no means of the Johnsonian school; so that less attention was paid to him than usual, which put him out of humour; and upon some imaginary offence from me, he attacked me with such rudeness, that I was vexed and angry, because it gave those persons an opportunity of enlarging upon his supposed ferocity, and ill treatment of his best friends. I was so much hurt, and had my pride so much roused, that I kept away from him for a week; and, perhaps, might have kept away much longer, nay, gone to Scotland without seeing him again, had not we fortunately met and been reconciled. To such unhappy chances are human friendships liable.

On Friday, May 8, I dined with him at Mr. Langton's. I was reserved and silent, which I suppose he perceived, and might recollect the cause. After dinner when Mr. Langton was called out of the room, and we were by ourselves, he drew his chair near to mine, and said, in a tone of conciliating courtesy, 'Well, how have you done?' BOSWELL. 'Sir, you have made me very uneasy by your behaviour to me when we were last at Sir Joshua Reynolds's. You know, my dear Sir, no man has a greater respect and affection for you, or would sooner go to the end of the world to serve you. Now to treat me so—.' He insisted that I had interrupted him, which I assured him was not the case; and proceeded—'But why treat me so before people who neither love you nor me?' JOHNSON. 'Well, I am sorry for it. I'll make it up to you twenty different ways, as you please.' BOSWELL. 'I said to-day to Sir Joshua, when he observed that you *tossed* me sometimes —I don't care how often, or how high he tosses me, when only friends are present, for then I fall upon soft ground: but I do not like falling on stones, which is the case when enemies are present.—I think this a pretty good image, Sir.' JOHNSON. 'Sir, it is one of the happiest I have ever heard.'

The truth is, there was no venom in the wounds which he inflicted at any time, unless they were irritated by some malignant infusion by other hands. We were instantly as cordial again as ever, and joined in hearty laugh at some ludicrous but innocent peculiarities of one of our friends. BOSWELL. 'Do you think, Sir, it is always culpable to laugh at a man to his face?' JOHNSON. 'Why, Sir, that depends upon the man and the thing. If it is a slight man, and a slight thing, you may; for you take nothing valuable from him.' . . .

When Mr. Langton returned to us, the 'flow of talk' went on. An eminent authour being mentioned;—JOHNSON. 'He is not a pleasant man. His conversation is neither instructive nor brilliant. He does not talk as if impelled by any fulness of knowledge or vivacity of imagination. His conversation is like that of any other sensible man. He talks with no wish either to inform or to hear, but only because he thinks it does not become ———— ———— to sit in a company and say nothing.'

Mr. Langton having repeated the anecdote of Addison having distinguished between his powers in conversation and in writing, by saying 'I have only nine-pence in my pocket; but I can draw for a thousand pounds;'—JOHNSON. 'He had not that retort ready, Sir; he had prepared it before-hand.' LANGTON. (turning to me,) 'A fine surmise. Set a thief to catch a thief.'

Johnson called the East-Indians barbarians. BOSWELL. 'You will except the Chinese, Sir?' JOHNSON. 'No, Sir.' BOSWELL. 'Have they not arts?' JOHNSON. 'They have pottery.' BOSWELL. 'What do you say to the written characters of their language?' JOHNSON. 'Sir, they have not an alphabet. They have not been able to form what all other nations have formed.' BOSWELL. 'There is more learning in their language than in any other, from the immense number of their characters.' JOHNSON. 'It is only more difficult from its rudeness; as there is more labour in hewing down a tree with a stone than with an axe.'

He said, 'I have been reading Lord Kames's *Sketches of the History of Man*. In treating of severity of punishment, he mentions that of Madame Lapouchin, in Russia, but he does not give it fairly; for I have looked at *Chappe D'Auteroche*, from whom he has taken it. He stops where it is said that the spectators thought her innocent, and leaves out what follows; that she nevertheless was guilty. Now this is being as culpable as one can conceive, to misrepresent fact in a book, and for what motive? It is like one of those lies which people tell, one cannot see why. The woman's life was spared; and no punishment was too great for the favourite of an Empress who had conspired to dethrone her mistress.' BOSWELL. 'He was only giving a picture of the lady in her sufferings.' JOHNSON. 'Nay, don't endeavour to palliate this. Guilt is a principal feature in the picture. Kames is puzzled with a question that puzzled me when I was a very young man. Why is it that the interest of money is lower, when money is plentiful; for five pounds has the same proportion of value to a hundred pounds when money is plentiful, as when it is scarce? A lady explained it to me. "It is (said she,) because when money is plentiful there are so many more who have money to lend, that they bid down one another. Many have then a hundred pounds; and one says,—Take mine rather than another's, and you shall have it at four *per cent.*" ' BOSWELL. 'Does Lord Kames decide the question?' JOHNSON. 'I think he leaves it as he found it. BOSWELL. 'This must have been an extraordinary lady who instructed you, Sir. May I ask who she was?' JOHNSON. 'Molly Aston, Sir, the sister of those ladies with whom you dined at Lichfield. I shall be at home to-morrow.' BOSWELL. 'Then let us dine by ourselves at the Mitre, to keep up the old custom, "the custom of the manor," the custom of the mitre.' JOHNSON. 'Sir, so it shall be.'

On Saturday, May 9, we fulfilled our purpose of dining by ourselves at the Mitre, according to old custom. There was, on these occasions, a little circumstance of kind attention to Mrs. Williams, which must not be omitted. Before coming out, and leaving her to dine alone, he gave her her choice of a chicken, a sweetbread, or any other little nice thing, which was carefully sent to her from the tavern, ready-drest.

Our conversation to-day, I know not how, turned, (I think for the only time at any length, during our long acquaintance,) upon the sensual intercourse between the sexes, the delight of which he ascribed chiefly to imagination. 'Were it not for imagination, Sir, (said he,) a man would be as happy in the arms of a chambermaid as of a Duchess. But such is the adventitious charm of fancy, that we find men who have violated the best principles of society, and ruined their fame and their fortune, that they might possess a woman of rank.' It would not be proper to record the particulars of such a conversation in moments of unreserved frankness, when nobody was present on whom it could have any hurtful effect. That subject, when philosophically treated, may surely employ the mind in as curious discussion, and as innocently, as anatomy; provided that those who do treat it keep clear of inflammatory incentives.

'From grave to gay, from lively to severe,'—we were soon engaged in very different speculation; humbly and reverently considering and wondering at the universal mystery of all things, as our imperfect faculties can now judge of them. 'There are (said he,) innumerable questions to which the inquisitive mind can in this state receive no answer: Why do you and I exist? Why was this world created? Since it was to be created, why was it not created sooner?'

On Sunday, May 10, I supped with him at Mr. Hoole's, with Sir Joshua Reynolds. I have neglected the memorial of this evening, so as to remember no more of it than two particulars; one, that he strenuously opposed an argument by Sir Joshua, that virtue was preferable to vice, considering this life only; and that a man would be virtuous were it only to preserve his character: and that he expressed much wonder at the curious formation of the bat, a mouse with wings; saying, that 'it was almost as strange a thing in physiology, as if the fabulous dragon could be seen.'

On Tuesday, May 12, I waited on the Earl of Marchmont, to know if his Lordship would favour Dr. Johnson with information concerning Pope, whose Life he was about to write. Johnson had not flattered himself with the hopes of receiving any civility from this nobleman; for he said to me, when I mentioned Lord Marchmont as one who could tell him a great deal about Pope,—'Sir, he will tell *me* nothing.' I had the honour of being known to his Lordship, and applied to him of myself, without being commissioned by Johnson. His Lordship behaved in the most polite and obliging manner, promised to tell all he recollected about Pope, and was so very courteous as to say, 'Tell Dr. Johnson I have a great respect for him, and am ready to shew it in any way I can. I am to be in the city to-morrow, and will call at his house as I return.' His Lordship however asked, 'Will he write the Lives of the Poets impartially? He was the first that brought Whig and Tory into a Dictionary. And what do you think of his definition of Excise? Do you know the history of his aversion to the word *transpire?*' Then taking down the folio *Dictionary*, he shewed it with this censure on its secondary sense: ' "To escape from secrecy to notice; a sense lately innovated from France, without necessity." The truth was Lord Bolingbroke, who left the Jacobites, first used it; therefore, it was to be condemned. He should have shewn what word would do for it, if it was unnecessary.' I afterwards put the question to Johnson: 'Why, Sir, (said he,) *get abroad.*' BOSWELL. 'That, Sir, is using two words.' JOHNSON. 'Sir, there is no end of this. You may as well insist to have a word for old age.' BOSWELL. 'Well, Sir, *Senectus.*' JOHNSON. 'Nay, Sir, to insist always that there should be one word to express a thing in English, because there is one in another language, is to change the language.'

I availed myself of this opportunity to hear from his Lordship many particulars both of Pope and Lord Bolingbroke, which I have in writing.

I proposed to Lord Marchmont that he should revise Johnson's *Life of Pope:* 'So (said his Lordship,) you would put me in a dangerous situation. You know he knocked down Osborne the bookseller.'

491

Elated with the success of my spontaneous exertion to procure material and respectable aid to Johnson for his very favourite work, *The Lives of the Poets,* I hastened down to Mr. Thrale's at Streatham, where he now was, that I might insure his being at home next day; and after dinner, when I thought he would receive the good news in the best humour, I announced it eagerly: 'I have been at work for you to-day, Sir. I have been with Lord Marchmont. He bade me tell you he has a great respect for you, and will call on you to-morrow at one o'clock, and communicate all he knows about Pope.'—Here I paused, in full expectation that he would be pleased with this intelligence, would praise my active merit, and would be alert to embrace such an offer from a nobleman. But whether I had shewn an over-exultation, which provoked his spleen; or whether he was seized with a suspicion that I had obtruded him on Lord Marchmont, and had humbled him too much; or whether there was any thing more than an unlucky fit of ill-humour, I know not; but, to my surprise, the result was,—JOHNSON. 'I shall not be in town to-morrow. I don't care to know about Pope.' MRS. THRALE. (surprized as I was, and a little angry,) 'I suppose, Sir, Mr. Boswell thought, that as you are to write *Pope's Life,* you would wish to know about him.' JOHNSON. 'Wish! why yes. If it rained knowledge I'd hold out my hand; but I would not give myself the trouble to go in quest of it.' There was no arguing with him at the moment. Some time afterwards he said, 'Lord Marchmont will call on me, and then I shall call on Lord Marchmont.' Mr. Thrale was uneasy at his unaccountable caprice; and told me, that if I did not take care to bring about a meeting betwen Lord Marchmont and him, it would never take place, which would be a great pity. I sent a card to his Lordship, to be left at Johnson's house, acquainting him, that Dr. Johnson could not be in town next day, but would do himself the honour of waiting on him at another time. I give this account fairly, as a specimen of that unhappy temper with which this great and good man had occasionally to struggle, from something morbid in his constitution. Let the most censorious of my readers suppose himself to have a violent fit of the tooth-ach, or to have received a severe stroke on the shin-bone, and when in such a state to be asked a question; and if he has any candour, he will not be surprized at the answers which Johnson sometimes gave in moments of irritation, which, let me assure them, is exquisitely painful. But it must not be erroneously supposed that he was, in the smallest degree, careless concerning any work which he undertook, or that he was generally thus peevish. It will be seen, that in the following year he had a very agreeable interview with Lord Marchmont, at his Lordship's house; and this very afternoon he soon forgot any fretfulness, and fell into conversation as usual.

I mentioned a reflection having been thrown out against four Peers for having presumed to rise in opposition to the opinion of the twelve Judges, in a cause in the House of Lords, as if that were indecent. JOHNSON. 'Sir, there is no ground for censure. The Peers are Judges themselves; and supposing them really to be of a different opinion, they might from duty be in opposition to the Judges, who were there only to be consulted.' . . .

Mrs. Thrale told us, that a curious clergyman of our acquaintance had discovered a licentious stanza, which Pope had originally in his *Universal Prayer,* before the stanza,

> 'What conscience dictates to be done,
>   Or warns us not to do,' &c.

It was this:—

> 'Can sins of moment claim the rod
>   Of everlasting fires?
> And that offend great Nature's GOD,
>   Which Nature's self inspires?'

and that Dr. Johnson observed, 'it had been borrowed from *Guarini.*' There are, indeed, in *Pastor Fido,* many such flimsy superficial reasonings, as that in the last two lines of this stanza.

BOSWELL. 'In that stanza of Pope's, *"Rod of fires"* is certainly a bad metaphor.' MRS. THRALE. 'And "sins of *moment*" is a faulty expression; for its true import is *momentous,* which cannot be intended.' JOHNSON. 'It must have been written "of *moments.*" Of *moment,* is *momentous;* of *moments, momentary.* I warrant you, however, Pope wrote this stanza, and some friend struck it out. Boileau wrote some such thing, and Arnaud struck it out, saying, "*Vous gagnerez deux ou trois impies, et perdrez je ne scais combien des honnettes gens.*" These fellows want to say a daring thing, and don't know how to go about it. Mere poets know no more of fundamental principles than——.' Here he was interrupted somehow. Mrs. Thrale mentioned Dryden. JOHNSON. 'He puzzled himself about predestination.——How foolish was it in Pope to give all his friendship to Lords, who thought they honoured him by being with him; and to choose such Lords as Burlington, and Cobham, and Bolingbroke! Bathurst was negative, a pleasing man; and I have heard no ill of Marchmont; and then always saying, "I do not value you for being a Lord;" which was a sure proof that he did. I never say, I do not

493

value Boswell more for being born to an estate, because I do not care.' BOSWELL. 'Nor for being a Scotchman?' JOHNSON. 'Nay, Sir, I do value you more for being a Scotchman. You are a Scotchman without the faults of a Scotchman. You would not have been so valuable as you are, had you not been a Scotchman.'

Talking of divorces, I asked if Othello's doctrine was not plausible?

> 'He that is robb'd, not wanting what is stolen,
> Let him not know't, and he's not robb'd at all.'

Dr. Johnson and Mrs. Thrale joined against this. JOHNSON. 'Ask any man if he'd wish not to know of such an injury.' BOSWELL. 'Would you tell your friend to make him unhappy?' JOHNSON. 'Perhaps, Sir, I should not; but that would be from prudence on my own account. A man would tell his father.' BOSWELL. 'Yes; because he would not have spurious children to get any share of the family inheritance.' MRS. THRALE. 'Or he would tell his brother.' BOSWELL. 'Certainly his *elder* brother.' JOHNSON. 'You would tell your friend of a woman's infamy, to prevent his marrying a whore: there is the same reason to tell him of his wife's infidelity, when he is married, to prevent the consequences of imposition. It is a breach of confidence not to tell a friend.' BOSWELL. 'Would you tell Mr. ————?' (naming a gentleman[1] who assuredly was not in the least danger of such a miserable disgrace, though married to a fine woman.) JOHNSON. 'No, Sir; because it would do no good: he is so sluggish, he'd never go to parliament and get through a divorce.'

He said of one of our friends, 'He is ruining himself without pleasure. A man who loses at play, or who runs out his fortune at court, makes his estate less, in hopes of making it bigger: (I am sure of this word, which was often used by him:) but it is a sad thing to pass through the quagmire of parsimony, to the gulph of ruin. To pass over the flowery path of extravagance is very well.'

Amongst the numerous prints pasted on the walls of the dining-room at Streatham, was Hogarth's 'Modern Midnight Conversation.' I asked him what he knew of Parson Ford, who makes a conspicuous figure in the riotous group. JOHNSON. 'Sir, he was my acquaintance and relation, my mother's nephew. He had purchased a living in the country, but not simoniacally. I never saw him but in the country. I have been told he was a man of great parts; very profligate, but I never heard he was impious.' BOSWELL. 'Was there not a story of

---

[1] Langton.

his ghost having appeared?' JOHNSON. 'Sir, it was believed. A waiter at the Hummums, in which house Ford died, had been absent for some time, and returned, not knowing that Ford was dead. Going down to the cellar, according to the story, he met him; going down again he met him a second time. When he came up, he asked some of the people of the house what Ford could be doing there. They told him Ford was dead. The waiter took a fever, in which he lay for some time. When he recovered, he said he had a message to deliver to some women from Ford; but he was not to tell what, or to whom. He walked out; he was followed; but somewhere about St. Paul's they lost him. He came back, and said he had delivered the message, and the women exclaimed, "Then we are all undone!" Dr. Pellet, who was not a credulous man, inquired into the truth of this story, and he said, the evidence was irresistible. My wife went to the Hummums; (it is a place where people get themselves cupped.) I believe she went with intention to hear about this story of Ford. At first they were unwilling to tell her; but, after they had talked to her, she came away satisfied that it was true. To be sure the man had a fever; and this vision may have been the beginning of it. But if the message to the women, and their behaviour upon it, were true as related, there was something supernatural. That rests upon his word; and there it remains.'

After Mrs. Thrale was gone to bed, Johnson and I sat up late. We resumed Sir Joshua Reynolds's argument on the preceding Sunday, that a man would be virtuous though he had no other motive than to preserve his character. JOHNSON. 'Sir, it is not true: for as to this world vice does not hurt a man's character.' BOSWELL. 'Yes, Sir, debauching a friend's wife will.' JOHNSON. 'No, Sir, who thinks the worse of ————[1] for it?' BOSWELL. 'Lord ————[2] was not his friend.' JOHNSON. 'That is only a circumstance, Sir; a slight distinction. He could not get into the house but by Lord ————. A man is chosen Knight of the shire, not the less for having debauched ladies.' BOSWELL. 'What, Sir, if he debauched the ladies of gentlemen in the county, will not there be a general resentment against him?' JOHNSON. 'No, Sir. He will lose those particular gentlemen; but the rest will not trouble their heads about it.' (warmly.) BOSWELL. 'Well, Sir, I cannot think so.' JOHNSON. 'Nay, Sir, there is no talking with a man who will dispute what every body knows, (angrily.) Don't you know this?' BOSWELL. 'No, Sir; and I wish to think better of your country than you represent it. I knew in Scotland

1 Beauclerk.
2 Henry St. John, 2nd Viscount Bolingbroke.

a gentleman obliged to leave it for debauching a lady; and in one of our counties an Earl's brother lost his election, because he had debauched the lady of another Earl in that county, and destroyed the peace of a noble family.'

Still he would not yield. He proceeded: 'Will you not allow, Sir, that vice does not hurt a man's character so as to obstruct his prosperity in life, when you know that —————[1] was loaded with wealth and honours; a man who had acquired his fortune by such crimes, that his consciousness of them impelled him to cut his own throat.' BOSWELL. 'You will recollect, Sir, that Dr. Robertson said, he cut his throat because he was weary of still life; little things not being sufficient to move his great mind.' JOHNSON. (very angry,) 'Nay, Sir, what stuff is this! You had no more this opinion after Robertson said it, than before. I know nothing more offensive than repeating what one knows to be foolish things, by way of continuing a dispute, to see what a man will answer, to make him your butt!' (angrier still.) BOSWELL. 'My dear Sir, I had no such intention as you seem to suspect; I had not indeed. Might not this nobleman have felt every thing "weary, stale, flat, and unprofitable," as Hamlet says?' JOHNSON. 'Nay, if you are to bring in gabble, I'll talk no more. I will not, upon my honour.'—My readers will decide upon this dispute.

Next morning I stated to Mrs. Thrale at breakfast, before he came down, the dispute of last night as to the influence of character upon success in life. She said he was certainly wrong; and told me, that a Baronet lost an election in Wales, because he had debauched the sister of a gentleman in the county, whom he made one of his daughters invite as her companion at his seat in the country, when his lady and his other children were in London. But she would not encounter Johnson upon the subject.

I staid all this day with him at Streatham. He talked a great deal, in very good humour.

Looking at Messrs. Dilly's splendid edition of Lord Chesterfield's miscellaneous works, he laughed, and said, 'Here now are two speeches ascribed to him, both of which were written by me: and the best of it is, they have found out that one is like Demosthenes, and the other like Cicero.'

He censured Lord Kames's *Sketches of the History of Man,* for misrepresenting Clarendon's account of the appearance of Sir George Villiers's ghost, as if Clarendon were weakly credulous; when the truth is, that Clarendon only says, that the story was upon a better foundation of credit, than usually

---

[1] Lord Clive.

such discourses are founded upon; nay, speaks thus of the person who was reported to have seen the vision, 'the poor man, *if he had been at all waking;*' which Lord Kames has omitted. He added, 'in this book it is maintained that virtue is natural to man, and that if we would but consult our own hearts we should be virtuous. Now after consulting our own hearts all we can, and with all the helps we have, we find how few of us are virtuous. This is saying a thing which all mankind know not to be true.' BOSWELL. 'Is not modesty natural?' JOHNSON. 'I cannot say, Sir, as we find no people quite in a state of nature; but I think the more they are taught, the more modest they are. The French are a gross, ill-bred, untaught people; a lady there will spit on the floor and rub it with her foot. What I gained by being in France was, learning to be better satisfied with my own country. Time may be employed to more advantage from nineteen to twenty-four almost in any way than in travelling; when you set travelling against mere negation, against doing nothing, it is better to be sure; but how much more would a young man improve were he to study during those years. Indeed, if a young man is wild, and must run after women and bad company, it is better this should be done abroad, as, on his return, he can break off such connections, and begin at home a new man, with a character to form, and acquaintances to make. How little does travelling supply to the conversation of any man who has travelled? how little to Beauclerk?' BOSWELL. 'What say you to Lord ———?' JOHNSON. 'I never but once heard him talk of what he had seen, and that was of a large serpent in one of the Pyramids of Egypt.' Boswell. 'Well, I happened to hear him tell the same thing, which made me mention him.'

I talked of a country life. JOHNSON. 'Were I to live in the country, I would not devote myself to the acquisition of popularity; I would live in a much better way, much more happily; I would have my time at my own command.' BOSWELL. 'But, Sir, is it not a sad thing to be at a distance from all our literary friends?' JOHNSON. 'Sir, you will by and by have enough of this conversation, which now delights you so much.'

As he was a zealous friend of subordination, he was at all times watchful to repress the vulgar cant against the manners of the great; 'High people, Sir, (said he,) are the best; take a hundred ladies of quality, you'll find them better wives, better mothers, more willing to sacrifice their own pleasure to their children than a hundred other women. Tradeswomen (I mean the wives of tradesmen) in the city, who are worth from ten to fifteen thousand pounds, are the worst creatures upon the earth, grossly ignorant, and thinking viciousness fashionable. Farmers, I think, are often worthless fellows. Few lords will cheat; and, if they do, they'll be ashamed of it: farmers cheat and are not ashamed of it: they have all the sensual vices too of the nobility, with cheating into the bargain. There is as much fornication and adultery among farmers as amongst noblemen.' BOSWELL. 'The notion of the world, Sir, however is, that the morals of women of quality are worse than those in lower stations.' JOHNSON. 'Yes, Sir, the licentiousness of one woman of quality makes more noise than that of a number of women in lower stations; then, Sir, you are to consider the malignity of women in the city against women of quality, which will make them believe any thing of them, such as that they call their coachmen to bed. No, Sir, so far as I have observed, the higher in rank, the richer ladies are, they are the better instructed and the more virtuous.'

This year the Reverend Mr. Horne published his *Letter to Mr. Dunning on the English Particle;* Johnson read it, and though not treated in it with sufficient respect, he had candour enough to say to Mr. Seward, 'Were I to make a new edition of my Dictionary, I would adopt several of Mr. Horne's etymologies; I hope they did not put the dog in the pillory for his libel; he has too much literature for that.'

On Saturday, May 16, I dined with him at Mr. Beauclerk's with Mr. Langton, Mr. Steevens, Dr. Higgins, and some others. I regret very feelingly every instance of my remissness in recording his *memorabilia;* I am afraid it is the condition of humanity (as Mr. Windham, of Norfolk, once observed to me, after having made an admirable speech in the House of Commons, which was highly applauded, but which he afterwards perceived might have been better:) 'that we are more uneasy from thinking of our wants, than happy in thinking of our acquisitions.' This is an unreasonable mode of disturbing our tranquillity, and should be corrected; let me then comfort myself with the large treasure of Johnson's conversation which I have preserved for my own enjoyment and that of the world, and let me exhibit what I have upon each occasion, whether more or less, whether a bulse, or only a few sparks of a diamond.

He said, 'Dr. Mead lived more in the broad sunshine of life than almost any man.'

The disaster of General Burgoyne's army was then the common topic of conversation. It was asked why piling their arms was insisted upon as a matter of such consequence, when it seemed to be a circumstance so inconsiderable in itself. JOHNSON. 'Why, Sir, a French authour says, "*Il y a beaucoup de puerilités dans la guerre."* All distinctions are trifles, because great things can seldom occur, and those distinctions are settled by custom. A savage would as willingly have his meat sent to him in the kitchen, as eat it at the table here; as men become civilized, various modes of denoting honourable preference are invented.' . . .

On Sunday, May 17, I presented to him Mr. Fullarton, of Fullarton, who has since distinguished himself so much in India, to whom he naturally talked of travels, as Mr. Brydone accompanied him in his tour to Sicily and Malta. He said, 'The information which we have from modern travellers is much more authentick than what we had from ancient travellers; ancient travellers guessed; modern travellers measure. The Swiss admit that there is but one errour in Stanyan. If Brydone were more attentive to his Bible, he would be a good traveller.'

He said, 'Lord Chatham was a Dictator; he possessed the power of putting the State in motion; now there is no power, all order is relaxed.' BOSWELL. 'Is there no hope of a change to the better?' JOHNSON. 'Why, yes, Sir, when we are weary of this relaxation. So the City of London will appoint its Mayors again by seniority.' BOSWELL. 'But is not that taking a mere chance for having a good or a bad Mayor?' JOHNSON. 'Yes, Sir; but the evil of competition is greater than that of the worst Mayor that can come; besides, there is no more reason to suppose that the choice of a rabble will be right, than that chance will be right.'

On Tuesday, May 19, I was to set out for Scotland in the evening. He was engaged to dine with me at Mr. Dilly's, I waited upon him to remind him of his appointment and attend him thither; he gave me some salutary counsel, and recommended vigorous resolution against any deviation from moral duty. BOSWELL. 'But you would not have me to bind myself by a solemn obligation?' JOHNSON. (much agitated,) 'What! a vow—O, no, Sir, a vow is a horrible thing, it is a snare for sin. The man who cannot go to Heaven without a vow—may go—' Here, standing erect, in the middle of his library, and rolling grand, his pause was truly a curious compound of the solemn and the ludicrous; he half-whistled in his usual way, when pleasant, and he paused, as if checked by religious awe. Methought he would have added—to Hell —but was restrained. I humoured the dilemma. 'What! Sir, (said I,) *In cælum jusseris ibit?*[1] alluding to his imitation of it,—

---

[1] 'And bid him go to heaven, to heaven he will go.' Juvenal, *Satires,* iii. 78. Johnson, *London,* 1, 116.

'And bid him go to Hell, to Hell he goes.'

I had mentioned to him a slight fault in his noble *Imitation of the Tenth Satire of Juvenal,* a too near recurrence of the verb *spread,* in his description of the young Enthusiast at College:—

'Through all his veins the fever of renown,
Spreads from the strong contagion of the gown;
O'er Bodley's dome his future labours *spread,*
And Bacon's mansion trembles o'er his head.'

He had desired me to change *spreads* to *burns,* but for perfect authenticity, I now had it done with his own hand. I thought this alteration not only cured the fault, but was more poetical, as it might carry an allusion to the shirt by which Hercules was inflamed.

We had a quiet comfortable meeting at Mr. Dilly's; nobody there but ourselves. Mr. Dilly mentioned somebody having wished that Milton's *Tractate on Education* should be printed along with his Poems in the edition of *The English Poets* then going on. JOHNSON. 'It would be breaking in upon the plan; but would be of no great consequence. So far as it would be any thing, it would be wrong. Education in England has been in danger of being hurt by two of its greatest men, Milton and Locke. Milton's plan is impracticable, and I suppose has never been tried. Locke's, I fancy, has been tried often enough, but is very imperfect; it gives too much to one side, and too little to the other; it gives too little to literature. —I shall do what I can for Dr. Watts; but my materials are very scanty. His poems are by no means his best works; I cannot praise his poetry itself highly; but I can praise its design.'

My illustrious friend and I parted with assurances of affectionate regard. . . .

Mr. Langton has been pleased, at my request, to favour me with some particulars of Dr. Johnson's visit to Warley-camp, where this gentleman was at the time stationed as a Captain in the Lincolnshire militia. I shall give them in his own words in a letter to me.

'It was in the summer of the year 1778, that he complied with my invitation to come down to the Camp at Warley, and he staid with me about a week; the scene appeared, notwithstanding a great degree of ill health that he seemed to labour under, to interest and amuse him, as agreeing with the disposition that I believe you know he constantly manifested towards enquiring into subjects of the military kind. He sate, with a patient degree of attention, to observe the proceedings of a regimental court-martial, that happened to be called, in the time of his stay with us; and one night, as late as at eleven o'clock, he accompanied the Major of the regiment in going what are styled the *Rounds*, where he might observe the forms of visiting the guards, for the seeing that they and their sentries are ready in their duty on their several posts. He took occasion to converse at times on military topicks, one in particular, that I see the mention of, in your *Journal of a Tour to the Hebrides*, which lies open before me, as to gun-powder; which he spoke of to the same effect, in part, that you relate.

'On one occasion, when the regiment were going through their exercise, he went quite close to the men at one of the extremities of it, and watched all their practices attentively; and, when he came away, his remark was, "The men indeed do load their muskets and fire with wonderful celerity." He was likewise particular in requiring to know what was the weight of the musquet balls in use, and within what distance they might be expected to take effect when fired off.

'In walking among the tents, and observing the difference between those of the officers and private men, he said that the superiority of accommodation of the better conditions of life, to that of the inferiour ones, was never exhibited to him in so distinct a view. The civilities paid to him in the camp were, from the gentlemen of the Lincolnshire regiment, one of the officers of which accommodated him with a tent in which he slept; and from General Hall, who very courteously invited him to dine with him, where he appeared to be very well pleased with his entertainment, and the civilities he received on the part of the General; the attention likewise, of the General's aide-de-camp, Captain Smith, seemed to be very welcome to him, as appeared by their engaging in a great deal of discourse together. The gentlemen of the East York regiment likewise on being informed of his coming, solicited his company at dinner, but by that time he had fixed his departure, so that he could not comply with the invitation.' . . .

In 1779, Johnson gave the world a luminous proof that the vigour of his mind in all its faculties, whether memory, judgement, or imagination, was not in the least abated; for this year came out the first four volumes of his *Prefaces, biographical and critical, to the most eminent of the English Poets,** published by the booksellers of London. The remaining volumes came out in the year 1780. The Poets were selected by the several booksellers who had the honorary copy right, which is still preserved among them by mutual compact, notwithstanding the decision of the House of Lords against the perpetuity of Literary Property. We have his own authority, that by his recommendation the poems of Blackmore, Watts, Pomfret, and Yalden, were added to the collection. . . .

This letter[1] crossed me on the road to London, where I arrived on Monday, March 15, and next morning at a late hour, found Dr. Johnson sitting over his tea, attended by Mrs. Desmoulins, Mr. Levett, and a clergyman, who had come to submit some poetical pieces to his revision. It is wonderful what a number and variety of writers, some of them even unknown to him, prevailed on his good-nature to look over their works, and suggest corrections and improvements. My arrival interrupted for a little while the important business of this true representative of Bayes; upon its being resumed, I found that the subject under immediate consideration was a translation, yet in manuscript, of the *Carmen Seculare* of Horace, which had this year been set to musick, and performed as a publick entertainment in London, for the joint benefit of Monsieur Philidor and Signor Baretti. When Johnson had done reading, the authour asked him bluntly, 'If upon the whole it was a good translation?' Johnson, whose regard for truth was uncommonly strict, seemed to be puzzled for a moment, what answer to make, as he certainly could not honestly commend the performance: with exquisite address he evaded the question thus, 'Sir, I do not say that it may not be made a very good translation.' Here nothing whatever in favour of the performance was affirmed, and yet the writer was not shocked. A printed *Ode to the Warlike Genius of Britain,* came next in review; the bard was a lank bony figure, with short black hair; he was writhing himself in agitation, while Johnson read, and shewing his teeth in a grin of earnestness, exclaimed in broken sentences, and in a keen sharp tone, 'Is that poetry, Sir?—Is it Pindar?' JOHNSON. 'Why, Sir, there is here a great deal of what is called poetry.' Then, turning to me, the poet cried, 'My muse has not been long upon the town, and (pointing to the *Ode*) it trembles under the hand of the great critick.' Johnson, in a tone of displeasure, asked him, 'Why do you praise Anson?' I did not trouble him by asking his reason for this question. He proceeded, 'Here is an errour, Sir; you have made Genius feminine.' 'Palpable, Sir; (cried the enthusiast,) I know it. But (in a lower tone,) it was to pay a compliment to the Duchess of Devonshire, with which her Grace was pleased. She is walking across Coxheath, in the military uniform, and I suppose her to be the Genius of Britain.' JOHNSON. 'Sir, you

[1] An exchange of letters between Boswell and Johnson is omitted.

are giving a reason for it; but that will not make it right. You may have a reason why two and two should make five; but they will still make but four.'

Although I was several times with him in the course of the following days, such it seems were my occupations, or such my negligence, that I have preserved no memorial of his conversation till Friday, March 26, when I visited him. He said he expected to be attacked on account of his *Lives of the Poets*. 'However (said he,) I would rather be attacked than unnoticed. For the worst thing you can do to an authour is to be silent as to his works. An assault upon a town is a bad thing; but starving it is still worse; an assault may be unsuccessful; you may have more men killed than you kill; but if you starve the town, you are sure of victory.'

Talking of a friend of ours[1] associating with persons of very discordant principles and characters; I said he was a very universal man, quite a man of the world. JOHNSON. 'Yes, Sir; but one may be so much a man of the world as to be nothing in the world. I remember a passage in Goldsmith's *Vicar of Wakefield*, which he was afterwards fool enough to expunge: "I do not love a man who is zealous for nothing."' BOSWELL. 'That was a fine passage.' JOHNSON. 'Yes, Sir: there was another fine passage too, which he struck out: "When I was a young man, being anxious to distinguish myself, I was perpetually starting new propositions. But I soon gave this over; for, I found that generally what was new was false."' I said I did not like to sit with people of whom I had not a good opinion. JOHNSON. 'But you must not indulge your delicacy too much; or you will be a *tête-à-tête* man all your life.'

During my stay in London this spring, I find I was unaccountably negligent in preserving Johnson's sayings, more so than at any time when I was happy enough to have an opportunity of hearing his wisdom and wit. There is no help for it now. I must content myself with presenting such scraps as I have. But I am nevertheless ashamed and vexed to think how much has been lost. It is not that there was a bad crop this year; but that I was not sufficiently careful in gathering it in. I, therefore, in some instances can only exhibit a few detached fragments.

Talking of the wonderful concealment of the authour of the celebrated letters signed *Junius;* he said, 'I should have believed Burke to be Junius, because I know no man but Burke who is capable of writing these letters; but Burke spontaneously denied it to me. The case would have been dif-

1 Reynolds.

ferent had I asked him if he was the authour; a man so questioned, as to an anonymous publication, may think he has a right to deny it.'

He observed that his old friend, Mr. Sheridan, had been honoured with extraordinary attention in his own country, by having had an exception made in his favour in an Irish Act of Parliament concerning insolvent debtors. 'Thus to be singled out (said he,) by a legislature, as an object of publick consideration and kindness, is a proof of no common merit.'

At Streatham, on Monday, March 29, at breakfast he maintained that a father had no right to control the inclinations of his daughters in marriage.

On Wednesday, March 31, when I visited him, and confessed an excess of which I had very seldom been guilty; that I had spent a whole night in playing at cards, and that I could not look back on it with satisfaction; instead of a harsh animadversion, he mildly said, 'Alas, Sir, on how few things can we look back with satisfaction.'

On Thursday, April 1, he commended one of the Dukes of Devonshire for 'a dogged veracity.' He said too, 'London is nothing to some people; but to a man whose pleasure is intellectual, London is the place. And there is no place where œconomy can be so well practised as in London. More can be had here for the money, even by ladies, than any where else. You cannot play tricks with your fortune in a small place; you must make an uniform appearance. Here a lady may have well-furnished apartments, and elegant dress, without any meat in her kitchen.'

I was amused by considering with how much ease and coolness he could write or talk to a friend, exhorting him not to suppose that happiness was not to be found as well in other places as in London; when he himself was at all times sensible of its being, comparatively speaking, a heaven upon earth. The truth is, that by those who from sagacity, attention, and experience, have learnt the full advantage of London, its pre-eminence over every other place, not only for variety of enjoyment, but for comfort, will be felt with a philosophical exultation. The freedom from remark and petty censure, with which life may be passed there, is a circumstance which a man who knows the teazing restraint of a narrow circle must relish highly. Mr. Burke, whose orderly and amiable domestic habits might make the eye of observation less irksome to him than to most men, said once very pleasantly, in my hearing, 'Though I have the honour to represent Bristol, I should not like to live there; I should be obliged to be so much *upon my good behaviour.*' In London, a man may live in splendid society at one time, and in frugal retirement at another, without animadversion. There, and there alone, a man's own house is truly his *castle,* in which he can be in perfect safety from intrusion whenever he pleases. I shall never forget how well this was expressed to me one day by Mr. Meynell: 'The chief advantage of London (said he,) is, that a man is always *so near his burrow.*'

He said of one of his old acquaintances, 'He is very fit for a travelling governour. He knows French very well. He is a man of good principles; and there would be no danger that a young gentleman should catch his manner; for it is so very bad, that it must be avoided. In that respect he would be like the drunken Helot.'

A gentleman has informed me, that Johnson said of the same person, 'Sir, he has the most *inverted* understanding of any man whom I have ever known.'

On Friday, April 2, being Good-Friday, I visited him in the morning as usual; and finding that we insensibly fell into a train of ridicule upon the foibles of one of our friends,[1] a very worthy man, I, by way of a check, quoted some good admonition from *The Government of the Tongue,* that very pious book. It happened also remarkably enough, that the subject of the sermon preached to us to-day by Dr. Burrows, the rector of St. Clement Danes, was the certainty that at the last day we must give an account of 'the deeds done in the body;' and, amongst various acts of culpability he mentioned evil-speaking. As we were moving slowly along in the crowd from church, Johnson jogged my elbow, and said, 'Did you attend to the sermon?' 'Yes, Sir, (said I,) it was very applicable to *us.*' He, however, stood upon the defensive. 'Why, Sir, the sense of ridicule is given us, and may be lawfully used. The authour of *The Government of the Tongue* would have us treat all men alike.'

In the interval between morning and evening service, he endeavoured to employ himself earnestly in devotional exercises; and, as he has mentioned in his *Prayers and Meditations,* gave me *Les Pensées de Pascal,* that I might not interrupt him. I preserve the book with reverence. His presenting it to me is marked upon it with his own hand, and I have found in it a truly divine unction. We went to church again in the afternoon.

On Saturday, April 3, I visited him at night, and found him sitting in Mrs. Williams's room, with her, and one who he afterwards told me was a natural son of the second Lord Southwell. The table had a singular appearance, being covered with a heterogeneous assemblage of oysters and porter

---

[1] Langton.

for his company, and tea for himself. I mentioned my having heard an eminent physician, who was himself a Chrisitan, argue in favour of universal toleration, and maintain, that no man could be hurt by another man's differing from him in opinion. JOHNSON. 'Sir, you are to a certain degree hurt by knowing that even one man does not believe.'

On Easter-day, after solemn service at St. Paul's, I dined with him: Mr. Allen the printer was also his guest. He was uncommonly silent; and I have not written down any thing, except a single curious fact, which, having the sanction of his inflexible veracity, may be received as a striking instance of human insensibility and inconsideration. As he was passing by a fishmonger who was skinning an eel alive, he heard him 'curse it, because it would not lye still.'

On Wednesday, April 7, I dined with him at Sir Joshua Reynolds's. I have not marked what company was there. Johnson harangued upon the qualities of different liquors; and spoke with great contempt of claret, as so weak, that 'a man would be drowned by it before it made him drunk.' He was persuaded to drink one glass of it, that he might judge, not from recollection, which might be dim, but from immediate sensation. He shook his head, and said, 'Poor stuff! No, Sir, claret is the liquor for boys; port, for men; but he who aspires to be a hero (smiling,) must drink brandy. In the first place, the flavour of brandy is most grateful to the palate; and then brandy will do soonest for a man what drinking *can* do for him. There are, indeed, few who are able to drink brandy. That is a power rather to be wished for than attained. And yet, (proceeded he,) as in all pleasure hope is a considerable part, I know not but fruition comes too quick by brandy. Florence wine I think the worst; it is wine only to the eye; it is wine neither while you are drinking it, nor after you have drunk it; it neither pleases the taste, nor exhilarates the spirits.' I reminded him how heartily he and I used to drink wine together, when we were first acquainted; and how I used to have a head-ache after sitting up with him. He did not like to have this recalled, or, perhaps, thinking that I boasted improperly, resolved to have a witty stroke at me: 'Nay, Sir, it was not the *wine* that made your head ache, but the *sense* that I put into it.' BOSWELL. 'What, Sir! will sense make the head ache?' JOHNSON. 'Yes, Sir, (with a smile,) when it is not used to it.'—No man who has a true relish of pleasantry could be offended at this; especially if Johnson in a long intimacy had given him repeated proofs of his regard and good estimation. I used to say, that as he had given me a thousand pounds in praise, he had a good right now and then to take a guinea from me.

On Thursday, April 8, I dined with him at Mr. Allan Ramsay's, with Lord Graham and some other company. We talked of Shakspeare's witches. JOHNSON. 'They are beings of his own creation; they are a compound of malignity and meanness, without any abilities; and are quite different from the Italian magician. King James says in his *Dæmonology*, 'Magicians command the devils: witches are their servants. The Italian magicians are elegant beings.' RAMSAY. 'Opera witches, not Drury-lane witches.' Johnson observed, that abilities might be employed in a narrow sphere, as in getting money, which he said he believed no man could do, without vigorous parts, though concentrated to a point. RAMSAY. 'Yes, like a strong horse in a mill; he pulls better.'

Lord Graham, while he praised the beauty of Lochlomond, on the banks of which is his family seat, complained of the climate, and said he could not bear it. JOHNSON. 'Nay, my Lord, don't talk so: you may bear it well enough. Your ancestors have borne it more years than I can tell.' This was a handsome compliment to the antiquity of the House of Montrose. His Lordship told me afterwards, that he had only affected to complain of the climate; lest, if he had spoken as favourably of his country as he really thought, Dr. Johnson might have attacked it. Johnson was very courteous to Lady Margaret Macdonald. 'Madam, (said he,) when I was in the Isle of Sky, I heard of the people running to take the stones off the road, lest Lady Margaret's horse should stumble.'

Lord Graham commended Dr. Drummond at Naples, as a man of extraordinary talents; and added, that he had a great love of liberty. JOHNSON. 'He is *young*, my Lord; (looking to his Lordship with an arch smile,) all *boys* love liberty, till experience convinces them they are not so fit to govern themselves as they imagined. We are all agreed as to our own liberty; we would have as much of it as we can get; but we are not agreed as to the liberty of others: for in proportion as we take, others must lose. I believe we hardly wish that the mob should have liberty to govern us. When that was the case some time ago, no man was at liberty not to have candles in his windows.' RAMSAY. 'The result is, that order is better than confusion.' JOHNSON. 'The result is, that order cannot be had but by subordination.'

On Friday, April 16, I had been present at the trial of the unfortunate Mr. Hackman, who, in a fit of frantick jealous love, had shot Miss Ray, the favourite of a nobleman.[1] Johnson, in whose company I dined to-day, with some other friends, was much interested by my account of what passed,

---

[1] John Montagu, 4th Earl of Sandwich.

and particularly with his prayer for the mercy of heaven. He said, in a solemn fervid tone, 'I hope he *shall* find mercy.'

This day a violent altercation arose between Johnson and Beauclerk, which having made much noise at the time, I think it proper, in order to prevent any future misrepresentation, to give a minute account of it.

In talking of Hackman, Johnson argued, as Judge Blackstone had done, that his being furnished with two pistols was a proof that he meant to shoot two persons. Mr. Beauclerk said, 'No; for that every wise man who intended to shoot himself, took two pistols, that he might be sure of doing it at once. Lord——— ———'s cook shot himself with one pistol, and lived ten days in great agony. Mr. ———, who loved buttered muffins, but durst not eat them because they disagreed with his stomach, resolved to shoot himself; and then he eat three buttered muffins for breakfast, before shooting himself, knowing that he should not be troubled with indigestion: *he* had two charged pistols; one was found lying charged upon the table by him, after he had shot himself with the other.' 'Well, (said Johnson, with an air of triumph,) you see here one pistol was sufficient.' Beauclerk replied smartly, 'Because it happened to kill him.' And either then, or a very little afterwards, being piqued at Johnson's triumphant remark, added, "This is what you don't know, and I do.' There was then a cessation of the dispute; and some minutes intervened, during which, dinner and the glass went on cheerfully; when Johnson suddenly and abruptly exclaimed, 'Mr. Beauclerk, how came you to talk so petulantly to me, as "This is what you don't know, but what I know"? One thing *I* know, which *you* don't seem to know, that you are very uncivil.' BEAUCLERK. 'Because *you* began by being uncivil, (which you always are.)' The words in parenthesis were, I believe, not heard by Mr. Johnson. Here again there was a cessation of arms. Johnson told me, that the reason why he waited at first some time without taking any notice of what Mr. Beauclerk said, was because he was thinking whether he should resent it. But when he considered that there were present a young Lord and an eminent traveller,[1] two men of the world with whom he had never dined before, he was apprehensive that they might think they had a right to take such liberties with him as Beauclerk did, and therefore resolved he would not let it pass; adding, that 'he would not appear a coward.' A little while after this, the conversation turned on the violence of Hackman's temper. Johnson then said, 'It was his business to *command* his temper, as my

[1] Viscount Althorp and Sir Joseph Banks.

friend, Mr. Beauclerk, should have done some time ago.'
BEAUCLERK. 'I should learn of *you*, Sir.' JOHNSON. 'Sir, you
have given *me* opportunities enough of learning, when I have
been in *your* company. No man loves to be treated with contempt.' BEAUCLERK. (with a polite inclination towards Johnson,) 'Sir, you have known me twenty years, and however I
may have treated others, you may be sure I could never treat
you with contempt.' JOHNSON. 'Sir, you have said more than
was necessary.' Thus it ended; and Beauclerk's coach not
having come for him till very late, Dr. Johnson and another
gentleman[1] sat with him a long time after the rest of the
company were gone; and he and I dined at Beauclerk's on the
Saturday se'nnight following.

After this tempest had subsided, I recollect the following
particulars of his conversation:—

'I am always for getting a boy forward in his learning; for
that is a sure good. I would let him at first read *any* English
book which happens to engage his attention; because you
have done a great deal when you have brought him to have
entertainment from a book. He'll get better books afterwards.' . . .

'To be contradicted, in order to force you to talk, is
mighty unpleasing. You *shine*, indeed; but it is by being
ground.' . . .

On Saturday, April 24, I dined with him at Mr. Beauclerk's, with Sir Joshua Reynolds, Mr. Jones, (afterwards Sir
William,) Mr. Langton, Mr. Steevens, Mr. Paradise, and Dr.
Higgins. I mentioned that Mr. Wilkes had attacked Garrick
to me, as a man who had no friend. 'I believe he is right, Sir.
. . . He had friends, but no friend. Garrick was so diffused,
he had no man to whom he wished to unbosom himself. He
found people always ready to applaud him, and that always
for the same thing: so he saw life with great uniformity.' I
took upon me, for once, to fight with Goliath's weapons, and
play the sophist.—'Garrick did not need a friend, as he got
from every body all he wanted. What is a friend? One who
supports you and comforts you, while others do not. Friendship, you know, Sir, is the cordial drop, "to make the nauseous
draught of life go down:" but if the draught be not nauseous,
if it be all sweet, there is no occasion for that drop.' JOHN-
SON. 'Many men would not be content to live so. I hope I
should not. They would wish to have an intimate friend, with
whom they might compare minds, and cherish private
virtues.' One of the company mentioned Lord Chesterfield, as
a man who had no friend. JOHNSON. 'There were more mate-

[1] Steevens.

rials to make friendship in Garrick, had he not been so diffused.' BOSWELL. 'Garrick was pure gold, but beat out to thin leaf. Lord Chesterfield was tinsel.' JOHNSON. 'Garrick was a very good man, the cheerfullest man of his age; a decent liver in a profession which is supposed to give indulgence to licentiousness; and a man who gave away, freely, money acquired by himself. He began the world with a great hunger for money; the son of a half-pay officer, bred in a family, whose study was to make four-pence do as much as others made four-pence halfpenny do. But, when he had got money, he was very liberal.' I presumed to animadvert on his eulogy on Garrick, in his *Lives of the Poets*. 'You say, Sir, his death eclipsed the gaiety of nations.' JOHNSON. 'I could not have said more nor less. It is the truth; *eclipsed,* not *extinguished;* and his death *did* eclipse; it was like a storm.' BOSWELL. 'But why nations? Did his gaiety extend farther than his own nation?' JOHNSON. 'Why, Sir, some exaggeration must be allowed. Besides, nations may be said—if we allow the Scotch to be a nation, and to have gaiety,—which they have not. *You* are an exception, though. Come, gentlemen, let us candidly admit that there is one Scotchman who is cheerful.' BEAUCLERK. 'But he is a very unnatural Scotchman.' I, however, continued to think the compliment to Garrick hyperbolically untrue. His acting had ceased some before his death; at any rate he had acted in Ireland but a short time, at an early period of his life, and never in Scotland. I objected also to what appears an anticlimax of praise, when contrasted with the preceding panegyrick,—'and diminished the public stock of harmless pleasure!'—'Is not *harmless pleasure* very tame?' JOHNSON. 'Nay, Sir, harmless pleasure is the highest praise. Pleasure is a word of dubious import; pleasure is in general dangerous, and pernicious to virtue; to be able therefore to furnish pleasure that is harmless, pleasure pure and unalloyed, is as great a power as man can possess.' This was, perhaps, as ingenious a defence as could be made; still, however, I was not satisfied.

A celebrated wit[1] being mentioned, he said, 'One may say of him as was said of a French wit, *Il n'a de l'esprit que contre Dieu.* I have been several times in company with him, but never perceived any strong power of wit. He produces a general effect by various means; he has a cheerful countenance and a gay voice. Besides his trade is wit. It would be as wild in him to come into company without merriment, as for a highwayman to take the road without his pistols.'

Talking of the effects of drinking, he said, 'Drinking may

[1] Wilkes.

be practised with great prudence; a man who exposes himself when he is intoxicated, has not the art of getting drunk; a sober man who happens occasionally to get drunk, readily enough goes into a new company, which a man who has been drinking should never do. Such a man will undertake any thing; he is without skill in inebriation. I used to slink home, when I had drunk too much. A man accustomed to self-examination will be conscious when he is drunk, though an habitual drunkard will not be conscious of it. I knew a physician[1] who for twenty years was not sober; yet in a pamphlet, which he wrote upon fevers, he appealed to Garrick and me for his vindication from a charge of drunkenness. A bookseller (naming him,)[2] who got a large fortune by trade, was so habitually and equably drunk, that his most intimate friends never perceived that he was more sober at one time than another.'

Talking of celebrated and successful irregular practisers in physick; he said, 'Taylor was the most ignorant man I ever knew; but sprightly. Ward the dullest. Taylor challenged me once to talk Latin with him; (laughing). I quoted some of Horace, which he took to be a part of my own speech. He said a few words well enough.' BEAUCLERK. 'I remember, Sir, you said that Taylor was an instance how far impudence could carry ignorance.' Mr. Beauclerk was very entertaining this day, and told us a number of short stories in a lively elegant manner, and with that air of *the world* which has I know not what impressive effect, as if there were something more than is expressed, or than perhaps we could perfectly understand. As Johnson and I accompanied Sir Joshua Reynolds in his coach, Johnson said, 'There is in Beauclerk a predominance over his company, that one does not like. But he is a man who has lived so much in the world, that he has a short story on every occasion; he is always ready to talk, and is never exhausted.'

Johnson and I passed the evening at Miss Reynolds's, Sir Joshua's sister. I mentioned that an eminent friend of ours,[3] talking of the common remark, that affection descends, said, that 'this was wisely contrived for the preservation of mankind; for which it was not so necessary that there should be affection from children to parents, as from parents to children; nay, there would be no harm in that view though children should at a certain age eat their parents.' JOHNSON. 'But, Sir, if this were known generally to be the case, parents

---

[1] Dr. Robert James.
[2] Andrew Millar.
[3] Burke.

would not have affection for children.' BOSWELL. 'True, Sir; for it is in expectation of a return that parents are so attentive to their children; and I know a very pretty instance of a little girl[1] of whom her father was very fond, who once when he was in a melancholy fit, and had gone to bed, persuaded him to rise in good humour by saying, "My dear papa, please to get up, and let me help you on with your clothes, that I may learn to do it when you are an old man."'

Soon after this time a little incident occurred, which I will not suppress, because I am desirous that my work should be, as much as is consistent with the strictest truth, an antidote to the false and injurious notions of his character, which have been given by others, and therefore I infuse every drop of genuine sweetness into my biographical cup.

'To DR. JOHNSON

'MY DEAR SIR,—I am in great pain with an inflamed foot, and obliged to keep my bed, so am prevented from having the pleasure to dine at Mr. Ramsay's to-day, which is very hard; and my spirits are sadly sunk. Will you be so friendly as to come and sit an hour with me in the evening. I am ever your most faithful, and affectionate humble servant,

 'South Audley-street,   'JAMES BOSWELL.'
 Monday, April 26.'

'To MR. BOSWELL

'Mr. Johnson laments the absence of Mr. Boswell, and will come to him.—Harley-street.'

He came to me in the evening, and brought Sir Joshua Reynolds. I need scarcely say, that their conversation, while they sate by my bedside, was the most pleasing opiate to pain that could have been administered.

Johnson being now better disposed to obtain information concerning Pope than he was last year, sent by me to my Lord Marchmont a present of those volumes of his *Lives of the Poets* which were at this time published, with a request to have permission to wait on him; and his Lordship, who had called on him twice, obligingly appointed Saturday, the first of May, for receiving us.

On that morning Johnson came to me from Streatham, and after drinking chocolate at General Paoli's, in South-Audley-street, we proceeded to Lord Marchmont's in Curzon-street. His Lordship met us at the door of his library, and with great politeness said to Johnson, 'I am not going to make an encomium upon *myself*, by telling you the high respect I have for

[1] Boswell's daughter, Veronica.

you, Sir.' Johnson was exceedingly courteous; and the interview, which lasted about two hours, during which the Earl communicated his anecdotes of Pope, was as agreeable as I could have wished. When we came out, I said to Johnson, that considering his Lordship's civility, I should have been vexed if he had again failed to come. 'Sir, (said he,) I would rather have given twenty pounds than not have come.' I accompanied him to Streatham, where we dined, and returned to town in the evening. . . .

My readers will not be displeased at being told every slight circumstance of the manner in which Dr. Johnson contrived to amuse his solitary hours. He sometimes employed himself in chymistry, sometimes in watering and pruning a vine, and sometimes in small experiments, at which those who may smile, should recollect that there are moments which admit of being soothed only by trifles. . . .

My friend Colonel James Stuart, second son of the Earl of Bute, who had distinguished himself as a good officer of the Bedfordshire militia, had taken a publick-spirited resolution to serve his country in its difficulties, by raising a regular regiment, and taking the command of it himself. This, in the heir of the immense property of Wortley, was highly honourable. Having been in Scotland recruiting, he obligingly asked me to accompany him to Leeds, then the head-quarters of his corps; from thence to London for a short time, and afterwards to other places to which the regiment might be ordered. Such an offer, at a time of the year when I had full leisure, was very pleasing; especially as I was to accompany a man of sterling good sense, information, discernment, and conviviality; and was to have a second crop, in one year, of London and Johnson. Of this I informed my illustrious friend, in characteristical warm terms, in a letter dated the 30th of September, from Leeds.

On Monday, October 4, I called at his house before he was up. He sent for me to his bedside, and expressed his satisfaction at this incidental meeting, with as much vivacity as if he had been in the gaiety of youth. He called briskly, 'Frank, go and get coffee, and let us breakfast *in splendour*.'

During this visit to London I had several interviews with him, which it is unnecessary to distinguish particularly. I consulted him as to the appointment of guardians to my children, in case of my death. 'Sir, (said he,) do not appoint a number of guardians. When there are many, they trust one to another, and the business is neglected. I would advise you to choose only one; let him be a man of respectable character, who, for his own credit, will do what is right; let him be a rich man, so that he may be under no temptation to take advantage; and let him be a man of business, who is used to conduct affairs with ability and expertness, to whom, therefore, the execution of the trust will not be burdensome.'

On Sunday, October 10, we dined together at Mr. Strahan's. The conversation having turned on the prevailing practice of going to the East-Indies in quest of wealth;—JOHNSON. 'A man had better have ten thousand pounds at the end of ten years passed in England, than twenty thousand pounds at the end of ten years passed in India, because you must compute what you *give* for money; and a man who has lived ten years in India, has given up ten years of social comfort and all those advantages which arise from living in England. The ingenious Mr. Brown, distinguished by the name of *Capability Brown*, told me, that he was once at the seat of Lord Clive, who had returned from India with great wealth; and that he shewed him at the door of his bed-chamber a large chest, which he said he had once had full of gold; upon which Brown observed, "I am glad you can bear it so near your bed-chamber." '

We talked of the state of the poor in London.—JOHNSON. 'Saunders Welch, the Justice, who was once High-Constable of Holborn, and had the best opportunities of knowing the state of the poor, told me, that I under-rated the number, when I computed that twenty a week, that is, above a thousand a year, died of hunger; not abolutely of immediate hunger; but of the wasting and other diseases which are the consequences of hunger. This happens only in so large a place as London, where people are not known. What we are told about the great sums got by begging is not true: the trade is overstocked. And, you may depend upon it, there are many who cannot get work. A particular kind of manufacture fails: those who have been used to work at it, can, for some time, work at nothing else. You meet a man begging; you charge him with idleness: he says, "I am willing to labour. Will you give me work?"— "I cannot."—"Why, then you have no right to charge me with idleness." '

We left Mr. Strahan's at seven, as Johnson had said he intended to go to evening prayers. As we walked along, he complained of a little gout in his toe, and said, 'I shan't go to prayers to-night; I shall go to-morrow: Whenever I miss church on a Sunday, I resolve to go another day. But I do not always do it.' This was a fair exhibition of that vibration between pious resolutions and indolence, which many of us have too often experienced.

I went home with him, and we had a long quiet conversation. . . .

BOSWELL. 'Why, Sir, do people play this trick which I observe now, when I look at your grate, putting the shovel against it to make the fire burn?' JOHNSON. 'They play the trick, but it does not make the fire burn. *There* is a better; (setting the poker perpendicularly up at right angles with the grate.) In days of superstition they thought, as it made a cross with the bars, it would drive away the witch.'

BOSWELL. 'By associating with you, Sir, I am always getting an accession of wisdom. But perhaps a man, after knowing his own character—the limited strength of his own mind, should not be desirous of having too much wisdom, considering, *quid valeant humeri,*[1] how little he can carry.' JOHNSON. 'Sir, be as wise as you can; let a man be *aliis lœtus, sapiens sibi:*[2]

> "Though pleas'd to see the dolphins play,
> I mind my compass and my way."

You may be wise in your study in the morning, and gay in company at a tavern in the evening. Every man is to take care of his own wisdom and his own virtue, without minding too much what others think.'

He said, 'Dodsley first mentioned to me the scheme of an English Dictionary; but I had long thought of it.' BOSWELL. 'You did not know what you were undertaking.' JOHNSON. 'Yes, Sir, I knew very well what I was undertaking,—and very well how to do it,—and have done it very well.' BOSWELL. 'An excellent climax! and it *has* availed you. In your Preface you say, "What would it avail me in this gloom of solitude?" You have been agreeably mistaken.' . . .

I mentioned to him a dispute between a friend of mine and his lady, concerning conjugal infidelity, which my friend had maintained was by no means so bad in the husband, as in the wife. JOHNSON 'Your friend was in the right, Sir. Between a man and his Maker it is a different question: but between a man and his wife, a husband's infidelity is nothing. They are connected by children, by fortune, by serious considerations of community. Wise married women don't trouble themselves about infidelity in their husbands.' BOSWELL. 'To be sure there is a great difference between the offence of infidelity in a man and that of his wife.' JOHNSON. 'The difference is boundless. The man imposes no bastards upon his wife.'

Here it may be questioned whether Johnson was entirely in the right. I suppose it will not be controverted that the difference in the degree of criminality is very great, on account of consequences: but still it may be maintained, that, independ-

---

[1] 'What your shoulders can support.' Horace, *Art of Poetry*, 1. 40.

[2] 'Happy with others, wise when alone.'

ent of moral obligation, infidelity is by no means a light offence in a husband; because it must hurt a delicate attachment, in which a mutual constancy is implied, with such refined sentiments as Massinger has exhibited in his play of *The Picture.*—Johnson probably at another time would have admitted this opinion. And let it be kept in remembrance, that he was very careful not to give any encouragement to irregular conduct. A gentleman,[1] not adverting to the distinction made by him upon this subject, supposed a case of singular perverseness in a wife, and heedlessly said, 'That then he thought a husband might do as he pleased with a safe conscience.' JOHNSON. 'Nay, Sir, this is wild indeed (smiling;) you must consider that fornication is a crime in a single man; and you cannot have more liberty by being married.'

He this evening expressed himself strongly against the Roman Catholics; observing, 'In every thing in which they differ from us they are wrong.' He was even against the invocation of Saints; in short, he was in the humour of opposition.

Having regretted to him that I had learnt little Greek, as is too generally the case in Scotland; that I had for a long time hardly applied at all to the study of that noble language, and that I was desirous of being told by him what method to follow; he recommended to me as easy helps, Sylvanus's *First Book of the Iliad;* Dawson's *Lexicon to the Greek New Testament;* and *Hesiod,* with *Pasoris Lexicon* at the end of it.

On Tuesday, October 12, I dined with him at Mr. Ramsay's, with Lord Newhaven, and some other company, none of whom I recollect, but a beautiful Miss Graham, a relation of his Lordship's, who asked Dr. Johnson to hob or nob with her. He was flattered by such pleasing attention, and politely told her, he never drank wine; but if she would drink a glass of water, he was much at her service. She accepted. 'Oho, Sir! (said Lord Newhaven,) you are caught.' JOHNSON. 'Nay, I do not see *how* I am *caught;* but if I am caught, I don't want to get free again. If I am caught, I hope to be kept.' Then when the two glasses of water were brought, smiling placidly to the young lady, he said, 'Madam, let us *reciprocate.'*

Lord Newhaven and Johnson carried on an argument for some time, concerning the Middlesex election. Johnson said, 'Parliament may be considered as bound by law as a man is bound where there is nobody to tie the knot. As it is clear that the House of Commons may expel, and expel again and again, why not allow of the power to incapacitate for that parliament, rather than have a perpetual contest kept up between parliament and the people.' Lord Newhaven took the opposite

[1] Boswell.

side; but respectfully said, 'I speak with great deference to you, Dr. Johnson; I speak to be instructed.' This had its full effect on my friend. He bowed his head almost as low as the table, to a complimenting nobleman; and called out, 'My Lord, my Lord, I do not desire all this ceremony; let us tell our minds to one another quietly.' After the debate was over, he said, 'I have got lights on the subject to-day, which I had not before.' This was a great deal from him, especially as he had written a pamphlet upon it.

He observed, 'The House of Commons was originally not a privilege of the people, but a check for the Crown on the House of Lords. I remember Henry the Eighth wanted them to do something; they hesitated in the morning, but did it in the afternoon. He told them, "It is well you did; or half your heads should have been upon Temple-bar." But the House of Commons is now no longer under the power of the crown, and therefore must be bribed.' He added, 'I have no delight in talking of publick affairs.'

Of his fellow-collegian, the celebrated Mr. George White-field, he said, 'Whitefield never drew as much attention as a mountebank does; he did not draw attention by doing better than others, but by doing what was strange. Were Astley to preach a sermon standing upon his head on a horse's back, he would collect a multitude to hear him; but no wise man would say he had made a better sermon for that. I never treated Whitefield's ministry with contempt; I believe he did good. He had devoted himself to the lower classes of mankind, and among them he was of use. But when familiarity and noise claim the praise due to knowledge, art, and elegance, we must beat down such pretensions.'

What I have preserved of his conversation during the re-mainder of my stay in London at this time, is only what fol-lows: I told him that when I objected to keeping company with a notorious infidel, a celebrated friend of ours said to me, 'I do not think that men who live laxly in the world, as you and I do, can with propriety assume such an authority. Dr. Johnson may, who is uniformly exemplary in his conduct. But it is not very consistent to shun an infidel to-day, and get drunk to-morrow.' JOHNSON. 'Nay, Sir, this is sad reasoning. Because a man cannot be right in all things, is he to be right in nothing? Because a man sometimes gets drunk, is he there-fore to steal? This doctrine would very soon bring a man to the gallows.' . . .

He, I know not why, shewed upon all occasions an aversion to go to Ireland, where I proposed to him that we should make a tour. JOHNSON. 'It is the last place where I should wish to travel.' BOSWELL. 'Should you not like to see Dublin,

Sir?' JOHNSON. 'No, Sir! Dublin is only a worse capital.' BOSWELL. 'Is not the Giant's-Causeway worth seeing?' JOHNSON. 'Worth seeing? yes; but not worth going to see.'

Yet he had a kindness for the Irish nation, and thus generously expressed himself to a gentleman from that country, on the subject of an UNION which artful Politicians have often had in view—'Do not make an union with us, Sir. We should unite with you, only to rob you. We should have robbed the Scotch, if they had had any thing of which we could have robbed them.'

Of an acquaintance of ours, whose manners and every thing about him, though expensive, were coarse, he said, 'Sir, you see in him vulgar prosperity.'

A foreign minister of no very high talents, who had been in his company for a considerable time quite overlooked, happened luckily to mention that he had read some of his *Rambler* in Italian, and admired it much. This pleased him greatly; he observed that the title had been translated, *Il Genio errante,* though I have been told it was rendered more ludicrously, *Il Vagabondo;* and finding that this minister gave such a proof of his taste, he was all attention to him, and on the first remark which he made, however simple, exclaimed, 'The Ambassadour says well—His Excellency observes—' And then he expanded and enriched the little that had been said, in so strong a manner, that it appeared something of consequence. This was exceedingly entertaining to the company who were present, and many a time afterwards it furnished a pleasant topick of merriment: *'The Ambassadour says well,'* became a laughable term of applause, when no mighty matter had been expressed.

I left London on Monday, October 18, and accompanied Colonel Stuart to Chester, where his regiment was to lye for some time. . . .

1780: ÆTAT. 71.]—IN 1780, the world was kept in impatience for the completion of his *Lives of the Poets,* upon which he was employed so far as his indolence allowed him to labour. . . .

On the 2nd of May I wrote to him, and requested that we might have another meeting somewhere in the North of England, in the autumn of this year.

From Mr. Langton I received soon after this time a letter, of which I extract a passage, relative both to Mr. Beauclerk and Dr. Johnson.

'The melancholy information you have received concerning Mr. Beauclerk's death is true. Had his talents been directed in any sufficient degree as they ought, I have always been strong-

518

ly of opinion that they were calculated to make an illustrious figure; and that opinion, as it had been in part formed upon Dr. Johnson's judgment, receives more and more confirmation by hearing what, since his death, Dr. Johnson has said concerning them; a few evenings ago, he was at Mr. Vesey's, where Lord Althorpe, who was one of a numerous company there, addressed Dr. Johnson on the subject of Mr. Beauclerk's death, saying, "Our CLUB has had a great loss since we met last." He replied, "A loss, that perhaps the whole nation could not repair!" The Doctor then went on to speak of his endowments, and particularly extolled the wonderful ease with which he uttered what was highly excellent. He said, that "no man ever was so free when he was going to say a good thing, from a *look* that expressed that it was coming; or, when he had said it, from a look that expressed that it *had* come." At Mr. Thrale's, some days before, when we were talking on the same subject, he said, referring to the same idea of his wonderful facility, "That Beauclerk's talents were those which he had felt himself more disposed to envy, than those of any whom he had known."

'On the evening I have spoken of above, at Mr. Vesey's, you would have been much gratified, as it exhibited an instance of the high importance in which Dr. Johnson's character is held, I think even beyond any I ever before was witness to. The company consisted chiefly of ladies, among whom were the Duchess Dowager of Portland, the Duchess of Beaufort, whom I suppose from her rank I must name before her mother Mrs. Boscawen, and her elder sister Mrs. Lewson, who was likewise there; Lady Lucan, Lady Clermont, and others of note both for their station and understandings. Among the gentlemen were Lord Althorpe, whom I have before named, Lord Macartney, Sir Joshua Reynolds, Lord Lucan, Mr. Wraxal, whose book you have probably seen, *The Tour to the Northern Parts of Europe;* a very agreeable ingenious man; Dr. Warren, Mr. Pepys, the Master in Chancery, whom I believe you know, and Dr. Barnard, the Provost of Eton. As soon as Dr. Johnson was come in and had taken a chair, the company began to collect round him, till they became not less than four, if not five, deep; those behind standing, and listening over the heads of those that were sitting near him. The conversation for some time was chiefly between Dr. Johnson and the Provost of Eton, while the others contributed occasionally their remarks. Without attempting to detail the particulars of the conversation, which perhaps if I did, I should spin my account out to a tedious length, I thought, my dear Sir, this general account of the respect with which our valued friend was attended to, might be acceptable.' . . .

Being disappointed in my hopes of meeting Johnson this year, so that I could hear none of his admirable sayings, I shall compensate for this want by inserting a collection of them, for which I am indebted to my worthy friend Mr. Langton, whose kind communications have been separately interwoven in many parts of this work. Very few articles of this collection were committed to writing by himself, he not having that habit; which he regrets, and which those who know the numerous opportunities he had of gathering the rich fruits of *Johnsonian* wit and wisdom, must ever regret. I however found, in conversations with him, that a good store of *Johnsoniana* was treasured in his mind; and I compared it to Herculaneum, or some old Roman field, which, when dug, fully rewards the labour employed. The authenticity of every article is unquestionable. For the expression, I, who wrote them down in his presence, am partly answerable. . . .

'It may be questioned, whether there is not some mistake as to the methods of employing the poor, seemingly on a supposition that there is a certain portion of work left undone for want of persons to do it; but if that is otherwise, and all the materials we have are actually worked up, or all the manufactures we can use or dispose of are already executed, then what is given to the poor, who are to be set at work, must be taken from some who now have it, as time must be taken for learning, according to Sir William Petty's observation; a certain part of those very materials that, as it is, are properly worked up, must be spoiled by the unskilfulness of novices. We may apply to well-meaning, but misjudging persons in particulars of this nature, what Giannone said to a monk, who wanted what he called to *convert* him: *"Tu sei santo, ma tu non sei filosofo."*[1]—It is an unhappy circumstance that one might give away five hundred pounds in a year to those that importune in the streets, and not do any good.'

'There is nothing more likely to betray a man into absurdity than *condescension;* when he seems to suppose his understanding too powerful for his company.'

'Having asked Mr. Langton if his father and mother had sat for their pictures, which he thought it right for each generation of a family to do, and being told they had opposed it, he said, "Sir, among the anfractuosities of the human mind, I know not if it may not be one, that there is a superstitious reluctance to sit for a picture."'

[1] 'You are a saint but not a philosopher.'

'John Gilbert Cooper related, that soon after the publication of his *Dictionary*, Garrick being asked by Johnson what people said of it, told him, that among other animadversions, it was objected that he cited authorities which were beneath the dignity of such a work, and mentioned Richardson. "Nay, (said Johnson,) I have done worse than that: I have cited *thee*, David." '

'Talking of expence, he observed, with what munificence a great merchant will spend his money, both from his having it at command, and from his enlarged views by calculation of a good effect upon the whole. "Whereas (said he,) you will hardly ever find a country gentleman who is not a good deal disconcerted at an unexpected occasion for his being obliged to lay out ten pounds." '

'When in good humour he would talk of his own writings with a wonderful frankness and candour, and would even criticise them with the closest severity. One day, having read over one of his *Ramblers*, Mr. Langton asked him, how he liked that paper; he shook his head, and answered, "too wordy." At another time, when one was reading his tragedy of *Irene* to a company at a house in the country, he left the room; and somebody having asked him the reason of this, he replied, "Sir, I thought it had been better." '

'Talking of a point of delicate scrupulosity of moral conduct, he said to Mr. Langton, "Men of harder minds than ours will do many things from which you and I would shrink; yet, Sir, they will, perhaps, do more good in life than we. But let us try to help one another. If there be a wrong twist it may be set right. It is not probable that two people can be wrong the same way." '

'Of the Preface to Capel's *Shakspeare*, he said, "If the man would have come to me, I would have endeavoured to endow his purposes with words; for, as it is, he doth gabble monstrously." '

'He related, that he had once in a dream a contest of wit with some other person, and that he was very much mortified by imagining that his opponent had the better of him. "Now, (said he,) one may mark here the effect of sleep in weakening the power of reflection; for had not my judgement failed me, I should have seen, that the wit of this supposed antagonist, by whose superiority I felt myself depressed, was as much furnished by me, as that which I thought I had been uttering in my own character." '

'One evening in company, an ingenious and learned gentleman read to him a letter of compliment which he had received from one of the Professors of a foreign University. Johnson, in an irritable fit, thinking there was too much ostentation, said, "I never receive any of these tributes of applause from abroad. One instance I recollect of a foreign publication, in which mention is made of *l'illustre Lockman.*" [1]

'Of Sir Joshua Reynolds, he said, "Sir, I know no man who has passed through life with more observation than Reynolds." '

'He repeated to Mr. Langton, with great energy, in the Greek, our SAVIOUR's gracious expression concerning the forgiveness of Mary Magdalen. . . . "Thy faith hath saved thee; go in peace." He said, "the manner of this dismission is exceedingly affecting." '

'He thus defined the difference between physical and moral truth; "Physical truth, is, when you tell a thing as it actually is. Moral truth, is, when you tell a thing sincerely and precisely as it appears to you. I say such a one walked across the street; if he really did so, I told a physical truth. If I thought so, though I should have been mistaken, I told a moral truth." ' . . .

'He used at one time to go occasionally to the green room of Drury-lane Theatre, where he was much regarded by the players, and was very easy and facetious with them. He had a very high opinion of Mrs. Clive's comick powers, and conversed more with her than with any of them. He said, "Clive, Sir, is a good thing to sit by; she always understands what you say." And she said of him, "I love to sit by Dr. Johnson; he always entertains me." One night, when *The Recruiting Officer* was acted, he said to Mr. Holland, who had been expressing an apprehension that Dr. Johnson would disdain the works of Farquhar; "No, Sir, I think Farquhar a man whose writings have considerable merit." '

'His friend Garrick was so busy in conducting the drama, that they could not have so much intercourse as Mr. Garrick used to profess an anxious wish that there should be. There might, indeed, be something in the contemptuous severity as to the merit of acting, which his old preceptor nourished in himself, that would mortify Garrick after the great applause which he received from the audience. For though Johnson said of him, "Sir, a man who has a nation to admire him every night, may well be expected to be somewhat elated;" yet he would treat theatrical matters with a ludicrous slight. He mentioned one evening, "I met David coming off the stage, drest in a woman's riding-hood, when he acted in *The*

---

[1] Secretary to the British Herring Fishery, remarkable for an extraordinary number of occasional verses, not of eminent merit—B.

522

Wonder; I came full upon him, and I believe he was not pleased." '

'Once he asked Tom Davies, whom he saw drest in a fine suit of clothes, "And what art thou to-night?" Tom answered, "The Thane of Ross;" (which it will be recollected is a very inconsiderable character.) "O brave!" said Johnson.' . . .

'Talking of the minuteness with which people will record the sayings of eminent persons, a story was told, that when Pope was on a visit to Spence at Oxford, as they looked from the window they saw a Gentleman Commoner, who was just come in from riding, amusing himself with whipping at a post. Pope took occasion to say, "That young gentleman seems to have little to do." Mr. Beauclerk observed, "Then, to be sure, Spence turned round and wrote that down;" and went on to say to Dr. Johnson, "Pope, Sir, would have said the same of you, if he had seen you distilling." JOHNSON. "Sir, if Pope had told me of my distilling, I would have told him of his grotto." '

'He would allow no settled indulgence of idleness upon principle, and always repelled every attempt to urge excuses for it. A friend one day suggested, that it was not wholesome to study soon after dinner. JOHNSON. "Ah, Sir, don't give way to such a fancy. At one time of my life I had taken it into my head that it was not wholesome to study between breakfast and dinner." '

'Mr. Beauclerk one day repeated to Dr. Johnson Pope's lines,

> "Let modest Foster, if he will, excel
> Ten metropolitans in preaching well:"

Then asked the Doctor, "Why did Pope say this?" JOHNSON. "Sir, he hoped it would vex somebody." '

'Dr. Goldsmith, upon occasion of Mrs. Lennox's bringing out a play, said to Dr. Johnson at THE CLUB, that a person[1] had advised him to go and hiss it, because she had attacked Shakspeare in her book called *Shakspeare Illustrated*. JOHNSON. "And did not you tell him he was a rascal? GOLDSMITH. "No, Sir, I did not. Perhaps he might not mean what he said." JOHNSON. "Nay, Sir, if he lied, it is a different thing." Colman slily said, (but it is believed Dr. Johnson did not hear him,) "Then the proper expression should have been,—Sir, if you don't lie, you're a rascal." '

'His affection for Topham Beauclerk was so great, that when Beauclerk was labouring under that severe illness which at last occasioned his death, Johnson said, (with a voice faul-

---

[1] Richard Cumberland.

tering with emotion,) "Sir, I would walk to the extent of the diameter of the earth to save Beauclerk." '

'One night at THE CLUB he produced a translation of an Epitaph which Lord Elibank had written in English, for his Lady, and requested of Johnson to turn into Latin for him. Having read *Domina de North et Gray,* he said to Dyer, "You see, Sir, what barbarisms we are compelled to make use of, when modern titles are to be specifically mentioned in Latin inscriptions." When he had read it once aloud, and there had been a general approbation expressed by the company, he addressed himself to Mr. Dyer in particular, and said, "Sir, I beg to have your judgement, for I know your nicety." Dyer then very properly desired to read it over again; which having done, he pointed out an incongruity in one of the sentences. Johnson immediately assented to the observation, and said, "Sir, this is owing to an alteration of a part of the sentence, from the form in which I had first written it; and I believe, Sir, you may have remarked, that the making a partial change, without a due regard to the general structure of the sentence, is a very frequent cause of errour in composition." '

'Johnson was well acquainted with Mr. Dossie, authour of a treatise on Agriculture: and said of him, "Sir, of the objects which the Society of Arts have chiefly in view, the chymical effects of bodies operating upon other bodies, he knows more than almost any man." Johnson, in order to give Mr. Dossie his vote to be a member of this Society, paid up an arrear which had run on for two years. On this occasion he mentioned a circumstance as characteristick of the Scotch. "One of that nation, (said he,) who had been a candidate, against whom I had voted, came up to me with a civil salutation. Now, Sir, this is their way. An Englishman would have stomached it, and been sulky, and never have taken further notice of you; but a Scotchman, Sir, though you vote nineteen times against him, will accost you with equal complaisance after each time, and the twentieth time, Sir, he will get your vote." '

'Talking on the subject of toleration, one day when some friends were with him in his study, he made his usual remark, that the State has a right to regulate the religion of the people, who are the children of the State. A clergyman having readily acquiesced in this, Johnson, who loved discussion, observed, "But, Sir, you must go round to other States than your own. You do not know what a Bramin has to say for himself. In short, Sir, I have got no further than this: Every man has a right to utter what he thinks truth, and every other man has a right to knock him down for it. Martyrdom is the test." '

'A man, he observed, should begin to write soon; for, if he waits till his judgement is matured, his inability, through want of practice to express his conceptions, will make the disproportion so great between what he sees, and what he can attain, that he will probably be discouraged from writing at all. As a proof of the justness of this remark, we may instance what is related of the great Lord Granville; that after he had written his letter, giving an account of the battle of Dettingen, he said, "Here is a letter, expressed in terms not good enough for a tallow-chandler to have used." '

'Talking of a Court-martial that was sitting upon a very momentous publick occasion, he expressed much doubt of an enlightened decision; and said, that perhaps there was not a member of it, who in the whole course of his life, had ever spent an hour by himself in balancing probabilities.'

'Goldsmith one day brought to THE CLUB a printed Ode, which he, with others, had been hearing read by its authour in a publick room at the rate of five shillings each for admission. One of the company[1] having read it aloud, Dr. Johnson said, "Bolder words and more timorous meaning, I think never were brought together." '

'Talking of Gray's *Odes,* he said, "They are forced plants raised in a hot-bed; and they are poor plants; they are but cucumbers after all." A gentleman present, who had been running down Ode-writing in general, as a bad species of poetry, unluckily said, "Had they been literally cucumbers, they had been better things than Odes."—"Yes, Sir, (said Johnson,) for a *hog.*" '

'His distinction of the different degrees of attainment of learning was thus marked upon two occasions. Of Queen Elizabeth he said, "She had learning enough to have given dignity to a bishop;" and of Mr. Thomas Davies he said, "Sir, Davies has learning enough to give credit to a clergyman." '

'He used to quote, with great warmth, the saying of Aristotle recorded by Diogenes Laertius; that there was the same difference between one learned and unlearned, as between the living and the dead.'

'It is very remarkable, that he retained in his memory very slight and trivial, as well as important things. As an instance of this, it seems that an inferiour domestick of the Duke of Leeds had attempted to celebrate his Grace's marriage in such homely rhimes as he could make; and this curious composition having been sung to Dr. Johnson he got it by heart,

[1] Burke.

and used to repeat it in a very pleasant manner. Two of the stanzas were these:—

> "When the Duke of Leeds shall married be
> To a fine young lady of high quality,
> How happy will that gentlewoman be
> In his Grace of Leeds's good company.
>
> She shall have all that's fine and fair,
> And the best of silk and sattin shall wear;
> And ride in a coach to take the air,
> And have a house in St. James's-square."

To hear a man, of the weight and dignity of Johnson, repeating such humble attempts at poetry, had a very amusing effect. He, however, seriously observed of the last stanza repeated by him, that it nearly comprized all the advantages that wealth can give.'

'An eminent foreigner, when he was shewn the British Museum, was very troublesome with many absurd inquiries. "Now there, Sir, (said he,) is the difference between an Englishman and a Frenchman. A Frenchman must be always talking, whether he knows any thing of the matter or not; an Englishman is content to say nothing, when he has nothing to say." '

'His unjust contempt for foreigners was, indeed, extreme. One evening, at old Slaughter's coffee-house, when a number of them were talking loud about little matters, he said, "Does not this confirm old Meynell's observation—*For any thing I see, foreigners are fools.*" '

'He said, that once, when he had a violent tooth-ach, a Frenchman accosted him thus:—"*Ah, Monsieur, vous étudiez trop.*" '

'Having spent an evening at Mr. Langton's with the Reverend Dr. Parr, he was much pleased with the conversation of that learned gentleman; and after he was gone, said to Mr. Langton, "Sir, I am obliged to you for having asked me this evening. Parr is a fair man. I do not know when I have had an occasion of such free controversy. It is remarkable how much of a man's life may pass without meeting with any instance of this kind of open discussion." '

'We may fairly institute a criticism between Shakspeare and Corneille, as they both had, though in a different degree, the lights of a latter age. It is not so just between the Greek dramatick writers and Shakspeare. It may be replied to what is said by one of the remarkers on Shakspeare, that though Darius's shade had *prescience*, it does not necessarily follow that he had all *past* particulars revealed to him.'

'Spanish plays, being wildly and improbably farcical, would please children here, as children are entertained with stories full of prodigies; their experience not being sufficient to cause them to be so readily startled at deviations from the natural course of life. The machinery of the pagans is uninteresting to us: when a Goddess appears in Homer or Virgil, we grow weary; still more so in the Grecian tragedies, as in that kind of composition a nearer approach to Nature is intended. Yet there are good reasons for reading romances; as—the fertility of invention, the beauty of style and expression, the curiosity of seeing with what kind of performances the age and country in which they were written was delighted: for it is to be apprehended, that at the time when very wild improbable tales were well received, the people were in a barbarous state, and so on the footing of children, as has been explained.'

'It is evident enough that no one who writes now can use the Pagan deities and mythology; the only machinery, therefore, seems that of ministering spirits, the ghosts of the departed, witches, and fairies, though these latter, as the vulgar superstition concerning them (which, while in its force, infected at least the imagination of those that had more advantage in education, though their reason set them free from it,) is every day wearing out, seem likely to be of little further assistance in the machinery of poetry. As I recollect, Hammond introduces a hag or witch into one of his love elegies, where the effect is unmeaning and disgusting.'

'The man who uses his talent of ridicule in creating or grossly exaggerating the instances he gives, who imputes absurdities that did not happen, or when a man was a little ridiculous describes him as having been very much so, abuses his talents greatly. The great use of delineating absurdities is, that we may know how far human folly can go; the account, therefore, ought of absolute necessity to be faithful. A certain character (naming the person) as to the general cast of it, is well described by Garrick, but a great deal of the phraseology he uses in it, is quite his own, particularly in the proverbial comparisons, "obstinate as a pig," &c., but I don't know whether it might not be true of Lord ———,[1] that from a too great eagerness for praise and popularity, and a politeness carried to a ridiculous excess, he was likely, after asserting a thing in general, to give it up again in parts. For instance, if he had said Reynolds was the first of painters, he was capable enough of giving up, as objections might happen to be severally made, first his outline,—then the grace in form,—then the

[1] Orrery.

colouring,—and lastly, to have owned that he was such a mannerist, that the disposition of his pictures was all alike.'

'For hospitality, as formerly practised, there is no longer the same reason; heretofore the poorer people were more numerous, and from want of commerce, their means of getting a livelihood more difficult; therefore the supporting them was an act of great benevolence; now that the poor can find maintenance for themselves, and their labour is wanted, a general undiscerning hospitality tends to ill, by withdrawing them from their work to idleness and drunkenness. Then, formerly rents were received in kind, so that there was a great abundance of provisions in possession of the owners of the lands, which, since the plenty of money afforded by commerce, is no longer the case.'

'Hospitality to strangers and foreigners in our country is now almost at an end, since, from the increase of them that come to us, there have been a sufficient number of people that have found an interest in providing inns and proper accommodations, which is in general a more expedient method for the entertainment of travellers. Where the travellers and strangers are few, more of that hospitality subsists, as it has not been worth while to provide places of accommodation. In Ireland there is still hospitality to strangers, in some degree; in Hungary and Poland probably more.'

'Colman, in a note on his translation of *Terence*, talking of Shakspeare's learning, asks, "What says Farmer to this? What says Johnson?" Upon this he observed. "Sir, let Farmer answer for himself: *I* never engaged in controversy. I always said, Shakspeare had Latin enough to grammaticise his English."'

'A clergyman, whom he characterised as one who loved to say little oddities, was affecting one day, at a Bishop's table, a sort of slyness and freedom not in character, and repeated, as if part of *The Old Man's Wish*, a song by Dr. Walter Pope, a verse bordering on licentiousness. Johnson rebuked him in the finest manner, by first shewing him that he did not know the passage he was aiming at, and thus humbling him: "Sir, that is not the song: it is thus." And he gave it right. Then looking stedfastly on him, "Sir, there is a part of that song which I should wish to exemplify in my own life:—

"May I govern my passions with absolute sway!"'

... 'He used frequently to observe, that men might be very eminent in a profession, without our perceiving any particular power of mind in them in conversation. "It seems strange (said he,) that a man should see so far to the right, who sees

528

so short a way to the left. Burke is the only man whose common conversation corresponds with the general fame which he has in the world. Take up whatever topick you please, he is ready to meet you." ' . . .

'Of Dodsley's *Publick Virtue, a Poem*, he said, "It was fine *blank* (meaning to express his usual contempt for blank verse); however, this miserable poem did not sell, and my poor friend Doddy said, Publick Virtue was not a subject to interest the age." '

'Mr. Langton, when a very young man, read Dodsley's *Cleone, a Tragedy*, to him, not aware of his extreme impatience to be read to. As it went on he turned his face to the back of his chair, and put himself into various attitudes, which marked his uneasiness. At the end of an act, however, he said, "Come let's have some more, let's go into the slaughter-house again, Lanky. But I am afraid there is more blood than brains." Yet he afterwards said, "When I heard you read it, I thought higher of its power of language: when I read it myself, I was more sensible of its pathetick effect;" and then he paid it a compliment which many will think very extravagant. "Sir, (said he,) if Otway had written this play, no other of his pieces would have been remembered." Dodsley himself, upon this being repeated to him, said, "It was too much:" it must be remembered, that Johnson always appeared not to be sufficiently sensible of the merit of Otway.'

'Snatches of reading (said he,) will not make a Bentley or a Clarke. They are, however, in a certain degree advantageous. I would put a child into a library (where no unfit books are) and let him read at his choice. A child should not be discouraged from reading any thing that he takes a liking to, from a notion that it is above his reach. If that be the case, the child will soon find it out and desist; if not, he of course gains the instruction; which is so much the more likely to come, from the inclination with which he takes up the study.'

'Though he used to censure carelessness with great vehemence, he owned, that he once, to avoid the trouble of locking up five guineas, hid them, he forgot where, so that he could not find them.'

'A gentleman who introduced his brother to Dr. Johnson was earnest to recommend him to the Doctor's notice, which he did by saying, "When we have sat together some time, you'll find my brother grow very entertaining."—"Sir, (said Johnson,) I can wait." '

'When the rumour was strong that we should have a war, because the French would assist the Americans, he rebuked a friend with some asperity for supposing it, saying, "No, Sir, national faith is not yet sunk so low." '

'In the latter part of his life, in order to satisfy himself whether his mental faculties were impaired, he resolved that he would try to learn a new language, and fixed upon the Low Dutch, for that purpose, and this he continued till he had read about one half of 'Thomas à Kempis'; and finding that there appeared no abatement of his power of acquisition, he then desisted, as thinking the experiment had been duly tried. Mr. Burke justly observed, that this was not the most vigorous trial, Low Dutch being a language so near to our own; had it been one of the languages entirely different, he might have been very soon satisfied.'

'Mr. Langton and he having gone to see a Freemason's funeral procession, when they were at Rochester, and some solemn musick being played on French horns, he said, "This is the first time that I have ever been affected by musical sounds;" adding, "that the impression made upon him was of a melancholy kind." Mr. Langton saying, that this effect was a fine one,—JOHNSON. "Yes, if it softens the mind, so as to prepare it for the reception of salutary feelings, it may be good: but inasmuch as it is melancholy *per se*, it is bad." '

'Goldsmith had long a visionary project, that some time or other when his circumstances should be easier, he would go to Aleppo, in order to acquire a knowledge as far as might be of any arts peculiar to the East, and introduce them into Britain. When this was talked of in Dr. Johnson's company, he said, "Of all men Goldsmith is the most unfit to go out upon such an inquiry; for he is utterly ignorant of such arts as we already possess, and consequently could not know what would be accessions to our present stock of mechanical knowledge. Sir, he would bring home a grinding barrow, which you see in every street of London, and think that he had furnished a wonderful improvement." '

'Greek, Sir, (said he,) is like lace; every man gets as much of it as he can.' . . .

'Johnson one day gave high praise to Dr. Bentley's verses in Dodsley's *Collection*, which he recited with his usual energy. Dr. Adam Smith, who was present, observed in his decisive professorial manner, "Very well—Very well." Johnson however added, "Yes, they *are* very well, Sir; but you may observe in what manner they are well. They are the forcible verses of a man of a strong mind, but not accustomed to write verse; for there is some uncouthness in the expression." '

'Drinking tea one day at Garrick's with Mr. Langton, he was questioned if he was not somewhat of a heretick as to Shakspeare; said Garrick, "I doubt he is a little of an infidel."

—"Sir, (said Johnson,) I will stand by the lines I have written on Shakspeare in my Prologue at the opening of your Theatre." Mr. Langton suggested, that in the line

> "And panting Time toil'd after him in vain,"

Johnson might have had in his eye the passage in *The Tempest*, where Prospero says of Miranda,

> "———She will outstrip all praise,
> And make it halt behind her."

Johnson said nothing. Garrick then ventured to observe, "I do not think that the happiest line in the praise of Shakspeare.' Johnson exclaimed (smiling,) "Prosaical rogues! Next time I write, I'll make both time and space pant." '

'It is well known that there was formerly a rude custom for those who were sailing upon the Thames, to accost each other as they passed, in the most abusive language they could invent, generally, however, with as much satirical humour as they were capable of producing. Addison gives a specimen of this ribaldry, in Number 383 of *The Spectator*, when Sir Roger de Coverley and he are going to Spring-garden. Johnson was once eminently successful in this species of contest; a fellow having attacked him with some coarse raillery, Johnson answered him, thus, "Sir, your wife, *under pretence of keeping a bawdy-house*, is a receiver of stolen goods." One evening when he and Mr. Burke and Mr. Langton were in company together, and the admirable scolding of Timon of Athens was mentioned, this instance of Johnson's was quoted, and thought to have at least equal excellence.'

'As Johnson always allowed the extraordinary talents of Mr. Burke, so Mr. Burke was fully sensible of the wonderful powers of Johnson. Mr. Langton recollects having passed an evening with both of them, when Mr. Burke repeatedly entered upon topicks which it was evident he would have illustrated with extensive knowledge and richness of expression; but Johnson always seized upon the conversation, in which, however, he acquitted himself in a most masterly manner. As Mr. Burke and Mr. Langton were walking home, Mr. Burke observed that Johnson had been very great that night; Mr. Langton joined in this, but added, he could have wished to hear more from another person; (plainly intimating that he meant Mr. Burke.) "O, no (said Mr. Burke,) it is enough for me to have rung the bell to him." '

'Beauclerk having observed to him of one of their friends, that he was aukward at counting money, "Why, Sir, (said Johnson,) I am likewise aukward at counting money. But then, Sir, the reason is plain; I have had very little money to count." '

'He had an abhorrence of affectation. Talking of old Mr. Langton, of whom he said, "Sir, you will seldom see such a gentleman, such are his stores of literature, such his knowledge in divinity, and such his exemplary life;" he added, 'and Sir, he has no grimace, no gesticulation, no bursts of admiration on trivial occasions; he never embraces you with an overacted cordiality." '

'Being in company with a gentleman who thought fit to maintain Dr. Berkeley's ingenious philosophy, that nothing exists but as perceived by some mind; when the gentleman was going away, Johnson said to him, "Pray, Sir, don't leave us; for we may perhaps forget to think of you, and then you will cease to exist." '

'Goldsmith, upon being visited by Johnson one day in the Temple, said to him with a little jealousy of the appearance of his accommodation, "I shall soon be in better chambers than these." Johnson at the same time checked him and paid him a handsome compliment, implying that a man of his talents should be above attention to such distinctions,—"Nay, Sir, never mind that. *Nil te quæsiveris extra.*" '[1]

'At the time when his pension was granted to him, he said, with a noble literary ambition, "Had this happened twenty years ago, I should have gone to Constantinople to learn Arabick, as Pococke did." ' . . .

'When Mr. Vesey was proposed as a member of the LITERARY CLUB, Mr. Burke began by saying that he was a man of gentle manners. "Sir, (said Johnson,) you need say no more. When you have said a man of gentle manners; you have said enough." '

'The late Mr. Fitzherbert told Mr. Langton that Johnson said to him, "Sir, a man has no more right to *say* an uncivil thing, than to *act* one; no more right to say a rude thing to another than to knock him down." '

'My dear friend Dr. Bathurst, (said he with a warmth of approbation,) declared he was glad that his father, who was a West-Indian planter, had left his affairs in total ruin, because having no estate, he was not under the temptation of having slaves.'

'Richardson had little conversation, except about his own works, of which Sir Joshua Reynolds said he was always willing to talk, and glad to have them introduced. Johnson when he carried Mr. Langton to see him, professed that he could

[1] 'Don't seek beyond yourself.' Adapted from Persius, *Satires*, i. 7.

bring him out into conversation, and used this allusive expression, "Sir, I can make him *rear*." But he failed; for in that interview Richardson said little else than that there lay in the room a translation of his *Clarissa* into German.'

'Once when somebody produced a newspaper in which there was a letter of stupid abuse of Sir Joshua Reynolds, of which Johnson himself came in for a share,—"Pray," said he, "let us have it read aloud from beginning to end;" which being done, he with a ludicrous earnestness, and not directing his look to any particular person, called out, "Are we alive after all this satire!"' . . .

'Depend upon it, said he, that if a man *talks* of his misfortunes, there is something in them that is not disagreeable to him; for where there is nothing but pure misery, there never is any recourse to the mention of it.'

'A man must be a poor beast that should *read* no more in quantity than he could *utter* aloud.'

'Imlac in *Rasselas,* I spelt with a *c* at the end, because it is less like English, which should always have the Saxon *k* added to the *c*.'

'Many a man is mad in certain instances, and goes through life without having it perceived: for example, a madness has seized a person of supposing himself obliged literally to pray continually—had the madness turned the opposite way and the person thought it a crime ever to pray, it might not improbably have continued unobserved.'

'He apprehended that the delineation of *characters* in the end of the first Book of the *Retreat of the Ten Thousand* was the first instance of the kind that was known.'

'Supposing (said he,) a wife to be of a studious or argumentative turn, it would be very troublesome: for instance, —if a woman should continually dwell upon the subject of the Arian heresy.'

'No man speaks concerning another, even suppose it be in his praise, if he thinks he does not hear him, exactly as he would, if he thought he was within hearing.'

' "The applause of a single human being is of great consequence." This he said to me with great earnestness of manner, very near the time of his decease, on occasion of having desired me to read a letter addressed to him from some person in the North of England; which when I had done, and he asked me what the contents were, as I thought being particular upon it might fatigue him, it being of great length, I only told him in general that it was highly in his praise;—and then he expressed himself as above.' . . .

'He observed once, at Sir Joshua Reynolds's, that a beggar in the street will more readily ask alms from a *man* though there should be no marks of wealth in his appearance, than from even a well-dressed *woman;* which he accounted for from the greater degree of carefulness as to money that is to be found in women; saying farther upon it, that the opportunities in general that they possess of improving their condition are much fewer than men have; and adding, as he looked round the company, which consisted of men only,—there is not one of us who does not think he might be richer if he would use his endeavour.'

'He thus characterised an ingenious writer of his acquaintance: "Sir, he is an enthusiast by rule." ' . . .

'An observation of Bathurst's may be mentioned, which Johnson repeated, appearing to acknowledge it to be well founded, namely, it was somewhat remarkable how seldom, on occasion of coming into the company of any new person, one felt any wish or inclination to see him again.' . . .

1781: ÆTAT. 72.]—IN 1781 Johnson at last completed his *Lives of the Poets,* of which he gives this account: 'Some time in March I finished the *Lives of the Poets,* which I wrote in my usual way, dilatorily and hastily, unwilling to work, and working with vigour and haste.' In a memorandum previous to this, he says of them: 'Written, I hope, in such a manner as may tend to the promotion of piety.'

This is the work which of all Dr. Johnson's writings will perhaps be read most generally, and with most pleasure. Philology and biography were his favourite pursuits, and those who lived most in intimacy with him, heard him upon all occasions, when there was a proper opportunity, take delight in expatiating upon the various merits of the English Poets: upon the niceties of their characters, and the events of their progress through the world which they contributed to illuminate. His mind was so full of that kind of information, and it was so well arranged in his memory, that in performing what he had undertaken in this way, he had little more to do than to put his thoughts upon paper, exhibiting first each Poet's life, and then subjoining a critical examination of his genius and works. But when he began to write, the subject swelled in such a manner, that instead of prefaces to each poet, of no more than a few pages, as he had originally intended, he produced an ample, rich, and most entertaining view of them in every respect. . . . The booksellers, justly sensible of the great additional value of the copy-right, presented him with another hundred pounds, over and above two hundred, for which his agreement was to furnish such prefaces as he thought fit.

This was, however, but a small recompence for such a collection of biography, and such principles and illustrations of criticism, as, if digested and arranged in one system, by some modern Aristotle or Longinus, might form a code upon that subject, such as no other nation can shew. As he was so good as to make me a present of the greatest part of the original, and indeed only manuscript of this admirable work, I have an opportunity of observing with wonder the correctness with which he rapidly struck off such glowing composition. . . .

That he, however, had a good deal of trouble, and some anxiety in carrying on the work, we see from a series of letters to Mr. Nichols the printer, whose variety of literary inquiry and obliging disposition, rendered him very useful to Johnson. Mr. Steevens appears, from the papers in my possession, to have supplied him with some anecdotes and quotations; and I observe the fair hand of Mrs. Thrale as one of his copyists of select passages. But he was principally indebted to my steady friend Mr. Isaac Reed, of Staple-inn, whose extensive and accurate knowledge of English literary history I do not express with exaggeration, when I say it is wonderful; indeed his labours have proved it to the world; and all who have the pleasure of his acquaintance can bear testimony to the frankness of his communications in private society. . . .

In drawing Dryden's character, Johnson has given, though I suppose unintentionally, some touches of his own. Thus:—'The power that predominated in his intellectual operations was rather strong reason than quick sensibility. Upon all occasions that were presented, he studied rather than felt; and produced sentiments not such as Nature enforces, but meditation supplies. With the simple and elemental passions as they spring separate in the mind, he seems not much acquainted. He is, therefore, with all his variety of excellence, not often pathetick; and had so little sensibility of the power of effusions purely natural, that he did not esteem them in others.' It may indeed be observed, that in all the numerous writings of Johnson, whether in prose or verse, and even in his Tragedy, of which the subject is the distress of an unfortunate Princess, there is not a single passage that ever drew a tear. . . .

The Life of POPE was written by Johnson *con amore,* both from the early possession which that writer had taken of his mind, and from the pleasure which he must have felt, in for ever silencing all attempts to lessen his poetical fame by demonstrating his excellence, and pronouncing the following triumphant eulogium:—'After all this, it is surely superfluous to answer the question that has once been asked, Whether Pope was a poet? otherwise than by asking in return, If Pope be not a poet, where is poetry to be found? To circumscribe poetry by a definition, will only shew the narrowness of the definer; though a definition which shall exclude Pope will not easily be made. Let us look round upon the present time, and back upon the past; let us enquire to whom the voice of mankind has decreed the wreath of poetry; let their productions be examined, and their claims stated, and the pretensions of Pope will be no more disputed.'

I remember once to have heard Johnson say, 'Sir, a thousand years may elapse before there shall appear another man with a power of versification equal to that of Pope.' That power must undoubtedly be allowed its due share in enhancing the value of his captivating composition. . . .

In the Life of SWIFT, it appears to me that Johnson had a certain degree of prejudice against that extraordinary man, of which I have elsewhere had occasion to speak. Mr. Thomas Sheridan imputed it to a supposed apprehension in Johnson, that Swift had not been sufficiently active in obtaining for him an Irish degree when it was solicited, but of this there was not sufficient evidence; and let me not presume to charge Johnson with injustice, because he did not think so highly of the writings of this authour, as I have done from my youth upwards. Yet that he had an unfavourable bias is evident, were it only from that passage in which he speaks of Swift's practice of saving, as, 'first ridiculous and at last detestable;' and yet after some examination of circumstances, finds himself obliged to own, that 'it will perhaps appear that he only liked one mode of expence better than another, and saved merely that he might have something to give.' . . .

While the world in general was filled with admiration of Johnson's *Lives of the Poets*, there were narrow circles in which prejudice and resentment were fostered, and from which attacks of different sorts issued against him. By some violent Whigs he was arraigned of injustice to Milton; by some Cambridge men of depreciating Gray; and his expressing with a dignified freedom what he really thought of George, Lord Lyttelton, gave offence to some of the friends of that nobleman, and particularly produced a declaration of war against him from Mrs. Montagu, the ingenious Essayist on Shakspeare, between whom and his Lordship a commerce of reciprocal compliments had long been carried on. In this war the smaller powers in alliance with him were of course led to engage, at least on the defensive, and thus I for one was excluded from the enjoyment of 'A Feast of Reason,' such as Mr. Cumberland has described, with a keen, yet just and delicate pen, in his *Observer*. These minute inconveniencies gave not the least disturbance to Johnson. He nobly said, when I talked to him of the feeble, though shrill outcry which had been raised, 'Sir, I considered myself as entrusted with a certain portion of truth. I have given my opinion sincerely; let them shew where they think me wrong.' . . .

I wrote to him in February, complaining of having been troubled by a recurrence of the perplexing question of Liberty and Necessity; and mentioning that I hoped soon to meet him again in London.

'To JAMES BOSWELL, ESQ.

'DEAR SIR,—I hoped you had got rid of all this hypocrisy of misery. What have you to do with Liberty and Necessity? Or what more than to hold your tongue about it? Do not doubt but I shall be most heartily glad to see you here again, for I love every part about you but your affectation of distress.

'I have at last finished my *Lives*, and have laid up for you a load of copy, all out of order, so that it will amuse you a long time to set it right. Come to me, my dear Bozzy, and let us be as happy as we can. We will go again to the Mitre, and talk old times over. I am, dear Sir, yours affectionately,

'March 14, 1781.'   'SAM. JOHNSON.'

On Monday, March 19, I arrived in London, and on Tuesday, the 20th, met him in Fleet-street, walking, or rather indeed moving along; for his peculiar march is thus described in a very just and picturesque manner, in a short Life of him published very soon after his death:—'When he walked the streets, what with the constant roll of his head, and the concomitant motion of his body, he appeared to make his way by that motion, independent of his feet.' That he was often much stared at while he advanced in this manner, may easily be believed; but it was not safe to make sport of one so robust as he was. Mr. Langton saw him one day, in a fit of absence, by a sudden start, drive the load off a porter's back, and walk forward briskly, without being conscious of what he had done. The porter was very angry, but stood still, and eyed the huge figure with much earnestness, till he was satisfied that his wisest course was to be quiet, and take up his burthen again.

Our accidental meeting in the street after a long separation was a pleasing surprize to us both. He stepped aside with me into Falcon-court, and made kind inquiries about my family, and as we were in a hurry going different ways, I promised to call on him next day; he said he was engaged to go out in the morning. 'Early, Sir?' said I. JOHNSON. 'Why, Sir, a London morning does not go with the sun.'

I waited on him next evening, and he gave me a great portion of his original manuscript of his *Lives of the Poets*, which he had preserved for me.

I found on visiting his friend, Mr. Thrale, that he was now very ill, and had removed, I suppose by the solicitation of Mrs. Thrale, to a house in Grosvenor-square. I was sorry to see him sadly changed in his appearance.

He told me I might now have the pleasure to see Dr. Johnson drink wine again, for he had lately returned to it. When I mentioned this to Johnson, he said, 'I drink it now sometimes, but not socially.' The first evening that I was with him at Thrale's, I observed he poured a quantity of it into a large glass, and swallowed it greedily. Every thing about his character and manners was forcible and violent; there never was any moderation; many a day did he fast, many a year did he refrain from wine; but when he did eat, it was voraciously; when he did drink wine, it was copiously. He could practise abstinence, but not temperance.

Mrs. Thrale and I had a dispute, whether Shakspeare or Milton had drawn the most admirable picture of a man. I was for Shakspeare; Mrs. Thrale for Milton; and after a fair hearing, Johnson decided for my opinion. . . .

He said, 'Mrs. Montagu has dropt me. Now, Sir, there are people whom one should like very well to drop, but would not wish to be dropped by.' He certainly was vain of the society of ladies, and could make himself very agreeable to them, when he chose it; Sir Joshua Reynolds agreed with me that he could. Mr. Gibbon, with his usual sneer, controverted it, perhaps in resentment of Johnson's having talked with some disgust of his ugliness, which one would think a *philosopher* would not mind. Dean Marlay wittily observed, 'A lady may be vain when she can turn a wolf-dog into a lap-dog.' . . .

Johnson's profound reverence for the Hierarchy made him expect from bishops the highest degree of decorum; he was offended even at their going to taverns; 'A bishop (said he,) has nothing to do at a tippling-house. It is not indeed immoral in him to go to a tavern; neither would it be immoral in him to whip a top in Grosvenor-square. But, if he did, I hope the boys would fall upon him and apply the whip to *him*. There are gradations in conduct; there is morality,—decency,—propriety. None of these should be violated by a bishop. A bishop should not go to a house where he may meet a young fellow leading out a wench.' BOSWELL. 'But, Sir, every tavern does not admit women.' JOHNSON. 'Depend upon it, Sir, any tavern will admit a well-drest man and a well-drest woman; they will not perhaps admit a woman whom they see every night walking by their door, in the street. But a well-drest man may lead in a well-drest woman to any tavern in London. Taverns sell meat and drink, and will sell them to any body who can eat and can drink. You may as well say that a mercer will not sell silks to a woman of the town.'

He also disapproved of bishops going to routs, at least of their staying at them longer than their presence commanded respect. He mentioned a particular bishop. 'Poh! (said Mrs. Thrale,) the Bishop of ————[1] is never minded at a rout.' BOSWELL. 'When a bishop places himself in a situation where he has no distinct character, and is of no consequence, he degrades the dignity of his order.' JOHNSON. 'Mr. Boswell, Madam, has said it as correctly as could be.'

Nor was it only in the dignitaries of the Church that Johnson required a particular decorum and delicacy of behaviour; he justly considered that the clergy, as persons set apart for the sacred office of serving at the altar, and impressing the minds of men with the aweful concerns of a future state, should be somewhat more serious than the generality of mankind, and have a suitable composure of manners. A due sense of the dignity of their profession, independent of higher motives, will ever prevent them from losing their distinction in an indiscriminate sociality; and did such as affect this, know how much it lessens them in the eyes of those whom they think to please by it, they would feel themselves much mortified.

Johnson and his friend, Beauclerk, were once together in company with several clergymen, who thought that they should appear to advantage, by assuming the lax jollity of *men of the world;* which, as it may be observed in similar cases, they carried to noisy excess. Johnson, who they expected would be *entertained,* sat grave and silent for some time; at last, turning to Beauclerk, he said, by no means in a whisper, 'This merriment of parsons is mighty offensive.' . . .

On Friday, March 30, I dined with him at Sir Joshua Reynolds's, with the Earl of Charlemont, Sir Annesley Stewart, Mr. Eliot of Port-Eliot, Mr. Burke, Dean Marlay, Mr. Langton; a most agreeable day, of which I regret that every circumstance is not preserved; but it is unreasonable to require such a multiplication of felicity.

Mr. Eliot, with whom Dr. Walter Harte had travelled, talked to us of his *History of Gustavus Adolphus,* which he said was a very good book in the German translation. JOHNSON. 'Harte was excessively vain. He put copies of his book in manuscript into the hands of Lord Chesterfield and Lord Granville, that they might revise it. Now, how absurd was it to suppose that two such noblemen would revise so big a

[1] Chester.

manuscript. Poor man! he left London the day of the publication of his book, that he might be out of the way of the great praise he was to receive; and he was ashamed to return, when he found how ill his book had succeeded. It was unlucky in coming out on the same day with Robertson's *History of Scotland*. His husbandry, however, is good.' BOSWELL. 'So he was fitter for that than for heroick history: he did well when he turned his sword into a ploughshare.'

Mr. Eliot mentioned a curious liquor peculiar to his country, which the Cornish fishermen drink. They call it *Mahogany;* and it is made of two parts gin, and one part treacle, well beaten together. I begged to have some of it made, which was done with proper skill by Mr. Eliot. I thought it very good liquor; and said it was a counterpart of what is called *Athol Porridge* in the Highlands of Scotland, which is a mixture of whisky and honey. Johnson said, 'that must be a better liquor than the Cornish, for both its component parts are better.' He also observed, '*Mahogany* must be a modern name; for it is not long since the wood called mahogany was known in this country.' I mentioned his scale of liquors;— claret for boys,—port for men,—brandy for heroes. 'Then (said Mr. Burke,) let me have claret: I love to be a boy; to have the careless gaiety of boyish days.' JOHNSON. 'I should drink claret too, if it would give me that; but it does not: it neither makes boys men, nor men boys. You'll be drowned by it, before it has any effect upon you.'

I ventured to mention a ludicrous paragraph in the newspapers, that Dr. Johnson was learning to dance of Vestris. Lord Charlemont, wishing to excite him to talk, proposed, in a whisper, that he should be asked, whether it was true. 'Shall I ask him?' said his Lordship. We were, by a great majority, clear for the experiment. Upon which his Lordship very gravely, and with a courteous air said, 'Pray, Sir, is it true that you are taking lessons of Vestris?' This was risking a good deal, and required the boldness of a General of Irish Volunteers to make the attempt. Johnson was at first startled, and in some heat answered, 'How can your Lordship ask so simple a question?' But immediately recovering himself, whether from unwillingness to be deceived, or to appear deceived, or whether from real good humour, he kept up the joke: 'Nay, but if any body were to answer the paragraph, and contradict it, I'd have a reply, and would say, that he who contradicted it was no friend either to Vestris or me. For why should not Dr. Johnson add to his other powers a little corporeal agility? Socrates learnt to dance at an advanced age, and Cato learnt Greek at an advanced age. Then it might proceed to say, that this Johnson, not content with dancing on the ground, might dance on the rope; and they might introduce the elephant dancing on the rope. A nobleman wrote a play, called *Love in a hollow Tree*. He found out that it was a bad one, and therefore wished to buy up all the copies, and burn them. The Duchess of Marlborough had kept one; and when he was against her at an election, she had a new edition of it printed, and prefixed to it, as a frontispiece, an elephant dancing on a rope; to shew, that his Lordship's writing comedy was as aukward as an elephant dancing on a rope.'

On Sunday, April 1, I dined with him at Mr. Thrale's, with Sir Philip Jennings Clerk and Mr. Perkins, who had the superintendence of Mr. Thrale's brewery, with a salary of five hundred pounds a year. Sir Philip had the appearance of a gentleman of ancient family, well advanced in life. He wore his own white hair in a bag of goodly size, a black velvet coat, with an embroidered waistcoat, and very rich laced ruffles; which Mrs. Thrale said were old fashioned, but which, for that reason, I thought the more respectable, more like a Tory; yet Sir Philip was then in Opposition in Parliament. 'Ah, Sir, (said Johnson,) ancient ruffles and modern principles do not agree.' Sir Philip defended the Opposition to the American war ably and with temper, and I joined him. He said, the majority of the nation was against the ministry. JOHNSON. '*I*, Sir, am against the ministry; but it is for having too little of that, of which Opposition thinks they have too much. Were I minister, if any man wagged his finger against me, he should be turned out; for that which it is in the power of Government to give at pleasure to one or to another, should be given to the supporters of Government. If you will not oppose at the expence of losing your place, your opposition will not be honest, you will feel no serious grievance; and the present opposition is only a contest to get what others have. Sir Robert Walpole acted as I would do. As to the American war, the *sense* of the nation is *with* the ministry. The majority of those who can *understand* is with it; the majority of those who can only *hear* is against it; and as those who can only hear are more numerous than those who can understand, and Opposition is always loudest, a majority of the rabble will be for Opposition.'

This boisterous vivacity entertained us; but the truth in my opinion was, that those who could understand the best were against the American war, as almost every man now is, when the question has been coolly considered.

Mrs. Thrale gave high praise to Mr. Dudley Long, (now North). JOHNSON. 'Nay, my dear lady, don't talk so. Mr. Long's character is very *short*. It is nothing, he fills a chair.

He is a man of genteel appearance, and that is all. I know nobody who blasts by praise as you do: for whenever there is exaggerated praise, every body is set against a character. They are provoked to attack it. Now there is Pepys; you praised that man with such disproportion, that I was incited to lessen him, perhaps more than he deserves. His blood is upon your head. By the same principle, your malice defeats itself; for your censure is too violent. And yet, (looking to her with a leering smile,) she is the first woman in the world, could she but restrain that wicked tongue of hers;—she would be the only woman, could she but command that little whirligig.'

Upon the subject of exaggerated praise I took the liberty to say, that I thought there might be very high praise given to a known character which deserved it, and therefore it would not be exaggerated. Thus, one might say of Mr. Edmund Burke, He is a very wonderful man. JOHNSON. 'No, Sir, you would not be safe if another man had a mind perversely to contradict. He might answer, "Where is all the wonder? Burke is, to be sure, a man of uncommon abilities, with a great quantity of matter in his mind, and a great fluency of language in his mouth. But we are not to be stunned and astonished by him." So you see, Sir, even Burke would suffer, not from any fault of his own, but from your folly.'

Mrs. Thrale mentioned a gentleman who had acquired a fortune of four thousand a year in trade, but was absolutely miserable, because he could not talk in company; so miserable, that he was impelled to lament his situation in the street to ******, whom he hates, and who he knows despises him. 'I am a most unhappy man, (said he). I am invited to conversations. I go to conversations; but, alas! I have no conversation.' JOHNSON. 'Man commonly cannot be successful in different ways. This gentleman has spent, in getting four thousand pounds a year, the time in which he might have learnt to talk; and now he cannot talk.' Mr. Perkins made a shrewd and droll remark: 'If he had got his four thousand a year as a mountebank, he might have learnt to talk at the same time that he was getting his fortune.'

Some other gentlemen came in. The conversation concerning the person whose character Dr. Johnson had treated so slightingly, as he did not know his merit, was resumed. Mrs. Thrale said, 'You think so of him, Sir, because he is quiet, and does not exert himself with force. You'll be saying the same thing of Mr. ***** there, who sits as quiet—.' This was not well-bred; and Johnson did not let it pass without correction. 'Nay, Madam, what right have you to talk thus? Both Mr. ***** and I have reason to take it ill. *You* may talk so of Mr. *****; but why do you make *me* do it? Have I said anything against Mr. *****? You have *set* him, that I might shoot him: but I have not shot him.'

One of the gentlemen said, he had seen three folio volumes of Dr. Johnson's sayings collected by me. 'I must put you right, Sir, (said I,) for I am very exact in authenticity. You could not see folio volumes, for I have none; you might have seen some in quarto and octavo. This is inattention which one should guard against.' JOHNSON. 'Sir, it is a want of concern about veracity. He does not know that he saw *any* volumes. If he had seen them he could have remembered their size.'

Mr. Thrale appeared very lethargick to-day. I saw him again on Monday evening, at which time he was not thought to be in immediate danger; but early in the morning of Wednesday, the 4th, he expired. Johnson was in the house, and thus mentions the event: 'I felt almost the last flutter of his pulse, and looked for the last time upon the face that for fifteen years had never been turned upon me but with respect and benignity.' Upon that day there was a *Call* of THE LITERARY CLUB; but Johnson apologised for his absence by the following note:—

'MR. JOHNSON knows that Sir Joshua Reynolds and the other gentlemen will excuse his incompliance with the call, when they are told that Mr. Thrale died this morning.— Wednesday.'

Mr. Thrale's death was a very essential loss to Johnson, who, although he did not foresee all that afterwards happened, was sufficiently convinced that the comforts which Mr. Thrale's family afforded him, would now in a great measure cease. He, however, continued to shew a kind attention to his widow and children as long as it was acceptable; and he took upon him, with a very earnest concern, the office of one of his executors, the importance of which seemed greater than usual to him, from his circumstances having been always such, that he had scarcely any share in the real business of life. His friends of THE CLUB were in hopes that Mr. Thrale might have made a liberal provision for him for his life, which, as Mr. Thrale left no son, and a very large fortune, it would have been highly to his honour to have done; and, considering Dr. Johnson's age, could not have been of long duration; but he bequeathed him only two hundred pounds, which was the legacy given to each of his executors. I could not but be somewhat diverted by hearing Johnson talk in a pompous manner of his new office, and particularly of the concerns of the brewery, which it was at last resolved should be sold. Lord Lucan tells a very good story, which, if not precisely exact, is certainly characteristical: that when the sale of Thrale's brewery was going forward, Johnson appeared bustling about, with an ink-horn and pen in his button-hole, like an excise-man; and on being asked what he really considered to be the value of the property which was to be disposed of, answered, 'We are not here to sell a parcel of boilers and vats, but the potentiality of growing rich, beyond the dreams of avarice.'

On Friday, April 6, he carried me to dine at a club, which, at his desire, had been lately formed at the Queen's Arms, in St. Paul's Church-yard. He told Mr. Hoole, that he wished to have a *City Club,* and asked him to collect one; but, said he, 'Don't let them be *patriots.*' The company to-day were very sensible, well-behaved men. I have preserved only two particulars of his conversation. He said he was glad Lord George Gordon had escaped, rather than that a precedent should be established for hanging a man for *constructive treason;* which, in consistency with his true, manly, constitutional Toryism, he considered would be a dangerous engine of arbitary power. And upon its being mentioned that an opulent and very indolent Scotch nobleman, who totally resigned the management of his affairs to a man of knowledge and abilities, had claimed some merit by saying, 'The next best thing to managing a man's own affairs well is being sensible of incapacity, and not attempting it, but having full confidence in one who can do it.' JOHNSON. 'Nay, Sir, this is paltry. There is a middle course. Let a man give application; and depend upon it he will soon get above a despicable state of helplessness, and attain the power of acting for himself.'

On Saturday, April 7, I dined with him at Mr. Hoole's, with Governour Bouchier and Captain Orme, both of whom had been long in the East-Indies; and being men of good sense and observation, were very entertaining. Johnson defended the oriental regulation of different *casts* of men, which was objected to as totally destructive of the hopes of rising in society by personal merit. He shewed that there was a *principle* in it sufficiently plausible by analogy. 'We see (said he,) in metals that there are different species; and so likewise in animals, though one species may not differ very widely from another, as in the species of dogs,—the cur, the spaniel, the mastiff. The Bramins are the mastiffs of mankind.'

On Thursday, April 12, I dined with him at a Bishop's,[1] where were Sir Joshua Reynolds, Mr. Berrenger, and some more company. He had dined the day before at another Bishop's.[2] I have unfortunately recorded none of his conver-

[1] The Bishop of Chester's.
[2] The Bishop of St. Asaph's.

sation at the Bishop's where we dined together: but I have preserved his ingenious defence of his dining twice abroad in Passion-week; a laxity, in which I am convinced he would not have indulged himself at the time when he wrote his solemn paper in *The Rambler,* upon that aweful season. It appeared to me, that by being much more in company, and enjoying more luxurious living, he had contracted a keener relish of pleasure, and was consequently less rigorous in his religious rites. This he would not acknowledge; but he reasoned, with admirable sophistry, as follows: 'Why, Sir, a Bishop's calling company together in this week is, to use the vulgar phrase, not *the thing.* But you must consider laxity is a bad thing; but preciseness is also a bad thing; and your general character may be more hurt by preciseness than by dining with a Bishop in Passion-week. There might be a handle for reflection. It might be said, "He refused to dine with a Bishop in Passion-week, but was three Sundays absent from Church." ' Boswell. 'Very true, Sir. But suppose a man to be uniformly of good conduct, would it not be better that he should refuse to dine with a Bishop in this week, and so not encourage a bad practice by his example?' Johnson. 'Why, Sir, you are to consider whether you might not do more harm by lessening the influence of a Bishop's character by your disapprobation in refusing him, than by going to him.' . . .

On Friday, April 13, being Good-Friday, I went to St. Clement's church with him, as usual. There I saw again his old fellow-collegian, Edwards, to whom I said, 'I think, Sir, Dr. Johnson and you meet only at Church.'—'Sir, (said he,) it is the best place we can meet in, except Heaven, and I hope we shall meet there too.' Dr. Johnson told me, that there was very little communication between Edwards and him, after their unexpected renewal of acquaintance. 'But, (said he, smiling), he met me once, and said, "I am told you have written a very pretty book called *The Rambler.*" I was unwilling that he should leave the world in total darkness, and sent him a set.'

Mr. Berenger visited him to-day, and was very pleasing. We talked of an evening society for conversation at a house in town, of which we were all members, but of which Johnson said, 'It will never do, Sir. There is nothing served about there, neither tea, nor coffee, nor lemonade, nor any thing whatever; and depend upon it, Sir, a man does not love to go to a place from whence he comes out exactly as he went in.' I endeavoured, for argument's sake, to maintain that men of learning and talents might have very good intellectual society, without the aid of any little gratifications of the senses. Ber-

545

enger joined with Johnson, and said, that without these any meeting would be dull and insipid. He would therefore have all the slight refreshments; nay, it would not amiss to have some cold meat, and a bottle of wine upon a side-board. 'Sir, (said Johnson to me, with an air of triumph,) Mr. Berenger knows the world. Every body loves to have good things furnished to them without any trouble. I told Mrs. Thrale once, that as she did not choose to have card tables, she should have a profusion of the best sweetmeats, and she would be sure to have company enough come to her.' I agreed with my illustrious friend upon this subject; for it has pleased God to make man a composite animal, and where there is nothing to refresh the body, the mind will languish.

On Sunday, April 15, being Easter-day, after solemn worship in St. Paul's church, I found him alone; Dr. Scott, of the Commons, came in. He talked of its having been said, that Addison wrote some of his best papers in *The Spectator* when warm with wine. Dr. Johnson did not seem willing to admit this. Dr. Scott, as a confirmation of it, related, that Blackstone, a sober man, composed his *Commentaries* with a bottle of port before him; and found his mind invigorated and supported in the fatigue of his great work, by a temperate use of it. . . .

We talked of the difference between the mode of education at Oxford, and that in those Colleges where instruction is chiefly conveyed by lectures. JOHNSON. 'Lectures were once useful; but now, when all can read, and books are so numerous, lectures are unnecessary. If your attention fails, and you miss a part of a lecture, it is lost; you cannot go back as you do upon a book.' Dr. Scott agreed with him. 'But yet (said I), Dr. Scott, you yourself gave lectures at Oxford.' He smiled. 'You laughed (then said I,) at those who came to you.'

Dr. Scott left us, and soon afterwards we went to dinner. Our company consisted of Mrs. Williams, Mrs. Desmoulins, Mr. Levett, Mr. Allen, the printer, and Mrs. Hall, sister of the Reverend Mr. John Wesley, and resembling him, as I thought, both in figure and manner. Johnson produced now, for the first time, some handsome silver salvers, which he told me he had bought fourteen years ago; so it was a great day. I was not a little amused by observing Allen perpetually struggling to talk in the manner of Johnson, like the little frog in the fable blowing himself up to resemble the stately ox.

I mentioned a kind religious Robinhood Society, which met every Sunday evening, at Coachmakers'-hall, for free debate; and that the subject for this night was, the text which relates, with other miracles, which happened at our SAVIOUR'S death, 'And the graves were opened, and many bodies of the saints which slept arose, and came out of the graves after his resurrection, and went into the holy city, and appeared unto many.' Mrs. Hall said it was a very curious subject, and she should like to hear it discussed. JOHNSON. (somewhat warmly,) 'One would not go to such a place to hear it,—one would not be seen in such a place—to give countenance to such a meeting.' I, however, resolved that I would go. 'But, Sir, (said she to Johnson,) I should like to hear *you* discuss it.' He seemed reluctant to engage in it. She talked of the resurrection of the human race in general, and maintained that we shall be raised with the same bodies. JOHNSON. 'Nay, Madam, we see that it is not to be the same body; for the Scripture uses the illustration of grain sown, and we know that the grain which grows is not the same with what is sown. You cannot suppose that we shall rise with a diseased body; it is enough if there be such a sameness as to distinguish identity of person.' She seemed desirous of knowing more, but he left the question in obscurity.

Of apparitions, he observed, 'A total disbelief of them is adverse to the opinion of the existence of the soul between death and the last day; the question simply is, whether departed spirits ever have the power of making themselves perceptible to us; a man who thinks he has seen an apparition, can only be convinced himself; his authority will not convince another, and his conviction, if rational, must be founded on being told something which cannot be known but by supernatural means.'

He mentioned a thing as not unfrequent, of which I had never heard before,—being *called,* that is, hearing one's name pronounced by the voice of a known person at a great distance, far beyond the possibility of being reached by any sound uttered by human organs. . . . Macbean asserted that this inexplicable *calling* was a thing very well known. Dr. Johnson said, that one day at Oxford, as he was turning the key of his chamber, he heard his mother distinctly call *Sam.* She was then at Lichfield; but nothing ensued. This phænomenon is, I think, as wonderful as any other mysterious fact, which many people are very slow to believe, or rather, indeed, reject with an obstinate contempt.

Some time after this, upon his making a remark which escaped my attention, Mrs. Williams and Mrs. Hall were both together striving to answer him. He grew angry, and called out loudly, 'Nay, when you both speak at once, it is intolerable.' But checking himself, and softening, he said, 'This one may say, though you *are* ladies.' Then he brightened into gay humour, and addressed them in the words of one of the songs in *The Beggar's Opera:*—

'What, Sir, (said I,) are you going to turn Captain Macheath?' There was something as pleasantly ludicrous in this scene as can be imagined. The contrast between Macheath, Polly, and Lucy—and Dr. Samuel Johnson, blind, peevish Mrs. Williams, and lean, lank, preaching Mrs. Hall, was exquisite. . . .

On Friday, April 20, I spent with him one of the happiest days that I remember to have enjoyed in the whole course of my life. Mrs. Garrick, whose grief for the loss of her husband was, I believe, as sincere as wounded affection and admiration could produce, had this day, for the first time since his death, a select party of his friends to dine with her. The company was Miss Hannah More, who lived with her, and whom she called her Chaplain; Mrs. Boscawen, Mrs. Elizabeth Carter, Sir Joshua Reynolds, Dr. Burney, Dr. Johnson, and myself. We found ourselves very elegantly entertained at her house in the Adelphi, where I have passed many a pleasing hour with him 'who gladdened life.' She looked very well, talked of her husband with complacency, and while she cast her eyes on his portrait, which hung over the chimney-piece, said, that 'death was now the most agreeable object to her.' The very semblance of David Garrick was cheering. . . .

We were all in fine spirits; and I whispered to Mrs. Boscawen, 'I believe this is as much as can be made of life.' In addition to a splendid entertainment, we were regaled with Lichfield ale, which had a peculiar appropriated value. Sir Joshua, and Dr. Burney, and I, drank cordially of it to Dr. Johnson's health; and though he would not join us, he as cordially answered, 'Gentlemen, I wish you all as well as you do me.'

The general effect of this day dwells upon my mind in fond remembrance; but I do not find much conversation recorded. What I have preserved shall be faithfully given.

One of the company mentioned Mr. Thomas Hollis, the strenuous Whig, who used to send over Europe presents of democratical books, with their boards stamped with daggers and caps of liberty. Mrs. Carter said, 'He was a bad man. He used to talk uncharitably.' JOHNSON. 'Poh! poh! Madam; who is the worse for being talked of uncharitably? Besides, he was a dull poor creature as ever lived: and I believe he would not have done harm to a man whom he knew to be of very opposite principles to his own. I remember once at the Society of Arts, when an advertisement was to be drawn up, he pointed me out as the man who could do it best. This, you will observe, was kindness to me. I however slipt away, and escaped it.'

Mrs. Carter having said of the same person, 'I doubt he

was an Atheist.' JOHNSON. 'I don't know that. He might perhaps have become one, if he had had time to ripen, (smiling.) He might have *exuberated* into an Atheist.'

Sir Joshua Reynolds praised *Mudge's Sermons*. JOHNSON. '*Mudge's Sermons* are good, but not practical. He grasps more sense than he can hold; he takes more corn than he can make into meal; he opens a wide prospect, but it is so distant, it is indistinct. I love *Blair's Sermons*. Though the dog is a Scotchman, and a Presbyterian, and every thing he should not be, I was the first to praise them. Such was my candour,' (smiling.) MRS. BOSCAWEN. 'Such his great merit to get the better of all your prejudices.' JOHNSON. 'Why, Madam, let us compound the matter; let us ascribe it to my candour, and his merit.'

In the evening we had a large company in the drawing-room, several ladies, the Bishop of Killaloe, Dr. Percy, Mr. Chamberlayne, of the Treasury, &c. &c. Somebody said the life of a mere literary man could not be very entertaining. JOHNSON. 'But it certainly may. This is a remark which has been made, and repeated, without justice; why should the life of a literary man be less entertaining than the life of any other man? Are there not as interesting varieties in such a life? As *a literary life* it may be very entertaining.' BOSWELL. 'But it must be better surely, when it is diversified with a little active variety—such as his having gone to Jamaica; or—his having gone to the Hebrides.' Johnson was not displeased at this.

Talking of a very respectable authour,[1] he told us a curious circumstance in his life, which was, that he had married a printer's devil. REYNOLDS. 'A printer's devil, Sir! Why, I thought a printer's devil was a creature with a black face and in rags.' JOHNSON. 'Yes, Sir. But I suppose, he had her face washed, and put clean clothes on her. (Then looking very serious, and very earnest.) And she did not disgrace him; the woman had a bottom of good sense.' The word *bottom* thus introduced, was so ludicrous when contrasted with his gravity, that most of us could not forbear tittering and laughing; though I recollect that the Bishop of Killaloe kept his countenance with perfect steadiness, while Miss Hannah More slyly hid her face behind a lady's back who sat on the same settee with her. His pride could not bear that any expression of his should excite ridicule, when he did not intend it; he therefore resolved to assume and exercise despotick power, glanced sternly around, and called out in a strong tone, 'Where's the merriment?' Then collecting himself, and looking aweful, to

[1] Dr. John Campbell.

make us feel how he could impose restraint, and as it were searching his mind for a still more ludicrous word, he slowly pronounced, 'I say the *woman* was *fundamentally* sensible;' as if he had said, hear this now, and laugh if you dare. We all sat composed as at a funeral.

He and I walked away together; we stopped a little while by the rails of the Adelphi, looking on the Thames, and I said to him with some emotion that I was now thinking of two friends we had lost, who once lived in the buildings behind us, Beauclerk and Garrick. 'Ay, Sir, (said he, tenderly,) and two such friends as cannot be supplied.'

For some time after this day I did not see him very often, and of the conversation which I did enjoy, I am sorry to find I have preserved but little. I was at this time engaged in a variety of other matters, which required exertion and assiduity, and necessarily occupied almost all my time.

One day having spoken very freely of those who were then in power, he said to me, 'Between ourselves, Sir, I do not like to give opposition the satisfaction of knowing how much I disapprove of the ministry.' And when I mentioned that Mr. Burke had boasted how quiet the nation was in George the Second's reign, when Whigs were in power, compared with the present reign, when Tories governed;—'Why, Sir, (said he,) you are to consider that Tories having more reverence for government, will not oppose with the same violence as Whigs, who being unrestrained by that principle, will oppose by any means.' . . .

On Tuesday, May 8, I had the pleasure of again dining with him and Mr. Wilkes, at Mr. Dilly's. No *negociation* was now required to bring them together; for Johnson was so well satisfied with the former interview, that he was very glad to meet Wilkes again, who was this day seated between Dr. Beattie and Dr. Johnson; (between *Truth* and *Reason,* as General Paoli said, when I told him of it.) WILKES. 'I have been thinking, Dr. Johnson, that there should be a bill brought into parliament that the controverted elections for Scotland should be tried in that country, at their own Abbey of Holy-Rood House, and not here; for the consequence of trying them here is, that we have an inundation of Scotchmen, who come up and never go back again. Now here is Boswell, who is come up upon the election for his own county, which will not last a fortnight.' JOHNSON. 'Nay, Sir, I see no reason why they should be tried at all; for, you know, one Scotchman is as good as another.' WILKES. 'Pray, Boswell, how much may be got in a year by an Advocate at the Scotch bar?' BOSWELL. 'I believe two thousand pounds.' WILKES. 'How can it be possible to spend that money in Scotland?' JOHNSON. 'Why, Sir, the money may be spent in England: but there is a harder question. If one man in Scotland gets possession of two thousand pounds, what remains for all the rest of the nation?' WILKES. 'You know, in the last war, the immense booty which Thurot carried off by the complete plunder of seven Scotch isles; he re-embarked with *three and six-pence.*' Here again Johnson and Wilkes joined in extravagant sportive raillery upon the supposed poverty of Scotland, which Dr. Beattie and I did not think it worth our while to dispute.

The subject of quotation being introduced, Mr. Wilkes censured it as pedantry. JOHNSON. 'No, Sir, it is a good thing; there is a community of mind in it. Classical quotation is the *parole* of literary men all over the world.' WILKES. 'Upon the continent they all quote the vulgate Bible. Shakspeare is chiefly quoted here; and we quote also Pope, Prior, Butler, Waller, and sometimes Cowley.'

We talked of Letter-writing. JOHNSON. 'It is now become so much the fashion to publish letters, that in order to avoid it, I put as little into mine as I can.' BOSWELL. 'Do what you will, Sir, you cannot avoid it. Should you even write as ill as you can, your letters would be published as curiosities:—

"Behold a miracle! instead of wit,
  See two dull lines with Stanhope's pencil writ." '

He gave us an entertaining account of *Bet Flint,* a woman of the town, who, with some eccentrick talents and much effrontery, forced herself upon his acquaintance. 'Bet (said he,) wrote her own Life in verse, which she brought to me, wishing that I would furnish her with a Preface to it, (laughing.) I used to say of her that she was generally slut and drunkard; occasionally, whore and thief. She had, however, genteel lodgings, a spinnet on which she played, and a boy that walked before her chair. Poor Bet was taken up on a charge of stealing a counterpane, and tried at the Old Bailey. Chief Justice ————, who loved a wench, summed up favourably, and she was acquitted. After which Bet said, with a gay and satisfied air, 'Now that the counterpane is *my own,* I shall make a petticoat of it.'

Talking of oratory, Mr. Wilkes described it as accompanied with all the charms of poetical expression. JOHNSON. 'No, Sir; oratory is the power of beating down your adversary's arguments, and putting better in their place.' WILKES. 'But this does not move the passions.' JOHNSON. 'He must be a weak man, who is to be so moved.' WILKES. (naming a celebrated orator,)[1] 'Amidst all the brilliancy of ————'s imagination, and the exuberance of his wit, there is a strange want of *taste*. It was observed of Apelles's Venus, that her flesh seemed as if she had been nourished by roses: his oratory would sometimes make one suspect that he eats potatoes and drinks whisky.'

Mr. Wilkes observed, how tenacious we are of forms in this country, and gave as an instance, the vote of the House of Commons for remitting money to pay the army in America *in Portugal pieces*, when, in reality, the remittance is made not in Portugal money, but in our own specie. JOHNSON. 'Is there not a law, Sir, against exporting the current coin of the realm?' WILKES. 'Yes, Sir: but might not the House of Commons, in case of real evident necessity, order our own current coin to be sent into our own colonies?' Here Johnson, with that quickness of recollection which distinguished him so eminently, gave the *Middlesex Patriot* an admirable retort upon his own ground. 'Sure, Sir, *you* don't think a *resolution of the House of Commons* equal to *the law of the land?*' WILKES. (at once perceiving the application,) 'GOD forbid, Sir.' To hear what had been treated with such violence in *The False Alarm*, now turned into pleasant repartee, was extremely agreeable. Johnson went on;—'Locke observes well, that a prohibition to export the current coin is impolitick; for when the balance of trade happens to be against a state, the current coin *must* be exported.'

Mr. Beauclerk's great library was this season sold in London by auction. Mr. Wilkes said, he wondered to find in it such a numerous collection of sermons; seeming to think it strange that a gentleman of Mr. Beauclerk's character in the gay world should have chosen to have many compositions of that kind. JOHNSON. 'Why, Sir, you are to consider, that sermons make a considerable branch of English literature; so that a library must be very imperfect if it has not a numerous collection of sermons: and in all collections, Sir, the desire of augmenting it grows stronger in proportion to the advance in acquisition; as motion is accelerated by the continuance of the *impetus*. Besides, Sir, (looking at Mr. Wilkes with a placid but significant smile,) a man may collect sermons with intention of making himself better by them. I hope Mr. Beauclerk intended, that some time or other that should be the case with him.'

Mr. Wilkes said to me, loud enough for Dr. Johnson to hear, 'Dr. Johnson should make me a present of his *Lives of the Poets*, as I am a poor patriot, who cannot afford to buy

[1] Burke.

them.' Johnson seemed to take no notice of this hint; but in a little while, he called to Mr. Dilly, 'Pray, Sir, be so good as to send a set of my *Lives* to Mr. Wilkes, with my compliments.' This was accordingly done; and Mr. Wilkes paid Dr. Johnson a visit, was courteously received, and sat with him a long time.

The company gradually dropped away. Mr. Dilly himself was called down stairs upon business; I left the room for some time; when I returned, I was struck with observing Dr. Samuel Johnson and John Wilkes, Esq., literally *tête-à-tête;* for they were reclined upon their chairs, with their heads leaning almost close to each other, and talking earnestly, in a kind of confidential whisper, of the personal quarrel between George the Second and the King of Prussia. Such a scene of perfectly easy sociality between two such opponents in the war of political controversy, as that which I now beheld, would have been an excellent subject for a picture. It presented to my mind the happy days which are foretold in Scripture, when the lion shall lie down with the kid.[1]

After this day there was another pretty long interval, during which Dr. Johnson and I did not meet. When I mentioned it to him with regret, he was pleased to say, 'Then, Sir, let us live double.'

About this time it was much the fashion for several ladies to have evening assemblies, where the fair sex might participate in conversation with literary and ingenious men, animated by a desire to please. These societies were denominated *Blue-stocking Clubs,* the origin of which title being little known, it may be worth while to relate it. One of the most eminent members of those societies, when they first commenced, was Mr. Stillingfleet, whose dress was remarkably grave, and in particular it was observed, that he wore blue stockings. Such was the excellence of his conversation, that his absence was felt as so great a loss, that it used to be said, 'We can do nothing without the *blue stockings;*' and thus by degrees the title was established. Miss Hannah More has admirably described a *Blue-stocking Club,* in her *Bas Bleu,* a poem in which many of the persons who were most conspicuous there are mentioned.

Johnson was prevailed with to come sometimes into these circles, and did not think himself too grave even for the lively Miss Monckton (now Countess of Corke), who used to

---

[1] When I mentioned this to the Bishop of Killaloe, 'With the *goat,*' said his Lordship. Such, however, is the engaging politeness and pleasantry of Mr. Wilkes, and such the social good humour of the Bishop, that when they dined together at Mr. Dilly's, where I also was, they were mutually agreeable—B.

have the finest *bit of blue* at the house of her mother, Lady Galway. Her vivacity enchanted the Sage, and they used to talk together with all imaginable ease. A singular instance happened one evening, when she insisted that some of Sterne's writings were very pathetick. Johnson bluntly denied it. 'I am sure (said she,) they have affected *me*.' 'Why, (said Johnson, smiling, and rolling himself about,) that is, because, dearest, you're a dunce.' When she some time afterwards mentioned this to him, he said with equal truth and politeness; 'Madam, if I had thought so, I certainly should not have said it.'

Another evening Johnson's kind indulgence towards me had a pretty difficult trial. I had dined at the Duke of Montroses's, with a very agreeable party, and his Grace, according to his usual custom, had circulated the bottle very freely. Lord Graham and I went together to Miss Monckton's, where I certainly was in extraordinary spirits, and above all fear or awe. In the midst of a great number of persons of the first rank, amongst whom I recollect with confusion, a noble lady of the most stately decorum, I placed myself next to Johnson, and thinking myself now fully his match, talked to him in a loud and boisterous manner, desirous to let the company know how I could contend with *Ajax*. I particularly remember pressing him upon the value of the pleasures of the imagination, and as an illustration of my argument, asking him, 'What, Sir, supposing I were to fancy that the —— (naming the most charming Duchess[1] in his Majesty's dominions) were in love with me, should I not be very happy?' My friend with much address evaded my interrogatories, and kept me as quiet as possible; but it may easily be conceived how he must have felt. However, when a few days afterwards I waited upon him and made an apology, he behaved with the most friendly gentleness.

While I remained in London this year, Johnson and I dined together at several places. I recollect a placid day at Dr. Butter's, who had now removed from Derby to Lower Grosvenor-street, London; but of his conversation on that and other occasions during this period, I neglected to keep any regular record, and shall therefore insert here some miscellaneous articles which I find in my Johnsonian notes.

His disorderly habits, when 'making provision for the day that was passing over him,' appear from the following anecdote, communicated to me by Mr. John Nichols:—'In the year 1763, a young bookseller, who was an apprentice to Mr. Whiston, waited on him with a subscription to his *Shaks-*

[1] The Duchess of Devonshire.

peare: and observing that the Doctor made no entry in any book of the subscriber's name, ventured diffidently to ask, whether he would please to have the gentleman's address, that it might be properly inserted in the printed list of subscribers. '*I shall print no list of subscribers;*' said Johnson, with great abruptness: but almost immediately recollecting himself, added, very complacently, 'Sir, I have two very cogent reasons for not printing any list of subscribers;—one, that I have lost all the names,—the other, that I have spent all the money.'

Johnson could not brook appearing to be worsted in argument, even when he had taken the wrong side, to shew the force and dexterity of his talents. When, therefore, he perceived that his opponent gained ground, he had recourse to some sudden mode of robust sophistry. Once when I was pressing upon him with visible advantage, he stopped me thus:—'My dear Boswell, let's have no more of this; you'll make nothing of it. I'd rather have you whistle a Scotch tune.'

Care, however, must be taken to distinguish between Johnson when he 'talked for victory,' and Johnson when he had no desire but to inform and illustrate. 'One of Johnson's principal talents (says an eminent friend of his)[1] was shewn in maintaining the wrong side of an argument, and in a splendid perversion of the truth. If you could contrive to have his fair opinion on a subject, and without any bias from personal prejudice, or from a wish to be victorious in argument, it was wisdom itself, not only convincing, but overpowering.'

He had, however, all his life habituated himself to consider conversation as a trial of intellectual vigour and skill; and to this, I think, we may venture to ascribe that unexampled richness and brilliancy which appeared in his own. As a proof at once of his eagerness for colloquial distinction, and his high notion of this eminent friend, he once addressed him thus:— '——, we now have been several hours together; and you have said but one thing for which I envied you.'

He disliked much all speculative desponding considerations, which tended to discourage men from diligence and exertion. He was in this like Dr. Shaw, the great traveller, who, Mr. Daines Barrington told me, used to say, 'I hate a *cui bono*[2] man.' Upon being asked by a friend what he should think of a man who was apt to say *non est tanti*,[3]—'That he's a stupid fellow, Sir; (answered Johnson): What would these

---

[1] William Gerard Hamilton.

[2] 'Who gains by it?'

[3] 'It is not worth while.'

tanti men be doing the while?' When I, in a low-spirited fit, was talking to him with indifference of the pursuits which generally engage us in a course of action, and inquiring a *reason* for taking so much trouble; 'Sir, (said he, in an animated tone) it is driving on the system of life.'

He told me, that he was glad that I had, by General Oglethorpe's means, become acquainted with Dr. Shebbeare. Indeed that gentleman, whatever objections were made to him, had knowledge and abilities much above the class of ordinary writers, and deserves to be remembered as a respectable name in literature, were it only for his admirable *Letters on the English Nation,* under the name of 'Battista Angeloni, a Jesuit.'

Johnson and Shebbeare[1] were frequently named together, as having in former reigns had no predilection for the family of Hanover. The authour of the celebrated *Heroick Epistle to Sir William Chambers,* introduces them in one line, in a list of those 'who tasted the sweets of his present Majesty's reign.' Such was Johnson's candid relish of the merit of that satire, that he allowed Dr. Goldsmith, as he told me, to read it to him from beginning to end, and did not refuse his praise to its execution.

Goldsmith could sometimes take adventurous liberties with him, and escape unpunished. Beauclerk told me that when Goldsmith talked of a project for having a third Theatre in London, solely for the exhibition of new plays, in order to deliver authours from the supposed tyranny of managers, Johnson treated it slightingly; upon which Goldsmith said, 'Ay, ay, this may be nothing to you, who can now shelter yourself behind the corner of a pension;' and that Johnson bore this with good-humour. . . .

Johnson had called twice on the Bishop of Killaloe before his Lordship set out for Ireland, having missed him the first time. He said, 'It would have hung heavy on my heart if I had not seen him. No man ever paid more attention to another than he has done to me; and I have neglected him, not wilfully, but from being otherwise occupied. Always, Sir, set a high value on spontaneous kindness. He whose inclination prompts him to cultivate your friendship of his own accord, will love you more than one whom you have been at pains to attach to you.'

Johnson told me, that he was once much pleased to find that a carpenter, who lived near him, was very ready to shew

[1] I recollect a ludicrous paragraph in the newspapers, that the King had pensioned both a *He*-bear and a *She*-bear—B.

him some things in his business which he wished to see: 'It was paying (said he,) respect to literature.'

I asked him if he was not dissatisfied with having so small a share of wealth, and none of those distinctions in the state which are the objects of ambition. He had only a pension of three hundred a year. Why was he not in such circumstances as to keep his coach? Why had he not some considerable office? JOHNSON. 'Sir, I have never complained of the world; nor do I think that I have reason to complain. It is rather to be wondered at that I have so much. My pension is more out of the usual course of things than any instance that I have known. Here, Sir, was a man avowedly no friend to Government at the time, who got a pension without asking for it. I never courted the great; they sent for me; but I think they now give me up. They are satisfied; they have seen enough of me.' Upon my observing that I could not believe this, for they must certainly be highly pleased by his conversation; conscious of his own superiority, he answered, 'No, Sir; great lords and great ladies don't love to have their mouths stopped.' This was very expressive of the effect which the force of his understanding and brilliancy of his fancy could not but produce; and, to be sure, they must have found themselves strangely diminished in his company. When I warmly declared how happy I was at all times to hear him;—'Yes, Sir, (said he); but if you were Lord Chancellor, it would not be so: you would then consider your own dignity.'

There was much truth and knowledge of human nature in this remark. But certainly one should think, that in whatever elevated state of life a man who *knew* the value of the conversation of Johnson might be placed, though he might prudently avoid a situation in which he might appear lessened by comparison; yet he would frequently gratify himself in private with the participation of the rich intellectual entertainment which Johnson could furnish. Strange, however, it is, to consider how few of the great sought his society; so that if one were disposed to take occasion for satire on that account, very conspicuous objects present themselves. His noble friend, Lord Elibank, well observed, that if a great man procured an interview with Johnson, and did not wish to see him more, it shewed a mere idle curiosity, and a wretched want of relish for extraordinary powers of mind. Mrs. Thrale justly and wittily accounted for such conduct by saying, that Johnson's conversation was by much too strong for a person accustomed to obsequiousness and flattery; it was *mustard in a young child's mouth!*

One day, when I told him that I was a zealous Tory, but not enough 'according to knowledge,' and should be obliged to him for 'a reason,' he was so candid, and expressed himself so well, that I begged of him to repeat what he had said, and I wrote down as follows:—

OF TORY AND WHIG.

'A wise Tory and a wise Whig, I believe, will agree. Their principles are the same, though their modes of thinking are different. A high Tory makes government unintelligible: it is lost in the clouds. A violent Whig makes it impracticable: he is for allowing so much liberty to every man, that there is not power enough to govern any man. The prejudice of the Tory is for establishment; the prejudice of the Whig is for innovation. A Tory does not wish to give more real power to Government; but that Government should have more reverence. Then they differ as to the Church. The Tory is not for giving more legal power to the Clergy, but wishes they should have a considerable influence, founded on the opinion of mankind; the Whig is for limiting and watching them with a narrow jealousy.' . . .

On Saturday, June 2, I set out for Scotland, and had promised to pay a visit in my way, as I sometimes did, at Southill, in Bedfordshire, at the hospitable mansion of 'Squire Dilly, the elder brother of my worthy friends, the booksellers, in the Poultry. Dr. Johnson agreed to be of the party this year, with Mr. Charles Dilly and me, and to go and see Lord Bute's seat at Luton Hoe. He talked little to us in the carriage, being chiefly occupied in reading Dr. Watson's second volume of *Chemical Essays,* which he liked very well, and his own *Prince of Abyssinia,* on which he seemed to be intensely fixed; having told us, that he had not looked at it since it was first published. I happened to take it out of my pocket this day, and he seized upon it with avidity. He pointed out to me the following remarkable passage:—

'By what means (said the prince) are the Europeans thus powerful; or why, since they can so easily visit Asia and Africa for trade or conquest, cannot the Asiaticks and Africans invade their coasts, plant colonies in their ports, and give laws to their natural princes? The same wind that carries them back would bring us thither.' 'They are more powerful, Sir, than we, (answered Imlac,) because they are wiser. Knowledge will always predominate over ignorance, as man governs the other animals. But why their knowledge is more than ours, I know not what reason can be given, but the unsearchable will of the Supreme Being.'

He said, 'This, Sir, no man can explain otherwise.'

We stopped at Welwyn, where I wished much to see, in company with Dr. Johnson, the residence of the authour of *Night Thoughts,* which was then possessed by his son, Mr. Young. Here some address was requisite, for I was not acquainted with Mr. Young, and had I proposed to Dr. Johnson that he should send to him, he would have checked my wish, and perhaps been offended. I therefore concerted with Mr. Dilly, that I should steal away from Dr. Johnson and him, and try what reception I could procure from Mr. Young; if unfavourable, nothing was to be said; but if agreeable, I should return and notify it to them. I hastened to Mr. Young's, found he was at home, sent in word that a gentleman desired to wait upon him, and was shewn into a parlour, where he and a young lady, his daughter, were sitting. He appeared to be a plain, civil, country gentleman; and when I begged pardon for presuming to trouble him, but that I wished much to see his place, if he would give me leave; he behaved very courteously and answered, 'By all means, Sir; we are just going to drink tea; will you sit down?' I thanked him, but said, that Dr. Johnson had come with me from London, and I must return to the inn and drink tea with him; that my name was Boswell, I had travelled with him in the Hebrides. 'Sir, (said he,) I should think it a great honour to see Dr. Johnson here. Will you allow me to send for him?' Availing myself of this opening, I said that 'I would go myself and bring him, when he had drunk tea; he knew nothing of my calling here.' Having been thus successful, I hastened back to the inn, and informed Dr. Johnson that 'Mr. Young, son of Dr. Young, the authour of *Night Thoughts,* whom I had just left, desired to have the honour of seeing him at the house where his father lived.' Dr. Johnson luckily made no inquiry how this invitation had arisen, but agreed to go, and when we entered Mr. Young's parlour, he addressed him with a very polite bow, 'Sir, I had a curiosity to come and see this place. I had the honour to know that great man, your father.' We went into the garden, where we found a gravel walk, on each side of which was a row of trees, planted by Dr. Young, which formed a handsome Gothick arch; Dr. Johnson called it a fine grove. I beheld it with reverence.

We sat some time in the summer-house, on the outside wall of which was inscribed, *'Ambulantes in horto audiebant vocem De;'*[1] and in reference to a brook by which it is situated, *'Vivendi rectè qui prorogat horam,'* &c.[2] I said to Mr.

[1] 'As they walked in the garden, they heard the voice of the Lord God.' Adapted from Genesis, iii. 8.

[2] 'He who postpones the hour of living rightly,' etc. Horace, *Epistles,* I. ii. 41.

Young, that I had been told his father was cheerful. 'Sir, (said he,) he was too well-bred a man not to be cheerful in company; but he was gloomy when alone. He never was cheerful after my mother's death, and he had met with many disappointments.' Dr. Johnson observed to me afterwards, 'That this was no favourable account of Dr. Young; for it is not becoming in a man to have so little acquiescence in the ways of Providence, as to be gloomy because he has not obtained as much preferment as he expected; nor to continue gloomy for the loss of his wife. Grief has its time.' The last part of this censure was theoretically made. Practically, we know that grief for the loss of a wife may be continued very long, in proportion as affection has been sincere. No man knew this better than Dr. Johnson. . . .

Upon the road we talked of the uncertainty of profit with which authours and booksellers engage in the publication of literary works. JOHNSON. 'My judgement I have found is no certain rule as to the sale of a book.' BOSWELL. 'Pray, Sir, have you been much plagued with authours sending you their works to revise?' JOHNSON. 'No, Sir; I have been thought a sour, surly fellow.' BOSWELL. 'Very lucky for you, Sir,—in that respect.' I must however observe, that notwithstanding what he now said, which he no doubt imagined at the time to be the fact, there was, perhaps, no man who more frequently yielded to the solicitations even of very obscure authours, to read their manuscripts, or more liberally assisted them with advice and correction.

He found himself very happy at 'Squire Dilly's, where there is always abundance of excellent fare, and hearty welcome.

On Sunday, June 3, we all went to Southill church, which is very near to Mr. Dilly's house. It being the first Sunday of the month, the holy sacrament was administered, and I staid to partake of it. When I came afterwards into Dr. Johnson's room, he said, 'You did right to stay and receive the communion; I had not thought of it.' This seemed to imply that he did not choose to approach the altar without a previous preparation, as to which good men entertain different opinions, some holding that it is irreverent to partake of that ordinance without considerable premeditation; others, that whoever is a sincere Christian, and in a proper frame of mind to discharge any other ritual duty of our religion, may, without scruple, discharge this most solemn one. A middle notion I believe to be the just one, which is, that communicants need not think a long train of preparatory forms indispensably necessary; but neither should they rashly and lightly venture upon so aweful and mysterious an institution. Christians must judge each for himself, what degree of retirement and self-examination is necessary upon each occasion.

Being in a frame of mind which, I hope for the felicity of human nature, many experience,—in fine weather,—at the country house of a friend,—consoled and elevated by pious exercises,—I expressed myself with an unrestrained fervour to my 'Guide, Philosopher, and Friend;' 'My dear Sir, I would fain be a good man; and I am very good now. I fear GOD, and honour the King, I wish to do no ill, and to be benevolent to all mankind.' He looked at me with a benignant indulgence; but took occasion to give me wise and salutary caution. 'Do not, Sir, accustom yourself to trust to *impressions*. There is a middle state of mind between conviction and hypocrisy, of which many are conscious. By trusting to impressions, a man may gradually come to yield to them, and at length be subject to them, so as not to be a free agent, or what is the same thing in effect, to *suppose* that he is not a free agent. A man who is in that state, should not be suffered to live; if he declares he cannot help acting in a particular way, and is irresistibly impelled, there can be no confidence in him, no more than in a tyger. But, Sir, no man believes himself to be impelled irresistibly; we know that he who says he believes it, lies. Favourable impressions at particular moments, as to the state of our souls, may be deceitful and dangerous. In general no man can be sure of his acceptance with God; some, indeed, may have had it revealed to them. St. Paul, who wrought miracles, may have had a miracle wrought on himself, and may have obtained supernatural assurance of pardon, and mercy, and beatitude; yet St. Paul, though he expresses strong hope, also expresses fear, lest having preached to others, he himself should be a cast-away.'

The opinion of a learned Bishop[1] of our acquaintance, as to there being merit in religious faith, being mentioned;— JOHNSON. 'Why, yes, Sir, the most licentious man, were hell open before him, would not take the most beautiful strumpet to his arms. We must, as the Apostle says, live by faith, not by sight.' . . .

The Reverend Mr. Palmer, Fellow of Queen's College, Cambridge, dined with us. He expressed a wish that a better provision were made for parish-clerks. JOHNSON. 'Yes, Sir, a parish-clerk should be a man who is able to make a will, or write a letter for any body in the parish.'

I mentioned Lord Monboddo's notion that the ancient Egyptians, with all their learning, and all their arts, were not only black, but woolly-haired. Mr. Palmer asked how did it

[1] The Bishop of Killaloe.

561

appear upon examining the mummies? Dr. Johnson approved of this test.

Although upon most occasions I never heard a more strenuous advocate for the advantages of wealth, than Dr. Johnson: he this day, I know not from what caprice, took the other side. 'I have not observed (said he,) that men of very large fortunes enjoy any thing extraordinary that makes happiness. What has the Duke of Bedford? What has the Duke of Devonshire? The only great instance that I have ever known of the enjoyment of wealth was, that of Jamaica Dawkins, who, going to visit Palmyra, and hearing that the way was infested by robbers, hired a troop of Turkish horse to guard him.'

Dr. Gibbons, the Dissenting minister, being mentioned, he said, 'I took to Dr. Gibbons.' And addressing himself to Mr. Charles Dilly, added, 'I shall be glad to see him. Tell him, if he'll call on me, and dawdle over a dish of tea in an afternoon, I shall take it kind.'

The Reverend Mr. Smith, Vicar of Southill, a very respectable man, with a very agreeable family, sent an invitation to us to drink tea. I remarked Dr. Johnson's very respectful politeness. Though always fond of changing the scene, he said, 'We must have Mr. Dilly's leave. We cannot go from your house, Sir, without your permission.' We all went, and were well satisfied with our visit. I however remember nothing particular, except a nice distinction which Dr. Johnson made with respect to the power of memory, maintaining that forgetfulness was a man's own fault. 'To remember and to recollect (said he,) are different things. A man has not the power to recollect what is not in his mind; but when a thing is in his mind he may remember it.' The remark was occasioned by my leaning back on a chair, which a little before I had perceived to be broken, and pleading forgetfulness as an excuse. 'Sir, (said he,) its being broken was certainly in your mind.'

When I observed that a housebreaker was in general very timorous; JOHNSON. 'No wonder, Sir; he is afraid of being shot getting *into* a house, or hanged when he has got *out* of it.'

He told us, that he had in one day written six sheets of a translation from the French, adding, 'I should be glad to see it now. I wish that I had copies of all the pamphlets written against me, as it is said Pope had. Had I known that I should make so much noise in the world, I should have been at pains to collect them. I believe there is hardly a day in which there is not something about me in the newspapers.'

On Monday, June 4, we all went to Luton-Hoe, to see

Lord Bute's magnificent seat, for which I had obtained a ticket. As we entered the park, I talked in a high style of my old friendship with Lord Mountstuart, and said, 'I shall probably be much at this place.' The Sage, aware of human vicissitudes, gently checked me: 'Don't you be too sure of that.' He made two or three peculiar observations; as when shewn the botanical garden, 'Is not *every* garden a botanical garden?' When told that there was a shrubbery to the extent of several miles: 'That is making a very foolish use of the ground; a little of it is very well.' When it was proposed that we should walk on the pleasure-ground; 'Don't let us fatigue ourselves. Why should we walk there? Here's a fine tree, let's get to the top of it.' But upon the whole, he was very much pleased. He said, 'This is one of the places I do not regret having come to see. It is a very stately place, indeed; in the house magnificence is not sacrificed to convenience, nor convenience to magnificence. The library is very splendid: the dignity of the rooms is very great; and the quantity of pictures is beyond expectation, beyond hope.'

It happened without any previous concert, that we visited the seat of Lord Bute upon the King's birthday; we dined and drank his Majesty's health at an inn, in the village of Luton.

In the evening I put him in mind of his promise to favour me with a copy of his celebrated Letter to the Earl of Chesterfield, and he was at last pleased to comply with this earnest request, by dictating it to me from his memory; for he believed that he himself had no copy. There was an animated glow in his countenance while he thus recalled his high-minded indignation. . . .

On Tuesday, June 5, Johnson was to return to London. He was very pleasant at breakfast; I mentioned a friend of mine[1] having resolved never to marry a pretty woman. JOHNSON. 'Sir, it is a very foolish resolution to resolve not to marry a pretty woman. Beauty is of itself very estimable. No, Sir, I would prefer a pretty woman, unless there are objections to her. A pretty woman may be foolish; a pretty woman may be wicked; a pretty woman may not like me. But there is no such danger in marrying a pretty woman as is apprehended: she will not be persecuted if she does not invite persecution. A pretty woman, if she has a mind to be wicked, can find a readier way than another; and that is all.'

I accompanied him in Mr. Dilly's chaise to Shefford, where talking of Lord Bute's never going to Scotland, he said, 'As an Englishman, I should wish all the Scotch gentlemen to be

---

[1] Charles Dilly.

educated in England; Scotland would become a province; they would spend all their rents in England.' . . .

At Shefford, I had another affectionate parting from my revered friend, who was taken up by the Bedford coach and carried to the metropolis. I went with Messieurs Dilly, to see some friends at Bedford; dined with the officers of the militia of the county, and next day proceeded on my journey. . . .

The following curious anecdote I insert in Dr. Burney's own words:—

'Dr. Burney related to Dr. Johnson the partiality which his writings had excited in a friend of Dr. Burney's, the late Mr. Bewley, well known in Norfolk by the name of the *Philosopher of Massingham:* who, from the *Ramblers* and the Plan of his *Dictionary*, and long before the authour's fame was established by the *Dictionary* itself, or any other work, had conceived such a reverence for him, that he urgently begged Dr. Burney to give him the cover of the first letter he had received from him, as a relick of so estimable a writer. This was in 1755. In 1760, when Dr. Burney visited Dr. Johnson at the Temple in London, where he had then chambers, he happened to arrive there before he was up; and being shewn into the room where he was to breakfast, finding himself alone, he examined the contents of the apartment, to try whether he could undiscovered steal anything to send to his friend Bewley, as another relick of the admirable Dr. Johnson. But finding nothing better to his purpose, he cut some bristles off his hearth-broom, and enclosed them in a letter to his country enthusiast, who received them with due reverence. The Doctor was so sensible of the honour done him by a man of genius and science, to whom he was an utter stranger, that he said to Dr. Burney, "Sir, there is no man possessed of the smallest portion of modesty, but must be flattered with the admiration of such a man. I'll give him a set of my *Lives*, if he will do me the honour to accept of them." In this he kept his word; and Dr. Burney had not only the pleasure of gratifying his friend with a present more worthy of his acceptance than the segment from the hearth-broom, but soon after of introducing him to Dr. Johnson himself in Boltcourt with whom he had the satisfaction of conversing a considerable time, not a fortnight before his death; which happened in St. Martin's-street, during his visit to Dr. Burney, in the house where the great Sir Isaac Newton had lived and died before.'

In one of his little memorandum-books is the following minute:—

'August 9, 3 P.M., ætat. 72, in the summer-house at Streatham.

'After innumerable resolutions formed and neglected, I have retired hither, to plan a life of greater diligence, in hope that I may yet be useful, and be daily better prepared to appear before my Creator and my Judge, from whose infinite mercy I humbly call for assistance and support.

'My purpose is,

'To pass eight hours every day in some serious employment.

'Having prayed, I purpose to employ the next six weeks upon the Italian language, for my settled study.'

How venerably pious does he appear in these moments of solitude, and how spirited are his resolutions for the improvement of his mind, even in elegant literature, at a very advanced period of life, and when afflicted with many complaints.

In autumn he went to Oxford, Birmingham, Lichfield, and Ashbourne, for which very good reasons might be given in the conjectural yet positive manner of writers, who are proud to account for every event which they relate. He himself, however, says, 'The motives of my journey I hardly know; I omitted it last year, and am not willing to miss it again.'

But some good considerations arise, amongst which is the kindly recollection of Mr. Hector, surgeon, at Birmingham: 'Hector is likewise an old friend, the only companion of my childhood that passed through the school with me. We have always loved one another; perhaps we may be made better by some serious conversation, of which however I have no distinct hope.' He says too, 'At Lichfield, my native place, I hope to shew a good example by frequent attendance on publick worship.' . . .

1782: ÆTAT. 73.]—IN 1782, his complaints increased, and the history of his life this year, is little more than a mournful recital of the variations of his illness, in the midst of which, however, it will appear from his letters, that the powers of his mind were in no degree impaired.

'To JAMES BOSWELL, ESQ.

'DEAR SIR,—I sit down to answer your letter on the same day in which I received it, and am pleased that my first letter of the year is to you. No man ought to be at ease while he knows himself in the wrong; and I have not satisfied myself with my long silence. . . .

'My health has been tottering this last year; and I can give no very laudable account of my time. I am always hoping to do better than I have ever hitherto done.

'My journey to Ashbourne and Staffordshire was not pleasant; for what enjoyment has a sick man visiting the sick?—Shall we ever have another frolick like our journey to the Hebrides?

'I hope that dear Mrs. Boswell will surmount her complaints; in losing her you would lose your anchor, and be tost, without stability, by the waves of life. I wish both her and you very many years, and very happy.

'For some months past I have been so withdrawn from the world, that I can send you nothing particular. All your friends, however, are well, and will be glad of your return to London. I am, dear Sir, yours most affectionately,

'January 5, 1782.'   'SAM. JOHNSON.'

At a time when he was less able than he had once been to sustain a shock, he was suddenly deprived of Mr. Levett, which event he thus communicated to Dr. Lawrence:—

'SIR,—Our old friend, Mr. Levett, who was last night eminently cheerful, died this morning. The man who lay in the same room, hearing an uncommon noise, got up and tried to make him speak, but without effect. He then called Mr. Holder, the apothecary, who, though when he came he thought him dead, opened a vein, but could draw no blood. So has ended the long life of a very useful and very blameless man. I am, Sir, your most humble servant,

'Jan. 17, 1782.'   'SAM. JOHNSON.'

In one of his memorandum-books in my possession, is the following entry:—'January 20, Sunday. Robert Levett was buried in the church-yard of Bridewell, between one and two in the afternoon. He died on Thursday 17, about seven in the morning, by an instantaneous death. He was an old and faithful friend; I have known him from about 46. *Commendavi.*[1] May GOD have mercy on him. May he have mercy on me.' . . .

In one of Johnson's registers of this year, there occurs the following curious passage:—'Jan. 20. The Ministry is dissolved. I prayed with Francis and gave thanks.'

It has been the subject of discussion, whether there are two distinct particulars mentioned here? or that we are to understand the giving of thanks to be in consequence of the dissolution of the Ministry? In support of the last of these conjectures may be urged his mean opinion of that Ministry, which

[1] 'I commended' (his soul to heaven).

566

has frequently appeared in the course of this work; and it is strongly confirmed by what he said on the subject to Mr. Seward:—'I am glad the Ministry is removed. Such a bunch of imbecility never disgraced a country. If they sent a messenger into the City to take up a printer, the messenger was taken up instead of the printer, and committed by the sitting Alderman. If they sent one army to the relief of another, the first army was defeated and taken before the second arrived. I will not say that what they did was always wrong; but it was always done at a wrong time.' . . .

The following letters require no extracts from mine to introduce them:—

'To JAMES BOSWELL, ESQ.

'DEAR SIR,—The earnestness and tenderness of your letter is such, that I cannot think myself shewing it more respect than it claims by sitting down to answer it the day on which I received it.

'This year has afflicted me with a very irksome and severe disorder. My respiration has been much impeded, and much blood has been taken away. I am now harassed by a catarrhous cough, from which my purpose is to seek relief by change of air; and I am, therefore, preparing to go to Oxford.

'Whether I did right in dissuading you from coming to London this spring, I will not determine. You have not lost much by missing my company; I have scarcely been well for a single week. I might have received comfort from your kindness; but you would have seen me afflicted, and, perhaps, found me peevish. Whatever might have been your pleasure or mine, I know not how I could have honestly advised you to come hither with borrowed money. Do not accustom yourself to consider debt only as an inconvenience; you will find it a calamity. Poverty takes away so many means of doing good, and produces so much inability to resist evil, both natural and moral, that it is by all virtuous means to be avoided. Consider a man whose fortune is very narrow; whatever be his rank by birth, or whatever his reputation by intellectual excellence, what good can he do? or what evil can he prevent? That he cannot help the needy is evident; he has nothing to spare. But, perhaps, his advice or admonition may be useful. His poverty will destroy his influence: many more can find that he is poor, than that he is wise, and few will reverence the understanding that is of so little advantage to its owner. I say nothing of the personal wretchedness of a debtor, which, however, has passed into a proverb. Of riches, it is not necessary to write the praise. Let it, however, be remembered, that he who has money to spare, has it always in his power to benefit others; and of such power a good man must always be desirous.

'I am pleased with your account of Easter. We shall meet, I hope, in Autumn, both well and both cheerful; and part each the better for the other's company.

'Make my compliments to Mrs. Boswell, and to the young charmers. I am, &c.

'London, June 3, 1782.'   'SAM. JOHNSON.'

... On the 30th of August, I informed him that my honoured father had died that morning; a complaint under which he had long laboured having suddenly come to a crisis, while I was upon a visit at the seat of Sir Charles Preston, from whence I had hastened the day before, upon receiving a letter by express.

'To JAMES BOSWELL, ESQ.

'DEAR SIR,—I have struggled through this year with so much infirmity of body, and such strong impressions of the fragility of life, that death, wherever it appears, fills me with melancholy; and I cannot hear without emotion, of the removal of any one, whom I have known, into another state.

'Your father's death had every circumstance that could enable you to bear it; it was at a mature age, and it was expected; and as his general life had been pious, his thoughts had doubtless for many years past been turned upon eternity. That you did not find him sensible must doubtless grieve you; his disposition towards you was undoubtedly that of a kind, though not of a fond father. Kindness, at least actual, is in our power, but fondness is not; and if by negligence or imprudence you had extinguished his fondness, he could not at will rekindle it. Nothing then remained between you but mutual forgiveness of each other's faults, and mutual desire of each other's happiness.

'I shall long to know his final disposition of his fortune.

'You, dear Sir, have now a new station, and have therefore new cares, and new employments. Life, as Cowley seems to say, ought to resemble a well-ordered poem; of which one rule generally received is, that the exordium should be simple, and should promise little. Begin your new course of life with the least show, and the least expence possible; you may at pleasure encrease both, but you cannot easily diminish them. Do not think your estate your own, while any man can call upon you for money which you cannot pay; therefore, begin with timorous parsimony. Let it be your first care not to be in any man's debt.

'When the thoughts are extended to a future state, the present life seems hardly worthy of all those principles of conduct, and maxims of prudence which one generation of men has transmitted to another; but upon a closer view, when it is perceived how much evil is produced, and how much good is impeded by embarrassment and distress, and how little room the expedients of poverty leave for the exercise of virtue, it grows manifest that the boundless importance of the next life enforces some attention to the interests of this.

'Be kind to the old servants, and secure the kindness of the agents and factors; do not disgust them by asperity, or unwelcome gaiety, or apparent suspicion. From them you must learn the real state of your affairs, the characters of your tenants, and the value of your lands.

'Make my compliments to Mrs. Boswell; I think her expectations from air and exercise are the best that she can form. I hope she will live long and happily. . . .

'I received your letters only this morning. I am, dear Sir, yours, &c.

'London, Sept. 7, 1782.'　　　　　　'SAM. JOHNSON.'

In answer to my next letter, I received one from him, dissuading me from hastening to him as I had proposed; what is proper for publication is the following paragraph, equally just and tender:—'One expence, however, I would not have you to spare: let nothing be omitted that can preserve Mrs. Boswell, though it should be necessary to transplant her for a time into a softer climate. She is the prop and stay of your life. How much must your children suffer by losing her.'

My wife was now so much convinced of his sincere friendship for me, and regard for her, that, without any suggestion on my part, she wrote him a very polite and grateful letter:—

'DR. JOHNSON to MRS. BOSWELL

'DEAR LADY,—I have not often received so much pleasure as from your invitation to Auchinleck. The journey thither and back is, indeed, too great for the latter part of the year; but if my health were fully recovered, I would suffer no little heat and cold, nor a wet or a rough road to keep me from you. I am, indeed, not without hope of seeing Auchinleck again; but to make it a pleasant place I must see its lady well, and brisk, and airy. For my sake, therefore, among many greater reasons, take care, dear Madam, of your health, spare no expence, and want no attendance that can procure ease, or preserve it. Be very careful to keep your mind quiet; and do

569

not think it too much to give an account of your recovery to, Madam, Yours, &c.

'London, Sept. 7, 1782.'[1]   'SAM. JOHNSON.'

. . . The death of Mr. Thrale had made a very material alteration with respect to Johnson's reception in that family. The manly authority of the husband no longer curbed the lively exuberance of the lady; and as her vanity had been fully gratified, by having the Colossus of Literature attached to her for many years, she gradually became less assiduous to please him. Whether her attachment to him was already divided by another object, I am unable to ascertain; but it is plain that Johnson's penetration was alive to her neglect or forced attention; for on the 6th of October this year, we find him making a 'parting use of the library' at Streatham, and pronouncing a prayer, which he composed 'On leaving Mr. Thrale's family.'

'Almighty God, Father of all mercy, help me by thy grace, that I may, with humble and sincere thankfulness, remember the comforts and conveniences which I have enjoyed at this place; and that I may resign them with holy submission, equally trusting in thy protection when thou givest, and when thou takest away. Have mercy upon me, O Lord, have mercy upon me.

'To thy fatherly protection, O Lord, I commend this family. Bless, guide, and defend them, that they may so pass through this world, as finally to enjoy in thy presence everlasting happiness, for Jesus Christ's sake. Amen.'

One cannot read this prayer, without some emotions not very favourable to the lady whose conduct occasioned it.

In one of his memorandum-books I find, 'Sunday, went to church at Streatham. *Templo valedixi cum osculo.*'[2]

He met Mr. Philip Metcalfe often at Sir Joshua Reynolds's, and other places, and was a good deal with him at Brighthelmston this autumn, being pleased at once with his excellent table and animated conversation. Mr. Metcalfe shewed him great respect, and sent him a note that he might have the use of his carriage whenever he pleased. Johnson (3rd October, 1782) returned this polite answer:—'Mr. Johnson is very much obliged by the kind offer of the carriage; but he has no desire of using Mr. Metcalfe's carriage, except when he can have the pleasure of Mr. Metcalfe's company.' Mr. Metcalfe could not but be highly pleased that his company was thus valued by Johnson, and he frequently attended him in airings. They also went together to Chichester, and they visited Petworth, and Cowdry, the venerable seat of the Lords Montacute. 'Sir,

[1] Actually, Dec. 7.

[2] 'I said good-bye to the church with a kiss.'

(said Johnson,) I should like to stay here four-and-twenty hours. We see here how our ancestors lived.' . . .

1783: ÆTAT. 74.]—IN 1783, he was more severely afflicted than ever, as will appear in the course of his correspondence; but still the same ardour for literature, the same constant piety, the same kindness for his friends, and the same vivacity both in conversation and writing, distinguished him. . . .

On Friday, March 21, having arrived in London the night before, I was glad to find him at Mrs. Thrale's house, in Argyll-street, appearances of friendship between them being still kept up. I was shewn into his room, and after the first salutation he said, 'I am glad you are come. I am very ill.' He looked pale, and was distressed with a difficulty of breathing; but after the common inquiries he assumed his usual strong animated style of conversation. Seeing me now for the first time as a *Laird,* or proprietor of land, he began thus: 'Sir, the superiority of a country-gentleman over the people upon his estate is very agreeable; and he who says he does not feel it to be agreeable, lies; for it must be agreeable to have a casual superiority over those who are by nature equal with us.' BOSWELL. 'Yet, Sir, we see great proprietors of land who prefer living in London.' JOHNSON. 'Why, Sir, the pleasure of living in London, the intellectual superiority that is enjoyed there, may counterbalance the other. Besides, Sir, a man may prefer the state of the country-gentleman upon the whole, and yet there may never be a moment when he is willing to make the change to quit London for it.' He said, 'It is better to have five *per cent.* out of land than out of money, because it is more secure; but the readiness of transfer, and promptness of interest, make many people rather choose the funds. Nay, there is another disadvantage belonging to land, compared with money. A man is not so much afraid of being a hard creditor, as of being a hard landlord.' BOSWELL. 'Because there is a sort of kindly connection between a landlord and his tenants.' JOHNSON. 'No, Sir; many landlords with us never see their tenants. It is because if a landlord drives away his tenants, he may not get others; whereas the demand for money is so great, it may always be lent.'

He talked with regret and indignation of the factious opposition to Government at this time, and imputed it, in a great measure, to the Revolution. 'Sir, (said he, in a low voice, having come nearer to me, while his old prejudices seemed to be fermenting in his mind,) this Hanoverian family is *isolée* here. They have no friends. Now the Stuarts had friends who stuck by them so late as 1745. When the right of the King is not reverenced, there will not be reverence for those appointed by the King.' . . .

He repeated to me his verses on Mr. Levett, with an emotion which gave them full effect; and then he was pleased to say, 'You must be as much with me as you can. You have done me good. You cannot think how much better I am since you came in.'

He sent a message to acquaint Mrs. Thrale that I was arrived. I had not seen her since her husband's death. She soon appeared, and favoured me with an invitation to stay to dinner, which I accepted. There was no other company but herself and three of her daughters, Dr. Johnson, and I. She too said, she was very glad I was come, for she was going to Bath, and should have been sorry to leave Dr. Johnson before I came. This seemed to be attentive and kind; and I who had not been informed of any change, imagined all to be as well as formerly. He was little inclined to talk at dinner, and went to sleep after it; but when he joined us in the drawing-room, he seemed revived, and was again himself.

Talking of conversation, he said, 'There must, in the first place, be knowledge, there must be materials; in the second place, there must be a command of words; in the third place, there must be imagination, to place things in such views as they are not commonly seen in; and in the fourth place, there must be presence of mind, and a resolution that is not to be overcome by failures: this last is an essential requisite; for want of it many people do not excel in conversation. Now *I* want it: I throw up the game upon losing a trick.' I wondered to hear him talk thus of himself, and said, 'I don't know, Sir, how this may be; but I am sure you beat other people's cards out of their hands.' I doubt whether he heard this remark. While he went on talking triumphantly, I was fixed in admiration, and said to Mrs. Thrale, 'O, for short-hand to take this down!' 'You'll carry it all in your head, (said she;) a long head is as good as short-hand.'

It has been observed and wondered at, that Mr. Charles Fox never talked with any freedom in the presence of Dr. Johnson, though it is well known, and I myself can witness, that his conversation is various, fluent, and exceedingly agreeable. Johnson's own experience, however, of that gentleman's reserve was a sufficient reason for his going on thus: 'Fox never talks in private company; not from any determination not to talk, but because he has not the first motion. A man who is used to the applause of the House of Commons, has no wish for that of a private company. A man accustomed to throw for a thousand pounds, if set down to throw for sixpence, would not be at the pains to count his dice. Burke's talk is the ebullition of his mind; he does not talk from a desire of distinction, but because his mind is full.'

He thus curiously characterised one of our old acquaintance:[1] '********* is a good man, Sir; but he is a vain man and a liar. He, however, only tells lies of vanity; of victories, for instance, in conversation, which never happened.' This alluded to a story which I had repeated from that gentleman, to entertain Johnson with its wild bravado: 'This Johnson, Sir, (said he,) whom you are all afraid of, will shrink if you come close to him in argument, and roar as loud as he. He once maintained the paradox, that there is no beauty but in utility. "Sir, (said I,) what say you to the peacock's tail, which is one of the most beautiful objects in nature, but would have as much utility if its feathers were all of one colour." He *felt* what I thus produced, and had recourse to his usual expedient, ridicule; exclaiming, "A peacock has a tail, and a fox has a tail;" and then he burst out into a laugh. "Well, Sir, (said I, with a strong voice, looking him full in the face,) you have unkennelled your fox; pursue him if you dare." He had not a word to say, Sir.' Johnson told me, that this was a fiction from beginning to end.

After musing for some time, he said, 'I wonder how I should have any enemies; for I do harm to nobody.'[2] BOSWELL. 'In the first place, Sir, you will be pleased to recollect, that you set out with attacking the Scotch; so you got a whole nation for your enemies.' JOHNSON. 'Why, I own, that by my definition of *oats* I meant to vex them.' BOSWELL. 'Pray, Sir, can you trace the cause of your antipathy to the Scotch?' JOHNSON. 'I cannot, Sir.' BOSWELL. 'Old Mr. Sheridan says, it was because they sold Charles the First.' JOHNSON. 'Then, Sir, old Mr. Sheridan has found out a very good reason.'

Surely the most obstinate and sulky nationality, the most determined aversion to this great and good man, must be cured, when he is seen thus playing with one of his prejudices, of which he candidly admitted that he could not tell the reason. It was, however, probably owing to his having had in his view the worst part of the Scottish nation, the needy adventurers, many of whom he thought were advanced above their merits by means which he did not approve. Had he in his early life been in Scotland, and seen the worthy, sensible, independent gentlemen, who live rationally and hospitably at home, he never could have entertained such unfavourable and unjust notions of his fellow-subjects. And accordingly we find, that

[1] Old Mr. Sheridan.

[2] This reflection was very natural in a man of a good heart, who was not conscious of any ill-will to mankind, though the sharp sayings which were sometimes produced by his discrimination and vivacity, and which he perhaps did not recollect, were, I am afraid, too often remembered with resentment—B.

when he did visit Scotland, in the latter period of his life, he was fully sensible of all that it deserved, as I have already pointed out, when speaking of his *Journey to the Western Islands*.

Next day, Saturday, March 22, I found him still at Mrs. Thrale's, but he told me that he was to go to his own house in the afternoon. He was better, but I perceived he was but an unruly patient, for Sir Lucas Pepys, who visited him, while I was with him said, 'If you were *tractable*, Sir, I should prescribe for you.'

I related to him a remark which a respectable friend[1] had made to me, upon the then state of Government, when those who had been long in opposition had attained to power, as it was supposed, against the inclination of the Sovereign. 'You need not be uneasy (said this gentleman,) about the King. He laughs at them all; he plays them one against another.' JOHNSON. 'Don't think so, Sir. The King is as much oppressed as a man can be. If he plays them one against another, he *wins* nothing.'

I had paid a visit to General Oglethorpe in the morning, and was told by him that Dr. Johnson saw company on Saturday evenings, and he would meet me at Johnson's, that night. When I mentioned this to Johnson, not doubting that it would please him, as he had a great value for Oglethorpe, the fretfulness of his disease unexpectedly shewed itself; his anger suddenly kindled, and he said, with vehemence, 'Did not you tell him not to come? Am I to be *hunted* in this manner?' I satisfied him that I could not divine that the visit would not be convenient, and that I certainly could not take it upon me of my own accord to forbid the General.

I found Dr. Johnson in the evening in Mrs. Williams's room, at tea and coffee with her and Mrs. Desmoulins, who were also both ill; it was a sad scene, and he was not in a very good humour. He said of a performance that had lately come out, 'Sir, if you should search all the mad-houses in England, you would not find ten men who would write so, and think it sense.'

I was glad when General Oglethorpe's arrival was announced, and we left the ladies. Dr. Johnson attended him in the parlour, and was as courteous as ever. The General said he was busy reading the writers of the middle age. Johnson said they were very curious. OGLETHORPE. 'The House of Commons has usurped the power of the nation's money, and used it tyrannically. Government is now carried on by corrupt influence, instead of the inherent right in the King.'

[1] General Paoli.

JOHNSON. 'Sir, the want of inherent right in the King occasions all this disturbance. What we did at the Revolution was necessary: but it broke our constitution.' OGLETHORPE. 'My father did not think it necessary.'

On Sunday, March 23, I breakfasted with Dr. Johnson, who seemed much relieved, having taken opium the night before. He however protested against it, as a remedy that should be given with the utmost reluctance, and only in extreme necessity. I mentioned how commonly it was used in Turkey, and that therefore it could not be so pernicious as he apprehended. He grew warm and said, 'Turks take opium, and Christians take opium; but Russel, in his account of Aleppo, tells us, that it is as disgraceful in Turkey to take too much opium, as it is with us to get drunk. Sir, it is amazing how things are exaggerated. A gentleman was lately telling in a company where I was present, that in France, as soon as a man of fashion marries, he takes an opera girl into keeping; and this he mentioned as a general custom. "Pray, Sir, (said I,) how many opera girls may there be?" He answered, "About fourscore." "Well then, Sir, (said I,) you see there can be no more than fourscore men of fashion who can do this." '

Mrs. Desmoulins made tea; and she and I talked before him upon a topick which he had once borne patiently from me when we were by ourselves,—his not complaining of the world, because he was not called to some great office, nor had attained to great wealth. He flew into a violent passion, I confess with some justice, and commanded us to have done. 'Nobody, (said he,) has a right to talk in this manner, to bring before a man his own character, and the events of his life, when he does not choose it should be done. I never have sought the world; the world was not to seek me. It is rather wonderful that so much has been done for me. All the complaints which are made of the world are unjust. I never knew a man of merit neglected: it was generally by his own fault that he failed of success. A man may hide his head in a hole: he may go into the country, and publish a book now and then, which nobody reads, and then complain he is neglected. There is no reason why any person should exert himself for a man who has written a good book: he has not written it for any individual. I may as well make a present to the postman who brings me a letter. When patronage was limited, an authour expected to find a Mæcenas, and complained if he did not find one. Why should he complain? This Mæcenas has others as good as he, or others who have got the start of him.' BOSWELL. 'But surely, Sir, you will allow that there are men of merit at the bar who never get practice.' JOHNSON. 'Sir, you

575

are sure that practice is got from an opinion that the person employed deserves it best; so that if a man of merit at the bar does not get practice, it is from errour, not from injustice. He is not neglected. A horse that is brought to market may not be bought, though he is a very good horse: but that is from ignorance, not from intention.' . . .

On the subject of the right employment of wealth, Johnson observed, 'A man cannot make a bad use of his money, so far as regards Society, if he does not hoard it; for if he either spends it or lends it out, Society has the benefit. It is in general better to spend money than to give it away; for industry is more promoted by spending money than by giving it away. A man who spends his money is sure he is doing good with it: he is not so sure when he gives it away. A man who spends ten thousand a year will do more good than a man who spends two thousand and gives away eight.'

In the evening I came to him again. He was somewhat fretful from his illness. A gentleman[1] asked him, whether he had been abroad to-day. 'Don't talk so childishly, (said he.) You may as well ask if I hanged myself to-day.' I mentioned politicks. JOHNSON. 'Sir, I'd as soon have a man to break my bones as talk to me of publick affairs, internal or external. I have lived to see things all as bad as they can be.'

Having mentioned his friend the second Lord Southwell, he said, 'Lord Southwell was the highest-bred man without insolence that I ever was in company with; the most *qualitied* I ever saw. Lord Orrery was not dignified: Lord Chesterfield was, but he was insolent. Lord ********[2] is a man of coarse manners, but a man of abilities and information. I don't say he is a man I would set at the head of a nation, though perhaps he may be as good as the next Prime Minister that comes; but he is a man to be at the head of a Club; I don't say *our* CLUB; for there's no such Club.' BOSWELL. 'But, Sir, was he not once a factious man?' JOHNSON. 'O yes, Sir; as factious a fellow as could be found: one who was for sinking us all into the mob.' BOSWELL. 'How then, Sir, did he get into favour with the King?' JOHNSON. 'Because, Sir, I suppose he promised the King to do whatever the King pleased.'

He said, 'Goldsmith's blundering speech to Lord Shelburne, which has been so often mentioned, and which he really did make to him, was only a blunder in emphasis: "I wonder they should call your Lordship *Malagrida*, for Malagrida was a very good man;" meant, I wonder they should use *Malagrida* as a term of reproach.'

[1] Boswell.
[2] Shelburne.

Soon after this time I had an opportunity of seeing, by means of one of his friends,[1] a proof that his talents, as well as his obliging service to authours, were ready as ever. He had revised *The Village,* an admirable poem, by the Reverend Mr. Crabbe. Its sentiments as to the false notions of rustick happiness and rustick virtue were quite congenial with his own; and he had taken the trouble not only to suggest slight corrections and variations, but to furnish some lines, when he thought he could give the writer's meaning better than in the words of the manuscript.

On Sunday, March 30, I found him at home in the evening, and had the pleasure to meet with Dr. Brocklesby, whose reading, and knowledge of life, and good spirits, supply him with a never-failing source of conversation. He mentioned a respectable gentleman, who became extremely penurious near the close of his life. Johnson said there must have been a degree of madness about him. 'Not at all, Sir, (said Dr. Brocklesby,) his judgement was entire.' Unluckily, however he mentioned that although he had a fortune of twenty-seven thousand pounds, he denied himself many comforts, from an apprehension that he could not afford them. 'Nay, Sir, (cried Johnson,) when the judgement is so disturbed that a man cannot count, that is pretty well.'

I shall here insert a few of Johnson's sayings, without the formality of dates, as they have no reference to any particular time or place.

'The more a man extends and varies his acquaintance the better.' This, however, was meant with a just restriction; for, he on another occasion said to me, 'Sir, a man may be so much of every thing, that he is nothing of any thing.'

'Raising the wages of day-labourers is wrong; for it does not make them live better, but only makes them idler, and idleness is a very bad thing for human nature.'

'It is a very good custom to keep a journal for a man's own use; he may write upon a card a day all that is necessary to be written, after he has had experience of life. At first there is a great deal to be written, because there is a great deal of novelty; but when once a man has settled his opinions, there is seldom much to be set down.'

'There is nothing wonderful in the journal which we see Swift kept in London, for it contains slight topicks, and it might soon be written.'

I praised the accuracy of an account-book of a lady whom I mentioned. JOHNSON. 'Keeping accounts, Sir, is of no use when a man is spending his own money, and has nobody to whom he is to account. You won't eat less beef to-day, because you have written down what it cost yesterday.' I mentioned another lady[1] who thought as he did, so that her husband could not get her to keep an account of the expence of the family, as she thought it enough that she never exceeded the sum allowed her. JOHNSON. 'Sir, it is fit she should keep an account, because her husband wishes it; but I do not see its use.' I maintained that keeping an account has this advantage, that it satisfies a man that his money has not been lost or stolen, which he might sometimes be apt to imagine, were there no written state of his expence; and besides, a calculation of œconomy so as not to exceed one's income, cannot be made without a view of the different articles in figures, that one may see how to retrench in some particulars less necessary than others. This he did not attempt to answer.

Talking of an acquaintance of ours,[2] whose narratives, which abounded in curious and interesting topicks, were unhappily found to be very fabulous; I mentioned Lord Mansfield's having said to me, 'Suppose we believe one *half* of what he tells.' JOHNSON. 'Ay; but we don't know *which* half to believe. By his lying we lose not only our reverence for him, but all comfort in his conversation.' BOSWELL. 'May we not take it as amusing fiction?' JOHNSON. 'Sir, the misfortune is, that you will insensibly believe as much of it as you incline to believe.'

It is remarkable, that notwithstanding their congeniality in politicks, he never was acquainted with a late eminent noble judge, whom I have heard speak of him as a writer, with great respect. Johnson, I know not upon what degree of investigation, entertained no exalted opinion of his Lordship's intellectual character. Talking of him to me one day, he said, 'It is wonderful, Sir, with how little real superiority of mind men can make an eminent figure in publick life.' He expressed himself to the same purpose concerning another law-Lord,[3] who, it seems, once took a fancy to associate with the wits of London; but with so little success, that Foote said, 'What can he mean by coming among us? He is not only dull himself, but the cause of dullness in others.' Trying him by the test of his colloquial powers, Johnson had found him very defective. He once said to Sir Joshua Reynolds, 'This man now has been ten years about town, and has made nothing of it;' meaning as a companion. He said to me, 'I never heard any thing from him in company that was at all striking; and

---

1 Mrs. Boswell.
2 Steevens.
3 Loughborough.

depend upon it, Sir, it is when you come close to a man in conversation, you discover what his real abilities are; to make a speech in a publick assembly is a knack. Now I honour Thurlow, Sir; Thurlow is a fine fellow; he fairly puts his mind to yours.'

After repeating to him some of his pointed, lively sayings, I said, 'It is a pity, Sir, you don't always remember your own good things, that you may have a laugh when you will.' JOHNSON. 'Nay, Sir, it is better that I forget them, that I may be reminded of them, and have a laugh on their being brought to my recollection.'

When I recalled to him his having said as we sailed upon Lochlomond, 'That if he wore any thing fine, it should be *very* fine;' I observed that all his thoughts were upon a great scale. JOHNSON. 'Depend upon it, Sir, every man will have as fine a thing as he can get; as a large diamond for his ring.' BOSWELL. 'Pardon me, Sir: a man of a narrow mind will not think of it, a slight trinket will satisfy him:

> *"Nec sufferre queat majoris pondera gemmæ."* '[1]

I told him I should send him some *Essays* which I had written, which I hoped he would be so good as to read, and pick out the good ones. JOHNSON. 'Nay, Sir, send me only the good ones; don't make *me* pick them.' . . .

As a small proof of his kindliness and delicacy of feeling, the following circumstance may be mentioned: One evening when we were in the street together, and I told him I was going to sup at Mr. Beauclerk's, he said, 'I'll go with you.' After having walked part of the way, seeming to recollect something he suddenly stopped and said, 'I cannot go,—but *I do not love Beauclerk the less.*'

On the frame of his portrait, Mr. Beauclerk had inscribed,—

> '————*Ingenium ingens*
> *Inculto latet hoc sub corpore.*'[2]

After Mr. Beauclerk's death, when it became Mr. Langton's property, he made the inscription be defaced. Johnson said complacently, 'It was kind in you to take it off;' and then after a short pause, added, 'and not unkind in him to put it on.'

He said, 'How few of his friends' houses would a man

---

[1] 'Unable to sustain a weighty jewel.' Juvenal, *Satires*, i. 29.

[2] 'An immense genius lies concealed within that uncouth person.' Horace, *Satires*, I. iii. 33-34.

choose to be at when he is sick.' He mentioned one or two. I recollect only Thrale's.

He observed, 'There is a wicked inclination in most people to suppose an old man decayed in his intellects. If a young or middle-aged man, when leaving a company, does not recollect where he laid his hat, it is nothing; but if the same inattention is discovered in an old man, people will shrug up their shoulders, and say "His memory is going."' . . .

I am very sorry that I did not take a note of an eloquent argument in which he maintained that the situation of Prince of Wales was the happiest of any person's in the kingdom, even beyond that of the Sovereign. I recollect only—the enjoyment of hope,—the high superiority of rank, without the anxious cares of government,—and a great degree of power, both from natural influence wisely used, and from the sanguine expectations of those who look forward to the chance of future favour.

Sir Joshua Reynolds communicated to me the following particulars:—

Johnson thought the poems published as translations from Ossian had so little merit, that he said, 'Sir, a man might write such stuff for ever, if he would *abandon* his mind to it.'

He said, 'A man should pass a part of his time with *the laughers*, by which means any thing ridiculous or particular about him might be presented to his view, and corrected.' I observed he must have been a bold laugher who would have ventured to tell Dr. Johnson of any of his particularities.[1]

Having observed the vain ostentatious importance of many people in quoting the authority of Dukes and Lords, as having been in their company, he said, he went to the other extreme, and did not mention his authority when he should have done it, had it not been that of a Duke or a Lord.

Dr. Goldsmith once said to Dr. Johnson, that he wished for some additional members to The Literary Club, to give it an agreeable variety; for (said he,) there can now be nothing new among us: we have travelled over one another's minds. Johnson seemed a little angry, and said, 'Sir, you have not travelled over *my* mind, I promise you.' Sir Joshua, however, thought Goldsmith right; observing, that 'when people

---

[1] I am happy, however, to mention a pleasing instance of his enduring with great gentleness to hear one of his most striking particularities pointed out:—Miss Hunter, a niece of his friend Christopher Smart, when a very young girl, struck by his extraordinary motions, said to him, 'Pray, Dr. Johnson, why do you make such strange gestures?' 'From bad habit,' he replied. 'Do you, my dear, take care to guard against bad habits.' This I was told by the young lady's brother at Margate—B.

have lived a great deal together, they know what each of them will say on every subject. A new understanding, therefore, is desirable; because though it may only furnish the same sense upon a question which would have been furnished by those with whom we are accustomed to live, yet this sense will have a different colouring; and colouring is of much effect in every thing else as well as in painting.'

Johnson used to say that he made it a constant rule to talk as well as he could both as to sentiment and expression, by which means, what had been originally effort became familiar and easy. The consequence of this, Sir Joshua observed, was, that his common conversation in all companies was such as to secure him universal attention, as something above the usual colloquial style was expected.

Yet, though Johnson had this habit in company, when another mode was necessary, in order to investigate truth, he could descend to a language intelligible to the meanest capacity. An instance of this was witnessed by Sir Joshua Reynolds, when they were present at an examination of a little blackguard boy, by Mr. Saunders Welch, the late Westminster Justice. Welch, who imagined that he was exalting himself in Dr. Johnson's eyes by using big words, spoke in a manner that was utterly unintelligible to the boy; Dr. Johnson perceiving it, addressed himself to the boy, and changed the pompous phraseology into colloquial language. Sir Joshua Reynolds, who was much amused by this procedure, which seemed a kind of reversing of what might have been expected from the two men, took notice of it to Dr. Johnson, as they walked away by themselves. Johnson said, that it was continually the case; and that he was always obliged to *translate* the Justice's swelling diction, (smiling,) so as that his meaning might be understood by the vulgar, from whom information was to be obtained.

Sir Joshua once observed to him, that he had talked above the capacity of some people with whom they had been in company together. 'No matter, Sir, (said Johnson;) they consider it as a compliment to be talked to, as if they were wiser than they are. So true is this, Sir, that Baxter made it a rule in every sermon that he preached, to say something that was above the capacity of his audience.'

Johnson's dexterity in retort, when he seemed to be driven to an extremity by his adversary, was very remarkable. Of his power in this respect, our common friend, Mr. Windham, of Norfolk, has been pleased to furnish me with an eminent instance. However unfavourable to Scotland, he uniformly gave liberal praise to George Buchanan, as a writer. In a conversation concerning the literary merits of the two countries, in which Buchanan was introduced, a Scotchman, imagining that on this ground he should have an undoubted triumph over him, exclaimed, 'Ah, Dr. Johnson, what would you have said of Buchanan, had he been an Englishman?' 'Why, Sir, (said Johnson, after a little pause,) I should *not* have said of Buchanan, had he been an *Englishman,* what I will now say of him as a *Scotchman,*—that he was the only man of genius his country ever produced.'

And this brings to my recollection another instance of the same nature. I once reminded him that when Dr. Adam Smith was expatiating on the beauty of Glasgow, he had cut him short by saying, 'Pray, Sir, have you ever seen Brentford?' and I took the liberty to add, 'My dear Sir, surely that was *shocking.*' 'Why, then, Sir, (he replied,) you have never seen Brentford.'

Though his usual phrase for conversation was *talk,* yet he made a distinction; for when he once told me that he dined the day before at a friend's house, with 'a very pretty company;' and I asked him if there was good conversation, he answered, 'No, Sir; we had *talk* enough, but no *conversation;* there was nothing *discussed.*'

Talking of the success of the Scotch in London, he imputed it in a considerable degree to their spirit of nationality. 'You know, Sir, (said he,) that no Scotchman publishes a book, or has a play brought upon the stage, but there are five hundred people ready to applaud him.' . . .

Such was his sensibility, and so much was he affected by pathetick poetry, that, when he was reading Dr. Beattie's *Hermit* in my presence, it brought tears into his eyes.

He disapproved much of mingling real facts with fiction. On this account he censured a book entitled *Love and Madness.*

Mr. Hoole told him, he was born in Moorfields, and had received part of his early instruction in Grub-street. 'Sir, (said Johnson, smiling,) you have been *regularly* educated.' Having asked who was his instructor, and Mr. Hoole having answered, 'My uncle, Sir, who was a taylor;' Johnson, recollecting himself, said, 'Sir, I knew him; we called him the *metaphysical taylor.* He was of a club in Old-street, with me and George Psalmanazar, and some others: but pray, Sir, was he a good taylor?' Mr. Hoole having answered that he believed he was too mathematical, and used to draw squares and triangles on his shop-board, so that he did not excel in the cut of a coat;—'I am sorry for it (said Johnson,) for I would have every man to be master of his own business.'

In pleasant reference to himself and Mr. Hoole, as brother

authours, he often said, 'Let you and I, Sir, go together, and eat a beef-steak in Grub-street.' . . .

He said to Sir William Scott, 'The age is running mad after innovation; all the business of the world is to be done in a new way; men are to be hanged in a new way; Tyburn itself is not safe from the fury of innovation.' It having been argued that this was an improvement,—'No, Sir, (said he, eagerly,) it is *not* an improvement: they object that the old method drew together a number of spectators. Sir, executions are intended to draw spectators. If they do not draw spectators they don't answer their purpose. The old method was most satisfactory to all parties; the publick was gratified by a procession; the criminal was supported by it. Why is all this to be swept away?' I perfectly agree with Dr. Johnson upon this head, and am persuaded that executions now, the solemn procession being discontinued, have not nearly the effect which they formerly had. Magistrates both in London, and elsewhere, have, I am afraid, in this had too much regard to their own ease.

Of Dr. Hurd, Bishop of Worcester, Johnson said to a friend, 'Hurd, Sir, is one of a set of men who account for everything systematically; for instance, it has been a fashion to wear scarlet breeches; these men would tell you, that according to causes and effects, no other wear could at that time have been chosen.' He, however, said of him at another time to the same gentleman, 'Hurd, Sir, is a man whose acquaintance is a valuable acquisition.'

That learned and ingenious Prelate, it is well known, published at one period of his life *Moral and Political Dialogues,* with a woefully whiggish cast. Afterwards, his Lordship having thought better, came to see his errour, and republished the work with a more constitutional spirit. Johnson, however, was unwilling to allow him full credit for his political conversion. I remember when his Lordship declined the honour of being Archbishop of Canterbury, Johnson said, 'I am glad he did not go to Lambeth; for, after all, I fear he is a Whig in his heart.'

Johnson's attention to precision and clearness in expression was very remarkable. He disapproved of parentheses; and I believe in all his voluminous writings, not half a dozen of them will be found. He never used the phrases *the former* and *the latter,* having observed, that they often occasioned obscurity; he therefore contrived to construct his sentences so as not to have occasion for them, and would even rather repeat the same words, in order to avoid them. Nothing is more common than to mistake surnames when we hear them carelessly uttered for the first time. To prevent this, he used not only to pronounce them slowly and distinctly, but to take the trouble of spelling them; a practice which I often followed; and which I wish were general.

Such was the heat and irritability of his blood, that not only did he pare his nails to the quick; but scraped the joints of his fingers with a pen-knife, till they seemed quite red and raw.

The heterogeneous composition of human nature was remarkably exemplified in Johnson. His liberality in giving his money to persons in distress was extraordinary. Yet there lurked about him a propensity to paltry saving. One day I owned to him that 'I was occasionally troubled with a fit of *narrowness*.' 'Why, Sir, (said he,) so am I. *But I do not tell it*.' He has now and then borrowed a shilling of me; and when I asked for it again, seemed to be rather out of humour. A droll little circumstance once occurred: as if he meant to reprimand my minute exactness as a creditor, as he thus addressed me;—'Boswell, *lend* me sixpence—*not to be repaid*.'

This great man's attention to small things was very remarkable. As an instance of it, he one day said to me, 'Sir, when you get silver in change for a guinea, look carefully at it; you may find some curious piece of coin.'

Though a stern *true-born Englishman*, and fully prejudiced against all other nations, he had discernment enough to see, and candour enough to censure, the cold reserve too common among Englishmen towards strangers: 'Sir, (said he,) two men of any other nation who are shewn into a room together, at a house where they are both visitors, will immediately find some conversation. But two Englishmen will probably go each to a different window, and remain in obstinate silence. Sir, we as yet do not enough understand the common rights of humanity.'

Johnson was at a certain period of his life a good deal with the Earl of Shelburne, now Marquis of Lansdown, as he doubtless could not but have a due value for that nobleman's activity of mind, and uncommon acquisitions of important knowledge, however much he might disapprove of other parts of his Lordship's character, which were widely different from his own.

Maurice Morgann, Esq., authour of the very ingenious *Essay on the character of Falstaff*, being a particular friend of his Lordship, had once an opportunity of entertaining Johnson for a day or two at Wickham, when its Lord was absent, and by him I have been favoured with two anecdotes.

One is not a little to the credit of Johnson's candour. Mr. Morgann and he had a dispute pretty late at night, in which

Johnson would not give up, though he had the wrong side, and in short, both kept the field. Next morning, when they met in the breakfasting-room, Dr. Johnson accosted Mr. Morgann thus:—'Sir, I have been thinking on our dispute last night— *You were in the right.*'

The other was as follows:—Johnson, for sport perhaps, or from the spirit of contradiction, eagerly maintained that Derrick had merit as a writer. Mr. Morgann argued with him directly, in vain. At length he had recourse to this device. 'Pray, Sir, (said he,) whether do you reckon Derrick or Smart the best poet?' Johnson at once felt himself rouzed; and answered, 'Sir, there is no settling point of precedency between a louse and a flea.'

Once, when checking my boasting too frequently of myself in company, he said to me, 'Boswell, you often vaunt so much as to provoke ridicule. You put me in mind of a man who was standing in the kitchen of an inn with his back to the fire, and thus accosted the person next him, "Do you know, Sir, who I am?" "No, Sir, (said the other,) I have not that advantage." "Sir, (said he,) I am the *great* TWALMLEY, who invented the New Flood-gate Iron."' . . .

He was pleased to say to me one morning when we were left alone in his study, 'Boswell, I think I am easier with you than with almost any body.'

He would not allow Mr. David Hume any credit for his political principles, though similar to his own; saying of him, 'Sir, he was a Tory by chance.'

His acute observation of human life made him remark, 'Sir, there is nothing by which a man exasperates most people more, than by displaying a superiour ability or brilliancy in conversation. They seem pleased at the time; but their envy makes them curse him in their hearts.'

My readers will probably be surprised to hear that the great Dr. Johnson could amuse himself with so slight and playful a species of compositions as a *Charade.* I have recovered one which he made on Dr. *Barnard,* now Lord Bishop of Killaloe; who has been pleased for many years to treat me with so much intimacy and social ease, that I may presume to call him not only my Right Reverend, but my very dear Friend. I therefore with peculiar pleasure give to the world a just and elegant compliment thus paid to his Lordship by Johnson.

CHARADE.

'My *first* shuts out thieves from your house or your room,
    My *second* expresses a Syrian perfume.
    My *whole* is a man in whose converse is shar'd,
    The strength of a Bar and the sweetness of Nard.'

Johnson asked Richard Owen Cambridge, Esq., if he had read the Spanish translation of *Sallust*, said to be written by a Prince of Spain, with the assistance of his tutor, who is professedly the authour of a treatise annexed, on the Phœnician language.

Mr. Cambridge commended the work particularly, as he thought the Translator understood his authour better than is commonly the case with Translators: but said, he was disappointed in the purpose for which he borrowed the book; to see whether a Spaniard could be better furnished with inscriptions from monuments, coins, or other antiquities which he might more probably find on a coast, so immediately opposite to Carthage than the Antiquaries of any other countries. JOHNSON. 'I am very sorry you was not gratified in your expectations.' CAMBRIDGE. 'The language would have been of little use, as there is no history existing in that tongue to balance the partial accounts which the Roman writers have left us.' JOHNSON. 'No, Sir. They have not been *partial*, they have told their own story, without shame or regard to equitable treatment of their injured enemy; they had no compunction, no feeling for a Carthaginian. Why, Sir, they would never have borne Virgil's description of Æneas's treatment of Dido, if she had not been a Carthaginian.' . . .

Johnson's love of little children, which he discovered upon all occasions, calling them 'pretty dears,' and giving them sweetmeats, was an undoubted proof of the real humanity and gentleness of his disposition.

His uncommon kindness to his servants, and serious concern, not only for their comfort in this world, but their happiness in the next, was another unquestionable evidence of what all, who were intimately acquainted with him, knew to be true.

Nor would it be just, under this head, to omit the fondness which he shewed for animals which he had taken under his protection. I never shall forget the indulgence with which he treated Hodge, his cat: for whom he himself used to go out and buy oysters, lest the servants having that trouble should take a dislike to the poor creature. I am, unluckily, one of those who have an antipathy to a cat, so that I am uneasy when in the room with one; and I own, I frequently suffered a good deal from the presence of this same Hodge. I recollect him one day scrambling up Dr. Johnson's breast, apparently with much satisfaction, while my friend smiling and half-whistling rubbed down his back, and pulled him by the tail; and when I observed he was a fine cat, saying, 'Why yes, Sir, but I have had cats whom I liked better than this;' and then as if perceiving Hodge to be out of countenance, adding, 'but he is a very fine cat, a very fine cat indeed.'

This reminds me of the ludicrous account which he gave Mr. Langton, of the despicable state of a young Gentleman of good family. 'Sir, when I heard of him last, he was running about town shooting cats.' And then in a sort of kindly reverie, he bethought himself of his own favourite cat and said, 'But Hodge shan't be shot; no, no, Hodge shall not be shot.'

He thought Mr. Beauclerk made a shrewd and judicious remark to Mr. Langton, who, after having been for the first time in company with a well-known wit about town, was warmly admiring and praising him, 'See him again,' said Beauclerk.

His respect for the Hierarchy, and particularly the Dignitaries of the Church, has been more than once exhibited in the course of this work. Mr. Seward saw him presented to the Archbishop of York, and described his *Bow to an* ARCHBISHOP, as such a studied elaboration of homage, such an extension of limb, such a flexion of body, as have seldom or ever been equalled. . . .

On Thursday, April 10, I introduced to him, at his house in Bolt-court, the Honourable and Reverend William Stuart, son of the Earl of Bute; a gentleman truly worthy of being known to Johnson; being, with all the advantages of high birth, learning, travel, and elegant manners, an exemplary parish priest in every respect.

After some compliments on both sides, the tour which Johnson and I had made to the Hebrides was mentioned. JOHNSON. 'I got an acquisition of more ideas by it than by any thing that I remember. I saw quite a different system of life.' BOSWELL. 'You would not like to make the same journey again?' JOHNSON. 'Why no, Sir; not the same: it is a tale told. Gravina, an Italian critick, observes that every man desires to see that of which he has read; but no man desires to read an account of what he has seen: so much does description fall short of reality. Description only excites curiosity: seeing satisfies it. Other people may go and see the Hebrides.' BOSWELL. 'I should wish to go and see some country totally different from what I have been used to; such as Turkey, where religion and everything else are different.' JOHNSON. 'Yes, Sir; there are two objects of curiosity,—the Christian world, and the Mahometan world. All the rest may be considered as barbarous.' . . .

BOSWELL. 'This has been a very factious reign, owing to the too great indulgence of Government.' JOHNSON. 'I think so, Sir. What at first was lenity, grew timidity. Yet this is

587

reasoning *à posteriori,* and may not be just. Supposing a few had at first been punished, I believe faction would have been crushed; but it might have been said, that it was a sanguinary reign. A man cannot tell *à priori* what will be best for Government to do. This reign has been very unfortunate. We have had an unsuccessful war; but that does not prove that we have been ill governed. One side or other must prevail in war, as one or other must win at play. When we beat Louis, we were not better governed; nor were the French better governed when Louis beat us.'

On Saturday, April 12, I visited him, in company with Mr. Windham, of Norfolk, whom, though a Whig, he highly valued. One of the best things he ever said was to this gentleman; who, before he set out for Ireland as Secretary to Lord Northington, when Lord Lieutenant, expressed to the Sage some modest and virtuous doubts, whether he could bring himself to practise those arts which it is supposed a person in that situation has occasion to employ. 'Don't be afraid, Sir, (said Johnson, with a pleasant smile,) you will soon make a very pretty rascal.'

He talked to-day a good deal of the wonderful extent and variety of London, and observed, that men of curious inquiry might see in it such modes of life as very few could even imagine. He in particular recommended to us to *explore Wapping,* which we resolved to do.[1]

Mr. Lowe, the painter, who was with him, was very much distressed that a large picture which he had painted was refused to be received into the Exhibition of the Royal Academy. Mrs. Thrale knew Johnson's character so superficially, as to represent him as unwilling to do small acts of benevolence; and mentions in particular, that he would hardly take the trouble to write a letter in favour of his friends. The truth, however, is, that he was remarkable, in an extraordinary degree, for what she denies to him; and, above all, for this very sort of kindness, writing letters for those to whom his solicitations might be of service. He now gave Mr. Lowe the following, of which I was diligent enough, with his permission, to take copies at the next coffeehouse, while Mr. Windham was so good as to stay by me.[2]

Such intercession was too powerful to be resisted; and Mr. Lowe's performance was admitted at Somerset Place. The subject, as I recollect, was the Deluge, at that point of time

[1] We accordingly carried our scheme into execution, in October, 1792; but whether from that uniformity which has in modern times, in a great degree, spread through every part of the Metropolis, or from our want of sufficient exertion, we were disappointed.—B.

[2] These letters, to Reynolds and Barry, are omitted.

when the water was verging to the top of the last uncovered mountain. Near to the spot was seen the last of the antediluvian race, exclusive of those who were saved in the ark of Noah. This was one of those giants, then the inhabitants of the earth, who had still strength to swim, and with one of his hands held aloft his infant child. Upon the small remaining dry spot appeared a famished lion, ready to spring at the child and devour it. Mr. Lowe told me that Johnson said to him, 'Sir, your picture is noble and probable.' 'A compliment, indeed, (said Mr. Lowe,) from a man who cannot lie, and cannot be mistaken.' . . .

On April 18, (being Good-Friday,) I found him at breakfast, in his usual manner upon that day, drinking tea without milk, and eating a cross-bun to prevent faintness; we went to St. Clement's church, as formerly. When we came home from church, he placed himself on one of the stone-seats at his garden-door, and I took the other, and thus in the open air and in a placid frame of mind, he talked away very easily. JOHNSON. 'Were I a country gentleman, I should not be very hospitable, I should not have crowds in my house.' BOSWELL. 'Sir Alexander Dick tells me, that he remembers having a thousand people in a year to dine at his house: that is, reckoning each person as one, each time that he dined there.' JOHNSON. 'That, Sir, is about three a day.' BOSWELL. 'How your statement lessens the idea.' JOHNSON. 'That, Sir, is the good of counting. It brings every thing to a certainty, which before floated in the mind indefinitely.' BOSWELL. 'But *Omne ignotum pro magnifico est:*[1] one is sorry to have this diminished.' JOHNSON. 'Sir, you should not allow yourself to be delighted with errour.' BOSWELL. 'Three a day seem but few.' JOHNSON. 'Nay, Sir, he who entertains three a day, does very liberally. And if there is a large family, the poor entertain those three, for they eat what the poor would get: there must be superfluous meat; it must be given to the poor, or thrown out.' BOSWELL. 'I observe in London, that the poor go about and gather bones, which I understand are manufactured.' JOHNSON. 'Yes, Sir; they boil them, and extract a grease from them for greasing wheels and other purposes. Of the best pieces they make a mock ivory, which is used for hafts to knives, and various other things; the coarser pieces they burn and pound, and sell the ashes.' BOSWELL. 'For what purpose, Sir?' JOHNSON. 'Why, Sir, for making a furnace for the chymists for melting iron. A paste made of burnt bones will stand a stronger heat than any thing else. Consider, Sir; if

[1] 'The unknown always passes for something great.' Tacitus, *Agricola,* ch. xxx.

you are to melt iron, you cannot line your pot with brass, because it is softer than iron, and would melt sooner; nor with iron, for though malleable iron is harder than cast iron, yet it would not do; but a paste of burnt-bones will not melt.' Boswell. 'Do you know, Sir, I have discovered a manufacture to a great extent, of what you only piddle at,—scraping and drying the peel of oranges. At a place in Newgate-street, there is a prodigious quantity prepared, which they sell to the distillers.' Johnson. 'Sir, I believe they make a higher thing out of them than a spirit; they make what is called orange-butter, the oil of the orange inspissated, which they mix perhaps with common pomatum, and make it fragrant. The oil does not fly off in the drying.'

Boswell. 'I wish to have a good walled garden.' Johnson. 'I don't think it would be worth the expence to you. We compute in England, a park wall at a thousand pounds a mile; now a garden-wall must cost at least as much. You intend your trees should grow higher than a deer will leap. Now let us see; for a hundred pounds you could only have forty-four square yards, which is very little; for two hundred pounds, you may have eighty-four square yards, which is very well. But when will you get the value of two hundred pounds of walls, in fruit, in your climate? No, Sir, such contention with Nature is not worth while. I would plant an orchard, and have plenty of such fruit as ripen well in your country. My friend, Dr. Madden, of Ireland, said, that "in an orchard there should be enough to eat, enough to lay up, enough to be stolen, and enough to rot upon the ground." Cherries are an early fruit, you may have them; and you may have the early apples and pears.' Boswell. 'We cannot have nonpareils.' Johnson. 'Sir, you can no more have nonpareils than you can have grapes.' Boswell. 'We have them, Sir; but they are very bad.' Johnson. 'Nay, Sir, never try to have a thing merely to shew that you *cannot* have it. From ground that would let for forty shillings you may have a large orchard; and you see it costs you only forty shillings. Nay, you may graze the ground when the trees are grown up; you cannot while they are young.' Boswell. 'Is not a good garden a very common thing in England, Sir?' Johnson. 'Not so common, Sir, as you imagine. In Lincolnshire there is hardly an orchard; in Staffordshire very little fruit.' Boswell. 'Has Langton no orchard?' Johnson. 'No, Sir.' Boswell. 'How so, Sir?' Johnson. 'Why, Sir, from the general negligence of the county. He has it not, because nobody else has it.' Boswell. 'A hot-house is a certain thing; I may have that.' Johnson. 'A hot-house is pretty certain; but you must first build it, then you must keep fires in it, and you must have a gardener to take care of it.' BOSWELL. 'But if I have a gardener at any rate?—' JOHNSON. 'Why, yes.' BOSWELL. 'I'd have it near my house; there is no need to have it in the orchard.' JOHNSON. 'Yes, I'd have it near my house. I would plant a great many currants; the fruit is good, and they make a pretty sweetmeat.'

I record this minute detail, which some may think trifling, in order to shew clearly how this great man, whose mind could grasp such large and extensive subjects, as he has shewn in his literary labours, was yet well-informed in the common affairs of life, and loved to illustrate them.

Mr. Walker, the celebrated master of elocution, came in, and then we went up stairs into the study. I asked him if he had taught many clergymen. JOHNSON. 'I hope not.' WALKER. 'I have taught only one, and he is the best reader I ever heard, not by my teaching, but by his own natural talents.' JOHNSON. 'Were he the best reader in the world, I would not have it told that he was taught.' Here was one of his peculiar prejudices. Could it be any disadvantage to the clergyman to have it known that he was taught an easy and graceful delivery? BOSWELL. 'Will you not allow, Sir, that a man may be taught to read well?' JOHNSON. 'Why, Sir, so far as to read better than he might do without being taught, yes. Formerly it was supposed that there was no difference in reading, but that one read as well as another.' BOSWELL. 'It is wonderful to see old Sheridan as enthusiastick about oratory as ever.' WALKER. 'His enthusiasm as to what oratory will do, may be too great: but he reads well.' JOHNSON. 'He reads well, but he reads low; and you know it is much easier to read low than to read high: for when you read high, you are much more limited, your loudest note can be but one, and so the variety is less in proportion to the loudness. Now some people have occasion to speak to an extensive audience, and must speak loud to be heard.' WALKER. 'The art is to read strong, though low.'

Talking of the origin of language; JOHNSON. 'It must have come by inspiration. A thousand, nay, a million of children could not invent a language. While the organs are pliable, there is not understanding enough to form a language; by the time that there is understanding enough, the organs are become stiff. We know that after a certain age we cannot learn to pronounce a new language. No foreigner, who comes to England when advanced in life, ever pronounces English tolerably well; at least such instances are very rare. When I maintain that language must have come by inspiration, I do not mean that inspiration is required for rhetorick, and all the beauties of language; for when once man has language, we can conceive that he may gradually form modifications of it. I mean only, that inspiration seems to me to be necessary to give man the faculty of speech; to inform him that he may have speech; which I think he could no more find out without inspiration, than cows or hogs would think of such a faculty.' WALKER. 'Do you think, Sir, that there are any perfect synonimes in any language?' JOHNSON. 'Originally there were not; but by using words negligently, or in poetry, one word comes to be confounded with another.'

He talked of Dr. Dodd. 'A friend of mine, (said he,) came to me and told me, that a lady wished to have Dr. Dodd's picture in a bracelet, and asked me for a motto. I said, I could think of no better than *Currat Lex*.[1] I was very willing to have him pardoned, that is, to have the sentence changed to transportation: but, when he was once hanged, I did not wish he should be made a saint.'

Mrs. Burney, wife of his friend Dr. Burney, came in, and he seemed to be entertained with her conversation.

Garrick's funeral was talked of as extravagantly expensive. Johnson, from his dislike to exaggeration, would not allow that it was distinguished by any extraordinary pomp. 'Were there not six horses to each coach?' said Mrs. Burney. JOHNSON. 'Madam, there were no more six horses than six phœnixes.'

Mrs. Burney wondered that some very beautiful new buildings should be erected in Moorfields, in so shocking a situation as between Bedlam and St. Luke's Hospital; and said she could not live there. JOHNSON. 'Nay, Madam, you see nothing there to hurt you. You no more think of madness by having windows that look to Bedlam, than you think of death by having windows that look to a church-yard.' MRS. BURNEY. 'We may look to a church-yard, Sir; for it is right that we should be kept in mind of death.' JOHNSON. 'Nay, Madam, if you go to that, it is right that we should be kept in mind of madness, which is occasioned by too much indulgence of imagination. I think a very moral use may be made of these new buildings: I would have those who have heated imaginations live there, and take warning.' MRS. BURNEY. 'But, Sir, many of the poor people that are mad, have become so from disease, or from distressing events. It is, therefore, not their fault, but their misfortune; and, therefore, to think of them is a melancholy consideration.'

Time passed on in conversation till it was too late for the service of the church at three o'clock. I took a walk, and left

---

[1] 'Let the law take its course.'

him alone for some time; then returned, and we had coffee and conversation again by ourselves.

I stated the character of a noble friend[1] of mine, as a curious case for his opinion:—'He is the most inexplicable man to me that I ever knew. Can you explain him, Sir? He is, I really believe, noble-minded, generous, and princely. But his most intimate friends may be separated from him for years, without his ever asking a question concerning them. He will meet them with a formality, a coldness, a stately indifference; but when they come close to him, and fairly engage him in conversation, they find him as easy, pleasant, and kind, as they could wish. One then supposes that what is so agreeable will soon be renewed; but stay away from him for half a year, and he will neither call on you, nor send to inquire about you.' JOHNSON. 'Why, Sir, I cannot ascertain his character exactly, as I do not know him; but I should not like to have such a man for my friend. He may love study, and wish not to be interrupted by his friends; *Amici fures temporis*.[2] He may be a frivolous man, and be so much occupied with petty pursuits, that he may not want friends. Or he may have a notion that there is a dignity in appearing indifferent, while he in fact may not be more indifferent at his heart than another.'

We went to evening prayers at St. Clement's, at seven, and then parted.

On Sunday, April 20, being Easter-day, after attending solemn service at St. Paul's, I came to Dr. Johnson, and found Mr. Lowe, the painter, sitting with him. Mr. Lowe mentioned the great number of new buildings of late in London, yet that Dr. Johnson had observed, that the number of inhabitants was not increased. JOHNSON. 'Why, Sir, the bills of mortality prove that no more people die now than formerly; so it is plain no more live. The register of births proves nothing, for not one tenth of the people of London are born there.' BOSWELL. 'I believe, Sir, a great many of the children born in London die early.' JOHNSON. 'Why, yes, Sir.' BOSWELL. 'But those who do live, are as stout and strong people as any: Dr. Price says, they must be naturally stronger to get through.' JOHNSON. 'That is system, Sir. A great traveller observes, that it is said there are no weak or deformed people among the Indians; but he with much sagacity assigns the reason of this, which is, that the hardship of their life as hunters and fishers does not allow weak or diseased children to grow up. Now had I been an Indian, I must have died early; my eyes would

[1] Lord Mountstuart.

[2] 'Friends are the thieves of time.' Bacon, *Advancement of Learning*, bk. ii.

not have served me to get food. I indeed now could fish, give me English tackle; but had I been an Indian I must have starved, or they would have knocked me on the head, when they saw I could do nothing.' BOSWELL. 'Perhaps they would have taken care of you: we are told they are fond of oratory, you would have talked to them.' JOHNSON. 'Nay, Sir, I should not have lived long enough to be fit to talk; I should have been dead before I was ten years old. Depend upon it, Sir, a savage, when he is hungry, will not carry about with him a looby of nine years old, who cannot help himself. They have no affection, Sir.' BOSWELL. 'I believe natural affection, of which we hear so much, is very small.' JOHNSON. 'Sir, natural affection is nothing: but affection from principle and established duty is sometimes wonderfully strong.' LOWE. 'A hen, Sir, will feed her chickens in preference to herself.' JOHNSON. 'But we don't know that the hen is hungry; let the hen be fairly hungry, and I'll warrant she'll peck the corn herself. A cock, I believe, will feed hens instead of himself; but we don't know that the cock is hungry.' BOSWELL. 'And that, Sir, is not from affection but gallantry. But some of the Indians have affection.' JOHNSON. 'Sir, that they help some of their children is plain; for some of them live, which they could not do without being helped.'

I dined with him; the company were, Mrs. Williams, Mrs. Desmoulins, and Mr. Lowe. He seemed not to be well, talked little, grew drowsy soon after dinner, and retired, upon which I went away.

Having next day gone to Mr. Burke's seat in the country, from whence I was recalled by an express, that a near relation of mine had killed his antagonist in a duel, and was himself dangerously wounded, I saw little of Dr. Johnson till Monday, April 28, when I spent a considerable part of the day with him, and introduced the subject, which then chiefly occupied my mind. JOHNSON. 'I do not see, Sir, that fighting is absolutely forbidden in Scripture; I see revenge forbidden, but not self-defence.' BOSWELL. 'The Quakers say it is; "Unto him that smiteth thee on one cheek, offer also the other."' JOHNSON. 'But stay, Sir; the text is meant only to have the effect of moderating passion; it is plain that we are not to take it in a literal sense. We see this from the context, where there are other recommendations, which I warrant you the Quaker will not take literally; as, for instance, "From him that would borrow of thee, turn thou not away." Let a man whose credit is bad, come to a Quaker, and say, "Well, Sir, lend me a hundred pounds;" he'll find him as unwilling as any other man. No, Sir, a man may shoot the man who invades his character, as he may shoot him who attempts to break into his house. So in 1745, my friend, Tom Cumming, the Quaker, said, he would not fight, but he would drive an ammunition cart; and we know that the Quakers have sent flannel waistcoats to our soldiers, to enable them to fight better.' BOSWELL. 'When a man is the aggressor, and by ill-usage forces on a duel in which he is killed, have we not little ground to hope that he is gone into a state of happiness?' JOHNSON. 'Sir, we are not to judge determinately of the state in which a man leaves this life. He may in a moment have repented effectually, and it is possible may have been accepted by GOD. There is in *Camden's Remains,* an epitaph upon a very wicked man, who was killed by a fall from his horse, in which he is supposed to say,

> "Between the stirrup and the ground,
>   I mercy ask'd, I mercy found." '

BOSWELL. 'Is not the expression in the Burial-service, "in the *sure* and *certain* hope of a blessed resurrection," too strong to be used indiscriminately, and, indeed, sometimes when those over whose bodies it is said, have been notoriously profane?' JOHNSON. 'It is sure and certain *hope,* Sir; not *belief.*' I did not insist further; but cannot help thinking that less positive words would be more proper.

Talking of a man who was grown very fat, so as to be incommoded with corpulency; he said, 'He eats too much, Sir.' BOSWELL. 'I don't know, Sir; you will see one man fat who eats moderately, and another lean who eats a great deal.' JOHNSON. 'Nay, Sir, whatever may be the quantity that a man eats, it is plain that if he is too fat, he has eaten more than he should have done. One man may have a digestion that consumes food better than common; but it is certain that solidity is encreased by putting something to it.' BOSWELL. 'But may not solids swell and be distended?' JOHNSON. 'Yes, Sir, they may swell and be distended; but that is not fat.'

We talked of the accusation against a gentleman for supposed delinquencies in India. JOHNSON. 'What foundation there is for accusation I know not, but they will not get at him. Where bad actions are committed at so great a distance, a delinquent can obscure the evidence till the scent becomes cold; there is a cloud between, which cannot be penetrated: therefore all distant power is bad. I am clear that the best plan for the government of India is a despotick governour; for if he be a good man, it is evidently the best government; and supposing him to be a bad man, it is better to have one plunderer than many. A governour whose power is checked, lets others plunder, that he himself may be allowed to plunder; but if despotick, he sees that the more he lets others plunder, the less there will be for himself, so he restrains them; and though he himself plunders, the country is a gainer, compared with being plundered by numbers.'

I mentioned the very liberal payment which had been received for reviewing; and, as evidence of this, that it had been proved in a trial, that Dr. Shebbeare had received six guineas a sheet for that kind of literary labour. JOHNSON. 'Sir, he might get six guineas for a particular sheet, but not *communibus sheetibus*.'[1] BOSWELL. 'Pray, Sir, by a sheet of review is it meant that it shall be all of the writer's own composition, or are extracts, made from the book reviewed, deducted?' JOHNSON. 'No, Sir; it is a sheet, no matter of what.' BOSWELL. 'I think that it is not reasonable.' JOHNSON. 'Yes, Sir, it is. A man will more easily write a sheet all his own, than read an octavo volume to get extracts.' To one of Johnson's wonderful fertility of mind I believe writing was really easier than reading and extracting; but with ordinary men the case is very different. . . .

Upon being told that old Mr. Sheridan, indignant at the neglect of his oratorical plans, had threatened to go to America; JOHNSON. 'I hope he will go to America.' BOSWELL. 'The Americans don't want oratory.' JOHNSON. 'But we can want Sheridan.'

On Monday, April 29,[2] I found him at home in the forenoon, and Mr. Seward with him. Horace having been mentioned; BOSWELL. 'There is a great deal of thinking in his works. One finds there almost every thing but religion.' SEWARD. 'He speaks of his returning to it, in his Ode *Parcus Deorum cultor et infrequens*.'[3] JOHNSON. 'Sir, he was not in earnest: this was merely poetical.' BOSWELL. 'There are, I am afraid, many people who have no religion at all.' SEWARD. 'And sensible people too.' JOHNSON. 'Why, Sir, not sensible in that respect. There must be either a natural or a moral stupidity, if one lives in a total neglect of so very important a concern.' SEWARD. 'I wonder that there should be people without religion.' JOHNSON. 'Sir, you need not wonder at this, when you consider how large a proportion of almost every man's life is passed without thinking of it. I myself was for some years totally regardless of religion. It had dropped out of my mind. It was at an early part of my life. Sickness brought it back, and I hope I have never lost it since.' BOSWELL. 'My dear Sir, what a man must you have been without religion! Why you must have gone on drinking, and swearing, and—' JOHNSON. (with a

[1] 'For average sheets.'
[2] Actually, Wednesday, April 30.
[3] 'A grudging and infrequent worshipper of the gods.' *Odes*, I. xxxiv. 1.

smile,) 'I drank enough and swore enough, to be sure.' SEW-ARD. 'One should think that sickness, and the view of death, would make more men religious.' JOHNSON. 'Sir, they do not know how to go about it: they have not the first notion. A man who has never had religion before, no more grows religious when he is sick, than a man who has never learnt figures can count when he has need of calculation.'

I mentioned a worthy friend[1] of ours whom we valued much, but observed that he was too ready to introduce religious discourse upon all occasions. JOHNSON. 'Why, yes, Sir, he will introduce religious discourse without seeing whether it will end in instruction and improvement, or produce some profane jest. He would introduce it in the company of Wilkes, and twenty more such.'

I mentioned Dr. Johnson's excellent distinction between liberty of conscience and liberty of teaching. JOHNSON. 'Consider, Sir; if you have children whom you wish to educate in the principles of the Church of England, and there comes a Quaker who tries to pervert them to his principles, you would drive away the Quaker. You would not trust to the predomination of right, which you believe is in your opinions; you would keep wrong out of their heads. Now the vulgar are the children of the State. If any one attempts to teach them doctrines contrary to what the State approves, the magistrate may and ought to restrain him.' SEWARD. 'Would you restrain private conversation, Sir?' JOHNSON. 'Why, Sir, it is difficult to say where private conversation begins, and where it ends. If we three should discuss even the great question concerning the existence of a Supreme Being by ourselves, we should not be restrained; for that would be to put an end to all improvement. But if we should discuss it in the presence of ten boarding-school girls, and as many boys, I think the magistrate would do well to put us in the stocks, to finish the debate there.'

Lord Hailes had sent him a present of a curious little printed poem, on repairing the University of Aberdeen, by David *Malloch*, which he thought would please Johnson, as affording clear evidence that Mallet had appeared even as a literary character by the name of *Malloch;* his changing which to one of softer sound, had given Johnson occasion to introduce him into his *Dictionary,* under the article *Alias*. This piece was, I suppose, one of Mallet's first essays. It is preserved in his works, with several variations. Johnson having read aloud, from the beginning of it, where there were some commonplace assertions as to the superiority of ancient times;—'How

[1] Langton.

false (said he,) is all this, to say that in ancient times learning was not a disgrace to a Peer as it is now. In ancient times a Peer was as ignorant as any one else. He would have been angry to have it thought he could write his name. Men in ancient times dared to stand forth with a degree of ignorance with which nobody would dare now to stand forth. I am always angry when I hear ancient times praised at the expence of modern times. There is now a great deal more learning in the world than there was formerly; for it is universally diffused. You have, perhaps, no man who knows as much Greek and Latin as Bentley; no man who knows as much mathematicks as Newton: but you have many more men who know Greek and Latin, and who know mathematicks.'

On Thursday, May 1, I visited him in the evening along with young Mr. Burke. He said, 'It is strange that there should be so little reading in the world, and so much writing. People in general do not willingly read, if they can have any thing else to amuse them. There must be an external impulse; emulation, or vanity, or avarice. The progress which the understanding makes through a book, has more pain than pleasure in it. Language is scanty, and inadequate to express the nice gradations and mixtures of our feelings. No man reads a book of science from pure inclination. The books that we do read with pleasure are light compositions, which contain a quick succession of events. However, I have this year read all Virgil through. I read a book of the *Æneid* every night, so it was done in twelve nights, and I had great delight in it. The *Georgicks* did not give me so much pleasure, except the fourth book. The *Eclogues* I have almost all by heart. I do not think the story of the *Æneid* interesting. I like the story of the *Odyssey* much better; and this not on account of the wonderful things which it contains; for there are wonderful things enough in the *Æneid*;—the ships of the Trojans turned to sea-nymphs,—the tree at Polydorus's tomb dropping blood. The story of the *Odyssey* is interesting, as a great part of it is domestick. It has been said, there is pleasure in writing, particularly in writing verses. I allow you may have pleasure from writing, after it is over, if you have written well; but you don't go willingly to it again. I know when I have been writing verses, I have run my finger down the margin, to see how many I had made, and how few I had to make.'

He seemed to be in a very placid humour, and although I have no note of the particulars of young Mr. Burke's conversation, it is but justice to mention in general, that it was such that Dr. Johnson said to me afterwards, 'He did very well indeed; I have a mind to tell his father.' . . .

598

I have no minute of any interview with Johnson till Thursday, May 15, when I find what follows:—BOSWELL. 'I wish much to be in Parliament, Sir.' JOHNSON. 'Why, Sir, unless you come resolved to support any administration, you would be the worse for being in Parliament, because you would be obliged to live more expensively.' BOSWELL. 'Perhaps, Sir, I should be the less happy for being in Parliament. I never would sell my vote, and I should be vexed if things went wrong.' JOHNSON. 'That's cant, Sir. It would not vex you more in the house, than in the gallery: publick affairs vex no man.' BOSWELL. 'Have not they vexed yourself a little, Sir? Have not you been vexed by all the turbulence of this reign, and by that absurd vote of the House of Commons, "That the influence of the Crown has increased, is increasing, and ought to be diminished?"' JOHNSON. 'Sir, I have never slept an hour less, nor eat an ounce less meat. I would have knocked the factious dogs on the head, to be sure; but I was not *vexed*.' BOSWELL. 'I declare, Sir, upon my honour, I did imagine I was vexed, and took a pride in it; but it *was*, perhaps, cant; for I own I neither ate less, nor slept less.' JOHNSON. 'My dear friend, clear your *mind* of cant. You may *talk* as other people do: you may say to a man, "Sir, I am your most humble servant." You are *not* his most humble servant. You may say, "These are sad times; it is a melancholy thing to be reserved to such times." You don't mind the times. You tell a man, "I am sorry you had such bad weather the last day of your journey, and were so much wet." You don't care six-pence whether he was wet or dry. You may *talk* in this manner; it is a mode of talking in Society: but don't *think* foolishly.'

I talked of living in the country. JOHNSON. 'Don't set up for what is called hospitality; it is a waste of time, and a waste of money; you are eaten up, and not the more respected for your liberality. If your house be like an inn, nobody cares for you. A man who stays a week with another, makes him a slave for a week.' BOSWELL. 'But there are people, Sir, who make their houses a home to their guests, and are themselves quite easy.' JOHNSON. 'Then, Sir, home must be the same to the guests, and they need not come.'

Here he discovered a notion common enough in persons not much accustomed to entertain company; that there must be a degree of elaborate attention, otherwise company will think themselves neglected; and such attention is no doubt very fatiguing. He proceeded: 'I would not, however, be a stranger in my own county; I would visit my neighbours, and receive their visits; but I would not be in haste to return visits. If a gentleman comes to see me, I tell him he does me a great deal of honour. I do not go to see him perhaps for ten weeks; then we are very complaisant to each other. No, Sir, you will have much more influence by giving or lending money where it is wanted, than by hospitality.'

On Saturday, May 17, I saw him for a short time. Having mentioned that I had that morning been with old Mr. Sheridan, he remembered their former intimacy with a cordial warmth, and said to me, 'Tell Mr. Sheridan, I shall be glad to see him, and shake hands with him.' BOSWELL. 'It is to me very wonderful that resentment should be kept up so long.' JOHNSON. 'Why, Sir, it is not altogether resentment that he does not visit me; it is partly falling out of the habit, —partly disgust, as one has at a drug that has made him sick. Besides, he knows that I laugh at his oratory.'

Another day I spoke of one of our friends,[1] of whom he, as well as I, had a very high opinion. He expatiated in his praise; but added, 'Sir, he is a cursed Whig, a *bottomless* Whig, as they all are now.'

I mentioned my expectations from the interest of an eminent person then in power; adding, 'but I have no claim but the claim of friendship; however, some people will go a great way from that motive.' JOHNSON. 'Sir, they will go all the way from that motive.' A gentleman talked of retiring. 'Never think of that,' said Johnson. The gentleman urged, 'I should then do no ill.' JOHNSON. 'Nor no good either, Sir, it would be a civil suicide.'

On Monday, May 26, I found him at tea, and the celebrated Miss Burney, the authour of *Evelina* and *Cecilia,* with him. I asked if there would be any speakers in Parliament, if there were no places to be obtained. JOHNSON. 'Yes, Sir. Why do you speak here? Either to instruct and entertain, which is a benevolent motive; or for distinction, which is a selfish motive.' I mentioned *Cecilia.* JOHNSON. (with an air of animated satisfaction,) 'Sir, if you talk of *Cecilia,* talk on.'

We talked of Mr. Barry's exhibition of his pictures. JOHNSON. 'Whatever the hand may have done, the mind has done its part. There is a grasp of mind there which you find nowhere else.'

I asked whether a man naturally virtuous, or one who has overcome wicked inclinations, is the best. JOHNSON. 'Sir, to *you,* the man who has overcome wicked inclinations is not the best. He has more merit to *himself.* I would rather trust my money to a man who has no hands, and so a physical impossibility to steal, than to a man of the most honest principles. There is a witty satirical story of Foote. He had a

<hr>

[1] Burke.

small bust of Garrick placed upon his bureau. "You may be surprized (said he,) that I allow him to be so near my gold; —but you will observe he has no hands." '

On Friday,[1] May 29, being to set out for Scotland next morning, I passed a part of the day with him in more than usual earnestness; as his health was in a more precarious state than at any time when I had parted from him. He, however, was quick and lively, and critical as usual. I mentioned one who was a very learned man.[2] JOHNSON. 'Yes, Sir, he has a great deal of learning; but it never lies straight. There is never one idea by the side of another; 'tis all entangled: and then he drives it so aukwardly upon conversation.'

I stated to him an anxious thought, by which a sincere Christian might be disturbed, even when conscious of having lived a good life, so far as is consistent with human infirmity; he might fear that he should afterwards fall away, and be guilty of such crimes as would render all his former religion vain. Could there be, upon this aweful subject, such a thing as balancing of accounts? Suppose a man who has led a good life for seven years, commits an act of wickedness, and instantly dies; will his former good life have any effect in his favour? JOHNSON. 'Sir, if a man has led a good life for seven years, and then is hurried by passion to do what is wrong, and is suddenly carried off, depend upon it he will have the reward of his seven years' good life; GOD will not take a catch of him. Upon this principle Richard Baxter believes that a Suicide may be saved. "If, (says he,) it should be objected that what I maintain may encourage suicide, I answer, I am not to tell a lie to prevent it."' BOSWELL. 'But does not the text say, "As the tree falls, so it must lie?"' JOHNSON. 'Yes, Sir; as the tree falls: but,—(after a little pause)—that is meant as to the general state of the tree, not what is the effect of a sudden blast.' In short, he interpreted the expression as referring to condition, not to position. The common notion, therefore, seems to be erroneous; and Shenstone's witty remark on Divines trying to give the tree a jerk upon a death-bed, to make it lie favourably, is not well founded. . . .

He said, 'Get as much force of mind as you can. Live within your income. Always have something saved at the end of the year. Let your imports be more than your exports, and you'll never go far wrong.'

I assured him, that in the extensive and various range of his acquaintance there never had been any one who had a

[1] Actually Thursday.
[2] Langton.

more sincere respect and affection for him than I had. He said, 'I believe it, Sir. Were I in distress, there is no man to whom I should sooner come than to you. I should like to come and have a cottage in your park, toddle about, live mostly on milk, and be taken care of by Mrs. Boswell. She and I are good friends now; are we not?'

Talking of devotion, he said, 'Though it be true that "GOD dwelleth not in temples made with hands," yet in this state of being, our minds are more piously affected in places appropriated to divine worship, than in others. Some people have a particular room in their house, where they say their prayers; of which I do not disapprove, as it may animate their devotion.'

He embraced me, and gave me his blessing, as usual when I was leaving him for any length of time. I walked from his door to-day, with a fearful apprehension of what might happen before I returned. . . .

My anxious apprehensions at parting with him this year proved to be but too well founded; for not long afterwards he had a dreadful stroke of the palsy, of which there are very full and accurate accounts in letters written by himself, which shew with what composure of mind, and resignation to the Divine Will, his steady piety enabled him to behave.

'To MR. EDMUND ALLEN

'DEAR SIR,—It has pleased GOD, this morning, to deprive me of the powers of speech; and as I do not know but that it may be his further good pleasure to deprive me soon of my senses, I request you will on the receipt of this note, come to me, and act for me, as the exigencies of my case may require. I am, sincerely yours,

'June 17, 1783.'   'SAM. JOHNSON.'

. . . Two days after he wrote thus to Mrs. Thrale:—

'On Monday, the 16th, I sat for my picture, and walked a considerable way with little inconvenience. In the afternoon and evening I felt myself light and easy, and began to plan schemes of life. Thus I went to bed, and in a short time waked and sat up, as has been long my custom, when I felt a confusion and indistinctness in my head, which lasted, I suppose, about half a minute. I was alarmed, and prayed God, that however he might afflict my body, he would spare my understanding. This prayer, that I might try the integrity of my faculties, I made in Latin verse. The lines were not very good, but I knew them not to be very good: I made them easily, and concluded myself to be unimpaired in my faculties.

'Soon after I perceived that I had suffered a paralytick stroke, and that my speech was taken from me. I had no pain, and so little dejection in this dreadful state, that I wondered at my own apathy, and considered that perhaps death itself, when it should come, would excite less horrour than seems now to attend it.

'In order to rouse the vocal organs, I took two drams. Wine has been celebrated for the production of eloquence. I put myself into violent motion, and I think repeated it; but all was vain. I then went to bed, and, strange as it may seem, I think, slept. When I saw light, it was time to contrive what I should do. Though God stopped my speech, he left me my hand; I enjoyed a mercy which was not granted to my dear friend Lawrence, who now perhaps overlooks me as I am writing, and rejoices that I have what he wanted. My first note was necessarily to my servant, who came in talking, and could not immediately comprehend why he should read what I put into his hands.

'I then wrote a card to Mr. Allen, that I might have a discreet friend at hand, to act as occasion should require. In penning this note, I had some difficulty; my hand, I knew not how nor why, made wrong letters. I then wrote to Dr. Taylor to come to me, and bring Dr. Heberden; and I sent to Dr. Brocklesby, who is my neighbour. My physicians are very friendly, and give me great hopes; but you may imagine my situation. I have so far recovered my vocal powers, as to repeat the Lord's Prayer with no very imperfect articulation. My memory, I hope, yet remains as it was; but such an attack produces solicitude for the safety of every faculty.' . . .

Such was the general vigour of his constitution, that he recovered from this alarming and severe attack with wonderful quickness; so that in July he was able to make a visit to Mr. Langton at Rochester, where he passed about a fortnight, and made little excursions as easily as at any time of his life. In August he went as far as the neighbourhood of Salisbury, to Heale, the seat of William Bowles, Esq., a gentleman whom I have heard him praise for exemplary religious order in his family. In his diary I find a short but honourable mention of this visit:—'August 28, I came to Heale without fatigue. 30, I am entertained quite to my mind.' . . .

While he was here he had a letter from Dr. Brocklesby, acquainting him of the death of Mrs. Williams, which affected him a good deal. Though for several years her temper had not been complacent, she had valuable qualities, and her departure left a blank in his house. Upon this occasion he, according to his habitual course of piety, composed a prayer.

I shall here insert a few particulars concerning him, with which I have been favoured by one of his friends.[1]

'He had once conceived the design of writing the Life of Oliver Cromwell, saying, that he thought it must be highly curious to trace his extraordinary rise to the supreme power, from so obscure a beginning. He at length laid aside his scheme, on discovering that all that can be told of him is already in print; and that it is impracticable to procure any authentick information in addition to what the world is already possessed of.

'He had likewise projected, but at what part of his life is not known, a work to shew how small a quantity of REAL FICTION there is in the world; and that the same images, with very little variation, have served all the authours who have ever written.'

'His thoughts in the latter part of his life were frequently employed on his deceased friends. He often muttered these, or such like sentences: "Poor man! and then he died." '

'Speaking of a certain literary friend, "He is a very pompous puzzling fellow, (said he;) he lent me a letter once that somebody had written to him, no matter what it was about; but he wanted to have the letter back, and expressed a mighty value for it; he hoped it was to be met with again, he would not lose it for a thousand pounds. I layed my hand upon it soon afterwards, and gave it him. I believe I said, I was very glad to have met with it. O, then he did not know that it signified any thing. So you see, when the letter was lost it was worth a thousand pounds, and when it was found it was not worth a farthing." '

'The style and character of his conversation is pretty generally known; it was certainly conducted in conformity with a precept of Lord Bacon, but it is not clear, I apprehend, that this conformity was either perceived or intended by Johnson. The precept alluded to is as follows: "In all kinds of speech, either pleasant, grave, severe, or ordinary, it is convenient to speak leisurely, and rather drawingly than hastily: because hasty speech confounds the memory, and oftentimes, besides the unseemliness, drives the man either to stammering, a non-plus, or harping on that which should follow; whereas a slow speech confirmeth the memory, addeth a conceit of wisdom to the hearers, besides a seemliness of speech and countenance." Dr. Johnson's method of conversation was certainly calculated to excite attention, and to amuse or instruct, (as it happened,) without wearying or confusing his company. He was always most perfectly clear and perspicuous;

[1] William Bowles.

and his language was so accurate, and his sentences so neatly constructed, that his conversation might have been all printed without any correction. At the same time, it was easy and natural; the accuracy of it had no appearance of labour, constraint, or stiffness; he seemed more correct than others, by the force of habit, and the customary exercises of his powerful mind.'

'He spoke often in praise of French literature. "The French are excellent in this, (he would say,) they have a book on every subject." From what he had seen of them he denied them the praise of superiour politeness, and mentioned, with very visible disgust, the custom they have of spitting on the floors of their apartments. "This, (said the Doctor,) is as gross a thing as can well be done; and one wonders how any man, or set of men, can persist in so offensive a practice for a whole day together; one should expect that the first effort toward civilization would remove it even amongst savages." '

'Baxter's *Reasons of the Christian Religion,* he thought contained the best collection of the evidence of the divinity of the Christian system.'

'Chymistry was always an interesting pursuit with Dr. Johnson. Whilst he was in Wiltshire, he attended some experiments that were made by a physician at Salisbury, on the new kinds of air. In the course of the experiments frequent mention being made of Dr. Priestley, Dr. Johnson knit his brows, and in a stern manner inquired, "Why do we hear so much of Dr. Priestley?" He was very properly answered, "Sir, because we are indebted to him for these important discoveries." On this, Dr. Johnson appeared well content; and replied, "Well, well, I believe we are; and let every man have the honour he has merited." '

'A friend was one day, about two years before his death, struck with some instance of Dr. Johnson's great candour. "Well, Sir, (said he,) I will always say that you are a very candid man." "Will you, (replied the Doctor,) I doubt then you will be very singular. But, indeed, Sir, (continued he,) I look upon myself to be a man very much misunderstood. I am not an uncandid, nor am I a severe man. I sometimes say more than I mean, in jest; and people are apt to believe me serious: however, I am more candid than I was when I was younger. As I know more of mankind I expect less of them, and am ready now to call a man *a good man,* upon easier terms than I was formerly." ' . . .

His fortitude and patience met with severe trials during this year. The stroke of the palsy has been related circumstantially; but he was also afflicted with the gout, and was besides troubled with a complaint which not only was attended with immediate inconvenience, but threatened him with a painful chirurgical operation, from which most men would shrink. The complaint was a *sarcocele,* which Johnson bore with uncommon firmness, and was not at all frightened while he looked forward to amputation. He was attended by Mr. Pott and Mr. Cruikshank. I have before me a letter of the 30th of July this year, to Mr. Cruikshank, in which he says, 'I am going to put myself into your hands;' and another, accompanying a set of his *Lives of the Poets,* in which he says, 'I beg your acceptance of these volumes, as an acknowledgement of the great favours which you have bestowed on, Sir, your most obliged and most humble servant.' . . .

Happily the complaint abated without his being put to the torture of amputation. But we must surely admire the manly resolution which he discovered while it hung over him. . . .

He this autumn received a visit from the celebrated Mrs. Siddons. He gives this account of it in one of his letters to Mrs. Thrale:—

'Mrs. Siddons, in her visit to me, behaved with great modesty and propriety, and left nothing behind her to be censured or despised. Neither praise nor money, the two powerful corrupters of mankind, seem to have depraved her. I shall be glad to see her again. Her brother Kemble calls on me, and pleases me very well. Mrs. Siddons and I talked of plays; and she told me her intention of exhibiting this winter the characters of Constance, Catharine, and Isabella, in Shakspeare.'

Mr. Kemble has favoured me with the following minute of what passed at this visit:—

'When Mrs. Siddons came into the room, there happened to be no chair ready for her, which he observing, said with a smile, "Madam, you who so often occasion a want of seats to other people, will the more easily excuse the want of one yourself."

'Having placed himself by her, he with great good-humour entered upon a consideration of the English drama; and, among other inquiries, particularly asked her which of Shakspeare's characters she was most pleased with. Upon her answering that she thought the character of Queen Catharine, in *Henry the Eighth,* the most natural:—"I think so too, Madam, (said he;) and whenever you perform it, I will once more hobble out to the theatre myself." Mrs. Siddons promised she would do herself the honour of acting his favourite part for him; but many circumstances happened to prevent the representation of *King Henry the Eighth* during the Doctor's life.

'In the course of the evening he thus gave his opinion upon

606

the merits of some of the principal performers whom he remembered to have seen upon the stage. "Mrs. Porter in the vehemence of rage, and Mrs. Clive in the sprightliness of humour, I have never seen equalled. What Clive did best, she did better than Garrick; but could not do half so many things well; she was a better romp than any I ever saw in nature. Pritchard, in common life, was a vulgar ideot; she would talk of her *gownd:* but, when she appeared upon the stage, seemed to be inspired by gentility and understanding. I once talked with Colley Cibber, and thought him ignorant of the principles of his art. Garrick, Madam, was no declaimer; there was not one of his own scene-shifters who could not have spoken *To be, or not to be,* better than he did; yet he was the only actor I ever saw whom I could call a master both in tragedy and comedy; though I liked him best in comedy. A true conception of character, and natural expression of it, were his distinguishing excellencies." Having expatiated, with his usual force and eloquence, on Mr. Garrick's extraordinary eminence as an actor, he concluded with this compliment to his social talents: "And after all, Madam, I thought him less to be envied on the stage than at the head of a table." '

Johnson, indeed, had thought more upon the subject of acting than might be generally supposed. Talking of it one day to Mr. Kemble, he said, 'Are you, Sir, one of those enthusiasts who believe yourself transformed into the very character you represent?' Upon Mr. Kemble's answering that he had never felt so strong a persuasion himself; 'To be sure not, Sir, (said Johnson;) the thing is impossible. And if Garrick really believed himself to be that monster, Richard the Third, he deserved to be hanged every time he performed it.' . . .

Notwithstanding the complication of disorders under which Johnson now laboured, he did not resign himself to despondency and discontent, but with wisdom and spirit endeavoured to console and amuse his mind with as many innocent enjoyments as he could procure. Sir John Hawkins has mentioned the cordiality with which he insisted that such of the members of the old club in Ivy-lane as survived, should meet again and dine together, which they did, twice at a tavern and once at his house: and in order to insure himself society in the evening for three days in the week, he instituted a club at the Essex Head, in Essex-street, then kept by Samuel Greaves, an old servant of Mr. Thrale's.

'To SIR JOSHUA REYNOLDS

'DEAR SIR,—It is inconvenient to me to come out, I should else have waited on you with an account of a little evening

607

Club which we are establishing in Essex-street, in the Strand, and of which you are desired to be one. It will be held at the Essex Head, now kept by an old servant of Thrale's. The company is numerous, and, as you will see by the list, miscellaneous. The terms are lax, and the expences light. Mr. Barry was adopted by Dr. Brocklesby, who joined with me in forming the plan. We meet thrice a week, and he who misses forfeits two-pence.

'If you are willing to become a member, draw a line under your name. Return the list. We meet for the first time on Monday at eight, I am, &c.

'Dec. 4, 1783.'   'SAM. JOHNSON.'

It did not suit Sir Joshua to be one of this Club. But when I mention only Mr. Daines Barrington, Dr. Brocklesby, Mr. Murphy, Mr. John Nichols, Mr. Cooke, Mr. Joddrel, Mr. Paradise, Dr. Horsley, Mr. Windham, I shall sufficiently obviate the misrepresentation of it by Sir John Hawkins, as if it had been a low ale-house association, by which Johnson was degraded. Johnson himself, like his namesake Old Ben, composed the Rules of his Club. . . .

1784: ÆTAT. 75.]—AND now I am arrived at the last year of the life of SAMUEL JOHNSON, a year in which, although passed in severe indisposition, he nevertheless gave many evidences of the continuance of those wondrous powers of mind, which raised him so high in the intellectual world. His conversation and his letters of this year were in no respect inferiour to those of former years. . . .

To Mr. Langton he wrote with that cordiality which was suitable to the long friendship which had subsisted between him and that gentleman.

March 27. 'Since you left me, I have continued in my own opinion, and in Dr. Brocklesby's, to grow better with respect to all my formidable and dangerous distempers: though to a body battered and shaken as mine has lately been, it is to be feared that weak attacks may be sometimes mischievous. I have, indeed, by standing carelessly at an open window, got a very troublesome cough, which it has been necessary to appease by opium, in larger quantities than I like to take, and I have not found it give way so readily as I expected; its obstinacy, however, seems at last disposed to submit to the remedy, and I know not whether I should then have a right to complain of any morbid sensation. My asthma is, I am afraid, constitutional and incurable; but it is only occasional, and unless it be excited by labour or by cold, gives me no molestation, nor does it lay very close siege to life; for Sir John Floyer, whom the physical race consider as authour of one of the best books upon it, panted on to ninety, as was supposed; and why were we content with supposing a fact so interesting, of a man so conspicuous, because he corrupted, at perhaps seventy or eighty, the register, that he might pass for younger than he was? He was not much less than eighty, when to a man of rank who modestly asked him his age, he answered, "Go look;" though he was in general a man of civility and elegance. . . .

What follows is a beautiful specimen of his gentleness and complacency to a young lady his god-child, one of the daughters of his friend Mr. Langton, then I think in her seventh year. He took the trouble to write it in a large round hand, nearly resembling printed characters, that she might have the satisfaction of reading it herself. The original lies before me, but shall be faithfully restored to her; and I dare say will be preserved by her as a jewel as long as she lives.

'To MISS JANE LANGTON, *in Rochester, Kent*

'MY DEAREST MISS JENNY,—I am sorry that your pretty letter has been so long without being answered; but, when I am not pretty well, I do not always write plain enough for young ladies. I am glad, my dear, to see that you write so well, and hope that you mind your pen, your book, and your needle, for they are all necessary. Your books will give you knowledge, and make you respected; and your needle will find you useful employment when you do not care to read. When you are a little older, I hope you will be very diligent in learning arithmetick, and, above all, that through your whole life you will carefully say your prayers, and read your Bible. I am, my dear, your most humble servant,

'May 10, 1784.'   'SAM. JOHNSON.'

On Wednesday, May 5, I arrived in London, and next morning had the pleasure to find Dr. Johnson greatly recovered. I but just saw him; for a coach was waiting to carry him to Islington, to the house of his friend the Reverend Mr. Strahan, where he went sometimes for the benefit of good air, which, notwithstanding his having formerly laughed at the general opinion upon the subject, he now acknowledged was conducive to health.

One morning afterwards, when I found him alone, he communicated to me, with solemn earnestness, a very remarkable circumstance which had happened in the course of his illness, when he was much distressed by the dropsy. He had shut himself up, and employed a day in particular exercises of religion—fasting, humiliation, and prayer. On a sudden he obtained extraordinary relief, for which he looked up to Heaven with grateful devotion. He made no direct inference from this fact; but from his manner of telling it, I could perceive that it appeared to him as something more than an incident in the common course of events. For my own part, I have no difficulty to avow that cast of thinking, which by many modern pretenders to wisdom is called *superstitious*. But here I think even men of dry rationality may believe, that there was an intermediate interposition of Divine Providence, and that 'the fervent prayer of this righteous man' availed.

On Sunday, May 9, I found Colonel Vallancy, the celebrated antiquarian and Engineer of Ireland, with him. On Monday, the 10th, I dined with him at Mr. Paradise's, where was a large company; Mr. Bryant, Mr. Joddrel, Mr. Hawkins Browne, &c. On Thursday, the 13th, I dined with him at Mr. Joddrel's, with another large company; the Bishop of Exeter, Lord Monboddo, Mr. Murphy, &c.

On Saturday, May 15, I dined with him at Dr. Brocklesby's, where were Colonel Vallancy, Mr. Murphy, and that ever-cheerful companion Mr. Devaynes, apothecary to his Majesty. Of these days, and others on which I saw him, I have no memorials, except the general recollection of his being able and animated in conversation, and appearing to relish society as much as the youngest man. I find only these three small particulars:—One, when a person was mentioned, who said, 'I have lived fifty-one years in this world without having had ten minutes of uneasiness;' he exclaimed, 'The man who says so, lies: he attempts to impose on human credulity.' The Bishop of Exeter in vain observed, that men were very different. His Lordship's manner was not impressive, and I learnt afterwards that Johnson did not find out that the person who talked to him was a Prelate; if he had, I doubt not that he would have treated him with more respect; for once talking of George Psalmanazar, whom he reverenced for his piety, he said, 'I should as soon think of contradicting a BISHOP.' One of the company provoked him greatly by doing what he could least of all bear, which was quoting something of his own writing, against what he then maintained. 'What, Sir, (cried the gentleman,) do you say to

> "The busy day, the peaceful night,
> Unfelt, uncounted, glided by?" '—

Johnson finding himself thus presented as giving an instance of a man who had lived without uneasiness, was much offended, for he looked upon such quotation as unfair. His anger burst out in an unjustifiable retort, insinuating that the gentleman's remark was a sally of ebriety; 'Sir, there is one passion I would advise you to command: when you have drunk out that glass, don't drink another.' Here was exemplified what Goldsmith said of him, with the aid of a very witty image from one of Cibber's Comedies: 'There is no arguing with Johnson; for if his pistol misses fire, he knocks you down with the butt end of it.' Another was this: when a gentleman of eminence[1] in the literary world was violently censured for attacking people by anonymous paragraphs in news-papers; he, from the spirit of contradiction as I thought, took up his defence, and said, 'Come, come, this is not so terrible a crime; he means only to vex them a little. I do not say that I should do it; but there is a great difference between him and me; what is fit for Hephæstion is not fit for Alexander.' Another, when I told him that a young and handsome Countess had said to me, 'I should think that to be praised by Dr. Johnson would make one a fool all one's life;' and that I answered, 'Madam, I shall make him a fool to-day, by repeating this to him,' he said, 'I am too old to be made a fool; but if you say I am made a fool, I shall not deny it. I am much pleased with a compliment, especially from a pretty woman.'

On the evening of Saturday, May 15, he was in fine spirits, at our Essex-Head Club. He told us, 'I dined yesterday at Mrs. Garrick's, with Mrs. Carter, Miss Hannah More, and Miss Fanny Burney. Three such women are not to be found: I know not where I could find a fourth, except Mrs. Lennox, who is superiour to them all. BOSWELL. 'What! had you them all to yourself, Sir?' JOHNSON. 'I had them all as much as they were had; but it might have been better had there been more company there.' BOSWELL. 'Might not Mrs. Montagu have been a fourth?' JOHNSON. 'Sir, Mrs. Montagu does not make a trade of her wit; but Mrs. Montagu is a very extraordinary woman; she has a constant stream of conversation, and it is always impregnated; it has always meaning.' BOSWELL. 'Mr. Burke has a constant stream of conversation.' JOHNSON. 'Yes, Sir; if a man were to go by chance at the same time with Burke under a shed, to shun a shower, he would say—"this is an extraordinary man." If Burke should go into a stable to see his horse drest, the ostler would say—"we have had an extraordinary man here." ' BOSWELL. 'Foote was a man who never failed in conversation. If he had gone into a stable—' JOHNSON. 'Sir, if he had gone into a stable, the ostler would have said, "here has been a comical fellow"; but he would not have respected him.' BOSWELL. 'And, Sir, the ostler would have answered him, would have given him as good as he brought, as the common saying is.' JOHNSON. 'Yes, Sir; and Foote would have answered the ostler.—When Burke does not descend to be merry, his conversation is very superiour indeed. There is no proportion between the powers which he shews in serious talk and in jocularity. When he lets himself down to that, he is in the kennel.' I have in another place opposed, and I hope with success, Dr. Johnson's very singular and erroneous notion as to Mr. Burke's pleasantry. Mr. Windham now said low to me, that he differed from our great friend in this observation; for that Mr. Burke was often very happy in his merriment. It would not have been right for either of us to have contradicted Johnson at this time, in a Society all of whom did not know and value Mr. Burke as much as we did. It might have occasioned something more rough, and at any rate would probably have checked the flow of Johnson's good-humour. He called to us with a sudden air of exultation, as the thought started into his mind, 'O! Gentlemen, I must tell you a very great thing. The Empress of Russia has ordered the *Rambler* to be translated into the Russian language: so I shall be read on the banks of the Wolga. Horace boasts that his fame would extend as far as the banks of the Rhone; now the Wolga is farther from me than the Rhone was from Horace.' BOSWELL. 'You must certainly be pleased with this, Sir.' JOHNSON. 'I am pleased, Sir, to be sure. A man is pleased to find he has succeeded in that which he has endeavoured to do.'

One of the company mentioned his having seen a noble person driving in his carriage, and looking exceedingly well, notwithstanding his great age. JOHNSON. 'Ah, Sir; that is nothing. Bacon observes, that a stout healthy old man is like a tower undermined.'

On Sunday, May 16, I found him alone; he talked of Mrs. Thrale with much concern, saying, 'Sir, she has done every thing wrong, since Thrale's bridle was off her neck;' and was proceeding to mention some circumstances which have since been the subject of publick discussion, when he was interrupted by the arrival of Dr. Douglas, now Bishop of Salisbury. . . .

Johnson, talking of the fear of death, said, 'Some people are not afraid, because they look upon salvation as the effect of an absolute decree, and think they feel in themselves the marks of sanctification. Others, and those the most rational in my opinion, look upon salvation as conditional; and as they never can be sure that they have complied with the conditions, they are afraid.'

In one of his little manuscript diaries, about this time, I find a short notice, which marks his amiable disposition more certainly than a thousand studied declarations.—'Afternoon spent cheerfully and elegantly, I hope without offence to GOD or man; though in no holy duty, yet in the general exercise and cultivation of benevolence.'

On Monday, May 17, I dined with him at Mr. Dilly's, where were Colonel Vallancy, the Reverend Dr. Gibbons, and Mr. Capel Lofft, who, though a most zealous Whig, has a mind so full of learning and knowledge, and so much exercised in various departments, and withal so much liberality, that the stupendous powers of the literary Goliath, though they did not frighten this little David of popular spirit, could not but excite his admiration. There was also Mr. Braithwaite of the Post-office, that amiable and friendly man, who, with modest and unassuming manners, has associated with many of the wits of the age. Johnson was very quiescent to-day. Perhaps too I was indolent. I find nothing more of him in my notes, but that when I mentioned that I had seen in the King's library sixty-three editions of my favourite *Thomas à Kempis,* amongst which it was in eight languages, Latin, German, French, Italian, Spanish, English, Arabick, and Armenian, he said, he thought it unnecessary to collect many editions of a book, which were all the same, except as to the paper and print; he would have the original, and all the translations, and all the editions which had any variations in the text. He approved of the famous collection of editions of Horace by Douglas, mentioned by Pope, who is said to have had a closet filled with them; and he added, 'every man should try to collect one book in that manner, and present it to a publick library.'

On Tuesday, May 18, I saw him for a short time in the morning. I told him that the mob had called out, as the King passed, 'No Fox—No Fox,' which I did not like. He said, 'They were right, Sir.' I said, I thought not; for it seemed to be making Mr. Fox the King's competitor. There being no audience, so that there could be no triumph in a victory, he fairly agreed with me. I said it might do very well, if explained thus:—'Let us have no Fox;' understanding it as a prayer to his Majesty not to appoint that gentleman minister.

On Wednesday, May 19, I sat a part of the evening with him, by ourselves. I observed, that the death of our friends might be a consolation against the fear of our own dissolution, because we might have more friends in the other world than in this. He perhaps felt this as a reflection upon his apprehension as to death; and said, with heat, 'How can a man know *where* his departed friends are, or whether they will be his friends in the other world? How many friendships have you known formed upon principles of virtue? Most friendships are formed by caprice or by chance, mere confederacies in vice or leagues in folly.'

We talked of our worthy friend Mr. Langton. He said, 'I know not who will go to Heaven if Langton does not. Sir, I could almost say, *Sit anima mea cum Langtono.*'[1] I mentioned a very eminent friend as a virtuous man. JOHNSON. 'Yes, Sir; but ———— has not the evangelical virtue of Langton. ————, I am afraid, would not scruple to pick up a wench.'

He however charged Mr. Langton with what he thought want of judgement upon an interesting occasion. 'When I was ill, (said he,) I desired he would tell me sincerely in what he thought my life was faulty. Sir, he brought me a sheet of paper, on which he had written down several texts of Scripture, recommending christian charity. And when I questioned him what occasion I had given for such an animadversion, all that he could say amounted to this,—that I sometimes contradicted people in conversation. Now what harm does it do to any man to be contradicted?' BOSWELL. 'I suppose he meant the *manner* of doing it; roughly,—and harshly.' JOHNSON. 'And who is the worse for that?' BOSWELL. 'It hurts people of weak nerves.' JOHNSON. 'I know no such weak-nerved people.' Mr. Burke, to whom I related this conference, said, 'It is well, if when a man comes to die, he has nothing heavier upon his conscience than having been a little rough in conversation.'

Johnson, at the time when the paper was presented to him, though at first pleased with the attention of his friend, whom he thanked in an earnest manner, soon exclaimed, in a loud and angry tone, 'What is your drift, Sir?' Sir Joshua Reynolds pleasantly observed, that it was a scene for a comedy, to see a penitent get into a violent passion and belabour his confessor.

I have preserved no more of his conversation at the times when I saw him during the rest of this month, till Sunday, the 30th of May, when I met him in the evening at Mr. Hoole's, where there was a large company both of ladies and gentlemen; Sir James Johnston happened to say, that he paid no regard to the arguments of counsel at the bar of the House of Commons, because they were paid for speaking. JOHNSON. 'Nay, Sir, argument is argument. You cannot help paying regard to their arguments, if they are good. If it were testimony, you might disregard it, if you knew that it were purchased. There is a beautiful image in Bacon upon this subject: testimony is like an arrow shot from a long bow;

[1] 'May my soul be with Langton.'

the force of it depends on the strength of the hand that draws it. Argument is like an arrow from a cross-bow, which has equal force though shot by a child.'

He had dined that day at Mr. Hoole's, and Miss Helen Maria Williams being expected in the evening, Mr. Hoole put into his hands her beautiful *Ode on the Peace:* Johnson read it over, and when this elegant and accomplished young lady was presented to him, he took her by the hand in the most courteous manner, and repeated the finest stanza of her poem; this was the most delicate and pleasing compliment he could pay. Her respectable friend, Dr. Kippis, from whom I had this anecdote, was standing by, and was not a little gratified.

Miss Williams told me, that the only other time she was fortunate enough to be in Dr. Johnson's company, he asked her to sit down by him, which she did, and upon her inquiring how he was, he answered, 'I am very ill indeed, Madam. I am very ill even when you are near me; what should I be were you at a distance?'

He had now a great desire to go to Oxford, as his first jaunt after his illness; we talked of it for some days, and I had promised to accompany him. He was impatient and fretful to-night, because I did not at once agree to go with him on Thursday. When I considered how ill he had been, and what allowance should be made for the influence of sickness upon his temper, I resolved to indulge him, though with some inconvenience to myself, as I wished to attend the musical meeting in honour of Handel, in Westminster-Abbey, on the following Saturday.

In the midst of his own diseases and pains, he was ever compassionate to the distresses of others, and actively earnest in procuring them aid, as appears from a note to Sir Joshua Reynolds, of June 1, in these words:—'I am ashamed to ask for some relief for a poor man, to whom, I hope, I have given what I can be expected to spare. The man importunes me, and the blow goes round. I am going to try another air on Thursday.'

On Thursday, June 3, the Oxford post-coach took us up in the morning at Bolt-court. The other two passengers were Mrs. Beresford and her daughter, two very agreeable ladies from America; they were going to Worcestershire, where they then resided. Frank had been sent by his master the day before to take places for us; and I found, from the waybill, that Dr. Johnson had made our names be put down. Mrs. Beresford, who had read it, whispered me, 'Is this the great Dr. Johnson?' I told her it was; so she was then prepared to listen. As she soon happened to mention in a voice so low that

Johnson did not hear it, that her husband had been a member of the American Congress, I cautioned her to beware of introducing that subject, as she must know how very violent Johnson was against the people of that country. He talked a great deal, but I am sorry I have preserved little of the conversation. Miss Beresford was so much charmed, that she said to me aside, 'How he does talk! Every sentence is an essay.' She amused herself in the coach with knotting; he would scarcely allow this species of employment any merit. 'Next to mere idleness (said he,) I think knotting is to be reckoned in the scale of insignificance; though I once attempted to learn knotting. Dempster's sister (looking to me,) endeavoured to teach me it; but I made no progress.'

I was surprised at his talking without reserve in the publick post-coach of the state of his affairs; 'I have (said he,) about the world I think above a thousand pounds, which I intend shall afford Frank an annuity of seventy pounds a year.' Indeed his openness with people at a first interview was remarkable. He said once to Mr. Langton, 'I think I am like Squire Richard in *The Journey to London*, "I'm never strange in a strange place."' He was truly *social*. He strongly censured what is much too common in England among persons of condition,—maintaining an absolute silence, when unknown to each other; as for instance, when occasionally brought together in a room before the master or mistress of the house has appeared. 'Sir, that is being so uncivilised as not to understand the common rights of humanity.'

At the inn where we stopped he was exceedingly dissatisfied with some roast mutton which we had for dinner. The ladies I saw wondered to see the great philosopher, whose wisdom and wit they had been admiring all the way, get into ill-humour from such a cause. He scolded the waiter, saying, 'It is as bad as bad can be: it is ill-fed, ill-killed, ill-kept, and ill-drest.'

He bore the journey very well, and seemed to feel himself elevated as he approached Oxford, that magnificent and venerable seat of learning, Orthodoxy, and Toryism. Frank came in the heavy coach, in readiness to attend him; and we were received with the most polite hospitality at the house of his old friend Dr. Adams, Master of Pembroke College, who had given us a kind invitation. Before we were set down, I communicated to Johnson my having engaged to return to London directly, for the reason I have mentioned, but that I would hasten back to him again. He was pleased that I had made this journey merely to keep him company. He was easy and placid, with Dr. Adams, Mrs. and Miss Adams, and Mrs. Kennicot, widow of the learned Hebræan, who was here on a

616

visit. He soon dispatched the inquiries which were made about his illness and recovery, by a short and distinct narrative; and then assuming a gay air, repeated from Swift,—

'Nor think on our approaching ills,
And talk of spectacles and pills.'

Dr. Newton, the Bishop of Bristol, having been mentioned, Johnson, recollecting the manner in which he had been censured by that Prelate, thus retaliated:—'Tom knew he should be dead before what he has said of me would appear. He durst not have printed it while he was alive.' DR. ADAMS. 'I believe his *Dissertations on the Prophecies* is his great work.' JOHNSON. 'Why, Sir, it is Tom's great work; but how far it is great, or how much of it is Tom's, are other questions. I fancy a considerable part of it was borrowed.' DR. ADAMS. 'He was a very successful man.' JOHNSON. 'I don't think so, Sir. He did not get very high. He was late in getting what he did get; and he did not get it by the best means. I believe he was a gross flatterer.'

I fulfilled my intention by going to London, and returned to Oxford on Wednesday, the 9th of June, when I was happy to find myself again in the same agreeable circle at Pembroke College, with the comfortable prospect of making some stay. Johnson welcomed my return with more than ordinary glee.

He talked with great regard of the Honourable Archibald Campbell, whose character he had given at the Duke of Argyll's table, when we were at Inverary; and at this time wrote out for me, in his own hand, a fuller account of that learned and venerable writer, which I have published in its proper place. Johnson made a remark this evening which struck me a good deal. 'I never (said he,) knew a non-juror who could reason.' . . .

Next morning at breakfast, he pointed out a passage in Savage's *Wanderer,* saying, 'These are fine verses.' 'If (said he,) I had written with hostility of Warburton in my *Shakspeare,* I should have quoted this couplet:—

"Here Learning, blinded first and then beguil'd,
Looks dark as Ignorance, as Fancy wild."

You see they'd have fitted him to a *T,*' (smiling.) DR. ADAMS. 'But you did not write against Warburton.' JOHNSON. 'No, Sir, I treated him with great respect both in my Preface and in my Notes.'

Mrs. Kennicot spoke of her brother, the Reverend Mr. Chamberlayne, who had given up great prospects in the Church of England on his conversion to the Roman Catholick faith. Johnson, who warmly admired every man who acted from a conscientious regard to principle, erroneous or not, exclaimed fervently, 'GOD bless him.'

Mrs. Kennicot, in confirmation of Dr. Johnson's opinion, that the present was not worse than former ages, mentioned that her brother assured her, there was now less infidelity on the Continent than there had been; Voltaire and Rousseau were less read. I asserted, from good authority, that Hume's infidelity was certainly less read. JOHNSON. 'All infidel writers drop into oblivion, when personal connections and the floridness of novelty are gone; though now and then a foolish fellow, who thinks he can be witty upon them, may bring them again into notice. There will sometimes start up a College joker, who does not consider that what is a joke in a College will not do in the world. To such defenders of Religion I would apply a stanza of a poem which I remember to have seen in some old collection:—

> "Henceforth be quiet and agree,
> Each kiss his empty brother;
> Religion scorns a foe like thee,
> But dreads a friend like t'other."

The point is well, though the expression is not correct; *one,* and not *thee,* should be opposed to *t'other.*'

On the Roman Catholick religion he said, 'If you join the Papists externally, they will not interrogate you strictly as to your belief in their tenets. No reasoning Papist believes every article of their faith. There is one side on which a good man might be persuaded to embrace it. A good man, of a timorous disposition, in great doubt of his acceptance with GOD, and pretty credulous, might be glad to be of a church where there are so many helps to get to Heaven. I would be a Papist if I could. I have fear enough; but an obstinate rationality prevents me. I shall never be a Papist, unless on the near approach of death, of which I have a very great terrour. I wonder that women are not all Papists.' BOSWELL. 'They are not more afraid of death than men are.' JOHNSON. 'Because they are less wicked.' DR. ADAMS. 'They are more pious.' JOHNSON. 'No, hang 'em, they are not more pious. A wicked fellow is the most pious when he takes to it. He'll beat you all at piety.'

He argued in defence of some of the peculiar tenets of the Church of Rome. As to the giving the bread only to the laity, he said, 'They may think, that in what is merely ritual, deviations from the primitive mode may be admitted on the ground of convenience, and I think they are as well warranted to make this alteration, as we are to substitute sprinkling in the room of the ancient baptism.' As to the invocation of saints, he said, 'Though I do not think it authorized, it appears to me, that "the communion of saints" in the Creed means the communion with the saints in Heaven, as connected with "The holy Catholick Church." ' He admitted the influence of evil spirits upon our minds, and said, 'Nobody who believes the New Testament can deny it.' . . .

After dinner, when one of us talked of there being a great enmity between Whig and Tory;—JOHNSON. 'Why not so much, I think, unless when they come into competition with each other. There is none when they are only common acquaintance, none when they are of different sexes. A Tory will marry into a Whig family, and a Whig into a Tory family, without any reluctance. But indeed, in a matter of much more concern than political tenets, and that is religion, men and women do not concern themselves much about difference of opinion; and ladies set no value on the moral character of men who pay their addresses to them; the greatest profligate will be as well received as the man of the greatest virtue, and this by a very good woman, by a woman who says her prayers three times a day.' Our ladies endeavoured to defend their sex from this charge; but he roared them down! 'No, no; a lady will take Jonathan Wild as readily as St. Austin, if he has threepence more; and, what is worse, her parents will give her to him. Women have a perpetual envy of our vices; they are less vicious than we, not from choice, but because we restrict them; they are the slaves of order and fashion; their virtue is of more consequence to us than our own, so far as concerns this world.'

Miss Adams mentioned a gentleman of licentious character, and said, 'Suppose I had a mind to marry that gentleman, would my parents consent?' JOHNSON. 'Yes, they'd consent, and you'd go. You'd go though they did not consent.' MISS ADAMS. 'Perhaps their opposing might make me go.' JOHNSON. 'O, very well; you'd take one whom you think a bad man, to have the pleasure of vexing your parents. You put me in mind of Dr. Barrowby, the physician, who was very fond of swine's flesh. One day, when he was eating it, he said, 'I wish I was a Jew.' 'Why so? (said somebody;) the Jews are not allowed to eat your favourite meat.' 'Because, (said he,) I should then have the gust of eating it, with the pleasure of sinning.' Johnson then proceeded in his declamation.

Miss Adams soon afterwards made an observation that I do not recollect, which pleased him much: he said with a good-humoured smile, 'That there should be so much excellence united with so much *depravity*, is strange.'

Indeed, this lady's good qualities, merit, and accomplishments, and her constant attention to Dr. Johnson, were not lost upon him. She happened to tell him that a little coffee-pot, in which she had made his coffee, was the only thing she could call her own. He turned to her with a complacent gallantry, 'Don't say so, my dear; I hope you don't reckon my heart as nothing.'

I asked him if it was true as reported, that he had said lately, 'I am for the King against Fox; but I am for Fox against Pitt.' JOHNSON. 'Yes, Sir; the King is my master; but I do not know Pitt; and Fox is my friend.'

'Fox, (added he,) is a most extraordinary man; here is a man (describing him in strong terms of objection in some respects according as he apprehended, but which exalted his abilities the more) who has divided the Kingdom with Cæsar; so that it was a doubt whether the nation should be ruled by the sceptre of George the Third, or the tongue of Fox.'

Dr. Wall, physician at Oxford, drank tea with us. Johnson had in general a peculiar pleasure in the company of physicians, which was certainly not abated by the conversation of this learned, ingenious, and pleasing gentleman. Johnson said, 'It is wonderful how little good Radcliffe's travelling fellowships have done. I know nothing that has been imported by them; yet many additions to our medical knowledge might be got in foreign countries. Inoculation, for instance, has saved more lives than war destroys: and the cures performed by the Peruvian-bark are innumerable. But it is in vain to send our travelling physicians to France, and Italy, and Germany, for all that is known there is known here; I'd send them out of Christendom; I'd send them among barbarous nations.'

On Friday, June 11, we talked at breakfast, of forms of prayer. JOHNSON. 'I know of no good prayers but those in the *Book of Common Prayer*.' DR. ADAMS. (in a very earnest manner:) 'I wish, Sir, you would compose some family prayers.' JOHNSON. 'I will not compose prayers for you, Sir, because you can do it for yourself. But I have thought of getting together all the books of prayers which I could, selecting those which should appear to me the best, putting out some, inserting others, adding some prayers of my own, and prefixing a discourse on prayer.' We all now gathered about him, and two or three of us at a time joined in pressing him to execute this plan. He seemed to be a little displeased at the manner of our importunity, and in great agitation called out, 'Do not talk thus of what is so aweful. I know not what time GOD will allow me in this world. There are many things which I wish to do.' Some of us persisted, and Dr. Adams said, 'I never was more serious about any thing in my life.' JOHNSON. 'Let me alone, let me alone; I am overpowered.' And then he put his hands before his face, and reclined for some time upon the table.

I mentioned Jeremy Taylor's using, in his forms of prayer, 'I am the chief of sinners,' and other such self-condemning expressions. 'Now, (said I,) this cannot be said with truth by every man, and therefore is improper for a general printed form. I myself cannot say that I am the worst of men; I *will* not say so.' JOHNSON. 'A man may know, that physically, that is, in the real state of things, he is not the worst man; but that morally he may be so. Law observes that "Every man knows something worse of himself, than he is sure of in others." You may not have committed such crimes as some men have done; but you do not know against what degree of light they have sinned. Besides, Sir, "the chief of sinners" is a mode of expression for "I am a great sinner." So St. Paul, speaking of our SAVIOUR's having died to save sinners, says, "of whom I am the chief;" yet he certainly did not think himself so bad as Judas Iscariot.' BOSWELL. 'But, Sir, Taylor means it literally, for he founds a conceit upon it. When praying for the conversion of sinners, and of himself in particular, he says, "LORD, thou wilt not leave thy *chief* work undone.' JOHNSON. 'I do not approve of figurative expressions in addressing the Supreme Being; and I never use them. Taylor gives a very good advice: "Never lie in your prayers; never confess more than you really believe; never promise more than you mean to perform." I recollected this precept in his *Golden Grove;* but his *example* for prayer contradicts his *precept.*'

Dr. Johnson and I went in Dr. Adams's coach to dine with Dr. Nowell, Principal of St. Mary Hall, at his beautiful villa at Iffley, on the banks of the Isis, about two miles from Oxford. While we were upon the road, I had the resolution to ask Johnson whether he thought that the roughness of his manner had been an advantage or not, and if he would not have done more good if he had been more gentle. I proceeded to answer myself thus: 'Perhaps it has been of advantage, as it has given weight to what you said: you could not, perhaps, have talked with such authority without it.' JOHNSON. 'No, Sir; I have done more good as I am. Obscenity and Impiety have always been repressed in my company.' BOSWELL. 'True, Sir; and that is more than can be said of every Bishop. Greater liberties have been taken in the presence of a Bishop, though a very good man, from his being milder, and therefore not commanding such awe. Yet, Sir, many people who might have been benefited by your conversation, have been frightened away. A worthy friend of ours has told me, that he has often been afraid to talk to you.' JOHNSON. 'Sir, he need not have been afraid, if he had any thing rational to say. If he had not, it was better he did not talk.'

Dr. Nowell is celebrated for having preached a sermon before the House of Commons, on the 30th of January, 1772, full of high Tory sentiments, for which he was thanked as usual, and printed it at their request; but, in the midst of that turbulence and faction which disgraced a part of the present reign, the thanks were afterwards ordered to be expunged. This strange conduct sufficiently exposes itself; and Dr. Nowell will ever have the honour which is due to a lofty friend of our monarchical constitution. Dr. Johnson said to me, 'Sir, the Court will be very much to blame, if he is not promoted.' I told this to Dr. Nowell, and asserting my humbler, though not less zealous exertions in the same cause, I suggested that whatever return we might receive, we should still have the consolation of being like Butler's steady and generous Royalist,

'True as the dial to the sun,
Although it be not shone upon.'

We were well entertained and very happy at Dr. Nowell's, where was a very agreeable company, and we drank 'Church and King' after dinner, with true Tory cordiality.

We talked of a certain clergyman of extraordinary character, who by exerting his talents in writing on temporary topicks, and displaying uncommon intrepidity, had raised himself to affluence. I maintained that we ought not to be indignant at his success; for merit of every sort was entitled to reward. JOHNSON. 'Sir, I will not allow this man to have merit. No, Sir; what he has is rather the contrary; I will, indeed, allow him courage, and on this account we so far give him credit. We have more respect for a man who robs boldly on the highway, than for a fellow who jumps out of a ditch, and knocks you down behind your back. Courage is a quality so necessary for maintaining virtue, that it is always respected, even when it is associated with vice.'

I censured the coarse invectives which were become fashionable in the House of Commons, and said that if members of parliament must attack each other personally in the heat of debate, it should be done more genteelly. JOHNSON. 'No, Sir; that would be much worse. Abuse is not so dangerous when there is no vehicle of wit or delicacy, no subtle conveyance. The difference between coarse and refined abuse is as the difference between being bruised by a club, and wounded by a poisoned arrow.' . . .

On Saturday, June 12, there drank tea with us at Dr. Adams's, Mr. John Henderson, student of Pembroke College, celebrated for his wonderful acquirements in Alchymy, Judicial Astrology, and other abstruse and curious learning; and the Reverend Herbert Croft, who, I am afraid, was somewhat mortified by Dr. Johnson's not being highly pleased with some *Family Discourses*, which he had printed; they were in too familiar a style to be approved of by so manly a mind. I have no note of this evening's conversation, except a single fragment. When I mentioned Thomas Lord Lyttelton's vision, the prediction of the time of his death, and its exact fulfilment;—JOHNSON. 'It is the most extraordinary thing that has happened in my day. I heard it with my own ears, from his uncle, Lord Westcote. I am so glad to have every evidence of the spiritual world, that I am willing to believe it.' DR. ADAMS. 'You have evidence enough; good evidence, which needs not such support.' JOHNSON. 'I like to have more.'

Mr. Henderson, with whom I had sauntered in the venerable walks of Merton College, and found him a very learned and pious man, supped with us. Dr. Johnson surprised him not a little, by acknowledging with a look of horrour, that he was much oppressed by the fear of death. The amiable Dr. Adams suggested that GOD was infinitely good. JOHNSON. 'That he is infinitely good, as far as the perfection of his nature will allow, I certainly believe; but it is necessary for good upon the whole, that individuals should be punished. As to an *individual*, therefore, he is not infinitely good; and as I cannot be *sure* that I have fulfilled the conditions on which salvation is granted, I am afraid I may be one of those who shall be damned' (looking dismally). DR. ADAMS. 'What do you mean by damned?' JOHNSON. (passionately and loudly,) 'Sent to Hell, Sir, and punished everlastingly!' DR. ADAMS. 'I don't believe that doctrine.' JOHNSON. 'Hold, Sir; do you believe that some will be punished at all?' DR. ADAMS. 'Being excluded from Heaven will be a punishment; yet there may be no great positive suffering.' JOHNSON. 'Well, Sir; but, if you admit any degree of punishment, there is an end of your argument for infinite goodness simply considered; for, infinite goodness would inflict no punishment whatever. There is not infinite goodness physically considered; morally there is.' BOSWELL. 'But may not a man attain to such a degree of hope as not to be uneasy from the fear of death?' JOHNSON. 'A man may have such a degree of hope as to keep him quiet. You see I am not quiet, from the vehemence with which I talk; but I do not despair.' MRS. ADAMS. 'You seem, Sir, to forget the merits of our Redeemer.' JOHNSON. 'Madam, I do not forget the merits of my Redeemer; but my Redeemer has said that he will get some on his right hand and some on his left.' He was in gloomy agitation, and said, 'I'll have no more on't.'

If what has now been stated should be urged by the enemies of Christianity, as if its influence on the mind were not benignant, let it be remembered, that Johnson's temperament was melancholy, of which such direful apprehensions of futurity are often a common effect. We shall presently see that when he approached nearer to his aweful change, his mind became tranquil, and he exhibited as much fortitude as becomes a thinking man in that situation.

From the subject of death we passed to discourse of life, whether it was upon the whole more happy or miserable. Johnson was decidedly for the balance of misery: in confirmation of which I maintained, that no man would choose to lead over again the life which he had experienced. Johnson acceded to that opinion in the strongest terms. This is an inquiry often made; and its being a subject of disquisition is a proof that much misery presses upon human feelings; for those who are conscious of a felicity of existence, would never hesitate to accept of a repetition of it. I have met with very few who would. I have heard Mr. Burke make use of a very ingenious and plausible argument on this subject;— 'Every man (said he,) would lead his life over again; for, every man is willing to go on and take an addition to his life, which, as he grows older, he has no reason to think will be better, or even so good as what has preceded.' I imagine, however, the truth is, that there is a deceitful hope that the next part of life will be free from the pains, and anxieties, and sorrows, which we have already felt. We are for wise purposes 'Condemn'd to Hope's delusive mine;' as Johnson finely says. . . .

It was observed to Dr. Johnson, that it seemed strange that he, who has so often delighted his company by his lively and brilliant conversation, should say he was miserable. JOHNSON. 'Alas! it is all outside; I may be cracking my joke, and cursing the sun. *Sun, how I hate thy beams!*' I knew not well what to think of this declaration; whether to hold it as a genuine picture of his mind, or as the effect of his persuading himself contrary to fact, that the position which he had assumed as to human unhappiness, was true. . . .

On Sunday, June 13, our philosopher was calm at breakfast. There was something exceedingly pleasing in our leading a College life, without restraint, and with superiour elegance, in consequence of our living in the Master's house, and having the company of ladies. Mrs. Kennicot related, in his presence, a lively saying of Dr. Johnson to Miss Hannah More, who had expressed a wonder that the poet who had written *Paradise Lost* should write such poor Sonnets:—'Milton, Madam, was a genius that could cut a Colossus from a rock; but could not carve heads upon cherry-stones.'

We talked of the casuistical question, Whether it was allowable at any time to depart from *Truth?* JOHNSON. 'The general rule is, that Truth should never be violated, because it is of the utmost importance to the comfort of life, that we should have a full security by mutual faith; and occasional inconveniencies should be willingly suffered that we may preserve it. There must, however, be some exceptions. If, for instance, a murderer should ask you which way a man is gone, you may tell him what is not true, because you are under a previous obligation not to betray a man to a murderer.' BOSWELL. 'Supposing the person who wrote *Junius* were asked whether he was the authour, might he deny it?' JOHNSON 'I don't know what to say to this. If you were *sure* that he wrote *Junius,* would you, if he denied it, think as well of him afterwards? Yet it may be urged, that what a man has no right to ask, you may refuse to communicate; and there is no other effectual mode of preserving a secret, and an important secret, the discovery of which may be very hurtful to you, but a flat denial; for if you are silent, or hesitate, or evade, it will be held equivalent to a confession. But stay, sir; here is another case. Supposing the authour had told me confidentially that he had written *Junius,* and I were asked if he had, I should hold myself at liberty to deny it, as being under a previous promise, express or implied, to conceal it. Now what I ought to do for the authour, may I not do for myself? But I deny the lawfulness of telling a lie to a sick man for fear of alarming him. You have no business with consequences, you are to tell the truth. Besides, you are not sure what effect your telling him that he is in danger may have. It may bring his distemper to a crisis, and that may cure him. Of all lying, I have the greatest abhorrence of this, because I believe it has been frequently practised on myself.' . . .

On Monday, June 14, and Tuesday, 15, Dr. Johnson and I dined, on one of them, I forget which, with Mr. Mickle, translator of the *Lusiad,* at Wheatley, a very pretty country place a few miles from Oxford; and on the other with Dr. Wetherell, Master of University College. From Dr. Wetherell's he went to visit Mr. Sackville Parker, the bookseller; and when he returned to us, gave the following account of his visit, saying, 'I have been to see my old friend, Sack. Parker; I find he has married his maid; he has done right. She had lived with him many years in great confidence, and they had mingled minds; I do not think he could have found any wife that would have made him so happy. The woman was very attentive and civil to me; she pressed me to fix a day for dining with them, and to say what I liked, and she would be sure to get it for me. Poor Sack! He is very ill, indeed. We parted as never to meet again. It has quite broke me down.' This pathetic narrative was strangely diversified with the grave and earnest defence of a man's having married his maid. I could not but feel it as in some degree ludicrous.

In the morning of Tuesday, June 15, while we sat at Dr. Adams's, we talked of a printed letter from the Reverend Herbert Croft, to a young gentleman who had been his pupil, in which he advised him to read to the end of whatever books he should begin to read. JOHNSON. 'This is surely a strange advice; you may as well resolve that whatever men you happen to get acquainted with, you are to keep to them for life. A book may be good for nothing; or there may be only one thing in it worth knowing; are we to read it all through? These Voyages, (pointing to the three large volumes of *Voyages to the South Sea*, which were just come out) *who* will read them through? A man had better work his way before the mast, than read them through; they will be eaten by rats and mice, before they are read through. There can be little entertainment in such books; one set of Savages is like another.' BOSWELL. 'I do not think the people of Otaheité can be reckoned Savages.' JOHNSON. 'Don't cant in defence of Savages.' BOSWELL. 'They have the art of navigation.' JOHNSON. 'A dog or a cat can swim.' BOSWELL. 'They carve very ingeniously.' JOHNSON. 'A cat can scratch, and a child with a nail can scratch.' I perceived this was none of the *mollia tempora fandi;* [1] so desisted.

Upon his mentioning that when he came to College he wrote his first exercise twice over; but never did so afterwards; MISS ADAMS. 'I suppose, Sir, you would not make them better?' JOHNSON. 'Yes, Madam, to be sure, I could make them better. Thought is better than no thought.' MISS ADAMS. 'Do you think, Sir, you could make your *Ramblers* better?' JOHNSON. 'Certainly I could.' BOSWELL. 'I'll lay a bet, Sir, you cannot.' JOHNSON. 'But I will, Sir, if I choose. I shall make the best of them you shall pick out, better.' BOSWELL. 'But you may add to them. I will not allow of that.' JOHNSON. 'Nay, Sir, there are three ways of making them better;—putting out,—adding,—or correcting.'

During our visit at Oxford, the following conversation passed between him and me on the subject of my trying my fortune at the English bar: Having asked whether a very extensive acquaintance in London, which was very valuable, and of great advantage to a man at large, might not be preju-

[1] 'The most propitious time to address him.' Adapted from Virgil, *Aeneid*, iv. 293.

dicial to a lawyer, by preventing him from giving sufficient attention to his business;—JOHNSON. 'Sir, you will attend to business, as business lays hold of you. When not actually employed, you may see your friends as much as you do now. You may dine at a Club every day, and sup with one of the members every night; and you may be as much at publick places as one who has seen them all would wish to be. But you must take care to attend constantly in Westminster-Hall; both to mind your business, as it is almost all learnt there, (for nobody reads now;) and to shew that you want to have business. And you must not be too often seen at publick places, that competitors may not have it to say, 'He is always at the Playhouse or at Ranelagh, and never to be found at his chambers.' And, Sir, there must be a kind of solemnity in the manner of a professional man. I have nothing particular to say to you on the subject. All this I should say to any one; I should have said it to Lord Thurlow twenty years ago.' . . .

On Wednesday, June 19,[1] Dr. Johnson and I returned to London; he was not well to-day, and said very little, employing himself chiefly in reading Euripides. He expressed some displeasure at me, for not observing sufficiently the various objects upon the road. 'If I had your eyes, Sir, (said he,) I should count the passengers.' It was wonderful how accurate his observation of visual objects was, notwithstanding his imperfect eyesight, owing to a habit of attention. That he was much satisfied with the respect paid to him at Dr. Adams's, is thus attested by himself: 'I returned last night from Oxford, after a fortnight's abode with Dr. Adams, who treated me as well as I could expect or wish; and he that contents a sick man, a man whom it is impossible to please, has surely done his part well.'

After his return to London from this excursion, I saw him frequently, but have few memorandums: I shall therefore here insert some particulars which I collected at various times. . . .

It having been mentioned to Dr. Johnson that a gentleman who had a son whom he imagined to have an extreme degree of timidity, resolved to send him to a publick school, that he might acquire confidence;—'Sir, (said Johnson,) this is a preposterous expedient for removing his infirmity; such a disposition should be cultivated in the shade. Placing him at a publick school is forcing an owl upon day.'

Speaking of a gentleman whose house was much frequented by low company; 'Rags, Sir, (said he,) will always make their appearance where they have a right to do it.'

[1] June 16.

Of the same gentleman's mode of living, he said, 'Sir, the servants, instead of doing what they are bid, stand round the table in idle clusters, gaping upon the guests; and seem as unfit to attend a company, as to steer a man of war.'

A dull country magistrate gave Johnson a long tedious account of his exercising his criminal jurisdiction, the result of which was his having sentenced four convicts to transportation. Johnson, in an agony of impatience to get rid of such a companion, exclaimed, 'I heartily wish, Sir, that I were a fifth.'

Johnson was present when a tragedy was read, in which there occurred this line:—

'Who rules o'er freemen should himself be free.'

The company having admired it much, 'I cannot agree with you (said Johnson). It might as well be said,—

'Who drives fat oxen should himself be fat.'

. . . Johnson having argued for some time with a pertinacious gentleman; his opponent, who had talked in a very puzzling manner, happened to say, 'I don't understand you, Sir:' upon which Johnson observed, 'Sir, I have found you an argument; but I am not obliged to find you an understanding.'

Talking to me of Horry Walpole, (as Horace late Earl of Orford was often called,) Johnson allowed that he got together a great many curious little things, and told them in an elegant manner. Mr. Walpole thought Johnson a more amiable character after reading his *Letters to Mrs. Thrale:* but never was one of the true admirers of that great man. We may suppose a prejudice conceived, if he ever heard Johnson's account to Sir George Staunton, that when he made the speeches in parliament for the *Gentleman's Magazine,* 'he always took care to put Sir Robert Walpole in the wrong, and to say every thing he could against the electorate of Hanover.' The celebrated *Heroick Epistle,* in which Johnson is satyrically introduced, has been ascribed both to Mr. Walpole and Mr. Mason. One day at Mr. Courtenay's, when a gentleman expressed his opinion that there was more energy in that poem than could be expected from Mr. Walpole; Mr. Warton, the late Laureat, observed, 'It may have been written by Walpole, and *buckram'd* by Mason.'

He disapproved of Lord Hailes, for having modernised the language of the ever-memorable John Hales of Eton, in an edition which his Lordship published of that writer's works. 'An authour's language, Sir, (said he,) is a characteristical part of his composition, and is also characteristical of the age in which he writes. Besides, Sir, when the language is changed we are not sure that the sense is the same. No, Sir; I am sorry Lord Hailes has done this.'

Here it may be observed, that his frequent use of the expression, *No, Sir*, was not always to intimate contradiction; for he would say so, when he was about to enforce an affirmative proposition which had not been denied, as in the instance last mentioned. I used to consider it as a kind of flag of defiance; as if he had said, 'Any argument you may offer against this, is not just. No, Sir, it is not.' It was like Falstaff's 'I deny your Major.'

Sir Joshua Reynolds having said that he took the altitude of a man's taste by his stories and his wit, and of his understanding by the remarks which he repeated; being always sure that he must be a weak man who quotes common things with an emphasis as if they were oracles; Johnson agreed with him; and Sir Joshua having also observed that the real character of a man was found out by his amusements,—Johnson added, 'Yes, Sir; no man is a hypocrite in his pleasures.—

I have mentioned Johnson's general aversion to a pun. He once, however, endured one of mine. When we were talking of a numerous company in which he had distinguished himself highly, I said, 'Sir, you were a COD surrounded by smelts. Is not this enough for you? at a time too when you were not *fishing* for a compliment?' He laughed at this with a complacent approbation. Old Mr. Sheridan observed, upon my mentioning it to him, 'He liked your compliment so well, he was willing to take it with *pun sauce*.' For my own part, I think no innocent species of wit or pleasantry should be suppressed; and that a good pun may be admitted among the smaller excellencies of lively conversation.

Had Johnson treated at large *De Claris Oratoribus*,[1] he might have given us an admirable work. When the Duke of Bedford attacked the ministry as vehemently as he could, for having taken upon them to extend the time for the importation of corn, Lord Chatham, in his first speech in the House of Lords, boldly avowed himself to be an adviser of that measure. 'My colleagues, (said he,) as I was confined by indisposition, did me the signal honour of coming to the bedside of a sick man, to ask his opinion. But, had they not thus condescended, I should have *taken up my bed and walked*, in order to have delivered that opinion at the Council-Board.' Mr. Langton, who was present, mentioned this to Johnson, who observed, 'Now, Sir, we see that he took these words as he found them; without considering, that though the expres-

---

[1] 'Of noted speakers.'

sion in Scripture, *take up thy bed and walk,* strictly suited the instance of the sick man restored to health and strength, who would of course be supposed to carry his bed with him, it could not be proper in the case of a man who was lying in a state of feebleness, and who certainly would not add to the difficulty of moving at all, that of carrying his bed.'

When I pointed out to him in the newspaper one of Mr. Grattan's animated and glowing speeches, in favour of the freedom of Ireland, in which this expression occurred (I know not if accurately taken): 'We will persevere, till there is not one link of the English chain left to clank upon the rags of the meanest beggar in Ireland;' Nay, Sir, (said Johnson,) don't you perceive that *one* link cannot clank?' . . .

Mr. Burke uniformly shewed Johnson the greatest respect; and when Mr. Townshend, now Lord Sydney, at a period when he was conspicuous in opposition, threw out some reflection in parliament upon the grant of a pension to a man of such political principles as Johnson; Mr. Burke, though then of the same party with Mr. Townshend, stood warmly forth in defence of his friend, to whom, he justly observed, the pension was granted solely on account of his eminent literary merit. I am well assured, that Mr. Townshend's attack upon Johnson was the occasion of his 'hitching in a rhyme;' for, that in the original copy of Goldsmith's character of Mr. Burke, in his *Retaliation,* another person's name stood in the couplet where Mr. Townshend is now introduced:—

'Though fraught with all learning kept straining his throat,
To persuade *Tommy Townshend* to lend him a vote.'

It may be worth remarking, among the *minutiæ* of my collection, that Johnson was once drawn to serve in the militia, the Trained Bands of the City of London, and that Mr. Rackstrow, of the Museum in Fleet-street, was his Colonel. It may be believed he did not serve in person; but the idea, with all its circumstances, is certainly laughable. He upon that occasion provided himself with a musket, and with a sword and belt, which I have seen hanging in his closet.

He was very constant to those whom he once employed, if they gave him no reason to be displeased. When somebody talked of being imposed on in the purchase of tea and sugar, and such articles: 'That will not be the case, (said he,) if you go to a *stately shop,* as I always do. In such a shop it is not worth their while to take a petty advantage.'

An authour of most anxious and restless vanity being mentioned, 'Sir, (said he,) there is not a young sapling upon Parnassus more severely blown about by every wind of criticism than that poor fellow.'

The difference, he observed, between a well-bred and an ill-bred man is this: 'One immediately attracts your liking, the other your aversion. You love the one till you find reason to hate him; you hate the other till you find reason to love him.'

The wife of one of his acquaintance had fraudulently made a purse for herself out of her husband's fortune. Feeling a proper compunction in her last moments, she confessed how much she had secreted; but before she could tell where it was placed, she was seized with a convulsive fit and expired. Her husband said, he was more hurt by her want of confidence in him, than by the loss of his money. 'I told him, (said Johnson,) that he should console himself: for *perhaps* the money might be *found*, and he was *sure* that his wife was *gone*.'

A foppish physician once reminded Johnson of his having been in company with him on a former occasion. 'I do not remember it, Sir.' The physician still insisted; adding that he that day wore so fine a coat that it must have attracted his notice. 'Sir, (said Johnson,) had you been dipt in Pactolus I should not have noticed you.'

He seemed to take a pleasure in speaking in his own style; for when he had carelessly missed it, he would repeat the thought translated into it. Talking of the Comedy of *The Rehearsal*, he said, 'It has not wit enough to keep it sweet.' This was easy; he therefore caught himself, and pronounced a more rounded sentence; 'It has not vitality enough to preserve it from putrefaction.'

He censured a writer of entertaining Travels for assuming a feigned character, saying, (in his sense of the word,) 'He carries out one lye; we know not how many he brings back.' At another time, talking of the same person, he observed, 'Sir, your assent to a man whom you have never known to falsify, is a debt: but after you have known a man to falsify, your assent to him then is a favour.'

Though he had no taste for painting, he admired much the manner in which Sir Joshua Reynolds treated of his art, in his *Discourses to the Royal Academy*. He observed one day of a passage in them, 'I think I might as well have said this myself:' and once when Mr. Langton was sitting by him, he read one of them very eagerly, and expressed himself thus: —'Very well, Master Reynolds; very well, indeed. But it will not be understood.'

When I observed to him that Painting was so far inferiour to Poetry, that the story or even emblem which it communicates must be previously known, and mentioned as a natural and laughable instance of this, that a little Miss on seeing a picture of Justice with the scales, had exclaimed to me, 'See, there's a woman selling sweetmeats;' he said, 'Painting, Sir, can illustrate, but cannot inform.'

No man was more ready to make an apology when he had censured unjustly, than Johnson. When a proof-sheet of one of his works was brought to him, he found fault with the mode in which a part of it was arranged, refused to read it, and in a passion desired that the compositor might be sent to him. The compositor was Mr. Manning, a decent sensible man, who had composed about one half of his *Dictionary*, when in Mr. Strahan's printing-house; and a great part of his *Lives of the Poets*, when in that of Mr. Nichols; and who (in his seventy-seventh year), when in Mr. Baldwin's printing-house, composed a part of the first edition of this work concerning him. By producing the manuscript, he at once satisfied Dr. Johnson that he was not to blame. Upon which Johnson candidly and earnestly said to him, 'Mr. Compositor, I ask your pardon. Mr. Compositor, I ask your pardon, again and again.'

His generous humanity to the miserable was almost beyond example. The following instance is well attested:—Coming home late one night, he found a poor woman lying in the street, so much exhausted that she could not walk; he took her upon his back, and carried her to his house, where he discovered that she was one of those wretched females who had fallen into the lowest state of vice, poverty, and disease. Instead of harshly upbraiding her, he had her taken care of with all tenderness for a long time, at considerable expence till she was restored to health, and endeavoured to put her into a virtuous way of living. . . .

He once in his life was known to have uttered what is called a *bull:* Sir Joshua Reynolds, when they were riding together in Devonshire, complained that he had a very bad horse, for that even when going down hill he moved slowly step by step. 'Ay (said Johnson,) and when he *goes* up hill, he *stands still*.'

He had a great aversion to gesticulating in company. He called once to a gentleman who offended him in that point, 'Don't *attitudenise*.' And when another gentleman thought he was giving additional force to what he uttered, by expressive movements of his hands, Johnson fairly seized them, and held them down.

An authour of considerable eminence having engrossed a good share of the conversation in the company of Johnson, and having said nothing but what was very trifling and insignificant; Johnson when he was gone, observed to us, 'It is wonderful what a difference there sometimes is between a man's powers of writing and of talking. ******* writes with great spirit, but is a poor talker; had he held his tongue we might have supposed him to have been restrained by modesty; but he has spoken a great deal to-day; and you have heard what stuff it was.' . . .

Mr. Steevens, who passed many a social hour with him during their long acquaintance, which commenced when they both lived in the Temple, has preserved a good number of particulars concerning him, most of which are to be found in the department of Apothegms, &c. in the Collection of *Johnson's Works*. But he has been pleased to favour me with the following, which are original:—

'One evening, previous to the trial of Baretti, a consultation of his friends was held at the house of Mr. Cox, the Solicitor, in Southampton-buildings, Chancery-lane. Among others present were, Mr. Burke and Dr. Johnson, who differed in sentiments concerning the tendency of some part of the defence the prisoner was to make. When the meeting was over, Mr. Steevens observed, that the question between him and his friend had been agitated with rather too much warmth. "It may be so, Sir, (replied the Doctor,) for Burke and I should have been of one opinion, if we had had no audience."

'Dr. Johnson once assumed a character in which perhaps even Mr. Boswell never saw him. His curiosity having been excited by the praises bestowed on the celebrated Torré's fireworks at Marybone-Gardens, he desired Mr. Steevens to accompany him thither. The evening had proved showery; and soon after the few people present were assembled, publick notice was given, that the conductors to the wheels, suns, stars, &c., were so thoroughly water-soaked, that it was impossible any part of the exhibition should be made. "This is a mere excuse, (says the Doctor,) to save their crackers for a more profitable company. Let us but hold up our sticks, and threaten to break those coloured lamps that surround the Orchestra, and we shall soon have our wishes gratified. The core of the fireworks cannot be injured; let the different pieces be touched in their respective centers, and they will do their offices as well as ever." Some young men who overheard him, immediately began the violence he had recommended, and an attempt was speedily made to fire some of the wheels which appeared to have received the smallest damage; but to little purpose were they lighted, for most of them completely failed. The authour of *The Rambler,* however, may be considered, on this occasion, as the ringleader of a successful riot, though not as skilful pyrotechnist.'

It has been supposed that Dr. Johnson, so far as fashion was concerned, was careless of his appearance in publick. But this is not altogether true, as the following slight instance may show:—Goldsmith's last Comedy was to be represented during some court-mourning: and Mr. Steevens appointed to call on Dr. Johnson, and carry him to the tavern where he was to dine with others of the Poet's friends. The Doctor was ready dressed, but in coloured cloaths; yet being told that he would find every one else in black, received the intelligence with a profusion of thanks, hastened to change his attire, all the while repeating his gratitude for the information that had saved him from an appearance so improper in the front row of a front box. "I would not (added he,) for ten pounds, have seemed so retrograde to any general observance."

'He would sometimes found his dislikes on very slender circumstances. Happening one day to mention Mr. Flexman, a Dissenting Minister, with some compliment to his exact memory in chronological matters; the Doctor replied, "Let me hear no more of him, Sir. That is the fellow who made the Index to my *Ramblers*, and set down the name of Milton thus: Milton, *Mr.* John." '

Mr. Steevens adds this testimony:—

'It is unfortunate, however, for Johnson, that his particularities and frailties can be more distinctly traced than his good and amiable exertions. Could the many bounties he studiously concealed, the many acts of humanity he performed in private, be displayed with equal circumstantiality, his defects would be so far lost in the blaze of his virtues, that the latter only would be regarded.'

Though from my very high admiration of Johnson, I have wondered that he was not courted by all the great and all the eminent persons of his time, it ought fairly to be considered, that no man of humble birth, who lived entirely by literature, in short no authour by profession, ever rose in this country into that personal notice which he did. In the course of this work a numerous variety of names has been mentioned, to which many might be added. I cannot omit Lord and Lady Lucan, at whose house he often enjoyed all that an elegant table and the best company can contribute to happiness; he found hospitality united with extraordinary accomplishments, and embellished with charms of which no man could be insensible.

On Tuesday, June 22, I dined with him at THE LITERARY CLUB, the last time of his being in that respectable society. The other members present were the Bishop of St. Asaph, Lord Eliot, Lord Palmerston, Dr. Fordyce, and Mr. Malone. He looked ill; but had such a manly fortitude, that he did not trouble the company with melancholy complaints. They all shewed evident marks of kind concern about him, with which he was much pleased, and he exerted himself to be as entertaining as his indisposition allowed him.

The anxiety of his friends to preserve so estimable a life, as long as human means might be supposed to have influence, made them plan for him a retreat from the severity of a British winter, to the mild climate of Italy. This scheme was at last brought to a serious resolution at General Paoli's, where I had often talked of it. One essential matter, however, I understood was necessary to be previously settled, which was obtaining such an addition to his income, as would be sufficient to enable him to defray the expence in a manner becoming the first literary character of a great nation, and, independent of all his other merits, the Authour of THE DICTIONARY OF THE ENGLISH LANGUAGE. The person to whom I above all others thought I should apply to negociate this business, was the Lord Chancellor, because I knew that he highly valued Johnson, and that Johnson highly valued his Lordship; so that it was no degradation of my illustrious friend to solicit for him the favour of such a man. I have mentioned what Johnson said of him to me when he was at the bar; and after his Lordship was advanced to the seals, he said of him, 'I would prepare myself for no man in England but Lord Thurlow. When I am to meet with him I should wish to know a day before.' How he would have prepared himself I cannot conjecture. Would he have selected certain topicks, and considered them in every view so as to be in readiness to argue them at all points? and what may we suppose those topicks to have been? I once started the curious inquiry to the great man who was the subject of this compliment: he smiled, but did not pursue it.

I first consulted with Sir Joshua Reynolds, who perfectly coincided in opinion with me; and I therefore, though personally very little known to his Lordship, wrote to him, stating the case, and requesting his good offices for Dr. Johnson. I mentioned that I was obliged to set out for Scotland early in the following week, so that if his Lordship should have any commands for me as to this pious negociation, he would be pleased to send them before that time; otherwise Sir Joshua Reynolds would give all attention to it.

This application was made not only without any suggestion on the part of Johnson himself, but was utterly unknown to him, nor had he the smallest suspicion of it. Any insinuations, therefore, which since his death have been thrown out, as if he had stooped to ask what was superfluous, are without any foundation. But, had he asked it, it would not have been superfluous; for though the money he had saved proved to be more than his friends imagined, or than I believe he himself, in his carelessness concerning worldly matters, knew it to be, had he travelled upon the Continent, an augmentation of his income would by no means have been unnecessary.

On Wednesday, June 23, I visited him in the morning, after having been present at the shocking sight of fifteen men executed before Newgate. I said to him, I was sure that human life was not machinery, that is to say, a chain of fatality planned and directed by the Supreme Being, as it had in it so much wickedness and misery, so many instances of both, as that by which my mind was now clouded. Were it machinery it would be better than it is in these respects, though less noble, as not being a system of moral government. He agreed with me now, as he always did, upon the great question of the liberty of the human will, which has been in all ages perplexed with so much sophistry. 'But, Sir, as to the doctrine of Necessity, no man believes it. If a man should give me arguments that I do not see, though I could not answer them, should I believe that I do not see?' It will be observed, that Johnson at all times made the just distinction between doctrines *contrary* to reason, and doctrines *above* reason.

Talking of the religious discipline proper for unhappy convicts, he said, 'Sir, one of our regular clergy will probably not impress their minds sufficiently: they should be attended by a Methodist preacher, or a Popish priest.' . . .

On Thursday, June 24, I dined with him at Mr. Dilly's, where were the Rev. Mr. (now Dr.) Knox, master of Tunbridge-school, Mr. Smith, Vicar of Southill, Dr. Beattie, Mr. Pinkerton, authour of various literary performances, and the Rev. Dr. Mayo. At my desire old Mr. Sheridan was invited, as I was earnest to have Johnson and him brought together again by chance, that a reconciliation might be effected. Mr. Sheridan happened to come early, and having learned that Dr. Johnson was to be there, went away; so I found, with sincere regret, that my friendly intentions were hopeless. I recollect nothing that passed this day, except Johnson's quickness, who, when Dr. Beattie observed, as something remarkable which had happened to him, that he had chanced to see both No. 1, and No. 1000, of the Hackney-coaches, the first and the last; 'Why, Sir, (said Johnson,) there is an equal chance for one's seeing those two numbers as any other two.' He was clearly right; yet the seeing of the two extremes, each of which is in some degree more conspicuous than the rest, could not but strike one in a stronger manner than the sight of any other two numbers. Though I have neglected to preserve his conversation, it was perhaps at this interview that Dr. Knox formed the notion of it which he has exhibited in his *Winter Evenings*.

On Friday, June 25, I dined with him at General Paoli's, where, he says in one of his letters to Mrs. Thrale, 'I love to dine.' There was a variety of dishes much to his taste, of all which he seemed to me to eat so much, that I was afraid he might be hurt by it; and I whispered to the General my fear, and begged he might not press him. 'Alas! (said the General,) see how very ill he looks; he can live but a very short time. Would you refuse any slight gratifications to a man under sentence of death? There is a humane custom in Italy, by which persons in that melancholy situation are indulged with having whatever they like best to eat and drink, even with expensive delicacies.'

I shewed him some verses on Lichfield by Miss Seward, which I had that day received from her, and had the pleasure to hear him approve of them. He confirmed to me the truth of a high compliment which I had been told he had paid to that lady, when she mentioned to him *The Colombiade*, an epick poem, by Madame du Boccage:—'Madam, there is not in it any thing equal to your description of the sea round the North Pole, in your Ode on the death of Captain Cook.'

On Sunday, June 27, I found him rather better. I mentioned to him a young man who was going to Jamaica with his wife and children, in expectation of being provided for by two of her brothers settled in that island, one a clergyman, and the other a physician. JOHNSON. 'It is a wild scheme, Sir, unless he has a positive and deliberate invitation. There was a poor girl, who used to come about me, who had a cousin in Barbadoes, that, in a letter to her, expressed a wish she should come out to that Island, and expatiated on the comforts and happiness of her situation. The poor girl went out: her cousin was much surprised, and asked her how she could think of coming. "Because, (said she,) you invited me." "Not I," answered the cousin. The letter was then produced. "I see it is true, (said she,) that I did invite you: but I did not think you would come." They lodged her in an out-house, where she passed her time miserably; and as soon as she had an opportunity she returned to England. Always tell this, when you hear of people going abroad to relations, upon a notion of being well received. In the case which you mention, it is probable the clergyman spends all he gets, and the physician does not know how much he is to get.'

We this day dined at Sir Joshua Reynolds's, with General Paoli, Lord Eliot, (formerly Mr. Eliot, of Port Eliot,) Dr. Beattie, and some other company. Talking of Lord Chesterfield;—JOHNSON. 'His manner was exquisitely elegant, and he had more knowledge than I expected.' BOSWELL. 'Did you find, Sir, his conversation to be of a superiour style?' JOHNson. 'Sir, in the conversation which I had with him I had the best right to superiority, for it was upon philology and literature.' Lord Eliot, who had travelled at the same time with Mr. Stanhope, Lord Chesterfield's natural son, justly observed, that it was strange that a man who shewed he had so much affection for his son as Lord Chesterfield did, by writing so many long and anxious letters to him, almost all of them when he was Secretary of State, which certainly was a proof of great goodness of disposition, should endeavour to make his son a rascal. His Lordship told us, that Foote had intended to bring on the stage a father who had thus tutored his son, and to shew the son an honest man to every one else, but practising his father's maxims upon him, and cheating him. JOHNSON. 'I am much pleased with this design; but I think there was no occasion to make the son honest at all. No; he should be a consummate rogue: the contrast between honesty and knavery would be the stronger. It should be contrived so that the father should be the only sufferer by the son's villainy, and thus there would be poetical justice.'

He put Lord Eliot in mind of Dr. Walter Harte. 'I know (said he,) Harte was your Lordship's tutor, and he was also tutor to the Peterborough family. Pray, my Lord, do you recollect any particulars that he told you of Lord Peterborough? He is a favourite of mine, and is not enough known; his character has been only ventilated in party pamphlets.' Lord Eliot said, if Dr. Johnson would be so good as to ask him any questions, he would tell what he could recollect. Accordingly some things were mentioned. 'But, (said his Lordship,) the best account of Lord Peterborough that I have happened to meet with, is in *Captain Carleton's Memoirs*. Carleton was descended of an ancestor who had distinguished himself at the siege of Derry. He was an officer; and, what was rare at that time, had some knowledge of engineering.' Johnson said, he had never heard of the book. Lord Eliot had it at Port Eliot; but, after a good deal of inquiry, procured a copy in London, and sent it to Johnson, who told Sir Joshua Reynolds that he was going to bed when it came, but was so much pleased with it, that he sat up till he had read it through, and found in it such an air of truth, that he could not doubt of its authenticity; adding, with a smile, (in allusion to Lord Eliot's having recently been raised to the peerage,) 'I did not think a *young Lord* could have mentioned to me a book in the English history that was not known to me.'

An addition to our company came after we went up to the drawing-room; Dr. Johnson seemed to rise in spirits as his audience increased. He said, 'He wished Lord Orford's pictures, and Sir Ashton Lever's Museum, might be purchased

638

by the publick, because both the money, and the pictures, and the curiosities, would remain in the country; whereas, if they were sold into another kingdom, the nation would indeed get some money, but would lose the pictures and curiosities, which it would be desirable we should have, for improvement in taste and natural history. The only question was, as the nation was much in want of money, whether it would not be better to take a large price from a foreign State?'

He entered upon a curious discussion of the difference between intuition and sagacity; one being immediate in its effect, the other requiring a circuitous process; one he observed was the *eye* of the mind, the other the *nose* of the mind.

A young gentleman[1] present took up the argument against him, and maintained that no man ever thinks of the *nose of the mind*, not adverting that though that figurative sense seems strange to us, as very unusual, it is truly not more forced than Hamlet's 'In my *mind's eye*, Horatio.' He persisted much too long, and appeared to Johnson as putting himself forward as his antagonist with too much presumption; upon which he called to him in a loud tone, 'What is it you are contending for, if you *be* contending?' And afterwards imagining that the gentleman retorted upon him with a kind of smart drollery, he said, 'Mr. *****, it does not become you to talk so to me. Besides, ridicule is not your talent; you have *there* neither intuition nor sagacity.' The gentleman protested that he had intended no improper freedom, but had the greatest respect for Dr. Johnson. After a short pause, during which we were somewhat uneasy,—Johnson. 'Give me your hand, Sir. You were too tedious, and I was too short.' Mr. *****. 'Sir, I am honoured by your attention in any way.' Johnson. 'Come, Sir, let's have no more of it. We offended one another by our contention; let us not offend the company by our compliments.'

He now said, 'He wished much to go to Italy, and that he dreaded passing the winter in England.' I said nothing; but enjoyed a secret satisfaction in thinking that I had taken the most effectual measures to make such a scheme practicable.

On Monday, June 28, I had the honour to receive from the Lord Chancellor the following letter:—

'To James Boswell, Esq.

'Sir,—I should have answered your letter immediately, if (being much engaged when I received it) I had not put it in my pocket, and forgot to open it till this morning.

[1] Burke's son, Richard.

'I am much obliged to you for the suggestion; and I will adopt and press it as far as I can. The best argument, I am sure, and I hope it is not likely to fail, is Dr. Johnson's merit. But it will be necessary, if I should be so unfortunate as to miss seeing you, to converse with Sir Joshua on the sum it will be proper to ask,—in short, upon the means of setting him out. It would be a reflection on us all, if such a man should perish for want of the means to take care of his health. Yours, &c.   'THURLOW.'

This letter gave me a very high satisfaction; I next day went and shewed it to Sir Joshua Reynolds, who was exceedingly pleased with it. He thought that I should now communicate the negociation to Dr. Johnson, who might afterwards complain if the attention with which he had been honoured, should be too long concealed from him. I intended to set out for Scotland next morning; but Sir Joshua cordially insisted that I should stay another day, that Johnson and I might dine with him, that we three might talk of his Italian Tour, and, as Sir Joshua expressed himself, 'have it all out.' I hastened to Johnson, and was told by him that he was rather better to-day. BOSWELL. 'I am very anxious about you, Sir, and particularly that you should go to Italy for the winter, which I believe is your own wish.' JOHNSON. 'It is, Sir.' BOSWELL. 'You have no objection, I presume, but the money it would require.' JOHNSON. 'Why, no, Sir.' Upon which I gave him a particular account of what had been done, and read to him the Lord Chancellor's letter. He listened with much attention; then warmly said, 'This is taking prodigious pains about a man.' 'O! Sir, (said I, with most sincere affection,) your friends would do every thing for you.' He paused, grew more and more agitated, till tears started into his eyes, and he exclaimed with fervent emotion, 'GOD bless you all.' I was so affected that I also shed tears. After a short silence he renewed and extended his grateful benediction, 'GOD bless you all, for JESUS CHRIST'S sake.' We both remained for some time unable to speak. He rose suddenly and quitted the room, quite melted in tenderness. He staid but a short time, till he had recovered his firmness; soon after he returned I left him, having first engaged him to dine at Sir Joshua Reynolds's, next day. I never was again under that roof which I had so long reverenced.

On Wednesday, June 30, the friendly confidential dinner with Sir Joshua Reynolds took place, no other company being present. Had I known that this was the last time that I should enjoy in this world, the conversation of a friend whom I so much respected, and from whom I derived so much instruction and entertainment, I should have been deeply affected. When I now look back to it, I am vexed that a single word should have been forgotten.

Both Sir Joshua and I were so sanguine in our expectations, that we expatiated with confidence on the liberal provision which we were sure would be made for him, conjecturing whether munificence would be displayed in one large donation, or in an ample increase of his pension. He himself catched so much of our enthusiasm, as to allow himself to suppose it not impossible that our hopes might in one way or other be realised. He said that he would rather have his pension doubled than a grant of a thousand pounds; 'For, (said he,) though probably I may not live to receive as much as a thousand pounds, a man would have the consciousness that he should pass the remainder of his life in splendour, how long soever it might be.' Considering what a moderate proportion an income of six hundred pounds a year bears to innumerable fortunes in this country, it is worthy of remark, that a man so truly great should think it splendour.

As an instance of extraordinary liberality of friendship, he told us, that Dr. Brocklesby had upon this occasion offered him a hundred a year for his life. A grateful tear started into his eye, as he spoke this in a faultering tone.

Sir Joshua and I endeavoured to flatter his imagination with agreeable prospects of happiness in Italy. 'Nay, (said he,) I must not expect much of that; when a man goes to Italy merely to feel how he breathes the air, he can enjoy very little.'

Our conversation turned upon living in the country, which Johnson, whose melancholy mind required the dissipation of quick successive variety, had habituated himself to consider as a kind of mental imprisonment. 'Yet, Sir, (said I,) there are many people who are content to live in the country.' JOHNSON. 'Sir, it is in the intellectual world as in the physical world; we are told by natural philosophers that a body is at rest in the place that is fit for it; they who are content to live in the country, are *fit* for the country.'

Talking of various enjoyments, I argued that a refinement of taste was a disadvantage, as they who have attained to it must be seldomer pleased than those who have no nice discrimination, and are therefore satisfied with every thing that comes in their way. JOHNSON. 'Nay, Sir; that is a paltry notion. Endeavour to be as perfect as you can in every respect.'

I accompanied him in Sir Joshua Reynolds's coach, to the entry of Bolt-court. He asked me whether I would not go with him to his house; I declined it, from an apprehension that my spirits would sink. We bade adieu to each other affectionately in the carriage. When he had got down upon the foot-pavement, he called out, 'Fare you well;' and without looking back, sprung away with a kind of pathetick briskness, if I may use that expression, which seemed to indicate a struggle to conceal uneasiness, and impressed me with a foreboding of our long, long separation.

I remained one day more in town, to have the chance of talking over my negociation with the Lord Chancellor; but the multiplicity of his Lordship's important engagements did not allow of it; so I left the management of the business in the hands of Sir Joshua Reynolds.

Soon after this time Dr. Johnson had the mortification of being informed by Mrs. Thrale, that, 'what she supposed he never believed,' was true; namely, that she was actually going to marry Signor Piozzi, an Italian musick-master. He endeavoured to prevent it; but in vain. If she would publish the whole of the correspondence that passed between Dr. Johnson and her on the subject, we should have a full view of his real sentiments. As it is, our judgement must be biassed by that characteristick specimen which Sir John Hawkins has given us: 'Poor Thrale! I thought that either her virtue or her vice would have restrained her from such a marriage. She is now become a subject for her enemies to exult over; and for her friends, if she has any left, to forget, or pity.'

It must be admitted that Johnson derived a considerable portion of happiness from the comforts and elegancies which he enjoyed in Mr. Thrale's family; but Mrs. Thrale assures us he was indebted for these to her husband alone, who certainly respected him sincerely. Her words are,—*Veneration for his virtue, reverence for his talents,* delight *in his conversation, and* habitual endurance of a yoke my husband first put upon me, *and of which he contentedly bore his share for sixteen or seventeen years, made me go on so long with* Mr. Johnson; *but the perpetual confinement I will own to have been* terrifying *in the first years of our friendship, and* irksome *in the last; nor could I pretend to* support *it without help, when my coadjutor was no more.'*

Alas! how different is this from the declarations which I have heard Mrs. Thrale make in his life-time, without a single murmur against any peculiarities, or against any one circumstance which attended their intimacy.

As a sincere friend of the great man whose *Life* I am writing, I think it necessary to guard my readers against the mistaken notion of Dr. Johnson's character, which this lady's *Anecdotes* of him suggest; for from the very nature and form of her book, 'it lends deception lighter wings to fly.'

'Let it be remembered, (says an eminent critick,)[1] that she has comprised in a small volume all that she could recollect of Dr. Johnson in *twenty years,* during which period, doubtless, some severe things were said by him; and they who read the book in *two hours,* naturally enough suppose that his whole conversation was of this complexion. But the fact is, I have been often in his company, and never *once* heard him say a severe thing to any one; and many others can attest the same. When he did say a severe thing, it was generally extorted by ignorance pretending to knowledge, or by extreme vanity or affectation. . . .

Having left the *pious negociation,* as I called it, in the best hands, I shall here insert what relates to it. Johnson wrote to Sir Joshua Reynolds on July 6, as follows:—

'I am going, I hope, in a few days, to try the air of Derbyshire, but hope to see you before I go. Let me, however, mention to you what I have much at heart. If the Chancellor should continue his attention to Mr. Boswell's request, and confer with you on the means of relieving my languid state, I am very desirous to avoid the appearance of asking money upon false pretences. I desire you to represent to his Lordship, what, as soon as it is suggested, he will perceive to be reasonable—That, if I grow much worse, I shall be afraid to leave my physicians, to suffer the inconveniences of travel, and pine in the solitude of a foreign country; That, if I grow much better, of which indeed there is now little appearance, I shall not wish to leave my friends and my domestick comforts; for I do not travel for pleasure or curiosity; yet if I should recover, curiosity would revive. In my present state, I am desirous to make a struggle for a little longer life, and hope to obtain some help from a softer climate. Do for me what you can.'

He wrote to me July 26:—'I wish your affairs could have permitted a longer and continued exertion of your zeal and kindness. They that have your kindness may want your ardour. In the mean time I am very feeble and very dejected.'

By a letter from Sir Joshua Reynolds I was informed, that the Lord Chancellor had called on him, and acquainted him that the application had not been successful; but that his Lordship, after speaking highly in praise of Johnson, as a man who was an honour to his country, desired Sir Joshua to let him know, that on granting a mortgage of his pension, he should draw on his Lordship to the amount of five or six hundred pounds; and that his Lordship explained the meaning of the mortgage to be, that he wished the business to be

[1] Malone.

conducted in such a manner, that Dr. Johnson should appear to be under the least possible obligation. Sir Joshua mentioned, that he had by the same post communicated all this to Dr. Johnson.

How Johnson was affected upon the occasion will appear from what he wrote to Sir Joshua Reynolds:——

'Ashbourne, Sept. 9. Many words I hope are not necessary between you and me, to convince you what gratitude is excited in my heart by the Chancellor's liberality, and your kind offices. . . .

'I have enclosed a letter to the Chancellor, which, when you have read it, you will be pleased to seal with a head, or any other general seal, and convey it to him: had I sent it directly to him, I should have seemed to overlook the favour of your intervention.'

'To THE LORD HIGH CHANCELLOR

'MY LORD,—After a long and not inattentive observation of mankind, the generosity of your Lordship's offer raises in me not less wonder than gratitude. Bounty, so liberally bestowed, I should gladly receive, if my condition made it necessary; for, to such a mind, who would not be proud to own his obligations? But it has pleased GOD to restore me to so great a measure of health, that if I should now appropriate so much of a fortune destined to do good, I could not escape from myself the charge of advancing a false claim. My journey to the continent, though I once thought it necessary, was never much encouraged by my physicians; and I was very desirous that your Lordship should be told of it by Sir Joshua Reynolds, as an event very uncertain; for if I grew much better, I should not be willing, if much worse, not able, to migrate. Your Lordship was first solicited without my knowledge; but, when I was told, that you were pleased to honour me with your patronage, I did not expect to hear of a refusal; yet, as I have had no long time to brood hope, and have not rioted in imaginary opulence, this cold reception has been scarce a disappointment; and, from your Lordship's kindness, I have received a benefit, which only men like you are able to bestow. I shall now live *mihi carior*,[1] with a higher opinion of my own merit. I am, my Lord, your Lordship's most obliged, most grateful, and most humble servant,

'September, 1784.'   'SAM. JOHNSON.'

... 'To THE REVEREND MR. BAGSHAW, *at Bromley*

'Sir,—Perhaps you may remember, that in the year 1753,[2]

---

[1] 'Dearer to myself.'
[2] Actually, 1752.

you committed to the ground my dear wife. I now entreat your permission to lay a stone upon her; and have sent the inscription, that, if you find it proper, you may signify your allowance.

'You will do me a great favour by showing the place where she lies, that the stone may protect her remains.

'Mr. Ryland will wait on you for the inscription, and procure it to be engraved. You will easily believe that I shrink from this mournful office. When it is done, if I have strength remaining, I will visit Bromley once again, and pay you part of the respect to which you have a right from, Reverend Sir, your most humble servant,

'July 12, 1784.'   'SAM. JOHNSON.'

. . . Next day he set out on a jaunt to Staffordshire and Derbyshire, flattering himself that he might be in some degree relieved. . . .

To MR. WINDHAM:—

AUGUST. 'The tenderness with which you have been pleased to treat me, through my long illness, neither health nor sickness can, I hope, make me forget; and you are not to suppose, that after we parted you were no longer in my mind. But what can a sick man say, but that he is sick? His thoughts are necessarily concentered in himself; he neither receives nor can give delight; his inquiries are after alleviations of pain, and his efforts are to catch some momentary comfort. Though I am now in the neighbourhood of the Peak, you must expect no account of its wonders, of its hills, its waters, its caverns, or its mines; but I will tell you, dear Sir, what I hope you will not hear with less satisfaction, that, for about a week past, my asthma has been less afflictive.'

LICHFIELD. OCTOBER 2. 'I believe you have been long enough acquainted with the *phænomena* of sickness, not to be surprised that a sick man wishes to be where he is not, and where it appears to every body but himself that he might easily be, without having the resolution to remove. I thought Ashbourne a solitary place, but did not come hither till last Monday. I have here more company, but my health has for this last week not advanced; and in the languor of disease how little can be done? Whither or when I shall make my next remove, I cannot tell; but I entreat you, dear Sir, to let me know, from time to time, where you may be found, for your residence is a very powerful attractive to, Sir, your most humble servant.' . . .

We now behold Johnson for the last time, in his native city,

645

for which he ever retained a warm affection, and which, by a sudden apostrophe, under the word *Lich*, he introduces with reverence, into his immortal Work, THE ENGLISH DICTIONARY: *Salve magna parens!*[1] . . .

To Mr. Henry White, a young clergyman, with whom he now formed an intimacy, so as to talk to him with great freedom, he mentioned that he could not in general accuse himself of having been an undutiful son. 'Once, indeed, (said he,) I was disobedient; I refused to attend my father to Uttoxeter-market. Pride was the source of that refusal, and the remembrance of it was painful. A few years ago, I desired to atone for this fault; I went to Uttoxeter in very bad weather, and stood for a considerable time bareheaded in the rain, on the spot where my father's stall used to stand. In contrition I stood, and I hope the penance was expiatory.'

'I told him (says Miss Seward) in one of my latest visits to him, of a wonderful learned pig, which I had seen at Nottingham; and which did all that we have observed exhibited by dogs and horses. The subject amused him.' 'Then, (said he,) the pigs are a race unjustly calumniated. *Pig* has, it seems, not been wanting to *man*, but *man* to *pig*. We do not allow *time* for his education, we kill him at a year old.' Mr. Henry White, who was present, observed that if this instance had happened in or before Pope's time, he would not have been justified in instancing the swine as the lowest degree of groveling instinct. Dr. Johnson seemed pleased with the observation, while the person who made it proceeded to remark, that great torture must have been employed, ere the indocility of the animal could have been subdued. 'Certainly, (said the Doctor;) but, (turning to me,) how old is your pig?' I told him, three years old. 'Then, (said he,) the pig has no cause to complain; he would have been killed the first year if he had not been *educated*, and protracted existence is a good recompence for very considerable degrees of torture.'

As Johnson had now very faint hopes of recovery, and as Mrs. Thrale was no longer devoted to him, it might have been supposed that he would naturally have chosen to remain in the comfortable house of his beloved wife's daughter, and end his life where he began it. But there was in him an animated and lofty spirit, and however complicated diseases might depress ordinary mortals, all who saw him, beheld and acknowledged the *invictum animum Catonis*.[2] Such was his intellectual ardour even at this time, that he said to one friend, 'Sir, I look upon every day to be lost, in which I do not make a new

---

[1] 'Hail, great mother.' Virgil, *Georgics*, ii. 173.

[2] 'The undaunted soul of Cato.' Altered from Horace, *Odes*, II. i. 24.

acquaintance;' and to another, when talking of his illness, 'I will be conquered; I will not capitulate.' And such was his love of London, so high a relish had he of its magnificent extent, and variety of intellectual entertainment, that he languished when absent from it, his mind having become quite luxurious from the long habit of enjoying the metropolis; and, therefore, although at Lichfield, surrounded with friends, who loved and revered him, and for whom he had a very sincere affection, he still found that such conversation as London affords, could be found no where else. These feelings, joined, probably, to some flattering hopes of aid from the eminent physicians and surgeons in London, who kindly and generously attended him without accepting of fees, made him resolve to return to the capital. . . .

He arrived in London on the 16th of November, and next day sent to Dr Burney the following note, which I insert as the last token of his remembrance of that ingenious and amiable man, and as another of the many proofs of the tenderness and benignity of his heart:—

'MR. JOHNSON, who came home last night, sends his respects to dear Dr. Burney, and all the dear Burneys, little and great.' . . .

I unfortunately was so much indisposed during a considerable part of the year, that it was not, or at least I thought it was not, in my power to write to my illustrious friend as formerly, or without expressing such complaints as offended him. Having conjured him not to do me the injustice of charging me with affection,[1] I was with much regret long silent. His last letter to me then came, and affected me very tenderly:—

'To JAMES BOSWELL, ESQ.

'DEAR SIR,—I have this summer sometimes amended, and sometimes relapsed, but, upon the whole, have lost ground, very much. My legs are extremely weak, and my breath very short, and the water is now encreasing upon me. In this uncomfortable state your letters used to relieve; what is the reason that I have them no longer? Are you sick, or are you sullen? Whatever be the reason, if it be less than necessity, drive it away; and of the short life that we have, make the best use for yourself and for your friends. . . . I am sometimes afraid that your omission to write has some real cause, and shall be glad to know that you are not sick, and that nothing ill has befallen dear Mrs. Boswell, or any of your family. I am, Sir, your, &c.

'Lichfield, Nov. 3, 1784.'   'SAM. JOHNSON.'

[1] Of melancholy.

Yet it was not a little painful to me to find, that in a paragraph of this letter, which I have omitted, he still persevered in arraigning me as before, which was strange in him who had so much experience of what I suffered. I, however, wrote to him two as kind letters as I could; the last of which came too late to be read by him, for his illness encreased more rapidly upon him than I had apprehended; but I had the consolation of being informed that he spoke of me on his death-bed, with affection, and I look forward with humble hope of renewing our friendship in a better world.

I now relieve the readers of this Work from any farther personal notice of its authour, who if he should be thought to have obtruded himself too much upon their attention, requests them to consider the peculiar plan of his biographical undertaking.

Soon after Johnson's return to the metropolis, both the asthma and dropsy became more violent and distressful. He had for some time kept a journal in Latin of the state of his illness, and the remedies which he used, under the title of *Ægri Ephemeris*,[1] which he began on the 6th of July, but continued it no longer than the 8th of November; finding, I suppose, that it was a mournful and unavailing register. It is in my possession; and is written with great care and accuracy. . . .

My readers are now, at last, to behold SAMUEL JOHNSON preparing himself for that doom, from which the most exalted powers afford no exemption to man. Death had always been to him an object of terrour; so that, though by no means happy, he still clung to life with an eagerness at which many have wondered. At any time when he was ill, he was very much pleased to be told that he looked better. An ingenious member of the *Eumelian Club*, informs me, that upon one occasion when he said to him that he saw health returning to his cheek, Johnson seized him by the hand and exclaimed, 'Sir, you are one of the kindest friends I ever had.'

His own state of his views of futurity will appear truly rational; and may, perhaps, impress the unthinking with seriousness.

'You know, (says he,) I never thought confidence with respect to futurity, any part of the character of a brave, a wise, or a good man. Bravery has no place where it can avail nothing; wisdom impresses strongly the consciousness of those faults, of which it is, perhaps, itself an aggravation; and goodness, always wishing to be better, and imputing every deficience to criminal negligence, and every fault to voluntary cor-

[1] 'A sick man's journal.'

ruption, never dares to suppose the condition of forgiveness fulfilled, nor what is wanting in the crime supplied by penitence.

'This is the state of the best; but what must be the condition of him whose heart will not suffer him to rank himself among the best, or among the good? Such must be his dread of the approaching trial, as will leave him little attention to the opinion of those whom he is leaving for ever; and the serenity that is not felt, it can be no virtue to feign.'

His great fear of death, and the strange dark manner in which Sir John Hawkins imparts the uneasiness which he expressed on account of offences with which he charged himself, may give occasion to injurious suspicions, as if there had been something of more than ordinary criminality weighing upon his conscience. On that account, therefore, as well as from the regard to truth which he inculcated, I am to mention, (with all possible respect and delicacy, however,) that his conduct, after he came to London, and had associated with Savage and others, was not so strictly virtuous, in one respect, as when he was a younger man. It was well known, that his amorous inclinations were uncommonly strong and impetuous. He owned to many of his friends, that he used to take women of the town to taverns, and hear them relate their history. In short, it must not be concealed, that, like many other good and pious men, among whom we may place the Apostle Paul upon his own authority, Johnson was not free from propensities which were ever 'warring against the law of his mind,'—and that in his combats with them, he was sometimes overcome.

Here let the profane and licentious pause; let them not thoughtlessly say that Johnson was an *hypocrite,* or that his *principles* were not firm, because his *practice* was not uniformly conformable to what he professed.

Let the question be considered independent of moral and religious association; and no man will deny that thousands, in many instances, act against conviction. Is a prodigal, for example, an *hypocrite,* when he owns he is satisfied that his extravagance will bring him to ruin and misery? We are *sure* he *believes* it; but immediate inclination, strengthened by indulgence, prevails over that belief in influencing his conduct. Why then shall credit be refused to the *sincerity* of those who acknowledge their persuasion of moral and religious duty, yet sometimes fail of living as it requires? I heard Dr. Johnson once observe, 'There is something noble in publishing truth though it condemns one's self.' And one who said in his presence, 'he had no notion of people being in earnest in their good professions, whose practice was not suitable to them,' was thus reprimanded by him:—'Sir, are you so grossly ignorant of human nature as not to know that a man may be very sincere in good principles, without having good practice?'

But let no man encourage or soothe himself in 'presumptuous sin,' from knowing that Johnson was sometimes hurried into indulgences which he thought criminal. I have exhibited this circumstance as a shade in so great a character, both from my sacred love of truth, and to shew that he was not so weakly scrupulous as he has been represented by those who imagine that the sins, of which a deep sense was upon his mind, were merely such little venial trifles as pouring milk into his tea on Good-Friday. His understanding will be defended by my statement, if his consistency of conduct be in some degree impaired. But what wise man would, for momentary gratifications, deliberately subject himself to suffer such uneasiness as we find was experienced by Johnson in reviewing his conduct as compared with his notion of the ethicks of the gospel? Let the following passages be kept in remembrance:—

'O, GOD, giver and preserver of all life, by whose power I was created, and by whose providence I am sustained, look down upon me with tenderness and mercy; grant that I may not have been created to be finally destroyed; that I may not be preserved to add wickedness to wickedness.' 'O, LORD, let me not sink into total depravity; look down upon me, and rescue me at last from the captivity of sin.' 'Almighty and most merciful Father, who hast continued my life from year to year, grant that by longer life I may become less desirous of sinful pleasures, and more careful of eternal happiness.' 'Let not my years be multiplied to increase my guilt; but as my age advances, let me become more pure in my thoughts, more regular in my desires, and more obedient to thy laws.' 'Forgive, O merciful LORD, whatever I have done contrary to thy laws. Give me such a sense of my wickedness as may produce true contrition and effectual repentance; so that when I shall be called into another state, I may be received among the sinners to whom sorrow and reformation have obtained pardon, for JESUS CHRIST's sake. Amen.'

Such was the distress of mind, such the penitence of Johnson, in his hours of privacy, and in his devout approaches to his Maker. His *sincerity*, therefore, must appear to every candid mind unquestionable.

It is of essential consequence to keep in view, that there was in this excellent man's conduct no false principle of *commutation*, no *deliberate* indulgence in sin, in consideration of a counterbalance of duty. His offending, and his repenting, were distinct and separate:[1] and when we consider his almost unex-

[1] Dr. Johnson related, with very earnest approbation, a story of a

ampled attention to truth, his inflexible integrity, his constant piety, who will dare to 'cast a stone' at him? Besides, let it never be forgotten, that he cannot be charged with any offence indicating badness of *heart,* any thing dishonest, base, or malignant; but that, on the contrary, he was charitable in an extraordinary degree: so that even in one of his own rigid judgements of himself, (Easter-eve, 1781,) while he says, 'I have corrected no external habits;' he is obliged to own, 'I hope that since my last communion I have advanced, by pious reflections in my submission to GOD, and my benevolence to man.'

I am conscious that this is the most difficult and dangerous part of my biographical work, and I cannot but be very anxious concerning it. I trust that I have got through it, preserving at once my regard to truth,—to my friend,—and to the interests of virtue and religion. Nor can I apprehend that more harm can ensue from the knowledge of the irregularity of Johnson, guarded as I have stated it, than from knowing that Addison and Parnell were intemperate in the use of wine; which he himself, in his *Lives* of those celebrated writers and pious men, has not forborne to record.

It is not my intention to give a very minute detail of the particulars of Johnson's remaining days, of whom it was now evident, that the crisis was fast approaching, when he must '*die like men, and fall like one of the Princes.*' Yet it will be instructive, as well as gratifying to the curiosity of my readers, to record a few circumstances, on the authenticity of which they may perfectly rely, as I have been at the utmost pains to obtain an accurate account of his last illness, from the best authority.

Dr. Heberden, Dr. Brocklesby, Dr. Warren, and Dr. Butter, physicians, generously attended him, without accepting of any fees, as did Mr. Cruikshank, surgeon; and all that could be done from professional skill and ability, was tried, to prolong a life so truly valuable. He himself, indeed, having, on account of his very bad constitution, been perpetually applying himself to medical inquiries, united his own efforts with those of the gentlemen who attended him; and imagining that the dropsical collection of water which oppressed him might be drawn off by making incisions in his body, he, with his usual resolute defiance of pain, cut deep, when he thought that his surgeon had done it too tenderly.

About eight or ten days before his death, when Dr. Brock-

---

gentleman, who, in an impulse of passion, overcame the virtue of a young woman. When she said to him, 'I am afraid we have done wrong!' he answered, 'Yes, we have done wrong;—for I would not *debauch her mind*'—B.

lesby paid him his morning visit, he seemed very low and desponding, and said, 'I have been as a dying man all night.' He then emphatically broke out, in the words of Shakspeare:—

> 'Can'st thou not minister to a mind diseas'd;
> Pluck from the memory a rooted sorrow;
> Raze out the written troubles of the brain;
> And, with some sweet oblivious antidote,
> Cleanse the stuff'd bosom of that perilous stuff,
> Which weighs upon the heart?'

To which Dr. Brocklesby readily answered, from the same great poet:—

> '———————— therein the patient
> Must minister to himself.'

Johnson expressed himself much satisfied with the application.

On another day after this, when talking on the subject of prayer, Dr. Brocklesby repeated from Juvenal,—

> '*Orandum est, ut sit mens sana in corpore sano.*'[1]

and so on to the end of the tenth satire; but in running it quickly over, he happened, in the line,

> '*Qui spatium vitæ extremum inter munera ponat,*'[2]

to pronounce *supremum* for *extremum;* at which Johnson's critical ear instantly took offence, and discoursing vehemently on the unmetrical effect of such a lapse, he shewed himself as full as ever of the spirit of the grammarian.

Having no near relations, it had been for some time Johnson's intention to make a liberal provision for his faithful servant, Mr. Francis Barber, whom he looked upon as particularly under his protection, and whom he had all along treated truly as an humble friend. Having asked Dr. Brocklesby what would be a proper annuity to bequeath to a favourite servant, and being answered that it must depend on the circumstances of the master; and, that in the case of a nobleman, fifty pounds a year was considered as an adequate reward for many years' faithful service; 'Then, (said Johnson,) shall I be *nobilissimus*,[3] for I mean to leave Frank seventy pounds a year, and I desire you to tell him so.' It is strange, however, to think, that Johnson was not free from that general weakness of being averse to execute a will, so that he delayed it from

---

[1] 'What should be prayed for is a sound mind in a sound body.' Juvenal, *Satires*, x. 356.

[2] 'Who holds long life the least of gifts.' x. 358.

[3] 'Most noble.'

time to time; and had it not been for Sir John Hawkins's repeatedly urging it, I think it is probable that his kind resolution would not have been fulfilled. After making one, which, as Sir John Hawkins informs us, extended no further than the promised annuity, Johnson's final disposition of his property was established by a Will and Codicil. . . .

The consideration of the numerous papers of which he was possessed, seems to have struck Johnson's mind with a sudden anxiety, and as they were in great confusion, it is much to be lamented that he had not entrusted some faithful and discreet person with the care and selection of them; instead of which, he, in a precipitate manner, burnt large masses of them, with little regard, as I apprehend, to discrimination. Not that I suppose we have thus been deprived of any compositions which he had ever intended for the publick eye; but, from what escaped the flames, I judge that many curious circumstances relating both to himself and other literary characters have perished.

Two very valuable articles, I am sure, we have lost, which were two quarto volumes, containing a full, fair, and most particular account of his own life, from his earliest recollection. I owned to him, that having accidentally seen them, I had read a great deal in them; and apologizing for the liberty I had taken, asked him if I could help it. He placidly answered, 'Why, Sir, I do not think you could have helped it.' I said that I had, for once in my life, felt half an inclination to commit theft. It had come into my mind to carry off those two volumes, and never see him more. Upon my inquiring how this would have affected him, 'Sir, (said he,) I believe I should have gone mad.'

During his last illness, Johnson experienced the steady and kind attachment of his numerous friends. Mr. Hoole has drawn up a narrative of what passed in the visits which he paid him during that time, from the 10th of November to the 13th of December, the day of his death, inclusive, and has favoured me with a perusal of it, with permission to make extracts, which I have done. Nobody was more attentive to him than Mr. Langton, to whom he tenderly said, *Te teneam moriens deficiente manu.*[1] And I think it highly to the honour of Mr. Windham, that his important occupations as an active statesman did not prevent him from paying assiduous respect to the dying Sage, whom he revered. Mr. Langton informs me that, 'one day he found Mr. Burke and four or five more friends sitting with Johnson. Mr. Burke said to him, "I am afraid, Sir, such a number of us may be oppressive to you."

[1] 'May I, dying, hold you with my failing hand.' Tibullus, *Elegies,* I. i. 61.

"No, Sir, (said Johnson,) it is not so; and I must be in a wretched state, indeed, when your company would not be a delight to me." Mr. Burke, in a tremulous voice, expressive of being very tenderly affected, replied, "My dear Sir, you have always been too good to me." Immediately afterwards he went away. This was the last circumstance in the acquaintance of these two eminent men.'

The following particulars of his conversation, within a few days of his death, I give on the authority of Mr. John Nichols:—

'He said, that the Parliamentary Debates were the only part of his writings which then gave him any compunction: but that at the time he wrote them, he had no conception he was imposing upon the world, though they were frequently written from very slender materials, and often from none at all,—the mere coinage of his own imagination. He never wrote any part of his works with equal velocity. Three columns of the *Magazine*, in an hour, was no uncommon effort, which was faster than most persons could have transcribed that quantity.

'Of his friend Cave, he always spoke with great affection. "Yet (said he,) Cave, (who never looked out of his window, but with a view to the *Gentleman's Magazine*,) was a penurious paymaster; he would contract for lines by the hundred, and expect the long hundred; but he was a good man, and always delighted to have his friends at his table."

'When talking of a regular edition of his own works, he said, "that he had power, [from the booksellers,] to print such an edition, if his health admitted it; but had no power to assign over any edition, unless he could add notes, and so alter them as to make them new works; which his state of health forbade him to think of. I may possibly live, (said he,) or rather breath, three days, or perhaps three weeks; but find myself daily and gradually weaker."

'He said at another time, three or four days only before his death, speaking of the little fear he had of undergoing a chirurgical operation, "I would give one of these legs for a year more of life, I mean of comfortable life, not such as that which I now suffer;"—and lamented much his inability to read during his hours of restlessness. "I used formerly, (he added,) when sleepless in bed, *to read like a Turk.*"

'Whilst confined by his last illness, it was his regular practice to have the church-service read to him, by some attentive and friendly Divine. The Rev. Mr. Hoole performed this kind office in my presence for the last time, when, by his own desire, no more than the Litany was read; in which his responses were in the deep and sonorous voice which Mr. Boswell has occasionally noticed, and with the most profound devotion that can be imagined. His hearing not being quite perfect, he more than once interrupted Mr. Hoole, with "Louder, my dear Sir, louder, I entreat you, or you pray in vain!"—and, when the service was ended, he, with great earnestness, turned round to an excellent lady who was present, saying, "I thank you, Madam, very heartily for your kindness in joining me in this solemn exercise. Live well, I conjure you; and you will not feel the compunction at the last, which I now feel." So truly humble were the thoughts which this great and good man entertained of his own approaches to religious perfection.

'He was earnestly invited to publish a volume of *Devotional Exercises;* but this, (though he listened to the proposal with much complacency, and a large sum of money was offered for it,) he declined, from motives of the sincerest modesty.'. . .

Amidst the melancholy clouds which hung over the dying Johnson, his characteristical manner shewed itself on different occasions.

When Dr. Warren, in the usual style, hoped that he was better; his answer was, 'No, Sir; you cannot conceive with what acceleration I advance towards death.'

A man whom he had never seen before was employed one night to sit up with him. Being asked next morning how he liked his attendant, his answer was, 'Not at all, Sir: the fellow's an ideot; he is as awkward as a turn-spit when first put into the wheel, and as sleepy as a dormouse.'

Mr. Windham having placed a pillow conveniently to support him, he thanked him for his kindness, and said, 'That will do,—all that a pillow can do.'

He repeated with great spirit a poem, consisting of several stanzas, in four lines, in alternate rhyme, which he said he had composed some years before, on occasion of a rich, extravagant young gentleman's coming of age; saying he had never repeated it but once since he composed it, and had given but one copy of it. That copy was given to Mrs. Thrale, now Piozzi, who has published it in a Book which she entitles *British Synonymy,* but which is truly a collection of entertaining remarks and stories, no matter whether accurate or not.[1] . . .

As he opened a note which his servant brought to him, he said, 'An odd thought strikes me: we shall receive no letters in the grave.'

He requested three things of Sir Joshua Reynolds:—To for-

---

[1] The poem is omitted here.

give him thirty pounds which he had borrowed of him; to read the Bible; and never to use his pencil on a Sunday. Sir Joshua readily acquiesced.

Indeed he shewed the greatest anxiety for the religious improvement of his friends, to whom he discoursed of its infinite consequence. He begged of Mr. Hoole to think of what he had said, and to commit it to writing: and, upon being afterwards assured that this was done, pressed his hands, and in an earnest tone thanked him. Dr. Brocklesby having attended him with the utmost assiduity and kindness as his physician and friend, he was peculiarly desirous that this gentleman should not entertain any loose speculative notions, but be confirmed in the truths of Christianity, and insisted on his writing down in his presence, as nearly as he could collect it, the import of what passed on the subject: and Dr. Brocklesby having complied with the request, he made him sign the paper, and urged him to keep it in his own custody as long as he lived.

Johnson, with that native fortitude, which, amidst all his bodily distress and mental sufferings, never forsook him, asked Dr. Brocklesby, as a man in whom he had confidence, to tell him plainly whether he could recover. 'Give me (said he,) a direct answer.' The Doctor having first asked him if he could bear the whole truth, which way soever it might lead, and being answered that he could, declared that, in his opinion, he could not recover without a miracle. 'Then, (said Johnson,) I will take no more physick, not even my opiates; for I have prayed that I may render up my soul to God unclouded.' In this resolution he persevered, and, at the same time, used only the weakest kinds of sustenance. Being pressed by Mr. Windham to take somewhat more generous nourishment, lest too low a diet should have the very effect which he dreaded, by debilitating his mind, he said, 'I will take any thing but inebriating sustenance.'

The Reverend Mr. Strahan, who was the son of his friend, and had been always one of his great favourites, had, during his last illness, the satisfaction of contributing to soothe and comfort him. That gentleman's house, at Islington, of which he is Vicar, afforded Johnson, occasionally and easily, an agreeable change of place and fresh air; and he attended also upon him in town in the discharge of the sacred offices of his profession.

Mr. Strahan has given me the agreeable assurance, that, after being in much agitation, Johnson became quite composed, and continued so till his death.

Dr. Brocklesby, who will not be suspected of fanaticism, obliged me with the following accounts:—

656

'For some time before his death, all his fears were calmed and absorbed by the prevalence of his faith, and his trust in the merits and *propitiation* of JESUS CHRIST.

'He talked often to me about the necessity of faith in the *sacrifice* of Jesus, as necessary beyond all good works whatever, for the salvation of mankind.

'He pressed me to study Dr. Clarke and to read his Sermons. I asked him why he pressed Dr. Clarke, an Arian. "Because, (said he,) he is fullest on the *propitiatory sacrifice.*" '

Johnson having thus in his mind the true Christian scheme, at once rational and consolatory, uniting justice and mercy in the DIVINITY, with the improvement of human nature, previous to his receiving the Holy Sacrament in his apartment, composed and fervently uttered this prayer:—

'Almighty and most merciful Father, I am now, as to human eyes, it seems, about to commemorate, for the last time, the death of thy Son JESUS CHRIST, our Saviour and Redeemer. Grant, O LORD, that my whole hope and confidence may be in his merits, and thy mercy; enforce and accept my imperfect repentance; make this commemoration available to the confirmation of my faith, the establishment of my hope, and the enlargement of my charity; and make the death of thy Son JESUS CHRIST effectual to my redemption. Have mercy upon me, and pardon the multitude of my offences. Bless my friends; have mercy upon all men. Support me, by thy Holy Spirit, in the days of weakness, and at the hour of death; and receive me, at my death, to everlasting happiness, for the sake of JESUS CHRIST. Amen.'

Having, as has been already mentioned, made his will on the 8th and 9th of December, and settled all his worldly affairs, he languished till Monday, the 13th of that month, when he expired, about seven o'clock in the evening, with so little apparent pain that his attendants hardly perceived when his dissolution took place.

Of his last moments, my brother, Thomas David, has furnished me with the following particulars:—

'The Doctor, from the time that he was certain his death was near, appeared to be perfectly resigned, was seldom or never fretful or out of temper, and often said to his faithful servant, who gave me this account, "Attend, Francis, to the salvation of your soul, which is the object of greatest importance:" he also explained to him passages in the scripture, and seemed to have pleasure in talking upon religious subjects.

'On Monday, the 13th of December, the day on which he died, a Miss Morris, daughter to a particular friend of his, called, and said to Francis, that she begged to be permitted to see the Doctor, that she might earnestly request him to give her his blessing. Francis went into his room, followed by the young lady, and delivered the message. The Doctor turned himself in the bed, and said, "GOD bless you, my dear!" These were the last words he spoke. His difficulty of breathing increased till about seven o'clock in the evening, when Mr. Barber and Mrs. Desmoulins, who were sitting in the room, observing that the noise he made in breathing had ceased, went to the bed, and found he was dead.'

About two days after his death, the following very agreeable account was communicated to Mr. Malone, in a letter by the Honourable John Byng, to whom I am much obliged for granting me permission to introduce it in my work.

'DEAR SIR,—Since I saw you, I have had a long conversation with Cawston,[1] who sat up with Dr. Johnson, from nine o'clock, on Sunday evening, till ten o'clock, on Monday morning. And, from what I can gather from him, it should seem, that Dr. Johnson was perfectly composed, steady in hope, and resigned to death. At the interval of each hour, they assisted him to sit up in his bed, and move his legs, which were in much pain; when he regularly addressed himself to fervent prayer; and though, sometimes, his voice failed him, his senses never did, during that time. The only sustenance he received, was cyder and water. He said his mind was prepared, and the time to his dissolution seemed long. At six in the morning, he inquired the hour, and, on being informed, said that all went on regularly, and he felt he had but a few hours to live.

'At ten o'clock in the morning, he parted from Cawston, saying, "You should not detain Mr. Windham's servant:—I thank you; bear my remembrance to your master." Cawston says, that no man could appear more collected, more devout, or less terrified at the thoughts of the approaching minute.

'This account, which is so much more agreeable than, and somewhat different from, yours, has given us the satisfaction of thinking that that great man died as he lived, full of resignation, strengthened in faith, and joyful in hope.'

A few days before his death, he had asked Sir John Hawkins, as one of his executors, where he should be buried; and on being answered, 'Doubtless, in Westminster-Abbey,' seemed to feel a satisfaction, very natural to a Poet; and indeed, in my opinion, very natural to every man of any imagination, who has no family sepulchre in which he can be laid with his fathers. Accordingly, upon Monday, December 20,

[1] Servant to the Right Honourable William Windham—B.

his remains were deposited in that noble and renowned edifice; and over his grave was placed a large blue flag-stone, with this inscription:—

'SAMUEL JOHNSON, LL.D.
Obiit XIII *die Decembris,*
Anno Domini
M.DCC.LXXXIV.
Ætatis suæ LXXV.'

His funeral was attended by a respectable number of his friends, particularly such of the members of the LITERARY CLUB as were then in town; and was also honoured with the presence of several of the Reverend Chapter of Westminster. Mr. Burke, Sir Joseph Banks, Mr. Windham, Mr. Langton, Sir Charles Bunbury, and Mr. Colman, bore his pall. His school-fellow, Dr. Taylor, performed the mournful office of reading the burial service.

I trust, I shall not be accused of affectation, when I declare, that I find myself unable to express all that I felt upon the loss of such a 'Guide, Philosopher, and Friend.' I shall, therefore, not say one word of my own, but adopt those of an eminent friend,[1] which he uttered with an abrupt felicity, superior to all studied compositions:—'He has made a chasm, which not only nothing can fill up, but which nothing has a tendency to fill up. Johnson is dead. Let us go to the next best:—there is nobody; no man can be said to put you in mind of Johnson.'

As Johnson had abundant homage paid to him during his life, so no writer in this nation ever had such an accumulation of literary honours after his death. A sermon upon that event was preached in St. Mary's Church, Oxford, before the University, by the Reverend Mr. Agutter, of Magdalen College. The *Lives,* the *Memoirs,* the *Essays,* both in prose and verse, which have been published concerning him, would make many volumes. The numerous attacks too upon him, I consider as part of his consequence, upon the principle which he himself so well knew and asserted. Many who trembled at his presence, were forward in assault, when they no longer apprehended danger. When one of his little pragmatical foes was invidiously snarling at his fame, at Sir Joshua Reynolds's table, the Reverend Dr. Parr exclaimed, with his usual bold animation, 'Ay, now that the old lion is dead, every ass thinks he may kick at him.'

A monument for him, in Westminster Abbey, was resolved upon soon after his death, and was supported by a most re-

[1] William Gerard Hamilton.

spectable contribution; but the Dean and Chapter of St. Paul's having come to a resolution of admitting monuments there, upon a liberal and magnificent plan, that Cathedral was afterwards fixed on, as the place in which a cenotaph should be erected to his memory: and in the cathedral of his native city of Lichfield, a smaller one is to be erected. To compose his epitaph, could not but excite the warmest competition of genius. If *laudari à laudato viro*[1] be praise which is highly estimable, I should not forgive myself were I to omit the following sepulchral verses on the authour of THE ENGLISH DICTIONARY, written by the Right Honourable Henry Flood:—

> 'No need of Latin or of Greek to grace
> Our JOHNSON's memory, or inscribe his grave;
> His native language claims this mournful space,
> To pay the Immortality he gave.'

The character of SAMUEL JOHNSON has, I trust, been so developed in the course of this work, that they who have honoured it with a perusal, may be considered as well acquainted with him. As, however, it may be expected that I should collect into one view the capital and distinguishing features of this extraordinary man, I shall endeavour to acquit myself of that part of my biographical undertaking, however difficult it may be to do that which many of my readers will do better for themselves.

His figure was large and well formed, and his countenance of the cast of an ancient statue; yet his appearance was rendered strange and somewhat uncouth, by convulsive cramps, by the scars of that distemper which it was once imagined the royal touch could cure, and by a slovenly mode of dress. He had the use only of one eye; yet so much does mind govern and even supply the deficiency of organs, that his visual perceptions, as far as they extended, were uncommonly quick and accurate. So morbid was his temperament, that he never knew the natural joy of a free and vigorous use of his limbs: when he walked, it was like the struggling gait of one in fetters; when he rode, he had no command or direction of his horse, but was carried as if in a balloon. That with his constitution and habits of life he should have lived seventy-five years, is a proof that an inherent *vivida vis*[2] is a powerful preservative of the human frame.

Man is, in general, made up of contradictory qualities; and these will ever shew themselves in strange succession, where a consistency in appearance at least, if not in reality, has not

---

[1] 'To be praised by one whom all praise.'

[2] 'Lively force.' Lucretius, *Of the Nature of Things*, i. 72.

been attained by long habits of philosophical discipline. In proportion to the native vigour of the mind, the contradictory qualities will be the more prominent, and more difficult to be adjusted; and, therefore, we are not to wonder, that Johnson exhibited an eminent example of this remark which I have made upon human nature. At different times, he seemed a different man, in some respects; not, however, in any great or essential article, upon which he had fully employed his mind, and settled certain principles of duty, but only in his manners, and in the display of argument and fancy in his talk. He was prone to superstition, but not to credulity. Though his imagination might incline him to a belief of the marvellous and the mysterious, his vigorous reason examined the evidence with jealousy. He was a sincere and zealous Christian, of high Church-of-England and monarchical principles, which he would not tamely suffer to be questioned; and had, perhaps, at an early period, narrowed his mind somewhat too much, both as to religion and politicks. His being impressed with the danger of extreme latitude in either, though he was of a very independent spirit, occasioned his appearing somewhat unfavourable to the prevalence of that noble freedom of sentiment which is the best possession of man. Nor can it be denied, that he had many prejudices; which, however, frequently suggested many of his pointed sayings, that rather shew a playfulness of fancy than any settled malignity. He was steady and inflexible in maintaining the obligations of religion and morality; both from a regard for the order of society, and from a veneration for the GREAT SOURCE of all order; correct, nay stern in his taste; hard to please, and easily offended; impetuous and irritable in his temper, but of a most humane and benevolent heart, which shewed itself not only in a most liberal charity, as far as his circumstances would allow, but in a thousand instances of active benevolence. He was afflicted with a bodily disease, which made him often restless and fretful; and with a constitutional melancholy, the clouds of which darkened the brightness of his fancy, and gave a gloomy cast to his whole course of thinking: we, therefore, ought not to wonder at his sallies of impatience and passion at any time; especially when provoked by obtrusive ignorance, or presuming petulance; and allowance must be made for his uttering hasty and satirical sallies, even against his best friends. And, surely, when it is considered, that, 'amidst sickness and sorrow,' he exerted his faculties in so many works for the benefit of mankind, and particularly that he atchieved the great and admirable DICTIONARY of our language, we must be astonished at his resolution. The solemn text, 'of him to whom much is given, much will be required,' seems to have been ever present to his mind, in a rigorous sense, and to have made him dissatisfied with his labours and acts of goodness, however comparatively great; so that the unavoidable consciousness of his superiority was, in that respect, a cause of disquiet. He suffered so much from this, and from the gloom which perpetually haunted him, and made solitude frightful, that it may be said of him, 'If in this life only he had hope, he was of all men most miserable.' He loved praise, when it was brought to him; but was too proud to seek for it. He was somewhat susceptible of flattery. As he was general and unconfined in his studies, he cannot be considered as master of any one particular science; but he had accumulated a vast and various collection of learning and knowledge, which was so arranged in his mind, as to be ever in readiness to be brought forth. But his superiority over other learned men consisted chiefly in what may be called the art of thinking, the art of using his mind; a certain continual power of seizing the useful substance of all that he knew, and exhibiting it in a clear and forcible manner; so that knowledge, which we often see to be no better than lumber in men of dull understanding, was, in him, true, evident, and actual wisdom. His moral precepts are practical; for they are drawn from an intimate acquaintance with human nature. His maxims carry conviction; for they are founded on the basis of common sense, and a very attentive and minute survey of real life. His mind was so full of imagery, that he might have been perpetually a poet; yet it is remarkable, that, however rich his prose is in this respect, his poetical pieces, in general, have not much of that splendour, but are rather distinguished by strong sentiment and acute observation, conveyed in harmonious and energetick verse, particularly in heroick couplets. Though usually grave, and even aweful, in his deportment, he possessed uncommon and peculiar powers of wit and humour; he frequently indulged himself in colloquial pleasantry; and the heartiest merriment was often enjoyed in his company; with this great advantage, that as it was entirely free from any poisonous tincture of vice or impiety, it was salutary to those who shared in it. He had accustomed himself to such accuracy in his common conversation, that he at all times expressed his thoughts with great force, and an elegant choice of language, the effect of which was aided by his having a loud voice, and a slow deliberate utterance. In him were united a most logical head with a most fertile imagination, which gave him an extraordinary advantage in arguing: for he could reason close or wide, as he saw best for the moment. Exulting in his intellectual strength and dexterity, he could, when he pleased, be the greatest sophist that ever contended in the lists of declamation; and, from a spirit of contradiction and a delight in shewing his powers, he would often maintain the wrong side with equal warmth and ingenuity; so that, when there was an audience, his real opinions could seldom be gathered from his talk; though when he was in company with a single friend, he would discuss a subject with genuine fairness: but he was too conscientious to make errour permanent and pernicious, by deliberately writing it; and, in all his numerous works, he earnestly inculcated what appeared to him to be the truth; his piety being constant, and the ruling principle of all his conduct.

Such was SAMUEL JOHNSON, a man whose talents, acquirements, and virtues, were so extraordinary, that the more his character is considered, the more he will be regarded by the present age, and by posterity, with admiration and reverence.

SELECTED BIBLIOGRAPHY

Works by Boswell

The Life of Samuel Johnson, ed. G. B. Hill, rev. L. F. Powell, 6 vols. New York: Oxford University Press, 1934–65. The standard edition. Volume 5 contains the *Journal of a Tour to the Hebrides* as Boswell printed it.

Journal of a Tour to the Hebrides, ed. F. A. Pottle and C. H. Bennett. New York: McGraw-Hill, rev. ed. 1962. An edition of the original manuscript.

Private Papers of James Boswell, ed. Geoffrey Scott and F. A. Pottle, 18 vols. plus Index. New York: Oxford University Press, 1928–37. Volume 6, Geoffrey Scott's "The Making of *The Life of Johnson,*" is of particular interest.

London Journal, 1762–1763, ed. F. A. Pottle. New York: McGraw-Hill, 1950. The first volume in the "trade" edition of the Yale editions of the *Private Papers of James Boswell.* Nine volumes in this series have been published so far.

Letters of James Boswell, ed. C. B. Tinker, 2 vols. New York: Oxford University Press, 1924.

Works about Boswell

Bronson, B. H. "Boswell's Boswell," in *Johnson Agonistes.* Berkeley: University of California Press, 1965.

Edel, Leon. *Literary Biography.* Toronto: University of Toronto Press, 1957.

Molin, S. E. "Boswell's Account of the Johnson-Wilkes Meeting," *Studies in English Literature,* 3 (1963).

Pottle, F. A. "Boswell Revalued," in *Literary Views,* ed. Carroll Camden. Chicago: University of Chicago Press, 1964.

———. *James Boswell: The Earlier Years.* New York: McGraw-Hill, 1966. The definitive biography of the first half of Boswell's life. The second and final volume of this biography by Frank Brady and F. A. Pottle is in preparation.

———. "James Boswell, Journalist," in *The Age of Johnson: Essays Presented to C. B. Tinker,* ed. F. W. Hilles. New Haven, Conn.: Yale University Press, 1949.

———. *The Literary Career of James Boswell, Esq.* New York: Oxford University Press, 1929. The standard bibliography of Boswell, which includes comments on the most interesting editions of the *Life.*

———. "The Power of Memory in Boswell and Scott," in *Essays on the 18th Century Presented to D. N. Smith.* London: Oxford University Press, 1945.

Wimsatt, W. K. "The Fact Revalued: James Boswell," in *Hateful Contraries.* Lexington: University of Kentucky Press, 1965.